The American Economy:
A Historical Encyclopedia

The American Economy: A Historical Encyclopedia

Volume One: Short Entries

edited by
Cynthia Clark Northrup

A B C ☰ C L I O

Santa Barbara, California   Denver, Colorado   Oxford, England

Library of Congress Cataloging-in-Publication Data
The American economy : a historical encyclopedia / edited by Cynthia
Clark Northrup.
     p. cm.
Includes bibliographical references and index.
  ISBN 1-57607-866-3 (2 vols. : hardcover : alk. paper)
  ISBN 1-57607-867-1 (eBook)
1. United States--Economic policy--Encyclopedias. 2. United
States--Economic conditions--Encyclopedias. 3. United States--Social
policy--Encyclopedias. 4. United States--Social
conditions--Encyclopedias. I. Northrup, Cynthia Clark, 1959-

   HC102.A66 2003
   330.973'003--dc22

                                              2003020334

07 06 05 04 03 10 9 8 7 6 5 4 3 2 1
This book is also available on the World Wide Web as an e-book. Visit www.abc-clio.com for details.

ABC-CLIO, Inc.
130 Cremona Drive, P.O. Box 1911
Santa Barbara, California 93116–1911

This book is printed on acid-free paper ∞.
Manufactured in the United States of America

Contents

The American Economy: A Historical Encyclopedia

List of Short Entries

List of Essays and Primary Source Documents

Acknowledgments

I would like to thank Dr. James Ciment, who recommended me to ABC-CLIO as editor for *The American Economy: A Historical Encyclopedia.* During the course of this project, numerous people have provided invaluable advice, assistance, and encouragement, for which I am grateful. I offer a special thanks to Drs. Walt Rostow, Sidney Weintraub, Robert Fairbanks, Alfred E. Eckes Jr., and Spencer Tucker for serving on the Board of Advisers.

Throughout the entire endeavor, I have had the support of the Department of History at the University of Texas at Arlington. I would like to extend a special thank-you to the reference librarians at Texas Christian University, the Dallas Public Library, and especially the University of Texas at Arlington, where I took advantage of an extensive library collection to verify the multitude of details and locate the primary source material for this work.

Without the support and impressive effort of the contributors, this work would not have been possible. Many of the authors took their time and energy away from other projects to ensure the success of the encyclopedia. A special thanks to those who assisted during the final stages by writing the last few entries on relatively short notice—and for doing so with such welcomed enthusiasm. For their assistance in typing many of the primary source documents, my deepest gratitude goes to Christopher Nichols and Vonnie Peach.

To my family a special thanks. Through months of telephone calls, correspondence, writing, and editing they continued to provide support and encouragement.

—*Cynthia Clark Northrup*

A Note on Using the Encyclopedia

During the last half of the twentieth century, scholars have tended to direct their attention away from economics to focus instead on social and cultural issues. But it is important for students and intellectuals to recognize the connection between economics and all other aspects of life. Without significant financial resources, the existence of which is determined by economic policy, the federal government cannot address social and cultural issues such as health care and Social Security. The shift in national economic policy that occurred primarily after the Civil War affected American life from immigration and settlement patterns to the manner in which business was conducted. The long-term effect of a specific act or policy is often complex.

Designed as a reference tool for anyone who wishes to learn more about the role of economic policy in American history, the encyclopedia includes numerous entries dealing with specific issues, longer essays that explore broader topics, and selected primary documents. The first volume contains more than 600 biographical and topical entries arranged alphabetically. The biographical entries provide brief but significant details about key individuals and concentrate on the specific role of each in U.S. economic history. Topical entries describe events, court cases, legislation, and so on in the light of their influence on the economic life of the nation.

Each entry in volume one includes references that lead to more thorough information about the topic and a "see also" section directing the reader to related entries in volumes one and two.

In volume two, essays explore broader topics such as the effect of economic policy on education, insurance, the judiciary, and science and technology. These in-depth essays explore topics from colonial times to the present. Also part of volume two are selected primary sources—the various acts and policies that have established economic policy throughout U.S. history—and a comprehensive bibliography with full citations. A list of biographical sketches of the contributors and a detailed subject index can be found at the end of volume two.

The encyclopedia contains detailed information about each economic policy act and about the individuals and debates that shaped the formation of economic policies in the United States from its infancy to the present day. Although the materials are extensive, space prohibits the inclusion of each individual or action connected to the process. This two-volume set addresses the most prominent matters and presents thorough, yet easy to understand, accounts of issues that continue to dictate both the domestic and foreign economic policies of the United States.

Introduction

The American Economy: A Historical Encyclopedia provides detailed information about the formation and development of economic policy throughout American history and describes its continued importance. Historically, economic issues have played a prominent role in U.S. policymaking. Economic policy has influenced social, cultural, political, and economic events from colonial times to the present.

Economic Policy

Economic policy has shifted many times over the course of American history. During colonial times, the British colonies operated under a mercantilist system in which all trade benefited the mother country. After the American Revolution, the fledgling United States attempted to operate under the Articles of Confederation, but the economic restrictions it placed on the national government caused that system to fail. Delegates meeting at the Constitutional Convention agreed that the federal government must have the power to tax. A decision to tax only imports, not exports or direct income, proved to be decisive in the development of domestic industry. Congress passed revenue tariffs (taxes on imports) during the early years of the Republic; after the War of 1812, a shift to protective tariffs occurred. These tariffs continued to increase reaching their apex during the Civil War under the Morrill Tariff. After the Civil War, tariff rates remained high, ensuring the rise of big business that did not have to compete against foreign manufacturers. The extreme wealth accumulated by captains of industry such as Andrew Carnegie and John D. Rockefeller stood in sharp contrast to the poverty of many Americans, especially new immigrants who crowded into tenements in major cities in the North and East. Public awareness of this economic inequity resulted in a movement to replace the tariff as the primary source of tax revenue with a direct personal income tax. However, Congress lacked constitutional authority to institute such a tax unless the states passed a constitutional amendment to allow direct taxation. Republicans finally agreed to lower the tariff rates if the amendment passed, thinking that the states would fail to pass it. The plan failed, and ratification in 1913 of the Sixteenth Amendment opened the door for direct taxation—a shift that has influenced capital accumulation, investment, and personal savings ever since.

After reducing the tariff rates and increasing personal income tax rates, Congress once again increased import duties because of World War I. After that conflict, European countries that had been carved out of the old empires raised their tariff rates to protect their own industries. Consequently, trade slowed at the same time that the U.S. stock market collapsed under the burden of overvaluation of company worth and market overstimulation due to purchases on margin. Within nine months of the crash, Congress passed the Hawley-Smoot Tariff, which raised tariff rates to a record high. Meanwhile, the Federal Reserve Board increased interest rates, contracting the money supply. The net effect was a prolonged depression that finally ended when the United States entered World War II.

The Great Depression and World War II mark a shift in U.S. economic policy. President Franklin D. Roosevelt followed the economic philosophy of John Maynard Keynes, who advocated deficit spending during periods of financial difficulty. Deficit spending would allow the federal government to initiate programs that politicians had traditionally shunned. For the first time, the federal government assumed the role of employer to thousands of the country's unemployed workers. Programs like the Civilian Conservation Corps and Works Progress Administration created jobs. Social Security was established to promote early retirement and so open up jobs to younger workers. In addition, the federal government funded projects such as the Rural Electrification Administration and the Tennessee Valley Authority to improve the lives of Americans in rural or poverty-stricken areas.

Welfare

From the 1930s to the present, the federal government has increasingly used economic policy to deal with social and cultural issues. In the immediate post–World War II period, Americans experienced an unprecedented period of prosperity because of the accumulation of personal savings and the expansion of industry during the war. But by the 1960s, it was apparent that although most Americans' standard of living had increased, African Americans and other groups had fallen deeper into poverty. President Lyndon B. Johnson attempted to correct the problem by using tax revenues to fund a new welfare state—the Great Society, which had programs ranging from Head Start to Medicaid that supported health, education, and community development. The Great Society redistributed the wealth but also created a group of people who became dependent on the federal government. After several decades, states including Wisconsin began to experiment with ways to eliminate this dependency on welfare. As of 2003, the number of people on the welfare rolls has dropped because similar efforts have also been undertaken at the federal level. This change in economic policy led to a drop in the number of births to unwed mothers and the number of abortions.

Education

The field of education has traditionally been the bailiwick of local and state governments rather than the federal government. By the second half of the twentieth century, however, the federal government had become a major participant in the education arena. After World War II, Congress passed the Servicemen's Readjustment Act (also known as the G.I. Bill), which gave returning veterans the opportunity to attend college at the government's expense and even to receive a small living allowance to help support themselves and their families during the process. As a result, during the 1950s and 1960s the number of professionals such as engineers, accountants, business executives, lawyers, and doctors increased dramatically. During the 1960s, Congress approved financial aid programs that gave all Americans, including those from poor families, the opportunity to attend college. By 2000, more Americans had attended college than ever before.

Settlement Patterns

Through various acts and economic policies, Congress has influenced settlement patterns. After the American Revolution, when the nation operated under the Articles of Confederation, the government began to encourage the settlement of the old northwest territory, which at the time encompassed the Ohio Valley region. Thomas Jefferson proposed surveying the land into townships and selling property to Americans in 160-acre parcels. Initially only wealthy investors could afford to purchase the land, and they then subdivided the properties into smaller farms and sold them. No credit terms existed between the government and the purchaser. The land sold very slowly, but gradually the population of the region increased.

After the purchase of the Louisiana Territory from France in 1803, Congress attempted to pass legislation to allow homesteaders to claim 160 acres of federal land in the newly acquired territory. The debate over the expansion of slavery prevented the passage of such legislation. Finally, during the Civil War, the Northern Republicans in Congress passed the Homestead Act of 1862, which encouraged western migration. During the 1870s Congress passed two additional acts—the Timber and Stone Culture Act and the Timber Culture Act—that helped more Americans claim land in the western part of the country. By the 1900s the federal government had initiated a series of dam projects to help supply both farms and cities with additional water so these communities could grow. Cities like Las Vegas, Nevada, could have not expanded without the water provided by the Hoover Dam. The government continues to influence settlement patterns by awarding contracts to employers like Lockheed-Martin and other defense contractors who can entice workers into an area like the Southwest by offering them jobs.

Although the government encouraged settlement of some areas, it restricted the use of other land. Beginning in the 1880s, presidents began setting aside public lands as national parks. Theodore Roosevelt set aside more land than all of his predecessors combined.

Science and Technology

Government spending during wartime has led to many breakthroughs in the fields of science and technology. In the post–Civil War period, medical professionals explored the cause of diseases and infections. By the 1900s army surgeons had discovered the cause of malaria and the public learned about germ theory. Wars also resulted in the development of penicillin and other antibiotic drugs. During World War I, Americans improved the airplane, and after World War II an entire aviation industry developed. During the cold war, the federal government funded the missile and space programs, which yielded such inventions as the computer chip and eventually the Internet.

Conclusion

All social, cultural, and political policies must be funded. The economic policies of the federal government affect all aspects of life in the United States. In the future, the nation will have to choose which economic policy to implement in connection with such issues as population growth and the increasing number of elderly citizens, which will place tremendous strain on the health care system. These economic decisions will affect the younger generation, which will have to pay the taxes to support these programs, and will determine the future history of this nation.

The American Economy:
A Historical Encyclopedia

A

A&M Records v. Napster Inc. (2001)

Court case that challenged federal copyright laws under *United States Code* Title 17.

In 2000, A&M Records and several other plaintiffs filed a civil case against Napster citing infringement of copyright laws. Napster, utilizing the latest MP3 digital music compression technology, allowed members to share music at no cost to the member. The founder, Shawn Fanning, established the Internet website for the purpose of providing "samples" of music from a variety of artists. When the recording industry filed charges against Napster, attorneys for the defendant argued that the company operated under the 1992 Audio Home Recording Act that allowed for the noncommercial reproduction of audio materials. Because Napster provided a free service allowing members to share music, the company argued that it complied with the existing copyright laws. Attorneys for A&M Records and various other plaintiffs within the music industry argued that Napster provided access to copyrighted music that individuals could download and then copy. The lower court ruled in favor of the plaintiffs, and an appeal was filed with the Ninth District Court of Appeals, which upheld the lower court's decision but returned the case to the lower court for the preparation of a revised injunction against Napster. According to the 2001 ruling, Napster must review its files and remove from its website all copyrighted music if the owner of the rights to that music objects to its use by Napster. Napster still retains the right to appeal the decision to the U.S. Supreme Court, but given the conservative nature of the Court, it appears improbable that Napster attorneys will pursue that course of action.

—Cynthia Clark Northrup

References

Mitten, Christopher. *Shawn Fanning: Napster and the Music Revolution.* Brookfield, CT: Twenty-First Century Books, 2002.

White, Ron, and Michael White. *MP3 Underground.* Indianapolis, IN: Que Corp., 2001.

See also Volume 2: Intellectual Property.

Acquired Immune Deficiency Syndrome (AIDS)

A disease caused by a retrovirus that mutates so rapidly that the B-lymphocytes and the body's natural antibodies cannot fight it off.

The introduction of AIDS (acquired immunodeficiency syndrome) in the United States occurred primarily in the homosexual and bisexual community. First diagnosed as a disease in 1981, it results in the vulnerability of the human body to disease and malignancies. As AIDS spread to include hemophiliacs and individuals who required blood transfusions, the public pressured the federal government for research funding. Symptoms appear initially like the flu but gradually develop into anxiety, weight loss, diarrhea, fatigue, shingles, and memory loss. Transmission of the disease occurs through the exchange of body fluids such as breast milk, semen, or vaginal secretions or through the exchange of blood and blood products. Kissing and the exchange of saliva do not appear to transmit the disease nor do urine, feces, or sweat.

The primarily economic implications of the disease include the increased health care cost associated with the care of AIDS patients as well as their medical treatments. As of 2002, physicians rely on three drugs—AZT (also known as Retrovir or Zidovudine), ddI (Videx® EC brand didanesine [delayed-release capsules]), and 3TC (Epivir® brand Iamivadine)—to delay the spread of symptoms in patients. In addition, another 30 alternative treatments are being tested. The enormous cost associated with the development of a cure for the disease has taxed the economic resources of private foundations established for that sole purpose as well as the federal government.

In the United States alone, the Centers for Disease Control and Prevention (CDC) estimates that about 850,000 to 950,000 Americans are infected by the human immunodeficiency virus, or HIV. HIV attacks the immune system cells. All individuals with AIDS have HIV, but not all people with HIV have AIDS. AIDS is a fatal disease caused by a rapidly mutating retrovirus that leaves the victim susceptible to infections, malignancies, and neurological disorders. Every year another 40,000 cases are reported. During the 1980s, a massive public awareness program resulted in a decline in new cases from 60,805 in 1996 to 40,766 in 2000. The majority of the new cases have occurred in the African American community—half of new cases among men and 65 percent of new cases among women occur among this group. As of the end of 2001, the CDC reported more than 467,910 deaths from the disease.

As a result of the continuing crisis, the federal government has appropriated millions of dollars for research. For the fiscal year 1999, Congress approved $110 million just for the African American community. The total figure for research, treatment, prevention, and educational programs amounted to $4.87 billion. During the last year of the Clinton administration that figure declined, but the incoming administration of George W. Bush increased the budget for AIDS once again.

—*Cynthia Clark Northrup*

References
Feldman, Douglas A., and Julia Wang Miller, eds. *The AIDS Crisis: A Documentary History.* Westport, CT: Greenwood Press, 1998.
See also Volume 1: Disease.

ADC
See Aid to Dependent Children.

Advanced Technology Office (ATO)
Office responsible for the integration of new and future technology into military systems.

In 1957, Congress created the Defense Advanced Research Projects Agency (DARPA) in response to the Soviet Union's launching of *Sputnik I*. The Advanced Technology Office (ATO), functioning under the authority and funding of DARPA, conducts research and integrates advanced technology into existing U.S. military systems. Researchers place special emphasis on maritime, communications, special operations, command and control, and information assurance and survivability mission areas. The goal of the ATO remains the most cost-effective use of technology to assist all branches of the military to fight against existing and future threats by outmaneuvering, gathering more intelligence, and reacting more quickly than the adversary. Current ATO programs include the development of artificial intelligence through the use of robotics, sensors, and satellites. Projects include Airborne Communications Node; Antipersonnel Landmine Alternative; Buoyant Cable Array Antenna; Center of Excellence for Research in Oceanographic Sciences; Future Combat Systems (FCS) Command and Control; FCS Communications; Metal Storm; Robust Passive Sonar; Submarine Payloads and Sensors Program; Tactical Mobile Robotics; Tactical Sensors; Undersea Littoral Warfare: Netted Search, Acquisition and Targeting (Net SAT); and Underwater Fighter (LOKI). Additional programs such as the Self-Healing Minefield system use the most advanced technology to prevent the breaching of minefields by the enemy. Instead of creating a static minefield, the program creates a dynamic minefield with the intelligent capability of physically reorganizing mines to prevent breaches by opposition forces. Government funding of the research has produced benefits for the American public as well because consumer applications for the technology exist and because ATO researchers continue to use high-tech devices developed by the private sector, which receives public funding for its research and development.

—*Cynthia Clark Northrup*

References
Keever, David B., ed. *Interactive Management and Defense Advanced Research Projects Agency.* Fairfax, VA: Institute for Advanced Study in the Integrative Sciences, George Mason University, 1990.
See also Volume 1: Defense Advanced Research Projects Agency.

AEA
See American Economic Association.

AFDC
See Aid to Families with Dependent Children.

Affirmative Action
Legislative attempt to eliminate economic discrimination by ensuring that blacks and other minorities play "on a level playing field."

Executive Order 10925, issued by President John F. Kennedy, recognized the need for affirmative action. After Kennedy's assassination, President Lyndon B. Johnson pushed the Civil Rights Act of 1964 through Congress. On September 24, 1965, Johnson signed Executive Order 11246, which provided for the enforcement of affirmative action, primarily in education and jobs. The federal government attempted to ensure that blacks and other minority groups played on a level playing field when it came to promotions, salaries, school admissions, scholarship, financial assistance, and participation in federal contracts. Although designed as a temporary measure, affirmative action assumed permanency after the introduction of quotas. (Racial quotas required employers to hire a percentage of their workers on the basis of race.)

Affirmative action's goals were met better in the educational realm than in the workplace. Colleges and universities reserved a specific number of positions for disadvantaged minorities, including women, under the quota system. As a result, some white males who qualified received rejection notices. In 1978, Allan Bakke sued the University of California for accepting less-qualified students to its medical school while refusing to accept him for two years in a row. In the landmark case *Regents of the University of California v. Bakke,* the U.S. Supreme Court ruled in 1978 that the inflexible quota system violated Title VI of the 1964 Civil Rights Act because it engaged in reverse discrimination. In 1986, the Court heard a second case, *Wygant v. Jackson Board of Education,* in which the justices ruled that white men could not be dismissed to make room for women or minority employees. The following year the Court heard *United States v. Paradise* and issued an opinion that allowed for a one-for-one promotion requirement—for every white male promoted, one minority employee must be promoted.

The debate over affirmative action continued through the 1990s. The federal government initiated programs that would economically support small businesses owned by women or minority groups. Employers attempted to achieve a reasonable diversity among employees without the rigid quotas. Congress even tried, unsuccessfully, to pass an affirmative action amendment to the Constitution, but the measure was defeated in 1979 by a 171 to 249 margin. Affirmative action has achieved some limited success—more women and minorities have reached senior-level positions, and student bodies in universities and colleges have become diverse.

Currently the U.S. Supreme Court is reviewing two cases concerning affirmative action—*Gratz v. Bollinger* and *Grutter v. Bollinger*—involving admission requirements or quotas used by the University of Michigan law school. The outcome of these cases will decide the future direction of affirmative action.

—*Cynthia Clark Northrup*

References
Altschiller, Donald, ed. *Affirmative Action.* New York: H. W. Wilson, 1991.
Cahn, Steven, ed. *The Affirmative Action Debate.* New York: Routledge, 2002.
See also Volume 1: Civil Rights Movement.

Affluence
Widespread prosperity.

A society in which a large proportion of members possess purchasing power in excess of that required for any necessary level of well-being is categorized as affluent. In an affluent society, most individuals satisfy their basic sustenance, accommodation, and entertainment needs. Beyond that level, sufficient wealth exists for many people to consume goods that offer only trivial value. An affluent society has resources to protect members from problems such as the loss of income and extra expense due to unemployment and health crises.

With the availability of a wide range of goods, many of which consumers do not need, producers are forced to create a demand through marketing and advertising. Continued economic growth requires the continuous creation of new demands to absorb the ever-increasing volume of production. Consumer purchases become increasingly influenced by the marketing of brand images rather than specific products.

Even in the midst of affluence, an inequality of wealth exists, with some people living in great poverty. As the requirements of producers evolve to take precedence over those of consumers, individuals who lack enough disposable income to afford the advertised lifestyle frequently buy on credit, leading them to live beyond their means. Demands by individual consumers, encouraged by marketing, may increase at the expense of the public good. Consumers who move to the suburbs for bigger, newer homes cause increased poverty in the inner urban areas and a crumbling infrastructure in many of the formerly tax-wealthy cities. The tax burden shifts to the expanding suburbs (for road, sanitation, water, and other systems) and lessens the amount of tax money available to major cities.

In the United States, the post–World War II era produced a period of affluence beginning in the 1950s. Most Americans realized an increase in disposable income, even though the majority of women remained outside the workforce. Families during this period purchased automobiles, homes in the suburbs, and modern appliances. Poverty did continue but remained overshadowed by the affluence of the majority.

During the 1960s it became apparent that not everyone in the United States enjoyed a prosperous lifestyle. President Lyndon B. Johnson attempted to address this disparity in wealth through the Great Society program. However, a gap continues to exist into the twenty-first century.

—*Tony Ward*

References
Galbraith, John Kenneth. *The Affluent Society.* 2d ed. Boston: Houghton Mifflin, 1969.
See also Volume 1: Consumer Spending.

AFL-CIO
See American Federation of Labor and Congress of Industrial Organizations.

Agricultural Adjustment Act of 1938
Legislation signed by President Franklin D. Roosevelt on February 16, 1938, that focused on the need for long-term consideration of agricultural production and soil conservation as well as the prevention of potential drought periods.

The Agricultural Adjustment Act (AAA) of 1938 was developed in 1937 as basic price-support legislation to replace the recently discredited AAA of 1933. Title I of the act amended the Soil Conservation and Domestic Allotment Act of 1936, and Title II authorized the secretary of agriculture to argue before the Commerce Commission regarding freight rates on agricultural commodities. The remaining three titles addressed loans and parity payments (government funds provided to farmers that help maintain a stable relationship between the level of farm prices and the general price level), cotton pool participation, and crop insurance.

The new act expanded the soil conservation features of the 1936 act with provisions for water conservation and erosion control in semiarid regions. The 1938 act sought to prevent the displacement of tenants and sharecroppers. Title III of the 1938 act redefined parity prices, creating a more precise formulation that included total interest payments and farm estate taxes as well as freight charges and shifts in prices of commodities. Congress also implemented changes in the method of figuring allotments for individual farmers to limit these to commercial growing areas.

This act provided the secretary of agriculture with three measures for controlling major crop surpluses: (1) Payments could be shifted from "soil-depleting" to "soil-conserving" crops by farming operations termed "cooperators" (those that limited production to established quotas); (2) the secretary could announce marketing quotas; or (3) the secretary could provide nonrecourse loans that enabled farmers and growers to hold market crops until the farmer could sell them at adequate prices. Congress authorized the secretary to continue parity payments after receiving congressional allocation of funds. The federal government sent these payments to cooperating producers to compensate them for the difference between market prices and established parity prices.

The AAA of 1938 included several other sections added as amendments to ensure that the legislation passed Congress. For example, Section 202 provided for four regional laboratories to conduct scientific research into new commercial uses of farm products.

—*Lisa L. Ossian*

References
Benedict, Murray R. *Farm Policies of the United States, 1790–1950: A Study of Their Origins and Development.* New York: Twentieth Century Fund, 1953.
Talbot, Ross B., and Don F. Hadwinger. *The Policy Process in American Agriculture.* San Francisco: Chandler Publishing, 1968.
See also Volume 2: Agricultural Policy.

Agricultural and Mechanical (A&M) Colleges

Postsecondary institutions established to promote the development of the practical arts and sciences.

Agricultural and mechanical (A&M) colleges were formed after the passage of the Morrill Land Grant Act in 1862. Congress granted the states 30,000 acres of federal land for each senator and representative that the state had in the national legislature for the purpose of establishing A&M colleges. The main curriculum would concentrate on agriculture, engineering, and home economics—the practical arts. The act, passed during the Civil War, also required the establishment of a Reserve Officers Training Corps (ROTC) at every land-grant institution. Most of the colleges implemented mandatory participation programs, but after the 1920s, membership in the ROTC became voluntary. Congress expanded the policy of assistance to A&M colleges in 1887 with the passage of the Hatch Act, which made funds available for research and experimental facilities. Additional

resources, allocated under the Smith-Lever Act of 1914, extended agricultural and home economics research.

The study and development of a variety of crops and the study of animal husbandry encouraged improved farming techniques, which in turn stimulated the economy through the increase in annual yield. But as farmers exceeded the demands of consumers, prices dropped. Agricultural depressions remained a recurrent theme from the late 1880s through the 1930s until the United States sought markets overseas and implemented domestic policies that included farm subsidies. In recent years, A&M colleges have shifted their emphasis to engineering. As of 1999, more than 10,000 universities and colleges, including 29 Native American tribal institutions, have achieved land-grant status as agricultural and engineering schools.

—*Cynthia Clark Northrup*

References
Parker, William B. *The Life and Public Services of Justin Smith Morrill.* New York: Da Capo Press, 1971.
Ross, Earle Dudley. *Democracy's College: The Land-Grant Movement in the Formative State.* New York: Arno Press, 1969.
See also Volume 2: Land Policies.

Agricultural Credit Act of 1987

Legislation that authorized $4 billion in a financial assistance for financially vulnerable institutions of the Farm Credit System (FCS) and protected many farmers whose loans fell delinquent.

Due to the 1980s farm crisis, which was brought on by tight credit and plummeting farm land prices, the FCS experienced deep financial problems. The Agricultural Credit Act required the FCS to establish a new Farm Credit System Assistance Board to take over bad loans and supervise financial assistance to system banks for the next five years (1987–1992). This board would allow these troubled institutions to issue preferred stock eventually purchased by the Farm Credit System Assistance Corporation. Troubled institutions could apply for this assistance when borrower stock, which makes up most of their capital reserves, failed to cover financial losses. The assistance board imposed several conditions on the institutions receiving these loans; it had power over debt issuance, interest rates on loans, and business and investment plans.

The act also required the Farmers Home Administration (FmHA) to modify delinquent loans to the maximum extent possible to avoid losses to the government. It required the secretary of agriculture to provide notice to each FmHA borrower of all loan-service programs available. If foreclosure happens, priority for purchasing goes to previous owners. The secretary also releases income from household and operating expenses for farmers who apply for loan restructuring.

The law mandated that the federal land bank and federal intermediate credit bank in each of the system's 12 districts merge. The 12 districts reorganized to allow for no fewer than 6 districts. This restructuring and consolidation allowed for more efficiency. Finally, the act created a secondary market for agricultural real estate and certain rural housing loans, establishing a Federal Agricultural Mortgage Corporation (Farmer Mac) within the FCS. System banks could package their agricultural real estate loans for resale to investors as tradable, interest-bearing securities. The Agricultural Credit Act of 1987 saved the FCS and made it financially sound in the 1990s. The FCS has continued to perform efficiently through 2003 and has received high marks from auditors.

—*T. Jason Soderstrum*

References

Harl, Neal. *The Farm Debt Crisis of the 1980s.* Ames: Iowa State University Press, 1990.

See also Volume 1: Farmer Mac Reform Act of 1995.

Agricultural Credit Improvement Act of 1992

Bill to assist beginning farmer to acquire his or her own farm.

This act required the U.S. Department of Agriculture's (USDA) Farm Service Agency (FSA) to target a percentage of its direct and guaranteed farm operating and farm ownership loans to beginning farmers and ranchers. In 1992, the average age of farmers had increased to 52 years of age. Twice as many farmers were 60 or older as were under the age of 35. The increased cost of farming since the 1970s and the farm crisis of the 1980s had washed many younger farmers out of the business.

To get the loans, the beginning farmer had to draw up a detailed 10-year plan of action for his or her farm. Once the USDA Farm Service Agency approved the plan, new farmers became eligible for direct, subsidized, operational loans from the FMHA for 10 years and federal loan guarantees for the next 5 years. After 15 years, these farmers became ineligible for the program. The federal government took up liability for 80 to 90 percent of these loans if they were defaulted on.

Another minor change in the law allowed banks, rather than the Farmers Home Administration (FmHA), to decide which farmers met eligibility requirements for this program. Members of Congress believed that this would get money to the farmer faster. The bill also called for special efforts to make loans more available to those who are "socially disadvantaged," including women.

—*T. Jason Soderstrum*

References

"Bill Easing Credit Designed to Recruit Young Farmers." *Congressional Quarterly* (August 8, 1992): 2351.

See also Volume 1: Agricultural Policy; Agricultural Credit Act of 1987.

Agricultural Government-Sponsored Enterprises (GSEs)

Organizations federally chartered, but privately owned and operated, that receive direct and indirect benefits from the government to improve credit availability and enhance market competition.

Congress charters a government-sponsored enterprise, or GSE, when perceived failures in private credit markets exist. Congress established GSEs to improve credit availability and enhance financial market competition in specific sectors of the economy.

GSEs can access a direct line of credit to the U.S. Treasury to achieve their goals, and Congress structures them so that they benefit from an implicit federal taxpayer guarantee on their obligations. The first GSE, the Farm Credit System, dealt primarily with agricultural and rural sectors. It was created by the Federal Farm Loan Act of 1916 (FFLA) and acts as a network of cooperative lending institutions that operates as a direct lender to agricultural producers, agricultural cooperatives, farm-related businesses, and rural residents. Another GSE, the Federal Agricultural Mortgage Corporation, was established in 1988 and acts as a secondary market for agricultural and rural housing mortgages.

—*Jonah Katz*

References

U.S. Department of Agriculture Economic Research Service. "Can Federal Action Improve Efficiency in the Market for Farm Loans?" Agriculture Information Bulletin no. 724-01, 1996.

See also Volume 1: Federal Agricultural Mortgage Corporation.

Agricultural Policy

The evolution of the federal government's efforts to stabilize agricultural markets.

The federal government had always maintained policies designed to encourage the development of agriculture, but not until the 1920s did it formulate policies to specifically regulate fundamental market forces in the agricultural sector.

Intensifying urbanization at the turn of the twentieth century generated increased demand for American farm products and subsequent improvements in the standard of living for American farmers. World War I further stimulated this expanding market as European allies began to depend on American agricultural exports. However, this wartime demand could not be sustained after the Armistice, and agricultural prices fell precipitously.

As falling commodity prices began to trigger bankruptcies in rural areas, Congress searched for the means to strengthen agricultural markets. An alteration of the mandate of the War Finance Corporation provided credit for farm exports; the Capper-Volstead Act (1922) protected agricultural cooperatives from antitrust prosecution; the Fordney-McCumber Tariff (1922) protected American farmers from foreign competition. The most controversial of these efforts came with the McNary-Haugen legislation. Beginning in 1924, members of Congress attempted to legislate a price support system in an effort to restore to farmers the purchasing power they had during the prewar boom. This system would guarantee domestic prices for key agricultural products and dump any surpluses on the international market. President Calvin Coolidge's two vetoes (in 1924 and 1928) of the McNary-Haugen legislation sparked a debate over farm policy that formed the groundwork for the New Deal's approach to agriculture in the administration of Franklin D. Roosevelt.

The farm crisis that began after World War I continued to deepen with the Great Depression. Under the New Deal, the federal government responded with the Agricultural Adjustment Act (1933). As it had done with the McNary-Haugen proposals, Congress designed the AAA to guarantee farmers a higher standard of living by enabling the federal government to set prices for key agricultural products. Unlike McNary-Haugen, the bill contained limits on agricultural production. By the end of the 1930s, the government's ability to set minimum prices for agricultural products and to limit the number of acres in production formed the core of federal agricultural policy.

This effort to create stability in prices coincided with support for modernization. Under the Rural Electrification Administration (REA), farmers in remote areas gained access to inexpensive electricity. The REA encouraged diversification by permitting extensive use of technologies, including refrigeration, irrigation pumps, and storage ventilation systems. The federal government built dams and levees to control flooding. These initiatives worked to improve the profitability of farming and raise the standard of living in rural areas.

The goals of agricultural policy set during the New Deal continued during World War II. As had been the case in World War I, demand for agricultural production increased tremendously. The federal government permitted farmers to put more land into production temporarily to meet wartime demand. However, at the end of the war, the government quickly reined in production to prevent agricultural surpluses that would have lowered commodity prices and farmers' income.

During the postwar period, efforts by the federal government to prevent overproduction became complicated due to continued improvements in farm technology. During the Eisenhower presidency, the administration initiated two major adjustments to compensate for this problem. Under the Agricultural Trade Development and Assistance Act of 1954 (PL 480), farmers could export agricultural surpluses to developing nations to alleviate food shortages. Exports under PL 480 projected American influence abroad while absorbing the surplus production of American farmers. To further limit the growing stocks of grain and cotton, the government created the Soil Bank, which permitted farmers to take land out of production for conservation purposes. The Soil Bank initiated a long-term pattern in which overproduction was curbed for reasons of ecological protection.

The construction of agricultural policy presented a conundrum in the postwar era. The ideal of the family farm permeated American culture, and the government remained committed to creating the circumstances under which family farms could provide a reasonable standard of living. However, the costs of agricultural programs remained high. As farmers made up a declining proportion of the American population, price support systems became harder to legitimize.

During the 1960s, federal agriculture policy continued to curtail surplus production and raise farm incomes, but it placed greater emphasis on guaranteeing low food prices to American consumers. The government dropped price support levels to reflect prevailing world market prices, not domestic spending patterns. This action by the government lowered food prices for American consumers and simultaneously pushed American farmers into more competition in the international market. The political effort to link low food prices and agricultural policy expanded under President Lyndon B. Johnson's Great Society, as the U.S. Department of Agriculture (USDA) supervised the food stamp and free school lunch programs.

The debate over farm subsidies intensified during the 1970s and 1980s, as American political rhetoric emphasized the importance of lowering food prices and limiting spending on farm subsidies. The Agricultural and Consumer Protection Act of 1973 reformulated the price support system. Under this new "deficiency payment" system, crop prices were compared with a USDA target price, and farmers received compensation for any shortfall. The deficiency payment system continued to form the basis for federal agricultural policy into the presidency of Bill Clinton, but it did little to curb overproduction or raise income levels for family farms. This failure was further complicated by increasing public support for balancing the federal budget by cutting spending for deficiency payments.

Dissatisfaction with the high costs resulting from federal agriculture policy led to the passage of the Federal Agricultural Improvement and Reform Act in 1996. The product of conservative rhetoric supporting "freedom to farm," the new policy—designed to eliminate federal subsidies and encourage diversification according to international market demands—returned American farmers to a free market system. The act marked the first legislative attempt to abandon the direction of marketplace regulation initiated in the 1920s.

—*Karen A. J. Miller*

References

Browne, William P. *Private Interests, Public Policy, and American Agriculture.* Lawrence: University Press of Kansas, 1988.

Hansen, John Mark. *Gaining Access: Congress and the Farm Lobby, 1919–1981.* Chicago: University of Chicago Press, 1991.

Robinson, Kenneth L. *Farm and Food Policies and Their Consequences.* Englewood Cliffs, NJ: Prentice-Hall, 1989.

Sheingate, Adam D. *The Rise of the Agricultural Welfare State: Institutions and Interest Group Power in the United States, France, and Japan.* Princeton, NJ: Princeton University Press, 2001.

See also Volume 1: Great Depression; McNary-Haugen Bill; Rural Electrification Administration.

Agricultural Programs Adjustment Act of 1984

Legislation that froze target price increases provided for in the 1981 act; authorized paid land diversions for upland cotton, rice, and feed; and provided a wheat payment-in-kind (PIK) program for 1984.

Signed into law on April 10, 1984, this overhaul of the federal crop program sparked controversy between the administration of President Ronald Reagan and members of Congress from the farm belt. With Reagan's approval, Senator Robert Dole (R-Kansas) and budget director David A. Stockman negotiated in private sessions to lessen federal spending by freezing target prices. However, farm groups lobbied for more aid to help with the recovery from the previous year's drought. With the exception of certain wheat interests, no one felt satisfied with the bill.

The act froze target prices so that the federal government paid farmers the difference if crop market prices dropped below a certain level (for example, $4.38 per bushel for wheat) over the next two years. It also maintained 1985 target levels for corn, cotton, and rice and authorized an acreage reduction program in which wheat farmers would take 20 percent of their land out of production to qualify for farm program benefits such as loans and price supports. A wheat farmer could receive compensation if he or she retired another 10 percent of his or her land. A farmer could set aside up to 20 percent more land and receive surplus wheat certificates (PIKs) at a rate of 85 percent of the expected yield. The hope was that this would lessen the nation's wheat surplus and increase prices well above target prices.

The law also stipulated that lenders value farm assets used as collateral for emergency disaster at their value prior to the disaster. Direct loans for economic emergencies such as drought, flooding, or falling land values increased by $250 million in 1984, providing farmers with $600 million in total loans ($310 million for direct loans and $290 for guaranteed loans). The secretary of agriculture made emergency loans available to farmers in counties touched by disaster. The ceiling on Farmers Home Administration (FmHA) farm operating loans increased from $200,000 to $400,000. Finally, the act required the lowering of the interest rate for the balance of rescheduled FmHA loans and the extension of the time period for repayment from 7 to 15 years. As awareness of the 1980s farm crisis deepened, subsequent legislation changed many components of the law and destroyed President Reagan's notion of withdrawing federal support of agriculture.

T. Jason Soderstrum

References
Harl, Neal. *The Farm Debt Crisis of the 1980s.* Ames: Iowa State University Press, 1990.
See also Volume 1: Agricultural Policy.

Aid to Dependent Children (ADC)

Mid- to late-twentieth-century government program that provided financial assistance to poor families with children.

Aid to Dependent Children (ADC), later known as Aid to Families with Dependent Children (AFDC), was a provision of the Social Security Act of 1935. Although the impulse to assist poor and orphaned children dates to after the Civil War, no formal federal government program aimed at alleviating poverty existed until President Franklin D. Roosevelt's New Deal. The Social Security Act called on states to develop plans to aid the poor, with the federal government matching up to one-third of these expenditures. The states had discretion to determine income eligibility and benefits levels, but they could not place a time limit on benefits or require recipients to work.

Originally intended to enable poor widows to care for their children, the program by the 1960s came to support mostly unmarried mothers. In fewer than 10 years, from 1961 to 1970, AFDC caseloads nearly tripled. Several Supreme Court cases decided in the late 1960s and early 1970s weakened state restrictions that had blocked some from receiving benefits, resulting in a further expansion in AFDC caseloads. Lower courts built on these precedents to expand the concept that citizens were entitled to receive welfare benefits, placing the burden on government to justify eligibility restrictions.

AFDC became the primary method of providing cash assistance to the poor for more than 60 years, and the term became synonymous with welfare. Critics of AFDC claimed that the absence of work requirements and time limits on benefits established a precedent for relief that fostered a culture of dependency. These concerns prompted several attempts at reform in the 1960s and 1970s, including President Richard Nixon's Family Assistance Plan and President Jimmy Carter's Program for Better Jobs and Income, but neither proposal passed Congress.

Passage of the Personal Responsibility and Work Opportunity Reconciliation Act of 1996 (PRWORA) eliminated the open-ended federal entitlement of AFDC by establishing time limits on benefits and by requiring recipients to work or participate in job training. Under the PRWORA, the federal government provided block grants to the states for the Temporary Assistance for Needy Families (TANF) program. Opponents of AFDC hailed the new measures and celebrated the precipitous decline in welfare caseloads in the late 1990s, while critics of the reforms of 1996 warned of rising poverty in poor economic times.

—Christopher A. Preble

References
Teles, Steven. *Whose Welfare? AFDC and Elite Politics.* Lawrence: University Press of Kansas, 1996.
See also Volume 1: Aid to Families with Dependent Children; Volume 2: Welfare State.

Aid to Families with Dependent Children (AFDC)

Welfare program in the United States intended to provide financial assistance to low-income families.

Initially created in 1935 under Title IV of the Social Security Act as Aid to Dependent Children, the program's principal objective focused on preventing poor families from placing their children in orphanages in exchange for direct cash payments. The program was renamed Aid to Families with Dependent Children (AFDC) in 1962, and the federal government matched state funds for the program. Although AFDC remained an entitlement of the federal government's budget, individual states determined eligibility and amount of benefits received, resulting in significant variation from state to state.

Typical recipients included single-parent families, especially unmarried mothers and their children. The basic eligibility requirement was that a family include a dependent child 18 years of age or younger, with an exception for 19-year-old high school students. The child must prove U.S. citizenship or possess a legal permanent alien status and must lack financial support from one parent. Two-parent families may receive benefits if one parent remains unemployed.

The American public perceived the ADFC program, customarily identified within the larger context of the welfare system, as flawed. It subsequently remained a target of bipartisan criticism that culminated in varied proposals to reform the system and to address the nation's poverty problem. These proposals typically sought to require the recipient to work, to assume personal responsibility, and to become self-sufficient. In 1988, Congress redefined AFDC through the Family Support Act, a comprehensive reform initiative that focused on employment rather than income support. Then, in 1996, Temporary Assistance for Needy Families (TANF), a component of the Personal Responsibility and Work Opportunity Reconciliation Act, replaced AFDC entirely. TANF differs from its predecessor on several levels. Primarily, it perceives welfare as a temporary circumstance rather than a lifelong situation, and consequently it establishes a five-year time limit for benefits. In addition, the program receives funding from federal block grants, which provide greater flexibility to the states and allow them to address their individual circumstances.

—*John Marino*

References

Amott, Teresa, and Michael D. Calhoun, with Don Reeves. *Let's Get Real about Welfare.* Silver Spring, MD: Bread for the World Occasional Paper no. 5, 1995.

See also Volume 1: Welfare Economics.

AIDS

See Acquired Immune Deficiency Syndrome.

Alaska

Forty-ninth state of the United States, known for the Trans-Alaska Pipeline.

"Seward's Folly" no longer has a place—if it ever did—in the lexicon as a nickname for Alaska, given the actual and potential reserves of Alaskan oil and gas, not to mention the abundance of coal. The oil field at Prudhoe Bay, discovered

by Atlantic Richfield in 1968, has the potential productive capacity of 10 billion barrels—twice as much as the next-largest field ever found in the United States, that of East Texas in 1930. As of 2000, the oil output of Alaska equaled 20 percent of the nation's yield.

During the global oil boom between 1973 and 1985, Alaska gloried in its oil revenues—so much so, in fact, that its legislature abolished the state's income tax in 1979, when oil prices neared their peak.

At the same time came the wrangling between oil companies and environmentalists over the proposal to build a pipeline from Alaska's North Slope 789 miles to the port of Valdez. In support of this objective, a consortium of oil companies formed, known first as the Trans-Alaska Pipeline System and then as the Alyeska Pipeline Service Company. The companies in the consortium saw the proposed pipeline as the most desirable way of solving a major problem—transporting the oil from Prudhoe Bay to distant markets.

Environmental activists protested the plan. They forced the national government to implement the National Environmental Policy Act of 1969, which called for an impact statement to precede the issuance of permits. A federal district court upheld this initiative by environmentalists when it forbade the secretary of the interior to issue the necessary permits.

The legal battle continued from August 1972 through April 1973, and in April 1973 the U.S. Supreme Court upheld a court of appeals decision, which delayed further the issuance of permits. At the insistence of environmentalists, the court of appeals had applied a provision of the Mineral Leasing Act of 1920, which limited rights-of-way across public lands to widths of 50 feet. The oil companies wanted widths up to three times that distance.

Congress then intervened. After a period of protracted debate, a bill finally cleared the Senate, then the House. Signed by President Richard Nixon in November 1973 under the title Trans-Alaska Pipeline Authorization Act, it permitted construction—the result being the completion of the Trans-Alaska Pipeline by 1977, which constituted an economic boon.

For the future, Alaska looks to further development of its petroleum resources, the mining of metals, tourism, and overseas trade with Asia as bases for prosperity. After the terrorist attacks on September 11, 2001, the administration of President G. W. Bush stepped up efforts to gain support for its proposal to drill for oil and gas in the Arctic National Wildlife Reserve, but the Senate rejected the measure April 18, 2003. New initiatives have been proposed to drill on Native American lands, but their future remains uncertain.

—*Keith L. Miller*

References

Brown, Thomas. *Oil on Ice: Alaskan Wilderness at the Crossroads.* San Francisco: Sierra Club, 1971.

Cicchetti, Charles J. *Alaskan Oil: Alternative Routes and Markets.* Baltimore, MD: Johns Hopkins University Press, 1972.

See also Volume 1: Energy; Oil.

Aldrich-Vreeland Act (1908)

Act meant to remedy perceived inadequacies of the U.S. banking structure revealed during the bank failures and panics of 1873, 1893, and 1907, which occurred because of the lack of regulatory federal legislation.

In January 1908, Senator Nelson Aldrich, Republican from Rhode Island, introduced a bill to permit the creation of emergency currency backed by state, municipal, and railroad bonds. But the currency commission of the American Bankers Association and other banking and merchant interests immediately opposed the Aldrich Bill, which many felt simply raised the value of railroad bonds and thus benefited the large eastern banks. In March, Aldrich—after meeting with George Perkins, a representative of the J. P. Morgan Company—removed railroad bonds as collateral for emergency currency. By the end of the month, the Senate had passed the bill. During the hearings in the House of Representatives, overwhelming opposition arose. Yet many wanted some type of regulation to prevent a financial panic similar to that in 1907. Congressman Edward B. Vreeland, speaking for the Republican caucus in the House, subsequently introduced a compromise bill.

Passed by Congress on May 30, 1908, the Aldrich-Vreeland Emergency Currency Act made available $500 million in emergency currency to certain national banks over the next six years by allowing them to issue circulating notes. The bill also allowed extra currency on bonds of towns, cities, counties, and states. But a graduated tax of up to 10 percent limited the issuance of currency. Moreover, the act established the National Monetary Commission, composed of nine members from the Senate and nine members from the House of Representatives, to investigate the deficiencies in the country's banking system. The commission, with Senator Aldrich as its chair, appointed experts to study the history of banking and the current condition of the industry in the United States. The commission subsequently issued a 49-volume report in 1911 that recommended the establishment of a national reserve association with branches to act as a central bank run by private bankers free of any real government control. The Aldrich-Vreeland Act preceded the Federal Reserve Act of 1913, which established a stable banking system in the United States.

—*Steven E. Siry*

References

Stephenson, Nathaniel Wright. *Nelson W. Aldrich: A Leader in American Politics.* New York: Scribner's, 1930.

See also Volume 1: Banking System, Federal Reserve Act; Volume 2: Banking.

Alliance for Progress

Economic program designed to improve relations between the United States and its southern neighbors, thereby combating the spread of communism.

Shortly after John F. Kennedy became president in 1961, he appointed Adolph Berle to establish a commission to investigate ways to improve relations between the United States and Latin American nations. This commission recommended expansive economic and social objectives that became the center of Kennedy's Latin American policy. In August 1961, the United States and the Organization of American States (OAS) signed the Charter of Punta del Este, which formally created the Alliance for Progress. The alliance would provide technical advice and financial assistance to Latin American nations interested in upgrading their economic positions, increasing their agricultural output, and improving their systems of education and health care.

The Alliance for Progress did not realize many of its stated objectives because of Kennedy's short time in office (he was assassinated in 1963), a lack of financial resources, and growing distrust of the United States by many Latin American nations. In the final analysis, the United States spent $10 billion in an unsuccessful effort to limit the influence of communism in Latin America in the decade following the Cuban Revolution and the Bay of Pigs invasion.

—*James T. Carroll*

References

Burner, David, and Thomas West. *The Torch Is Passed: The Kennedy Brothers and American Liberalism.* New York: Brandywine Press, 1984.

See also Volume 1: Organization of American States.

American Economic Association (AEA)

Organization of professional economists established in 1885.

Founded primarily by a group of younger professors led by Richard Ely of Johns Hopkins University, the American Economic Association (AEA) challenged the economic orthodoxy of laissez-faire espoused by David Ricardo. However, to attract membership from a wide range of academics (including the organization's first president, the Massachusetts Institute of Technology's Francis Walker), the organization soon adopted a policy concentrating on the promotion of scholarly and scientific activities while studiously avoiding partisanship and official positions on policy issues. Although individual members have frequently signed petitions and called for the government to adopt or alter specific economic policies, the AEA has consistently maintained its stance of neutrality for more than a century—much more so than professional organizations in other social sciences. The association remains an open society, with no significant membership restrictions such as nationality, education, or ideology.

The AEA holds annual meetings at which economists can socialize, present their research findings, comment on the ideas of others, and search for jobs and job candidates. The organization focuses on the dissemination of research findings. The AEA's publications include the prestigious *American Economic Review,* established in 1911, which includes technical research articles; the *Journal of Economic Literature,* established in 1963, which includes book reviews and surveys of recent research; and the *Journal of Economic Perspectives,* established in 1987, which aims to put economic research into the hands of college students and educated readers.

Since its early days, the AEA has repeatedly provided expert advice in the design and development of the census and other government statistics. During both world wars, the AEA played a notable role in organizing professional expertise for government service. Presidents of the AEA have included the profession's most noted researchers—including Nobel Prize recipients and governmental advisers.

—*Robert Whaples*

References

Coats, A. W. "The American Economic Association and the Economics Profession." *Journal of Economic Literature*, vol. 23 (1985): 1697–1727.

American Economic Association. http://www.vanderbilt. edu/AEA/; accessed January 15, 2003.

See also Volume 2: Economic Theories.

American Federation of Labor and Congress of Industrial Organizations (AFL-CIO)

Largest labor union in the United States.

The AFL-CIO formed in 1955 when the American Federation of Labor and the Congress of Industrial Organizations merged. During the 1950s and 1960s, the AFL-CIO concentrated on increasing the wages of union members and on improving employee benefits. Collective bargaining, legal under the Wagner Act, provided labor with a powerful bargaining tool, and the prosperity of the times resulted in employers agreeing to most union demands. However, by the 1970s economic stagflation (the coexistence of high unemployment and high inflation) resulted in many workers being laid off.

One of the most difficult challenges faced by the union was that the Japanese automakers flooded the U.S. market with their smaller, more fuel-efficient cars just when the Organization of Petroleum Exporting Countries (OPEC) placed embargoes on oil shipped to western nations. For the first time, AFL-CIO officials petitioned Congress to raise tariff rates on Japanese imports. Congress did not acquiesce to an increase, because tariff officials agreed that Americans wanted smaller vehicles and the Japanese had not engaged in unfair trade practices. The AFL-CIO continued to pressure the government, fearing the loss of American jobs. The Japanese agreed to voluntary export restrictions and began building plants in the United States to address the issue of lost jobs. Since the late 1980s, the union has opposed free trade. During the negotiating process for the North American Free Trade Agreement (NAFTA), the AFL-CIO pushed for provisions that would protect American workers and the environment and expressed its disapproval when Congress ratified the agreement without such provisions.

—*Cynthia Clark Northrup*

References

Sweeney, John J., and David Kusnet. *America Needs a Raise: Fighting for Economic Security and Social Justice.* New York: Replica Books, 2000.

Zieger, Robert. H. *American Workers, American Unions, 1920–1985.* Baltimore, MD: Johns Hopkins University Press, 1994.

See also Volume 1: Wagner Act; Volume 2: Labor.

American Inventors Protection Act of 1999

Act passed to modify existing patent law.

In November 1999, Congress passed the Intellectual Property and Communication Omnibus Act of 1999. Title IV of the act contains the American Inventors Protection Act. President Bill Clinton signed the bill on November 29, 1999, and it became effective in 2000. The American Inventors Protection Act established a first-to-invent infringement defense that allows inventors who have used the invention for one year prior to the filing date of the patent to defend themselves against this purported infringement. This clause is restricted to methods of doing business, not production or methods of manufacture. The act also authorizes the publication of foreign applications after 18 months and requires filers to make application to the U.S. Patent Office if they wish to restrict publication of their application within a specific time period. If the applicant agrees to have the patent application published, penalties for infringements prior to the issuance of the patent remain restricted to a reasonable royalty. In addition, Congress approved grant extensions of patents due to delays arising from the Patent and Trademark Office. The American Inventors Protection Act reduces patent fees and restricts disclosure of sensitive military or intelligence patent information. It also allows third parties to challenge the validity of a patent but restricts the involvement of third parties—they cannot participate in, nor will they receive a full transcript of, the interview of the patentee, and they cannot file a suit in civil court after the patent board issues a ruling that upholds the validity of the patent.

—*Cynthia Clark Northrup*

References

Elias, Stephen, and Richard Stim. *Patent, Copyright, and Trademark.* Berkeley, CA: Nolo, 2002.

See also Volume 2: Intellectual Property.

American Revolution (1775–1783)

Event that severed the political ties between Great Britain and its 13 North American colonies, setting the stage for the development of the United States of America.

In its Navigational Acts of the latter half of the seventeenth century, England created a closed mercantile system designed to control, regulate, and tax trade with its American colonies and to ensure that New World wealth flowed back to England. This system benefited the English state and economy, but for the American colonies it created problems, as their specie (gold and silver coin used as money) flowed back to England. As the trans-Atlantic trade flourished, the British encountered difficulties enforcing the restrictions on their distant colonies and failed to maintain a truly mercantile closed system that benefited the mother country. The American colonies quickly discovered that throughout the Atlantic trading world, trading partners other than the English were ready and willing to purchase their commodities. This illegal trade proved extremely profitable, and thus in the late seventeenth and eighteenth centuries, Americans engaged in smuggling on a regular basis. The profits provided Americans with money to consume English goods, while English merchants extended credit to Americans, thus allowing them to purchase even more products.

In 1763, the French and Indian War ended, with Britain as the victorious master of North America. A long series of wars had left the British state deeply in debt and ready to reexamine its empire for new sources of revenue. Parliament and the king's ministers decided that the colonies had not paid enough in taxes for their own support and maintenance. In 1764, Minister George Grenville and the British Parliament passed the Sugar Act as a way to curtail America's smuggling and increase Britain's revenue. This act reduced the tax on molasses, making it cheaper to purchase it legally. Parliament then passed the Currency Act, forbidding the use of paper money as legal tender. For Americans, these acts were intrusive and damaging interference in their economic growth and, when Parliament passed the Stamp Act in 1765, resistance began. The Stamp Act taxed all printed documents in the colonies, such as newspapers, legal documents, and playing cards—another example of England's increasing tyranny.

American resistance stemmed from the slogan "No taxation without representation." Americans believed that when the government created a new tax it took private property away from its citizens. Government could only do this with the permission of the people. Because the colonies held no seats in Britain's Parliament, they lacked representation and therefore could not be taxed. Parliament responded with the argument that all colonies received "virtual representation," as each member of Parliament represented all of the British Empire. Americans resisted the Stamp Act and argued against Britain's tyranny by effectively employing the strategy of non-importation, refusing to purchase any new British commodities or to pay their debts to British creditors. The Marquis of Rockingham repealed the Stamp Act for this reason.

During the Stamp Act crisis, Americans argued that there was a difference between a tax for revenue and a tax for the regulation of trade—Parliament, the Americans said, lacked the authority to pass the former but not the latter. The Townshend Acts (1767) were Parliament's attempt to establish an external regulatory tax against the colonies, but the Americans responded by implementing a boycott of British goods, as they had done during the previous attempt to implement an external tax. The Townshend Duties hurt British manufacturers and Britain's internal economy.

The Americans continued to combine their political and economic arguments against Britain's tyranny in the years leading up to the American Revolution. Colonists realized that to improve economically they needed a voice in the political process. The events that led to the Declaration of Independence and the war allowed American patriots to reject an imperial motherland thousands of miles away in favor of developing a political and economic ideology that better suited their needs. Americans fought against Britain to gain control over their own destiny, realizing that political sovereignty would eventually provide economic prosperity.

During the American Revolution, Americans struggled with a limited supply of specie (gold and silver). At the same time, many long-established trade relations between England and the colonists were disrupted, creating a trade deficit. Americans attempted to negotiate favorable trade relations with France and Spain, but the lack of economic and political strength forced the struggling U.S. government to accept terms that were less than favorable.

—*Ty M. Reese*

References
Becker, Robert A. *Revolution, Reform, and the Politics of American Taxation.* Baton Rouge: Louisiana State University Press, 1980.
Middlekauff, Robert. *The Glorious Cause: The American Revolution, 1763–1789.* New York: Oxford University Press, 1982.
See also Volume 1: Colonial Administration; Mercantilism; Navigation Acts; Non-Importation Act; Smuggling; Stamp Act; Stamp Act Congress; Sugar Act of 1764; Volume 2: Taxation.

American Stock Exchange (AMEX)

Second-oldest stock exchange in the United States.

The American Stock Exchange (AMEX) originally began as an outdoor trading center for government securities and for other companies in the mid-1850s. Known initially as "the Curb" because all transaction occurred outside, by 1908 it organized formally under the name of the New York Curb Agency after federal legislation tightened control over trading activities. In 1921, the exchange moved indoors to its present location at 86 Trinity Place in New York City. The New York Curb Agency traded commodities, monetary instruments, and the stocks of smaller companies not traded on the New York Stock Exchange. In 1953 the name changed again, this time to the American Stock Exchange. By the 1960s, the exchange had introduced state-of-the-art computer technology that by the 1970s included display screens with data about the equities market. Always aware of the need to remain on the cutting edge, the American Stock Exchange entered into an agreement in 2000 that allows investors to trade in AMEX stocks through the Singapore Exchange. The exchange continues to move toward the decimalization of price quotes from eighths to tenths of a point, a system commonly used in the United States. The major index of the American Stock Exchange is the American Composite. The exchange currently lists more than 800 companies.

—*Cynthia Clark Northrup*

References
Sobel, Robert. *AMEX: A History of the American Stock Exchange, 1921–1971.* New York: Weybright and Talley, 1972.
See also Volume 1: Nasdaq; New York Stock Exchange.

American System

Term used by Henry Clay, representative from Kentucky, in a speech before the House of Representatives on March 31, 1824, in favor of a protective tariff and a federal program designed to stimulate the nation's economic growth and reduce economic dependency on Europe.

During the "Era of Good Feelings" from 1816 to 1824, businesspeople in the North implemented the factory system, which was characterized by water-powered machinery and interchangeable parts. Factory owners wanted protection against European-made goods. At the same time, a transportation revolution occurred, with the extensive use of steamboats on major inland waterways and the state-supported construction of canals to link these waterways with coastal rivers that emptied into the Atlantic Ocean. The admission of six new western states also motivated public support for economic nationalism and the use of federal power to stimulate the expanding frontier.

Clay's speech on the 1824 protective tariff bill helped to ensure its passage in the House of Representatives by the narrow vote of 107 to 102. A conservative Senate modified the bill, but the average rate ended up at 37 percent—although some items, like imported wool, were as low as 30 percent. Clay believed that a protective tariff would greatly assist the growth of American industries and also provide a domestic market for farm produce. Because the protective tariff would generate surplus revenue for the federal treasury, Congress could use the funds to extend the National Road and construct turnpikes and canals to link northern factories to distant western markets.

Earlier, in 1816, to further promote economic nationalism, Clay had joined John C. Calhoun of South Carolina to recharter a Second Bank of the United States. Stepping down from the Speaker's chair, Clay told his colleagues that although he had opposed the rechartering of the First Bank of the United States in 1811, he believed Congress possessed the "constructive power" to incorporate such an institution. The House passed the bank bill by 80 to 71, and President James Madison signed it into law on April 10, 1816.

Clay's American System of protective tariffs, federal internal improvements, and a national bank aroused increasing opposition after the panic of 1819—a depression exceeded in severity only by the Great Depression of the 1930s—among planters, farmers, and land speculators, all of whom feared the consolidating power of the national government. They embraced an agrarian philosophy that feared the federal government growing stronger and aligning itself with manufacturing and financial interests against the interests of the farmer. Beginning in 1824, a political realignment began over the American System that led to the creation of two new political parties out of the old Jeffersonian-Republican consensus of the "Era of Good Feelings." One group, led by Clay, John Quincy Adams, and Daniel Webster, eventually called themselves Whigs; they believed in the American System and its economic nationalism. The Democrats, led by Andrew Jackson, Martin Van Buren, and John Calhoun, championed agrarian interests and states' rights against federal consolidation. In the 1832 presidential election Henry Clay, the Whig

candidate, ran against incumbent Andrew Jackson on the strength of the American System, with a special focus on Jackson's veto of the rechartering of the Second Bank of the United States. But Clay carried only six states: Massachusetts, Rhode Island, Connecticut, Maryland, Delaware, and Kentucky. A third-party candidate, William Wirt of the Antimasonic Party, won Vermont. Jackson carried all the rest. The American System, as a viable political program, never recovered from the defeat.

—*Robert P. Sutton*

References

Dangerfield, George. *The Era of Good Feelings.* New York: Harcourt, Brace and World, 1952.

———. *The Awakening of American Nationalism 1815–1828.* New York: Harper and Row, 1965.

Van Deusen, Glyndon G. *The Jacksonian Era 1828–1848.* Prospect Heights, IL: Waveland Press, 1992.

See also Volume 1: Clay, Henry; Jackson, Andrew; Panic of 1819.

AMEX

See American Stock Exchange.

Antidumping

Preventing the placing of goods on the market in large quantities at a price below normal cost to eliminate competition.

Dumping of goods into the United States by foreign manufacturers dates back to the early 1800s. After the Napoleonic Wars, both the British and the French dumped products on the U.S. market, and Congress responded by passing protectionist tariffs. The practice continued sporadically throughout the remainder of the nineteenth century, although not on a large scale. After World War I, American manufacturers and legislators once again feared an increase in dumping. Congress responded by passing the Fordney-McCumber Tariff, which returned the protectionist rates to their prewar level and provided for remedies against unfair foreign competition. The U.S. Antidumping Act of 1921 remained in effect until the adoption in 1967 of the international dumping code during the Kennedy Round of the General Agreement on Tariffs and Trade (GATT). This provision was included in GATT to ensure the acceptance by the signatories of the negotiations and to prevent foreign countries from using antidumping laws as tariff barriers against American manufacturers. In 1979 Congress authorized the secretary of the treasury to use broad discretionary powers to investigate antidumping claims and determine fair value and injury. Traditionally, antidumping laws have dealt with goods; changes in trade during the twentieth century forced Congress to address the social dumping of large labor-intensive surpluses produced overseas—by Japan during the first part of the twentieth century and, more recently, by China.

—*Cynthia Clark Northrup*

References
Eckes, Alfred E. *Opening America's Market: U.S. Foreign
    Policy since 1776.* Chapel Hill: University of North
    Carolina Press, 1995.
See also Volume 1: General Agreement on Tariffs and Trade;
    Protective Tariffs; World War I.

Anti-Imperialist League

Organization composed mainly of old-fashioned liberal New England politicians, publicists, and intellectuals, who challenged America's overseas territorial expansion at the close of the nineteenth century.

Members founded the Anti-Imperialist League at a meeting in Faneuil Hall in Boston on June 15, 1898, in direct response to U.S. expansion in the Caribbean and Pacific at the dawn of the new century. At the conclusion of the Spanish-American War of 1898, the government secured possession of Puerto Rico, Hawaii, and the Philippines. Many Americans feared that the nation's industrial growth would lead to an imperialist course of action in foreign affairs.

The center of the movement remained located in Boston, although local branches existed in Chicago, which became national headquarters briefly before the movement relocated back to Boston, St. Louis, San Francisco, and other cities. League leaders stoutly defended the Declaration of Independence and believed that all government derived its power from the consent of the governed. Gamaliel Bradford, Moorfield Storey, Edward Atkinson, Erving Winslow, and William A. Croffut led the battle against overseas territorial expansion. Political allies such as George S. Boutwell, Senator George F. Hoar, Representative Samuel W. McCall, and William Jennings Bryan combined forces with other prominent figures including David Starr Jordan, Samuel Gompers, William James, Andrew Carnegie, Carl Schurz, William Graham Sumner, and General Nelson A. Miles to argue that imperialism remained detrimental to the free-trade basis of competitive capitalism and diverted attention from the urgent need for domestic reform.

Writers William Vaughn Moody and Mark Twain lent their pens to the cause. Twain's powerful essay "To the Person Sitting in the Darkness" remains one of the most persuasive pieces of anti-imperialist literature published in support of the league's objectives.

Specifically, the league sought to discourage the McKinley administration from seizing the Philippines. Senate ratification of the Treaty of Peace Between the United States and Spain (known as the Paris Peace Treaty) on February 6, 1899, however—followed two days later by the eruption of the Filipino-American War—transformed the league into a national movement with a mass constituency. The league worked with other anti-imperialist elements, and its membership expanded to more than 30,000 members. By October 1898, its campaign had reached close to 30 states. Finding receptive audiences, anti-imperialists distributed literature and placed speakers around the country as they pursued two simple goals: an immediate suspension of hostilities in the Philippines and a congressional pledge of Philippine independence.

The league's periodical, the *Anti-Imperialist,* and pamphlets like Atkinson's *The Cost of a National Crime* and *The Hell of War and Its Penalties* provided ample illustrations of the "repulsive and ghastly slaughter in the guerilla warfare in the Philippines." But the league's most original and compelling arguments focused on economic issues. Atkinson, a retired textile manufacturer, refuted the arguments of businesspeople who maintained that America's industrial economy would profit from the nation's outward thrust. He pointed out that American sugar and hemp growers would face competition from Philippine producers and that American laborers would experience competition as well. New England jurist Storey boldly declared his opposition to the use of foreign capital to develop the Philippines since it would impose foreign influence on the islands. General Miles weighed in by observing that Wall Street would benefit the most from U.S. control of the Philippines.

Despite leveling a multitude of compelling economic arguments, the league's movement had several contradictory elements. Southern anti-imperialists observed that American boys had not enlisted "to fight niggers" (referring to nonwhite Filipinos), while in Chicago the Black Man's Burden Association objected strenuously to the Filipino-American War's Anglo-Saxon racist overtones. Many in the movement had supported the Spanish-American War and failed to object to the colonial annexation of nearby Puerto Rico. Others opposed to colonial annexation rested their beliefs not so much on the principle of self-determination but rather in the conviction that economic imperialism would proceed more safely and smoothly if it was not burdened by the tasks of colonial administration. Whatever the position, the anti-imperialist effort rested more on abstract political and ideological principles than on strictly economic, religious, constitutional, or humanitarian considerations.

Marked by contradictory positions, the Anti-Imperialist League and its accompanying movement quickly dissolved, even with the revelation of atrocities committed in the Philippines by American troops. During the winter of 1899–1900, anti-imperialist efforts slipped from a campaign of mass mobilization into the utter confusion of electoral politics. Unable to halt war through popular agitation, the leaders of the league toyed with the prospect of mounting a third-party effort for the 1900 presidential election.

Surprisingly, most decided to support the candidacy of William Jennings Bryan, the Democratic leader who, though grudgingly, supported Senate ratification of the Paris treaty, which granted the United States control over the Philippines. This fact, combined with the rejection of Bryan's candidacy by noted industrialist Andrew Carnegie (who thought Bryan a demagogue) and the success of American military forces in grinding down the "insurrection," resulted in a McKinley victory even more decisive than in the election of 1896.

Between 250,000 and 600,000 Filipinos died as a result of the war, compared with 7,000 American troops. Early in February 1902, U.S. troops captured Filipino leader Emilio Aquinaldo. Within a few months Theodore Roosevelt, who had become president upon McKinley's assassination the previous year, declared the war over. Congress immediately declared that the Philippines were to be constituted an unorganized territory of the United States. The Anti-Imperialist League's influence proved ineffective in subsequent matters involving foreign policy.

—Charles F. Howlett

References

Beisner, Robert L. *Twelve against Empire: The Anti-Imperialists, 1898–1900.* Chicago: University of Chicago Press, 1985.

Chatfield, Charles. *The American Peace Movement: Ideals and Activism.* New York: Twayne Publishers, 1992.

Herman, Sondra R. *Eleven against Empire: Studies in American Internationalist Thought, 1898–1921.* Stanford, CA: Stanford University Press, 1969.

Schirmer, Daniel B. *Republic or Empire: American Resistance to the Philippine War.* Cambridge, MA: Schenkman, 1972.

Tompkins, E. Berkeley. "The Old Guard: A Study of Anti-Imperialist Leadership." *Historian,* vol. 30 (May 1968): 360–388.

Welch, Richard E. *Response to Imperialism: The United States and the Philippine American War, 1898–1902.* Chapel Hill: University of North Carolina Press, 1972.

See also Volume 1: Philippines; Roosevelt, Theodore; Spanish-American War.

Anti-Inflation Act of 1942

See Emergency Price Control Act, 1942.

Antitrust Suits

Lawsuits arising when competitors engage in prohibited practices like fixing prices, rigging bids, or allocating customers, which causes prices to rise to artificially high levels or reduces competition.

Antitrust laws prohibit practices restraining trade, reducing competition, and promoting or maintaining monopoly power in virtually all industries. The Sherman Anti-Trust Act, the Clayton Anti-Trust Act, and the Federal Trade Commission Act enable the Department of Justice to enforce federal antitrust laws through criminal and civil actions. The Federal Trade Commission (FTC) and private citizens may also sue civilly. Similar laws ratified as early as 1880 in some states are enforced through the offices of state attorneys general. The 1890 Sherman Act outlaws all contracts, combinations, and conspiracies that unreasonably restrain interstate and foreign trade. Violations are usually punished as criminal felonies. The 1914 Clayton Act prohibits mergers or acquisitions likely to lesson competition. The Federal Trade Commission Act, implemented in 1914, empowers the president or Congress to investigate and report facts regarding alleged antitrust violations by any corporation.

Antitrust acts embodied popular political viewpoints in the late nineteenth and early twentieth centuries. Presidents Benjamin Harrison, Theodore Roosevelt, William Taft, and Woodrow Wilson advocated government oversight of large corporations and trust busting. In 1912 Supreme Court Justice Louis Brandeis argued that industrial giants were potentially dangerous forces capable of controlling politicians and undermining consumer interests.

Greater resources bolstered the Justice Department's antitrust enforcement in the 1930s. Under Chief Thurman Arnold, a Roosevelt appointee, the division's budget quadrupled within three years. Cartels and monopolies were investigated, and a landmark 1945 case against Alcoa found that the company unlawfully wielded monopoly power over the aluminum industry. In the 1950s and 1960s, the Warren Supreme Court interpreted the Celler-Kefauver Act of 1950 as establishing a presumption of illegality for mergers in concentrated industries between competitors with a combined market share as low as 30 percent. Some mergers with combined market shares below 10 percent were condemned. Historian Richard Hofstadter noted in the mid-1960s that businesspeople are always cognizant of antitrust laws.

The Johnson, Nixon, Ford, and Carter administrations proceeded with vigorous antitrust enforcement. Seed money for state investigations provided by the Ford administration in the mid-1970s established a formidable army of populist state attorneys general under the umbrella of the National Association of Attorneys General (NAAG). They challenged mergers approved by federal agencies and launched *parens patraie* (the state acting as "the father of the country") suits against manufacturers guilty of vertical price maintenance. The conservative, antipopulist "Chicago School" of antitrust theory also surfaced in the 1970s. Robert Bork's 1978 book, *The Antitrust Paradox: A Policy at War with Itself,* recommended that the sole objective of antitrust law should be maximization of "consumer welfare." The Chicago School viewed attempts to curtail industrial consolidation as undermining economic efficiency.

The Reagan administration consistently appointed Chicago School scholars to federal courts, and Justice Department Antitrust Division Chief William Baxter disposed of a massive case against IBM and announced the settlement of the historic AT&T breakup. He also called for "merger guidelines" designed to determine whether prices were unilaterally or collectively raised above competitive levels. Beginning in the early 1990s, antitrust policy shifted toward moderate domestic pursuits and aggressive international protections. Federal and state interaction was encouraged, and United States officials asserted the right to employ federal antitrust laws against anticompetitive foreign conduct, which critics labeled antitrust imperialism. In 1991 the Antitrust Division of the Justice Department, the FTC, and the European Union's competition authority jointly announced the execution of an Antitrust Enforcement Cooperation Agreement.

Clinton administration appointees advocated the "post-Chicago School"—a movement championing consumer welfare standards to preserve competition rather than unfettered freedom for producers. In the late 1990s the Antitrust Division pursued Microsoft Corporation with the help of state attorneys general, signaling the most significant government legal challenge in more than 20 years.

Issues of intellectual property complicate modern antitrust designations. Although past antitrust attention focused on exorbitant prices and the reduction of competition, scholars in the twenty-first century are investigating whether high-technology mergers result in less innovation. In the early nineteenth century, Standard Oil Company violated antitrust rules by controlling petroleum transportation, refining, and distribution. Conversely, software maker Microsoft protects the source code to its computer operating system and all adjoining application interfaces, leading to claims of predatory abuses. Determining how to assess the consequences of this power and the implications for competitive firms will decide which companies struggle or survive in emerging markets that dominate the domestic and world economies.

—*R. Jake Sudderth*

References

Brodley, Joseph F. "Post-Chicago Economics and Workable Legal Policy." *Antitrust Law Journal,* vol. 63, no. 2 (1995): 683.

Hofstadter, Richard, ed. *The Paranoid Style in American Politics and Other Essays.* New York: Alfred A. Knopf, 1965.

Roy, William G. *Socializing Capital: The Rise of The Large Industrial Corporation in America.* Princeton, NJ: Princeton University Press, 1997.

Skitol, Robert A. "The Shifting Sands of Antitrust Policy: Where It Has Been, Where It Is Now, Where It Will Be in Its Third Century." *Cornell Journal of Law and Public Policy,* vol. 9, no. 1 (Fall 1999): 239–266.

Sullivan, Lawrence A. "Post-Chicago Economics: Economists, Lawyers, Judges, and Enforcement Officials in a Less Determinate Theoretical World." *Antitrust Law Journal,* vol. 63, no. 2 (1995): 669–674.

See also Volume 1: Clayton Anti-Trust Act; Federal Trade Commission Act; Microsoft; Roosevelt, Theodore; Sherman Anti-Trust Act; Standard Oil; Wilson, Woodrow.

Antiunion Policies

Position taken by the federal government toward labor unions during the nineteenth century.

After the Civil War the start of the industrial revolution in the United States led to dramatic changes in labor. Traditionally, Americans owned small proprietorships or worked as apprentices for a skilled master. With the introduction of automated machinery and the specialization of tasks, workers found their economic position declining. Employers hired unskilled laborers for many of the positions and increasingly demanded longer and longer hours at a lower wage from their workers. Consequently, various occupations formed societies similar to the guilds of Europe. At first these organizations focused on a particular skilled craft, but eventually unions accepted unskilled workers to their ranks as well.

The rise of labor unions led to an increase in demands on the part of the workers for shorter hours, better pay, and safer working conditions. Employers realized that any concessions to labor would ultimately reduce profits, so negotiations usually proved futile to the labor unions. By the 1880s labor strikes began to occur with some frequency, often resulting in violence and bloodshed. The first of the big strikes occurred in 1892 at Andrew Carnegie's Homestead Steel Plant, where workers staged a sit-in until management agreed to their demands. The manager of the plant called in Pinkerton detectives to remove the strikers, and violence erupted. When the management asked the federal government for assistance, the president authorized the use of the National Guard. From this first involvement through the end of the nineteenth century, the federal government continued this policy of assisting business owners against the workers.

The Supreme Court maintained a similar policy. As reformers within the government fought for increased restrictions on the monopolistic practices of big business, Congress debated and passed the Sherman Anti-Trust Act, which outlawed such monopolies. On several occasions the Supreme Court heard cases involving alleged monopolistic practices, the most famous being *United States v. E. C. Knight & Co.* In this case, the high Court ruled that the company had not violated the Sherman Anti-Trust Act since it only controlled 98 percent of the sugar market—that left 2 percent for the competition. Yet when the American Railways Union went on strike against the Pullman Palace Car Company in 1894, the Court ruled that the union had violated the act and held the union president, Eugene V. Debs, responsible. The majority opinion declared that because the union had joined with other unions to shut down the entire railroad, it had in essence created a monopoly.

As the era of big business passed and legislative reformers successfully reduced the high tariffs that had protected these businesses, labor unions earned more respect from the government. By the time of the Great Depression, Congress had passed measures such as Section 7a of the National Industrial Recovery Act, allowing unions to picket, strike, and engage in collective bargaining. The Supreme Court declared the entire act unconstitutional, but Congress replaced Section 7a with the Wagner Act, thus ensuring continued protection of union activities. Although the federal government restricted some of the power of the unions in the immediate post–World War II period, no efforts have occurred to deny unions protection under federal law.

—*Cynthia Clark Northrup*

References

Dubofsky, Melvyn. *Hard Work: The Making of Labor History.* Urbana: University of Illinois Press, 2000.

See also Volume 1: National Industrial Recovery Act; New Deal; Pullman Strike; Sherman Anti-Trust Act; *United States v. E. C. Knight & Co.;* Wagner Act.

Arab Oil Embargo (1973–1974)

An embargo—a stoppage of oil shipments from OPEC countries to the West—that created a severe energy crisis among the western industrialized nations.

Arab displeasure with the pro-Israeli policy of the United States and some European countries during the October 1973 Yom Kippur war in the Middle East occasioned the imposition of an oil embargo by the Organization of Petroleum Exporting Countries (OPEC) on October 18, 1973. This embargo remained in effect until March 18, 1974.

The ramifications, especially for the United States, soon became evident. The most visible sign in the United States was long lines at service stations, many of which, if not all, began to close on Sundays as their supplies of gasoline dwindled.

Another major consequence of the embargo involved the phenomenal increase in the per-barrel price of crude oil worldwide. That inflation, while important during the five months of the actual embargo, continued to affect prices until the end of 1985, when the per-barrel cost of oil finally began to moderate. Oil prices reached their peak levels in 1980 and 1981, when they ranged between $35 and $40 per barrel—the latter figure prevailing during the Iranian Revolution of 1981.

With this global oil boom triggered by the Arab oil embargo, oil companies, particularly in the United States, garnered tremendous earnings. American companies showed record profits in 1973, up on average 48 percent from 1972. Profits continued to rise, too. In the first six months of 1974 they jumped 82 percent over their level a year earlier.

The American public, including most of its congressional representatives, raised a groundswell of opposition. Congress implemented two pieces of legislation of paramount importance. The first came in 1975, when Congress disallowed the 27 percent depletion allowance for the major oil companies, retaining it only for small producers. This allowance, dating from 1926, had permitted American oil companies to reduce their taxable income by as much as 27 percent per company. The second action took place during the administration of President Jimmy Carter. In 1980 Congress, responding to recurring energy shortages, rising energy costs, and the reports of record profits by major American oil companies, imposed the Windfall Profits Tax. The act included the largest tax ever imposed on a single industry and was expected to increase federal revenues by at least $227 billion during the 1980s.

Congress also created the Strategic Petroleum Reserve (SPR) in 1976. The SPR provided for the storage of crude in underground reservoirs to be held in reserve and used only in the event of a future crisis in oil supplies. The SPR attained its maximum storage in 1994 of 592 million barrels.

—*Keith L. Miller*

References

Energy Information Administration. *Twenty-fifth Anniversary of the 1973 Oil Embargo: Energy Trends since the First Major U.S. Energy Crisis.* Washington, DC: U.S. Government Printing Office, 1998.

Grotton, Martha V., ed. *Congress and the Nation.* Vol. 5, 1977–1980, Government Series. Washington, DC: Congressional Quarterly Press, 1981.

O'Conner, Patricia Ann, ed. "Congress and the Nation." *Congressional Quarterly,* vol. 4 (1977): 201, 203.

See also Volume 1: Energy.

Articles of Confederation (1776–1789)

Document that established the interim government in power from the American Revolution in 1777 until the ratification of the U.S. Constitution in 1789.

The Confederation operated as a loose arrangement, rather than a federal system. It was a central government that could ask for funds, supplies, and troops but had no method to compel the states to comply. The executive under the Confederation, an elected leader of the Congress who held a one-year term, remained extraordinarily weak. Amendments to the Confederation required a unanimous vote of the participants, making it difficult to add measures like federal courts, trade regulations, or uniform taxes. This system, given time, might have matured into one resembling the British parliamentary cabinet, with increasingly powerful departments.

Financial pressures doomed the Confederation. With the central government unable to dictate trade policy, the colonies engaged separately with foreign powers, much to their detriment. Meanwhile, the colonies issued separate money, competed for resources, and laid different tariffs on incoming foreign goods. The shortage of cash and lack of infrastructure hindered growing industry, while foreclosures on mortgages outraged many war veterans, and debtors demanded increased circulation of paper money. Shays' Rebellion, an uprising in Massachusetts against poll and land taxes and protesting that citizens were unable to pay for goods using commodities like corn and whiskey, illustrated the flaws of the Confederation and sparked calls for a stronger central government.

The revolutionary spirit that had prompted the Confederation and that feared the tyranny of a strong central authority faded when merchants, bankers, and crafts workers demanded a steady money supply, central planning, and use of resources to encourage American manufacturing and business. Additionally, some of the revolution's leaders, for example, John Adams, George Washington, and James Madison, disapproved of the regionalism and ruthless competition among the new states, reevaluating their assumptions that the new nation would be governed best by being governed least. Against the wishes of the Anti-Federalists, many of them farmers, the Articles of Confederation were eventually relegated to retirement in favor of the new U.S. Constitution. Interim steps toward a federal government included the 1786 Annapolis Convention, arranged by George Washington to decide the navigation rights to the Potomac River and Chesapeake Bay, and the Constitutional Convention of 1787.

Despite its weaknesses, the Confederation calmed Americans' fears of tyranny, provided a government through the Revolutionary War, negotiated the Treaty of 1783, and prevented the seizure of the infant state by any clique of politicians. Although economically disadvantageous, the Confederation survived the fires of the revolution and 12 years of execution before being replaced by a stronger, centralized system.

—*Margaret Sankey*

References

Jensen, Merrill. *The Articles of Confederation*. Madison: University of Wisconsin Press, 1940.

Ketchem, Ralph, ed. *The Anti-Federalist Papers and the Constitutional Convention Debates*. New York: New American Library, 1986.

See also Volume 1: American Revolution; Constitution.

ATO

See Advanced Technology Office.

Automobile

A typically four-wheeled automotive vehicle designed for transportation invented in the late nineteenth century and destined to have a profound influence on the American economy.

The modern automobile first appeared on the market in the 1880s, although it is impossible to credit a single inventor with its creation. Key inventors included Germans Gottlieb Daimler, who produced the first modern gas engine and mounted it on a carriage in 1886, and Karl Benz, who patented a gas-powered vehicle that same year and integrated it into a three-, then four-wheel, chassis. Though Panhard and Levassor became the world's first automobile company, the Benz Company became the world's largest producer of automobiles by 1900. Charles and Frank Duryea started making automobiles in the United States as early as 1888, but the U.S. automobile industry did not really start until the turn of the twentieth century. In 1899, Ransom Olds moved to Detroit and started the Olds Motor Works, and in 1901 he began to manufacture a standard, relatively affordable, automobile. In 1903, Henry Ford formed his own company, and in 1908 he revolutionized the American automobile industry with his Model T. Ford designed the Model T for the average American, seeking to sell the car to farmers and small business people. This design became even more affordable when Ford moved production to a new assembly-line factory in Highland Park, Michigan. With this new system of production, which he coined "mass production," the Model T became increasingly affordable, even to the factory workers who produced the cars. By 1922 it cost just $225. Nearly as important as the Model T's mass-producible design was the network of local dealers and consumer loan opportunities Ford created. Ford brought production of the Model T to an end in 1927 after 15 million Model Ts had rolled off the assembly line. Ford and the Model T inspired a host of competitors, including General Motors (1908).

By 1925 a majority of Americans owned cars. The proliferation of the automobile in the United States led to fundamental cultural, social, and economic changes. Because the car made cities accessible from greater distances, suburbs dependent on automobile traffic began to develop in the 1920s; they had another explosive growth period after World War II. The car spawned a host of leisure and lifestyle institutions, from the self-service grocery store (1916) to the shopping mall (1923) to the drive-in movie (1933). Car travel became a vacation activity, and in 1926 the first motel opened in San Luis Obispo, California.

With the flood of cars came the need for new infrastructure and regulation. The Federal Road Act of 1916 began the federal government's effort to transform muddy roads into a network of interconnected paved highways. In the 1954 Federal-Aid Highway Act, President Dwight D. Eisenhower authorized $175 million in federal funds on a 60–40 matching basis to states for the construction of the interstate highway system.

Cars themselves became the target of increased safety engineering in the 1950s and 1960s with the introduction of technologies borrowed from race cars, such as seat belts, disc brakes, the collapsible steering column, and head rests. Following the lead of California, the first state to pass emission controls, Congress passed the 1970 Clean Air Act banning leaded gasoline and requiring catalytic converters to reduce the toxic emissions of automobiles. Taking advantage of this legislation and the oil crises of the 1970s, smaller, more fuel-efficient Japanese cars challenged Detroit, and by 1980 they had captured nearly 30 percent of the American market.

American manufacturers regained a portion of their former market share in the 1980s as consumers demanded larger, more powerful cars. Through mergers and partnerships with German and Japanese automakers, American manufacturers introduced cars designed with German influence and produced using Japanese quality control techniques. In addition, globalization has redistributed the American automobile industry to new regions such as Toyota's Kentucky plant, BMW's South Carolina operations, and Daimler-Chrysler's Alabama factory. American manufacturers also moved some production to Mexico and Canada. A major trade policy issue arose in the 1990s with U.S. interests pushing for access to protected Asian markets.

—*Ann Johnson*

References

Flink, James J. *The Automobile Age*. Cambridge, MA: MIT Press, 1990.

Jennings, Jan, ed. *Roadside America: The Car in Design and Culture*. Ames: Iowa State University Press, 1990.

Motor Vehicles Manufacturers Association. *Motor Vehicle Facts and Figures*. Detroit, MI: Automobile Manufacturers Association, annual publication.

See also Volume 1: Federal Highway Act of 1956; North American Free Trade Agreement.

Aviation

An industry focused on the manufacture, design, development, and operation of aircraft that had its birth in the early years of the twentieth century.

From 1917 to 2002, the American aviation industry consisted of a relatively small number of firms that enjoyed a high degree of government patronage. These industries benefited from a de facto industrial policy: The U.S. government has, subsidized plant construction, funded research and development (R&D), provided guaranteed markets, protected weak firms, promoted the industry's global competitiveness, and collaborated with it on strategic planning.

Before 1914, aircraft were essentially produced by hand. The outbreak of World War I precipitated the creation of an aviation industry, which produced some 14,000 aircraft and 20,000 engines from 1917 to 1919 (compared with 411 aircraft in 1916). Government procurement imploded in 1919 with the end of the war, and commercial aviation was as yet economically unavailable. Thus, government contracts to deliver mail by air and to produce military aircraft provided an essential subsidy, constituting 60 to 90 percent of the aviation industry's total sales between the world wars. This patronage permitted nine airframe and two engine manufacturers to dominate the industry, but it encouraged tremendous innovation in the production of long-range, all-metal monoplanes with excellent engines and instruments.

During World War II, American production rose from 2,141 aircraft in 1939 to 96,318 in 1944. The U.S. wartime total of 300,000 aircraft far exceeded that for the other Allies and for the Allies' opponents. The aviation industry hired more than 2 million workers (12 percent of the workforce), including many women and blacks, and built massive production facilities, particularly in the South and West. Infrastructure and skilled labor that developed during the war placed American aviation in a commanding postwar position, and companies that produced bombers soon retooled to build passenger transports.

After the war, military aviation sales contracted dramatically, and the workforce shrank to 10 percent of wartime levels. However, the onset of the cold war and expanding commercial markets partly offset these difficulties. Demand for civil aviation doubled in the 1950s and increased again when jet transports entered service in 1958. America produced 87 percent of all jet airliners from 1958 to 1985. Nevertheless, most aerospace firms depended on military contracts for 50 to 90 percent of their business during the cold war. These contracts centered on the production of supersonic fighters, long-range jet bombers, and ballistic missiles. Aerospace companies absorbed 20 to 30 percent of all government R&D expenditures until 1965, and the aerospace industry became the nation's largest employer. Aerospace also drove a major expansion of the related computer, communications, and electronics industries, giving rise to the integrated circuit chip, among other products.

The 1990s brought new challenges to the aerospace industry, as military budgets fell after the cold war. Major corporations were forced to merge (e.g., Northrop and Grumman, Lockheed and Martin Marietta) and the workforce declined 40 percent (to 790,000) between 1990 and 2001. Aerospace corporations often "teamed" with ostensible competitors and collaborated with foreign companies to penetrate foreign markets. The industry sought to shift emphasis to commercial production (government contracts accounted for 40 percent of total revenue in 2001, down from 60 percent in 1990), and exports proved particularly important (commercial exports accounted for about 27 percent of aerospace revenue in 2001). This strategy may prove difficult to sustain in the face of increasing competition from heavily subsidized European and Japanese manufacturers.

—*James D. Perry*

References

Bilstein, Roger E. *The American Aerospace Industry.* New York: Twayne Publishers, 1996.

Markusen, Ann, and Joel Yudken. *Dismantling the Cold War Economy.* New York: Basic Books, 1992.

See also Volume 1: World War I; World War II.

B

Baby Boom

Explosive population increase that occurred between 1946 and 1964.

After World War II, the United States experienced an abnormal number of births per year. In 1940, records indicate that about 2.6 million Americans were born. As servicemen and servicewomen returned home after World War II, married, and had more children, traditional living arrangements changed. Previously, young married couples had lived with their parents, but the availability of affordable housing in the suburbs created a demographic shift. By 1946, the number of births had increased to 3.4 million, and it peaked in 1957 with 4.3 million births. In 1964 the number of children born remained high (4 million); the following year, the figure dropped to 3.7 million, signaling the end of the baby boom generation.

This population expansion produced numerous economic consequences. As the baby boom generation entered the workplace, their wages generated more wealth in the United States, and the deduction of their Social Security tax ensured the continuation of the program for elderly Americans. In 1964, the baby boomers made up 40 percent of the population. Such a large concentration of young people altered American culture and society in ways ranging from rock and roll music to increased use of the automobile. Because there were more consumers and more disposable income, marketing techniques also changed to create a need for more consumer goods, which in turn fueled the economy.

Between 1940 and 1994, 202 million Americans were born, about 28 percent of the population as of the year 2002. Another major economic impact of this generation will most likely be felt as these workers retire. Because Congress has continuously (since the 1960s) borrowed money from the Social Security fund, payout of future benefits will place an added burden on the federal budget over the next several decades. Consequently, younger Americans will be forced to pay higher taxes, which will reduce their disposable income and reduce consumer spending.

—*Cynthia Clark Northrup*

References

Smith, Olivia J., ed. *Aging in America*. New York: H. W. Wilson, 2000.

See also Volume 1: Levittown; World War II.

Bacon, Nathaniel (1647–1676)

Colonist responsible for the outbreak of Bacon's rebellion in the Virginia Colony in the 1670s.

Born January 2, 1647, in Suffolk, England, to wealthy parents, Nathaniel Bacon graduated from Cambridge University. His family, staunch supporters of Oliver Cromwell and the Puritans, who gained control in England after the beheading of Charles I during the Great Civil War, fell out of favor, and Bacon himself had already earned the reputation of being a hot-tempered, landless young man with little future. Unwelcome in England, Bacon was sent to the Virginia Colony to make his fortune. He arrived well-connected in 1674—his cousin was the wife of the governor, William Berkeley. Bacon soon had a seat on the governor's council and a generous land grant. But he gravitated toward the rivals of the long-serving, royalist Berkeley, especially those newly arrived in the colonies or recently freed from indenture. Many of these people became squatters on the Western frontier, and they clashed with Berkeley over his policy of fur trade with the Native Americans, a policy that limited new settlement on Indian lands.

Following a series of squabbles between settlers and Indians in 1676, in which his overseer died, Bacon assumed command of a large force of vigilantes who pushed for all-out war on the local Native American population after the government refused to retaliate against an Indian attack. When Berkeley refused to grant Bacon official command and declared him a rebel against the colonial government, Bacon attacked Jamestown and burned it, forcing Berkeley to flee to safety and summon help from England. Meanwhile, Bacon and his men ruthlessly pursued all of the natives they could find to fight, pushing the Pamunkey into the Great Dismal Swamp, where Bacon caught a terrible swamp fever and died on October 26, 1676. Without Bacon, the movement fell apart, and Berkeley executed many of its leaders. Although Bacon's rebellion failed, it opened new lands on the frontier belonging to the defeated Indian tribes, and it opened the corridors of power in Virginia to newer arrivals because the Crown removed Governor Berkeley from office after the rebellion.

—*Margaret Sankey*

References

Middlekauff, Robert. *Bacon's Rebellion.* Chicago: Rand McNally, 1964.

Washburn, Wilcomb A. *The Governor and the Rebel: A History of Bacon's Rebellion.* Chapel Hill: University of North Carolina Press, published for the Institute of Early American History and Culture at Williamsburg, Virginia, 1957.

Web, Stephen Saunders. *1676: The End of American Independence.* New York: Alfred A. Knopf, 1984.

See also Volume 1: Bacon's Rebellion.

Bacon's Rebellion (1676)

Uprising in the Virginia Colony over the government's refusal to retaliate against an Indian attack—the rebellion ultimately opened up Western lands for the settlers.

By the 1670s, Virginia society suffered under the strain of new immigration from England, which pushed the frontiers of the colony into land belonging to the Powhatan Confederation and other Native American neighbors. The former indentured servants and new arrivals had little patience with the policies of long-serving royalist governor William Berkeley, who advocated a policy of trade with the tribes, particularly in fur, from which he and his political allies profited. Under the leadership of a young, Cambridge-educated émigré, Nathaniel Bacon, whose plantation overseer had died in a raid by the Doeg tribe (a raid stemming from a series of misunderstandings and attacks by settlers), many discontented Virginia settlers wanted to wage war against the Indians and seize their land.

Berkeley refused, citing cost and the disruption of relations with the natives. Bacon responded by marching his vigilante army on the capitol at Jamestown, capturing it, and driving the governor from his residence into the safety of a sheltered plantation, where he waited for help from England. Meanwhile, Bacon burned Jamestown and led his men on an all-out attack on the Pamunkey Indians, who had nothing to do with the attacks that had provoked Bacon in the first place. The rebels chased the Pamunkey into the Great Dismal Swamp, where Bacon and many of his men caught swamp fever, of which Bacon died shortly thereafter. Berkeley restored order with the help of troops from England and hung 23 of the rebels before being retired by Charles II. Bacon's rebellion failed, but it opened Virginia politics and land to new arrivals and the recently freed indentured servants, who took much of the land conquered by Bacon from surrounding tribes.

Paranoia like that of Bacon's toward the natives also broke out in 1692 in Salem, Massachusetts, manifesting itself in the Salem witch trials, which targeted recently emigrated settlers who were considered outsiders by the Puritan colonists.

—*Margaret Sankey*

References

Middlekauff, Robert. *Bacon's Rebellion.* Chicago: Rand McNally, 1964.

Washburn, Wilcomb A. *The Governor and the Rebel: A History of Bacon's Rebellion.* Chapel Hill: University of North Carolina Press, published for the Institute of Early American History and Culture at Williamsburg, Virginia, 1957.

Web, Stephen Saunders. *1676: The End of American Independence.* New York: Alfred A. Knopf, 1984.

See also Volume 1: Bacon, Nathaniel.

Bakke v. Board of Regents of California (June 28, 1978)

Controversial 5 to 4 decision handed down June 28, 1978, in which the Supreme Court declared unconstitutional rigid racial quotas, or "set-asides," for admission to a university medical school.

Seeking greater racial diversity, in 1978 the University of California Medical School at Davis set aside 16 of the 100 freshman slots (out of 2,664 applicants) for African American, Asian, Native American, and Latino applicants, and the school established lower academic requirements for these individuals than for the 84 regular-admission candidates. Alan Bakke, a white male, had twice applied to the medical school, and both times the admissions board rejected his application. He then discovered that he had higher scores on the medical school examination than those who had been admitted under the set-aside quotas. He filed a lawsuit that went to the California Superior Court, arguing that the set-aside program violated his rights under Title VI of the 1964 Civil Rights Act, which forbids racial or ethnic quotas in any state program receiving federal funds. He also claimed that the Davis admissions program violated the equal protection clause of the Fourteenth Amendment. The California court agreed with Bakke but refused to order the university to admit him, claiming he had not proven that he would have qualified for admission without the restrictions of the quotas.

Bakke appealed to the U.S. Supreme Court, which heard arguments on October 12, 1977. Although the Court issued six opinions, Justice F. Lewis Powell Jr. announced the decision. He wrote that the "plain meaning" of Title VI of the 1964 Civil Rights Act prohibited the exclusion of any individual solely on racial grounds in federally funded state programs. He further asserted that the set-aside program at the Davis medical school "totally excluded" Bakke from competing "with applicants from the preferred groups for the special admission seats" and therefore denied him the "equal protection" required by the Fourteenth Amendment. However, Powell justified a less rigid, competitive program of admission in which the university could consider race and ethnicity as one of many factors in the goal of establishing a "diverse student body."

The decision had little immediate impact on set-aside programs at other university postgraduate schools. It only restricted the use of quotas in admissions in state medical schools and left open later challenges of quotas in law schools and graduate schools.

—*Robert P. Sutton*

References

Jeffries, John C. *Justice Lewis F. Powell, Jr.: Biography*. New York: Scribner's, 1994.

O'Neill, Timothy J. *Bakke and the Politics of Equality*. Middletown, CT: Wesleyan University Press, 1985.

Wilkinson, J. Harvie. *From Brown to Bakke: The Supreme Court and School Integration*. New York: Oxford University Press, 1979.

See also Volume 2: Education.

Balance of Payments

Financial summary of all international transactions.

The Bureau of Economic Analysis (BEA) under the U.S. Department of Commerce records transactions involving the international transfer of goods, services, income, financial claims, or gifts. Used as an indicator of the flow of goods and services between the United States and other parts of the world, the strength of the balance of payments affects the credit standing of the federal government. The stronger the financial statistics, the better the nation's position.

The transfer of goods and services—or unilateral transfers—is recorded in the current account; the capital account consists of the transfer of financial assets and liabilities. Using the traditional accounting method of double-entry record keeping, entries are recorded in a manner in which the debits and credits always balance. When recording the balance of payments for the United States, the BEA includes all transactions for the 50 states, the District of Columbia, the Commonwealth of Puerto Rico, American Samoa, Guam, Midway Island, the Virgin Islands, Wake Island, and all other U.S. territories and possessions (Marshall Islands, Federated States of Micronesia, Northern Marianas, and Palau). Under the terms of the Bretton Woods agreement signed in 1945, section 8, the U.S. government has the legal authority to collect the data on the balance of payments. The Office of Management and Budget publishes the balance of payments report on a quarterly basis ten weeks after the end of each quarter. The International Monetary Fund uses the information provided by the BEA to establish currency conversion rates.

—*Cynthia Clark Northrup*

References

Bureau of Economic Analysis. *Balance of Payments of the United States: Concepts, Data Sources, and Estimating Procedures*. Washington, DC: U.S. Government Printing Office, 1990.

See also Volume 2: Trade Policy.

Balance of Trade

Difference between the value of total imports and exports of a country over a specific period of time.

The merchandise balance of trade refers to the difference between a country's merchandise exports and merchandise imports. If exports exceed imports, a trade surplus or favorable balance of trade is being realized. If imports exceed exports, a trade deficit or unfavorable balance of trade occurs. Since the early 1980s, the United States has experienced a rapidly growing international trade deficit, in which imports exceed exports. The *Survey of Current Business*, published in March 1985, showed that during the previous year the U.S. merchandise exports of $220 billion did not earn the nation enough foreign monies to finance its merchandise imports of $328 billion. In March 2003 the United States imported $126.3 billion and exported $82.8 billion for a trade deficit of $43.5 billion.

Causes of the trade deficit included an appreciated dollar, relatively rapid expansion of the American economy, and curtailed purchases of U.S. exports by less-developed countries. The effects of this expanding trade deficit have been manifold. It has had a contractionary, anti-inflationary impact on the U.S. domestic economy. American export-dependent industries have experienced declines in output, employment, and profits, thereby generating political pressures for protection. However, the trade deficit has also meant an increase in the living standards of American consumers.

The basic theory of trade explains trade patterns in terms of competitive supply and demand. Three variants of the basic theory emphasizing the supply side are Adam Smith's theory of absolute advantage, David Ricardo's principle of comparative advantage, and the Heckscher-Ohlin theory stressing factor proportions. Smith challenged the principles of mercantilism, which promoted the interests of the mother country at the expense of the colonies, and argued for free trade on the basis of cost-efficiency, with the only exception being national defense. Ricardo argued that, under the principle of comparative advantage, a country benefits by producing more of those goods in which it is relatively efficient and exporting them in return for goods that could only be produced inefficiently. The principle of comparative advantage assumed constant marginal costs (a rate that barely covers cost). Dropping Ricardo's constant-cost assumption to allow for increasing marginal costs makes it easier to explain why countries do not specialize completely. Heckscher-Ohlin explained trade patterns based on the fact that different goods use the factors of production (such as cost of raw materials and labor) in different ratios and that nations differ in their relative factor endowments. The theory also explains that trade patterns predict that nations tend to export the goods that use their abundant factors more intensively in exchange for the goods that use their scarce factors less intensively.

International trade has been slowly drifting toward trade among similar countries and toward trade in similar goods rather than trade between very different industrial sectors. A greater and greater share of world trade consists of intra-industry trade (IIT), or two-way trade within industrial categories. A challenge for trade theorists is to explain what is special about trade of knowledge-intensive goods such as software, why we have so much IIT, and whether the conclusions of the standard model (used to determine the standard for profits) about the gains from trade still hold in a world of IIT in knowledge-intensive goods.

—*Albert Atkins*

References

Lindert, Peter H. *International Economics.* Homewood, IL: R. D. Irwin, 1991.

McConnell, Campbell R. *Economics: Principles, Problems, and Policies.* New York: McGraw-Hill, 1963.

See also Volume 1: Export Control Act; Free Trade.

Bank Failures

Recurring problem in the United States until the creation of the Federal Reserve Bank.

Bank failures occurred often throughout American history as a result of the federal government's reliance on the states to regulate banking activities. The first major bank crisis occurred during the panic of 1819. The director of the Second Bank of the United States, Captain William Jones, allowed and participated in the speculation of bank stocks (the purchase of stocks with the expectation of increased value), and so value of the stock in the national bank dropped. State banks responded by printing unsecured paper currency. Langdon Cheves, the new director, implemented strict policies calling in loans owed by the state banks. The state banks, scrambling to cover their responsibilities, called in the notes of their customers, many of whom were Western and Southern farmers. Although the Bank of the United States survived, many of the state banks faced difficult times, and some were forced to close. Western farmers had the most difficulty because of the constricted economy.

After President Andrew Jackson did away with the Second Bank of the United States, the federal government deposited millions of dollars from its funds in state banks. This money was lost in the panic of 1837, during which hundreds of state banks failed; for the next three years, the remaining banks struggled. Federal money was finally placed in an Independent Treasury—basically a safe for federal funds that did not allow the circulation of currency—but only until after the 1840 election, which Whig candidate William Henry Harrison won. They repealed the act that had created the Independent Treasury, and the federal funds were returned to the state banks.

In the post–Civil War period, banks failed more frequently. As speculators sought to take advantage of the advances in technology and business, bankers loaned money carelessly. No federal authority or oversight existed. After the panics of 1873, 1893, and 1907, Congress began examining the issue. During the presidential election campaign of 1912, successful Democratic candidate Woodrow Wilson pledged to create a new banking system designed to create elasticity in the money supply and to be a lender of last resort for banks when no other sources of funds are available. In 1914 Congress passed the Federal Reserve Act. The legislation created 12 branch banks, all equal in status, with shares owned by the federal government and the national banks. Stricter accounting methods and lending requirements, as well as the requirement that a minimum amount of funds be held in reserve, created new confidence in the banking system. Although these federal regulations have prevented panics of the type experienced in the nineteenth century, even they did not prevent another banking crisis during the Great Depression.

After Franklin D. Roosevelt's election to the presidency in 1932 and before he took the oath of office, many financial investors and businesspeople voiced concern over the radical New Deal that he had promised, and their rising pessimism resulted in runs on a few banks. To prevent the situation from becoming a crisis, Roosevelt closed all U.S. banks for a four-day bank holiday. Institutions found financially solvent reopened at the end of four days, while other banks opened later, and some were forced to close their doors. Roosevelt then asked for legislation that would protect depositors' funds, and Congress created the Federal Deposit Insurance Corporation (FDIC). With confidence restored and the continuation of government oversight, the United States has not experienced another mass bank failure since the Great Depression of 1932. The widespread failure of savings and loan institutions in the 1970s was not originally covered by the FDIC; these institutions are different than banks. They are now covered.

—*Cynthia Clark Northrup*

References

Hammond, Bray. *Banks and Politics in America from the Revolution to the Civil War.* Princeton, NJ: Princeton University Press, 1957.

See also Volume 1: Federal Reserve Act; Great Depression; Panic of 1819; Panic of 1837; Panic of 1873; Panic of 1893; Panic of 1907; Wilson, Woodrow.

Bank of the United States (BUS), First: 1791–1811

Central federal bank that was an integral part of Secretary of the Treasury Alexander Hamilton's economic recovery program for the new nation during the administration of the first American president, George Washington.

Treasury Secretary Alexander Hamilton submitted a "Report on the Bank of the United States" to Congress on December 13, 1790, almost a year after he sent legislators his "Report on Public Credit," a plan to fund federal and state debts at face value. He argued that this debt—$38 million for the federal government and $25 million for the states—needed a central bank to carry through on the funding of the debts. Hamilton also believed in the necessity of a national bank because the existing medium for circulating currency remained inadequate and private businesspeople needed a better way to get credit. He wanted Congress to charter a bank with a capital of $10 million, one-fifth of the funds to be provided by the federal government and the other four-fifths by private investors. On the basis of this capitalization, the bank could issue its own bank notes up to $10 million. A board of directors of 25 people, 5 of them named by Congress, would govern the bank at its Philadelphia headquarters and through the presidents of eight state branches. Lastly, the BUS could act as an agent for the federal government and be the depository for federal funds.

Hamilton's plan was for an institution with a mixture of public and private aspects—essentially a private institution with a special relationship to the federal government. Despite the opposition of James Madison and others in the House of Representatives, the bill establishing the First Bank of the United States passed Congress and went to President Washington on February 25, 1791. In the ensuing Cabinet discussion, Secretary of State Thomas Jefferson continued the opposition and advised Washington not to sign the bill because it was unconstitutional; that is, Congress had exercised a power not specifically given to it by the Constitution. Hamilton argued that it was constitutional because the federal government could do anything not specifically prohibited by the Constitution if it was "necessary and proper." Washington agreed with Hamilton and signed the bill into law. The first BUS proved salutary and stimulated investment, especially in the North. It also ushered in a period of growth for state banks and served as a safe depository for federal funds. Despite the contributions of the first BUS to the economy, Congress allowed its charter to expire in 1811, largely because of the approaching War of 1812.

—*Robert P. Sutton*

References

Appleby, Joyce. *Capitalism and a New Social Order: The Republican Vision of the 1790s.* New York: New York University Press, 1984.

Cunningham, Noble E. *The Jeffersonian Republicans: The Formation of Party Organization, 1789–1801.* Chapel Hill: University of North Carolina Press, published for the Institute of Early American History and Culture at Williamsburg, Virginia, 1957.

Frisch, Morton. *Alexander Hamilton and the Political Order.* Lanham, MD: University Press of America, 1991.

Hammond, Bray. *Banks and Politics in America from the Revolution to the Civil War.* Princeton, NJ: Princeton University Press, 1957.

Nelson, John R., Jr. *Liberty and Property: Political Economy and Policy Making in the New Nation 1789–1812.* Baltimore, MD: Johns Hopkins University Press, 1987.

See also Volume 1: Constitution; Hamilton, Alexander; War of 1812.

Second BUS tripled the capitalization of its predecessor, with $35 million in funds invested. The bank was severely criticized because of the panic of 1819, particularly in the West, where many Americans held it responsible for a large number of foreclosures. The reputation of the Second BUS improved under the able management of its president, Nicholas Biddle, from 1822 to 1836.

Unfortunately, Biddle's political connections with President Andrew Jackson's opponents, Whig leaders Henry Clay and Daniel Webster, caused Jackson to view the power of the bank suspiciously. Biddle, urged by Clay, submitted for an early rechartering of the bank in the summer of 1832—hoping that, on the eve of the upcoming presidential election, Jackson would not risk a veto. But Jackson perceived this move as a personal challenge and issued a precedent-making veto that he justified by declaring the BUS unconstitutional, calling it a monopoly uncontrolled by the people and a "hydra of corruption." The veto was sustained and, in 1833, President Jackson removed all federal funds from the BUS, effectively forcing it to close its doors, and distributed the money to numerous "pet" state banks in regions that had supported him in the 1832 election. This transfer led to runaway speculation in the purchase of federal lands and in part brought on the panic of 1837, when the economy experienced the "Great Contraction." After the federal charter for the Second BUS expired in 1836, Biddle had Pennsylvania charter the bank as a state institution. It was an important financial institution in that state's economy until 1841.

—*Robert P. Sutton*

References

Latner, Richard B. *The Presidency of Andrew Jackson.* Athens: University of Georgia Press, 1979.

Remini, Robert V. *Andrew Jackson and the Bank War: A Study in the Growth of Presidential Power.* New York: W. W. Norton, 1967.

Taylor, George Rogers, ed. *Jackson vs. Biddle's Bank: The Struggle over the Second Bank of the United States.* Lexington, MA: D. C. Heath, 1972.

Temin, Peter. *The Jacksonian Economy.* New York: W. W. Norton, 1969.

Watson, Harry L. *Liberty and Power: The Politics of Jacksonian America.* New York: Hill and Wang, 1990.

Wilburn, Jean Alexander. *Biddle's Bank: The Crucial Years.* New York: Columbia University Press, 1967.

See also Volume 1: Clay, Henry; Jackson, Andrew; Panic of 1837.

Bank of the United States (BUS), Second: 1816–1836

Central bank modeled on the First Bank of the United States and signed into law by President James Madison, who stated that the bank had justified its constitutionality "by usage."

Three years after the Bank of the United States (BUS) received its second charter, the Supreme Court in *McCulloch v. Maryland* confirmed the bank's constitutionality. The Second BUS resembled the first in structure but not size; the

Bank Protection Act (1968)

Act established in 1968 with the agenda to maintain minimum-security measures for banks.

The principal objective of the Bank Protection Act focuses on discouraging robberies, burglaries, and larcenies and aiding in the capture and prosecution of those who commit such acts. This measure attempts to deter future crimes and to protect banking institutions and society. The act initially outlined detailed provisions for installation, maintenance, and operation of security devices, and it specified limitations on the amount of time taken to accomplish this.

Federal supervisory agencies enforce the rules establishing minimum standards for protection. These regulations demanded that all banks and savings and loan associations follow the regulations on installation, maintenance, and operation of security devices and procedures. They also included the expectation that all banking institutions would address the stated matters with efficiency and with reasonable cost. New amendments to the act have recently addressed two issues: requirements for using surveillance cameras and restrictions on cyber-banking (banking over the Internet).

In 1981, both minor and major changes occurred when the act was further amended. One new provision eliminated the need for mandatory annual reports. This action helped reduce the complexity of constantly updating the required security devices because of changes in technology. The Bank Protection Act now requires that each institution designate a security officer to launch a security program that would require the installation of specific security devices in banking establishments. The minimum requirements stated by the Bank Protection Act require resources to protect liquid assets, a lighting system for nighttime hours, an alarm system, and tamper-resistant locks. Congress also required the documentation of all suspicious activity in banking institutions—such as unusually large transactions, apparent money laundering, and other curious acts.

—*Sandra L. Willett*

References
Fein, Melanie L. "What Does It Mean to Banking: Regulating Cyberspace?" *Bank Management*, vol. 71 (September–October 1995): 8–14.
See also Volume 1: Banking System; Volume 2: Money Laundering.

Banking Act (1933)

A federal statute signed into law by President Franklin D. Roosevelt on June 16, 1933, to help stabilize America's banking system and promote recovery during the Great Depression.

After the stock market crash in 1929, many people who had deposited money in banks began withdrawing their funds. However, because of the decentralized nature of American banking in the 1920s, many banks had overextended their loans or lost depositors' money by speculating in the stock market. To preserve their liquidity (their ability to convert assets to cash), banks began calling in their loans in the early 1930s—but because they had made loans to people now unable to repay them because of the Great Depression, many financial institutions ran out of money and shut down or were left barely solvent. Consequently, many Americans lost their savings, and the nation's banking system neared collapse.

President Herbert Hoover attempted to resolve the crisis by creating the National Credit Administration and later the Reconstruction Finance Corporation (RFC) to stabilize banks and other institutions. But these efforts failed to stem the tide of bank failures, and the crisis became the problem of

the newly elected president, Franklin D. Roosevelt. Once in office, Roosevelt immediately declared a national bank holiday and convened a special session of Congress to consider emergency banking legislation. The Emergency Banking Act, which Congress passed on March 9, 1933, used RFC loans to increase the liquidity of struggling banks, authorized the government to issue emergency currency, and allowed the secretary of the Treasury to determine which banks were sound and should reopen.

Although confidence in American banking rose, many people argued that the Emergency Banking Act did not correct the underlying flaws in the nation's banking system. Thus, in May 1933, Democratic Senator Carter Glass of Virginia and Democratic Congressman Henry Steagall of Alabama introduced the Banking Act of 1933 in Congress. This act separated commercial and investment banking, increased the powers of the Federal Reserve, recognized the Open Market Committee (a Federal Reserve committee that decides economic policy), and more effectively coordinated the Federal Reserve's open market operations. It also gave commercial banks until July 1, 1935, to relinquish their private securities, prohibited them from underwriting additional private securities, and created the Federal Deposit Insurance Corporation (FDIC) to protect depositors' savings.

Although many bankers believed that the Banking Act was an unwarranted federal intrusion into the banking system, public opinion favored these reforms. Two years later, Congress modified and extended the Banking Act of 1933 when it passed the Banking Act of 1935.

—*David W. Waltrop*

References
Burns, Helen M. *The American Banking Community and New Deal Banking Reforms: 1933–1935*. Westport, CT: Greenwood Press, 1974.
Kennedy, Susan Estabrook. *The Banking Crisis of 1933*. Lexington: University of Kentucky Press, 1973.
See also Volume 1: Banking System; Volume 2: Banking.

Banking System

Largest financial intermediary with historically important role in money supply process and transmission of monetary policy.

Commercial banks received state charters primarily between 1789 and 1863. Their liabilities (sources of funds) consisted mostly of banknotes but included some deposits. Their assets (uses of funds) consisted of specie (gold and silver) and short-term commercial loans intended for financing inventories or accounts receivable.

The federal government chartered the First Bank of the United States (1791–1811) and the Second Bank of the United States (1816–1836). These banks attempted to control the money supply and improve the soundness of commercial banks by redeeming banknotes of state banks. Particularly in western and southern states, bankers disliked these activities and successfully prevented an extension of the Second Bank's federal charter.

Between 1837 and 1863, states exclusively regulated banks. Banking regulations and the extent of supervision differed substantially among states, resulting in a heterogeneous currency with numerous banknotes circulating at varying discounts. The federal government reestablished a regulatory role through passage of the National Banking Act of 1863 and its subsequent amendments. The act's objectives included providing a uniform national currency and strengthening the government bond market. It established nationally chartered banks, the reserves of which included gold and United States government bonds. It imposed a 10 percent tax on state banknotes, thereby eliminating banknotes as a source of funds for state-chartered banks.

However, state-chartered banks survived by acquiring funds through deposits. They thrived after 1880 because many bankers saw profit opportunities in obtaining a state bank charter, which had lower capital requirements, lower reserve requirements, more flexibility regarding loans, and less supervision than national banks. A dual banking system developed in which a bank could have either a national charter or a state charter.

The dual banking system resulted in a complex structure of regulation as each state established its own set of rules for banks operating in that state. Many states became unit-banking states, in which a bank could operate at only one location, because many people feared that large banks would engage in monopolistic practices if allowed to expand geographically. Restrictions on national banks reinforced these state banking laws. Because this legal environment limited where a bank could operate, the United States developed a system with many more commercial banks—and typically smaller banks—than banking systems of other industrialized nations.

The national banking system provided a uniform currency, which reduced transactions costs, but it remained subject to significant fluctuations in the money supply and frequent bank panics that resulted in many bankruptcies and business failures. In 1913, Congress established the Federal Reserve System to act as a lender of last resort when no other sources of funds are available to ensure the banking system's stability.

Between 1930 and 1933, the Federal Reserve failed to prevent a financial collapse as approximately one-third of commercial banks went bankrupt. To rebuild the banking system and to prevent its future collapse, Congress passed the Glass-Steagall Act (1933) and the Banking Act of 1935. This New Deal economic legislation of President Franklin D. Roosevelt, reflecting the view that too much competition existed in the banking industry, separated commercial banking from the investment banking and securities industry, created the Federal Deposit Insurance Corporation (FDIC), restricted checkable deposits to commercial banks, and regulated interest rates paid on deposits.

The legislation established a restrictive legal environment in which commercial banks operated during the next five decades. Although commercial banks gradually lost market share among financial intermediaries, the banking system would not substantially change until the 1970s. Ultimately financial innovation resulted from improved technology that lowered costs of providing certain financial services/instruments, from banks seeking improved profit by avoiding existing regulations, and from rising and more variable inflation, which increased both interest rate risk and cost of regulations.

The problems caused by rising inflation throughout the 1970s forced major changes in the legal environment in which banks operated. Some savers withdrew funds from depository institutions to purchase direct claims by borrowers (for example, certificates of deposit or money market accounts) as market interest rates rose above legal interest rate ceilings placed on banks; the rapid growth of money market mutual funds intensified loss of deposits. As many banks faced dwindling profits and even bankruptcy, Congress passed the Depository Institutions Deregulation and Monetary Control Act (1980) and Garn–St. Germain Depository Institutions Act (1982). These acts allowed depository institutions to provide interest-bearing checkable deposits, to issue more competitive savings accounts, and to broaden permissible activities of thrifts (mutual savings banks/saving and loan associations).

The legislation was too late to prevent numerous bankruptcies among thrifts, which had losses from withdrawal of funds or bad loans. Bankruptcies became less common among commercial banks, which were concentrated in oil-producing states. These banks had poorly diversified loan portfolios and had to deal with fluctuating oil prices, but because oil was in short supply in the 1970s the banks did not experience a withdrawal of funds. Congress passed the Financial Institutions Reform, Recovery, and Enforcement Act (1989) to bail out thrifts and passed the Federal Deposit Insurance Corporation Improvement Act (1991) to improve soundness of commercial banks by establishing new categories of capital adequacy.

During the 1970s and 1980s, banks expanded across state lines as interstate compacts developed. During the 1990s, they obtained greater flexibility, expanding geographically and broadening their range of activities. The Riegle-Neal Interstate Banking and Efficiency Act (1994) established nationwide interstate banking. During the 1980s and 1990s, the Federal Reserve allowed specific bank holding companies to expand activities. Because restrictions on commercial banks' securities and insurance activities placed U.S. banks at a competitive disadvantage to foreign banks, bills to repeal Glass-Steagall appeared regularly in Congress during the 1990s. The Gramm-Leach-Bliley Financial Services Modernization Act (1999) repealed Glass-Steagall to allow consolidation of financial services. Numerous mergers among banks from the mid-1990s to 2003 indicate that some banks believe their best strategy is to become large diversified financial service firms by growing geographically and increasing the range of products they offer. However, other banks stress local ownership and personal service as their strategy for survival.

The share of assets in financial intermediaries such as commercial banks and securities dealers has continued to fall, particularly since 1985, because of the rising importance of mutual funds and pension plans. However, banks remain the most important source of funding for small and medium-sized businesses, the financial intermediary used most often by the general public, and a major player in the money supply process. Although credit unions have existed in the United States since 1909, their primary function is to serve members as credit cooperatives. Credit unions were healthy into 2003, but they do not fulfill many of the functions of banks.

—*Robert Herren*

References
Friedman, Milton, and Anna J. Schwartz. *A Monetary History of the United States, 1867–1960.* Princeton, NJ: Princeton University Press, 1963.
Klebaner, Benjamin J. *American Commercial Banking: A History.* Boston: Twayne Publishers, 1990.
Rockoff, Hugh. "Banking and Finance, 1789–1914." In Stanley L. Engerman and Robert E. Gallman, eds., *The Cambridge Economic History of the United States.* Vol. 2: *The Long Nineteenth Century.* New York: Cambridge University Press, 2000.
White, Eugene N. "Banking and Finance in the Twentieth Century." In Stanley L. Engerman and Robert E. Gallman, eds., *The Cambridge Economic History of the United States.* Vol. 3: *The Twentieth Century.* New York: Cambridge University Press, 2000.
See also Volume 1: Bank of the United States, First; Bank of the United States, Second; Bank Protection Act; Banking Act; Federal Reserve Act; Glass-Steagall Banking Act; Volume 2: Banking.

Beard, Charles Austin (1874–1949)

Author of *American Government and Politics,* supporter of the New Deal, and remembered for emphasizing the impact of other fields, including economics, on history.

Born November 27, 1874, to a prosperous farmer in Knightstown, Indiana, Charles Beard grew up discussing and debating public affairs. Beard's father bought his son the town newspaper, the weekly *Knightstown Sun,* when Beard was just 18. After four years as a newspaperman, Beard attended DePauw College, graduating in 1898. He spent the next few years enrolled in graduate study divided between Columbia in New York and Oxford in England.

Beard received his doctorate from Columbia in 1904 and began a career teaching at Columbia. Although credited with founding Columbia's school of politics, Beard's academic career ended abruptly. He believed firmly in the principles of academic freedom and resigned after the college dismissed three of his colleagues for disagreeing with the college president's views on American participation in World War I. Beard did not take another academic appointment.

Throughout his career Beard authored several books that would become standard texts in political science and history including *Economic Interpretation of the Constitution.* His textbook *American Government and Politics* had ten editions in Beard's lifetime. He also wrote a series of history books with his wife, historian Mary Ritter Beard, geared toward the general public.

Beard supported President Franklin D. Roosevelt's New Deal program during the depression. However, he soundly rejected Roosevelt's foreign policy and began supporting an isolationist stance on World War II. At one point, he accused Roosevelt of manipulating the Japanese attack on Pearl Harbor.

Beard continued to write and speak publicly until his death September 1, 1949. His views and mountain of work changed the way professors have taught history and political science. By emphasizing the impact of other fields, including economics, on history, Beard demonstrated the importance of a broad view of the past to the study of any field.

—*Lisa A. Ennis*

References
Martin, James J. "Charles Beard: A Tribute." *Journal of Historical Review.* 1981. Available: http://www.ihr.org/jhr/v03/v03p239_Martin.html; accessed September 6, 2001.
See also Volume 1: Constitution; *Economic Interpretation of the Constitution.*

Berlin Wall

Physical barrier separating East and West Berlin that was a symbol of cold war between the United States and the Soviet Union.

A few months after settling into the White House, President John F. Kennedy met Soviet Premier Nikita Khrushchev at Vienna in June 1961. During that meeting, Kennedy sought cooperation, but the tough-talking Russian adopted a belligerent attitude, threatening to make a treaty with East Germany and cut off Western access to Berlin. Kennedy was visibly shaken but refused to be bullied. On returning to the United States, he requested an increase in the military budget and called up reserve troops for the possible defense of Berlin. The Soviets backed off from their most bellicose threats but suddenly began to construct the Berlin Wall August 13, 1961; it was built virtually overnight. Until 1961 East German citizens had been able travel to West Berlin, although it became difficult after the Soviets closed the border between East and West Germany in 1952. A barbed wire and concrete barrier, the Berlin Wall was designed to stop the heavy population drain of skilled workers from East Germany to West Germany (more than 2.6 million East Germans from a total population of about 17 million escaped to West Berlin or West Germany from 1949 to 1961). After the construction of the Berlin Wall, many East Germans attempted to scale the wall and flee to West Berlin. On August 24, 1961, Günter Litwin became the first of 171 people who died trying to escape by scaling the wall or tunneling under it. Another 5,000 people managed to escape to freedom.

Another problem involved the two currencies in Germany and especially in Berlin. Germans exchanged the West German DM into East German DM at a rate of 1:6 (1 DM West = 6 DM East) in West Berlin. People with West German DM could get goods very cheaply in the eastern part of Berlin. The East German government saw no other way to prevent funds and people from escaping to the West via

Berlin than closing the border between East and West Berlin on August 13, 1961.

In 1984, Mikhail Gorbachev started to change the Soviet Union's policies by instituting *perestroika* (a reorganization and movement toward an open economy) and *glasnost* (openness that included a movement toward free speech and a loosening of control by the USSR national police, the KGB). The Soviet reforms also influenced other communist countries, especially Poland and Hungary, which had established a nonphysical but effective Iron Curtain that prevented free travel out of those countries. On August 23, 1989, Hungary opened the Iron Curtain to Austria, allowing East German tourists to escape to Austria through Hungary, and in September 1989 more than 13,000 East German escaped via Hungary within three days. The event marked the first mass exodus of East Germans after the erection of the Berlin Wall in 1961. Mass demonstrations against the government and the economic system occurred in East Germany starting at the end of September and finally ending in November 1989. Erich Honecker, East Germany's head of state, finally resigned on October 18, 1989, and the new government issued a new law that lifted travel restrictions for East German citizens.

At 6:53 P.M. on November 9, 1989, a member of the new East German government responded to a press conference question about when the new East German travel law would take effect. The official answered: "Well, as far as I can see, . . . straightaway, immediately." That moment signaled the end of the Berlin Wall. That night East Germans opened the deadly border peacefully at 10:30 P.M. During the ensuing weeks, citizens helped tear down the wall. Official demolition began on June 13, 1990, and most work was completed by November 30, 1990.

—*Albert Atkins*

References
Flemming, Thomas. *The Berlin Wall.* Munich: Hagen Koch, 1988.
Isaacs, Jeremy, and Taylor Downing. *The Cold War.* Boston: Little, Brown, 1999.
See also Volume 1: Cold War.

BIA
See Bureau of Indian Affairs.

Biddle, Nicholas (1786–1844)
Director of the Second Bank of the United States.

Born January 8, 1786, in Philadelphia to a wealthy Quaker family, Nicholas Biddle entered the University of Pennsylvania at the age of 10 and graduated three years later. Biddle then enrolled in the College of New Jersey at Princeton to study classics and was graduated as valedictorian in 1801. Although his family expected him to pursue writing, Biddle decided to pursue law and went to work with his brother William, also a lawyer.

In 1804, Biddle accompanied General John Armstrong to France as his secretary. Only 18 years old, he received the responsibility of the monies associated with claims from the Napoleonic Wars. He spent the next few years traveling through Europe. In 1807 he returned to the United States and resumed his law studies; in 1809, he rediscovered writing, joined a literary group, and wrote his *History of the Expedition of Captains Lewis and Clark* (1814).

Biddle helped Secretary of War James Madison secure loans for the War of 1812. He assisted Madison in securing the recharter for the Second Bank of the United States (BUS). In 1819, President James Madison appointed him as one of the government directors of the Second Bank of the United States. At Madison's request, Biddle compiled a digest of international exchange, *Commercial Regulations* (1819), and he served five years as a BUS director, working to keep the bank politically neutral.

Under President Andrew Jackson, Biddle pushed bank issues to the center of the presidential campaign. Jackson, believing the bank to be unconstitutional, strongly opposed renewing its charter. An effort in 1832 to renew the bank's national charter failed, but Biddle obtained a state charter and the bank continued as the Bank of the United States of Pennsylvania. Biddle retired in 1839 to Delaware, where he busied himself with intellectual pursuits. He died on February 27, 1844, at the age of 58.

—*Lisa A. Ennis*

References
Johnson, Allen, ed. *Dictionary of American Biography.* Vols. 2, 3, and 5. New York: Scribner's, 1929.
See also Volume 1: Bank of the United States, Second.

Bison (Buffalo)
Largest mammal in North America extensively slaughtered in the 1870s and 1880s for hides, meat, and tongues.

When Europeans arrived in the new world, two subspecies of bison roamed much of the North American continent—north to south from present-day Canada into northern Mexico and west to east from present-day California to the Appalachian Mountains, northern Florida, and Pennsylvania. The most prolific of the species was the Plains bison *(Bison, bison, bison)*, which roamed the plains and prairies. The wood or mountain bison *(Bison, bison, athabascae)* thrived in the Rocky Mountains. Bison population peaked in the mid-nineteenth century. Although scientists and historians have had difficulty determining exact numbers, most accept that the plains species totaled between 30 and 70 million and the mountain variety between 3 and 5 million.

The bison was critical to the survival, advancement, and development—both physical and spiritual—of the indigenous populations of the North American plains. Native peoples organized massive hunts and then used all parts of the animals for everything from food to shelter to utensils. Immediately following a kill, the tribes had what some have described as a feeding frenzy, eating some parts of the bison raw. They made jerky and pemmican via a process somewhat like canning that used the hide as the container and fat for curing. Hides provided clothing, shelter, canoe-like floating vessels, and even shield and decoy material in battle. Dung proved an excellent source of fuel. Hair, horns, tails, and other body parts made cooking utensils, shoes, saddles, tools, containers, and much more. Bison hair made jewelry and rope, and the heads were used for ceremonial dress. Perhaps no animal proved more important to the development of North American indigenous populations than did the bison.

When white settlers began the westward rush to the plains, they, too, recognized the utility of the Great Plains animals. Most of the great travel routes were trails that the bison had trekked for centuries. Railroads, too, followed the overland trails of the great bison herds, and bison were food for the men who built the rails. Soon after the land rush of the mid-nineteenth century, buffalo robes and the delicacy of bison tongues became popular in both the Eastern U.S. and European cities.

With leather supplies from the South American market dwindling, bison products filled consumer needs. Between 1870 and 1883, hide hunters decimated the plains bison population. Between 1872 and 1874 the major rail companies shipped more than 1,378,000 hides and 6,751,000 pounds of meat to Eastern markets, representing $4,823,000 in hides alone, which sold for $3.50 apiece. These shipments represented more than 3,158,700 slaughtered bison. The carcasses proved useful as well: they attracted wolves, which were dangerous to cattle operations booming in the West, so ranchers laced the decaying bison with poison and helped eradicate the predator from the plains. Entrepreneurs also shipped carcasses east, where bones were used for fertilizer, horns for sugar refining, and hoofs for glue. Between 1872 and 1874, the major rail lines shipped roughly 32,380,000 pounds of bison bones, representing approximately 550,000 animals and more than $161,900 in revenue (at an average of $10 per ton).

By 1880, a few well-intentioned laws forbade the hunting of bison in several Western states, but by all accounts the legislation was too little, too late. In 1900 only a handful of bison remained on the Great Plains. Private individuals began to ask for federal intervention in saving the nearly extinct animals; success came slowly and at the expense of the mountain species when the U.S. Army introduced a tame herd of plains animals into Yellowstone National Park in 1902. They eventually mixed with the mountain herd to form a hybrid species. Today Yellowstone boasts the largest free-ranging bison herd in the world, with a population of more than 3,000.

The nineteenth-century market for buffalo robes and meat died as quickly as the herds had died. Several marketing operations have developed since, including the raising and sale of "cattalo," a mixed breed of domestic cattle and bison, and the breeding and selling of domestic bison.

—*Elaine C. Prange Turney*

References
Isenberg, Andrew C. *The Destruction of the Bison: An Environmental History, 1750–1920.* New York: Cambridge University Press, 2000.
McHugh, Tom. *The Time of the Buffalo.* New York: Alfred A. Knopf, 1972.
See also Volume 1: Homestead Act; Timber and Stone Act; Timber Culture Act.

Bland-Allison Act (1878)

Legislation that provided for the freer coinage of silver and placed the money supply of the United States on a bimetal standard.

Authored by Democratic Representative Richard P. Bland of Missouri and passed in 1878, the Bland-Allison Act attempted to satisfy the demands of Western interests for the free and unlimited coinage of silver. The bill passed the House of Representatives but underwent major modifications by Republican Senator William B. Allison of Iowa. The final version of the act, passed over the veto of President Rutherford B. Hayes, required the U.S. Treasury to purchase between $2 and $4 million worth of silver bullion each month at market prices. The government would use this silver to coin a limited number of silver dollars at a ratio of 16 to 1 with gold and to back the issuance of paper money called silver certificates.

Reversing the Coinage Act of 1873, which had placed the country on the gold standard, the Bland-Allison Act provided a compromise for conflicting sectional interests in monetary policy. The financial forces of the East favored the contraction of the money supply and the gold standard. The indebted agrarian classes in the South and West demanded inflation and cheap money to ease the burden of debt caused by falling prices for farm products. Also, Western silver miners favored bimetalism (the use of silver as well as gold as specie, or hard metal currency) because the price of silver had declined drastically because of overproduction, and they required a steady and reliable market.

The act did not have the effects that conservatives feared or "silverites" hoped. Its provisions proved insufficient to halt the decline of silver prices or to increase the amount of money in circulation, primarily because government officials purchased only the minimum amount of bullion required by law. The Sherman Silver Purchase Act of 1890 replaced this act.

—*Peter S. Genovese*

References
Timberlake, Richard. *Monetary Policy in the United States: An Intellectual and Institutional History.* Chicago: University of Chicago Press, 1993.
See also Volume 1: Populist Party.

Block Grants

Federal funding and regulation that combine several categorical grants into one grant.

Block grants incorporate categorical grants into a larger package called grants-in-aid, in effect reducing the regulations formerly attached to each individual categorical grant. Block grants have fewer regulations because they remain administered under general, less-specific guidelines. State and local governments receive less money through block grants, but they have increased latitude to administer funds in the deregulated policy environment and to craft their own strategies for using the funds. The relative decreases in funding and the increased responsibility create incentives for local governments to use funding more strategically as incentives or subsidies to encourage private-sector participation in areas where the public sector had formerly performed.

Block grants were significant in the administration of President Ronald Reagan, reflecting the broader strategy of the Omnibus Budget Reconciliation Act (1981) to decrease the federal budget and deregulate funding. The block grant as used by Reagan served as a model for efficiency to consolidate categorical funds, eliminate regulations, and devolve responsibility for programs from the federal government to the local government. Devolution meant that Congress cut or eliminated programs that directly assisted the poor, instead encouraging private and public partnerships that included local business interests. Local governments administered their own programs with less federal support money, relying more heavily on markets and less heavily on the public sector to solve the nation's economic problems. The August 1981 publication of the *Governor's Bulletin* reported that block grants "represent some progress toward greater flexibility for state and local officials at a time when aid to the state and local governments is shrinking."

The effects of federal funding in the form of block grants in the 1980s remain institutionalized 20 years later. Actions by Congress under the Reagan administration consolidated more than 57 federal categorical programs into nine block grants. Congress also created six new block grants, three of which involved the transfer of federal funds to state administration in the existing block grant programs. In terms of policy areas, four of the block grants deal with health services, two focus on social services, and one addresses low-income energy assistance, education, and community development.

—*Eileen Robertson-Rehberg*

References

Cope, Megan. "Responsibility, Regulation, and Retrenchment: The End of Welfare?" In Lynn A. Staeheli, Janet E. Kodras, and Colin Flint, eds., *State Devolution in America*. Beverly Hills, CA: Sage Publications, 1997.

See also Volume 1: Reagan, Ronald.

Board of Governors of the Federal Reserve System

The highest authority in U.S. central banking since 1914, with members appointed by the president.

The Federal Reserve System, consisting of 12 regional reserve banks and a central Federal Reserve Board, began operation in 1914 as lender of last resort for banks when no other sources of funds are available during periods of economic stringency. The Federal Reserve Board consisted initially of five members appointed by the president (subject to Senate confirmation) for 10-year terms, the first members serving for terms of 2, 4, 6, 8, and 10 years. The board includes a governor and vice governor, two ex-officio members, the secretary of the Treasury, and the comptroller of the currency. The number of appointed members increased to six in 1922, and Congress lengthened the terms to 12 years in 1933.

The Banking Act of 1935 changed the formal name to Board of Governors of the Federal Reserve System, with 7 members appointed for 14-year terms, 2 being designated for four-year terms as chair and vice chair. The ex-officio members ceased to serve from February 1, 1936, and voting membership was increased to 12. The board remains popularly known as the Federal Reserve Board. Its 12 voting members—the president of the Federal Reserve Bank of New York, and four of the presidents of the other 11 reserve banks, chosen by rotation (with the other reserve bank presidents as observers)—make up the Federal Reserve's Open Market Committee, which decides economic policy.

The 12 regional Federal Reserve banks had considerable independence in setting discount rates (the rates they charged for loans they made to commercial banks and other depository institutions) until integration of financial markets during World War I forced uniform discount rates. In the 1920s, the Federal Reserve Board disclaimed any responsibility for inflation or deflation, claiming to passively accommodate the needs of trade.

Benjamin Strong was president of the Federal Reserve Bank of New York and a member of the Federal Reserve Board from the bank's inception until his death in 1928. He overshadowed the board's decision-making process during the entire time. Under Marriner Eccles, governor and chair from 1934 to 1948, the board became both more prominent within the Federal Reserve system and more concerned with macroeconomic stability—that is, stability in overall aspects of the economy such as income and output and the interrelationship among such aspects. Ironically, Treasury Department pressure on the board increased after the Treasury secretary ceased to be an ex-officio member, and during World War II monetary policy remained dominated by the government's financing needs. The Treasury–Federal Reserve accord of March 1951 freed the Federal Reserve from the wartime commitment to maintain the market value of government securities (and thus peg interest rates at a certain level). Paul Volcker and Allan Greenspan, the successive chairs of the Board since 1979, have dominated the Federal Reserve System and have become influential public figures, promoting central bank independence and acting to diminish and control inflation.

—*Robert Dimand*

References

Anderson, Clay J. *A Half-Century of Federal Reserve Policymaking, 1914–1964*. Philadelphia: Federal Reserve Bank of Philadelphia, 1964.

Friedman, Milton, and Anna J. Schwartz. *A Monetary History of the United States, 1867–1960*. Princeton, NJ: Princeton University Press, 1963.

Meulendyke, Ann-Marie. *U.S. Monetary Policy and Financial Markets*. 3d ed. New York: Federal Reserve Bank of New York, 1998.

See also Volume 1: Federal Reserve Act (Owen-Glass Act) of 1913; Volume 2: Federal Reserve Bank.

Bond Sales

Sales of treasury bonds, notes, and bills, which play an integral role in fiscal and monetary policy.

The conventional view assumes the government must sell securities to finance the difference between its spending and its tax revenues (deficit spending). However, this view overlooks the crucial role that bond sales play in managing aggregate bank reserves and in the administration of short-term (overnight interbank) interest rates.

When government spends, recipients of Department of the Treasury checks deposit them into banks, which adds reserves to the banking system. When government taxes, reserves decrease. The Federal Reserve does not pay interest on reserves, so if government deficit spending (spending that exceeds tax revenues) causes excess total bank reserves, the overnight interbank interest rate quickly falls to 0 percent. To maintain a positive overnight rate, the government can sell securities to drain the excess reserves from the system. Thus, logically, government spending precedes bond sales and functions to support interest rates, not to fund expenditures as generally assumed. In this sense, the imperative of treasury bond sales should not be thought of as borrowing, since the sales do not finance or fund government expenditure.

The national debt in this sense provides a record of government action to maintain a positive short-term interest rate and functions as an interest rate maintenance account.

Modern (state) money remains fiat currency (irredeemable paper currency that derives its purchasing power from the declaratory fiat of the issuing government), with the national government the monopoly issuer. Treasury bonds thus differ from other, nongovernment types of debt, because no financial constraint restricts the issuer of the currency. Government debt denominated in another currency or debt issued by parties not acting as currency monopolists constitute very different matters.

—*Mathew Forstater*

References

Bell, Stephanie. "Can Taxes and Bonds Finance Government Spending?" *Journal of Economic Issues,* vol. 34, no. 3 (2000): 603–620.

Mosler, Warren. *Soft Currency Economics.* West Palm Beach, FL: AVM, 1995.

Wray, L. Randall, *Understanding Modern Money.* Cheltenham, England: Edward Elgar, 1998.

See also Volume 1: Deficit Spending.

Bonus March (1932)

Depression-era protest.

In 1924, Congress approved a deferred $1,000 bonus for veterans of the American Expeditionary Force as a reward for their service during World War I. The government scheduled payment of the money to begin in 1945, but financial hardships brought on by the Great Depression led many veterans to demand their payments early. In 1932, President Herbert Hoover, concerned with balancing the federal budget and overwhelmed by the nation's economic woes, refused to support the early disbursal of the bonus funds and effectively killed off the required legislation. In response, a group of unemployed veterans, led by ex-sergeant Walter Williams and calling itself the Bonus Expeditionary Force, marched on Washington in protest in May 1932. They built crude camps around the city and vowed to remain in the nation's capital until the government paid the bonuses. By June 1932, the "Bonus Army" numbered about 20,000 men, many of whom had their wives and children with them. After Congress refused to comply with their request, many of the veterans left the city, but several thousand remained to continue the lobbying effort.

By mid-July the veterans' camps had become a political embarrassment to Hoover, and he issued orders to have the protestors evicted from the capital. He first called in the Washington police, but their efforts only led to a riot during which two veterans died. Hoover then called in the U.S. Army. Hurling tear gas and brandishing bayonets, federal troops led by General Douglas MacArthur chased the overmatched protestors out of town, burning their camps and injuring more than 100 veterans. The idea of U.S. soldiers attacking U.S. war veterans appalled the general public, and the political consequences for Hoover were disastrous. Though MacArthur had exceeded the president's orders with regard to excessive use of force, many Americans blamed Hoover personally for the entire episode, further damaging his already tarnished political image.

—*Ben Wynne*

References

Liebovich, Louis W. *Bylines in Despair: Herbert Hoover, the Great Depression, and the U.S. Media.* Westport, CT: Praeger, 1994.

See also Volume 1: Great Depression.

Boston Tea Party (December 16, 1773)

Protest against English taxation that sparked the American Revolution.

The British East India Company, facing severe financial reverses, convinced the British Parliament to allow it to sell tea in the American colonies at a price that would undercut even smuggled Dutch tea and would raise revenue while clearing the company's warehouses of a huge surplus. Unfortunately, this tea would still carry the despised perpound tax, which had remained as a token duty, and would be sold through only a handful of dealers in America. This high-handed policy united small merchants who were left out of the deal with patriot organizations that protested the tax. The arrival of the tea ships *Eleanor, Dartmouth,* and *Beaver* sparked public protest in Boston, including public meetings, distribution of fliers, and harassment of the consignees, who took shelter in Castle William (a fort on an island in Boston Harbor) to avoid the crowds.

The Sons of Liberty, led by Samuel Adams, decided on December 13, 1773, that no one could unload the tea, nor could it remain on board 20 days, at which time customs officials would seize the tea for sale. On December 16, the night the Sons of Liberty planned their raid on the ships to destroy the tea, a public protest at the Old South Meeting House turned rowdy after several people suggested dumping the tea in the harbor. As protesters stormed out of the meetinghouse, they met Sons of Liberty, costumed as Narragansett Indians, on their way to do the same thing. Followed by a huge crowd of perhaps 1,000 Bostonians, the "Indians" and volunteers stormed the three ships and, in a three-hour fracas lasting from 6:00 until 9:00 P.M., broke open all of the tea chests and dumped them into the harbor.

The attack had been conscientiously planned, and the protesters disturbed no other ship or cargo. Only one injury occurred, when a collapsing winch knocked a man unconscious. However, participants had ruined £18,000 worth of tea and infuriated the British government and particularly the king. Boston authorities arrested a barber named Eckley who had been caught bragging about his participation, but they could not find anyone who could identify the protestors, and sympathizers tarred and feathered Eckley's accuser in retaliation. George III specifically noted the Tea Party in his address to Parliament, and he and Lord North pushed through the Coercive Acts by April 1774, sparking further protests and eventually war between Britain and its American colonies.

—*Margaret Sankey*

References
Griswold, Wesley S. *The Night the Revolution Began.* Brattleboro, VT: Stephen Green Press, 1972.
Labarre, Benjamin Woods. *The Boston Tea Party.* New York: Oxford University Press, 1964.
See also Volume 1: American Revolution.

Boxer Rebellion (1898–1900)

A violent antiforeign revolt that occurred in north and northeast China between 1898 and 1900, launched by "the Righteous Harmony Fists" (*Yihequan* in Chinese) or Boxers.

A secret society that originally emerged in Shandong Province, the Boxers represented rural Chinese nativist resentment against increased Western enterprise and missionary activity, which it saw as posing a fatal threat to traditional Chinese village life. With peasants and lower classes as the backbone of membership, the Boxers detested the weak-kneed policy that the Qing (Manchu) government pursued toward foreign powers. The organization deemed Chinese martial arts and traditional superstitious rituals as the means to terminate foreign presence and influence in China. Pressed by foreign powers, the Qing court austerely suppressed the antiforeign terror committed by the Boxers under the slogan "Oppose the Qing Dynasty, Exterminate the Foreigners." In 1900, the main forces of the Boxers shifted to Hebei Province, especially the Beijing and Tianjin regions, and undertook as their the strategy "Uphold the Qing, Exterminate the Foreigners." This attitude won the support of conservatives in the Qing nobility and officialdom then under the ruling Empress Dowager Cixi, who seized the opportunity to rid China of foreign powers through this rebel group. With the

Qing government's connivance and acquiescence, the Boxers launched a large-scale rebellion against railroads and telegraph lines that stood as symbols of Western imperialism, burned churches, and massacred foreign diplomats, missionaries, Chinese Christians, and other Chinese with foreign ties. The uprising culminated in a siege of foreign diplomatic legations in Beijing. To protect their interests and citizens, foreign powers including the United States dispatched an international expeditionary force to China in June 1900 and broke the siege in August. They forced the Qing government to accept the Protocol of 1900, which banned antiforeign activities in China and allowed foreign troops to be stationed in Beijing to protect the diplomatic legation and in 12 other major cities along the railroad from Beijing to Shanghai Guan Pass. In addition, it called for China to pay for the damages caused by the Boxers.

—*Guoqiang Zheng*

References
Preston, Diana. *The Boxer Rebellion: The Dramatic Story of China's War on Foreigners That Shook the World in the Summer of 1900.* New York: Walker, 2000.
See also Volume 1: China; Foreign Policy.

Boycotts, Colonial

Method used by colonists to protest and influence British commercial policies.

A boycott is the act of abstaining from using, buying, or dealing with something or someone as a means of protest and coercion. During the late colonial era, Americans commonly used boycotts as a powerful way of expressing disagreement with and anger over England's attempt to regulate commerce and increase its revenue. As the colonies grew, Americans came to realize that they provided a major market for English manufactures and believed they could easily exert real leverage on economic policy by boycotting British products rather than appealing through political channels. Boycotts spread through nonimportation agreements, in which groups organized in opposition to British actions and persuaded individuals not to buy, or merchants not to sell, British goods. These "agreements" appealed to a person's sense of patriotism but were also commonly enforced via threats and overt acts of violence against violators.

The influence of boycotts on British policymaking remained indirect yet effective. The Stamp Act provides the best example of a boycott influencing imperial policy. Generally, Parliament demonstrated little concern with colonial opinions about fiscal measures or commercial regulation. However, government officials remained sensitive to and greatly influenced by the economic interests of British merchants and manufacturers, who suffered economically when American colonists boycotted British goods. The widespread colonial boycott that emerged in 1765 coincided with an economic depression in England, which compounded problems for British industry and shipping. With profits plummeting and warehouses full of unsold merchandise, British merchants generated strong political opposition to the act, forcing Parliament to repeal it the following year. The repeal of the Stamp Act by the British further fueled the belief among colonists that economic coercion would influence commercial policy. Colonists repeatedly implemented boycotts over the next decade in response to Parliament's tightening of the imperial system.

Although they were ineffective in changing the long-term course of British policy concerning taxation, boycotts remained important to the development of social and political cohesion in the 1760s and 1770s. Boycotts politicized the population by making the individual's decision to import or purchase an item a political statement and proved crucial to creating widespread opposition to British rule. They enabled leaders to consolidate and direct opposition to the imperial system. Although boycotts were initially local efforts in seaport cities, after 1765 they became government policy as colonial legislatures imposed nonimportation acts. These acts forged a sense of common identity across colonial borders and stimulated a commitment to domestic manufacturing and economic self-sufficiency.

—*Peter S. Genovese*

References

Maier, Pauline. *From Resistance to Revolution: Colonial Radicals and the Development of American Opposition to Britain, 1765–1776.* New York: Alfred A. Knopf, 1972.

See also Volume 1: Non-Importation Act; Non-Intercourse Act of 1809.

Bretton Woods Agreement (1945)

Post–World War II agreement for international economic cooperation.

Bretton Woods, New Hampshire, was the site of the 1944 United Nations Monetary and Financial Conference in which the United States, the United Kingdom, and 44 of their allies (plus Argentina) agreed to establish international monetary and financial institutions to promote peace and prosperity in response to the destruction wrought by World War II. The agreement was actually signed in 1945. Much of the conference was dominated by the emergence of two rival plans, one put forth by Henry Dexter White of the U.S. Treasury Department and the other by John Maynard Keynes of the United Kingdom. The compromise that emerged after the negotiations reflected the dominance of the preeminent postwar power, the United States.

In principle, the countries agreed to establish a multilateral institutional framework that created an international monetary system based on stable and adjustable exchange rates. Nations agreed to (1) submit their exchange rates to international discipline; (2) avoid the classical medicine of deflating their domestic economy when faced with balance-of-payment deficits; (3) establish the U.S. dollar as the standard to which other currencies were pegged, and; (4) create supranatural organizations—the International Monetary Fund (IMF) and the World Bank—whereby member countries could establish protocol and procedures to coordinate international monetary cooperation. These four points would become known as the "Bretton Woods System" that governed international monetary cooperation.

In the years after World War II, the IMF would come to regulate currency values and convertibility, supply monetary liquidity (ability to convert assets to cash), and serve as a consultative forum for its members. In fact, the Bretton Woods system soon became equivalent to the dollar exchange standard, a system under which dollars could be traded for gold at the Federal Reserve. The United States became the source of global liquidity growth through the deficits in its own balance of payments. Then, in the late 1960s, America's net gold reserves dropped, undermining the confidence of investors, who feared that the dollar was overvalued and not convertible to gold. The Bretton Woods system eventually broke down on August 15, 1971, when President Richard Nixon suspended the convertibility of the dollar into gold, thus floating the dollar against other currencies.

—*Keith A. Leitich*

References

James, Harold. *International Monetary Cooperation since Bretton Woods.* New York: Oxford University Press, 1996.

Mikesell, Raymond Frech. *The Bretton Woods Debates: A Memoir.* Princeton, NJ: International Finance Section, Department of Economics, Princeton University, 1994.

Schild, Georg. *Bretton Woods and Dumbarton Oaks: American Economic and Political Postwar Planning in the Summer of 1944.* New York: St. Martin's Press, 1995.

Stevenson, Jonathon. *Preventing Conflict: The Role of the Bretton Woods Institutions.* New York: Oxford University Press, 2000.

You, Jong-il. *The Bretton Woods Institutions: Evolution, Reform, and Change.* Seoul: Korea Development Institute, 2000.

See also Volume 1: Cold War; World War II.

Budget and Accounting Act of 1921

Legislation that delineated the responsibility and authority for the annual federal budget between the executive and legislative branches of the federal government.

Before the passage of the Budget and Accounting Act of 1921, the president and Congress each had sought to exercise increased control over the budget process. The Budget and Accounting Act of 1921 eliminated that recurring struggle by establishing specific mechanisms and procedures to be used. It calls for the Bureau of the Budget (now the Office of Management and Budget) to accept requests from government departments for funds. This information is reviewed before it goes to the president, who then formulates the annual budget ultimately submitted to Congress. Because Congress receives the proposed budget from the president, legislators may adjust it, but the budget's overall structure remains shaped by the executive branch. Between 1921 and 1974, Congress had to contend with the power of the president to appropriate funds at whatever rate he deemed appropriate—a power that has often led to a delay or termination of funded programs. Congress finally corrected this flaw with the passage of the Budget and Impoundment Control Act of

1974. Another issue that has arisen as a result of this budget process involves the inconsistency between the spending budget and revenue budget. Because the two budgets are arrived at separately, the spending budget often exceeds annual revenue projections—a trend that contributes to deficit spending.

The Budget and Accounting Act also established the General Accounting Office (GAO—an agency that conducts independent audits of government expenditures), which reports to Congress.

—*Cynthia Clark Northrup*

References
Savage, James D. *Balanced Budgets and American Politics.* Ithaca, NY: Cornell University Press, 1988.
See also Volume 1: Budget Deficits and Surpluses.

Budget Deficits and Surpluses

Discrepancies, either actual or structural, between government expenditures and tax revenues over a delineated period of time.

Since the popularization of the Keynesian idea of the "full-employment budget" (and its corollary, stabilization analysis) in the late 1940s, the Committee on Economic Development (CED), budget planners, and economists have emphasized the need to gear the federal budget for full employment (defined in terms of the nonaccelerating inflation rate of unemployment, or NAIRU). Accordingly, budget planners have distinguished between the actual and structural dimensions of the federal budget. Whereas the actual budget accounts for the variation of tax revenues and transfer payments with the cyclical fluctuations of the economy, the structural budget represents discretionary fiscal policy (that is, the domain of tax rates, government spending on goods and services, and transfer payments).

As a rule, actual (cyclical) deficits emerge when the economy is functioning below full employment. Under such conditions, tax revenues decrease while transfer payments (for example, unemployment compensation and welfare benefits) increase. In contrast, actual (cyclical) surpluses emerge when the economy is functioning above full employment. Under such conditions, tax revenues increase while transfer payments decrease. Finally, the actual (cyclical) budget is considered "balanced" when the economy is functioning at full employment (NAIRU).

Setting aside the impact of cyclical economic fluctuations, the structural budget estimates the deficit or surplus under the following conditions: the continuation of existing spending and tax policies; the maintenance of a given trend in gross domestic product; and the perpetuation of full employment (NAIRU). Thus, in principle, the structural budget can be used to anticipate the influence of government fiscal policy on the performance of the economy. In addition, budget planners use the structural budget to assess the extent to which increased public investment reduces private investment (a phenomenon known as the "crowding-out effect").

Throughout the postwar period (1945–1973), the U.S. economy operated beyond full employment. As a consequence, the United States maintained relatively negligible actual deficits (despite the ascendancy of Keynesian economics, increased expenditures on the social programs of the Great Society, and, ultimately, the high cost of the Vietnam conflict). Only with the fiscal crisis of the 1970s did the United States experience higher actual deficits. In fact, owing to the recession of 1981–1982, tax cuts during the administration of Ronald Reagan, and the augmentation of defense spending, the actual deficit reached unprecedented levels in the early 1980s. Since the 1980s there has been considerable debate on the effects—desirable and pernicious—of actual deficits. These debates culminated in the passage of a series of legislative initiatives designed to institutionalize a balanced budget: the Balanced Budget and Emergency Deficit Control Act of 1985, the Balanced Budget and Emergency Deficit Control Reaffirmation Act of 1987, and the Budget Enforcement Act of 1990.

Since the recession of 2001 and the terrorist attacks of September 11, 2001, the economy has experienced difficulty. President George W. Bush has proposed tax cuts and deficit spending to stimulate the economy. Although a balanced budget is ideal under normal circumstances, the domestic and international events of the past several years have shifted priorities.

—*Mark Frezzo*

References
Brown, E. Cary. "Fiscal Policy in the Thirties: A Reappraisal." *American Economic Review,* vol. 46, no. 5 (1956): 875–879.
Eisner, Robert. *How Real Is the Federal Deficit?* New York: Free Press, 1986.
Levy, Michael E., et al. *Federal Budget Deficits and the U.S. Economy.* New York: The Conference Board, 1984.
See also Volume 1: Deficit Spending; Keynesian Economics.

Buffalo
See Bison.

Bunau-Varilla, Philippe Jean (1859–1940)

French engineer who helped to orchestrate the separation of Panama from Colombia and the construction of the Panama Canal.

Philippe Bunau-Varilla worked his way up to become the head engineer for the French company that held the rights to construct a canal through Panama, which was a possession of Colombia. When this company went bankrupt in 1889, he formed a new company that obtained the rights of the failed enterprise. Technical difficulties, disease (men building the canal died from yellow fever and malaria), and funding problems led Bunau-Varilla to turn to the United States. He persuaded President William McKinley—and after McKinley's assassination, President Theodore Roosevelt—to pursue the idea of the United States purchasing the rights of the company and constructing the canal. When negotiations between the United States and Colombia failed, Bunau-Varilla coordinated efforts with insurrectionists within Panama. When the rebels declared their independence from Colombia, Roosevelt ensured the success of the revolution by sending U.S. warships to protect Panama City. Bunau-Varilla appointed himself Panamanian Minister to the United States and proceeded to negotiate the Hay-Bunau-Varilla Treaty, which granted the United States the authority to construct the canal. The completion of the canal substantially shortened oceanic voyages from the West Coast of the United States to the East Coast, increasing trade and development throughout the nation and the world.

—*Cynthia Clark Northrup*

References
Anguizola, G. A. *Philippe Bunau-Varilla: The Man behind the Panama Canal*. Chicago: Nelson-Hall, 1980.
See also Volume 1: Panama and the Panama Canal; Roosevelt, Theodore.

Bureau of Corporations

Bureau established in 1903 to determine whether U.S. companies were acting in the public interest.

Congress established the Bureau of Corporations as a division of the Department of Commerce and Labor on February 14, 1903. The bureau was assigned to gather information about companies and to determine whether they were acting in the public interest.

As a repository of industry data, the Bureau of Corporations deterred illicit business activities by sharing corporate information. It was empowered to inspect and publish reports about the operation of interstate corporations (except common carriers of people or property), predating the Federal Trade Commission (FTC). When the Department of Commerce and Labor was divided into two departments in 1913, the Bureau of Corporations was assigned to the Department of Commerce.

The bureau's inspection power provided evidence for antitrust lawsuits. Following the passage of the Sherman Anti-Trust Act in 1890, courts were tolerant of vertical integration. However, in 1906 bureau officials conducted an in-depth investigation of Standard Oil Company of New Jersey that resulted in the company facing charges of monopolization in United States Circuit Court. In May 1911, the court ruled that Standard Oil was guilty of gaining through its stocks as a result of its monopoly, a violation of the Sherman Act. The decision forced Standard Oil to release the stocks of 36 independent companies and ended its domination.

In 1909, Bureau of Corporations officials concluded that the American Tobacco Company (ATC) prevailed against competitors because of astounding financial resources as opposed to superior organization or technology. The Supreme Court agreed in 1911, finding that the ATC had unfairly used vertical integration (a business structure in which a company owns its suppliers and buyers) to facilitate the creation of a monopoly by "foreclosing" competitors from sources for materials or outlets.

Detractors criticized the bureau for providing "sunshine" regulation, a system in which the regulator disingenuously cleansed corporate practices through the medium of public scrutiny while simultaneously educating the business community about efficient methods of competition. In 1914, the bureau was abolished and superseded by the FTC.

—*R. Jake Sudderth*

References
McCraw, Thomas K. *Prophets of Regulation*. Cambridge, MA: Harvard University Press, 1984.
Roy, William G. "The Politics of Bureaucratization and the United States Bureau of Corporations." *Journal of Political and Military Sociology,* vol. 10 (1982).
Sklar, Martin J. *The Corporate Reconstruction of American Capitalism, 1890–1916: The Market, the Law, and Politics*. New York: Cambridge University Press, 1988.
Thorelli, Hans B. *The Federal Antitrust Policy: The Origination of an American Tradition*. Baltimore, MD: Johns Hopkins University Press, 1955.
See also Volume 1: Carnegie, Andrew; Rockefeller, John D.; Standard Oil.

Bureau of Freedmen, Refugees, and Abandoned Lands

Reconstruction-era relief agency.

Congress established this temporary agency, commonly called the Freedmen's Bureau, in March of 1865 as part of the U.S. War Department. Its primary function was to provide practical assistance to four million former slaves as they made the transition from bondage to freedom. The task proved daunting, to say the least. The bureau operated in a region ravaged by war and acutely conflicted by competing visions of postwar Southern society, one white and one black. Although Southern whites accepted the act of emancipation, they feared a new order that included full social and political equality for African Americans. The former slaves craved true freedom, which they interpreted as independence from white control through land ownership, franchise, and the establishment of their own institutions.

General Oliver Otis Howard, a devout Evangelical Christian wounded during the Civil War, led the bureau as commissioner with the aid of assistant commissioners in each Southern state. Although the agency distributed badly needed food and medical supplies to destitute blacks and whites alike, insufficient resources coupled with the highly charged political climate of the period retarded its long-term effectiveness. Nevertheless, the bureau played an active role in the lives of the freedmen for several years. Freedmen's Bureau agents negotiated labor contracts between whites and blacks, adjudicated labor disputes between white landowners and their black employees, supervised state and local courts in their general treatment of the freedmen, and helped reunite black families separated by slavery and the war. The greatest accomplishments of the bureau were in the field of education: It paid teachers' salaries, supported school construction, and established black colleges and a system of schools that would survive Reconstruction and lay the foundation for public education in the South.

With the notable exception of its education programs, the bureau's efforts to provide long-term aid to former slaves lasted only a short time. Ambitious plans to redistribute land never materialized. By the time he left office, President Andrew Johnson, who opposed the bureau, had pardoned most of the ex-Confederates and restored to them hundreds of thousands of confiscated acres once earmarked for sale to freedmen. In 1866 the Supreme Court unanimously ruled in *ex parte Milligan* that military courts had no authority in areas where civilian courts functioned, thus casting serious doubts on the legality of martial law and the Freedmen's Bureau courts. A lack of funding and staff (for instance, at any given time no more than 20 agents operated in the state of Alabama) continued to plague the agency, as did growing apathy among Northern politicians with regard to the entire Reconstruction process. As the white Democratic Party grew stronger in the South, its leaders stepped up their resistance to the bureau, disparaging it as nothing more than a corrupt political tool of the Republican Congress. Ultimately crushed under the weight of the social and political struggles of the period, the Freedmen's Bureau ceased operation in 1872, leaving a mixed legacy.

—*Ben Wynne*

References
Foner, Eric. *Reconstruction: America's Unfinished Revolution, 1863–1877.* New York: Harper and Row, 1988.
Nieman, Donald G., ed. *The Freedmen's Bureau and Black Freedom.* Vol. 2, *African-American Life in the Post-Emancipation South, 1861–1900.* New York: Garland Publishing, 1994.
See also Volume 1: Education; Volume 2: Education.

Bureau of Indian Affairs (BIA)
Agency responsible for planning and executing federal policies concerning Native Americans.

Congress established the Bureau of Indian Affairs (BIA) in 1824 as part of the War Department. In 1849 it became part of the newly formed Department of Interior. In the nineteenth century, the BIA negotiated treaties with various Indian tribes, supervised Indian agents and other employees, formulated federal Indian policies, conducted on- and off-reservation Indian schools, monitored annuity payments, and protected Indian interests with federal and state authorities. Until 1933 the Bureau of Indian Affairs focused on programs of cultural assimilation intended to eventually break down the barriers between Native Americans and their Euro-American counterparts. After the passage of the Indian Reorganization Act in 1934, the BIA focused on preserving and cultivating Native American culture and identity. Today it remains committed to providing technical assistance to more than 500 federally recognized Indian tribes without compromising the government-to-government relationship that exists between tribal authorities and the federal government.

The BIA is headed by an assistant secretary of the interior who holds the title Commissioner of Indian Affairs and supervises 84 agency offices on Indian reservations and more than 14,000 employees.

—*James T. Carroll*

References
Prucha, Paul. *The Great Father: The United States Government and the American Indians.* Lincoln: University of Nebraska Press, 1984.
See also Volume 1: Indian Policy.

BUS
See Bank of the United States, First: 1791–1811; Bank of the United States, Second: 1816–1836.

Bush, George Herbert Walker (1924–)
American statesman, forty-first president of the United States (1989–1993), Republican.

The presidency of George H. W. Bush provides a vivid recent example of how lack of success in dealing with economic problems can dramatically erode political support for a leader despite his effectiveness in other spheres of statecraft.

Born June 12, 1924, in Milton, Massachusetts, Bush earned a degree in economics from Yale University in 1948, moved to Texas, and went successfully into the oil business. Between 1948 and 1950 he worked as a salesman for Idec, an oil-field equipment supply company. He founded Bush-Overly Oil Development Co. and Zapata Petroleum Corp. From 1964 to 1966 he worked as a chief executive officer of Zapata Petroleum Off Shore. Bush served as a Congressman (1967–1971), U.S. ambassador to the United Nations (1971–1973), chair of the Republican National Committee (1973–1974), chief of the U.S. liaison office (a quasi-embassy) in Peking (1974–1975), and director of the Central Intelligence Service (1976–1977).

During the Republican presidential primary campaign of 1980, Bush ran as a moderate candidate, criticizing the conservative economic program of Ronald Reagan and advocating governmental activism in the social sphere. Reagan won the party's nomination and Bush compromised his approach with Reagan's program, accepting the nomination for vice presidency. Serving as vice president from 1981 through 1989 in the Reagan administration, he contributed to the success of Reaganomics (or supply-side economics), particularly in heading a task force to reduce federal regulations. In 1988, Bush won his second bid for the Republican presidential nomination and defeated Democrat Michael S. Dukakis in the election. Bush lost the 1992 election to Bill Clinton.

As president, George H. W. Bush tried to consolidate the main accomplishments of the Reagan era. The end of the cold war in 1989 allowed him to cancel the annual inflation-adjustment spending increase of the military budget. He also initiated some important social measures including an increase in the minimum wage (from $3.80 per hour in 1990 to $4.25 per hour in 1991), and he championed two laws that imposed significant requirements on business: the Americans with Disabilities Act, which broadened the rights of disabled Americans; and a comprehensive Clean Air Act, which envisaged tighter control on auto emissions, use of fuel, emissions by utility plants, and so on, and would cost business more than $20 billion annually.

As the lengthy recession began in the summer of 1990, the economy also experienced some long-range negative consequences of the Reagan era, particularly a huge deficit. Hoping to spark a solid economic recovery, the Bush administration tried to negotiate a deficit-cutting budget with Congress, which was controlled by the Democrats. Bush had to accept tax increases, particularly for those paying top individual tax rates, as well as taxes on gasoline, beer, and luxury items, as a part of the budget compromise—even though during the campaign of 1988 he had issued a categorical pledge not to raise taxes.

Although the weakened economy kept tax receipts down and precluded expected deficit reductions in 1991 and 1992, the president's tax concessions to the Democrats alienated his conservative Republican supporters. These factors highlighted his ineffectiveness in dealing with domestic issues despite his strong leadership at the end of the cold war (the Berlin Wall fell in 1989, and the Soviet Union ended in December 1991) and after the U.S. victory in the Gulf War of 1991, and he lost his bid for reelection in 1992 to Bill Clinton.

In the international arena, Bush tried to manage commercial economic conflicts with main U.S. rivals (particularly Japan), promoted global economic coordination within the Group of Seven (the world's seven largest industrialized nations), and supported the idea of free trade. On December 17, 1992, he signed the North American Free Trade Agreement with Canada and Mexico, which created a free trade zone in the northern part of the Western Hemisphere.

—*Peter Rainow*

References

Greene, John Robert. *The Presidency of George Bush.* Lawrence: University Press of Kansas, 2000.

Parmet, Herbert. *George Bush: The Life of a Lone Star Yankee.* New York: Scribner's, 1997.

See also Volume 2: Trade Policy.

Bush, George W. (1946–)

Forty-third president of the United States, the son of former President George Herbert Walker Bush, Republican.

Born in New Haven, Connecticut, July 6, 1946, George W. Bush moved with his family to Midland, Texas, and then to Houston, where his father, George H. W. Bush, owned and operated an oil company. George W. Bush attended Yale University, receiving a bachelor's degree in 1968. After serving in the Texas Air National Guard during the Vietnam conflict, he earned his master's degree in business from Harvard Business School in 1975. He returned to Texas, worked in the energy industry, and helped his father win the presidency in 1988. Bush then formed a partnership that purchased the Texas Rangers baseball team in 1989. He became the general manager of the team and remained in that position until he won the Texas governor's race in 1994 and again in 1998. In 2000, Bush was the Republican candidate in the national presidential election, facing Democrat Al Gore. The election was close and, after a court battle that went to the Supreme Court, Bush was awarded Florida's winning Electoral College votes. His opponents charged him with "stealing" the election. Bush was inaugurated in 2001.

In 2001 the economy was in a recession that had begun the previous year when technology stocks plummeted, and Bush proposed a tax cut as a means of stimulating the economy. But before the tax cut could be implemented, terrorists attacked in New York City and Washington, D.C., on September 11, 2001, using passenger jets as weapons. The economy suffered as the country fought to rebound after the attacks. The airline industry was particularly hard hit. Bush insisted on a tax cut, and rebate checks were issued to many taxpayers in 2002. On May 28, 2003, Bush signed the Jobs and Growth Plan, which increased child tax credits from $600 to $1,000 per child; in July 2003 the Internal Revenue Service was to begin issuing checks for the difference to 25 million eligible families. The legislation also reduced the "marriage penalty," in which married couples pay a higher tax rate than two single individuals filing two separate returns. It reduced the amount of taxes withheld from employees' paychecks; this reduction applied to everyone who has to pay taxes based on wages. By June 2003 the Federal Reserve Board indicated that the U.S. economy is showing signs of recovery.

Bush has also implemented several other economic policies including those to expand home ownership (through creation of a federal fund to assist low-income families with down payments, a tax credit for the construction of single-family housing in the inner city, and simplification of the home closing process), increase international trade (through negotiations with foreign countries on free trade and the reduction of trade barriers), and develop a sound energy policy that encourages the development of alternative energy and reduces the dependence on foreign oil. The House of Representatives passed a comprehensive energy bill in April 2003 but at this writing the Senate continues to debate the issue. Meanwhile, the price of oil has dropped slightly. After the 2003 war in Iraq and the lifting of a UN embargo against that country, Iraqi oil can now freely be sold on the international market.

After accounting scandals at Enron (December 2001) and several other U.S. corporations revealed profiteering by top executives and the loss of retirement funds of workers, Bush introduced legislation designed to improve corporate responsibility. In 2002 Congress passed the Public Company Accounting Reform and Investor Protection Act, which charges the Securities and Exchange Commission with stricter enforcement of accounting and stock market practices and requires stiff penalties for violators. Bush has proposed health care reforms including improved availability of affordable prescription drugs for the elderly. Education reforms, including an early childhood initiative and school vouchers (which allow parents to use tax money to send their children to the school of their choice) are also on the president's agenda. Many of these policies are still being debated by Congress. Meanwhile, the Bush administration continues the international "war on terrorism," which began with the destruction of terrorist training camps in Afghanistan following terrorist attacks on the United States in 2001. Additional resources are being allocated to the new Homeland Security Agency, which now operates as the umbrella agency for many other departments in the domestic war against terrorism.

—*Cynthia Clark Northrup*

References
White House. Available: http://www.whitehouse.gov; accessed June 1, 2003.
See also Volume 1: Education; Volume 2: Education; Energy Policy.

Business

Companies that generate revenue and employee labor and that pay many of the taxes that fund the operation of the American government.

Historically, the business community maintained the tax base in the United States through the twentieth century and as the twenty-first century began. Companies that imported goods paid an import duty ranging from about 2 percent to more than 50 percent depending on the product. After ratification of the U.S. Constitution, the federal government relied on these revenue tariffs to pay off the fledgling nation's debt. As early as 1792, Secretary of the Treasury Alexander Hamilton in his *Report on the Subject of Manufactures* encouraged Congress to assist businesses, especially manufacturers, by erecting high protective tariffs. Although Congress rejected Hamilton's recommendations, by 1816 it recognized the need for a stronger manufacturing base in the United States to provide for the home market. Passage of the first protective tariff in 1816 signaled the beginning of a period of high protectionism that intensified during and after the Civil War.

When the United States emerged from the Civil War, Congress continued to repeatedly increase tariff duties and thus stimulate business, even though the government experienced many years of fiscal surpluses. As a result, big business flourished. Individuals such as Andrew Carnegie, John D. Rockefeller, and J. P. Morgan operated businesses freely without the threat of foreign competition. However, abuses experienced by laborers during this period eventually created a backlash against business that pushed Congress into passing such acts as the Sherman Anti-Trust Act and the Clayton Anti-Trust Act. Even with government prohibition of monopolies, the tendency remained to encourage big business, especially up to 1913, when a large portion of government revenue shifted from the tariff to a graduated personal income tax. Ratification in 1913 of the Sixteenth Amendment, which authorized a personal income tax, transferred a large portion of the burden of taxation from the business community to individuals. However, business continues to constitute a large portion of the taxes. During the Great Depression, despite the fact that the government now collected the personal income tax, tariff rates again increased as a result of the Hawley-Smoot Tariff—reaching an average level of about 50 percent on many items. Because many economists believed that the Hawley-Smoot Tariff of 1930 led to World War II because of the disruption of international trade and a worldwide depression, American officials after that war advocated free trade over protectionism. By this time, however, business in the United States had matured and no longer required government protection.

Because the United States operates under a capitalist system and business continues both to stimulate the economy and to provide revenue for the federal government, business will continue to enjoy a position of importance in the United States.

—*Cynthia Clark Northrup*

References
Eckes, Alfred E. *Opening America's Market: U.S. Foreign Policy since 1776.* Chapel Hill: University of North Carolina Press, 1995.
See also Volume 1: Antiunion Policies; Clayton Anti-Trust Act; Protective Tariffs; Sherman Anti-Trust Act; Sixteenth Amendment; Volume 2 (Documents): *Report on the Subject of Manufactures.*

C

Canada, Invasion of (1812–1813)

Attempt by the United States to acquire Canada in the early nineteenth century.

In the first years of the nineteenth century, many Americans, especially westerners, enviously eyed the natural resources of their northern neighbor, Canada. The lands around Lake Erie and Lake Ontario were a prime timber region, and those along the St. Lawrence River were exceedingly fertile. In November 1811, a new group of southern and western representatives arrived at the Twelfth Congress in Washington, D.C. Led by Henry Clay of Kentucky, John C. Calhoun of South Carolina, Peter B. Porter of New York, and Felix Grundy of Tennessee, this faction fanned the flames of the coming War of 1812 with Britain. They were outspoken advocates of defending American honor at sea, ending the threat of Indian attacks on the frontier, and incorporating Canada into the United States. Thus one element of the War of 1812 was a feeble, poorly planned, and uncoordinated attempt by U.S. forces to capture Canada. The strategy was to make a three-pronged attack against Montreal. All three attacks, carried out in the fall of 1813, failed. In the first, General William Hull ended his advance and returned to Detroit, fearing attacks by Indians in both countries. A second attempt failed when New York militiamen refused to enter Canada, and the final invasion under General Henry Dearborn ended for the same reason. Although these attempts failed, the desire to acquire more territory remained important to the United States.

The attempted invasion of Canada demonstrated the importance that territorial expansion played in America's vision of economic development. Acquiring new land would increase agricultural production and expand the nation's economy. The invasion also reflected the growing hunger for land among western farmers and speculators and the role their interest played in fueling the nation's expansion across the continent.

—*Peter S. Genovese*

References
Hickey, Donald R. *The War of 1812: A Forgotten Conflict.* Urbana: University of Illinois Press, 1989.
See also Volume 1: War of 1812.

Capitalism

An economic system stressing free markets and enterprise that played a vital role in the development of the United States.

Capitalism first arose in Europe and stemmed from the decline of feudalism, the rise of private property, and the placing of the individual good over the common good. It developed over hundreds of years in combination with various internal and external factors including state building, an agricultural revolution, a demographic revolution, a price revolution, and, in the 1800s, the Industrial Revolution.

Elements of capitalism have always existed, but beginning in the 1400s, as Europe started to expand outward, the means of production and mercantile activity slowly concentrated in the hands of private individuals. Europe's expansion into the Indian and Atlantic Oceans integrated its economy into those of the Far East and the Americas while introducing it to new sources of wealth, commodities, raw materials, markets, and consumers. The wealth of New Spain, for example, flowed back to Europe, initiating a price revolution as Europe moved away from a subsistence and barter economic system to a moneyed and market-driven economic system. This increase in the money supply corresponded with growth in the European population, which created both more workers and more consumers.

As more European states became involved in colonizing the Americas, they developed an economic system—termed *mercantilism* by economic theorist Adam Smith—designed to increase the power of the state. This system saw land, gold, and silver as the major forms of wealth and believed that wealth remained finite. Therefore, if a state gained or lost wealth, it gained or lost power. One issue stressed by Smith and many other early theorists was that a nation could increase its power by establishing colonies and foreign trade. They believed that monopolies allowed the state to acquire its revenues but that they limited the full potential of this developing economic system. In the mid-seventeenth and early eighteenth centuries in England, a debate began between supporters of monopolies and supporters of free trade. This debate culminated in the 1776 publication of Adam Smith's

Wealth of Nations exploring this new capitalist economic system. In his work, Smith argued that wealth, in the form of commodities, remained infinite and that a free market system created more wealth than a closed system. Smith and the political economists who built upon his work created the theoretical foundations of capitalism and expanded our understanding of how the economy works.

England's economic development set the stage for the rise of capitalism in the Americas. During the American Revolution, the American colonists hoped to establish free enterprise. After the creation of the U.S. Constitution, Secretary of the Treasury Alexander Hamilton used the powers it granted to further expand America's economic development. From the eighteenth century onward, capitalism played an important role in forming the American political, economic, social, ideological, and cultural system.

—*Ty M. Reese*

References
Smith, Adam. *An Inquiry into the Nature and Causes of the Wealth of Nations.* London, 1776.
Wallerstein, Immanuel. *Mercantilism and the Consolidation of the European World Economy, 1600–1750.* New York: Academic Press, 1980.
See also Volume 1: Hamilton, Alexander; Industrial Revolution.

Captains of Industry

Business leaders, industrial magnates, and entrepreneurs of the late nineteenth century.

Men like John D. Rockefeller, Andrew Carnegie, and John Pierpont (J. P.) Morgan, among many others, owned and coordinated large business enterprises such as oil production, steel manufacture, and investment banking. These captains of industry introduced products and employed methods of organization that fostered national economic growth while allowing them to accumulate massive fortunes and wield tremendous power. Though they achieved great wealth, status, and power, these men routinely risked significant financial loss. Ironically, a primary motivation for their risk-taking included their desire to bring order to an environment of chaotic competition.

The original entrepreneurs of sixteenth-century France did not take risks in commerce but operated rather as "fortune captains" who hired mercenaries for wars of gain and plunder. American captains of industry often pursued their economic goals with the same creativity and ruthlessness of military leaders. Via innovation, intense competition, and new organizational processes, captains of industry both eliminated competitors and changed the rules of doing business. Sociologist Joseph Schumpeter argued that, although entrepreneurs differed fundamentally from military leaders, they nevertheless acted out of a desire for conquest and control and remained capable of astounding innovation. The captains of industry generally did not create the industries in which they excelled, but they achieved success because of organizational, promotional, and administrative skill.

John D. Rockefeller manifested these skills at his company, Standard Oil. By eliminating competitors through horizontal integration (that is, merging with or controlling other organizations that produce the same product), Rockefeller mastered the use of the holding company, in which one company controls other companies by holding the majority of their stock. Rockefeller also achieved astounding success through vertical integration by controlling the sources of production and outlets of sale for a particular product. For instance, in addition to building his own tankers and pipelines, Rockefeller obtained railroad rebates that gave him a significant cost advantage over competitors.

Few captains of industry proved more skillful than Andrew Carnegie, who used vertical integration to outmaneuver competitors and create Carnegie Steel, the largest steel business in the world. Obsessed with reducing costs, Carnegie acquired not only his own sources for the raw materials used in steel production but also sales outlets for that production.

The investor and financier J. P. Morgan imposed a similar order on his business environment through investments and financial control. Morgan provided capital for the nation's rapidly expanding industries, thereby acquiring control of company management decisions and ultimately controlling entire economic sectors. Believing that unfettered economic competition led to chaos, Morgan acquired partial or full control of such key economic concerns as railroads, American Telephone and Telegraph, a host of financial and banking concerns, and even Carnegie's steel empire.

Through horizontal or vertical integration or through financial maneuvering, Rockefeller, Carnegie, and Morgan imposed stability and predictability on the highly competitive business environment of the late nineteenth century.

—*Eric Pullin*

References
Heilbroner, Robert L., and Aaron Singer. *The Economic Transformation of America: 1600 to Present.* San Diego, CA: Harcourt Brace Jovanovich, 1984.
Livesay, Harold C. *Andrew Carnegie and the Rise of Big Business.* Boston: Little, Brown, 1975.
Nevins, Allan. *John D. Rockefeller.* New York: Scribner's, 1940.
Strouse, Jean. *Morgan: American Financier.* New York: Random House, 1999.
See also Volume 1: Carnegie, Andrew; Morgan, John Pierpont; Rockefeller, John D.

Carey Act (1894)

The federal government's inadequate first effort to underwrite water reclamation projects by selling public lands and blending federal and state responsibilities.

After the Civil War, the growing agricultural needs of industrial America and the population's westward surge encountered a harsh reality—arid lands beyond the 100th meridian could not sustain eastern forms of agriculture. Inspired by Jeffersonian ideals of an agrarian society, generous rains in the 1870s and 1880s, and a fantasy that "water follows the plow" (and forests), the federal government determined to promote irrigation. The Timber Culture Act (1873) gave land to anyone planting trees; the Desert Land Act (1877) bestowed additional acres on those irrigating land. These measures benefited mostly speculators; individual farmers lacked the capital necessary to purchase any land.

John Wesley Powell's *Report on the Lands of the Arid Region of the United States* (1878) advocated that laws be appropriate to the environment. Arid land required larger homesteads, whose shape and location must depend on available water—irrigation remained essential. By the 1880s and 1890s, droughts and the panic of 1893 gave his proposals urgency.

Irrigation advocates feuded. Should the federal government undertake reclamation (as many western congressional representatives wanted) or simply support reclamation by land cessions? Eastern states feared the reclamation cost, so in 1894 U.S. Senator Joseph Carey (Wyoming) authored a law mixing federal and state responsibilities. Any arid state might receive up to one million acres for reclamation, though neither it nor its assignees (such as an heir or prospective buyer) could receive title to that land until after 10 years of irrigation. State or private companies could build the reclamation projects using the land as collateral. Settlers must irrigate 20 of every 160 acres. The federal government approved all plans, and states chose the land, supervised settlement (preventing monopolies and speculation), and regulated water prices. Several projects started, most notably one by William F. "Buffalo Bill" Cody. Yet this experiment in cooperative federalism failed. By 1958, only a million acres had been distributed. States feared indebtedness as in the canal debacles of the 1830s; Populist suspicions of big government, localism, and sectionalism hampered progress; and projects exceeded westerners' technical and capital resources. It remained for the federal government to undertake reclamation itself after the passage of the Newlands Reclamation Act of 1902.

—*Everett W. Kindig*

References
Pisani, Donald J. *To Reclaim a Divided West: Water, Law, and Public Policy, 1848–1902*. Albuquerque: University of New Mexico Press, 1992.
U.S. Statutes at Large 28 (1895): 422–423.
See also Volume 2: Land Policies.

Carnegie, Andrew (1835–1919)
Scottish-born immigrant who made a fortune in the iron business but is best remembered for his generosity and philanthropy.

Andrew Carnegie was born November 25, 1835. In 1848, the Carnegie family left the poverty of Scotland in hopes of a better life in America. They joined other family members in Pittsburgh, Pennsylvania, where young Andrew held a series of odd jobs. At age 14 he acquired a job with the telegraph, where he excelled, earning an astounding $4 a week. In the telegraph office Andrew met Thomas A. Scott, who had just started his railroad career as a station agent with the Pennsylvania Railroad. Scott hired Andrew as his secretary and personal telegraph messenger at a salary of $35 a week.

Carnegie remained with Pennsylvania Railroad for 12 years, working his way up until he succeeded Scott as superintendent. He acquired his first large profit from his stock in the Woodruff Company, holder of the Pullman sleeping car patent. In 1865, he resigned from the Pennsylvania Railroad to take advantage of a new field that had blossomed during the Civil War—the iron industry. Using his connections in Europe and the railroad business, Carnegie amassed a fortune in iron and steel.

A shrewd and talented businessman, Carnegie had a passion for learning and reading. He wrote several books and papers on wealth and its uses. In 1901 he sold his company, Carnegie Steel, to J. P. Morgan's United States Steel Corporation. With the money from the sale, he established a retirement and benefit fund for his employees.

Carnegie believed any wealth above $50,000 per year should be spent giving back to the community. He donated money to colleges, trusts, and other causes he felt were important. The Carnegie Library Project remains one of his most visible projects. Many small and rural libraries throughout the country were gifts from the Carnegie Foundation. Carnegie continued his good works until his death August 11, 1919, at the age of 83. He had been so influential that his life reflected the development of industrial history as a whole.

—*Lisa A. Ennis*

References
Johnson, Allen, ed. *Dictionary of American Biography*. Vols. 2, 3, and 5. New York: Scribner's, 1929.
See also Volume 1: Steel.

Carpetbaggers
Term given to Northerners who traveled south during Reconstruction hoping to make a fortune by taking advantage of the South's weakened economy following the Civil War.

Southern states, essentially bankrupt and starved for capital at the close of the Civil War, hoped Northern investors would revitalize the Southern economy. Reassured by the Southern press that the Northerners meant no harm, Southerners welcomed Northern investors, who were drawn to the potential for wealth. Among these "carpetbaggers" were well-educated businesspeople, political leaders, teachers, and soldiers who worked in partnerships with southern planters. Some bought abandoned or repossessed land, hoping to take advantage of the South's agricultural opportunities. Northern investments helped raise land prices and allowed the Southern planters to maintain their standard of living. Some carpetbaggers became involved in reform and politics, seeking to modernize the South through various internal improvements. Several carpetbaggers served in Congress during Reconstruction.

Although most people recognized the importance of the carpetbaggers in stabilizing the Southern economy, they remained unpopular outsiders in many areas. The carpetbaggers' confidence and their disregard for Southern opinions and culture often created tensions. Another area of strain involved race. Carpetbaggers and their Southern counterpart, Scalawags, tended to vote along Republican lines aligned with the newly freed slaves, some working as Freedmen's Bureau agents. This antagonism helped promote the vicious image associated with the carpetbagger. (The name itself was negative and came from rumors that the Northerners were from lowest class and moved south with everything they owned put in one bag made of carpet.) Most carpetbaggers either returned to the North or joined Southern society after the compromise of 1877, which resulted in Rutherford B. Hayes becoming president with the understanding that Reconstruction would end.

—*Lisa A. Ennis*

References
Foner, Eric. *Reconstruction: America's Unfinished Revolution, 1863–1877.* New York: Harper and Row, 1988.
See also Volumes 1, 2: Slavery.

CCC

See Civilian Conservation Corps.

CCW

See Committee on the Conduct of the War.

CEA

See Council of Economic Advisers.

Census

A systematic accounting of persons, demographics, and economic resources of the nation.

Since ancient times, governments have recorded census information in an effort to determine the composition and condition of the nation or empire, primarily for taxation purposes. Under the U.S. Constitution, the United States conducted its first census in 1790 and has continued to do so every 10 years. Early census records focused primarily on population statistics—for example, the number of free persons and slaves, family size, and average age groups. Not until the 1820s did the government include additional categories to glean information about agriculture, commerce, and manufacturing. (Just four years prior to the 1820 census, the government had enacted the first of many protective tariffs designed to encourage the growth of manufacturing. Consequently, the figures were important as the government sought to track economic changes.)

By 1840, the census expanded to include information on transportation (sea navigation, canals, and lakes), mining, churches, libraries, schools, education, literacy, marriages, births, and deaths. Also included was information pertaining to newspapers and printing. The inclusion of these facts reflects the onset of the market revolution and its accompanying transportation, communication, and social revolutions. The 1840s and 1850s were a period of tremendous change as a result of the move from subsistence to a market economy, and through the census the government attempted to record these changes.

The next major change in the census occurred in 1870, when categories were added for race and place of birth in an effort to track the origins of foreign-born peoples residing in the United States. Other categories added concerned taxation (federal, state, and local) and property. Significantly, it was not until the 1900 census that adequate figures appear on labor—not surprisingly, well after the major labor strikes of the late 1800s. After a period in which divorce rates increased rapidly, the government included questions about the marital status of Americans in the 1930 census. By the 1940s, the census questionnaire also included categories for retail and wholesale establishments, reflecting expansion of the nation's commerce during World War II. By the 1960s the census sought a wealth of information that enabled the government to discern the economic and social condition of the country. Congress uses the statistics to determine the allocation of funds and programs. The primary concern in recent decades is the undercounting of homeless and minority groups, a fact that could reduce federal expenditures in the areas most in need of funds.

—*Cynthia Clark Northrup*

References
Kassinger, Ruth. *U.S. Census: A Mirror of America.* Austin, TX: Raintree Steck-Vaughn, 1999.
See also Volume 1: Population; Slavery; Volume 2: Labor; Slavery.

CENTO

See Central Treaty Organization.

Central Treaty Organization (CENTO)

Organization in existence from 1955 until 1979 that attempted to unite the northern tier of Middle Eastern states in the face of the Soviet threat to the region during the cold war.

The Central Treaty Organization (CENTO) grew out of the Baghdad Pact, a mutual assistance and defense arrangement signed by Iraq and Turkey on February 24, 1955; the United Kingdom on April 5, 1955; Pakistan on September 23, 1955; and Iran on November 3, 1955. Originally dubbed the Middle East Treaty Organization (METO) and then called the Baghdad Pact, CENTO also reflected the West's growing concerns over potential threats emerging from within the region—for example, Gamal Abdel Nasser's Egypt with its pro-Soviet leanings. The United States actively promoted the Baghdad Pact as a key indicator of the West's commitment to the region and induced Pakistan to join the Baghdad Pact in 1955. The United States became an associate member of

METO in 1956, revealing its overt interest in supporting the organization. Following Iraq's withdrawal from the Baghdad Pact in the aftermath of its 1958 revolution, METO headquarters moved from Baghdad to Ankara, Turkey, and the organization changed its name to CENTO.

Conceived as a part of U.S. Secretary of State John Foster Dulles's "pactomania" along with the formation of the North Atlantic Treaty Organization and the Southeast Asia Treaty Organization, CENTO attempted to surround the Soviet Union with defensive alliances. The organization closed the geostrategic gap between NATO and SEATO that exposed to potential attack Persian Gulf oilfields and vital transit routes like the Suez Canal. Never challenged militarily, CENTO proved a reliable though not always effective conduit for U.S. financial assistance to CENTO members. USAID (the United States Agency for International Development) remained CENTO's most significant American contributor, underscoring the U.S. government position that CENTO operated primarily as a political tool and, at best, a marginal military alliance. CENTO collapsed in 1979 during the Iranian Revolution when Iran, Pakistan, and Turkey withdrew.

—*Robert Rook*

References
Kuniholm, Bruce R. *The Origins of the Cold War in the Near East: Great-Power Conflict and Diplomacy in Iran, Turkey, and Greece.* Princeton, NJ: Princeton University Press, 1980.
See also Volume 1: Cold War.

Charles River Bridge v. Warren Bridge (1837)

A court case pitting the public good against private property rights.

In 1785, the Massachusetts legislature granted a corporate charter to John Hancock and other investors to build a toll bridge over the Charles River from Boston in the south to Charlestown in the north. The bridge quickly proved a profitable venture, and the value of the original shares increased tenfold. The high profits of the Charles River Bridge Company were threatened in 1828 when the Massachusetts legislature granted a corporate charter to the Warren Bridge Company to build another bridge across the Charles River. The new bridge would charge a toll only until the original investors had recouped their initial investment. The Warren Bridge would then be free to all travelers who crossed it.

The owners of the Charles River Bridge sued the owners of the Warren Bridge, arguing that their original corporate charter gave them a vested right to control bridge traffic across the Charles River. Because the new Warren Bridge would eventually charge no tolls, it would inevitably destroy the business of the Charles River Bridge and thus impair the original charter. Massachusetts, argued owners of the Charles River Bridge, had therefore violated the contract clause of the U.S. Constitution that clearly states in Article 1, Section 10: "No State shall ... pass any Law impairing the Obligation of Contracts." The owners of the Charles River Bridge hoped that the Supreme Court would follow the precedent set in *Dartmouth College v. Woodward* (1819) and decide the case in their favor.

Although the case was originally argued in 1831 before the Court of Chief Justice John Marshall, the justices could never reach a decision. When Roger B. Taney became chief justice in 1836, he ordered that the case be reargued in January 1837 and ruled in favor of the Warren Bridge on February 12, 1837. In a 4-to-3 decision, Taney held that the 1785 charter did not explicitly state that the Charles River Bridge had an exclusive right to carry traffic. He reasoned that if monopoly rights were read into every corporate charter, the American people would be unable to benefit from technological improvements in the future. Taney laid down an even more important precedent when he ruled that the public good must prevail whenever the rights of the community conflict with the rights of private property. Justice Taney's decision did much to promote the growth of American business in the early nineteenth century.

—*Mary Stockwell*

References
Siegel, Martin. *The Taney Court, 1836–1864.* Millwood, NY: Associated Faculty Press, 1987.
See also Volume 2: Judiciary.

Checkers Speech (September 23, 1952)

Nationally televised speech delivered by Republican vice presidential candidate Richard Nixon.

During the 1952 presidential election campaign, in which he ran as Dwight D. Eisenhower's vice presidential candidate, Richard Nixon appeared on national television in response to Democratic charges that he had accepted payments for political expenses from a secret fund managed by a group of dubious businesspeople. The fund and the transactions associated with it were legal and commonplace, but the publicity generated by the charges threatened Nixon's place on the Republican ticket and his long-term political plans. Nixon gave a masterful performance. He disclosed his financial situation to the television audience, assuring millions of viewers that he was not a wealthy man and that he had never profited from public service. He also boasted that his wife Pat, in contrast to the mink-coated wives of officials in President Harry S Truman's administration, wore a "respectable Republican cloth coat." The speech received its name because of Nixon's admission that his family did plan to keep one political contribution—a black and white cocker spaniel that his young daughter Tricia named Checkers. The televised appearance was a great success for Nixon. He remained on the Republican ticket and served as vice president under President Dwight D. Eisenhower for eight years. Throughout the rest of Nixon's political career, his detractors would recall the performance as a brazen exercise in manipulation.

—*Ben Wynne*

References
Ambrose, Stephen E. *The Education of a Politician.* Vol. 1, *Nixon.* New York: Simon and Schuster, 1987–1991.
See also Volume 1: Corruption.

Checks and Balances

A system designed to protect individual rights against possible violation by government; part of the theory of balanced government in which powers are separated, a theory that can be traced back to ancient times.

The theory of checks and balances rests on a system of separation of powers or balanced government. Historians can trace government consisting of a separation of powers back to the ancient Greeks. Aristotle prescribed a system of "mixed government" composed of monarchy, aristocracy, and democracy. The system of the ancient Romans relied on a "balance of interests" among the monarchical, aristocratic, and democratic parts of the government.

The American system achieves a balance of powers or functions among the three branches of government: the executive (the president), the legislative (the two houses of Congress), and the judicial (the Supreme Court). This system predates independence from England. It operated in several of the colonial provincial governments, including those of Virginia, Massachusetts, and New Hampshire. During the period of the Articles of Confederation, Thomas Jefferson advocated a system of balanced government to avoid corruption, tyranny, and despotism.

The Americans, when drafting the U.S. Constitution, adopted these ideas from the eighteenth-century French philosopher Charles de Secondat, Baron de Montesquieu (1689–1755), who wrote *The Spirit of the Laws* (1748). Montesquieu bequeathed to the American founding fathers the principle of separation of powers necessary for the system of checks and balances to function.

The founding fathers believed that to maintain a government that is free from tyranny and corruption, the government must have more than simple separation of powers. Thus, they prescribed a system of checks (each government branch watches the other two to restrain them from usurping power) and balances (power remains equally divided among the three government branches). The U.S. Constitution specifically delineates these checks and balances: The two houses of Congress, the Senate and the House of Representatives, legislate separately but require at least minimal cooperation of the other. Congress can pass a bill into law, but the president can veto it. The Congress and president can agree on passing a law, but the judiciary can declare it unconstitutional. The president is in charge of foreign and military policy, but the Senate must ratify the president's treaties if they are to become law. Congress must agree to raise the funds to support the military. Under this system, each branch of government has its own authority to make decisions on specific issues; however, it often requires the consent of the other two branches.

The American system of a federal government further ensures the working of a system of checks and balances. State governments share power with the federal government; thus, neither has supreme power. The fact that the people directly elect politicians is another check on power.

—*Leigh Whaley*

References

Merry, Henry J. *Five-Branch Government: The Full Measure of Constitutional Checks and Balances.* Urbana: University of Illinois Press, 1980.

Panogopoulos, E. P. *Essays on the History and Meaning of Checks and Balances.* Lanham, MD: University Press of America, 1986.

See also Volume 1: Constitution.

Child Labor

The employment of youths under the age of 18 years.

From colonial times through the mid-1840s, the United States experienced a scarcity of laborers. Families relied on their children to assist with agricultural chores or with the family-owned business. Usually young boys between the ages of 10 and 14 would be apprenticed outside the home for additional wages. This system remained in place and unchallenged until the 1840s, when educational reformers sought to regulate work hours in an effort to ensure that children would have enough time to attend school and complete their studies. The beginning of the movement for child labor regulation coincides with the transformation from a subsistence economy to a market economy in the United States—a change that demanded a literate citizenry. States including Connecticut and Massachusetts passed legislation requiring employers to provide a minimum of three hours of educational instruction to children, but these laws remained relatively ineffective because of a lack of enforcement.

Just as factories began to expand rapidly, a wave of immigrants arrived in the United States. Employers often hired adult immigrants who had many children so that their children would also be available as laborers. In these factories, children worked from 10- to 13-hour days in unhealthy conditions. Because women filled most of the positions in the textile industry, children moved into other, more hazardous, occupations, such as coal mining. Employers realized that children could be paid a lower wage and that they usually proved more controllable than adults, especially because unions had a difficult time organizing them.

By the beginning of the twentieth century, the Progressives, who advocated a wide range of political, social, and economic reforms, began advocating the regulation of child labor at the federal level. They championed their cause by initiating a public awareness campaign, distributing photographs of the deplorable conditions under which many children worked, and raising the level of public sympathy for the children. Proponents of federal legislation distributed pamphlets, lobbied Congress, and employed experts to conduct studies. Congress finally passed child labor laws in 1916 and 1918, but the U.S. Supreme Court declared the laws unconstitutional.

As a result of increased unemployment during the Great Depression, Congress passed the Fair Labor Standards Act of 1938, which proved to be the first effective measure that would regulate the number of hours worked by, and wages paid to, children. Upheld by the U.S. Supreme Court as constitutional, the act meant to ensure that adults had jobs by restricting the employment of children. Children under the age of 14 were forbidden to work for commercial agriculture or in other places of employment other than their family farm or business. Children between 14 and 16 could only work 18 hours a week during the school year and 40 hours a week during the summer. In addition, the Department of Labor in 1938 issued a list of hazardous occupations in which child labor is prohibited, with the imposition of stiff penalties for violators. Currently, federal law allows for the minimum payment of $4.25 an hour for the first 90 days of employment for youths, with an increase to the minimum wage standard after the probationary period. Children cannot work prior to 7 A.M. or after 7 P.M. except in the summer, when the latter time is extended to 9 P.M.

Restriction of child labor has resulted in a general increase in wages for the lower-paying jobs. It has also encouraged children to concentrate on their education. Consequently, more employment opportunities exist for adults. Overall, the legislation has proved effective except for migratory agricultural laborers and in the textile industry, where the children of illegal immigrants work long hours for less than the minimum wage.

—*Cynthia Clark Northrup*

References
Trattner, Walter. *Crusade for the Children: A History of the National Child Labor Committee and Child Labor Reform in America*. Chicago: Quadrangle Books, 1970.
See also Volume 2: Labor.

China

World's most populous country and third-largest country in size, with increasing importance for U.S. trade and investment since the 1880s.

Formal U.S.-China economic relations began with the 1844 Treaty of Wangxia, which granted most-favored-nation trading status to the United States. American economic interests rapidly expanded in China during the late nineteenth century, when the United States emerged as a major world power and its influence grew in the Pacific. By acquiring the Philippines in the Spanish-American War of 1898, the United States founded a stronghold for American trade in Asia and gained convenient proximity for American commercial gains in China. But given the exclusive spheres of influence that other Western powers and Japan had carved out based on the unequal treaties with the Qing government since 1840, the United States faced the danger of being cut off from the China trade. To protect American interests without risking conflict, U.S. Secretary of State John Hay, in 1899 and 1900, respectively, delivered diplomatic notes to the major powers (England, Germany, Russia, France, Japan, and Italy) that possessed spheres of influence in China. He demanded equal and fair chances for all nations that wanted to compete in the China market and asked the major powers for their commitment to Chinese sovereignty and territorial integrity. These notes established an "open door" as the international policy

pursued by the United States toward China until 1949, and they were important for U.S. relations with other imperial powers in East Asia until World War II. When the Communist Party of China (CPC) defeated the Nationalist Chinese forces and took power in China's mainland in 1949, economic contact between mainland China (the People's Republic of China) and the United States was suspended, not to be renewed until 1978.

After the fall of mainland China to communist forces under Mao Zedong, the United States formally recognized Taiwan as the legitimate government of China under Chiang Kai-Shek, the leader of the Nationalist Chinese forces. Although Richard Nixon visited the People's Republic of China in 1972 after the U.S. government initiated a policy of détente toward communist countries, the United States continued to recognize Taiwan as the legitimate government of China until 1979. In 1979 the United States transferred recognition to the government of the People's Republic of China.

Chinese-American economic relations developed rapidly in the 1980s when the new CPC leadership under Deng Xiaoping pursued pragmatic modernization for China and initiated continuous economic reforms in the name of building "socialism" with Chinese characteristics. Through economic decentralization and by opening up to foreign investments, China has improved its productivity and its people's living standard and has made its national strength more comprehensive.

Vital to China's economic growth are exports to the United States and American investment in Chinese technology. Since 1980 the United States has become a foremost market for Chinese exports, and China has generated increasing trade surplus—more than $103 billion in 2002. Meanwhile, American investment in China has been growing rapidly. In 1997 alone, Americans had investments in 22,240 Chinese projects the total contractual value of which was worth $35.17 billion. Despite the trend toward greater economic intercourse with China, the United States has long been protesting China's unfair trade practices (high tariffs and market closings to certain American industries) and piracy of intellectual property rights (especially in U.S. movies, computer software, and compact discs). Contention on these issues led the United States to threaten tariff retaliation against China in 1992. To avoid a trade war, the two countries negotiated and signed the 1992 Intellectual Property Protection Memorandum. In 1995, China promised to lower certain tariff barriers and open markets to several American products in exchange for American support of China's entry into the World Trade Organization (WTO). In 2000, the U.S. Congress voted to give China permanent most-favored-nation status.

—*Guoqiang Zheng*

References
Vohra, Ranbir. *China's Path to Modernization*. Upper Saddle River, NJ: Prentice-Hall, 2000.
See also Volume 1: Boxer Rebellion; Open Door Notes; World Trade Organization.

Civil Rights Act of 1968

Act that reinforced the end of racial segregation.

The Civil Rights Act of 1968 passed Congress on April 11, 1968, after a two-year struggle to include an open housing act under the broad umbrella of civil rights. The assassination of civil rights leader Martin Luther King on April 4, 1968, guaranteed the passage of this law and prompted members of Congress to attach a provision to the act that made crossing state lines for purposes of inciting disorder a federal crime.

This legislation prohibits housing discrimination in sales and rentals based on race, color, national origin, or religion. It also eliminated a major legal obstacle to racial equality and concluded an important legislative epoch that began with the U.S. Supreme Court decision in *Brown v. Board of Education* (1954) that ended segregation in public schools.

—*James T. Carroll*

References
Patterson, James. *Grand Expectations: The United States, 1945–1974.* New York: Oxford University Press, 1996.
See also Volume 1: Civil Rights Movement.

Civil Rights Movement (1955–1968)

Attempts by the African American community to achieve political and economic equality.

Although the Civil War ended with the freeing of all Africans from the institution of slavery and the passage of the Thirteenth and Fourteenth Amendments, which ended slavery and defined citizenship, due process, and equal protection, blacks in the United States continued to experience discrimination. Jim Crow laws in the South between the 1880s and 1960s, which enforced segregation, and the 1896 Supreme Court decision in *Plessy v. Ferguson,* which determined that blacks must have equal facilities even if they were separate facilities, resulted in widespread discrimination against black citizens. Not until after World War II and the dismantling of the colonial empires of the world did the United States begin the slow process of ending segregation. In 1954, the Supreme Court heard arguments in the case of *Brown v. Board of Education,* in which attorneys for the plaintiffs argued that separate schools for black children could not provide an education equal to that available to white children. They based their arguments on a study conducted among black and white children in which the children invariably favored white dolls over black dolls because they were "prettier" or "richer" or "better." The Supreme Court accepted the argument and ordered that the states desegregate the public schools. This decision was later extended to higher education. Access to better educational opportunities became a key economic tool for advancement by African Americans.

Brown v. Board of Education provided an impetus to the Civil Rights movement. On December 1, 1955, Rosa Parks, a black seamstress, refused to give up her seat to a white passenger on a public bus in Montgomery, Alabama. Parks, a member of the National Association for the Advancement of Colored People, was arrested. Blacks in Montgomery, led by a charismatic young preacher named Martin Luther King Jr., initiated a boycott of the Montgomery bus system that lasted for a year and ceased only after an edict was issued ending segregation on public transportation. The boycott's success can be attributed to economic pressure placed on the municipality by loss of revenue, because blacks comprised the largest percentage of fare-paying passengers.

Nonviolent civil disobedience became the hallmark of the Civil Rights movement throughout the rest of the 1950s and the first half of the 1960s. Students engaged in sit-ins at lunch counters after being refused service based on the color of their skin. The first of these occurred in 1960 when students of the North Carolina Agricultural and Technical College refused to leave a drugstore lunch counter or offer resistance when white patrons spat at them, poured drinks and catsup on them, and verbally harassed them. In the meantime, the lunch counter lost revenue because the seats were occupied.

The Civil Rights movement gained national attention in 1963 when the Student Nonviolent Coordinating Committee (SNCC) organized a campaign in Birmingham, Alabama. Television cameras captured the events as police used dogs, fire hoses, and clubs against nonviolent demonstrators, some of whom were children. The violence in Birmingham led President John F. Kennedy to push for legislation that would ensure rights for black citizens. After Kennedy's assassination, President Lyndon B. Johnson secured passage of the Civil Rights Act of 1964, which prohibited discrimination based on race, sex, or creed, and the Voting Rights Act of 1965. After Johnson's Great Society speech in which he demanded an end to poverty and injustice, many blacks believed that the federal government would move quickly to improve their economic plight. When new economic opportunities failed to materialize and both Martin Luther King and former Attorney General Robert F. Kennedy, a powerful supporter of civil rights, were assassinated in 1968, several U.S. cities experienced riots. After 1968, the Civil Rights movement became more violent with the rise of groups like the Black Panthers, who advocated a more militant approach.

During the 1970s, the Supreme Court once again became involved in civil rights, ordering school busing of children as a way of ending school segregation caused by "white flight," in which great numbers of white families left cities to move to more expensive suburbs, leaving the urban core to poorer black families. Over the past several decades, the national Civil Rights movement has declined as more black Americans have achieved new levels of economic, social, and political acceptance.

—*Cynthia Clark Northrup*

References
Davis, Jack E. *The Civil Rights Movement.* Malden, MA: Blackwell, 2001.
See also Volume 1: Montgomery Bus Boycott.

Civil Works Administration (CWA)

A federal depression-era program that put out-of-work Americans to work on public projects.

President Franklin D. Roosevelt signed Executive Order 6420-B creating the Civil Works Administration (CWA) on November 9, 1933. This entirely federal program was headed by Harry L. Hopkins, a federal emergency relief administrator who recruited people from relief and unemployment lists. Keeping in mind people's emotional and psychological well-being, Hopkins created a system in which people worked on public works projects throughout the nation rather than simply receiving a regular relief check. By early 1943, the CWA employed 4.2 million people. Roosevelt would remember this successful model in future relief projects. The program became an extraordinary and immediate success. In the West, CWA workers helped cope with a serious drought. With help from Eleanor Roosevelt, the president's wife, Hopkins also focused on providing work for artists and actors, despite the president's doubts about the idea's validity. For instance, Hopkins sent opera singers on tour in the Ozark Mountains, providing people in an economically disadvantaged region with a cultural event they would otherwise never have experienced. Unemployed teachers also benefited from the CWA. Overall, the CWA remains responsible for building 40,000 schools, 469 airports, and miles of streets and roads. The most important result of the program, however, was the morale boost it gave the nation.

Hopkins and Roosevelt tried to keep politics out of the CWA, but it was hurt by rumors of political patronage and illegal profits. During the harsh winter of 1933–1934, Roosevelt wanted to end the program despite its success, worried about the political problems and enormous cost associated with the program and about creating a permanent poor class dependent on welfare. Overall, the program infused the economy with more than $1 billion dollars and played an important part in helping the American people survive the 1933 winter. In 1939 the CWA became known as the Works Progress Administration.

—*Lisa A. Ennis*

References

Olson, James Stuart, ed. *Historical Dictionary of the New Deal: From Inauguration to Preparation for War.* Westport, CT: Greenwood Press, 1985.
See also Volume 1: New Deal; Roosevelt, Franklin D.

Civilian Conservation Corps (CCC)

A depression-era program designed to provide employment relief for young men and as an emergency conservation measure.

On March 21, 1933, President Franklin D. Roosevelt asked Congress to create the Civilian Conservation Corps (CCC). One of the first and most successful of the New Deal programs, which were designed to initiate political, social, and economic reforms, the CCC provided jobs for 17- to 24-year-old single men whose families already received some sort of relief. Eventually, some 2.5 million young men would serve in the CCC. Organized and administered by the U.S. Army, the CCC consisted of companies of 200 men. Each volunteer received a monthly paycheck of $30, a portion of which they

sent home. Much like army recruits, the CCC volunteers lived in camps or barracks and received uniforms, meals, and medical care. The agency stressed education, and many men learned to read and write in CCC camps. When Congress removed age and marital restrictions in 1935, participation in the CCC increased markedly. The Corps was open to all races, and many Native Americans and African Americans volunteered. However, African Americans were segregated in all-black camps.

One of the most expensive of the New Deal programs, the CCC was also one of the most beneficial. CCC volunteers restored national historic sites, built various facilities in national parks, worked on dams and reservoirs, and helped fight forest fires. The group receives credit for their reforestation efforts; nicknamed "Roosevelt's Tree Army," the CCC planted more than two billion trees. Under the authority of the Tennessee Valley Authority, the CCC also worked to prevent topsoil erosion. As the economy improved, the CCC's numbers began to decline, and in 1942 Congress cut funding.

—*Lisa A. Ennis*

References

Olson, James Stuart, ed. *Historical Dictionary of the New Deal: From Inauguration to Preparation for War.* Westport, CT: Greenwood Press, 1985.
See also Volume 1: New Deal; Roosevelt, Franklin D.

Class

Collection of people with commensurate economic or social standing.

The term *class* was known to the Romans, who categorized people according to wealth. During the modern period, which began in the eighteenth century, the term's definition was refined by Physiocrats, classical political economists, and Marxists. In the writings of the Physiocratic School, particularly in François Quesnay's *Tableau Oeconomique* (1758), the term was used to designate farmers (*classe productive*), landlords (*classe distributive*), and merchants (*classe sterile*). Though familiar with the works of the Physiocrats, economic theorist Adam Smith preferred to describe social relations in terms of ranks and orders. Thereafter, David Ricardo's *Principles of Political Economy* (1817), written during the economic, political, and social ferment of the Industrial Revolution, demarcated the classes of capital and labor. Finally, Karl Marx's critique of classical political economy, which reworked the categories of Smith and Ricardo, emphasized the irreducible conflict between the capitalist class (the owners of the means of production) and the working class (the sellers of labor power).

In Marx's view, the existence of classes was linked inextricably to "particular, historic phases in the development of production." Accordingly, Marx anticipated the intensification of class struggle (and hence the progressive polarization of society). In theory, this historical process would produce a socialist revolution followed by the consolidation of a provisional workers' state. However, the electoral success of socialist parties (for example, the German Social Democratic Party) dampened the revolutionary fervor of the working-class movement. Consequently, Eduard Bernstein and other revisionists came not only to advocate the parliamentary path to socialism but also to elaborate a more nuanced conception of class conflict. In essence, Bernstein argued that the rising standard of living of the working class and the growth of the middle class testified to the success of parliamentary socialism. (Arguably, Bernstein's vision was vindicated by the advent of the welfare state—the historic compromise between capital and labor—in the aftermath of World War II.)

With the emergence of sociology as an academic discipline early in the twentieth century, the concept of class received further elaboration. Fittingly, the putative founders of sociology, Emile Durkheim and Max Weber, engaged in an implicit dialogue with Marxism. Durkheim—influenced by the positivism of Auguste Comte, who created the field of sociology, and the utopian socialism of philosopher Claude Henri de Rouvroy, Comte de Saint-Simon—isolated two forms of social cohesion: mechanical solidarity (deriving from common beliefs, sentiments, rituals, and routines) and organic solidarity (deriving from participation in the division of labor). Influenced by neo-Kantianism, Weber introduced three terms to designate social standing: class situation (i.e., economic or material prospects), status situation (i.e., honor or prestige), and power (i.e., access to the legitimate use of force). Thus, in effect, the contributions of Durkheim and Weber compensated for the class reductionism inherent in orthodox Marxism.

In the United States, the absence of a significant socialist movement led sociologists to postulate "American exceptionalism." Though indebted to Marx, C. Wright Mills rejected the idea of the working class as the motor of social change. His intervention had a lasting influence on American sociology.

—Mark Frezzo

References

Bottomore, Tom. *Classes in Modern Society.* New York: Vintage Books, 1991.

Foster, John. *Class Struggle and the Industrial Revolution.* London: Weidenfeld and Nicolson, 1974.

Giddens, Anthony. *The Class Structure of Modern Society.* London: Hutchinson, 1973.

Hall, John, and Patrick Joyce, eds. *Reworking Class.* Ithaca, NY: Cornell University Press, 1987.

Poulantzas, Nicos. *Political Power and Social Classes.* London: New Left Books, 1973.

Wright, Eric Olin. *Class, Crisis, and the State.* London: New Left Books, 1978.

See also Volume 1: Marxism; Socialism.

Clay, Henry (1777–1852)

American politician and diplomat who dominated U.S. politics during the antebellum period (the years preceding the Civil War).

Henry Clay was born April 12, 1777. He was first elected to Congress in 1806 as a senator from Kentucky, Henry Clay represented the state for nearly 30 years, serving both as a senator and a representative. Clay typified the ardent nationalist and, during his early career, advocated a staunch defense of American territorial and trade rights against British interference. In 1812, as Speaker of the House, Clay joined other "War Hawks" in supporting America's declaration of war against England. An economic nationalist, Clay supported an active government intervention in the economy. He supported federal assistance for roads and canals, the Second Bank of the United States, and a protective tariff in the belief they could bring the American people "additional security to their liberties and the Union." This program, called the American System, became a central feature of the Whig Party's political platform in the 1830s. It also furnished targets for American politicians, like Andrew Jackson, concerned about the potentially intrusive and unconstitutional role of the federal government.

Clay ran for the presidency on five separate occasions but failed in each of his attempts. Although unsuccessful as a presidential candidate, Clay proved a masterful and prescient politician, particularly with regard to America's future social and economic development. A slaveholder, Clay regarded the institution as a necessary but temporary evil, one to be ended by gradual emancipation. He also advocated economic development as a means of uniting the nation and reducing its dependence on imports.

Clay's leadership of the Whig Party in the 1830s and 1840s remains a testament to his belief in economic expansion and political union, concepts that he considered were threatened by escalating sectionalism, in which different geographic regions competed for political and economic dominance. Clay regarded any potential dissolution of the union as "the greatest of all calamities" and worked assiduously to defuse several crises during the antebellum period. Instrumental in crafting the Missouri Compromise of 1820 that temporarily settled the issue of slavery in the Louisiana Territory, Clay also played a key role in negotiating a compromise tariff bill in 1833 that ended the South Carolina nullification crisis, during which South Carolina threatened to secede from the Union because of its objection to a large increase in tariff rates that discriminated against Southern agricultural states. In 1850, Clay cobbled together a series of proposals to quell a sectional crisis generated by the Mexican-American War—a war that he opposed because he foresaw, correctly, its potential to increase tensions between the North and South. This final effort, the Compromise of 1850, once again temporarily reduced sectional tensions but ultimately failed to forestall a civil war. Nonetheless, Clay's history of success in crafting political compromise amidst national crisis won him the monikers "the Great Compromiser" and "the Great Pacificator." He died June 29, 1852.

—Robert Rook

References

Peterson, Merrill D. *The Great Triumvirate: Webster, Clay, and Calhoun.* New York: Oxford University Press, 1987.

Remini, Robert V. *Henry Clay: Statesman for the Union.* New York: W. W. Norton, 1991.

See also Volume 1: American System.

Clayton Anti-Trust Act (1914)

Act meant to reinforce the Sherman Anti-Trust Act of 1890.

In 1914, when Congress passed the Clayton Anti-Trust Act, it completed the initial New Freedom legislative program of President Woodrow Wilson, who had campaigned in 1912 on a platform to renew competition in the economy by creating more specific prohibitions against restraint of trade. Congress passed the act partly as a response to revelations of the Pujo committee in the House of Representatives, which documented how the financial empire of J. P. Morgan and John D. Rockefeller sat atop a massive power structure of interlocking directorates in control of companies worth one-tenth of the national wealth. The Clayton Anti-Trust Act, drafted by congressman and jurist Henry De Lamar Clayton, prohibited interlocking directorates in industrial corporations capitalized at $1 million or more and in banks with assets of more than $5 million. In addition, it banned unfair trade practices, such as pricing policies that created a monopoly. But legislators exempted trade unions and agricultural organizations seeking legitimate goals from the provisions of the act. Indeed, the act limited the use of injunctions and restraining orders in labor disputes, while also seeking to legalize boycotts, picketing, and peaceful strikes. Decisions by federal courts soon rendered these provisions of the act almost useless. By the time Congress passed the Clayton Act, President Wilson had appeared to lose interest in the measure and almost completely accepted Theodore Roosevelt's New Nationalism idea of a powerful trade commission to regulate business.

—*Steven E. Siry*

References

Clements, Kendrick A. *The Presidency of Woodrow Wilson.* Lawrence: University Press of Kansas, 1992.

See also Volume 1: Sherman Anti-Trust Act; Volume 2 (Documents): Clayton Anti-Trust Act..

Cleveland, Grover (1837–1908)

An American statesman, twenty-second (1885–1889) and twenty-fourth (1893–1897) president of the United States, first Democratic president after the social and economic turmoil of the Civil War and Reconstruction.

Born March 18, 1837, in Caldwell, New Jersey, Grover Cleveland studied law in Buffalo, New York, and in 1859 commenced his law practice. He represented many clients including Standard Oil; Merchants and Traders Bank; and Buffalo, Rochester and Pittsburgh Railroad. He served as a mayor of Buffalo (1881–1882) and governor of New York (1883–1884).

During his first presidential administration, Cleveland expanded federal involvement in economic and commercial affairs. On February 4, 1887, Congress passed the Interstate Commerce Act, and on March 22, 1887, the first Interstate Commerce Commission received its appointments to administer it. Although the act primarily regulated railway transportation, it also served as the first major step in establishing federal control over business. In February 1889 Cleveland created the Department of Agriculture as an executive department. To strengthen the Treasury Department,

Cleveland tried to reevaluate and limit expenditures for pensions, particularly for Union army veterans. His numerous vetoes on pension bills antagonized influential veteran interest groups. This policy, as well as his unsuccessful fight to lower protective tariff rates in 1887 and 1888, contributed to his defeat to Benjamin Harrison in 1888.

During his second presidential term (1893–1897), Cleveland faced a severe nationwide economic and financial crisis and the worst economic depression up to that time following the panic of 1893. Viewing the economic and financial policy of the Harrison administration as the major cause of lowering governmental revenues and the dangerous depletion of the U.S. Treasury, Cleveland in 1893 persuaded a special session of Congress controlled by the Democrats to repeal the Sherman Silver Purchase Act of 1890. The revision of the protectionist McKinley Tariff of 1890, also initiated by the president, led to bitter strife in the Senate. The compromise Wilson-Gorman Tariff Act, which appeared in 1894, combined some adjustments in the tariff rates with important concessions to protectionism. Cleveland denounced the final tariff bill while allowing it to become law without his signature.

To keep the nation on the gold standard and strengthen U.S. finances, Cleveland placed bank loans with the J. P. Morgan syndicate and August Belmont Jr., the representative for the Rothschild Bank in America in 1895. Although Cleveland's anticrisis measures brought about some relief to the Treasury, at the same time they alienated western and southern farmers and split the Democratic Party. Cleveland also alienated labor by remaining reluctant to provide direct governmental help to a growing number of unemployed. He also took a hard line toward a series of labor protests when public order or federal interests became endangered. In July 1894, federal troops dispatched by the president, despite opposition from the governor of Illinois, put down riots in the Chicago area that developed from the Pullman strike.

The Cleveland administration also believed that the enlarged American foreign trade could provide a key to economic revival for the nation, and he tried to expand U.S. commerce in Latin America. In doing so, between 1893 and 1895, the U.S. clashed with European rivals in Brazil, Nicaragua, Santo Domingo, and Venezuela. Grover Cleveland died in Princeton, New Jersey, on June 24, 1908.

—*Peter Rainow*

References

Brodsky, Alyn. *Grover Cleveland: A Study in Character.* New York: St. Martin's Press, 2000.

Jeffers, Harry Paul. *An Honest President: The Life and Presidencies of Grover Cleveland.* New York: William Morrow, 2000.

See also Volume 1: Morgan, John Pierpont; Protective Tariffs; Sherman Anti-Trust Act; Wilson-Gorman Tariff.

Clinton, William Jefferson (1946–)

Forty-second president of the United States, who came to office as a "new Democrat" and ended up completing the Reagan revolution in economic policy.

William Jefferson Clinton was born August 19, 1946. He graduated from Georgetown University and earned a law degree from Yale University in 1973. In 1976 he became attorney general for the state of Arkansas, and in 1978 he was elected governor. He lost a reelection bid for the governorship but later regained the office; he was Arkansas governor when he ran for the U.S. presidency in 1992.

During his presidential campaign and immediately after the election, Bill Clinton identified five failures of the economic policies of the 12 previous years from 1981 to 1992: (1) the anemic nature of the economic recovery from the 1990 recession; (2) stagnation in the standard of living for the majority of the population since the early 1970s; (3) increased income inequality and the shrinking of the middle class; (4) the run-up of the national debt as a result of high deficit spending, even in years of prosperity; and (5) the failure of the government to use borrowed funds productively during the same period—more specifically, the neglect of infrastructure and education. He promised to fix these problems and to deliver sweeping reforms in the delivery of health care and in the welfare (Aid to Families with Dependent Children, or AFDC) system.

Clinton focused on the following to address these issues:

1. To accelerate the recovery, he proposed a stimulus package that would add $30 billion in spending increases and tax cuts to the government budget during the fiscal years of 1993 and 1994.
2. To raise income for the majority of the population, he proposed to vigorously pursue a full employment policy. He promised to promote education and training to prepare low-income workers for good, high-paying jobs.
3. To combat the worsening economic inequality, he proposed raising taxes on high-income people and expanding the earned income tax credit, which cut taxes and increased transfer payments (a form of wealth redistribution) to low-income workers.
4. Even while proposing the stimulus package, he made a commitment to reducing the federal budget deficit by combining tax increases and spending cuts that would reduce the budget deficit over five years by $148 billion—still not enough to bring the budget into balance.
5. Although focusing on deficit reduction, he promised to redirect government expenditure to what he called "investments"—infrastructure, training, aid to education, and targeted tax cuts.

Faced with unanimous opposition from Senate Republicans, who all signed a letter promising to filibuster the stimulus package, Clinton quickly abandoned that part of his program and devoted his entire attention in his first year to getting a deficit reduction plan passed. He succeeded without a vote to spare. This victory actually masked an important change in American economic policymaking. The argument that in 12 previous years the government had not provided the solution but instead remained the problem and that deficit reduction should only come from spending cuts instead of tax increases obviously had an effect. This Democratic president, working with Democratic majorities in both house of Congress, found himself shackled by the intellectual baggage from the so-called Reagan revolution in economic policymaking. Even tax increases that focused on very few Americans, those who had experienced dramatic increases in their incomes in the previous dozen years, barely won approval from that Democratic majority. This experience set the stage for Clinton's failures in achieving a balanced budget and surrender to budget cuts over the next three years.

In 1994, Clinton proposed a sweeping reform of the delivery of health care to all Americans. Rejecting the simple but radical idea of a Canadian-style single-payer system of health insurance, which would effectively eliminate the role of the private insurance industry in the delivery of health care, the administration opted for a system of universal coverage through that same private insurance industry—a fatal mistake. Instead of frightening the insurance industry into supporting a rather moderate health care reform proposal that limited their incomes but left them with at least half a loaf, the proposal emboldened them to opt for no change at all because it posed no real threat to them. This reaction was despite the fact that all scientifically conducted studies of the attitudes of ordinary Americans indicated they remained quite sympathetic to the specifics of the Canadian single-payer plan, absent the pejorative socialist label that ideologues and shills for the insurance industry hung on it. The result was predictable. The complicated Clinton proposal confused people so much that they fell prey to television advertisements featuring an Everyman and his wife ("Harry and Louise") discussing the Clinton plan with worried looks on their faces, exclaiming, "There's got to be a better way!" It never even came to a vote in Congress.

Welfare reform began for Clinton as a program to move able-bodied welfare recipients into the labor force with a carrot and a stick. The carrot increased expenditures on education, job training, and particularly child care. The stick placed time limits on how long an individual could continue to collect AFDC payments. The proposal never even came to a Congressional hearing.

With memories of the tax increases of 1993 and the failure to accomplish anything on health care reform in 1994 fresh in their minds, voters decided by the 1994 midterm Republican Congressional and Senatorial campaigns (under the banner "contract with America," which set forth a Republican agenda for dealing with a variety of issues) to "throw the rascals out." The Democrats lost control of both houses of Congress for the first time since 1954. The Republicans immediately proposed a massive tax cut combined with even bigger spending cuts (most of the actual dollars would come from reductions in the Medicare budget), which—based on the projection of 2 percent growth in gross domestic product (GDP) per year for seven years—would lead to a balanced budget by 2002. Republicans also passed a much more draconian version of welfare reform. President Clinton vetoed both bills. With no agreement on the budget for fiscal year 1996, government shutdowns in December 1995 and January

1996 occurred before public opinion forced the two sides to compromise. Although all eyes focused on the supposed "overreaching" of the Republicans, the Clinton administration accepted the goal of budget balance by 2002. In 1996 President Clinton also signed a slightly modified version of the Personal Responsibility Act (the Republican version of welfare reform) that he had previously vetoed. These two actions, one in February and the other in June, ensured Clinton's reelection and guaranteed that virtually everything he had promised in terms of reversing the 12 years of failure against which he had campaigned would be forgotten. By 1996, the economy had started to grow much more quickly than it had in Clinton's first three years, and he did claim responsibility for that rapid growth because he had created what he called "fiscal discipline." Certainly, there is strong support for the view that holding down spending and raising taxes pointed the economy toward a budgeted balance and caused long-term interest rates to decline, which stimulated investment. However, much of the investment that it spurred remained purely financial investment in the stock market and in start-up companies (the so-called "dot-coms"). The result was what became known as "irrational exuberance," which fueled a stock market boom that raised price:earnings ratios to historic highs. Although the stock market rose between 1996 and 2000 (it peaked in early 2000), consumption also rose as a percentage of GDP. In 1999 and 2000, in fact, consumption exceeded personal income. This stock market boom produced a consumption boom that also produced a windfall of increased revenues for the federal government, resulting in a balanced budget in 1998 instead of 2002.

By the time Clinton left office, the economy appeared to be in great shape, but income inequality had barely moderated. The federal government deficit had become a surplus, but private borrowing both by individuals and businesses increased faster than government borrowing decreased, thereby reducing national savings. The stock market boom that caused the dramatic increase in consumption pushed price:earnings ratios to three times their previous historic highs—a clearly unsustainable situation.

Some take issue with this rather negative judgment. For them, the fact that poverty rates declined, that low-wage Americans increased their incomes faster than the average American, and that unemployment fell to a 30-year low without accelerating inflation provides evidence of the correctness of Clinton's economic policies. Only time will tell whether these were short-run phenomena built on the unsustainable run-up in private debt and a giant stock market bubble or whether something significant had changed in the economy. Only with the hindsight of history will we know what in Clinton's policies contributed to these positive trends or whether he was just lucky to occupy the White House at the right time.

—*Michael A. Meeropol*

References

Meeropol, Michael. *Surrender, How the Clinton Administration Completed the Reagan Revolution.* Ann Arbor: University of Michigan Press, 1998.
See also Volume 1: North American Free Trade Agreement.

CoCom

See Coordinating Committee for Multilateral Export Controls

Cohens v. Virginia (1821)

Case resulting in decision that Supreme Court may rule on state court decisions.

Even though Virginia had banned all lotteries not approved by its state legislature, Philip and Mendes Cohen of Baltimore, Maryland, sold tickets in Norfolk for a lottery approved by Congress to benefit the District of Columbia. They were subsequently arrested and convicted under the Virginia state law. Although the state courts ruled in favor of Virginia, the Cohens took their case to the U.S. Supreme Court in the hope that the Court would rule a national law must always take precedence over a state law. They also argued that the Court had the authority to rule on the constitutionality of a state court decision under the Judiciary Act of 1793. The state of Virginia countered that the Supreme Court was precluded from hearing the case under the Eleventh Amendment, which states that a federal court cannot rule on suits brought against a state by citizens of another state or by foreign nationals.

Issuing the Court's decision in a 6-to-0 decision, Chief Justice John Marshall used the case to make one of the strongest statements of his career on the nature of the federal union. Although he ruled against the Cohens on the grounds that the lottery in question applied only to the District of Columbia, he reminded Virginia and all other states that they belonged to a union under the rule of the Constitution. "We are one people," wrote Justice Marshall, "in commerce, in war and peace, and in so many other ways." Marshall also stated that all federal questions must ultimately be decided in the federal courts. Even when a state court has ruled on the constitutionality of a state law, the Supreme Court must have the final word if the underlying issue is federal. The Eleventh Amendment does not preclude the Supreme Court from ruling in such cases.

—*Mary Stockwell*

References

Siegel, Adrienne. *The Marshall Court, 1801–1835.* Millwood, NY: Associated Faculty Press, 1987.
See also Volume 2: Judiciary.

Coin's Financial School (1894)

A 1894 tract in support of bimetalism that sold a million copies.

In the post–Civil War period, the U.S. government used both gold and silver as specie (coined money) until 1873 when only gold was accepted. This policy hurt farmers and the poorer classes, who wanted silver used again because it would expand the money supply and lower interest rates. William H. Harvey's *Coin's Financial School,* published by the author in June 1894, became the most effective and most widely read free-silver tract, laying the foundations for William Jennings Bryan's "cross of gold" speech and 1896 presidential campaign. The author wrote the book while Jacob Coxey's "army" of the unemployed marched in protest on Washington, and he published it the same month the Pullman strike began, at a time of economic depression and falling prices. *Coin's Financial School* advocated raising prices by increasing the quantity of money and recommended accomplishing this by coining silver as well as gold at a mint ratio of 16 ounces of silver to 1 ounce of gold. The book contains six public lectures on the money question given by the fictitious Coin, a young financier wise beyond his years. In addition to the lectures, the author interspersed dialogues in which Coin bested advocates of the gold standard, including businessmen Phillip Armour and Marshall Field, banker and future Treasury Secretary Lyman Gage, Senator Shelby Collum, and J. Laurence Laughlin, founder of the Economics Department of the University of Chicago. Stung by being made the butt of a fictitious character's arguments, Laughlin engaged Harvey in a genuine public debate in 1895 and wrote one of many replies to *Coin's Financial School,* none of which sold nearly as well as the original. Laughlin and other economists denied that a higher price level would produce lasting real benefits or that the government (especially the government of one country acting unilaterally) could fix the relative price of two metals without driving one out of circulation.

Harvey and his readers remained unimpressed by such criticisms. The National Silver Party (the executive committee of which included Harvey) bought and distributed 125,000 copies of *Coin's Financial School* during the Bryan campaign of 1896. Gold discoveries in South Africa and the Alaskan Klondike and the new cyanide process of extracting gold from low-grade ores caused price levels to rise under the gold standard after 1896, muting the agitation for free silver. In 1900, the Virginia-born Harvey moved from Chicago to Rogers, Arkansas, later founding the Ozark Trails Association to mark and promote interstate highways. In his last years, Harvey denounced Franklin Roosevelt's silver purchase policy, designed to increase the price of silver by inflating the currency, as too timid and therefore unable to achieve the desired goal.

—*Robert Dimand*

References

Harvey, William H. *Coin's Financial School up to Date.* Chicago: Coin Publishing, 1895.

———. *Coin's Financial School.* Reprinted with introduction by Richard Hofstadter. Cambridge, MA: Harvard University Press, 1963.

Nichols, Jeannette P. "Bryan's Benefactor: Coin Harvey and His World." *Ohio Historical Quarterly,* vol. 67 (October 1958): 299–325.

See also Volume 1: Populist Party.

Cold War (1947–1991)

A global conflict between the United States and the Soviet Union, the two superpowers that emerged from World War II, that for more than four decades had a central bearing on the political, economic, and strategic nature of international relations.

The cold war was a lengthy struggle from 1947 to 1991 between the United States and the Union of Soviet Socialist Republics (USSR, or Soviet Union), two superpowers that perceived a post–World War II international order differently. Washington, with a vision for a U.S.-led liberal capitalist structure for world peace and prosperity, resented the communist totalitarianism that Moscow imposed on Eastern Europe and feared growing Soviet ideological hostility toward the capitalist West, as exemplified by the formation of a Soviet-dominated Communist Information Bureau in 1947. Based on its Marxist-Leninist ideology, meanwhile, Moscow resented the aggressive advance of capitalism in the postwar world in areas such as the Middle East, Western Europe, and Southeast Asia. The Soviet leadership believed that the USSR's survival as a socialist state relied on a solid sphere of Eastern European communism under Soviet control. At the same time, the Soviet Union would do its utmost to ensure its national security and compete for the upper hand in a global struggle between the progressive forces of communism and the reactionary forces of imperialism.

The Truman Doctrine emerged in March 1947 as America's fundamental policy to contain Soviet expansion, occasioned by the crisis of civil war in Greece between the oppressive but pro-Western government in place and communist guerrillas. The Marshall Plan ensued as one dimension of containment; it entailed America's all-out approach for Western European economic recovery and unity. In response, Moscow imposed its own communist command economy on the Eastern European nations. Following the failed Berlin blockade initiated by Moscow in late 1948, in which the Soviet Union attacked to prevent Western democracies from having access to West Berlin, the United States created the North Atlantic Treaty Organization (NATO) in 1949 to rival Soviet strategic strength in Europe. The United States initiated an airlift to resupply West Berlin from June 1948 to May 1949, when the Soviet Union ended the blockade.

The cold war spread to Asia with the rise to power of the Chinese Communist Party in 1949 and was particularly manifest in the Korean War (1950–1953), which was brought on by the communist North Korean invasion of South Korea. To stop the thrust of Soviet-backed communist aggression in Asia, the United States enforced both its military commitment and substantial economic assistance to the safety and welfare of friendly pro-American governments like Taiwan, South Korea, and Japan. Nourished by American economic aid and protected under the American military umbrella, Japan—a former enemy but now a front-line ally—began its journey toward becoming a major world economic power.

For six years following the death in March 1953 of Soviet leader Joseph Stalin, the United States and the Soviet Union de-escalated their contentious relationship, replacing conflict with peaceful coexistence and competition toward the capitalist West. Intending to confront each other without threatening the survival of the world with nuclear war, Moscow and Washington worked through diplomatic channels, ultimately holding the Camp David talks in 1959 between President Dwight D. Eisenhower and Soviet Premier Nikita Khruschev. These talks resulted in a statement that renounced the use of force. Meanwhile, though, the two superpowers covertly and overtly intensified their struggle for influence in the Third World, where the collapse of old colonial system left a vacuum.

The early 1960s brimmed with crises as the scope of U.S.-Soviet rivalry extended. The threat to cut off access to West Berlin (1960–1961) provoked Washington into a dangerous face-off with the potential for open armed conflict. After the Soviets launched the first *Sputnik* in 1957, the United States strengthened its effort to blunt the advantage in outer space technology that Moscow had allegedly gained. In 1962 as a result of an intensified race for nuclear deterrence, the USSR attempted to position nuclear weapons in Cuba, and the resulting Cuban missile crisis brought the two countries to the brink of a nuclear war. This crisis was eased through an agreement whereby the USSR would remove missiles under construction in Cuba and the United States would remove its intermediate-range missiles located in Turkey.

After that crisis, to allay the danger of direct confrontation and nuclear catastrophe, both governments felt it appropriate to ease tensions via negotiations and to contest each other in areas where neither had vital interests at stake. The United States, for instance, turned to Vietnam, but U.S. involvement in the Vietnam conflict (1954–1973) drained American resources and undermined American prestige in world opinion. The price of fighting in this peripheral region, coupled with U.S. economic policies of the late 1960s and early 1970s, largely triggered the lessening of the U.S. competitive lead in the world economy, whereas Japan and Western Europe assumed a growing edge.

The cold war eased during the 1970s when the United States pursued the flexible policy of détente with the Soviet Union and China. In the 1980s, the administration of President Ronald Reagan resolved to use America's economic and military strength (through Reagan's Strategic Defense Initiative [SDI]) as well as moral leadership in a renewed bid to win the cold war. At the same time, reforms by the new Soviet leader, Mikhail Gorbachev, failed to rejuvenate the Soviet Union's decadent political and economic system. Although costly for the United States, the SDI drove the Soviet Union into bankruptcy; the USSR could not afford to keep up with the United States in the arms race while also waging a costly war in Afghanistan. This situation quickened the Soviet Union's collapse and caused the downfall of Soviet domination in Eastern Europe. The breakup of the Soviet Union in 1991 finally concluded the cold war and left the United States as the sole—but wounded—superpower in the world.

—*Guoqiang Zheng*

References

Judge, Edward H., and John W. Langdon. *A Hard and Bitter Peace: A Global History of the Cold War.* Englewood Cliffs, NJ: Prentice-Hall, 1996.

Leebaert, Derek. *The Fifty-Year Wound: The True Price of America's Cold War Victory.* New York: Little, Brown, 2002.

See also Volume 1: World War II.

Colonial Administration

System by which England attempted to exert commercial and fiscal control over its American colonies and eventually led to the separation of the colonies from Britain.

The ideological foundation of the British imperial system rested on mercantilism, which dictates that the state direct all economic activity within its borders, subordinate private profit to public good, and increase national wealth by encouraging exports over imports. Mercantilism required England to maintain continuous supervision and control over all economic activities in the colonies. Although England passed measures to control colonial trade, a consistent policy developed slowly because of the distance between England and America, British indifference toward the colonies prior to the end of the French and Indian War in 1763, and the conflict between the Crown and Parliament over political authority.

By the mid-seventeenth century, England began to create a coherent system designed to increase government revenues and to benefit certain special-interest groups in Britain. Although altered over time, the Navigation Acts of 1660 and 1663 provided the foundations of this new system. They required the carrying of colonial trade in English ships, the direct shipment of a list of enumerated goods to England, and the strict regulation of colonial imports. These and other acts attempted to establish the control required by mercantilism.

Problems of enforcement plagued the imperial system. Corruption, bribery, and colonial political structures hindered the Crown's ability to exert its authority. In the last half of the seventeenth century, England attempted to address this failing. In 1675, King Charles II appointed a special committee of the Privy Council (the King's advisory council) called the Lords of Trade to assess and enforce colonial policies. The committee recommended more stringent measures and, in 1686, under King James II, created the Dominion of New England, an administrative division that stretched from Massachusetts to New Jersey. As governor of the Dominion, Sir Edmund Andros revoked colonial charters, dissolved assemblies, and generated fervent opposition from the colonists.

The Glorious Revolution of 1688, in which Parliament replaced King James II with King William and Queen Mary, overturned this policy, but Britain's concern with enforcement did not wane. In 1696, Parliament provided stricter enforcement by requiring governors to take an oath to enforce the Navigation Acts, establishing a custom service with increased authority, and organizing admiralty courts to try violators. Also in 1696, the Privy Council created the Lord Commissioners of Trade and Plantations, or the Board of Trade, to inform and advise the king on colonial matters. This group played a crucial role in shaping policy for the rest of the period. Although completely restructured, the system did not greatly limit the economic opportunities open to colonists.

This system remained fundamentally unchanged until after the French and Indian War (1756–1763). In 1763, because of war-related increased national debt, Britain began to view the colonies as a source of revenue. Over the next decade, Parliament passed numerous acts to regulate trade and generate revenues. The tightening of the system after midcentury clashed with the growing desire of colonists to exert greater control over their own economic activity. This clash exacerbated tensions that already existed in the system and led to the separation of the American colonies from England.

—*Peter S. Genovese*

References

Christie, Ian R. *Crisis of Empire: Great Britain and the American Colonies, 1754–1783.* New York: W. W. Norton, 1966.

Steele, Ian K. *Politics of Colonial Policy: The Board of Trade in Colonial Administration 1696–1720.* Oxford: Clarendon Press, 1968.

See also Volume 1: American Revolution; Stamp Act; Sugar Act of 1764.

Commission Government

A form of municipal government that consolidates administrative and legislative power in a single body.

Commission government is an alternative to the traditional mayor-council form of municipal government and was pioneered by Galveston, Texas, and Des Moines, Iowa. A product of the municipal reform movements of the Progressive Era in the late nineteenth century, commission government remained modeled on the business corporation and touted for its putative enhancement of economy, efficiency, and expertise. Its essential feature involved the consolidation of administrative and legislative power in a single body—the commission as a whole making ordinances and each individual commissioner simultaneously managing a specific department. Municipalities frequently adopted commission government as part of a reform package that also included the short ballot, at-large and nonpartisan elections, the separation of local from state and national contests, civil service, initiative, referendum, recall, and home rule.

The coupling of commission government with at-large, nonpartisan elections separate from state and national contests virtually guaranteed that the commissioners would be businesspeople and professionals. Although early reformers (e.g., the National Municipal League) contented themselves with modifications to the mayor-council system, the hurricane that devastated Galveston in 1901 provided the opportunity for more drastic restructuring of that city's government. Buoyed by the apparent success of that experiment, municipal reformers in Des Moines adopted a slightly modified version after a protracted and often bitter political campaign. By 1917, nearly 500 cities had adopted some form of commission government. However, adoptions remained largely limited to small and medium-sized cities, many of which eventually abandoned the experiment. Larger cities generally stuck with the mayor-council system, while the number of municipalities adopting the newer city manager system rapidly outpaced those with commission government. By 1976, only 215 cities, with a combined population of about 5 million, still used the commission form, compared with the council manager form, which prevailed in 2,441 cities, including 70 in the over–100,000 population class.

—*John D. Buenker*

References

Holli, Melvin G. "Urban Reform." In Lewis L. Gould, ed., *The Progressive Era.* Syracuse, NY: Syracuse University Press, 1974.

Rice, Bradley Robert. *Progressive Cities: The Commission Government Movement in America, 1901–1920.* Austin: University of Texas Press, 1977.

See also Volume 2: Urbanization.

Committee on the Conduct of the War (CCW)

Committee created in response to early Civil War military disasters.

Early Civil War military disasters provoked Congress to create the Joint Select Committee on the Conduct of the War (CCW) in December 1861. Radical Republicans dominated the CCW, membership of which consisted of Senators Benjamin Wade, Zachariah Chandler, and Andrew Johnson and Representatives George Julian, John Covode, and Daniel Gooch. Moses Odell was the single Democrat on the committee. From 1861 until 1865, the CCW investigated the conduct of military operations, military contracts, alleged enemy atrocities, treatment of prisoners, confiscation of enemy property, and government corruption. It agitated relentlessly for a more energetic prosecution of the war, for emancipation, and for the use of black troops.

The initial CCW investigations of the Battles of Bull Run and Ball's Bluff showed that the Republicans intended to use the CCW for partisan purposes. The CCW excoriated conciliatory Union officers—like Generals Robert Patterson and Charles Stone—who considered that respecting Southern property and the institution of slavery would convince Southerners to reenter the Union. The CCW severely criticized West Point graduates, many of whom were conservative Democrats. The CCW successfully lobbied on behalf of General John C. Fremont, who favored freeing slaves and confiscating Southern property. Fremont had been relieved for corruption and incompetence, but after the outcry from the CCW, President Abraham Lincoln appointed him to a minor post.

In 1862, the CCW focused its wrath on General George McClellan, commander of the army of the Potomac, whose conciliatory views infuriated the committee. McClellan devoted considerable time to organizing, training, and supplying the army, and CCW criticism of his "inaction"—which was interpreted as cowardice or disloyalty—reflected vast ignorance of the difficulties of this process. McClellan's cautious prosecution of the Peninsula campaign against Richmond that led to the Battle of Seven Pines and the campaign's ultimate failure prompted Lincoln to remove McClellan from command. The CCW sought to blame the failures of his successors on subordinate commanders who remained loyal to McClellan.

In 1864 and 1865, the CCW attempted to boost Northern morale by publicizing radical views that focused on Southern battlefield atrocities and mistreatment of prisoners. The CCW continued to agitate on behalf of military leaders such as Benjamin Butler, who endorsed these radical views, and attacked those who favored a "soft peace" with the South.

CCW investigations exposed cases of venality, mismanagement, and war crimes. However, CCW ideological bias, reflected in attacks on Democratic generals and support for incompetent Republican generals like Fremont and Butler, promoted discord and undermined the Union war effort.

—*James D. Perry*

References

Tap, Bruce. *Over Lincoln's Shoulder.* Lawrence: University Press of Kansas, 1998.

Trefousee, Hans L. *The Radical Republicans.* New York: Alfred A. Knopf, 1969.

Williams, T. Harry. *Lincoln and the Radicals.* Madison: University of Wisconsin Press, 1941.

See also Volume 1: War and Warfare.

Commonwealth v. Hunt (March 1842)

Supreme Court decision declaring that labor unions are legal.

The first labor unions in the United States were organized in the early national period (1800–1830) among skilled workers in trades such as shoemaking, weaving, and printing. These unions worked to keep wages high in the face of growing industries that relied on cheap labor. Employers reacted to the rise of labor unions by arguing in the courts that these organizations were conspiracies and therefore illegal. Following precedents set in English common law, lawyers hired by employers defined a conspiracy as a combination of two or more persons who banded together to harm society. Influenced by Adam Smith's *The Wealth of Nations,* they reasoned that unions hurt society by demanding higher wages, which in turn raised the price of goods, slowed demand, and eventually brought unemployment.

The first conspiracy case was brought against the shoemakers of Philadelphia in 1806. The prosecutor argued that while one man could set the price of his own labor, a group of men could not do the same without harming society. Men grouped together in unions hurt society in two ways. First, unions drove up the price of goods by demanding higher wages. Second, union members intimidated workers who refused to join. The prosecutor also argued that unions should be outlawed in the United States because they were illegal under English common law. Lawyers for the Philadelphia shoemakers countered that no evidence had been provided to prove that unions harmed society. Instead, a case could be made that unions actually helped society by raising wages and so improving the lives of workers. They also argued that English common law no longer applied to the United States. The jury, comprising mainly merchants and shopkeepers, agreed with the prosecution and ruled that the union was illegal.

The precedent set in Philadelphia in 1806 was followed in other eastern cities including Baltimore and New York during the next 30 years. Juries handed down numerous decisions finding unions to be illegal conspiracies. However, unions continued to grow and even won the support of Andrew Jackson and the rising Democratic Party. By the late 1830s, many Americans openly sympathized with the plight of the unions. Workers even had enough public support to organize mass demonstrations in New York and Washington against judges who had condemned labor unions. The nation's changing political climate came into play when members of the Boston Journeymen Bootmakers Society went on trial for conspiracy in 1842. The bootmakers had walked off the job when a shop employed nonunion members. Found guilty of conspiracy, the bootmakers appealed to the Supreme Judicial Court of Massachusetts and then to the U.S. Supreme Court.

After hearing many of the same arguments that had been debated for more than 30 years, Chief Justice Lemuel Shaw handed down the most important ruling in American labor history to date in *Commonwealth v. Hunt.* He argued that the case posed two questions: First, were unions illegal? Second, were the actions of this union illegal? Shaw answered that although an organization of workers might exist for "pernicious" reasons, it might also exist for "highly meritorious and public-spirited" ones. Although a union's battle to raise wages might harm some, its true purpose was to improve the lives of the workers and so improve society. He further explained that even if an individual union member committed illegal acts, the union could not be blamed. The individual must be prosecuted, and not the union. Although Shaw's ruling in *Commonwealth v. Hunt* served as a precedent for unions to organize and collectively bargain, American workers did not fully win these rights until the passage of the Wagner Act in 1935.

—*Mary Stockwell*

References

Taylor, Benjamin, and Fred Witney. *Labor Relations Law.* Englewood Cliffs, NJ: Prentice-Hall, 1987.

See also Volume 1: National Recovery Administration; Wagner Act.

Communism

Political ideology developed by V. I. Lenin and installed in Russia after the Revolution of November 1917 in which labor is organized for the advantage of the worker and there is collective ownership of property. Opposition to communism throughout the world shaped the direction of the U.S. economy from 1950 to 1990.

The United States in 1917 appropriated troops and weapons to assist the White Army in overthrowing the usurping Bolshevik power in Russia. However, the United States would not become preoccupied with communism until after World War II, which left the world in an economic vacuum. Great Britain, which in the past had assumed the role of the economic giant that both assisted and profited from the rest of the world, found itself unable to remain in that position.

Two nations with separate political ideologies emerged: the Union of Soviet Socialist Republics (USSR) and the United States. If the United States was to ensure that it would assume the role of economic superpower, it would need to support reconstruction of the nations that World War II decimated and would need to install a free market economy in these nations.

The USSR began making great strides in expanding communism to the rest of Europe after World War II through active political participation and organization in countries devastated by war. Realizing that the United States lagged behind in its efforts to combat the spread of communism, President Harry S Truman proclaimed the Truman Doctrine in 1947 that gave economic and military aid to any nation of free people threatened by a foreign power. The United States appropriated $400 million for Greece and Turkey, two countries struggling against communists within their respective borders. The Truman Doctrine led to the Marshall Plan (1948), also known as the Economic Cooperation Act. Under this act, countries devastated by World War II qualified for funds from the United States after they had met and coordinated expenditures to achieve recovery through a free market system. Congress appropriated $34 billion for the Marshall Plan.

European countries responded favorably to the Marshall Plan, and their positive response prompted other U.S. economic aid programs for Europe and Asia. These were established under the Foreign Assistance Act (FAA) in April 1948, which supplemented the Marshall Plan. The FAA appropriated $5.3 billion for the first year of recovery, of which China received $338 million. The Columbo Plan of 1950, an international and British legislative effort, provided military and economic relief specifically for Asia and Southeast Asia; the plan appropriated $203 million in economic aid. The United States during this time continued to promote free trade, which would benefit the United States, while attempting to stifle the USSR and its communist aims.

The United States also set up military protection for the states under the Marshall Plan. Congress appropriated $1.34 billion for the Mutual Defense Assistance Act (MDAA) in 1949, which supplied the countries with weapons, training, and other military needs. Along with MDAA, the United States asked the countries that received monetary assistance to join the North Atlantic Treaty Organization (NATO), which was formed in 1949. NATO kept the free market nations under the sphere of influence of the United States. Therefore, NATO protected the U.S. economic investment while assuring the economic growth of its economy.

The U.S. economy, after these acts, appropriated funds to fight communism in the Chinese Civil War (1947–1949), the Korean War (1950–1953), and the Vietnam conflict (1954–1973). Congress approved President John F. Kennedy's request for funds to close the missile gap, a perceived disparity in missile technology that developed after the launching by the USSR of *Sputnik*. This spending sparked a strategic arms race that, even through President Richard Nixon's détente, or thawing of relations, continued with fervor until Soviet communism collapsed in 1989 after Soviet Premier

Mikhail Gorbachev initiated a policy of openness and economic restructuring.

—*Shannon Daniel O'Bryan*

References
Leopold, Richard W. *The Growth of American Foreign Policy.* New York: Alfred A. Knopf, 1962.
Patterson, Thomas G., and Dennis Merrill, eds. *Major Problems in American Foreign Relations since 1914.* Vol. 2. Lexington, MA: D. C. Heath, 1995.
See also Volume 1: Cold War; Marshall Plan; North Atlantic Treaty Organization; Truman Doctrine.

Community Action Programs

A policy initiative in the mid-1960s that sought to empower the poor by granting them a major stake in the implementation of antipoverty measures.

The concept of using community-based initiatives to address social problems traces its origins to the Progressive Era in the late nineteenth century, but community action remained untested until the early 1960s. Drawing on the findings of Columbia University scholars Lloyd Ohlin and Richard Cloward, who developed the Mobilization for Youth test program for the slums of New York City, the administration of President John F. Kennedy employed community action in a program begun in 1962 aimed at reducing juvenile delinquency. David Hackett, an aide to Attorney General Robert F. Kennedy in the Justice Department who participated in the Kennedy administration's Committee on Juvenile Delinquency and Youth Crime, championed the concept.

In the administration of President Lyndon B. Johnson, the national War on Poverty incorporated many principles of community action. The keystone of the Community Action Program included within the Economic Opportunity Act (EOA) of 1964 (one piece of the legislation that became known as the War on Poverty) was the stipulation that the poor be afforded "maximum feasible participation" in the design, implementation, and administration of community-based antipoverty programs. The ramifications of community action included within the EOA legislation remained unclear to many who initially supported its passage. Within short order, however, the "maximum feasible participation" provisions aroused the ire of local leaders who had expected to use War on Poverty funds to reward political allies. These seasoned politicians especially distrusted the notion of granting political power to the dispossessed, which included many racial and ethnic minorities many of whom pledged to overthrow established political institutions dominated by white men.

Due largely to the political threat posed to individuals who would have normally championed antipoverty measures, a firestorm of controversy erupted around community action in its many forms, tarnishing the historical record of the War on Poverty, as well as the image of R. Sargent Shriver, the former Peace Corps director named head of the Office of Economic Opportunity in 1964 who had achieved a successful record in his former position.

Although the War on Poverty ultimately failed to achieve the lofty goals suggested by Lyndon Johnson's rhetoric, the Community Action Program spawned the creation of nearly 2,000 Community Action Agencies in cities and towns across the United States. More than 1,000 of these remain active in the twenty-first century, promoting antipoverty measures and acting as advocates for the poor.

—*Christopher A. Preble*

References

Matusow, Allen J. *The Unraveling of America: A History of Liberalism in the 1960s.* New York: Harper and Row, 1984.

Moynihan, Daniel Patrick. *Maximum Feasible Misunderstanding: Community Action in the War on Poverty.* New York: Free Press, 1969.

See also Volume 1: Civil Rights Movement; Economic Opportunity Act.

Company Towns

Company-owned settlements (built around company-owned industries) that became embroiled in labor disputes during an era of rapid unionization in response to employer domination over workers.

Company towns, owned by and built near industries, were a phenomenon of the Industrial Revolution and grew up along with industries burgeoning in the late nineteenth and early twentieth centuries. Company towns existed widely in the textile mills of the Southeast, the coal mines of the Appalachians, western oilfields, steel mills, and lumberyards. Located in far-flung places, the companies needed to establish permanent settlements to accommodate a daily workforce. To promote good worker relations, companies leased housing to workers and their families and sometimes provided stores, schools, groceries, doctors, and churches. Company bosses often adopted paternalistic attitudes toward their workers, who inevitably became quite dependent on the company.

Working and living conditions in company towns, although not squalid, were often extremely difficult and unsafe. Workers could do little about their lot, however, because the boss directly controlled leases and employment. During the 1920s, as workers tried to form unions within companies, company towns became hot spots for labor disputes. In some cases, as in the towns of the Borderland Coal Company, bosses resorted to evictions and violence to subvert unionization, as well as layoffs. The National Labor Relations Act of 1935 legally ended such abuses by outlawing yellow-dog contracts (in which employers required workers to sign a pledge that they were not, nor would they become, a union member) and establishing the National Labor Relations Board to hear workers' complaints against owners and to end antiunion practices. Company towns began to give way in the 1950s because of industry depression, increases in worker mobility, and ultimately the mechanization of manufacturing processes.

—*John Grady Powell*

References

Crawford, Margaret L. *Building the Workingman's Paradise: The Design of American Company Towns.* New York: Verso, 1993.

See also Volume 1: National Labor Relations Board.

Computer

An electronic programmable device that can store, process, and retrieve data and that has its roots principally in devices produced during World War II.

Although the computer has antecedents in the business machines of the nineteenth and early twentieth century, the electronic computer's origins date to World War II. Several machines were simultaneously produced during that war, intended for such military tasks as calculating ballistics tables; the computational work of the Manhattan Project, which resulted in the atomic bomb; and code breaking. The United States, Great Britain, Germany, and the Soviet Union created computers. J. Presper Eckert and John Mauchly designed the most important of these—the electronic numerical integrator and computer, or ENIAC (1946)—at the University of Pennsylvania. Like other machines of the era, ENIAC was a behemoth, filling a large room and requiring immense electrical power. It required several operators to program it. John von Neumann became inspired by this machine to invent a new conception of the computer, allowing the program to be stored in the computer's memory along with the data. Von Neuman's "architecture," as this arrangement is called, persists to the present day.

After the war, Eckert and Mauchly formed UNIVAC, a private company, to produce computers for commercial use. The federal government's Census Bureau became their first customer. The business difficulties of producing a computer with limited time and financial resources proved more complicated than Eckert and Mauchly anticipated, and in 1951 they sold their company to Remington Rand.

A competing business machine company's interest in computing, plus the Korean War, drove Tom Watson Sr., the president of International Business Machines (IBM), to invest in computer design and production in the 1950s. In 1953, IBM introduced the 701 Defense Calculator, IBM's first commercially available scientific computer. IBM also announced it would produce a smaller computer for accounting applications, the 650. The 650 became the best-selling computer of the 1950s; nearly 2,000 were sold. In 1957, IBM introduced the FORTRAN programming language, which allowed programmers to write their instructions in a code similar to English or algebra. Although not the only programming language of the 1950s by any means, FORTRAN dominated scientific computing and helped lead IBM to a dominant position in the computer industry.

The first computers relied on electronic tubes. In the 1950s, small transistors replaced the tubes and made computers not only considerably smaller but also more reliable and cheaper. In the 1960s, companies like Fairchild and Intel pioneered the design of integrated circuits, in which hundreds of transistors are etched onto a single silicon chip. In 1971 Intel announced with its 4004 microprocessor the production of the first computer on a chip. With these developments, computers became cheap enough to use in dedicated industrial applications, beginning with electronic systems for spacecraft and aircraft navigation and guidance, spreading to automobiles and industrial machinery in the 1970s, and then moving to home appliances in the 1980s.

In 1975, the Altair 8800 appeared as the first microprocessor-based computer. At less than $400, this unit became the first computer cheap enough for individuals, although the user actually purchased a kit from which to build the machine. Although the Altair remained extremely limited in its functions, it developed into the personal computer (PC). Within two years, several companies were competing for the new PC market—the best-known being Tandy, Commodore, and Apple Computer.

By 1980 these upstart companies threatened the business market of established companies, particularly IBM. If IBM was to enter and successfully compete in the rapidly changing PC market, its bureaucracy had to change. To compete with Apple and other small computer manufacturers, IBM needed to speed production of new designs, outsource components, and use retail outlets instead of its own sales force. IBM launched the sale of its PC in summer 1981. The product used the Intel 8088 microprocessor, which operates on a central processing unit (CPU) contained on one integrated circuit and came packaged with an operating system and BASIC compiler from Microsoft, a leading software manufacturer. The consumer also received software programs that run applications for a spreadsheet, word processing, and a game. IBM's entry into the PC market proved so successful that it quadrupled production almost immediately. Some competitors, like Compaq, took advantage of the hot market and produced "clones" of the IBM PC, which used the same Intel microprocessor and ran the same Microsoft software.

The key developments of the 1980s were in software, not the machines (hardware) themselves. In 1981 the market for PC software was $140 million; by 1985 it topped $1.6 billion. The software industry developed on different business models than did the hardware industry, depending more on the marketing than on manufacturing—analogous to entertainment, not machines. Microsoft remains the great success story of the 1980s software boom. Because manufacturers packaged its operating system with every IBM PC and every clone, Microsoft constituted the link between hardware and software. MS-DOS (Microsoft disk operating system) acted as Microsoft's revenue engine, creating $10 million in revenue within just two years. With MS-DOS as a guaranteed revenue source, Microsoft's software failures simply faded into the background.

Two machines launched in the early 1980s offered different kinds of operating systems, systems that provided users with more than a blinking cursor ready to accept formal commands. The Xerox Star and Apple Macintosh introduced graphical user interfaces, or GUIs, to the PC market. Neither became especially successful—the Macintosh was slightly more successful—but they generated a series of projects in other companies to create a GUI operating system for the dominant IBM PC. Although several companies made such operating systems, Microsoft held a distinct advantage because of its existing contractual connection to IBM. In 1985 Microsoft launched Windows, a GUI-based operating system for the PC. A second version, Windows 2.0, appeared in 1987. But the hardware of the PC was not yet powerful or fast enough to make the early Windows operating system practical. That limitation did not stop Apple from filing a copyright infringement suit against Microsoft in 1988 for copying the appearance of the Macintosh interface. Still, Microsoft grew rapidly with the continued success of MS-DOS, new spreadsheet and word processing programs, and new versions of Windows capitalizing on the growing power and speed of new hardware. Later in 1988 Apple dropped its suit.

In 1990, Microsoft's legal problems escalated when the Federal Trade Commission announced it would investigate Microsoft on the grounds of antitrust violations. Although the Justice Department reached an agreement with Microsoft in 1994 requiring Microsoft to change some of its business practices, Microsoft has continued to be vulnerable to antitrust suits and investigations from governments (including the European Union) and competitors.

Since the use of PCs has become widespread, more than 21 million workers complete their office work at home, although most are not paid for this additional time. Also, many workers employed by businesses now telecommute—that is, they work mainly from home. In 2003, 4.1 million self-employed workers used computers in their home-based businesses, and 1.8 million people work at a second job from home using their computers. Scheduling flexibility and the reduction in travel time and cost have helped to increase the work-related use of computers outside the workplace. Overall, computers have not replaced people in the workplace but have increased the functions that people perform.

—*Ann Johnson*

References

Bassett, Ross Knox. *To the Digital Age: Research Labs, Start-up Companies, and the Rise of MOS Technology.* Baltimore, MD: Johns Hopkins University Press, 2002.

Campbell-Kelly, Martin, and William Aspray. *Computer: A History of the Information Machine.* New York: Basic Books, 1996.

See also Volume 1: Microsoft.

Confiscation Acts (1861–1864)

Several acts passed during the Civil War that dealt with the confiscation of property (August 6, 1861; July 17, 1862; March 12, 1863; July 2, 1864).

Before the Civil War began, the North and the South had already split over the issue of slavery. Many Northerners opposed the Federal Fugitive Slave Act, which transferred trials involving supposed runaway slaves from state to federal courts. They actively promoted personal liberty laws, which made it difficult for supposed runaway slaves to be returned to the South, and the Underground Railroad, a network of sympathizers that helped runaway slaves escape. After the Southern states (Confederates) seceded from the Union in 1860 and 1861, Northerners, who now dominated Congress, seized the opportunity to pass a series of confiscation acts. On August 6, 1861, Congress authorized the seizure of Confederate property and declared that any slaves who fought with or otherwise assisted the Confederate army would be declared free. Because Union forces had not yet won a major victory, and fearing the secession of border states that still had slavery, President Abraham Lincoln opposed the first confiscation act and urged a program of gradual emancipation of the slaves instead. The following year, Congress passed a second confiscation act. On July 17, 1862, Congress declared that all slaves of military or civilian Confederate officials were free forever, but the act was only enforced in areas controlled by Union forces. Once again, Lincoln opposed the measure on the grounds of possible secession by the border states. By January 1, 1963, Lincoln finally issued the Emancipation Proclamation, which freed all slaves who lived in areas that were in open rebellion against the Union. Two more confiscation acts—one on March 12, 1863, and one on July 2, 1864—combined with the Emancipation Proclamation resulted in freedom for slaves who had been worth $2 billion to the economy of the South.

—*Cynthia Clark Northrup*

References

Guelzo, Allen G. *Lincoln: Redeemer President.* Grand Rapids, MI: W. B. Eerdmans, 1999.

See also Volume 2: Slavery.

Congress

Every piece of legislation passed by the U.S. Congress—the supreme legislative body of the federal government, made up of the House of Representatives and the Senate—produces economic consequences.

The framers of the U.S. Constitution included in it Article I, Section 8, which grants Congress power to tax, grant copyrights, and regulate interstate and foreign commerce—that is, the power of the "purse." Traditionally, certain congressional committees have been particularly attuned to economic policy, most notably the prestigious Ways and Means Committee of the U.S. House of Representatives, which can trace its lineage to the late eighteenth century, and the Senate Finance Committee, formed as a standing committee in 1861 and is considered the most prestigious and powerful committee in the U.S. Senate. The Constitution requires that all money bills originate in the U.S. House of Representatives, and so the Ways and Means Committee, which determines which bills will be sent to the full House for a vote, typically acts before the Senate Finance Committee. Interest groups, or lobbyists (those representing business associations are generally the best financed and most influential), observe what has been produced and then lobby the Senate Finance Committee accordingly. At this writing, Democratic Senator Max Baucus of Montana chairs the Senate Finance Committee.

The state of Louisiana, which beginning in the twentieth century became dependent on oil and natural gas for much of its economic strength, has for decades maintained a seat on the Senate Finance Committee—a fine perch from which to look after the oil depletion allowance, which allows a 15 percent deduction for fossil fuels. Louisiana Democrat Russell Long (son of Louisiana Governor Huey Long, who formed the Win or Lose Oil Company, which reputedly never lost) chaired the committee for many years. During his last six-year term (1981 to 1987), when the Republicans controlled the U.S. Senate, Long served as ranking minority member on the committee. His direct successor, Democrat John Breaux of Louisiana, serves on the committee at this writing. Recent Republican chairs of the Senate Finance Committee have included Bill Roth of Delaware (best remembered for lending his name to the Roth Individual Retirement Account, which allows investments to be tax-free at retirement), who lost his bid for reelection in 2000, and Republican Charles Grassley of Iowa, who served four months in 2001 before turning the reins of the committee over to Baucus. Presidential candidates who have served on the committee include Democrat Bill Bradley of New Jersey and Republican Bob Dole of Kansas.

An issue that dominated Congress in the last two decades of the twentieth century but that has disappeared in the twenty-first century is passage of a constitutional amendment requiring a balanced budget. Ironically (because the president did not push a balanced budget), two members of the administration of President Ronald Reagan—Director of the Office of Management and Budget David A. Stockman, himself a former Michigan representative, and U.S. Secretary of the Treasury Donald T. Regan, who presided over massive peacetime increases in the national deficit—testified in favor of such an amendment in 1982. Adoption of the proposed amendment became part of the Republican Party's "Contract with America" in 1994, an agenda that dealt with various issues and was credited with helping the Republicans take control of the U.S. House of Representatives for the first time in 40 years. In 1997, a balanced budget amendment missed being sent to the states by a one-vote margin when Democratic U.S. Senator Robert Torricelli of New Jersey switched his position from one he had held in an earlier Congress.

Since the formation of the federal government under the U.S. Constitution, Congress has addressed a multitude of economic issues. Until the 1930s it handled trade issues exclusively; since then, the executive branch has assumed more responsibility for negotiating trade agreements. During the nineteenth century, Congress supported western migration by providing inexpensive or free land for Americans, land grants for agricultural colleges, and financing and land for railroad companies. Congress has continued to support business, because most congressional representatives believe that a strong economy must be protected to ensure the economic well-being of the country. By the mid-1900s, Congress finally began addressing social issues, resulting in dramatic economic consequences. The Social Security Act guarantees financial protection for the elderly; Aid to Dependent Children (later known as Aid to Families with Dependent

Children) protects single mothers and children; the Civil Rights Act and affirmative action safeguard minority groups against discrimination in hiring or admission to universities; and the Americans with Disabilities Act ensures that individuals with physical or mental disabilities can enjoy basic human rights including the right to work if they are able. Congress has also stimulated the economy through acts that promote transportation and protect labor. Most recently, Congress has engaged in the North American Free Trade Agreement, the World Trade Organization, and the World Intellectual Property Organization in an effort to encourage trade and protect property rights. Congress continues to struggle with health care and environmental issues, both of which affect American society economically.

—*Henry B. Sirgo*

References

Chamberlain, Lawrence H. *The President, Congress, and Legislation.* New York: Columbia University Press, 1946.

See also Volume 1: Aid to Dependent Children; General Agreement on Tariffs and Trade; North American Free Trade Agreement; Sherman Anti-Trust Act; Social Security Act of 1935; Wagner Act; World Intellectual Property Organization; World Trade Organization; Volume 2: Trade Policy.

Conservation

Policy of using natural resources judiciously to ensure perpetual sustainability of the commodities and services on which humans depend.

Conservation involves both restrictions on demand for resources and efforts to replenish supply whenever possible. As such, it necessitates management based on sound ecological and economic principles, emphasizing the role of processes and interconnections. Touching on every variety of threatened natural resource, conservation often requires consideration of entire habitats or ecosystems. It mandates efficiency and cost-effectiveness and requires constant data collection and monitoring.

The policy of conservation emerged during the Progressive Era in the late nineteenth century, when industrial growth strained supplies of valuable raw materials such as minerals and timber. The western frontier, once assumed limitless, appeared almost depleted, prompting a reform movement culminating in the administration of President Theodore Roosevelt, conservation's earliest champion. Out of this era emerged the National Park Service and the U.S. Forest Service—the former created to ensure protection of sites historically and ecologically significant and the latter meant to ensure reforestation and a continual supply of lumber. Irrigation and other reclamation efforts sought to use water wisely. During the administration of President Franklin D. Roosevelt, as the dust bowl ravished much of the Great Plains, soil conservation became a national priority.

The need to conserve natural resources is extensive today, and a wide array of federal, state, and local agencies implement conservation initiatives. These agencies range from the Fish and Wildlife Service, charged with protecting threatened species in a system of wildlife refuges, to the National Oceanic and Atmospheric Administration, charged with managing ocean resources. The Bureau of Land Management controls almost one-third of America's land, constantly balancing the needs of ranchers, miners, and others seeking to utilize its extensive holdings. Several private industries also practice conservation, either for their own economic self-interest or because of legal requirements dictated by agencies such as the Environmental Protection Agency. Conservation legislation at all levels of government influences the lives of millions, regulating every activity from hunting to the use of electricity. Laws designed to stimulate recycling of plastics, paper, and tin, for example, have created new industries. As economic growth continues to deplete finite energy resources, conservation will grow in importance as a national priority.

Balancing the needs of conflicting interests, conservation has often provoked debate. This conflict has pertained not only to questions of utility—who, when, and how the resource in question should be used—but more basic issues such as whether the resource should be used at all. Finding value in undisturbed nature, preservationists often challenge conservationists. Today many federal agencies operate under "multiple-use" mandates, attempts to define clearly and balance priorities, facilitating conservation and, it is hoped, diminishing conflict.

—*Brooks Flippen*

References

Hays, Samuel P. *Conservation and the Gospel of Efficiency: The Progressive Conservation Movement, 1890–1920.* Cambridge, MA: Harvard University Press, 1959.

Helms, Douglas, and Susan Flader, eds. *The History of Soil and Water Conservation.* Berkeley: University of California Press, 1985.

Opie, John. *Nature's Nation: An Environmental History of the United States.* Ft. Worth, TX: Harcourt, Brace, 1998.

Petulla, Joseph M. *American Environmental History.* 2d ed. Columbus, OH: Merrill Publishing, 1988.

Worster, Donald, ed. *American Environmentalism: The Formative Period, 1860–1915.* New York: John Wiley and Sons, 1973.

See also Volume 1: Roosevelt, Theodore.

Constitution (1788)

The document that serves as the basis for the American political system while clearly delegating most economic policy decisions to the congressional branch.

A convention created the Constitution in 1787 (ratified by the required number of states in 1788) to alleviate the problems caused by the American Revolution and to resolve the inadequacies of the Articles of Confederation, under which the fledgling country had been governed. Although some have argued that the founding fathers drafted the Constitution as an economic document designed to protect minority interests, most see it as a republican document that allowed for the rise of democracy. The first mention of the federal government's economic power occurs in Article 1,

Section 2, in the "3/5ths Compromise." This compromise allowed direct taxation apportioned to the states in relation to population, with a slave counting as 3/5ths of a person. Section 7 mandates that all bills concerning revenue taxes must begin in the House of Representatives and receive approval by the Senate. Section 8 and 9 define the federal government's economic power. Section 8 grants Congress the power to create and collect a variety of taxes, duties, and excises equally spread throughout the Union. Congress also receives the power to borrow money, create trade agreements with foreign nations, develop universal bankruptcy rules, mint coins, regulate the value of America's currency, standardize weights and measures, punish those who counterfeit currency, allow people to patent their inventions, and punish piracy. Section 9 further defines Congress's ability to tax while limiting its ability to withdraw money from the Treasury unless allowed by law. This section requires the federal government to keep and publish records concerning its spending of public money.

One of the most debated aspects of Section 9, at its creation, involved the slave trade. Here the Constitution prohibited the federal government from stopping the importation of slaves until 1808 and allowed Congress to tax each imported slave in an amount not to exceed $10. The last section of Article 1, Section 10, defines how these federal economic powers will relate to economic powers possessed by each individual state. This section clearly asserts that federal economic policy remains superior to state economic policy. Article 6 deals with economic policy and guarantees that all debts created under the Articles of Confederation would be transferred to the new government. The framers of the Constitution believed that if they refused to pay these previous debts, creditors would remain reluctant to lend the government money.

Although the Constitution spelled out the economic powers of the federal government, it did not specify what type of economy the new nation needed. The discussion over interpreting the Constitution in this regard was best exemplified by the debate between Secretary of State Thomas Jefferson and Secretary of the Treasury Alexander Hamilton. Jefferson believed that the Constitution best served an agrarian state, while Hamilton believed it supported a manufacturing and mercantile state.

—*Ty M. Reese*

References
Brown, Roger H. *Redeeming the Republic: Federalists, Taxation, and the Origins of the Constitution.* Baltimore, MD: Johns Hopkins University Press, 1993.
See also Volume 1: Articles of Confederation.

Consumer Credit Protection Act, Title I
See Truth-in-Lending Act.

Consumer Price Index (CPI)
Index that measures the average level of prices of the goods and services bought by a typical family.

The chief purpose of the consumer price index (CPI) is to calculate the rate of inflation facing consumers. Economists first select a base period and measure consumer spending patterns to determine the contents and cost of a "basket" of goods and services that people bought during the base period. Economists define the cost of this basket as 100. Prices of the items in the basket are updated as years pass, and occasionally the items in the basket must be changed to account for changing buying patterns. The Bureau of Labor Statistics (BLS) first began measuring prices early in the twentieth century and publishes the official CPI for the United States, which goes back to 1913 and which is updated monthly. Economic historians have extended unofficial consumer price indices for the United States back to 1665 (available online at http://www.eh.net/hmit/).

Historical price indexes show that overall relative costs remain fairly constant during much of American history, with prices rising during wartime and generally drifting downward between wars. In 1900, the CPI remained about the same as it had been during the late 1600s and most of the 1700s, but it was half of what the rate was at the end of the Civil War. During the twentieth century, the CPI rose tremendously—consumer prices were about 18 times higher in 2001 than in 1913, having risen strongly during the world wars and from the late 1960s to the early 1980s. Although the CPI does not provide a true cost-of-living index, economists often use it for calculating inflation-adjusted wages and incomes, thus measuring changes in the standard of living over time.

There is no perfect way to measure the overall consumer price level, and the official CPI has received criticism over the years because of inadequacies. In 1996 the Senate Finance Committee established a commission of leading economists, headed by Stanford University's Michael Boskin, to examine flaws in the official CPI. The commission estimated that the CPI overstated inflation by about 1.1 percentage points per year, primarily because of three types of bias: (1) substitution bias (overstatement of inflation, because consumers actually have the ability to switch away from goods the prices of which rise the most quickly), (2) new goods bias (overstatement because of the introduction of new goods into the standard consumption basket several years after they become available), and (3) quality change bias (failure to account for improvements in goods and services over time). Before adjustments were made in 1985, the CPI also received criticism for overstating inflation through its assumption that homeowners' costs remained directly tied to interest rates.

Federal law has required that, unlike other macroeconomic measures, the BLS cannot revise the CPI after its publication because many governmental policies remained tied to the CPI, including payments of Social Security benefits (beginning in 1972), Supplemental Security Income, and military and civil service retirement. Since 1981, the government has indexed individual income tax brackets and personal exemptions to the CPI's rate of inflation. Private contracts, especially union contracts, have also been indexed to changes in the CPI.

—*Robert Whaples*

References
McCusker, John J. *How Much Is That in Real Money? A Historical Price Index for Use as a Deflator of Money Values in the Economy of the United States.* 2d ed. Worcester, MA: American Antiquarian Society, 2001.
See also Volume 1: Macroeconomics.

Consumer Spending

The value of individual or household expenditures on final goods and services.

The Bureau of Labor Statistics' most recent consumer expenditure survey (CES) tells us that in 2000, the average American "consuming unit" (which included 2.5 persons, of whom 1.4 earned some sort of income and 0.7 were children) received $41,532 in after-tax income and consumed $38,045 of this income. Of this amount, 13.6 percent ($5,158) was spent on food, 32.4 percent ($12,319) was spent on housing, and 5.4 percent ($2,066) was spent on health care.

How does the level of consumption or the pattern of expenditure shares compare with those in the past? Drawing on Jacobs and Shipp's (1990) historical review of CES data, household expenditures at the turn of the twentieth century were $791, based on a pretax income of $827. Of this amount, 43.0 percent ($340) was spent on food and alcohol, 22.5 percent ($178) was spent on housing, and 2.7 percent ($21) was spent on health care. By mid-century, the average household consumed $3,925, of which 32.5 percent ($1,275) was spent on food, 25.8 percent ($1,101) was spent on housing, and 5.1 percent ($200) was spent on health care.

This does not mean, of course, that household consumption increased fifty-fold between 1901 and 2000. In real or price-adjusted terms, the actual increase for the representative household was less than five-fold. However, the decline in household size— from 5.3 persons in 1901 to 3.4 persons in 1950 to 2.5 persons in 2000—implies that consumption per member rose more than this. An increase in the number of household members in the labor force was required to support the increase in consumption.

Reckoned in either current or constant prices, it is clear that on the one hand the proportion of household expenditures devoted to food has decreased over time, to much less than half its 1901 value. The share devoted to shelter, on the other hand, has increased from about one-fifth of the household budget to one-third. The share devoted to health care more than doubled between 1901 and 1950 but has not increased much since then. It is important to interpret these data with care: The last of these, for example, does not mean that the share of national income spent on health care has also remained constant, but rather that much of the increase assumes the form of job-based insurance premiums.

In addition to this sort of descriptive data, the Bureau of Labor Statistics and other government agencies also construct prescriptive consumption data for the purposes of economic policy. The earliest consumer expenditure surveys, for example, calculated the costs of minimum and fair standards of living for a representative "working man" and his dependents and led to the construction of the first consumer price index (CPI). One of the most famous prescriptive measures is the Social Security Administration's poverty line, which defines the threshold to be three times the cost of a minimum adequate diet for all the members of a household. In 2001, 13.4 percent of all families with children under 18 fell short of this threshold, but this number obscures some disturbing differences: for African Americans, the proportion was 26.6 percent, and for those of Hispanic origin, the proportion was 23.7 percent.

—*Peter Hans Matthews*

References
Fisher, Gordon M. "The Development and History of the Poverty Thresholds." *Social Security Bulletin,* vol. 55 (Winter 1992): 3–14.
Jacobs, Eva, and Stephanie Shipp. "How Family Spending Has Changed in the U.S."*Monthly Labor Review,* vol. 113, no. 3 (March 1990): 20–27.
Johnson, David S., John M. Rogers, and Lucilla Tan. "A Century of Family Budgets in the United States." *Monthly Labor Review,* vol. 124, no. 5 (May 2001): 28–45.
See also Volume 1: Economic Indicators.

Continental Congress

The confederate system of government that led America through its revolution, while its weaknesses set the stage for the creation of the Constitution.

The First Continental Congress met in September 1774 at Philadelphia in response to the British Parliament's passing of the Intolerable Acts (known as the Coercive Acts in Great Britain) in response to the Boston Tea Party. At the congress, 55 delegates from 12 colonies (no delegate arrived to represent Georgia) met to decide the best course of colonial action. The calling of the congress signaled the culmination of years of colonial resistance and organization, and very early on they debated the creation of a union. One action the delegates agreed on involved the establishment of the Continental Association, which recommended that each community form a committee to boycott English commodities. The Continental Congress then recommended the mobilization of the local militia and started to prepare for war.

The Second Continental Congress began in May 1775 after the hostilities of Lexington and Concord, and it quickly faced the challenges of fighting a war for independence. It created an army, making George Washington commander, and then quickly searched for ways to pay for this army. Soon after the publication of Thomas Paine's "Common Sense," which argued that the Americans would be better off economically if they broke away from England, the second congress created, debated, and passed the Declaration of Independence, which served as a formal declaration of war. The major war-related problems that the congress encountered centered on finance and supply. The supplies needed, both food and military, remained expensive and hard to come by, and as the British mercantile system forbade the development of American industry, most colonial military supplies came from abroad. The congress supported its operations by making each state provide supplies, by giving certificates to farmers whose crops quartermasters confiscated for the army's use, and by using the printing presses to print documents such as "Common Sense." Another cost the congress had to deal with was paying its soldiers and, when fewer people than necessary willingly enlisted, it needed to create enlistment bonuses. The congress succeeded in creating an alliance with France, which provided America with money and supplies.

The Continental Congress faced a major problem in that it operated as an ad hoc body that needed to create a national system of government. In 1781, members ratified the Articles of Confederation, under which the government operated until 1789. The Continental Congress served its purpose in holding the colonies together and winning the Revolutionary War.

—*Ty M. Reese*

References

Middlekauff, Robert. *The Glorious Cause: The American Revolution, 1763–1789*. New York: Oxford University Press, 1982.

See also Volume 1: American Revolution.

Continental Impost

Tax measure proposed during the Confederation Era (1777–1789) to supply Congress with a consistent source of revenue and increased powers.

By 1780, Congress, deep in debt to foreign and domestic creditors, believed that the requisition system of taxation had proven inadequate to meet the demands that had been placed on the new U.S. government by the Revolutionary War against England. That year, Congress debated various financial schemes to alleviate the government's desperate situation. In a political environment wary of taxes, an impost (or import tax) provided the only method of raising revenue agreeable to the majority of states. In 1781, Congress proposed to place a 5 percent duty, or tariff, on all goods imported into the country. Because the Articles of Confederation, under which the government operated, did not grant Congress the right to regulate trade, the measure required unanimous consent of the states. In 1781, Rhode Island's opposition defeated the impost and, in 1783, New York's refusal to ratify ended the impost's political viability.

The controversy over the impost reflected the tensions in American politics that resulted from the Revolutionary War. Supporters argued that the impost would provide Congress with a source of income under its own control, which would facilitate and guarantee regular payments of its debts and place the United States in good standing with foreign governments. Opponents, however, rightly believed that passage would lead to an attempt by a powerful aristocratic element within the national government to increase the powers of Congress. Because of difficulties in fighting the war, the impost's strongest advocates envisioned the measure as the first step in creating a more powerful and fiscally independent central government to overcome the government's shortcomings. Their adversaries feared this concentration of authority and believed that the attempt to subvert the role of the states posed a threat to the liberties of the American people.

—*Peter S. Genovese*

References

Ferguson, E. James. *The Power of the Purse: A History of American Public Finance, 1776–1789*. Chapel Hill: University of North Carolina Press, 1961.

See also Volume 1: Congress.

Continental System

A method of economic warfare in the early 1800s in Europe during the Napoleonic Wars that forced the United States to fight Great Britain for its economic independence.

The Continental System emerged from Napoleon's 1806 Berlin Decrees, which declared Britain under blockade, forbade all commerce with Britain, and ordered the seizure of British goods and all vessels trading with the British Empire. Britain responded with the Orders in Council, which declared a blockade of the Continent and required neutral vessels to obtain licenses to trade with France. France countered with the 1807 Milan Decrees, which ordained confiscation of all ships and goods complying with the Orders in Council. In sum, Britain and France hoped to use economic pressure to bankrupt each other, to force other powers into conflict with their opponent, and to transfer some of the financial burdens of war from themselves to the rest of the world.

The Continental System permitted France to exploit Europe economically and politically. French ministers dictated foreign and trade policies, and even the laws, of subject countries, and forced them to open their markets to French goods while maintaining French trade barriers. European trade and maritime industries suffered serious losses, especially in northern Germany, and prices and shortages of various consumer goods increased. However, the Continental System promoted European industrialization and construction of nonmaritime infrastructure.

Extensive smuggling undermined the system, which France never enforced effectively. In 1810, to generate revenue, Napoleon even permitted French trade with Britain. Although denied access to the Continent, Britain expanded into new markets, especially in South America after France occupied Spain in 1807. Most significantly, the Continental System created considerable friction between France and other powers. Russia defected from the system in 1810 and increased duties on French imports. Franco-Russian relations quickly deteriorated, leading to war in 1812. War led to the collapse of the system in 1813 and the fall of Napoleon in 1814. In short, from 1807 to 1813, Britain's credit and financial system proved superior to France's, and thus the Continental System as a method of economic warfare proved a failure.

—*James D. Perry*

References
Marcus, G. J. *The Age of Nelson.* New York: Viking, 1971.
Schroeder, Paul W. *The Transformation of European Politics,
    1763–1848.* Oxford: Oxford University Press, 1994.
See also Volume 1: War of 1812.

Convict Lease

System of involuntary labor that developed after the Civil
War in the South.

At the close of the Civil War, Southern states found themselves essentially bankrupt. The emancipation of slaves had
dissolved the South's workforce in one motion. Practically
overnight, the free population of the South more than doubled. Coping with double the number of free persons
strained the South's economy and justice and political systems. The already weakened prison system now dealt with
black as well as white lawbreakers. With few or no resources
remaining, the South and Reconstruction governments
attempted to rebuild the region physically and financially.

With the loss of slaves as a workforce and a growing prison
population, Southern states decided to use prisoners as a
cheap labor force. Individual states turned the potential
financial drain of rebuilding their prison system on a larger
scale into a money-making venture by leasing convicts. States
leased convicts to private companies for use as labor. The
companies in turn took over the maintenance of the convicts.
Thus, the state spent nothing on the convicts. Convicts usually worked for plantation owners, railroad companies, and
mining companies, but any operation that needed a large
labor force could lease convicts. In Georgia, for example, the
governor leased the entire population of the state penitentiary in Milledgeville to a railroad company. Even the disabled, women, and the aged could be leased for less physically
demanding work such as that of camp cook.

Although the convict lease system proved a perfect solution for the financially pressed South, the system had little or
no state supervision. The convicts were abused and neglected
and received minimal care and sustenance. Extreme working
and living conditions coupled with a wholly inadequate diet
ensured high mortality. Eventually, reformers began to publi-
cize the abuses and misuses of convict labor. The system did
not end, however, until Herbert Hoover's bid for the presidency in 1928.

—*Lisa A. Ennis*

References
Coleman, Kenneth, ed. *A History of Georgia.* Athens:
    University of Georgia Press, 1977.
Tindall, George Brown, and David Emory Shi. *America: A
    Narrative History.* New York: W. W. Norton, 1999.
See also Volume 1: Slavery.

Coordinating Committee for Multilateral Export Controls (CoCom)

A nontreaty organization formed by the United States with
its allies to prevent the transfer of western technology and
hardware that would augment the military strength of communist nations.

In the opening phase of the cold war, the Marshall Plan
(1947) bestowed on the United States enormous authority to
channel the economic life of Europe in a manner that reflected U.S. concerns over the Union of Soviet Socialist
Republics (USSR) and the Soviet bloc of eastern European
countries under Soviet control. One manifestation of this
authority appeared in November 1949 when France, Great
Britain, Italy, and the Low Countries (Belgium and the
Netherlands) agreed to join the United States in founding the
Coordinating Committee for Multilateral Export Controls
(CoCom). Membership in the unchartered, informal group
extended to include Canada, Denmark, Japan, Norway,
Portugal, and West Germany in 1950. In August 1953, Greece
and Turkey also joined.

CoCom recognized the West's boycott of military-related
technologies imposed against the USSR and its allies in
Europe and Asia. It received direction for its work when the
U.S. Congress approved the Mutual Defense Assistance Act in
1951 (called the Battle Act in honor of its sponsor,
Democratic Congressman Laurie C. Battle of Alabama). The
legislation mandated that the executive branch withhold military and economic aid from any country that ships strategic
goods to a nation or group of nations that threatened the
security of the United States. Understandably, most
American products denied the Soviet Union through the
Export Control Act (February 1949) reappeared on CoCom's
commodities list of embargoed items that were prohibited.

As the cold war matured and Western Europe recovered
from the economic devastation of World War II, U.S. leadership of CoCom declined. The United States simply failed to
understand its allies' opinion on the subject of commerce
with communist nations. American policymakers from the
late 1940s to the late 1980s viewed such trade almost exclusively in political terms, whereas the non-U.S. CoCom members favorably weighed trade's economic benefits. The most
egregious violation of CoCom's policy occurred between
1981 and 1984 when the USSR bought several proscribed
computer-controlled milling machines from a subsidiary of
Toshiba Corporation of Japan and numerical controls from
the state-owned Kongsberg-Vaapenfabrikk of Norway. Soviet
industry employed the machines and controls to manufacture silent propellers for submarines. With the collapse of the
Soviet bloc in 1989 and the Soviet Union in 1991, the rationale for CoCom evaporated, and the organization disbanded
in 1994.

—*James K. Libbey*

References
Adler-Karlsson, Gunnar. *Western Economic Warfare
    1947–1967.* Stockholm: Almquist and Wiksell, 1968.
Libbey, James K. *Russian-American Economic Relations.* Gulf
    Breeze, FL: Academic International Press, 1999.
Mastanduno, Michael. *Economic Containment: CoCom and
    the Politics of East-West Trade.* Ithaca, NY: Cornell
    University Press, 1992.
Mutual Defense Assistance Control Act. U.S. Statutes at Large
    65 (1952): 644.
See also Volume 1: Cold War.

Corruption

Bribery, smuggling, graft, extortion, or other illegal activity.

Since colonial times Americans have engaged in various forms of corruption. During the period of the Navigation Acts, these activities usually involved smuggling goods into the country to avoid the payment of customs duties. The practice, which resulted in a net loss of £700,000 a year to the British treasury, led to the passage by Great Britain of the Sugar Act, which authorized trials for suspected smugglers in vice admiralty courts.

Government officials operating under the new Constitution, some of whom had engaged in smuggling during their prerevolutionary days, feared corruption. The founding fathers instituted a series of checks and balances among the three branches of government that were designed to prevent corruption at the federal level. During the early years of the republic, the system worked well, but as the nation moved from subsistence to a market economy, the opportunity for corruption resurfaced.

During the administration of President Andrew Jackson (1828–1836), the issue of the spoils system—that is, the political appointment of supporters—was raised. Jackson ordered an audit of all government departments—a move that frightened anti-Jackson forces because they feared he would fire all political opponents. Fewer than 300 employees were fired, or 9 percent of the total government bureaucratic positions. During Jackson's time, the area in which theft and graft occurred most often was the Customs Service. Several collectors in the larger port cities of New York, Boston, and New Orleans were charged with theft, and a couple of them fled the country with $1 million of public monies.

In the post–Civil War period, during the administration of President Ulysses S. Grant, the practice of patronage became the primary corruption issue. During the presidency of Chester Arthur, Congress passed the Pendleton Civil Service Act. The legislation, limited at first to a small percentage of positions, required that applicants for government jobs take a civil service exam and that employment be based on merit instead of bribes, kickbacks, or patronage. Eventually under this act, most nonappointment jobs fell into this category. Elimination of corruption among political appointees at the federal level coincided with the rise of political party bosses who controlled local politics. The "boss system" dominated state and local politics, with Tammany Hall in New York City operating as the most powerful boss ring in the country, controlling politics in the city through bribery and corruption. Many bosses courted new immigrants, who were unfamiliar with the democratic process—most had arrived from countries ruled by autocratic leaders and readily accepted this familiar form of governing. By the end of the 1800s, many governors and city mayors had initiated political reforms to counter bossism. Both Grover Cleveland, as mayor of Buffalo and then as governor of New York, and Theodore Roosevelt, as the head of the U.S. Civil Service Commission and as the president of the New York City Police Commission, gained national recognition for their efforts to root out bossism.

Early in the twentieth century, the anti-immigrant sentiment that developed as immigrants flooded into the United States after World War I, coupled with an existing Prohibition movement that focused on the drinking of Europeans, led to the ratification in 1920 of the Eghteenth Amendment prohibiting the manufacture, sale, or distribution of alcohol. In 1920 Congress passed the Volstead Act to enforce the amendment. The federal government hired 1,500 agents to patrol U.S. borders and investigate illegal activities. In the major cities, gangsters found it very profitable to smuggle in liquor from Canada. When rival gangs competed for distribution areas (such as in Chicago, where Al Capone was powerful) the situation often became deadly as rival suppliers fought over distribution territory. Local police and customs officials accepted bribes, and corruption became rampant.

Crime and corruption decreased in 1933 with the ratification of the Twenty-first Amendment to the Constitution repealing Prohibition. During the period of corruption prior to the passage of this amendment, the U.S. Treasury lost tax revenues while having to spend scarce resources on the enforcement of the Volstead Act. Corruption occurred again in the last two decades of the twentieth century in connection with the "War on Drugs," when the government pursued drug sellers and users in an effort to reduce crime, which led to the illegal importation of marijuana, cocaine, and heroin. Local customs officials, members of law enforcement, and judges accepted bribes in exchange for protecting drug traffickers from prosecution. In 1988 alone, the estimated gross sales of illicit drugs exceeded $120 billion.

At the federal level, the issue of corruption led to the passage of the 1978 Ethics in Government Act. Brought on primarily because of obstruction-of-justice charges stemming from the Watergate political scandal and the bribery charges that led to the resignation of Vice President Spiro Agnew, the act sought to prevent officials from engaging in illegal activities. Since then, many government officials have been accused of and charged with corruption on charges including mail fraud, check kiting (in which checks are written without funds available and are covered by the deposit of another check from an account that also lacks sufficient funds at the time), bribery, and illegal lobbying. Strict financial disclosures under the Ethics in Government Act have resulted in closer scrutiny of officials by government agencies. During the 1990s, campaign finance reform attempted to deal with corruption related to excessive political contributions, in which contributors of large amounts gained influence over politicians whereas other groups were denied such access. Individuals and political action committees (U.S. corporations, labor unions, or associations formed to raise money for political purposes) were forced to limit their contributions, thus restricting their influence on politicians. Although Congress continues to deal with the issue of corruption, the number of corruption cases has diminished in recent years.

—*Cynthia Clark Northrup*

References

Cordery, Stacy A. *Theodore Roosevelt: In the Vanguard of the Modern.* Belmont, CA: Wadsworth, 2003.

Joseph, Joan. *Political Corruption.* New York: Pocket Books, 1974.

Zink, Harry. *City Bosses in the United States: A Study of Twenty Municipal Bosses.* Durham, NC: Duke University Press, 1930.

See also Volume 1: Cleveland, Grover; Pendleton Act; Roosevelt, Theodore.

Cotton

A plant that produces a soft fibrous substance that can be processed into cloth, arguably the single most significant agricultural commodity influencing U.S. political, economic, and social development.

Cotton, more than any other single agricultural commodity, is identified with an entire socioeconomic system: the plantation system and concomitant slavery of the Deep South from 1800 until the end of the Civil War. Slavery had started to decline in the South when Eli Whitney invented the cotton gin in 1792. The widespread adoption of the cotton gin and expansionist land policies combined to stimulate both the cotton and slave trades. By 1820, cotton had eclipsed tobacco as the nation's top export commodity. Exports rose dramatically from approximately 20 million pounds in 1800 to 128 million pounds in 1820, peaking at 1.8 billion pounds in 1860. To put these numbers in context, cotton comprised 42 percent of all American exports in 1820, rising to 67 percent of total exports in 1840. After 1840, manufactured products from the Northeast began to comprise a larger share of total exports. Nonetheless, cotton remained the dominant export commodity until 1880.

Expansion of cotton production paralleled the rise of slavery and the large plantation system in the Deep South states of Georgia, Mississippi, and Alabama. Large plantations subsidized production costs through slavery. The long summers and mild winters of the Deep South meant that the costs of social reproduction—that is, the goods and infrastructure needed to maintain the political and economic lifestyle of the area—were quite low, enabling large plantations to operate almost self-sufficiently. This occurred at the long-term expense of the region, however, as the plantation-system did not require investment in social and physical infrastructure. This self-sufficiency operated in contradistinction to the mid-Atlantic and especially New England states, which benefited in less direct, but more substantial ways from the slave and cotton industries, as the South supplied the raw material for New England's textile mills.

Cotton's role as the top export commodity of the early 1800s should not be underestimated. Cotton strengthened U.S. economic bonds with England. The rapid expansion of cotton exports to the English Midlands meant rapid expansion of the plantation system, which required ships and financial services (financing, insuring, and marketing) provided primarily by New England and the mid-Atlantic states. This commerce stimulated their economic development and urbanization and funded many of their industrial and academic centers. Strong global demand for cotton cloth, technological innovations in processing, the expansion of lands favorable to cotton production, and slavery combined to make cotton a global commodity within a few years.

Cotton production and productivity did not undergo significant change until the 1940s, when mechanized harvesting was introduced in the form of single-row pickers pulled behind tractors. The 1950s and 1960s saw a significant rise in productivity (the amount of labor required per acre dropped from about 150 hours to almost 25 hours) as larger, self-propelled cotton pickers were widely adopted. Likewise, yield per acre increased slowly from 174.2 pounds in 1870 to 185.5 pounds in 1935, increasing rapidly with mechanization to 508.0 pounds per acre in 1965. Cotton declined in socioeconomic significance as the United States became the world's dominant manufacturing power after World War I.

—*W. Chad Futrell*

References

Cochrane, Willard W. *The Development of American Agriculture: A Historical Analysis.* Minneapolis: University of Minnesota Press, 1993.

See also Volume 1: Protective Tariffs; Volumes 1, 2: Slavery.

Council-Manager Government

A popular form of city government in the early twentieth century.

The council-manager form of government became a popular form of government in the early twentieth century and has persisted into the twenty-first with no signs of abatement. It stands in contrast to the commission form of government introduced in Galveston, Texas, following the devastation of a hurricane and that no longer functions even in the city of its origin.

The rise of the council-manager form of government coincided with the massive industrialization and urbanization that marked life in the United States in the first decades of the twentieth century. It was part of a series of ideas prevalent in business and municipal government that included Frederick Taylor's theory of scientific management, nonpartisan elections, and the use of direct party primary for the nomination of candidates. Political scientist and future Democratic president Woodrow Wilson argued that politics and administration could be separated, an idea that no longer holds sway in the field of public administration. Rather, citizens assume that city managers will have considerable input into the policymaking process.

Middle- and upper-class reformers of the early twentieth century believed that there was neither a Republican nor a Democratic way to dig a ditch—one of the mundane but essential functions of local government. Upper- and middle-class policymakers had little use for the social welfare services that political machines provided for working-class and lower-class individuals. The municipal corporation ideally would be run as a business and optimize efficiency.

The council-manager form of government has been most commonly employed in medium-sized cities averaging a homogenous population of 80,000 residents of middle- and upper-class income. Frequently these medium-sized cities are bedroom communities where white-collar and blue-collar workers live who commute to larger nearby cities in which they are employed.

Large cities and most municipalities with heterogeneous populations have found the coalition-building skills of elected mayors to be indispensable. Villages and towns have not had substantial enough budgets to adequately compensate full-time city managers with advanced degrees. In Louisiana, no municipality uses the council-manager form of government.

On average, the city manager holds her or his position for about seven years before moving on to a similar position in another city. Educational attainment by city managers increased over the course of the past century as their focus of study shifted from a focus on engineering skills to a greater emphasis on management and organizational skills. City managers usually hold a master of public administration (MPA) degree. The major professional organization for both public administrators and practitioners, including many city managers, is the American Society for Public Administration. Among its regional affiliates is the Southeastern Conference of Public Administration (SECoPA).

The council-manager form of government resembles the structures routinely used to govern school districts throughout the United States. Just as the elected school board members hire and usually defer to a full-time superintendent, who typically holds a master's or more advanced degree in education, the city council hires and usually defers to the city manager. Council-manager forms of government commonly have a mayor, who, however, is usually a council member who for a certain period of time serves when needed at ceremonial functions.

Responsibilities that have been increasingly added to the work of city managers since the 1960s include the need to engage in collective bargaining with municipal employees and to reorganize and consolidate management structures in response to increased resistance to property tax burdens on the citizenry and business. A spillover effect of Executive Order 10988 issued by President John F. Kennedy on January 17, 1962, included increased collective bargaining at the local level of government. A. E. Bent and R. A. Rossum (1976) observed that "it required federal agencies to deal with employee organizations and to grant them official recognition for negotiation or consultation." As is frequently the case in a federal system, what takes place at one level is emulated at another level. A fairly typical organizational scheme, as noted by R. T. Golembiewski and Michael White (1983), would have the city manager responsible for supervising her or his assistant, the city attorney, the finance department, the planning department, the public works department, the police department, the fire department, and the housing department. The council-manager form of government promises to persist as a common structure of municipal governance well into the twenty-first century, although its responsibilities may change.

—Henry B. Sirgo

References
Bent, A. E., and R. A. Rossum. "Urban Administration and Collective Bargaining." In Alan Edward Bent and Ralph A. Rossum, eds., *Urban Administration: Management, Politics, and Change.* Port Washington, NY: Kennikat Press, 1976.
Golembiewski, R. T., and M. White. *Cases in Public Management.* Boston: Houghton Mifflin, 1983.
See also Volume 2: Urbanization.

Council of Economic Advisers (CEA)

Group that provides expert information to the president about the future of the economy.

New Dealers, who sought to address economic problems during the Great Depression through the implementation of government programs, passed the Employment Act of 1946. Although they saw a need for a full employment bill, the 1946 legislation shifted the policy emphasis to economic growth and away from the entitlement of a job for every citizen. The mature economy thesis, a legacy from the Great Depression concerning the means of attaining economic growth, remained the major ideological concern of the supporters of the law. Leon H. Keyserling, a Keynesian economist, suggested forming a special committee that eventually became the Council of Economic Advisers (CEA). Historically, the CEA expressed the concern about the future of the economy. As progressives, CEA members assumed that experts could play a major role in governmental policies. The council's first staff consisted of one statistician and nine economists. The CEA became operational by August 1946, six months after the Employment Act became law.

Not as far-reaching as many reformers desired, the law provided a policy and ideological battleground for struggles over the federal government's response to the business cycle.

After 1946, the CEA dealt with the issue of "guns and butter." The "guns" referred to the need for a strong military budget as the cold war emerged from the ashes of World War II. The "butter" was slang for domestic reform, for extending the New Deal to the Fair Deal (Harry S Truman's policies promoting full and fair employment and economic assistance for farmers and the elderly) and beyond. Members of the CEA expressed concern over the threat of a major economic recession.

A moderate economist from the Brookings Institution, Edwin G. Nourse, served as the CEA's first chair. Leon H. Keyserling, a New Dealer, assumed the office of vice-chair, and John D. Black, a wealthy businessman who had a successful academic career, became the third member. From the beginning, Nourse and the other members clashed over issues dealing with the nature of their advice to the president, their relationship to politics, and finally whether the administration should focus on price stability (Nourse's fear of inflation) or economic growth (Keyserling's concern about economic maturity). By October 1949 Nourse had resigned, and Keyserling became chair for the remainder of the presidency of Harry S Truman.

Under Keyserling's leadership, the CEA proved instrumental in holding down inflation during the Korean War. Keyserling also supplied data and narrative for a document known as NSC-68, which was the economic basis for the containment policy against communist expansion. That document also argued that the American economy could provide both guns and butter.

The CEA lost favor in presidential administrations after the Truman administration. The more conservative presidents disliked its New Deal/Fair Deal origins. Until the late 1960s the CEA figured prominently in disputes about the federal government's response to the business cycle. As the post-1968 years brought stagflation—increased unemployment and inflation simultaneously—the conservative supply-side ("trickle-down") "revolution" curtailed the CEA's appeal to politicians, and political and cultural conservatism reduced the CEA's influence. The Federal Reserve Board became the center of economic forecasting for the public and for politicians.

—*Donald K. Pickens*

References
Collins, Robert M. *More: The Politics of Economic Growth in Postwar America.* New York: Oxford University Press, 2000.
Hargrove, Edwin C., and Samuel A. Morley, eds. *The President and the Council of Economic Advisers: Interviews with CEA Chairmen.* Boulder, CO: Westview Press, 1984.
Pickens, Donald K. "Truman's Council of Economic Advisers and the Legacy of New Deal Liberalism." In William T. Levantrosser, ed., *Harry S. Truman, the Man from Independence.* New York: Greenwood Press, 1986, pp. 245–263.
———. "The CEA and the Burden of New Deal Liberalism." In Bernard J. Firestone and Robert C. Vogt, eds., *Lyndon Baines Johnson.* New York: Greenwood Press, 1988, pp. 191–204.
See also Volume 1: Federal Reserve Act; Keyserling, Leon; New Deal.

Coxey's Army (April 1894)

A movement that called for government action to alleviate the problems of the economic depression of 1893.

In April 1894, Populist Jacob Coxey led his army of 400 into Washington, D.C., to demand that the federal government help the unemployed. Coxey, a wealthy Ohio quarry owner, had passionately debated monetary reform. In 1893, at a Chicago monetary reform meeting, he encountered a man named Carl Browne and found that they shared common views on the subject of monetary reform. Browne returned with Coxey to his home in Ohio, and the two—who cofounded an organization called the Commonweal of Christ—developed a plan to march on Washington to focus awareness on America's economic problems and spur government action.

The federal government believed in an economic "invisible hand" and thus believed the depression was a natural event that it could not change. Thus, during the 1893 depression, also known as the panic of 1893, America's unemployed relied upon private charity that, although it tried, failed to meet their needs. Coxey and Browne hoped to convince the federal government to begin a public works program that would provide jobs for America's unemployed. Their plans remained small until a local Ohio reporter sent the story to the national wire, where it was quickly picked up by America's largest newspapers. This publicity created nationwide interest in the Commonweal of Christ, and letters of support, financial assistance, and recruits started to arrive. The march was small to begin with—it did include Coxey's son, whose name was Legal Tender, and 44 journalists. But as it moved toward Washington, its numbers expanded. When the army finally arrived, many government officials feared violence and, when Coxey attempted to read his speech on the U.S. Capitol's steps, officers arrested him for walking on the grass. Coxey's march focused national attention on the plight of America's poor and stressed the belief that the federal government could end a depression.

—*Ty M. Reese*

References
Schwantes, Carlos A. *Coxey's Army: An American Odyssey.* Lincoln: University of Nebraska Press, 1985.
See also Volume 1: Panic of 1893.

CPI

See Consumer Price Index.

Credit

An agreement that allows a buyer to take possession of goods, services, or funds with the understanding that in the future he or she will compensate the seller.

In the United States until the beginning of the twentieth century, extension of credit consisted primarily of business credit or personal loans granted by banking institutions or private individuals. The scarcity of specie such as gold and silver restricted the use of credit for the most part to purchases of goods for resale or of land. Beginning with Henry Ford's establishment of an installment plan for the purchase of automobiles in 1916, consumers started purchasing all types of household items on installment credit. During the 1920s, with the employment rate high and most Americans experiencing prosperity, retailers offered durable goods such as appliances, radios, and furniture on credit. During the Great Depression, the availability of credit diminished, and during World War II the rationing of goods continued to restrict its use. During the prosperous 1950s, use of credit expanded, primarily for home purchases and automobiles. The government provided low-interest home loans to veterans through the Servicemen's Readjustment Act (1944), but nonveterans could obtain credit on easy terms as well.

The use of credit cards began in 1950 when Diner's Club made a card available that could be used at 27 New York City restaurants. By 1958, Americans could charge their purchases on their BankAmericard (Visa). By the mid-1960s, more than 5 million credit cards were being used in the United States. That number has continued to increase and by 2002 over 1.4 billion cards were used to purchase more than $991 billion worth of goods annually. Total U.S. credit card debt in 2002 amounted to $60 billion. Technological advances have resulted in the widespread use of credit cards for purchases via the Internet. The low monthly payment allows consumers to enjoy more conveniences, but the interest rate remains high on most cards, and in the long run consumers' purchasing power is diminished. The abuse of credit cards accounts for a large percentage of bankruptcies filed each year in the United States.

—*Cynthia Clark Northrup*

References
Compton, Eric N. *The New World of Commercial Banking.* Lexington, MA: Lexington Books, 1987.
Dunkman, William E. *Money, Credit, and Banking.* New York: Random House, 1970.
See also Volume 1: Ford, Henry; Great Depression; Volume 2: Banking.

Crédit Mobilier

An 1872 scandal, one of the most notorious financial scandals of American history involving governmental corruption.

During the mid-nineteenth century, both commercial interests and government—spurred by the new technology of steam locomotives, the intense public desire to construct and promote public improvements, and the push to develop the West following the acquisition of Oregon and California—promoted transcontinental railroads linking the Atlantic and Pacific seaboards. To facilitate construction, Congress passed the Pacific Railway Acts of 1862 and 1864, permitting the national government to make direct land grants of 20 sections of public land for every mile of track laid as well as a 30-year guaranteed, subsidized loan to private construction companies at below market interest rates.

The Union Pacific Railroad Company, organized in 1862, laid track from Omaha to the state line of California. The Union Pacific trustees knew that construction fees provided the true profits; therefore, they contracted with themselves—through a separate construction company—to build the railroad and maximize their profits. They chose an already existing corporation, the Pennsylvania Fiscal Agency, to achieve that goal. The trustees of the Union Pacific, who controlled the majority of the stock in the newly purchased company, changed the name to Crédit Mobilier.

Oakes Ames, a member of the House of Representatives Committee on Railroads, invested heavily in the company and played a key role in financial affairs. Ames sold or assigned Crédit Mobilier stock to members of Congress at prices substantially below market value in an apparent attempt to influence them in the corporation's favor. Information identifying those members of Congress came to light during the 1872 presidential election (five or six years after the events) and triggered an intensive congressional investigation. The revelations badly damaged the reputations of leading government officials including Vice President Schuyler Colfax, Republican Speaker of the House James Blaine, Democratic Representative James Brooks of New York, and Republican Senator James W. Patterson of New Hampshire. No prosecutions occurred.

The direct effects of this scheme produced immense profits ($30 to $40 million) for the investors—coming primarily from public funds—and smeared the reputations of several national leaders. The public, disgusted about the bloated profits and perceived waste of taxpayers' money and repulsed by the political corruption, had an lingering distrust of corporate influence on public officials. It also contributed to the judicially created rule that restricted the use of public money for public purposes only.

—*Susan Coleman*

References
Rubin, Dale F. "Public Aid to Professional Sports Teams." *Toledo Law Review,* vol. 30 (Spring 1999): 393–418.
White, Henry K. "The Pacific Railway Debts." *Journal of Political Economy,* vol. 2 (June 1894): 424–452.
See also Volume 1: Corruption; Railroads.

Crime

Unlawful activities ranging from violent crimes such as murder and rape to nonviolent "white-collar" crimes.

During colonial days, public humiliation served as the primary form of deterrence for nonviolent crimes. Time confined to the public stocks, dunking, or the wearing of a scarlet letter "A" for adultery dissuaded many from engaging in unacceptable social behavior. Murderers were confined in a stone structure until they had served their time or were executed. Society expended very few resources on the construction or maintenance of jails. As the U.S. population increased during the nineteenth century, crime rates edged upward, and prisoners were forced to perform hard labor as punishment for their crimes. During the Jacksonian Era (1828–1836), several reforms such as the asylum and reform school movements occurred, including the penitentiary movement, which was favored by reformers who believed that criminals who had a chance to reflect on the error of their ways while confined in solitary cells would become penitent and would not want to commit future crimes. Extended periods of confinement without human interaction produced severe psychological problems among the prisoners, a flaw corrected by placing two men in the same cell and initiating programs that included periods of exercise as well as work. Since federal and state penitentiaries were first formed in the mid-1800s, the system has required the allocation of resources for the construction, maintenance, and staffing of the facilities. Billions of dollars per year are spent on a system that has largely proven ineffective; the number of repeat offenders remain high.

Beginning in the 1960s and especially during the 1990s, the number of prisoners in the system dramatically increased because of the prosecution of drug offenders. By 2001 more than 1.96 million Americans were incarcerated in federal, state, and local prison facilities. That figure represents an increase between 1995 and 2001 of 3.8 percent annually. In 1989, 57 percent of the prison population were confined as a result of the War on Drugs initiated by President George H. W. Bush. The government loses tax revenues when drug dealers commit their crimes while at the same time the taxpayers must pay for the additional law enforcement personnel and facilities necessary to combat the problem.

Another financial drain on the public treasury involves the detention of illegal immigrants. Between 1990 and 2000, the number of immigration violators within the system increased by 691 percent, again resulting in increased expenditures within the Immigration and Naturalization Service.

Based on recent statistics, a disproportionate number of African American males are incarcerated—46.5 percent of all prisoners are African American, although only 10 percent of the U.S. population is African American. Crime has become a class issue.

—*Cynthia Clark Northrup*

References
Jones, David A. *History of Criminology: A Philosophical Perspective.* Westport, CT: Greenwood Press, 1986.
See also Volume 1: Class; Poverty.

Cuba

Caribbean nation south of Florida that for several centuries was part of the Spanish empire.

Spain claimed possession of Cuba from 1492 through 1898, managing to hold the island longer than it held most of its other colonies. However, a rebellion against Spanish control began in Cuba in 1895. The Spanish used brutal tactics against the revolutionaries, and the conflict was much written about in American newspapers. Without a solution to the fighting in sight, the United States went to war against Spain in 1898 in support of Cuban independence fighters, quickly defeating Spain but giving the Cubans little credit for their role in the fighting. United States troops remained in Cuba after the war, but the Teller Amendment (passed in April 1898 before hostilities began) prohibited American annexation of the island. Therefore, the United States gave Cuba independence but insisted that the Cubans incorporate into their constitution the Platt Amendment, which gave the United States the authority to intervene in Cuban affairs if the American government believed Cuba's independence was in jeopardy. It also prohibited the Cuban government from contracting a debt, and it gave the United States the rights to a naval base at Guantanamo Bay on the western end of the island.

In 1934, the Platt Amendment was abrogated, and the United States passed the Jones-Castigan Act, which lowered the tariff on Cuban sugar entering the United States. Cuban sugar output increased dramatically, but the island became dependent on American sugar purchases and failed to develop a diverse economy. Because of mismanagement and lack of diversification, the Cuban economy began to steadily decline throughout the 1940s. Even so, Havana became famous for its nightlife and was a popular destination for American travelers.

In the face of a sinking economy and charges of government corruption in the mid-1950s, a rebel guerrilla movement led by Fidel Castro moved against the Cuban leader, Fulgencio Batista. In 1959, Castro took control of the government, and economic reforms soon followed. Castro reduced utility rates and raised workers' wages. Of more interest to the United States, his government seized property and began import restrictions on luxury items that Cuba typically imported from the United States.

Cuba, still largely dependent on the United States, avoided offending its northern neighbor until it began to receive Soviet economic assistance in 1960. Once Cuba developed close ties to the Soviet Union, the administration of President Dwight D. Eisenhower slashed the Cuban sugar quota to zero and the United States stopped importing the product. Cuba remained a communist nation and, in 1962, the United States instigated a full economic boycott against the island following the Cuban missile crisis in October 1962. The crisis occurred when the United States initiated a quarantine of the island after spy flights discovered the construction of ballistic missile silos for which the Soviet Union was providing missiles. After a tense standoff, the Soviets removed all missiles from Cuba in exchange for the United States removing its missiles from Turkey. In the early 1980s, the administration of Ronald Reagan tightened the blockade. The United States refused to import goods that had been transshipped through Cuba or even finished goods that contained materials originating in Cuba. Even travel to and from Cuba was prohibited. The boycott has had a disastrous effect on the Cuban economy that has only increased since the collapse of the Soviet Union in 1991. The embargo and travel restrictions remain in effect. Only academics conducting research, U.S. and international politicians, athletes performing at recognized events, journalists, and family members returning one time per year are allowed to travel to the country.

—*John K. Franklin*

References
Pérez, Louis A. *Cuba: Between Reform and Revolution.* New York: Oxford University Press, 1988.
See also Volume 1: Cold War; Spanish-American War; Sugar.

Currency Act (1764)

British act that restricted the ability of colonists to conduct economic transactions.

The British government, lobbied by merchants in London, worried about the circulation of paper currency in the American colonies. Following the Seven Years' War between Britain and France, most of the colonies issued paper bills, a practice tolerated during the war for its convenience in purchasing supplies and paying colonial militia troops. In 1751, Parliament had passed the Currency Reform Act, which regulated colonial paper currency, but in the war years from 1754 to 1763, New York, Pennsylvania, and Maryland had issued technically illegal currency. However, by 1764, much of this currency fluctuated so wildly in value that it threatened the stability of the trade and debts between colonists and the trading houses in England that handled their accounts. To make matters worse, many private banks and companies issued paper money that depreciated even more rapidly than that of the colonial governments.

The Currency Act, passed by British Parliament September 1, 1764, prohibited any colony from issuing paper currency in any form, including bills of exchange. This action met with colonial protest, since a shortage of hard currency existed, particularly on the frontier, which sometimes made paper currency necessary for any trade to take place at all. It also frustrated tobacco planters accustomed to storing their crops in government warehouses while receiving bills of exchange with which they paid tithes, taxes, and salaries. The harshest criticism occurred because of the bills' enforcement measures, which included a fine of £1,000 and the dismissal of any governor whose administration allowed the circulation of paper money.

—*Margaret Sankey*

References

Doerflinger, Thomas. *A Vigorous Spirit of Enterprise: Merchants and Economic Development in Revolutionary Philadelphia.* Chapel Hill: University of North Carolina Press, 1986.

Maier, Pauline. *From Resistance to Revolution: Colonial Radicals and the Development of American Opposition to Britain, 1765–1776.* New York: Alfred A. Knopf, 1972.

See also Volume 1: American Revolution.

Currency Act of 1900

Act through which the United States abandoned a bimetal (silver and gold) backing of the currency and converted to gold.

The Currency Act of 1900 dominated and affected the economic growth of the country for three decades. It reduced by 50 percent the minimum capital needed for a small national bank, thus increasing the number of bank establishments, and it increased the limitations on the issue of banknotes. In 1878, with the discovery of silver in the West and the Free Silver Movement advocating the unlimited coinage of silver, the federal government passed the Bland-Allison Act, which authorized it to buy a limited amount of silver, between $2 million and $4 million, each month and convert it into dollars. In an attempt to pacify silverites (silver mine owners, western farmers, and the lower laboring classes that benefited from an expanded currency) and not alienate eastern investors, Republicans passed the Sherman Silver Purchase Act of 1890, which doubled the amount of silver purchased. Because money is a medium of both domestic and foreign exchange, many Republicans felt it was essential to maintain the gold standard if U.S. businesses were to compete internationally. They also believed that Gresham's Law (overvalued species will drive out undervalued species) would lead to a depletion of gold in federal mints as individuals sold gold in European markets.

With the discovery of gold in Alaska, which increased the nation's currency supply, President William McKinley persuaded Congress to pass the Currency Act of 1900. The government backed all currency with gold and fixed the price at $20.67 an ounce. By going to this standard, the nation found itself facing several disadvantages in the first three decades of the twentieth century. A growing economy needs a growing gold reserve to back it up. If such reserves decline, the money supply slows and economic growth is restricted. People can also decide to convert their currency into gold in a speculative move, thereby draining the federal reserve of gold and reducing the money supply. Many historians and economists contend that the gold standard led to the Great Depression. In 1933, the federal government feared a depletion of its gold supply, and President Franklin D. Roosevelt decided to go off the gold standard.

—*T. Jason Soderstrum*

References

Weber, Christopher. *". . . Good as Gold"? How We Lost Our Gold Reserves and Destroyed the Dollar.* Berryville, VA: George Edward Durell Foundation, 1988.

See also Volume 1: Bland-Allison Act; Gold versus Silver.

CWA

See Civil Works Administration.

D

Dams, Construction of

The building of barriers across a water source that results in the formation of a reservoir to store water; in the United States, stored water provided irrigation, drinking water, and electricity to 17 western states and allowed for the production of crops and the growth of cities and industries in previously uninhabited areas.

The construction of dams in the United States became a coordinated federal goal with the passage of the Reclamation Act of 1902. Congress created the U.S. Bureau of Reclamation to oversee the development of water resources in the semiarid and arid region of the western United States. Although the Homestead, Timber Culture, and Timber and Stone acts had attracted settlers farther west, hundreds of thousands of acres remained uninhabitable or uncultivable because of the lack of water. The bureau designed a system of dams on numerous rivers to be used both for irrigation and the generation of hydroelectric power. Working with the U.S. Army Corps of Engineers, the Bureau of Reclamation constructed most of these dams between 1909 and 1947. On the North Platte River, the Pathfinder Dam (1909) and the Guernsey Dam (1927) provide water and power to western Nebraska and eastern Wyoming. The Shoshone Project, which includes the Buffalo Bill Dam (1910), services northwestern Wyoming. In Colorado a series of dams including the Granby and the Green Mountain dams form reservoirs from which water is pumped into a tunnel that descends the slope of the Continental Divide, providing water and power to the eastern slope of the Rocky Mountains.

Between 1933 and 1943, the U.S. Corps of Engineers constructed the Bonneville Dam and the Grand Coulee Dam on the Columbia River between Oregon and Washington. Special consideration for the salmon that spawn upriver resulted in the inclusion of fish ladders. In California the dams along the Sacramento and San Joaquin rivers provide water for the farmlands of the Central Valley and for municipalities that desperately need water and power for their growing populations. In 1944 Congress authorized the construction of the series of 112 dams throughout the Missouri River basin that provided water and power to Nebraska, Montana, South Dakota, North Dakota, Wyoming, Kansas, Missouri, Colorado, Iowa, and Minnesota. Since the 1950s the North Platte, Shoshone, Colorado, and Missouri projects have been integrated. One of the most dramatic results of dam construction was in Nevada, where the U.S. Corps of Engineers built the Hoover Dam (1933–1947), one of the world's largest. Designed to harness the Colorado River, the dam created Lake Mead, which provides water for the growing Las Vegas area as well as other parts of Nevada—area that would have otherwise remained a barren desert.

The two largest dam projects in the United States were the Tennessee Valley Authority (TVA) and the St. Lawrence Seaway. The TVA, built during the Great Depression, provided irrigation and inexpensive hydroelectric power for one of the country's poorest regions. The project has proven successful in terms of providing local inhabitants with a higher standard of living through the creation of jobs, education programs, and soil conservation. The St. Lawrence Seaway, authorized in 1954 and constructed jointly with Canada, opened up the American industrial and agricultural heartland to oceangoing vessels. A series of canals, dams, and locks allows ships to travel the Great Lakes all the way to Chicago. Other major cities that benefit from the seaway include Buffalo, Duluth, Milwaukee, Detroit, Toledo, and Cleveland. Important commodities shipped through the seaway include iron ore from Michigan and Minnesota as well as wheat and coal. In addition to opening up a new trade route, the St. Lawrence Seaway also generates power for New York and Ontario.

—*Cynthia Clark Northrup*

References

Jackson, Donald. *Great American Bridges and Dams*. New York: John Wiley and Sons, 1988.

Stevens, Joseph E. *Hoover Dam: An American Adventure*. Norman: University of Oklahoma Press, 1988.

Sussman, Gennifer. *The St. Lawrence Seaway: History and Analysis of a Joint Water Highway*. Washington, DC: National Planning Association, 1978.

See also Volume 1: Electricity; Homestead Act; Tennessee Valley Authority; Timber and Stone Act; Timber Culture Act.

DARPA

See Defense Advanced Research Projects Agency.

Dartmouth College v. Woodward (1819)

Early Supreme Court case that upheld the validity of contracts under the U.S. Constitution.

In 1769, King George III granted a charter to Dartmouth College in the colony of New Hampshire. The charter established that 12 trustees and their successors would direct the college "forever." By the early nineteenth century, the trustees of Dartmouth College were well known as staunch supporters of the Federalist Party during a period involving a power struggle between the Federalists and the newly dominant Democratic-Republican Party—a fact that William Plumer, the newly elected Democratic-Republican governor of the state, decided to no longer tolerate. With the support of a Democratic-Republican majority in the legislature, Governor Plumer passed a series of laws in 1816 that changed Dartmouth from a private college to a public university. The new laws would allow the governor to appoint more trustees to the college, as well as a board of overseers. The college immediately sued the state of New Hampshire for impairing its original charter and hired Daniel Webster to argue its case before the Supreme Court.

Webster believed that New Hampshire had clearly violated the contract clause of the Constitution, which says that no state may pass a law "impairing the Obligation of Contracts." Ruling for the Court in a 5-to-1 decision, Chief Justice John Marshall agreed with Webster and went even further by extending the protection of the contract clause to all private corporations. Marshall first argued that Dartmouth College was a private and not a public corporation, since its founders were individuals who hoped to spread the Christian faith among the Indians. As a private corporation, Dartmouth College had the right to direct itself through its trustees in accordance with the original charter. The new laws passed by the state of New Hampshire had impaired the original charter and thus violated the Constitution. By extending the protection of the contract clause, Marshall helped to make private corporations the main tool of business expansion in America.

—*Mary Stockwell*

References
Siegel, Adrienne. *The Marshall Court, 1801–1835.* Millwood, NY: Associated Faculty Press, 1987.
See also Volume 2: Judiciary.

Dawes Plan

A plan designed to stabilize the European economy after World War I by facilitating monetary stabilization in Germany.

After World War I, the Reparations Commission, an Allied-controlled agency created under the Versailles Treaty, established the system of reparations. The German hyperinflation that emerged after the French occupation of the industrial center of the Ruhr River valley forced European leaders to reconsider that system.

In November 1923 the Reparations Commission called for the formation of two independent advisory panels comprising financial experts from the United States and Europe. At the suggestion of the administration of President Calvin Coolidge, the Reparations Commission invited the American banker, Charles G. Dawes, to lead the effort.

The Americans dominated this effort to reconfigure German reparations. They convinced the Europeans to adopt a system based on German "capacity to pay." Germany would pay in full, but only at a rate consistent with the elimination of inflation. By stabilizing the German monetary system, investor confidence would increase, restoring trade balances and improving economic conditions for all of western and central Europe.

The Dawes Plan required that Germany return to the gold standard and establish a new central bank. These reforms would curb inflation, discourage German deficit spending, and encourage foreign investment in Germany. A new office, agent general, determined rates for reparations payments that would not provoke inflation or reduce the standard of living in Germany.

The Dawes Plan did temporarily stabilize the German economy. However, it did not make the German economy strong enough to withstand a series of global financial shocks between 1929 and 1931.

—*Karen A. J. Miller*

References
McNeil, William C. *American Money and the Weimar Republic: Economics and Politics on the Eve of the Great Depression.* New York: Columbia University Press, 1986.
See also Volume 1: World War II.

Dawes Severalty Act (1887)

Act ending policies that had provided reservations to Indian tribes, instead providing 160-acre tracts of land to individual Native Americans and weakening the cohesiveness of the tribes.

By the late 1880s, a series of wars with Native Americans had convinced many reformers that programs designed to concentrate Indians on reservations had failed. Without access to traditional lands and cultural practices and with the decline of the buffalo, tribes slowly became dangerously dependent on governmental aid for their survival. Moreover, whenever whites wanted access to Indian lands, they often violated treaties with impunity, as railroad companies so often did when they ran tracks across a reservation. Against this backdrop Congress passed the Dawes Severalty Act in 1887. The act ended the policy of placing tribes on reservations, attempting instead to assimilate Native Americans into the cultural and economic habits of mainstream white Americans by undermining their communal structure, parceling out and privatizing their land, and setting them up as farmers. To prevent whites from swindling Indians out of their land, the Dawes Severalty Act placed the federal government in a position to hold title to the land for 25 years. The stipulation worked poorly, however, as Indians "leased" land to unscrupulous speculators, and any reservation land not given to Indians remained available to non-Indian homesteaders. Native Americans also proved fiercely loyal to their languages, religions, and cultures. Few succeeded as traditional farmers and, by 1933, almost half of the Native Americans living on reservations whose land had been allotted found themselves landless. Many who retained allotments found themselves working mainly desert land. Under the Dawes Severalty Act, Indian poverty only deepened, as assimilation efforts continued apace, culminating in the 1920s with the Bureau of Indian Affairs outlawing Indian religious ceremonies, banning polygamy, and even imposing limits on the length of a man's hair.

—*James E. McWilliams*

References

Carlson, Leonard A. *Indians, Bureaucrats, and Land: The Dawes Act and the Decline of Indian Farming.* Westport, CT: Greenwood Press, 1981.

See also Volume 1: Indian Policy.

Debs, Eugene Victor (1855–1926)

Popular labor union activist, founder of the Social Democratic Party, and 1919 presidential candidate.

Born November 5, 1855, in Terre Haute, Indiana, to French immigrant parents, Eugene Debs had nine siblings. He attended a local school until he turned 14, when he went to work on the railroad, eventually becoming a locomotive fireman. He left the railroad four years later to work as a grocery clerk. Debs stayed active in railroad, however, first by joining and participating in the Brotherhood of Locomotive Firemen and then as editor of the *Firemen's Magazine.* Debs married Katherine Mezel in 1885 and served briefly in the Indiana legislature.

Debs remains most remembered for his work with labor unions. In 1893 he helped to form an industrial labor society called the American Railway Union (ARU), and he was the organization's first president. The ARU gained national exposure during the Pullman strike of 1894, which turned into a walkout of all ARU members who served the Great Northern Railway out of Chicago. When all railroad employees went out on strike, the courts—under the Sherman Anti-Trust Act—convicted Debs and others for obstructing the mail. Debs served six months in jail, during which time he read and studied, emerging from his jail term a socialist. He then organized the Social Democratic Party of America from what little remained of the ARU; the union had lost many members after the government issued an injunction against it.

Debs made several runs for president as the Socialist Party candidate. He also wrote for and edited socialist publications. On June 16, 1918, during a speech at a socialist convention in Canton, Ohio, he encouraged listeners to oppose the war by any means. Charged with sedition and indicted for violating the Espionage Act, Debs received a 10-year sentence on two counts of disobeying an injunction issued by the federal government that ordered workers to return to their jobs or be in violation of the Sherman Anti-Trust Act. In 1919 Debs, while still a prisoner, received the nomination for president by the Socialist Party; he received 919,799 votes. President Warren G. Harding paroled Debs in 1922, but the Atlanta penitentiary had taken a toll on his health. Debs returned home to Indiana and continued to write. His syndicated column on prison life was compiled and published as a book, *Walls and Bars,* in 1927. Debs died October 20, 1926, at a sanitarium; more than 10,000 people attended his funeral.

—*Lisa A. Ennis*

References

Johnson, Allen, ed. *Dictionary of American Biography.* Vols. 2, 3, and 5. New York: Scribner's, 1929.

See also Volume 1: Railroads.

Defense Advanced Research Projects Agency (DARPA)

Federal agency established in 1958 to ensure U.S. world leadership in military technology; the agency that originated the Internet.

DARPA's mission ("to engage in such advanced projects, essential to the Defense Department's responsibilities in the field of basic applied research and development") and organizational structure are unique among government agencies. DARPA reported directly to the secretary of defense but remained independent of the military research and development divisions. One of DARPA's primary objectives was to deliberately avoid traditional ways of thinking and approaches to problems. Acceptance of the possibility of failure is another important founding principal of DARPA. These characteristics allow the agency to work quickly and decisively.

Throughout its history, DARPA has clung to most of its original principles and ideals. The organization remains small and flexible with a flat organizational structure with few levels of management, and it has retained its autonomy from traditional bureaucratic entanglements. The technical staff includes world-class scientists who rotate in and out every three to five years.

The organization has changed little, except in terms of its reporting chain and its name. DARPA has reported to secretary, deputy secretary, and undersecretary of defense; most recently DARPA reports to the director for defense research and engineering. The name changes are more complicated. Established in 1958 by Department of Defense directive 5105.15 in response to the Soviet launch of *Sputnik,* it was called the Advanced Research Projects Agency (ARPA). In 1972 the name changed to Defense Advanced Research Projects Agency (DARPA), and it became a separate defense agency. In 1993, President Bill Clinton changed the name back to ARPA in an effort to focus on its role in general economic growth, and in 1996 the name reverted back to DARPA under Title IX of the Defense Authorization Act. Its operating philosophy has also changed over time—originally it focused on microelectronics and computing and network technologies, then on research and development business practices, and most recently on joint-service solutions that coordinate efforts among various agencies.

DARPA's most visible influence has been on the evolution of computing and computer networks. Its structure and flexibility allowed for the creation and promotion of ARPANet, a means by which scientists and researchers could share information over computer networks using packet switching—a procedure in which "packets" of information are transmitted over various routes and then reassembled at the destination in complete form. The success of ARPANet and other DARPA research led to the creation and development of the Internet. Within 35 years, computers had spread beyond the highly expensive realm of a few and were connecting millions through desktop PCs. Consumers gained access to a multitude of Internet services from purchasing products to paying bills online.

The success of DARPA, however, is derived from the implementation of its technology and ideas into military abilities. For instance, the F-117 stealth fighter, the Joint Surveillance Target and Attack Radar System (JSTARS), and Uncooled Infrared Sensors—all used in the 1991 Gulf War—had their origins in DARPA research. The M-16 assault rifle, the standard issue for all U.S. troops, also has its roots in DARPA. From the military standpoint DARPA has proven highly successful.

—*Lisa A. Ennis*

References

"ARPA-DARPA: The History of the Name." April 18, 2001. Available: http://www.darpa.mil/; accessed September 17, 2001.

"DARPA over the Years." April 18, 2001. Available: http://www.darpa.mil/; accessed September 17, 2001.

DARPA. "Technology Transition." January 1997. Available: http://www.darpa.mil/; accessed September 17, 2001.

See also Volume 1: Computer; Volume 2: Communications.

Defense Plant Corporation (DPC)

A federal agency and subsidiary of the U.S. government's Reconstruction Finance Corporation (RFC) that led to acquisition by the federal government of a dominant position in several large industries.

On August 22, 1940, Congress chartered the Defense Plant Corporation (DPC) in anticipation of war hostilities and assigned it the task of expanding production capabilities for military equipment. Its charter permitted both the building and equipping of new facilities and the expansion of existing structures.

Previously, in 1932, Congress had established the RFC as an independent government agency whose original purpose was to facilitate economic activity by lending during the Great Depression. The RFC would make and collect loans and buy and sell securities. At first it lent money only to financial, industrial, and agricultural institutions, but the scope of its operations widened greatly as a result of revised legislative amendments. These amendments allowed for the making of loans to foreign governments, providing protec-

tion against war and disaster damages, and financing the construction and operation of war plants. Approximately two-thirds or $20 billion of RFC disbursements went toward U.S. national defense, especially during World War II.

The RFC financed much of American industrial expansion during World War II. Various government departments such as the War and Navy Departments, the Office of Production Management, the War Production Board, and the Maritime Commission would request what they needed from the RFC, and in turn the DPC would ensure that the plants (mostly new factories and mills) were constructed, equipped, and operated. Jesse H. Jones, with Emil Schram and Sam Husbands, managed the DPC. From its inception in 1940 through 1945, the DPC disbursed over $9 billion on 2,300 projects in 46 states and in foreign countries. In general, the government owned the plants and then leased them to private companies to operate. In spending these billions of dollars, the government acquired a dominant position in several industries including aircraft manufacture, nonferrous metals, machine tools, synthetic rubber, and shipping. The materials and supplies produced during the war ranged from bearings to giant guns, tanks, ships, and airplanes. About half of the spending of funds went directly or indirectly for aviation. One of the DPC's largest projects involved a $176 million Dodge-Chicago plant that manufactured aircraft engines for the B-29 and B-32 airplanes. The plant's 19 one-story buildings stretched over 1,545 acres of floor space. It was so large that it had its own steel forge and aluminum foundry and could take in raw materials at one end and turn out finished engines at the other. Congress dissolved the DPC on July 1, 1945.

—*Albert Atkins*

References

Defense Manufacturing in 2010 and Beyond, Meeting the Changing Needs of National Defense. Appendix A. National Academy Press, 1999. Available: http://www.nap.edu.readingroom/books/defman/app_appa.html; accessed September 17, 2001.

See also Volume 1: World War II.

Defense Sciences

An agency under the Defense Advanced Research Project Agency that develops military technologies.

The tremendous influence of science and technology on war during the second half of the twentieth century mirrored the equally momentous influence that war had on science and technology. The U.S. Army Research Laboratory (ARL) played a key role in the Department of Defense and army research and development programs. The dynamic organizational structure of ARL provides insight into army research and development programs and technological core competencies including some basic research, a substantial exploratory development program, and a continuing effort to "field" technology through a succession of advanced technology demonstrations.

Other agencies draw on expertise in computer science, mathematics, operations research, electrical engineering, and physics. The Advanced Information Technology Center concentrates on access to the Defense Information Systems Agency (DISA), College Financial System (CFS), and Information Technology Standards Library. In addition, the DISA mission is to plan, engineer, develop, test, and manage programs; to acquire, implement, operate, and maintain information systems for C4I (an Air Force geographic information system for communication planning and modeling); and to provide mission support under all conditions of peace and war. It also contains information about the Defense Research and Engineering Network, which is the networking component of the Department of Defense (DOD) High Performance Computing Modernization Program.

The Defense Technology Information Center provides access to and transfer of scientific and technical information for DOD personnel, for example, to the Office of Naval Research (ONR). The ONR coordinates, executes, and promotes the science and technology programs of the United States Navy and Marine Corps through universities, government laboratories, and nonprofit organizations.

—*Albert Atkins*

References

Chambers, John Whiteclay, II. *The American Military History.* New York: Oxford University Press, 1999.
See also Volume 1: World War II.

Deficit Spending

Government expenditure in excess of tax revenue over a specific period of time.

By definition, deficit spending entails recourse to government borrowing (typically through the sale of bonds). Since 1945, it has been widely acknowledged that the Keynesian revolution, which witnessed the overthrow of classical economics, produced a theoretical justification for deficit spending. Nevertheless, there has been considerable debate on the extent to which John Maynard Keynes himself favored deficit spending as a policy option. In contributing to the debate, J. A. Kregel has contended that Keynes never explicitly proposed "government deficits as a tool of stabilization policy." It is necessary, therefore, to trace the evolution of Keynes's ideas on the subject.

Amidst the economic chaos produced by World War I and the draconian Treaty of Versailles, Keynes critiqued not just classical economic theory but also British economic policy. In the 1920s, Keynes attacked the "treasury view," held by Ralph Hawtrey and Winston Churchill, that increased public expenditure would crowd out private expenditure. Accordingly, he advocated loan-financed public works as a remedy for unemployment. Subsequently, in "An Open Letter to President Roosevelt" (1933), Keynes criticized the U.S. government for striving to maintain a balanced budget in the midst of an unprecedented crisis. More precisely, Keynes pointed to "the increase of national purchasing power resulting from governmental expenditure . . . financed by loans and not by taxing present incomes." Finally, in *The General Theory*

of Employment, Interest and Money (1936), Keynes attributed the Great Depression to deficient aggregate demand. Thus, in an effort to explain the multiplier effect (in which the monetary supply expands through banks' lending), he argued that "public works even of doubtful utility [would] pay for themselves over and over again in times of severe unemployment." It is not surprising that Alvin Hansen's *Full Recovery or Stagnation* (1938) stressed the "income-stimulating expenditures of the federal government." In a similar vein, Abba Lerner's "Functional Finance and the Public Debt" (1943) attributed the idea of functional finance (as distinguished from the more orthodox sound finance) to Keynes.

To recapitulate, owing to the exigencies of the depression, Keynesian revolutionaries (especially in the United States) interpreted Keynes's *General Theory* as a justification for countercyclical demand management (or stabilization policy). In the Keynesian view, stabilization would be achieved by manipulating the balance between spending and taxation. Thus, faced with the threat of recession, the government would increase public spending and/or decrease taxes. Conversely, faced with the threat of inflationary expansion, the government would decrease public spending and/or increase taxes. By alternating between deficit and surplus, the government would regulate the business cycle.

Throughout the "Keynesian consensus"—a period of time between the end of World War II (1945) and the year the United States went off the gold standard (1973) when scholars and economists believed that deficit spending would help the economy—the United States employed a version of functional finance in the regulation of the business cycle (despite the inflationary pressures the policy seemed to produce). In recent years, however, deficit spending has fallen into disrepute across the political spectrum (not least because deficits have been equated with deferred taxation).

—*Mark Frezzo*

References

Buchanan, James, and Richard Wagner. *Democracy in Deficit.* New York: Academic Press, 1977.
Hansen, Alvin. *Full Recovery or Stagnation.* New York: Norton and Norton, 1938.
Kregel, J. A. "Budget Deficits, Stabilization Policy, and Liquidity Preference." In Fausto Vicarelli, ed. *Keynes's Relevance Today.* Philadelphia: University of Pennsylvania Press, 1985.
Lerner, Abba. *The Economics of Employment.* New York: McGraw-Hill, 1951.
See also Volume 1: Budget Deficits and Surpluses; Keynes, John Maynard.

DeLima v. Bidwell (1901)

Case that determined if newly acquired territories were foreign governments and therefore subject to import taxes.

The case of *DeLima v. Bidwell* questioned if newly acquired territories were considered foreign governments, therefore subject to import taxes, or if they were part of the United States. The firm of D. A. DeLima & Co. sued George

Bidwell, the New York port tax collector, in 1899 to recover import taxes collected on Puerto Rican sugar. In early January 1901, the Supreme Court heard the case along with *Downes v. Bidwell* and, on May 27, 1901, it decided both cases. DeLima received a 5-to-4 vote stating Puerto Rico was not a foreign country and therefore not subject to foreign import duties, entitling DeLima to recover the exacted duties. The decision of the Court was debated publicly and bitterly. The way the decision read, Congress would need to incorporate any acquired territory into the general revenue system to eliminate any questions about the territory's statutes in trading partnerships. Only issued Congressional legislation could make the territory "domestic" and part of the internal trading system.

This case is one of the Insular Cases, a collection of Court cases heard between 1900 and 1904 that established how the U.S. Constitution would apply to acquired island territories. In 1957 the Insular Cases were seemingly overturned by *Reid v. Covert*, which determined that U.S. citizens residing abroad are under the same jurisdiction as U.S. citizens at home in matters of their civil and legal rights. The assumption that citizens are under U.S. laws was endorsed by *Examining Board of Architects, Engineers and Surveyors v. Flores de Otero* in 1976, which stated that a dependent of a U.S. citizen can be tried by U.S. courts. However, with *United States v. Verduigo-Urquidez* in 1990, the Supreme Court declared that the Insular Cases still governed how the U.S. Constitution applied to island territories and that property owned by a nonresident alien located in a foreign country is not subject to U.S. search and seizure laws.

—*Deana Covel*

References
MacMeekin, Dan. *Island Law: The Insular Cases.* November 26, 2002. Available: http://www.macmeekin.com/Library/Insular%20Cases.htm#Verdugo; accessed December 28, 2002.
See also Volume 2: Judiciary.

Democracy

Political concept denoting a form of government by and for the people, exercised either directly or through elected representatives, and essential for the functioning of a modern capitalist economy.

In a democracy, the sovereign power resides in the people rather than in an elite group. In the case of U.S. democracy, the people on the basis of universal suffrage elect both the executive and the legislative branches of government. Modern democracy is characterized by individual freedom, including economic freedom. This freedom allows citizens of democratic nations such as the United States to engage freely in economic pursuits.

American democracy rests on the revolutionary democratic principle of "no taxation without representation." The colonists who revolted against Great Britain did so on the premise that Parliament had violated their economic interests. Economic freedom involved the freedom of trade and the freedom of a people to tax itself rather than being taxed by an outside power. This principle of economic freedom lies at the heart of the American Revolution. Ordinary people in colonial ports formed democratic organizations such as the Sons of Liberty in the 1760s. These mechanics, tradesmen, and artisans came together to boycott British goods.

American democracy has evolved over the 225 years since the signing of the Declaration of Independence. However, the essential features proclaimed in this founding historic document, which asserted the right to life, liberty, and the pursuit of happiness, and which included the freedom to own private property, remain key to American democracy to this day. The crucial concept is the freedom of the individual to be the owner of goods and services intended for sale. Individuals and private corporations also control the dynamic of production.

Today the American economy functions as a part of a democratic system of government comprising free and equal people; a free marketplace; and complex businesses, labor unions, and social organizations. The economy remains democratic in the sense that people can vote as citizens on public issues and for the political leaders who set policies that have a major effect on the economy.

—*Leigh Whaley*

References
de Tocqueville, Alexis. *Democracy in America,* ed. J. P. Mayer; trans. George Lawrence. New York: Perennial Library, 1988.
Foner, Eric. *The Story of American Freedom.* New York: Norton, 1999.
See also Volume 1: Constitution.

Democratic Party

Political party formed in 1792 by Governor George Clinton of New York and Virginians Thomas Jefferson and James Madison.

The economic policy of the Democratic Party favored the small yeoman farmer. Originally called the Jeffersonian Democratic-Republican Party, the group dropped "Republican" during the age of Andrew Jackson (1828–1836) when property-holding requirements for voting vanished throughout most of the United States. In Thomas Jefferson's view, an individual who worked for an employer lost his or her freedom. This favoring of modest folks continued as President Andrew Jackson fought the establishment of the Second National Bank of the United States, although Democratic-Republican president James Madison had come to support the idea of a national bank. Democrats had little in the way of electoral competition in the first half of the nineteenth century as the merchant-oriented Federalists fell from favor because of their support for such unpopular measures as the Alien and Sedition Act, which overturned the right to freedom of speech and the press. The Whigs, the successors of the Federalists, only managed to win a couple of presidential elections.

A new Republican Party, founded in 1854, competed strongly with the Democrats from the beginning and achieved hegemony in the late nineteenth century that endured until 1930, when Democrats assumed control of the U.S. House of Representatives. The competitiveness of the Democratic Party was dampened because of an economic downturn during the second administration of President Grover Cleveland and the populist campaign of 1896 Democratic presidential nominee William Jennings Bryan, who supported helping alienated city dwellers—mostly underpaid workers and immigrants who operated outside the mainstream political system—in a rapidly urbanizing nation. Following the economic crash of 1929, which came during a period of unified Republican control of the national government, the Democratic Party gained favorable recognition.

Although Americans continued to perceive the Republican Party as better able to conduct foreign policy during most of the twentieth century, the Democrats had the edge on handling the economy, and this doubtless contributed to the pattern in U.S. politics after the 1930 midterm elections. For the remainder of the century, the Republicans controlled both the presidency and both houses of Congress for a total of just four years—whereas the Democrats dominated Congress for 32 years running at the end of the twentieth century. Key to Democratic success was disproportionate support for its candidates by members of the working class, many of whom lived in large urban areas. In presidential elections where class polarization existed, such as in 1936, 1940, and 1976, Democratic candidates emerged victorious. In the presidential election of 1972, when the correlation of voter choice with class status approached zero, Republican Richard M. Nixon handily defeated Democratic U.S. Senator George McGovern. Interestingly, Nixon identified himself as a Keynesian, a theory of economics more closely identified with Democratic policies than with Republican ones. The Republican Party continues to define itself as a party that recognizes Keynesian economics but within a balanced budget.

—*Henry B. Sirgo*

References

Goldman, Ralph Morris. *The Democratic Party in American Politics.* New York: Macmillan, 1966.

Kent, Frank R. *The Democratic Party: A History.* New York: Century Co., 1928.

See also Volume 1: Great Depression; Republican Party.

Depression, The

See Great Depression.

Depression of the 1890s

Severe economic downturn after cotton-growing regions of the South and agricultural areas of the Great Plains began experiencing significant decline in prices, increases in expenses, and a precipitous spike in farm foreclosures.

The depression of the 1890s arrived at Wall Street on May 5, 1893, when stock prices declined in the face of uncertainty about the gold supply and the failure of the Philadelphia and Reading Railroad. This economic crisis reached its nadir in 1894 but endured until mid-1897. A depression in Europe, low agricultural prices, deflated monetary prices, watered railroad stocks, and a lack of government regulation precipitated this economic crisis. The Panic of 1893 began because of a financial crisis in the railroad industry, the most important component of the national economy, and quickly affected virtually every sector of American economic life. The unemployment rate reached 20 percent, 156 railroads and 400 banks failed, and 16,000 businesses went bankrupt.

This economic crisis revealed class differences when Jacob Coxey's army of unemployed Americans marched toward Washington, D.C., in March and April 1893 in search of jobs and government relief. The desperation of union members became evident in Chicago during the Homestead (1892) and Pullman (1894) strikes.

—*James T. Carroll*

References

Steeples, Douglas, and David Whitten. *Democracy in Desperation: The Depression of 1893.* Westport, CT: Greenwood Press, 1998.

See also Volume 1: Pullman Strike; Railroads; Volume 2: Labor.

Depressions

Sustained periods of economic contraction, characterized by high and persistent levels of unemployment accompanied by falling prices, investment contraction, financial crises, reduced demand, and general decline in business activity.

Although some economists view depressions as random aberrations, most agree that they remain inherent to capitalist economies. Throughout the long-term evolution of capitalism, the type and nature of depressions has changed. The structural and institutional development of the economy has played an important role in the types of depressions that have emerged. The United States has experienced six major depressions in its economic history since the early 1800s—all similar in length and severity. Prior to that, economic declines had occurred largely because of wars, natural disasters, and other noneconomic factors.

During the early nineteenth century, merchant capitalism, in which depressions remain largely commercial and speculative in character, ended. Small proprietorships made up the economy at this time. This raw-materials economy resulted in depressions accompanied by speculation and sharp declines in prices for agricultural and raw materials. With the advent of the Industrial Revolution in the late nineteenth century and diminished contribution of agriculture to economic growth, crisis became associated with the rise, expansion, and financing of industrial activity. The profit incentive became even more important in an era of increased demand

and mass production. Corporations replaced proprietorships, and new financial institutions emerged to facilitate factory production. The development of competitive markets frequently led companies into price wars, which undermined profitability and hence firms' ability to meet financial obligations. This uncertainty led to the emergence of a different type of company—one with great market power and control characterized by cartels, trusts, and mergers. Investment banking evolved to service these organizations, acquiring a large stake in their control by securing a large number of firm shares and positions on governing boards. The depressions in the era of what may be called "banker capitalism" during the 1920s occurred as a result of the aggressive expansion of these firms and accompanying financial speculation. The authority of investment banking over the firms and lack of internal control are closely related to the massive financial speculation that brought about market instability and played a pivotal role in the deepest and most severe depression of our time, also referred to as the Great Depression, in the 1930s. In the post–World War II era, financial sector development and innovation, increasing globalization, and increasing financial instability have triggered several global financial crises or recessions, but no depressions.

Although economists disagree on the exact causes of each depression, the nature of depressions has changed with the evolution of capitalism. Whether linked to a collapse in agricultural prices or speculative financial attacks, all depressions include a sharp decline in demand. Each of the six major U.S. depressions has followed periods of sustained government surpluses and sharp debt reductions, thereby stifling aggregate demand. Price shocks, stock market crashes, and banking-sector crises act as catalysts that bring about the fast, sharp decline in economic activity that is typical of depressions.

Depressions are protracted and severe because it takes a while for business confidence to return. Sharp declines in demand or overinvestment (or both) lead to cutbacks in production, involuntary inventory accumulation, and massive layoffs. Declines in employment further depress aggregate demand, leading to a downward spiral in economic activity. Business confidence falls so that expected future returns do not warrant any new investment, even in the face of falling prices, wages, and interest rates. As markets fail to bring about a recovery, policy proposals have emerged for governments to implement countercyclical measures. The suggested remedial policy responses include "priming the pump," large public infrastructure investment, public service employment programs like those of the New Deal era, and job guarantee schemes, such as making the government an employer of last resort or making public service employment available. The emergence of big government, in which the federal government assumes control over a major portion of the U.S. economy, has contributed to the lack of depressions since World War II.

—*Pavlina R. Tcherneva and Mathew Forstater*

References

Galbraith, John Kenneth. *The Great Crash, 1929.* Boston: Houghton Mifflin, 1972.

Minsky, Hyman P. *Can "It" Happen Again?* Armonk, NY: M. E. Sharpe, 1982.

See also Volume 1: Captains of Industry; Great Depression.

Deregulation

The loosening of government controls over vital industries such as the airline, utility, and communications industries.

The legal cartel theory (in which some companies control pricing and supply although competitors exist), increasing evidence of waste and inefficiency in regulated industries, and the contention that government was regulating potentially competitive industries all contributed to the deregulation movement of the 1970s and 1980s. Since 1980, important legislation has been passed that deregulates in varying degrees the airline, trucking, banking, railroad, and television broadcasting industries.

Deregulation has proven controversial, and the nature of the controversy remains quite predictable. Basing their arguments on the legal cartel theory, in which certain companies control a near monopoly but some competitors exist, proponents of deregulation contend that it will result in lower prices, more output, and the elimination of bureaucratic inefficiencies. Some critics of deregulation, embracing the public interest theory, argue that deregulation will result in the gradual monopolization of the industry by one or two firms, which in turn will lead to higher prices and diminished output or service. Other critics contend that deregulation may lead to excessive competition and industry instability, and that vital services (for example, transportation) may be withdrawn from smaller communities. Still other critics stress that as increased competition reduces each firm's revenues, companies may lower their standards with respect to safety and risk as they try to reduce costs and remain profitable.

Perhaps the most publicized case of deregulation involves the airlines. The Airmail Act of 1925 provided for the encouragement of the air carrier industry; the Civil Aeronautics Act in 1938 established economic and other regulations upon which the industry matured and developed. Many factions and individuals representing the aviation industry, government, and the general public continued to express dissatisfaction after Congress passed the Civil Aeronautics Act in 1938 and again after the Federal Aviation Act became law in 1958. Dissent against and criticism of federal aviation regulation continued with increasing force until the 1970s. As early as 1975 a law was proposed that was also known as the Federal Aviation Act. Congress did not pass the act, but opposition grew regarding the economic regulation of the aviation industry. In the early 1970s, many academic economists questioned the need for economic regulation of air carriers. As a result, President Gerald Ford began to press for deregulation. Then President Jimmy Carter appointed Alfred Khan as Chairman of the Civil Aeronautics Board, and he moved quickly toward deregulation in areas of pricing, entry, and exit.

In 1975, Senator Edward Kennedy began an investigation of the regulatory practices of the Civil Aeronautics Board and the effects of these practices upon the air carrier industry. As a result, President Carter signed the Airline Deregulation Act of 1978 into law on October 24, 1978. Some believe that deregulation is the best thing to ever happen to the United States air transportation industry, whereas others believe that it is the most disastrous. Airline fares have decreased in the face of competition within the industry. At the same time, with fewer passengers flying after the terrorist attacks on September 11, 2001, rates dropped to a level that forced some airlines near or into bankruptcy, required the permanent reduction of staff, and required wage concessions from union members who remained with the airlines. External factors have contributed more to the industry's decline than has deregulation.

During the past 25 years, the federal government, in an effort to reduce the cost of government bureaucracies overseeing specific industries, initiated a policy of deregulation in areas other than the airline industry. The trucking industry was deregulated in 1980, and rates were adjusted from below market price to become competitive. The telecommunications industry was deregulated in the early 1980s, resulting in a variety of new providers—for example, Sprint, MCI, and later the cellular networks—entering the marketplace. The natural gas industry was deregulated in 1985. Also in the 1980s, the railroad industry deregulated to maintain control over its market share of freight and passenger services. Deregulation is designed to encourage competition and reduce prices for the consumer. In all but the energy industry, costs appear to be trending downward.

—*Albert Atkins*

References

MacAvoy, Paul W., ed. *Deregulation and Privatization in the United States.* Edinburgh, Scotland: Edinburgh University Press, 1995.
See also Volume 1: Aviation.

Desert Land Act (1877)

Legislation to encourage settlement and irrigation of western arid lands.

In 1877, Congress passed the Desert Land Act. Any citizen, person who had applied to become a naturalized citizen, head of household, or male over the age of 21 who had never been an enemy or aided an enemy of the United States could claim 160 acres of land in the public domain for a cost of $1.25 per acre. At the time the claim was placed, the claimant had to pay 25 cents, with the balance due in two years. Unlike the Homestead Act, the Desert Land Act did not include a residency requirement, but it did stipulate that title would be transferred after three years if irrigation had been accomplished within that time. Whereas the amount of land granted under the Homestead Act exceeded 287.5 million acres, the Desert Land Act failed to entice large number of settlers into the vast territory of the West and resulted in the granting of only 10.7 million acres to settlers. Consequently, Congress later passed the Newlands Reclamation Act of 1902, which provided that 95 percent of the funds derived from the sale of public lands in the western states would be used for irrigation projects such as the construction of dams, which would entice more settlers.

—*Cynthia Clark Northrup*

References

Hibbard, Benjamin Horace. *A History of the Public Land Policies.* Madison: University of Wisconsin Press, 1965.
See also Volume 2: Land Policies.

Digital Millennium Copyright Act of 1998

U.S. act that implemented two world treaties—World Intellectual Property Organization (WIPO) Copyright Treaty and the WIPO Performances and Phonograms Treaty—and also dealt with other copyright-related matters.

Legal recognition of the commercial value of the products of the intellect and the need to protect that value are often attributed to the guilds of the Middle Ages and their proprietary attitudes toward craft knowledge. The U.S. Constitution provides that Congress "promote the progress of science and useful arts by securing for limited times to authors and inventors the exclusive right to their respective writings and discoveries." Since 1790 Congress has passed many statutes to meet that responsibility, with the Digital Millennium Copyright Act (DMCA) the most recent.

The chief exception to copyright infringement is the "fair use" doctrine, which permits others to copy and distribute the creator's work within limits. In determining if a work is fair use, courts consider such factors as nature of the copyrighted work, purpose and character of the use, the relative proportion of the work used, and the effect of the use on the potential market of the work. However, advanced computer technology and the inherent openness of the World Wide Web (an Internet communication system that allows individuals to communicate and share information via the computer) pose unique problems for protection of an author's work when copyright can be infringed simply by clicking a computer mouse.

The DCMA limits the liability of online Internet service providers (companies that operate computers that facilitate the connection of PC users to the Internet) and nonprofit educational institutions for copyright infringement when they merely act as a data conduit or conduct system cacheing, when the information resides on the system or network at the direction of users, or when referrals to websites such as search engines or hyperlinks contain infringing material. The remedy remains an injunction preventing further use of the material, but the awarding of monetary damages is not legislated. Yet the DMCA does not offer much guidance for Web users and website managers or for those seeking to prevent copyright infringement on the Internet. For example, are the standards for fair use the same for the Web as elsewhere?

Under the WIPO treaties, the United States recognizes copyrights from other nations that have not fallen into the public domain, just as other signatories must accept U.S. copyrights. In addition, nations must prevent circumvention of technological measures used to protect copyrighted works. The DCMA is the start of that effort.

—Susan Coleman

References

Carothers, Jo Dale. "Protection of Intellectual Property on the World Wide Web: Is the Digital Millennium Copyright Act Sufficient?" *Arizona Law Review,* vol. 41 (Fall 1999): 937–961.

Digital Millennium Copyright Act. U.S. Statutes at Large 112 (1998): 2860.

U.S. Copyright Office. "The Digital Millennium Copyright Act of 1998 Summary." December 1998. Available: www.loc.gov/copyright/legislation/dmca.pdf; accessed September 15, 2001.

See also Volume 2: Intellectual Property.

Dingley Tariff (1897)

Legislation that created a record level of tariff duties.

By 1897 nearly all factions of the Republican Party wanted the prompt passage of a new protective tariff to restore confidence in the economy following the panic of 1893 (precipitated by a crisis in the railroad industry) and the subsequent depression. Nelson Dingley Jr., a Republican congressman from Maine, developed a tariff bill that removed raw wool from the free list but left hides and copper on the list. It also placed high duties on linens, woolens, and silks while leaving the main steel and iron tariff schedules mostly untouched. The bill's most significant change involved the doubling of the duty on sugar, an important revenue-producing item, as a way to end the treasury deficits created by the panic of 1893.

The Senate, however, added 872 mostly insignificant amendments and in the process altered the House's tariff rates. In conference committee, the more protectionist House resisted the Senate changes, and the final bill closely resembled Dingley's original proposal. Signed into law by President William McKinley on July 24, 1897, the Dingley Tariff raised average duties to a record level of 52 percent, mainly because of the new sugar duty. With the return of prosperity in the latter half of 1897, many high-tariff Republicans became convinced that the Dingley Tariff remained essential for maintaining the nation's economic health. Representing a final burst of nineteenth-century protectionism, the tariff remained in effect until the passage of the Payne-Aldrich Tariff Act in 1909.

—Steven E. Siry

References

Terrill, Tom E. *The Tariff, Politics, and American Foreign Policy: 1874–1901.* Westport, CT: Greenwood Press, 1973.

See also Volume 1: Sugar.

Disarmament

Reduction or limitation of weaponry, specifically nuclear arms, among world powers designed to reduce worldwide tensions.

The objectives of disarmament are to reduce the likelihood of war, to reduce military costs in peacetime, and to reduce the destructiveness of war should it occur. The theoretical basis for disarmament is the belief that arms races involve action/reaction cycles that escalate international tensions, and in times of crisis these tensions become destabilizing—they combine with accidents or misperceptions to cause wars. Many disarmament advocates regard World War I as the classic example of an arms race leading to an accidental war.

In the interwar period (1919 to 1939), forced disarmament of a defeated enemy and a voluntary disarmament through international agreement both occurred. The Versailles Treaty demilitarized the Rhineland, limited the size of Germany's army and navy, and prohibited Germany from operating tanks, combat aircraft, and submarines. The 1922 Washington Naval Conference limited the size of battleships, proclaimed a ten-year moratorium on expending capital to build new battleships, and set a 5:5:3 ratio for British, American, and Japanese battleships and aircraft carriers. The 1930 London Naval Conference awarded Japan a 7:10 ratio compared with the United States and Britain in cruisers and destroyers and awarded Japan parity with the United States in submarines. Germany and Japan first violated and then abrogated these treaties, and Britain and the United States lacked the will to enforce the treaties or to rearm. Thus, interwar agreements disarmed the democracies and emboldened the dictatorships, contributing to the outbreak of World War II.

During the cold war, U.S. negotiators sought to prevent or limit the Soviet counterforce threat to U.S. land-based intercontinental ballistic missiles (ICBMs). The Strategic Arms Limitations Talks (SALT) I and II, both treaties of the 1970s, failed to achieve this goal, instead only codifying the buildup in Soviet offensive forces. However, the superpowers agreed to disarm themselves of biological weapons and antiballistic missile forces in 1972 and of intermediate-range nuclear forces in 1988. Multilateral treaties prohibited placing nuclear weapons in Antarctica (1961), outer space (1967), or the seabed (1970). The 1963 Test Ban Treaty prohibited nuclear testing in the atmosphere, outer space, or the seabed, and the 1968 Non-Proliferation Treaty obligated states with nuclear weapons not to transfer the weapons or their technology to third parties.

On the whole, cold war disarmament remained hostage to the political relationship between the two superpowers. Once the Soviet Union collapsed, large-scale disarmament was not merely possible, but inevitable. The 1992 Conventional Forces in Europe (CFE) Treaty established a formula for the reduction of nonnuclear forces in Europe, and the Strategic Arms Reductions Treaties (START) negotiated during the 1990s called for the United States and Russia to both reduce their nuclear arsenals to about 2,000 strategic warheads each over the decade to come. Moreover, significant multilateral disarmament treaties were negotiated in the 1990s, including regional nuclear-free zones, bans on chemical weapons and land mines, and a Comprehensive Test Ban Treaty. Multilateral export control agreements seek to prevent proliferation of nuclear, biological, chemical, and ballistic missile technologies—and "dual-use items" such as nuclear power—to certain countries.

Unfortunately, despite these agreements, several "rogue states" including North Korea, Iran, Iraq, and Libya continue to seek nuclear, biological, and chemical (NBC) capabilities. NBC technology and expertise continue to flow from Russia and China to these countries and possibly to terrorist groups. The problems of how to verify violations of these agreements—and how to respond once violation has been proven—remain unresolved.

—*James D. Perry*

References

Freedman, Lawrence. *The Evolution of Nuclear Strategy.* New York: St. Martin's Press, 1989.

Glynn, Patrick. *Closing Pandora's Box.* New York: New Republic Books, 1992.

Gray, Colin S. *House of Cards.* Ithaca, NY: Cornell University Press, 1992.

Schelling, Thomas C., and Morton H. Halperin. *Strategy and Arms Control.* New York: Twentieth Century Fund, 1961.

See also Volume 1: Cold War; Strategic Defense Initiative (SDI).

Disaster Assistance Act of 1988

Amendment to the Stafford Act of 1974 that provided new guidelines for federal funding of natural or emergency disasters.

Under the Disaster Assistance Act of 1988, the federal government assumed liability for funding not less than 75 percent of the cost of a natural disaster or an emergency disaster in any given state under the direction of the Federal Emergency Management Agency. That amount could increase to 100 percent for the first ten days of the emergency, but Congress placed a limit of $5 million on that portion of the assistance package, to be exceeded only if the president declared that continued assistance was required or that there was a sustained threat to life, property, health, or safety or that no other timely assistance could be provided. The federal government could also assume responsibility for 100 percent of the cost of temporary housing as well as other associated expenses.

Although the act was designed to shift financial responsibility more toward the states and local communities, the net result has been a greater expenditure on the part of the federal government. Much of this increase has occurred because of the rise in the number of disasters that have occurred. Between 1985 and 1989 more than 119 disasters were declared, whereas between 1990 and 1994 more than 195 declared disasters occurred. In addition, the dollar value of each disaster has substantially increased over time because of increased population density and inflation.

—*Cynthia Clark Northrup*

References

Binns, Tristan Boyer. *FEMA: Federal Emergency Management Agency.* Chicago: Heinemann, 2002.

See also Volume 1: Federal Emergency Management Agency.

Disease

A medical disorder with recognizable symptoms that may or may not have a known source and that creates an economic burden on society, including the medical community.

During the colonial period, colonists experienced relatively few outbreaks of disease. Low population levels combined with distribution of cities and farms over a large geographical area prevented the spread of infections. Northern regions, where the temperature falls to freezing or below, had fewer outbreaks than the southern colonies, where the temperature reaches near-tropical levels during a substantial portion of the year. In the southern colonies, especially in South Carolina, the diseases that appeared most frequently were yellow fever and malaria—both carried by the mosquito. African slaves who carried the sickle-cell trait proved resistant to malaria, so southern planters invested in the costs of slaves as workers in the low, swampy regions throughout the South.

Another disease, smallpox, decimated the Native American population in particular. Entire villages in New England were often wiped out by the disease, leaving the land open for European settlement. In some instances, it was reported by colonial authorities and government agents that the blankets and other items given to the Indians were purposely infected with the smallpox virus.

As the population of the country multiplied and urban areas grew during the late eighteenth and early nineteenth centuries, disease became more frequent. Unsanitary conditions, for example, the lack of clean water and sewage systems, aided the spread of diseases such as cholera, an often fatal intestinal disease that results in severe diarrhea, vomiting, dehydration, and gastric pain. These outbreaks spread throughout the country either along rivers or along the coast since the primary mode of transportation was still by ship. Inadequate food preservation and unsanitary conditions also led to increased outbreaks of diseases such as diphtheria, whooping cough, fevers, and influenza. Mortality rates climbed to levels comparable to those in Europe for the first time since colonization had begun in the early 1600s.

During the late nineteenth century, urban areas experienced a high incidence of tuberculosis, especially in overcrowded tenements where immigrants congregated. Efforts to prevent the disease proved somewhat successful by the end of the 1880s, although it has not yet been eradicated in the twenty-first century.

After the Civil War, the U.S. Army initiated a series of experiments that led to significant breakthroughs in disease control. After the Spanish-American War, funded by the federal government, American surgeon Walter Reed focused on the problem of typhoid; his research yielded positive results and future outbreaks were prevented.

Next, Reed assembled a team of army doctors, including Major James Carroll, Major Jesse W. Lazear, and Major Aristides Agramonte of Havana (a Cuban national who was a member of the U.S. Army Medical Corps), to investigate the cause of yellow fever, which was a serious problem in late nineteenth-century Cuba, especially after the Spanish-American War. Basing their investigations on previous research by Dr. Carlos Juan Finley, they discovered that the mosquito carried the disease. Specifically, the mosquito had to bite an infected person during the first 3 days of the person's illness, and the disease had to mature in the mosquito for 12 days before it could be transmitted to another host. Reed announced the findings at the 1900 meeting of the American Public Health Association. The army successfully eradicated yellow fever from Cuba through the systematic destruction of mosquitoes on the island; it initiated a similar program in Panama during the construction of the Panama Canal. The French had experienced extremely high death rates from yellow fever when they began construction on the canal. As a result of the work of Walter Reed, the Americans experienced dramatically fewer fatalities after they assumed control of canal construction from the French in 1903. Reed's work emphasized the need for future research to discover the cause and the epidemiology (spread) of epidemic diseases.

From 1918 to 1920, the United States experienced an influenza epidemic. In 1918 and 1919 more than 400,000 Americans died of the disease—more than the number of U.S. soldiers killed during World War I. Infectious diseases such as whooping cough, measles, mumps, and polio spread throughout the nation between World War I and World War II. Outbreaks of these diseases affected children primarily, although polio hit old and young alike. With the beginning of World War II, the federal government funded medical research on a much larger scale. Sulfa drugs, penicillin, and antibiotics yielded promising results. The discovery of the polio vaccine by Jonas Salk and Albert Sabin, in which patients developed immunity to polio after receiving injections of small doses of the disease, lessened the number of people who were infected.

By the 1960s, the U.S. medical profession was focusing on noncontagious diseases such as heart disease, cancer, and strokes. Funding for research into these diseases expanded the medical field and created new jobs, but the costs for operations and treatments strained the existing health system and health care costs began to increase. Then, in the 1980s, the medical profession faced one of its greatest challenges with the outbreak of acquired immune deficiency syndrome (AIDS). At first the disease primarily affected gay men and intravenous drug users, and society placed a lower priority on funding research. However, as AIDS spread to the heterosexual population—and to children during birth via their infected mothers or through the use of tainted blood used for transfusions—society recognized the need for research into its cause and prevention. As of 2000, the Centers for Disease Control and Prevention estimated that between 850,000 and 950,000 Americans were infected with the virus. That same year, the United States spent about $4.87 billion on research,

treatment, prevention, and education for this disease alone. During the administration of President George W. Bush, funding for AIDS research increased after a reduction in funding during the administration of President Bill Clinton.

The medical profession faces another challenge, Alzheimer's disease, which is suffered by prominent individuals including President Ronald Reagan and actor Charlton Heston and so is in the forefront of public attention. As of 2003, medical research has yielded few results, and costs to businesses and caregivers have continued to skyrocket. Businesses contribute about $176 million annually for research into Alzheimer's while spending an additional $24.5 billion annually on health care treatment. In addition, the cost to caregivers—counting time lost from work, lost jobs, and sale of homes and other assets to pay the costs of medical care—has reached about $36.5 billion. As the baby boom generation ages and as medical research finds cures for other diseases, research into Alzheimer's—which has replaced heart disease and cancer as the number-one killer of elderly Americans—must expand to prevent the escalation of health costs for the elderly.

—*Cynthia Clark Northrup*

References

Bean, William Bennett. *Walter Reed: A Biography.* Charlottesville: University Press of Virginia, 1982.

Feldman, Douglas A., and Julia Wang Miller, eds. *The AIDS Crisis: A Documentary History.* Westport, CT: Greenwood Press, 1998.

Groh, Lynn. *Walter Reed, Pioneer in Medicine.* Champaign, IL: Garrard Publishing, 1971.

Koppel, Ross. *Alzheimer's Disease: The Costs to U.S. Businesses in 2002.* Wyncote, PA: Alzheimer's Association, 2002.

See also Volume 1: Acquired Immune Deficiency Syndrome (AIDS); Medicaid; Medicare.

Distribution Act (1836)

Act to distribute federal surpluses to select state banks passed by Congress on June 23, 1836, after the charter of the Second Bank of the United States expired.

The Distribution Act of 1836, spearheaded by Senator Henry Clay, provided for a system of distributing federal surpluses to state banks and restricting legal tender to gold and silver. This plan received support by those who wanted to quickly replace the functions performed by the Bank of the United States, whose charter had expired in 1836. Supporters of hard money (or specie, i.e., gold and silver) opposed the bill, fearing speculative banking and the contraction of the money supply.

The law stipulated that $5 million in surplus treasury funds be distributed to the state banks beginning January 1, 1837, in four quarterly installments as interest-free, unsecured loans. No one expected the repayment of the loans. The influx of federal monies to the states further stimulated an overheated economy in 1836 and early 1837. The panic of 1837 occurred because of overspeculation in western lands, poor banking procedures, and a decline in farm prices, all of which the distribution system (which called for the distribution of surplus funds to the states) further compounded. Americans abandoned the provisions of the act in 1842 when Congress passed the protectionist Tariff of 1842, which greatly slashed federal revenues.

—James T. Carroll

References
Sellers, Charles. *The Market Revolution: Jacksonian America, 1815–1846.* New York: Oxford University Press, 1991.
See also Volume 1: Bank of the United States (BUS), First; Bank of the United States (BUS), Second.

Divorce

The dissolution of a marriage and the separation of economic interaction between the spouses.

Throughout most of American history, it was not easy to obtain a divorce. Courts required evidence that one partner had breached the contract of marriage as a result of adultery, desertion, abuse (either physical or mental), mental incapacity, incarceration, nonsupport, or substance abuse. Each state determined the requirements for divorce. Divorce rates soared during the prosperous 1920s, and the number of divorces has escalated since 1945, when 35 percent of marriages ended in divorce. By 1979, 53 percent of marriages ended in divorce. Since then the divorce rate has remained constant at between 43 percent and 47 percent of marriages. Beginning in the late 1900s, states began granting "no-fault" divorces based on grounds of incompatibility.

Divorce financially affects the family as well as society. Mothers with young children and no adequate job skills find themselves in a downward economic spiral, especially if the father fails to pay court-ordered child support. (In 1998, more than 16 million noncustodial parents owed back child support to more than 32 million children.) These women turn to government-sponsored entitlement programs such as Aid to Dependent Children and Aid to Families with Dependent Children for assistance. Until recent changes in the laws following the passage of the Personal Responsibility Act of 1996, once in the welfare system women found it difficult to break the cycle of economic dependency on the government. The children of divorced parents also suffer. Many of them experience difficulty in school or simply drop out. During the 1990s the dropout rate declined, but it was still more than 381,000 students annually out of 3.4 million students. Most of these children are forced to accept jobs at minimum wage or slightly above. Consequently, their economic opportunities are limited. Fathers also suffer financially if they remarry and have to assist in supporting both their previous and current households. Many divorces result in one or both partners being forced to file for bankruptcy. In 1980 only 300,000 divorces resulted in bankruptcy, but by 1998 more than 1.4 million divorces ended in bankruptcy proceedings.

—Cynthia Clark Northrup

References
Arendell, Terry. *Mothers and Divorce: Legal, Economic, and Social Dilemmas.* Berkeley: University of California Press, 1986.
See also Volume 1: Aid to Dependent Children; Aid to Families with Dependent Children.

DOD

See U.S. Department of Defense.

Dollar Diplomacy

Term used to describe certain elements of U.S. foreign policy during the presidency of William Howard Taft (1909–1913).

President William Howard Taft, like his predecessor Theodore Roosevelt, sought to increase America's influence as a world power. Part of his foreign policy strategy involved extending American financial investments and institutions into less-developed regions. To accomplish these goals, the Taft administration concentrated on promoting and protecting American corporate interests in Central America and the Far East. Theoretically, by "substituting dollars for bullets," as Taft phrased it, both the United States and the underdeveloped nations would benefit. United States trade would increase while the smaller countries would enter a new era of political stability and improved social conditions. Taft chose Philander C. Knox as his secretary of state and charged him with implementing the policy of dollar diplomacy. Knox, a wealthy conservative corporate lawyer who had represented the Carnegie Steel Corporation, remained sympathetic to the needs and goals of big business.

Taft and Knox believed that the best way to control Central American countries involved taking over their customs houses where import duties are collected and arranging for the countries to repay European debts through loans from American businesses. The United States introduced financing schemes in Honduras, Guatemala, and Haiti. Nicaragua provided the clearest example of the practical value of dollar diplomacy. Taft and Knox believed the small nation had great strategic importance because of its proximity to the Panama Canal. The United States helped topple longtime Nicaraguan dictator Jose Santos Zelaya, who had refused to cooperate with the administration's plans to establish a neutral Honduras, in 1907. The United States subsequently supported Adolfo Diaz as the head of the Nicaraguan government, made loans to the new regime, and seized control of the country's customs houses. The situation left Nicaragua a virtual U.S. protectorate and generated resentment among the Nicaraguan people. The American policy failed to create stability in the country, and sporadic violence led Taft to send in troops that would remain in Nicaragua for years.

Under pressure from American bankers, Taft and Knox also sought to implement dollar diplomacy in China. There they hoped to dilute Japanese and Russian influence in

Manchuria, strengthening both the Open Door Policy (which called for the territorial integration of China and the establishment of free trade in China) and the weak Chinese government. Knox worked to include the United States in a consortium of western powers formed to construct railroads in Manchuria. When English, French, and German bankers reluctantly agreed with the plan, Knox carried it a step further by trying to exclude the Japanese completely from any role in the enterprise. The Japanese responded by forming a loose alliance with Russia, and the railroad project quickly collapsed in 1910.

Taft abandoned dollar diplomacy during the final year of his administration, and in 1913 his successor, Woodrow Wilson, publicly repudiated the policy. Taft's economic interventionism had been an outright failure in China and created ill will and social turmoil in Central America that would last for decades. Today the term *dollar diplomacy* has negative connotations and is used to refer to the needless manipulation of foreign affairs for economic gain.

—*Ben Wynne*

References

Coletta, Paola E. *The Presidency of William Howard Taft.* Lawrence: University Press of Kansas, 1973.

Schoultz, Lars. *Beneath the United States: A History of U.S. Policy toward Latin America.* Cambridge, MA: Harvard University Press, 1998.

See also Volumes 1, 2: Foreign Policy.

Dominican Republic

Nation located on the eastern half of the island of Hispaniola in the Caribbean Sea.

The Dominican Republic declared its independence in 1844 after more than two centuries as a Spanish colony and a brief stint as part of Haiti. In its early years of independence in the latter nineteenth century, the Dominican Republic experienced a great deal of chaos and government instability. The instability created poor economic conditions, and the nation was unable to make debt payments to European lenders. With the beginning of construction on the Panama Canal in 1904, the United States had a strategic interest in the Caribbean, and American leaders believed that the fighting and poor economic conditions in the Dominican Republic could lead to European military action there. As a result, in 1905, the United States convinced the Dominican Republic to sign an agreement that gave the United States responsibility for all Dominican Republic debt and the right to collect customs duties in order to repay that debt. Many citizens of the Dominican Republic protested, and the chaos worsened. To protect American interests, U.S. Marines occupied the island, and the U.S. maintained military control from 1916 until 1924. The United States gained several economic benefits from this intervention. Previously the republic had exported most of its tobacco, cocoa, and sugar to Europe, but after U.S. intervention it exported these goods to the United States. Additionally, American sugar companies took control of large portions of the Dominican Republic's economy. After

American withdrawal, the Dominican Republic continued to have close economic ties with the United States, and throughout much of the twentieth century, sugar exports to the United States were a mainstay of the Dominican Republic's economy.

—*John K. Franklin*

References

Haggerty, Richard A., ed. *Dominican Republic and Haiti: Country Studies.* 2d ed. Washington DC: U.S. Government Printing Office, 1991.

See also Volume 1: Panama and the Panama Canal; Wilson, Woodrow.

Dow Jones Industrial Average

Economic indicator for stocks.

Charles Dow and Edward Davis Jones created the Dow Jones Industrial Average in 1884 to measure 11 blue-chip stocks, most of which involved railroad companies. On May 26, 1896, they published the first Dow-Jones average, which consisted of 12 stocks. (The railroad stocks were made part of a separate transportation index in 1970.) The Dow originally equaled an average of the stock price for each company divided by the number of companies. However, with the passage of time, stock splits and other changes made comparisons of averages both impractical and unreliable. (When a company splits its stock, it decreases the cost of a share by half, making share purchase more attractive to smaller investors. However, the number of stocks is doubled in this illusionary tactic, and market capitalization remains the same.) On December 31, 1927, the editors of the *Wall Street Journal* modified the Dow-Jones index with a divisor that made allowances for stock splits and to ensure comparative continuity among stock prices. On October 1, 1928, the Dow expanded to include 30 stocks which, except for the transportation and utilities sectors, represented the U.S. economy.

The utilities average appeared in 1929. The railroad average created in 1896 was renamed the transportation average in 1970. The Dow Jones Industrial Average with the railroad and utilities averages provides a broad overview of the U.S. economy and remains the most popular index of market growth and contraction.

—*James T. Carroll*

References

Prestbo, John, ed. *Markets Measure: An Illustrated History of America Told through the Dow Jones Industrial Average.* New York: Dow Jones, 1999.

See also Volume 2: Stock Market.

Downes v. Bidwell (1901)

One of several Supreme Court "Insular Cases" that determined the legal relationship between the United States and several of its territories.

Congress passed the Foraker Act in November 1900, which provided a temporary civil government in Puerto Rico and provided it with revenue without declaring it a territory of the United States. However, the act also imposed a 15 percent tariff on items from foreign countries, leaving unclear whether Puerto Rico was considered a foreign country. The case of *Downes v. Bidwell* questioned if Puerto Rico and other territories were subject to Article I, Section 8 of the United States Constitution, which requires that "all duties, imposts, and excises shall be uniform throughout the United States."

Downes v. Bidwell was heard at the same time as *DeLima v. Bidwell.* In *DeLima* in a 5-to-4 decision, the Court decided that Puerto Rico was not a foreign country and therefore not subject to foreign duties. *Downes* extended the question to if new territories had the same rights as the states. On May 27, 1901, in *Downes,* the Supreme Court ruled 5–4 that Puerto Rico was not part of the United States but was subject to its jurisdiction. Therefore, the revenue tariff clause did not apply, and duties could be collected on items coming from Puerto Rico that could not be collected on items shipped between states.

This case is one of the Insular Cases, which are a collection of Supreme Court cases heard between 1900 and 1904 that established how the United States Constitution would apply to island territories that were acquired during the Spanish-American War.

It seemed that the Insular Cases were overturned by *Reid v. Covert* in 1957, when their continuing vitality was questioned for U.S. citizens and dependents living abroad. The assumption that anyone in a foreign country fell outside the jurisdiction of the United States government was endorsed by *Examining Board of Architects, Engineers and Surveyors v. Flores de Otero* in 1976, which stated that the Insular Cases were overturned. However, with *United States v. Verduigo-Urquidez* in 1990, which also considered the issue of how far the Constitution extended, the Supreme Court declared that the Insular Cases still governed how the U.S. Constitution applied to island territories.

—*Deana Covel*

References
MacMeekin, Dan. *Island Law: The Insular Cases.* November 26, 2002. Available: http://www.macmeekin.com/Library/Insular%20Cases.htm#Verdugo; accessed December 28, 2002.
See also Volume 1: Insular Cases; Volume 2: Judiciary.

Dust Bowl
An environmental and economic disaster that occurred because of drought and poor farming practices in the Southwest.

Little rain fell over the United States in the summer of 1930, and fulvous dirt began to blow. The center of drought shifted to the Great Plains by early 1931, combining with both dust storms and intense heat to batter a bowl-shaped area of Kansas, Colorado, New Mexico, Oklahoma, and Texas. Various areas were affected from year to year during the "dirty thirties," as the weather pattern occasionally moved as far north as Nebraska and the Dakotas. Dust storms in 1935 carried away wheat—half of the crop in Kansas, one-fourth in Oklahoma, and the entire Nebraska planting. By 1938, the peak year for wind erosion, 10 million acres had lost at least the upper five inches of topsoil and another 13.5 million acres had lost at least two and one-half inches. One sample of dirt deposited in Iowa contained 10 times as much organic matter and nitrogen—the basics of plant fertility—as did the sand dunes left behind in Dallas County, Texas. Oklahoma law allowed farmers to take out a chattel mortgage (third-party financing) on crops not yet planted, and many did so. Because of the widespread crop failures, many farmers were now hopelessly in debt, and many declared bankruptcy and placed all their possessions on the auction block. Others simply loaded what they could into a truck and drove away during the 1930s—the "Okies" famously portrayed in John Steinbeck's *The Grapes of Wrath.* Under the New Deal of President Franklin D. Roosevelt, the dust bowl states received more federal dollars than any other region, most coming from the Agricultural Adjustment Act of 1933. Farmers who stayed on were encouraged by the government to practice scientific farming methods including the planting of shelterbelts of trees to protect crops from the wind and the contouring of furrows, which allowed rain and snow to stay in the soil rather than disappearing as runoff.

—*Caryn E. Neumann*

References
Worster, Donald. *Dust Bowl: The Southern Plains in the 1930s.* Oxford: Oxford University Press, 1979.
See also Volume 1: Great Depression.

DPC
See Defense Plant Corporation.

E

Earnings

The real or inflation-adjusted pretax wages, salaries, and benefits that workers receive.

A complete picture of the historical evolution of earnings in the United States, and of the effects of economic policies on this evolution, must distinguish among the earnings' level, rate of change, and distribution. Expressed in constant 1988 dollars, for example, the mean wage was $12,225 in 1927 and $31,422 in 1998, consistent with an average annual growth rate of 1.6 percent. However, earnings have sometimes increased more or less quickly than this. Between 1950 and 1970, a period some have called the golden age of American capitalism, mean wages increased more than 2 percent per annum, a rate that, if sustained, would have allowed earnings to double from one generation to the next. Between 1970 and 1995, on the other hand, the average annual growth rate was less than 0.5 percent.

Conventional economic wisdom holds that much, perhaps most, of the growth in mean earnings is the result of technological change. In this context, it comes as no surprise that the period of slow earnings growth between 1970 and 1995 coincides with a productivity slowdown. Unfortunately, it is difficult to influence the rate of technological change, even with targeted economic policies.

The effect of economic policies on the distribution of earnings is perhaps more visible, and there are three distinct historical episodes to be explained. From the Civil War to the Great Depression, earnings distribution tended to become more unequal, but this inequality was reversed in the subsequent great compression of the economy, the effects of which continued to resonate until the 1970s, after which the distribution again became more lopsided—a trend that has lasted to and intensified in the present. Those in the top 10 percent of earnings level received 30.3 percent of all wage income in 1932, 25.2 percent in 1950, 25.7 percent in 1970, 31.8 percent in 1990, and more than 35 percent in 2000.

A list of the immediate institutional causes of the great compression would include both the National Industrial Recovery Act of 1933 and the National War Labor Board (NWLB), which was established in 1942 and dissolved in 1945. What is more difficult to explain is the persistence of wartime compression decades after the end of the war. Some recent research suggests that a robust set of compensation norms (the average expected compensation) emerged in the aftermath of the Great Depression and World War II and that these norms persisted even if their codification—in the "little steel formula" (which allowed wage increases to 15 percent of January 1941 levels during a period of rapid inflation at the beginning of World War II) and other practices of the NLWB—proved to be short-lived.

Both the slowdown in the growth of earnings since the 1970s, which was mirrored in the experiences of other advanced capitalist economies, and the increasing unevenness of the earnings distribution, which was not mirrored in other economies, have also received considerable attention from social scientists. The second of these seems to contradict the hypothesis of Simon Kuznets (1955), which claims that after some threshold level of economic development has been attained, the distribution of earnings tends to become more equal.

—*Peter Hans Matthews*

References

Denison, Edward F. *Trends in American Economic Growth, 1915–1982.* Washington, DC: Brookings Institution, 1982.

Goldin, Claudia, and Robert A. Margo. "The Great Compression: The Wage Structure in the United States at Mid-Century." *Quarterly Journal of Economics,* vol. 107 (February 1992): 1–34.

Kuznets, Simon. "Economic Growth and Income Inequality." *American Economic Review,* vol. 45, no. 1 (March 1955): 1–28.

Piketty, Thomas, and Emmanuel Saez. "Income Inequality in the United States, 1913–1998." National Bureau of Economic Research Working Paper no. 8467, September 2001.

See also Volume 1: Great Depression; National Labor Relations Board.

Economic Cooperation Administration (ECA)

U.S. agency created by the Economic Recovery Act of April 1948 to administer postwar American aid to Western Europe; widely known as the agency that administers the Marshall Plan.

U.S. Secretary of State General George G. Marshall announced the Marshall Plan in a famous speech at Harvard University June 5, 1947. The plan sought to stabilize Europe politically and to help Western European economies recover by integrating them in a U.S-dominated international economic order. The provision of financial aid to Europe is framed within this broader context and defines U.S. foreign economic relations after World War II. Before the creation of ECA, in July 1947, 16 Western European nations created the Committee of European Economic Cooperation (CEEC), later renamed Organization for European Economic Cooperation (OEEC), a body charged with assembling a coordinated proposal for the use of funds in Europe. Throughout the autumn and winter of 1947, the U.S. administration and Congress discussed the best way to help Western Europe and decided to grant both interim and long-term aid. Congress approved the European Recovery Program (ERP) on April 3, 1948, and called for the plan to be administered by the ECA, the government oversight agency, and the OEEC, which would actually distribute funds in Europe. Over the next four years, the ECA administered $12 billion in aid. Basically, the ECA granted the OEEC two kinds of aid—on one hand a great number of direct grants (food, fertilizer, machinery, shipping, raw materials, and fuel) and on the other the equivalent of more than $4.3 billion in counterpart funds—that is, the local currency receipt of sales of ERP supplies on national markets. These currency receipts were placed in a special fund used to invest in the industrial sector and aid the recovery of European infrastructure under agreements between European governments and the ECA.

The ECA administrators encompassed both liberal academics and politicians working according to Keynesian ideas and forward-looking businessmen like ECA's first administrator, Paul Hoffmann. He hoped to modernize the Western European economies and help them to recover, both to support social stability and to shape a continent-sized market. In turn, setting up intra-European trade would have reduced Europe's need for American aid and increased European productivity. However, European nations did not see the OEEC as a supranational body that would distribute aid across the continent on a rational basis and improve national economies by building intra-European trade. Instead, each European nation tended to help its own economy to recover by using OEEC funds within its own nation.

In 1951, Congress replaced the ECA with the Mutual Security Agency (MSA), which had an aid policy aimed at increasing military supplies and coordinating economic and military plans. The MSA was abolished in 1953 when its functions were transferred to the Foreign Operations Administration.

—*Simone Selva*

References
Arkes, Adley. *Bureaucracy, the Marshall Plan, and the National Interest.* Princeton, NJ: Princeton University Press, 1973.
Killick, John. *The United States and European Reconstruction, 1945–1960.* Edinburgh, UK: Keele University Press, 1997.

Economic Indicators

Statistical measures of economic activity used to gauge the health of the economy.

In the United States, the federal government and private agencies generate more than 250 economic indicators. The most notable include the consumer price index (CPI), producer price index (PPI), unemployment rate, corporate profits, industrial production index, money supply, interest rates, personal income and saving, inventory:sales ratios, consumer confidence index, productivity, import and export indexes, and gross domestic product (GDP). The Bureau of Labor Statistics (BLS), Bureau of Economic Analysis (BEA), Bureau of the Census, Internal Revenue Service (IRS), National Bureau for Economic Research (NBER), and the Conference Board publish economic indicators monthly, quarterly, and yearly.

Economic indicators are used to identify, analyze, and evaluate current and past economic performances with the ultimate goal of predicting and controlling business cycles. However, economic indicators are more than statistics. They lie at the heart of all public policy. People's economic and social well-being depend on the accuracy of these indicators and on the way policymakers use them. Expectations concerning changes in these indicators are also of critical importance for corporations and investors.

For the United States, the NBER has selected 30 leading economic indicators that reach peaks or troughs before the peak or trough in economic activity. These leading indicators are used by the NBER to predict economic performance. The NBER's prediction is based on a diffusion index (DI). When the DI is higher than 50, the economy is said to be in an expansion; when the DI is lower than 50, the economy is said to be in a decline. The larger the DI number, the stronger the basis for predicting expansions.

Economic indicators have improved economic analysis a great deal with regard to business performance. However, these indicators are more useful when their users are aware of their limitations. In fact, economic indicators are highly aggregated and averaged numbers. Even though they do tell us about past economic conditions, we must not assume that these conditions will remain the same in the future. Therefore prediction involves more than the mere reliance on economic indicators; it involves a lot of common-sense judgments based on expectations of future economic conditions.

—*Fadhel Kaboub*

References
Frumkin, Norman. *Guide to Economic Indicators*. Armonk,
    NY: M. E. Sharpe, 1994.
See also Volume 1: Consumer Price Index.

References
McGuire, Robert A. *To Form a More Perfect Union: A New
    Economic Interpretation of the Constitution of the United
    States*. New York: Oxford University Press, 2001.
See also Volume 1: Constitution.

Economic Interpretation of the Constitution (1913)

A 1913 study by Charles Beard that initiated a firestorm of debate over one of America's most cherished documents.

Charles Beard, part of a group of professional historians known as the Progressives who were greatly influenced by the Populist movement, ascribed to the theory of economic determinism. In his work *An Economic Interpretation of the Constitution,* Beard challenged the idea that the founding fathers, placing the nation's common good over their own individual interests, designed the Constitution to create a democratic and equal society. Instead, Beard argued, four groups—the money, public securities, manufacturers, and trade and shipping interests—called for and supported the Constitution's creation because they thought it in their best interest, and those who created the Constitution planned to gain economically from it. Even though it could be accepted that the founders had an economic motivation, Beard argued that the process of creating the Constitution thwarted the democratic process by disenfranchising a large group of Americans. He noted that a popular vote never occurred to see if American society wanted a new government. Consequently, a small group of private interests, not the common good, guided this political change. When the founding fathers assembled at the Constitutional Convention in 1787 in Philadelphia, the majority of Americans enjoyed no form of representation and thus their ideas and hopes remained silent. Beard also argued that the framers of the Constitution all shared the belief that they must protect private property at all costs; hence, the wealth of a minority must remain protected against the basic needs of a majority. Finally, Beard argued that most American voters (at this time adult white males) refused to vote for their convention delegates and refused to vote on the issue of ratification or could not vote because they did not meet property qualifications. Beard believed that approximately one-sixth of America's voters ratified the Constitution and that the document offered neither a democratic nor representative expression of the desires of American society as a whole.

Beard's work created a maelstrom of controversy and was publicly both praised and condemned. President William Howard Taft, especially, hated it. Since the publication of Beard's book, scholars have continually worked both to expand and refute his argument. But what Beard wrote made many people aware of the private motivations that lie behind public decisions.

—*Ty M. Reese*

Economic Liberalism

Doctrine of nonintervention by state in economy.

Economic liberalism developed as a reaction against an older system called mercantilism, in which government controlled commerce, industry, and trade. Under economic liberalism, industry, agriculture, and trade operate free from governmental supervision and regulation (free trade). The doctrine seeks maximum freedom for individual entrepreneurs; removal of tariffs, monopolies, and trade restrictions; and opposition to factory legislation (which benefits labor through concessions on wages or working conditions) and to trade unions. The doctrine originated with the work of Adam Smith in the late eighteenth century and the French economic philosophers of the Enlightenment, commonly known as the Physiocrats. Smith's *Inquiry into the Nature and Causes of the Wealth of Nations* (1776) put forth the idea of an invisible hand that operated in the economy, permitting self-interest (if enlightened) to work for man's good—in short, laissez-faire economics. (Smith was not the first person to use this term: it had been introduced before the end of the seventeenth century by Pierre Boisguillebert, a wealthy French landowner and economist, who spoke of laissez-faire and laissez-passez [unrestricted travel].)

A group of Englishmen including the utilitarian Jeremy Bentham developed the classic doctrine of free trade. Economist David Ricardo, author of *Principles of Moral Economy* (1817), provided the basic labor theory of value, which ties the value of a product to the cost of labor. Ricardo apparently believed much less than Smith in a natural order of harmony in economic affairs. But his passionate support for free trade and his hostility to landlords helped give classical political economy an even firmer place in liberal ideology.

The liberal thinker John Stuart Mill also wrote on the subject of economics in his *Principles of Political Economy* (1848). Mill recognized the significant role played by the entrepreneur—what he called the "undertaker" in economic development. Profit rewarded hard work and skill.

—*Leigh Whaley*

References
Brittan, Samuel. *A Restatement of Economic Liberalism*.
    Atlantic Highlands, NJ: Humanities Press International,
    1988.
McNamara, Peter. *Political Economy and Statesmanship:
    Smith, Hamilton, and the Foundation of the Commercial
    Republic*. DeKalb: Northern Illinois University Press,
    1998.

Economic Opportunity Act of 1964

Major legislation designed to achieve the promises of the Great Society of President Lyndon B. Johnson.

When Lyndon B. Johnson assumed the presidency after the assassination of President John F. Kennedy, he announced his desire to create a Great Society, in which all citizens could share in the wealth of the United States. Working with lawmakers to achieve this goal, Johnson persuaded Congress to pass the Economic Opportunity Act of 1964. The act established the Economic Opportunity Office and created several federally funded programs designed to "eliminate the paradox of poverty in the midst of plenty in this Nation by opening to everyone the opportunity for education and training, the opportunity to work, and the opportunity to live in decency and dignity." Agencies established included the Job Corps, the Neighborhood Youth Corps, Head Start, Adult Basic Education, Family Planning, Community Health Centers, Congregate Meal Preparation, Economic Development, Foster Grandparents, Legal Services, Neighborhood Centers, Summer Youth Programs, and Senior Centers. Between 1964 and 1968, more than 1,600 Community Action Centers were built around the country to encourage maximum participation from the community to help realize the Great Society. By the late 1960s, when minority groups realized that the promises of the federal government had not been realized, Congress passed several amendments to the Economic Opportunity Act. In 1981 the Economic Opportunity Office was abolished, although many of its programs still exist after being transferred to other agencies.

—*Cynthia Clark Northrup*

References
Davidson, Roger H., and Sar A. Levitan. *Antipoverty Housekeeping: The Administration of the Economic Opportunity Act.* Ann Arbor, MI: Institute of Labor and Industrial Relations, 1968.
Economic Opportunity Act of 1964. U.S. Statutes at Large 78 (1965).
See also Volume 1: Great Society.

Economic Stabilization Act of 1970

Law that gave the president power to impose wage and price controls to stem inflation caused by the Vietnam conflict and by escalating transfer payments (funds distributed to an individual or organization without an equivalent exchange of goods or services).

Signed on August 15, 1970, during the administration of Richard Nixon, the Economic Stabilization Act gave the president power to impose wage and price controls to stem inflation caused by federal efforts to finance its operations. It extended a law that had provided the executive with similar authority during the Korean War; the earlier law, in turn, had precedents in controls imposed during World Wars I and II.

Richard Nixon, a Republican and economic conservative, declared when he signed the Democrat-inspired bill that he would not exercise the authority granted. In his memoirs, he would disavow wage and price controls on the grounds that

"tampering with the orthodox economic mechanisms" remained unwise. Nevertheless, on August 15, 1971, he announced a new economic policy that included a 90-day freeze on all wages and prices except those for raw agricultural products and finished imports. He initiated the action at the urging of Secretary of the Treasury John Connolly and Arthur Burns, who headed the Council of Economic Advisers; it enjoyed substantial support among consumers who wanted price relief and business leaders who wished to curb wages. Moreover, Nixon was operating under pressure to show improvement in the economy before his bid for reelection in 1972.

The Cost of Living Council, the Office of Emergency Preparedness, and the Internal Revenue Service administered the controls, followed later by a Price Commission and Pay Board. After the 90-day period, the initial sweeping controls shifted to somewhat more limited sector controls. In January 1973, the first attempt to remove controls altogether saw a sharp increase in prices—particularly food, which shot up 4.5 percent in two months. This increase resulted in a second 60-day freeze. Controls were gradually phased out by April 1974.

—*Laura Seeley Pangallozzi*

References
Rockoff, Hugh. *Drastic Measures: A History of Wage and Price Controls in the United States.* New York: Cambridge University Press, 1984.
See also Volume 1: Wage and Price Freeze.

Economy Act (1933)

A federal statute signed into law by President Franklin D. Roosevelt on March 20, 1933, to help reduce the federal budget and promote economic recovery during the Great Depression.

By the time Franklin D. Roosevelt assumed the presidency in March 1933, the United States had been suffering through the Great Depression for nearly three years, and many of the nation's key institutions were on the verge of financial collapse. Believing that the expanding federal budget during the administration of President Herbert Hoover was hampering economic recovery, President Roosevelt sent an emergency measure to Congress on March 10, 1933, requesting the authority to cut $500 million from the federal budget. Drafted largely by budget director Lewis Douglas and Grenville Clark, a private lawyer and presidential adviser, the Economy Act called for the elimination and reorganization of several federal agencies, a 15 percent pay cut for the vice-president and members of Congress, additional salary cuts for other military and civilian federal employees, and a nearly 50 percent cut in veterans' benefits.

However, the bill was extremely controversial. Veterans' benefits represented almost one-quarter of the nation's $3.6 billion budget, and many people, including the House Democratic caucus, refused to support the bill on the grounds that large cuts in these benefits were unduly cruel to America's World War I veterans. Indeed, many lawmakers remembered the political backlash that occurred when U.S. troops forcibly expelled the Bonus Army (a group of veterans who demanded concessions from Congress at the beginning of the depression) from Washington, D.C., in July 1932, and they wanted to avoid antagonizing this politically powerful constituency.

Yet, despite this controversy and the fact that 92 House Democrats voted against the bill, the Economy Act passed through Congress and became law. The Economy Act successfully cut about $243 million from the federal budget, far less than the $500 million the president had intended, but many of these reductions in federal spending were offset by the large increases in federal relief spending during Roosevelt's first term. In 1934, Congress rescinded some of these cuts when it passed the Independent Officers Appropriation Act, which increased the salaries of government employees and raised veterans' benefits. Although President Roosevelt vetoed this bill, claiming that it would unnecessarily expand the federal budget, the election-year demands of veterans and government employees were too powerful, and Congress overrode the President's veto.

—David W. Waltrop

References

Leuchtenburg, William Edward. *Franklin D. Roosevelt and the New Deal, 1932–1940.* New York: Harper and Row, 1963.

See also Volume 1: Great Depression.

Ecosocialism

Social movement and body of thought developed in the 1970s that views capitalism as inherently unsustainable and promotes a socialist society based on principles of ecological sustainability.

Ecosocialists view capitalism much as did Karl Marx—competition requires that firms expand or go bust, where "expand" means to earn profits and reinvest them in production on an ever-larger scale. Maximizing profits by whatever means results in tremendous social costs in the form of environmental degradation, pollution, and unsustainable use of exhaustible and renewable resources. Ecosocialists also emphasize capitalism's negative impact on the social as well as natural environment. Capitalist social relations are alienating, with unemployment and poverty the usual state of affairs. According to ecosocialists, these aspects of capitalism remain unreformable, and democratic socialism provides the only alternative.

Ecosocialists recognize that Soviet-style socialist economies, like capitalist economies, also had a bad record on the environment, as well as other problems. Large-scale industrialization remains problematic worldwide, whether private companies or the government owns the means of production. Ecosocialists often look to some writers and activists in the anarchist tradition, such as Peter Kropotkin, an early proponent of small-scale sustainable production and alternative relations of production, and they anticipated later authors

such as E. F. Schumacher (author of *Small is Beautiful,* 1973) and Murray Bookchin (author of *The Ecology of Freedom,* 1982). But ecosocialists tend to see a much greater role for the state than do ecological anarchists.

Ecosocialism has been criticized for assigning privilege to class relations, overemphasizing the environmental crisis, and overlooking the ways in which a postcapitalist society might still fail to address racial domination and patriarchy—which could also prevent a full transition to sustainability. These shortcomings have led to the development of ecosocialist feminism, and ties have developed to the environmental justice movement, which focuses on environmental racism.

—Mathew Forstater

References

Benton, Ted, ed. *The Greening of Marxism.* New York: Guilford Press, 1996.

O'Connor, Martin, ed. *Is Capitalism Sustainable? Political Economy and the Politics of Ecology.* New York: Guilford Press, 1994.

See also Volume 1: Capitalism.

Edison, Thomas Alva (1847–1931)

Self-educated inventor who became famous for applying the principles of chemistry and electricity to America's industrial development in the late nineteenth and early twentieth centuries.

Born in Milan, Ohio, on February 11, 1847, Thomas Edison was the youngest of seven children. His father owned a prosperous shingle manufacturing business, and his mother was a former schoolteacher. In 1854 the family moved to Fort Huron, Michigan. Educated by his mother because his public school teachers considered him "too slow," Edison developed an early interest in chemistry. At age 15 he set up his own basement laboratory where he dabbled regularly in scientific experiments.

During the Civil War, Edison worked as a telegraph operator in various parts of the Midwest. At the same time, his inventive genius took shape. He invented electrical machines such as a vote recorder, pneumatic stencil pen, and stock printer, while also perfecting the stock ticker and typewriter. His practical inventiveness enabled him to improve the functioning of the automatic telegraph as well. In 1869, he became a partner in a New York City electrical engineering company and the following year established his own business.

Between 1870 and 1890, Edison invented numerous and widespread products. During his lifetime he applied for 1,093 patents. Although he discovered the application of alternating current (AC), he did not see its advantage over direct current (DC). His abandoning the "Edison effect" (the discovery that an independent wire placed between two filament legs would control the flow of current) would cost him dearly later on. Yet he continued working, devising a carbon transmitter to improve telephone communications and inventing the phonograph, and, most importantly, the incandescent lamp. In 1887, he built a large research plant in West Orange, New Jersey, where he and his team of experts—including mechanical engineers, clockmakers, and glassblowers—continued overseeing a host of inventions and promoting sales of his products.

Edison achieved fame in the field of applied electricity, and the Edison General Electric Company amassed a huge fortune for its namesake. Although first and foremost a practical inventor, Edison also became a shrewd businessman who jealously guarded his fortunes. In the late 1880s and early 1890s, when Westinghouse Electric promoted the use of AC as being more efficient and cheaper—thus becoming Edison's chief rival in the industry—Edison responded harshly. Edison, who had built the first central electric station in New York City in 1881 using DC, feared that his transmission system stood to lose millions of dollars if AC took over. At West Orange, Edison set up an experimental laboratory and invited visitors from the metropolitan area to witness the electrocution by AC of cats, dogs, and even an elephant. The "electrical shootout," which was set up to illustrate which form of current was safer, became so intense that chief scientists from both companies hooked themselves up to their type of electrical transmission to see who would last the longest. The challenge using human guinea pigs ended, but Edison's scare tactics failed. AC proved more economically efficient, and New York City eventually converted to its use. In 1892, in need of finances, Edison sold the rights to many of his inventions to the General Electric Company.

Though smarting from his defeat by Westinghouse, Edison continued working on new patents as the century turned. He made a motion picture machine and a fluoroscope still used by the medical profession today; manufactured Portland cement to build highways and houses; produced the alkaline nickel/iron storage battery, a dictating machine, a mimeograph machine, and disk records; and devised his own processes for manufacturing phenol and benzol. During World War I, Edison worked on improving the operation of submarines and methods of torpedo detection. A few years before his death he collaborated with Henry Ford and Harvey S. Firestone to produce rubber from domestic plants.

Edison's contributions significantly influenced American economic life. His contribution of applied science to industry helped to streamline labor (many of his inventions, including electricity to move the assembly line, reduced manufacturing time) and to improve the areas of communications, transportation, and housing. The invention of the incandescent lamp helped eliminate the dangers associated with petroleum or gas lighting. In 1923 his inventions were worth $16 million. On August 1, 1931, still working in his lab, he collapsed from a stroke. He died on October 18, 1931, and his family buried him in Orange, New Jersey. When asked to describe genius, he once remarked that it consisted of "one percent inspiration and ninety-nine percent perspiration."

—*Charles F. Howlett*

References

Clark, Ronald W. *Edison: The Man Who Made the Future.* New York: G. P. Putnam, 1977.

Conot, Robert E. *A Streak of Luck: The Life and Legend of Thomas Alva Edison.* New York: Seaview Books, 1979.

Josephson, Matthew. *Edison: A Biography.* New York: McGraw-Hill, 1959.

Starr, Chauncey, and Philip C. Ritterbush. *Science, Technology, and the Human Prospect: Proceedings of the Edison Centennial Symposium.* New York: Pergamon Press, 1980.

Wachhorst, Wyn. *Thomas Alva Edison: An American Myth.* Cambridge, MA: MIT Press, 1980.

See also Volume 1: Electricity.

Education

A learning process that develops a skill or knowledge and is one of the primary mechanisms for socialization and the driver of technological innovation and economic expansion.

The philosophical basis, policy relevance, and implementation of education in the United States have evolved tremendously over the last 200 years. Originally based on the Bible, education was seen as the safeguard of liberty by Thomas Jefferson, and it has been seminal in creating America's national identity as well as its technological and economic prowess.

Education has been and continues to be one of the most contentious areas of politics. Thomas Jefferson, Benjamin Franklin, educator Horace Mann, and philosopher and educator John Dewey are just a few who have debated the need for public school education. These ideological battles have continued in part because the states, not the federal government, have historically controlled education. Because schools in colonial times were decentralized and rural, the founding fathers failed to expressly delegate federal authority over education in the Constitution. Local and state governments have provided the majority of funds for education and have thus wielded an immense amount of power in terms of educational practices and curriculum.

Small schools in rural areas, where one teacher taught students of all ages in the same classroom, characterized education in the eighteenth and nineteenth centuries. The rise of free publicly funded elementary schools in the Common School Era (1820s and 1830s) and the spread of compulsory education to high school during the Progressive Era in the late 1800s both led to greater standardization in education. By 1918, all states had compulsory education laws for all children. Unfortunately, the Supreme Court's infamous ruling in *Plessy v. Ferguson* in 1896 meant that schools operated under a policy of racial segregation; the schools remained separate but certainly were not equal. The Supreme Court attempted to remedy this inequality through its landmark 1954 decision in *Brown v. Topeka Board of Education,* an example of the federal government superseding states' sovereignty to right a social injustice. The Elementary and Secondary Education Act of 1965 continued this shift toward a greater emphasis on equity and equal educational opportunity.

In 1974, in *Swann v. Charlotte-Mecklenberg Board of Education,* the U.S. Supreme Court ordered busing—the transporting of students from ill-equipped, primarily African American schools in poor urban black neighborhoods to better-equipped schools in middle-class, primarily white neighborhoods, and vice versa. Busing would have ended segregation in schools while leaving housing patterns segregated. By the 1970s, whites had begun to leave the major cities for the suburbs—a phenomenon called "white flight"—in an attempt to circumvent the Court-ordered busing. During the last 25 years of the twentieth century, busing continued among schools in primarily African American school districts, and few white suburbs were integrated in the process. Currently, many urban school districts are arguing that their schools have become as integrated as they can be without the inclusion of students from the suburbs. Equal educational opportunity has still not been fully achieved.

Finally, the *Sputnik* launch in 1957 led to a greater emphasis on mathematics, science, and engineering in U.S. schools as the United States attempted to close the perceived missile gap (difference in rocket technology between the United States and the Soviet Union). President John F. Kennedy vowed in 1992 that the United States would land a man on the moon by the end of the 1960s—a feat that was accomplished in July 1969. The space program was the source of a wealth of new inventions, from the calculator to the personal computer.

Regarding higher education, the Morrill Act of 1862 expanded the number of public universities by creating a system of land grant universities. These provided a remarkable investment in the national economy as they raised agricultural and industrial productivity by encouraging the discovery of technological innovations. And after World War II, the GI Bill enabled those who otherwise could not afford it access to a university education. This rapid expansion of higher education fueled much of the economic prosperity of the last half of the twentieth century.

Given education's central role in the social and economic progress of the United States, it is not surprising that education continues to be a controversial subject. One contentious issue is school vouchers, which would allow parents to spend federal tax money intended for the public schools on private-school tuition for their children. Democrats have argued against the plan on the basis that the public school system needs more, not less, funding if it is to excel. Republicans, on the other hand, have pushed for school vouchers so parents in poorer and middle-class areas have the option of providing the best possible education for their children. On July 27, 2002, the U.S. Supreme Court upheld the constitutionality of school vouchers. Public schools will have to compete and prove they offer an excellent educational program to attract students under this competitive arrangement. Debates about vouchers and national standards that compel students to meet basic requirements in science, math, and technology remind us that many of the issues raised by educators including Horace Mann and John Dewey, two pioneers in the field of modern education, remain relevant today.

—*W. Chad Futrell*

References

Vinovskis, Maris A. *Education, Society, and Economic Opportunity: A Historical Perspective on Persistent Issues.* New Haven, CT: Yale University Press, 1995.

See also Volume 1: Cold War; Servicemen's Readjustment Act; U.S. Department of Health and Human Services.

Electricity

Source of power that propels the U.S. economy.

Electricity is generated in the United States by two kinds of utilities: investor-owned (privately owned) and public. With the advent of the Great Depression, privately owned facilities generated most of the electricity. A wave of regulatory reform in the 1930s saw Congress pass, among other legislation, the Public Utilities Holding Company Act of 1935, which restrained geographical integration (concentration of raw materials, processing facilities, and distribution facilities), vertical integration (control of upstream suppliers and downstream buyers), and horizontal integration (control of two or more companies in the same line of business) ostensibly to ensure that electric utilities, among others, remained unable to evade regulation at the state level. This "anticapitalist" measure virtually froze the organizational form of electricity generation in the United States for almost six decades, although there was a shift in type of energy source from coal- to oil-fired plants between the 1930s and 1960s and a later shift to the present oil-gas-coal-nuclear mix.

In 1978 Congress passed the Public Utility Regulatory Policy Act (PURPA). This act provided tax benefits that encouraged the building of small-scale electricity plants that ran on alternative energy sources like wind, solar, and small hydroelectric. PURPA also required utilities to buy this power—and power generated from industrial cogeneration units (which use multiple fuel sources to produce power cheaply)—at rates as high as the most expensive source of marginal power available to the utility. PURPA encouraged diversifying the mix of energy sources. Many cogeneration projects are competitive at today's electricity rates even without tax or other benefits. However, some states applied PURPA in a way that encouraged an oversupply of uneconomic energy. This practice caused the problem of stranded costs (costs that cannot be recovered in a competitive marketplace).

The Federal Energy Policy Act (FEPA) of 1992 required utilities to permit their customers to have access to other utilities and to a growing number of independent power producers. This change signaled the beginning of a new era of competition in electricity markets. Customers served by a local utility at high rates could buy power from other lower-cost sources by paying a small transmission user fee.

The FEPA of 1992 paved the way for restructuring and deregulating energy markets at the state level. In 1996 California enacted a comprehensive deregulation act (Assembly Bill No. 1890), and restructuring has spread; half of U.S. states have issued restructuring legislation or regulatory orders at the Public Utilities Commission (PUC) level. A major rationale for electricity restructuring remains to provide stronger incentives for efficiency in both generation and distribution than is possible under the regulated monopoly regime. However, results vary among the deregulating states. In California, the state legislature deregulated the energy industry in 1996, requiring electricity providers to sell off much of their generating capacity, prohibiting companies from signing long-term contracts for supplies, and restricting customer rate increases until 2002. During 2001, California experienced an energy shortage and rolling brownouts that critics of deregulation blamed on deregulation. However, subsequent investigations into the Texas-based energy company Enron, after its financial collapse in 2001, revealed that Enron had hidden energy reserves until the restriction against rate increases expired in 2002. As of 2003, only eight states have begun electricity deregulation, and in all eight—California, Texas, Pennsylvania, Rhode Island, New York, Illinois, Maine, and Massachusetts—the cost of electricity exceeds the national average. The United States provides a fascinating test case for deregulation policy, because each state is largely free to determine its own restructuring subject to approval by the Federal Electricity Regulatory Commission.

—*Warren Young and Eli Goldstein*

References

Newbery, David M. *Privatization, Restructuring, and Regulation of Network Utilities.* Cambridge, MA: MIT Press, 1999.

Vietor, Richard. *Contrived Competition: Regulation and Deregulation in America.* Cambridge, MA: Harvard University Press, 1994.

Young, Warren. *Atomic Energy Costing.* Norwell, MA: Kluwer Press, 1998.

See also Volume 1: Energy.

Electronic Commerce (E-Commerce)

Business-to-consumer trade and business-to-business transactions using the Internet platform, particularly the World Wide Web.

Between 1995 and 2001, e-commerce became the fastest-growing form of commerce in the world. In the United States alone, it grew from virtually nothing in 1995 to a volume of almost $65 billion in business-to-consumer trade and roughly $700 billion in business-to-business transactions in 2001. Despite astoundingly rapid growth, e-commerce had mixed success. In 1994, entrepreneur Jeff Bezos launched Amazon.com, an Internet book retailer that lacked the traditional "brick and mortar" infrastructure. Although Amazon.com had annual sales of over $2 billion by 2000, it suffered significant losses from its inception until the fourth quarter of 2001, when it finally reported a "pro forma operating profit" (a profit that excludes amortization of goodwill stock–based compensation and any restructuring costs).

Amazon.com's troubles were not unique. Between 1995 and 2000 more than $125 billion of venture capital was invested in more than 12,500 Internet start-up companies, or "dot-coms." However, by 2001 only 10 percent of those start-ups had survived as independent companies and, of those that survived, few operated profitably. Expectations for initial public offerings (IPOs) of dot-coms remained high, and many

investors hoped these IPOs would yield great profits. Between 1986 and 1995, only 1 percent of dot-com stocks traded at less than $1 per share. By 2001, 12 percent of the dot-coms that had gone public between 1998 and 2000 traded at $1 or less per share. For instance, Ask Jeeves.com and IVillage.com, once trading at highs of $190.50 and $130.00 per share respectively, both fell to less than $1.00 per share in April 2001 because of overvaluation in the high-tech stocks that had become apparent by the beginning of the year.

Business-to-consumer e-commerce developed in the early 1980s, when Prodigy (the largest Internet service provider in the United States) and Boston's Citinet (a communications provider that closed in March 2003), among other innovators, began offering information services such as electronic mail, real estate listings, and home banking. However, given the limited access of consumers to personal computers (PCs) at the time, e-commerce remained unpopular. Promising joint ventures like the collaboration between Chase Manhattan Bank and AT&T, which would have used telephone lines for electronic communication, failed because consumers rejected the high costs and awkward technology. In the 1990s, the reduced price and improved quality of PCs (by 2000, more than 60 percent of U.S. households had PCs), along with the increasing availability of Internet connections and bandwidth, changed consumer attitudes and created numerous opportunities for the growth of e-commerce.

Business-to-business e-commerce developed in the 1960s as companies realized that electronically exchanging common pieces of information such as bills of lading, invoices, and shipping orders could result in great savings compared with repeatedly producing the same information on paper. Businesses such as American Airlines, General Electric, Wal-Mart, and American Hospital Supply and Products (AHSP) established electronic data interchanges or interorganizational systems to exchange information with other firms with whom they did business. For instance, AHSP set up an e-commerce system in which customers, not AHSP employees, made and tracked product orders. This system enhanced operational efficiency by improving customer relations and saving AHSP significant time, labor, and shipping costs. In the 1990s, companies such as SAP, Cisco, and Federal Express improved on these pioneering efforts by providing direct access to services and retail outlets, creating information exchange networks, and establishing customer tracking systems.

—*Eric Pullin*

References

Laudon, Kenneth, and Carol Guercio Traver. *E-Commerce: Business, Technology, Society.* Boston: Addison-Wesley, 2002.

Rayport, Jeffrey, and Bernard Jaworski. *e-Commerce.* Boston: McGraw-Hill, 2001.

Schneider, Gary, and James Perry. *Electronic Commerce.* Boston: Thompson Learning, 2001.

See also Volume 1: Computer.

Emancipation Proclamation (January 1, 1863)

A proclamation by President Abraham Lincoln freeing slaves in states still in rebellion against the United States and designed to keep Great Britain, which had abolished slavery within the British Empire, from providing economic and political support to the Confederate states, with which Britain had traditionally had a strong trading relationship.

At the beginning of the Civil War, President Abraham Lincoln's major objective remained the restoration of the Union—not the abolition of slavery. Although personally opposed to slavery, he believed it was important politically to consider the feelings of those in loyal slave states as well as those who favored abolition. Although most people in the North opposed slavery, many Northerners believed that blacks were an inferior race and therefore were not willing to fight to end slavery. As the war progressed, some of Lincoln's abolitionist friends urged him to free the slaves. He was advised by members of Congress and his own Cabinet that such a move would destabilize the South's economy. Confederate slaves had been working in the South's farms and factories, allowing whites to serve in the military. Slaves produced the cotton crops that the South was trying to sell overseas. They had also seen frontline service as orderlies and military laborers. With the war going against the North in the first part of 1862, Lincoln began drafting, in the latter part of the year, a proclamation to free slaves.

On August 6, 1861, Congress passed the First Confiscation Act, which authorized Union forces to seize rebel property and freed slaves who had worked as cooks or laborers for Confederate forces. In 1862 Congress passed the Second Confiscation Act, which freed slaves living in rebel states. But Lincoln rejected both acts as emancipation proclamations for fear of alienating the border states. A preliminary emancipation document from Lincoln initially warned that slaves would receive their freedom on January 1, 1863. The final proclamation did not free all slaves but kept slavery intact in the loyal states of Delaware, Missouri, Kentucky, and Maryland. Slave owners remained exempted in the 48 counties now known as West Virginia and in several parishes and cities in Louisiana and Virginia.

The proclamation had the desired effect. The South's economy collapsed, and more than 500,000 slaves fled to Northern states. About 200,000 former slaves served the North in the Civil War, offsetting diminishing manpower in the Northern forces. Congress eliminated the presence of slavery anywhere in the United States after the states ratified the Thirteenth Amendment to the Constitution in December 1865.

—*David E. Walker*

References

Jones, Howard. *Abraham Lincoln and a New Birth of Freedom.* Lincoln: University of Nebraska Press, 1999.

Trefousee, Hans L. *Lincoln's Design for Emancipation.* Philadelphia: Lippincott, 1975.

See also Volumes 1, 2: Slavery; Volume 2 (Documents): Emancipation Proclamation.

Embargo of 1807

Act that restricted U.S. trade with Great Britain and France and led to the War of 1812.

During the Napoleonic Wars in which France and Great Britain were enemies, the United States became increasingly frustrated by demands from France and Great Britain for the United States to cease trade with one or the other, limiting American ability to realize a profit from both sides as well as from neutral countries. Napoleon's Continental System (which blockaded Great Britain and threatened to confiscate American ships that refused to trade with France) and the British practice of impressing American sailors and seizing ships thought to carry war material outraged the American public. Then, in 1807, the British HMS *Leopard* fired on the USS *Chesapeake,* forcing President Thomas Jefferson into action. Jefferson, who opposed a war, believed that an embargo against both France and Britain (which Congress passed in December 1807) would impress foreign nations with the value of neutral American trade and that Americans would willingly accept the inconvenience.

Instead, American exports fell from $108 million in 1807 to $22 million in 1808, while U.S. ships lay idle and many lost their jobs. The embargo also encouraged smuggling and evasion by otherwise law-abiding Americans and bitterly alienated the seafaring states of New England. The 1806 Non-Importation Act had removed British goods from the American market, and the embargo simply pushed the nation into economic recession. The president lifted the embargo three days before he left office. President James Madison replaced it in 1809 with the Non-Intercourse Act, which allowed the U.S. to trade with all countries except Britain and France unless either country promised to stop harassing American trade. Napoleon Bonaparte, the leader of France, issued such a promise, and Madison then asked Congress for a declaration of war against Great Britain. The War of 1812 was fought over issues of national honor, freedom to trade on the high seas, and U.S. economic independence.

—*Margaret Sankey*

References

Stuart, Reginald. *Half-Way Pacifist: Thomas Jefferson's View of War.* Toronto: University of Toronto Press, 1978.

Tucker, Robert. *Empire of Liberty: The Statecraft of Thomas Jefferson.* New York: Oxford University Press, 1990.

See also Volume 1: Non-Importation Act; Non-Intercourse Act; War of 1812.

Embargoes

Prohibition by one country of the importation of goods by and/or exportation of goods to another country.

When Great Britain attempted to exercise tighter control over the American colonies after the French and Indian War, colonists used embargoes several times between 1763 and 1776 to pressure Great Britain to repeal the hated Stamp Act and Townshend Duties. After the American Revolution, as the United States attempted to remain neutral in the conflict between Great Britain and France during the Napoleonic Wars, the only option that seemed available was to place an embargo against both countries. Although the embargo lasted more than a year, it created financial difficulties for American citizens and merchants while proving ineffective against the intended targets. The severity of the economic losses resulted in the delegates to the Hartford Convention—a meeting of Federalists held during the War of 1812—to demand that Congress pass any future embargoes by a two-thirds vote, not a simply majority, and restrict embargoes to 60 days. These demands were never implemented; the Federalists were completely discredited by the end of the conflict because of what most Americans perceived as traitorous activity during wartime.

After the U.S. embargo of 1809 on Great Britain and France in response to those countries' violation of American neutrality during the Napoleonic Wars, the United States rejected embargoes as a diplomatic tool until the twentieth century, when it used the embargo as a diplomatic tool against aggressor nations. In 1941 the United States placed an embargo on the shipment of oil and scrap metal to Japan that ended in the attack on Pearl Harbor. In 1962, an embargo was placed on Cuba after the Cuban missile crisis, in which the Soviet Union attempted to place in Cuba intermediate-range missiles that could reach U.S. soil. Other Central and South American countries joined in the embargo but have since repealed the measure. As of 2003 the U.S. embargo continues. Another international embargo that included members of the United Nations began against Iraq after the Persian Gulf War in 1991. The United Nations modified the embargo in 1996 to allow the sale of oil for food and medical supplies. As of May 2003, after the toppling of Saddam Hussein's government, the UN sanctions have been lifted. Other embargoes have existed between the United States and Yugoslavia (1992), Rhodesia (1970s), and South Africa (1980s). All failed to achieve the level of success officials had hoped for.

—*Cynthia Clark Northrup*

References

Dobson, Alan P. *U.S. Economic Statecraft for Survival, 1933–1991: Of Sanctions, Embargoes, and Economic Warfare.* New York: Routledge, 2002.
Schweitzer, Robert L., ed. *United States Policy toward Cuba: Tighten or Lift the Embargo?* Washington, DC: United States Global Strategy Council, 1995.
See also Volume 1: Embargo of 1807; War of 1812; United Nations.

Emergency Price Control Act (1942)

An effort on the part of the federal government during World War II to limit the severity of wartime inflation that had plagued the nation during World War I.

Congress charged the Office of Price Administration (OPA), established on April 11, 1942, with the responsibility of controlling prices and wages during World War II. On January 30, 1942, President Franklin D. Roosevelt signed the Emergency Price Control Act, which gave OPA the authority to impose price ceilings on a wide range of consumer items, fine those in violation of the law, and impose rent controls in defense areas, where plants producing military equipment were located. In April 1942, OPA issued a memorandum, "General Maximum Price Regulation," which froze prices at their March 1942 levels. The policies related to wage controls and rationing proved unpopular, but nearly 90 percent of Americans approved of price controls. During World War II this legislation limited inflation to a little over 2 percent, and many considered the act one of the great home-front successes of the war. This legislation expired on May 29, 1947.

—*James T. Carroll*

References

Rockoff, Hugh. *Drastic Measures: A History of Wage and Price Controls in the United States.* New York: Cambridge University Press, 1984.
See also Volume 1: Office of Price Administration; Roosevelt, Franklin D.; World War II.

Employment Act of 1946

Legislation that indicated the concerns of twentieth-century economic policy and that called for full employment, an end to racial discrimination in hiring, and an increased minimum wage.

The Great Depression was the impetus for the Employment Act of 1946. In the 1930s, economists feared a mature economy, which is characterized by chronic unemployment and underemployment. Economic growth had stopped. New Deal theorists began a campaign for a full employment policy in which the federal government played a major role. Because the New Deal equaled "groceries plus liberty," the idea developed that a job remained not only a necessity for economic recovery but also an entitlement for every citizen.

Congressional New Dealers after World War II wanted a bill in which the government guaranteed the full employment ideal. Fearing a major recession, elements of the Roosevelt coalition sought legislation. A full employment bill passed the Senate, but the House compromise bill—the version that was enacted—adopted only the goals of maximum employment, production, and purchasing power, not full employment. Drawing on the notion that expert advice is valuable, Congress created the Council of Economic Advisers (CEA), established by the Employment Act of 1946, to help President Harry S Truman draft economic polices. The CEA worked with a Joint Economic Committee to generate an *Economic Report of the President* regarding the economy's future.

Ironically, the failure of a full employment bill created a vacuum in postwar economic policy in which forms of military Keynesianism, resulting from the cold war, dominated the public agenda until end of the twentieth century. The Congressional Budget and Impoundment Act of 1974 effectively reduced the power of the congressional Joint Economic Committee in formulating policy, although, in the tradition of the Employment Act of 1946, the Humphrey-Hawkins Bill (the Full Employment and Balanced Growth Act of 1978) became law and the 1974 act was subsequently ignored. Legislative compromise, administrative disregard of the law, and cold war Keynesianism reduced the high idealism of the full employment ideal to a very limited role in American economic policy.

—*Donald K. Pickens*

References

Bailey, Stephen K. *Congress Makes a Law: The Story behind the Employment Act of 1946.* New York: Columbia University Press, 1950.

Mucciaroni, Gary. *The Political Failure of Employment Policy, 1945–1982.* Pittsburgh, PA: University of Pittsburgh Press, 1990.

Norton, Hugh S. *The Employment Act and the Council of Economic Advisers, 1946–1976.* Columbia: University of South Carolina Press, 1977.

See also Volume 1: Council of Economic Advisers; Great Depression; Keynesian Economics; New Deal.

Energy

A source of usable heat or power such as petroleum or coal.

Human civilization depends on energy. Until the 1770s, the only available energy sources were manpower, animal power, lumber, water, and wind. The invention of the steam engine ignited the Industrial Revolution initially fueled by wood, which remained the dominant energy source until about 1885. Coal then became the primary energy source, replaced by oil in the 1950s. Coal and oil are burned today to generate electricity, which is the primary engine that drives the modern economy. Each energy transition has had revolutionary social and economic consequences.

Heavily forested America was relatively slow to switch from wood to coal. Exploitation of the Pennsylvania coalfields after 1850 to fuel railroads and steel mills enabled America to become the world's leading industrial power by 1900. Coal first powered transportation and industry, but after 1960 it primarily powered electric utilities. In 2000, the United States produced more than a billion tons of coal, and coal accounted for one-third of U.S. energy production and one-third of U.S. generation of carbon dioxide.

Subsurface oil was first extracted in Pennsylvania in 1859. Used primarily as an illuminant and lubricant, oil proved more versatile and transportable than coal, and manufacturers quickly adapted it for industrial use. Oil fueled mass-produced automobiles and the vehicles of modern military forces after 1914, and the world's great powers—the United States, Great Britain, the Soviet Union, Germany, and France—thus struggled to control world oil supplies. The United States dominated world oil production for decades but became a net importer in the 1960s. Some argue that oil prices must soon rise dramatically, as new discoveries cannot keep pace with increased demand, especially in Asia. Oil production, controlled for decades by the Organization of Petroleum Exporting Countries (OPEC), may change as the United States takes a more active role in the Middle East in countries such as Iraq and Kuwait in 2003.

Natural gas remains clean and cheap but requires extensive pipelines for distribution. First used for illumination, today natural gas is primarily used in industry and for home heating and cooking. Gas use increased dramatically in the 1990s, but reserves for 93 years remain in North America.

Nuclear energy as a source of electric power became popular in the 1960s as dependence on imported oil grew, but its popularity declined in the 1970s due to safety and environmental concerns. Construction of many proposed nuclear plants was canceled after 1980, partly because fossil power plants remained cheaper to build and operate. Nuclear energy produced 20 percent of U.S. electricity in 2000, but nuclear power will diminish in importance as plants are retired and not replaced. In 2003, 104 nuclear units continue to operate; 28 units have been permanently shut down. No new nuclear plants are scheduled to be built in the next few years. Nuclear energy continues to power large ships and submarines that travel long distances before refueling or that need the stronger propulsion capabilities that nuclear power provides. At the end of the cold war, there were 400 nuclear-powered military vessels around the world; in 2003 only 160 remain, and half of those belong to the United States.

Estimates of fossil fuel reserves vary widely, but approximately 40 years' reserve of oil, 93 years of natural gas, 250 years of coal, and thousands of years of uranium exist at current rates of consumption. Oil shale (a black or brown shale containing hydrocarbons that yield petroleum by distillation) may provide additional energy. Improved technology for finding, extracting, and using fossil fuels will extend effective reserves even further. Ultimately, however, scarcity of fossil fuel and environmental concerns, particularly over greenhouse gas emissions, which trap solar radiation and cause global warming, will force a transition to renewable energy sources—wind, solar, and geothermal power, which are not now cost-competitive—in the near future.

—*James D. Perry*

References

Chandler, Alfred Dupont. *The Visible Hand: The Managerial Revolution in American Business.* Cambridge, MA: Harvard University Press, Belknap Press, 1977.

Schurr, Sam H., and Bruce C. Netschert. *Energy in the American Economy, 1850–1975: An Economic Study of Its History and Prospects.* Baltimore, MD: Johns Hopkins University Press, 1960.

U.S. Department of Energy. *Energy in the United States, 1635–2000.* April 2002. Available: http://www.eia.doe.gov/emeu/aer; accessed June 20, 2002.

Yergin, Daniel. *The Prize: The Epic Quest for Oil, Money, and Power.* New York: Simon and Schuster, 1991.

See also Volume 1: Electricity; Oil.

Energy Crisis

Twentieth and twenty-first century problem involving a reduced production of oil.

The energy crisis dates from October 1973, when the Arab

oil embargo, which prohibited sale of Arab oil to Western industrial nations, began. Since then, industrialized countries have experienced a certain uneasiness from time to time regarding future supplies of energy, especially of oil.

The United States continues to depend on coal and oil for its energy needs. As recently as 1999, oil supplied 34 percent of the Earth's energy. Natural gas furnished another 23 percent, while coal contributed 22 percent of mankind's energy needs. Despite efforts, especially in recent years, to harness more power from the wind, water, sun and, in certain circumstances, from nuclear reactors, fossil fuels (oil, gas, and coal) still supply 79 percent of the world's requirements.

We must prepare for a much different energy future, particularly through governmental action including legislation. That will mean lesser reliance on fossil fuels (other than natural gas) and a greater recourse to alternative energy sources, especially from solar power, biomass (the processing of plant life into fuel), the wind, and water. If these efforts are successful, carbon emissions (from carbon dioxide, methane, and nitrous oxide) into the global atmosphere would be greatly abated, if not eliminated, and so would the fears of a growing number of people regarding the effects of the so-called greenhouse gases on the climate.

Until the world's peoples reduce their heavy dependence on coal and oil and at the same time begin to use renewable, nonpolluting forms of energy, natural gas should provide for a period of transition. It remains an abundant (the Earth's proven reserves amounted to 5,145 trillion cubic feet as of January 1, 1999) and relatively clean-burning fuel. Moreover, processes exist for converting it into liquid fuel. In fact, enough recoverable natural gas exists to supply the world with 500 billion barrels of synthetic crude oil—more than twice the total of oil ever produced in the United States.

Another potential supply of gas (mainly methane) exists in the form of hydrates—gas locked in an icelike, crystalline condition beneath the continental margins of the oceans and in permafrost regions on land. These hydrates may well make up the world's greatest single storehouse of usable energy.

—*Keith L. Miller*

References

Fouda, Safaa A. "Liquid Fuels from Natural Gas." *Scientific American,* vol. 278, no. 3 (March 1998): 74–77.

Lowrie, Allen, and Michael D. Max. "The Extraordinary Promise and Challenge of Gas Hydrates." *World Oil,* vol. 220, no. 9 (September 1999): 49–57.

Vaitheeswaran, Vejay. "Energy: A Brighter Future." *The Economist,* February 10, 2001.

Weeks, Lewis G. "Where Will Energy Come from in 2059?" *Petroleum Engineer for Management,* vol. 31 (August 1959): 53–69.

See also Volume 1: Oil; Oil Embargoes.

Entitlement Programs

Government-sponsored benefits provided for individuals based on their age, need, or other criteria.

In the United States, the federal government established the first entitlement program in 1935 with the passage of the Social Security Act. Not surprisingly, this initial program was designed to be self-funding through the additional tax paid on income by all income-generating Americans. The first Social Security checks were sent out in 1939, and from then on the number of elderly who receive benefits under the program has continued to mushroom. Social Security taxes are placed in a trust that would have provided enough revenue for the large baby boom generation born in the late 1940s and 1950s, except that Congress has repeatedly used the funds to meet other budgetary needs; Social Security is expected to become insolvent by 2032. Retirees from some occupations, for example, government worker and teacher, will be covered by non–Social Security programs.

Entitlement programs that followed the Social Security Act were not self-supporting. During the administration of President John F. Kennedy, the United States set up the Medicare program, which was designed to provide limited medical assistance to the nation's elderly. More than 40 million Americans including individuals 65 or older, disabled individuals of all ages, and people with end-stage renal disease have Medicare coverage. The coverage pays for long-term care, hospice care for terminally ill patients, doctors' visits, hospital stays, surgery, and durable medical equipment such as wheelchairs for qualifying recipients. During the 1980s and 1990s Congress revised the Medicare program, and participants now pay a small fee to participate in the program, which covers a percentage of the health care costs. In 1999 federal net outlays for Medicare amounted to $190.5 billion. During the administration of President Lyndon B. Johnson a similar program, Medicaid, was established to provide health benefits for qualified low-income families. Although Medicaid is a federally funded program, states establish their own eligibility guidelines. During the 1960s, the number of children born out of wedlock or living in single-family homes due to divorce prompted the federal government to also establish the Aid to Dependent Children (ADC) and the Aid to Families with Dependent Children (AFDC) programs. AFDC issues cash payments to recipients for rent, transportation, and other basic needs. The system was designed in such a way that a mother would lose benefits if she was married to or lived with the father or if the father earned more than a certain state-defined income. In some cases, as many as three generations of women on assistance chose to live together and pool their assistance checks to avoid such penalties. In this way, women were forced into a cycle of dependency once they became pregnant. This situation forced state legislators who controlled the program to reform the AFDC benefits eligibility in September 1997. Wisconsin initiated the first welfare-to-work AFDC program, which required women to actively look for work and restricted the number of eligible benefit years. Opponents argued that the measure would create a disaster when the time limit arrived, but the program's success has resulted in most states adopting this approach. The program continues to assist with child care for women employed in low-paying jobs, and it also provides some training assistance. In 1999 Congress appropriated $2.3 billion for AFDC; $16.5 million went for child care and $319.5 million for block grants to states to fund the welfare-to-work programs. In addition to AFDC, low-income families are also eligible for food stamps. Initially recipients received coupons that could be exchanged for food, but the sale or exchange of the coupons for drugs or nonfood items led states to establish a system in which a card similar to a credit card is scanned at the checkout counter and the balance deducted electronically. In 2002 Congress earmarked $1.3 billion for the food stamp program.

Since the 1960s, Congress has established many entitlement programs. Federal Housing Assistance, known as Section 8 housing, provides low-cost dwellings for eligible Americans. School breakfast and lunch programs ensure that children receive proper nutrition so they are capable of learning. Special Supplemental Nutrition Programs for Women, Infants, and Children (WIC) operates for the same purpose but for pre- and postnatal women and young children. The Head Start program provides opportunities for early childhood learning so that when the children begin kindergarten they have the fundamental knowledge required to function at the appropriate level. The government also provides energy assistance through the Low-Income Home Energy Assistance Program.

Veterans also receive health, education, and other benefits through a variety of acts. Veterans Administration (VA) hospitals provide essential medical services to a high concentration of disabled veterans. Veterans can also receive up to $1,000 a month toward a college education and can qualify for low-interest mortgages through VA programs.

Each year the federal government expends billions of dollars on entitlement programs. Some are funded by special taxes or employer contributions, but many are paid for with taxpayers' dollars.

—*Cynthia Clark Northrup*

References

Bruce, Neil. *Public Finance and the American Economy.* Boston, MA: Addison-Wesley, 2001.

Samuelson, Robert J. *The Good Life and Its Discontents: The American Dream in the Age of Entitlement, 1945–1995.* New York: Time Books, 1995.

See also Volume 1: Aid to Dependent Children; Aid to Families with Dependent Children; Medicaid; Medicare; Social Security Act of 1935; Volume 2: Welfare State.

Environment

External physical conditions that affect growth, development, and survival of plant and animal organisms.

Industrial growth characteristic of post–World War II affluence threatened the nation's natural environment and made environmental quality an overriding national value with significant import for the economy. Environmental protection, previously the domain of state and local governments, became a federal mandate during the 1960s and 1970s, primarily during the administrations of Presidents Lyndon B. Johnson and Richard Nixon. In the early 1970s, as the first wave of environmental regulations took hold, total capital outlays plus operating expenditures for pollution con-

trol amounted to about 15 percent of the gross domestic product. Thirty years later, this figure has risen to over 20 percent and is expected to increase in the future. The Environmental Protection Agency (USEPA), the chief regulatory body for environmental protection, today employs about 18,000 people and has an annual budget of more than $7 billion. As such, it ranks as one of the largest federal agencies, its regulatory functions emulated by similar agencies at the state level.

Environmental legislation over the past 40 years has established a regulatory framework that touches on almost every aspect of the economy. Modern clean water and air laws, for example, regulate emissions from factories and automobiles, often at considerable cost to the regulated industry. The National Environmental Policy Act established a clean environment as a national priority and mandated extensive environmental impact statements before the completion of any large federal program. Unlike most of the previous federal legislation in American history, this wave of environmental legislation applied to all industries, and environmental regulators were not held responsible for the economic impact of regulations on specific industries. This regulatory climate helped to exacerbate a growing tension between the nation's two stated goals: a healthy environment and a growing economy. The effect of economic policies on environmental quality and the effect of pollution control on the nation's economy and industrial competitiveness have been controversial from the outset, often pitting competing environmental and industry lobbies in a struggle for public opinion and congressional votes. In addition, local and state governments often complain of "unfunded mandates" from Washington, in which Congress imposes administrative and fiscal burdens without compensating financial support.

In another respect, environmental protection also demands international cooperation. Considerable diplomacy remains necessary, as Third World and developing nations perceive international environmental controls as a hindrance to their economic advancement. To these nations, developed countries such as those in Western Europe and North America are the principal environmental polluters. Under the Kyoto Protocol, industrialized countries must reduce emissions by 5.2 percent of 1990 levels. Only 1 country out of the 55 countries required to implement the agreement has ratified the agreement—in the case of the United States, the Senate voted 95 to 0 against ratification. In March 2001, the administration of President George W. Bush abandoned the Kyoto Protocol entirely because it did not require India and China to reduce their emissions and because, the administration claimed, it was not in the best interests of the United States to operate under the protocol. Despite these objections to the 1997 protocol, negotiations among participants of the General Agreement on Tariffs and Trade have continued. As of 2001, 156 countries had signed the agreement.

Today, industries and governments at all levels struggle to reconcile these two legitimate preconditions—a healthy environment and a growing economy—for human prosperity and happiness. Many government agencies, including the USEPA, conduct extensive cost-benefit and risk assessment analyses before they implement a policy. Others perceive environmental regulations as providing tremendous economic opportunity in "environment-friendly" industries. There is a way, they claim, to have both economic growth and environmental protection.

—*Brooks Flippen*

References

Hays, Samuel P. *Beauty, Health, and Permanence: Environmental Politics in the United States, 1955–1985.* New York: Cambridge University Press, 1987.

Rothman, Hal. *The Greening of a Nation? Environmentalism in the United States since 1945.* Ft. Worth, TX: Harcourt, Brace, 1998.

Sale, Kirkpatrick. *The Green Revolution: The American Environmental Movement, 1962–1992.* New York: Hill and Wang, 1993.

See also Volume 1: Conservation; U.S. Environmental Protection Agency.

Environmental Protection Agency

See U.S. Environmental Protection Agency.

EPA

See U.S. Environmental Protection Agency.

Equal Pay Act of 1963

Legislation mandating that women and men would receive equal pay for the same work.

The Equal Pay Act had its roots in anger among women at the ongoing and widespread practice of paying women half the wages of men, a practice that dates from the early 1800s, when factories were founded in the United States. Many male workers opposed equal pay because they believed that if employers had to pay the same for women workers as for men, they would hire women. However, supporters including feminists and their sympathizers sought fairness in the workplace, calling for equal pay for equal work. In 1945, feminists introduced a bill to protect women's pay, but the measure gathered little support. In 1963, president John F. Kennedy's Commission on the Status of Women (CSW) was established, championed by Esther Peterson, head of the Women's Bureau of the Department of Labor. The CSW agreed that fairness demanded equal pay and it endorsed the concept. Debate soon arose over whether equal pay meant that all workers at a particular job or a particular level would receive the same wages. Employers opposed the bill, and members of Congress voiced fears that equal pay would take jobs away from men, but the bill's opponents surrendered when they became convinced that the bill would be more symbolic than effective because of widespread job segregation by sex. The Equal Pay Act (1963) provides that employers may not pay workers of one sex at rates lower than they pay employees of the opposite sex employed in the same establishment for equal work. It applies to jobs that require substantially equal skill, effort, and responsibility and that are performed under similar working conditions. Exceptions permitted under the law include when sex differences in pay occur due to seniority, merit, quantity or quality of production, or any factor other than sex. In 1972, the provisions of the law extended to cover management and professional employees and state and local government workers. Employers with fewer than 25 employees remain exempt.

—*Caryn E. Neumann*

References

Bureau of National Affairs (BNA). *Equal Pay for Equal Work: Federal Equal Pay Law of 1963.* Washington, DC: BNA, 1963.

See also Volume 2: Labor.

European Recovery Plan

See Economic Cooperation Administration; Marshall Plan.

Export Control Act (1949)

First post-World War II legislation authorizing the U.S. government to restrict exports via a system of licenses.

Although the U.S. Congress had enacted export control measures in wartime, the national legislature approved and President Harry S Truman signed into law in February 1949 the first bill to hand the government broad powers over exports in peacetime. The legislation can only be understood within the context of the cold war, which pitted the United States against the Union of Soviet Socialist Republics (USSR). Twelve months earlier, the USSR had backed a communist coup in Czechoslovakia that removed the last semiautonomous government in the Soviet sphere of influence in Eastern Europe. On the heels of this event the Soviets challenged American, French, and British access rights to Berlin between June 1948 and May 1949 (a blockade of Berlin, in effect, in which the USSR cut off land access to West Berlin).

The Czech coup and Berlin blockade provoked sharp restrictions on the shipment of American goods to the Soviet Union and its communist allies. The USSR retaliated against U.S. export policies by curbing in December 1948 the sale of such items as manganese and platinum. These Soviet materials possessed strategic value through their use in U.S. armaments, aircraft, and communications equipment. The Soviet reprisal encouraged Congress to sanction the sweeping Export Control Act. It established, through the U.S. Department of Commerce, comprehensive licensing procedures for all exports. It also created commodities lists to limit or prevent the sale or transfer of specific products or technologies that might enhance the strength of U.S. adversaries.

In the hothouse atmosphere of confrontation over Berlin—the United States had to airlift supplies to the city for more than a year—American officials deemed most U.S. products to be of military value. By 1950, U.S. sales to the USSR fell below $1 million, marking the virtual end to

America's export trade with the world's largest country. Congress reapproved the Export Control Act in 1962 and then revised or reauthorized it through the Export Administration Acts of 1969, 1979, and 1985. Each adjustment reflected shifts in U.S. policy that mirrored the evolution over time of America's relations with communist nations. Despite the collapse of the Soviet bloc in 1989 and the Soviet Union in 1991, U.S. economic controls continued to prevent the transfer of cutting-edge technologies to other countries and the sale of military hardware to so-called rogue nations. Congress, for example, renewed the Export Administration Act in 1999 to prevent the proliferation of weapons of mass destruction and their means of delivery to the nations of Iran, Iraq, Libya, and North Korea.

—*James K. Libbey*

References

Funigiello, Philip J. *American-Soviet Trade in the Cold War.* Chapel Hill: University of North Carolina Press, 1988.

Libbey, James K. *Russian-American Economic Relations.* Gulf Breeze, FL: Academic International Press, 1999.

Export Control Act. U.S. Statutes at Large 63 (1949): 7.

Senate Subcommittee on International Trade and Finance. *Reauthorization of the Export Administration Act.* Washington, DC: U.S. Government Printing Office, 2000.

See also Volume 1: Cold War: Coordinating Committee for Multilateral Export Controls.

F

FAIR Act of 1996

See Federal Agricultural Improvement and Reform Act of 1996.

Family Assistance Plan (FAP)

Welfare reform proposal first introduced by President Richard Nixon in 1969 that would have guaranteed a minimum income for poor families.

The idea of a guaranteed minimum income gained acceptability in conservative circles in the mid-1960s when libertarian economist Milton Friedman suggested adopting a negative income tax to provide a safety net for the poor while also rewarding work. President Nixon liked the boldness of a proposal that would abolish the current welfare system, and he presented the Family Assistance Plan (FAP) in a nationally televised address on August 8, 1969.

The FAP included an increase of about $2.5 billion in federal welfare spending, with the average family of four expected to receive $1,600 in monthly benefits. The plan also promised to provide benefits for more than 13 million working men and women whose wages remained insufficient to lift them above the poverty line but who failed to pass eligibility requirements for other federal welfare benefits.

Nixon's public support for the FAP was not matched by decisive action to ensure passage of the FAP. The proposal failed to pass Congress in 1970 and again in 1972, as the votes in support of the plan proved insufficient to overcome the opposition from both sides of the ideological spectrum: Conservatives thought the proposal too generous, but liberal politicians and welfare rights activists, most notably the National Welfare Rights Organization, characterized the benefits under FAP as being too stingy. Liberals also opposed the work requirements inherent in FAP, the very feature of the program that conservatives found most appealing.

Although the Family Assistance Plan never became law, efforts to raise the incomes of low-wage workers persisted. The Earned Income Tax Credit (EITC), first enacted in 1975, followed in the ideological tradition of the FAP by seeking to provide working families with greater after-tax income.

—*Christopher A. Preble*

References

Unger, Irwin. *The Best of Intentions: The Triumph and Failure of the Great Society under Kennedy, Johnson, and Nixon.* New York: Doubleday, 1996.

Zundel, Alan F. *Declarations of Dependency: The Civic Republican Tradition in U.S. Poverty Policy.* Albany, NY: State University of New York Press, 2000.

See also Volume 2: Welfare State.

Fannie Mae

See Federal National Mortgage Association.

FAP

See Family Assistance Plan.

Farm Credit Amendments Act of 1985

Act that reorganized and rescued the Farm Credit System, a network of borrower-owned lending institutions and service organizations for farmers, ranchers, producers, or harvesters of agricultural products.

Because of the 1980s farm crisis in rural America—caused by farming overexpansion, overinvestment in land and technology, and a 1979 wheat embargo against the Soviet Union that hurt U.S. wheat farmers—the Farm Credit System (FSC) remained in a precarious situation. Congress designed the Farm Credit Amendments Act of 1985 to centralize the process for obtaining credit and to optimize lending efficiency among the Farm Credit System's five credit banks and one agricultural bank. The Farm Credit Administration (FCA) assumed responsibility for regulating the FSC. A three-member board of directors nominated by the president and confirmed by the Congress, each of whom serves a single six-year term, governs the FCA. The board regulates the Farm Credit System in much the same way that the Federal Deposit Insurance Corporation regulates commercial banks. The president names a chair to oversee the agency instead of the board appointing a FCA governor. The three-member board of directors has become an advisory panel stripped of almost all its power. The FCA sets loan security requirements and interest rates, regulates the transfer of funds, oversees annual independent audits of each institution, and approves bond issues. The act establishes and enforces minimum levels of capital reserves for each member institution. The FCA can also issue cease-and-desist orders against officers or institutions for violation of regulations and can correct these violations. It can remove any directors or officers of the institutions as it deems necessary.

The act also created a new institution called the Farm Credit System Capital Corporation, owned and controlled by participating banking institutions, which has the power to redistribute capital resources among the institutions to resolve financial problems. The Farm Credit System Capital Corporation took over bad loans and centralized about $7 million in surplus reserve. A five-member board of directors—including three members elected by the farm credit banks, which own voting stock in the corporation, and two members appoint the FSC chair—oversees the corporation's operations. This basic system currently governs the Farm Credit System.

—*T. Jason Soderstrum*

References
Harl, Neal. *The Farm Debt Crisis of the 1980s.* Ames: Iowa State University Press, 1990.
See also Volumes 1, 2: Agricultural Policy.

Farm Credit System Reform Act of 1996

Act that permitted the Federal Agricultural Mortgage Corporation (Farmer Mac) to serve as an agricultural mortgage marketing facility.

In the aftermath of the 1980s farm crisis, which was set off by the wheat embargo against the Soviet Union in 1979, Congress created Farmer Mac (the Federal Agricultural Mortgage Corporation) in 1987. Its purpose was to help bail out the Farm Credit System—which was designed to provide low-interest loans to farmers—with the purpose of forming a secondary market for, and to guarantee securities based on, farm real estate loans. These securities failed to establish a growing niche in farm credit markets, and the Farmer Mac capital base began to decline by the mid-1990s. The Farmer Mac charter required changes to allow it to become more beneficial.

Signed into law on February 10, 1996, the Farm Credit System Reform Act (1996 Reform Act) allowed Farmer Mac to become a direct purchaser of mortgages in order to form pools of financial resources. Previously Farmer Mac had just guaranteed securities formed from loan pools. The 1996 Reform Act amended the Farm Credit Act of 1971 by modifying the definition of *certified facility* to allow Farmer Mac to

purchase loans for pooling (collecting) and securitization (backing) directly from sellers. It also eliminated the rule that Farmer Mac must keep a 10 percent subordinated interest [funds under the control of another authority] or cash reserves for loan pools. Farmer Mac now uses Federal Reserve banks as depositories, fiscal agents, or custodians. Regulatory oversight has increased, and timetables for recapitalization have been set. All of these measures made it more attractive for banks to participate in Farmer Mac.

In 2001, farmers and ranchers have more than $3.1 billion in mortgages that back securities guaranteed by Farmer Mac. The 1996 Reform Act allowed Farmer Mac to achieve profitability for the first time in its history, and its performance has improved every year since. It increased its capital from $12 million in 1995 to more than $100 million by 2001.

—*T. Jason Soderstrum*

References
U.S. Department of Agriculture. *Credit in Rural America.* Washington, DC: U.S. Government Printing Office, 2001.
See also Volumes 1, 2: Agricultural Policy.

Farm Crisis of 1982

An economic crisis in rural America in the 1980s caused because the U.S. government had encouraged farming overexpansion and overinvestment in land and technology during the previous decade and exacerbated by the Soviet wheat embargo of 1979, which resulted in oversupply and devalued farm prices.

In light of expanding markets in the 1970s, the federal government urged farmers to farm "fencerow to fencerow." Land used in corn production increased by 38 percent from the late 1960s to 1981, climbing from 56 million acres to 74.6 million acres. Wheat-cultivated land made a similar jump of 48 percent. Improved technology enormously increased the cost of items such as tractors. From 1970 to 1980, non–real estate debt of U.S. farmers increased by $67 billion, almost tripling. Yet as farming costs increased, so did the value of the land. Between 1970 and 1982, in some areas of the country, land values increased by 400 percent. In the 1970s, banks also liberalized their lending practices toward the agricultural community. Bankers, like farmers, assumed that land prices would keep increasing at the double-digit rate of inflation of up to 20 percent. Based on this assumption, many banks made shaky loans.

On October 9, 1979, the Federal Reserve Board implemented several policies to reduce inflation. These changes made farmland less attractive as an investment, contributed to the decline in land value, caused lower returns on farmers' equity, and adversely affected exports. By the end of 1981, leveraged landowners, whose loans were based on inflated land rates, began to realize that they could not make their high-interest-rate loan payments. Lending institutions began to retract their easy credit policies and called in their problem loans. As the value of farm acreage decreased, those in risky credit positions began to wash out—generally younger, more progressive farmers.

In reaction to the credit problem, the federal government began several programs to reduce production and provide financial assistance to farmers. One of the most famous of these acts, the Food Security Act of 1985, authorized more than $52 billion in farm supports. By that point, however, most of the farmers in financial straits had already left the land. The farm crisis of 1982 devastated rural America, forcing family farms out of the picture and replacing them with large agribusiness corporations.

—*T. Jason Soderstrum*

References

Harl, Neal. *The Farm Debt Crisis of the 1980s.* Ames: Iowa State University Press, 1990.

See also Volumes 1, 2: Agricultural Policy.

Farm Disaster Assistance Act of 1987

Law that provided assistance to farmers who lost crops because of natural disasters in 1986.

The Farm Disaster Assistance Act of 1987 expanded the number of farmers who were eligible to receive disaster relief assistance. This measure was the first legislation that Congressional opponents to the administration of President Ronald Reagan and the 1985 Farm Bill could use to boost farmers' incomes. The Democratic leadership opposed the president's plan to cut back and restructure basic price and income supports for agriculture.

The Farm Disaster Assistance Act provided a one-time disaster payment of payment-in-kind (PIK) certificates, redeemed from government-owned grain, to farms in counties designated as disaster areas. Farmers could get up to $100,000 in a PIK certificate to cover any losses that exceeded 50 percent of their 1986 harvest. Those who farmed federally subsidized crops such as wheat, cotton, rice, and feed grains could apply, as well as those raising "nonprogram" specialty crops. Farmers only had to prove that "drought, excessive heat, flood, hail, or excessive moisture" afflicted their crops.

Two hundred thousand farmers in 38 states applied for the $400 million in benefits, most of them residents of the drought-ridden Southeast or flooded areas in the Midwest. The amount they applied for exceeded $500 million, and Oklahoma winter wheat farmers had not originally been part of the program, so Congress agreed to provide an additional $135 million to cover the shortfalls. It also gave PIK certificates to those unable to plant their winter crops. Although many in Congress tried to help farmers hurt by the farm crisis of 1982 (a period of depressed agricultural prices and overproduction), most such farmers had given up farming by 1987. The Reagan administration and Democratic members of Congress both understood that the Farm Disaster Assistance Act only signaled the first step in reversing the administration's "decoupling" plan to reduce farmers' reliance on the federal government.

—*T. Jason Soderstrum*

References

Harl, Neal. *The Farm Debt Crisis of the 1980s.* Ames: Iowa State University Press, 1990.

See also Volumes 1, 2: Agricultural Policy.

Farm Security Administration (FSA)

One of several programs of President Franklin D. Roosevelt's New Deal designed to ease hardships endured by farmers and sharecroppers during the Great Depression.

The Farm Security Administration (FSA) was created by the Bankhead-Jones Farm Tenancy Act of 1937, itself inspired by an alarming report on the spread of farm tenancy filed earlier that year by the Special Committee on Farm Tenancy chaired by Secretary of Agriculture Henry A. Wallace. (In farm tenancy, farmers remain in debt to landowners and exchange a portion of the harvest for use of the land, seed, and supplies.) Rexford G. Tugwell, a close adviser to President Franklin D. Roosevelt and a professor of economics at Columbia University, headed the FSA. Along with taking over the work of the 1935 Resettlement Administration, which had as its purpose the elimination of migrant and tenant farming, the FSA set up decent migrant labor camps and helped to establish cooperative homestead communities to assist farmers driven off their land by bankruptcy and foreclosure and exploited by large growers. It also extended long-term, low-interest loans to farmers and sharecroppers to help them regain their independence, although these loans were spread thinly over more than 650,000 recipients.

The historical section of the FSA's Information Division became well known during the Great Depression by employing more than a dozen first-rate photographers to generate sympathy and support for the FSA by documenting harsh rural conditions. Led by Roy Emerson Stryker, this notable group included John Collier, Jack Delano, Walker Evans, Dorothea Lange, Russell Lee, Carl Mydans, Arthur Rothstein, John Vachon, and Marion Post Wolcott. Lange's "Migrant Mother" became arguably the most famous image from the Great Depression.

The FSA attracted sharp criticism, especially from large commercial farmers who feared losing cheap labor. In reaction, in 1941, Stryker's photographers shifted their focus from farming to patriotic subjects related to the impending world war. The agency's funding was cut dramatically in 1942, and it was abolished in 1946, its programs taken over by the Farmers Home Administration.

—*David B. Sicilia*

References

Baldwin, Sidney. *Poverty and Politics: The Rise and Decline of the Farm Security Administration.* Chapel Hill: University of North Carolina Press, 1968.

Curtis, James. *Mind's Eye, Mind's Truth: FSA Photography Reconsidered.* Philadelphia: Temple University Press, 1989.

See also Volume 1: Great Depression; New Deal; Roosevelt, Franklin D.

Farmer Mac

See Federal Agricultural Mortgage Corporation.

Farmer Mac Reform Act of 1995

Act that eased the regulatory requirements for the Farm Credit System and gave the Federal Agricultural Mortgage Company, or Farmer Mac, the authority to pool (collect) loans.

Designed to improve the efficiency and operation of the Farmer Mac (Federal Agricultural Mortgage Corporation), the Farmer Mac Reform Act of 1995 made substantial changes to the Farm Credit Act of 1971, which governed agricultural real estate and rural housing loans. Farmer Mac guaranteed these loans from commercial banks, insurance companies, and the cooperative farm credit system.

Congress had originally established Farmer Mac to bring lower-cost, long-term real estate financing to farmers and ranchers who had survived the 1980s farm crisis, a period of higher interest rates and lower agricultural prices. The federal government intended Farmer Mac to become a new source of credit by creating government-supported programs for farm mortgages, as other government-sponsored enterprises such as Fannie Mae and Freddie Mac had done for the housing sector. Farmer Mac failed in its goals. Initially capitalized with $21 million in private investments by nonprofit institutions, that equity declined by more than $9.5 million, and the Office of Secondary Market Oversight (OSMO) estimated that Farmer Mac would fall short of sufficient core capital by the end of 1996.

The Farmer Mac Reform Act liberalized Farmer Mac's charter. It eliminated the requirement that banks back each pool of loans by 10 percent subordinated interest [funds under the control of another authority] or cash reserves. During three years following the enactment of the Farmer Mac Reform Act, Congress also liberalized the statutory minimum capital requirements. The Farm Credit Administration (FCA) and the OSMO received an additional three years to implement risk-based capital requirements for Farmer Mac. In addition, the legislation required Farmer Mac institutions to streamline their business operations, for example, by requiring Federal Reserve banks to act as depositories and fiscal agents for Farmer Mac's securities and providing for Farmer Mac's access to the book-entry system of the Federal Reserve system.

—*T. Jason Soderstrum*

References

U.S. House of Representatives. *Farmer Mac Reform Act of 1995.* Washington, DC: U.S. Government Printing Office, 1996.

See also Volume 1: Federal Agricultural Mortgage Corporation (Farmer Mac).

FDA

See Food and Drug Administration.

FDIC

See Federal Deposit Insurance Corporation.

Federal Agricultural Improvement and Reform Act of 1996 (FAIR Act of 1996)

Legislation that scaled back government-subsidized agricultural production and gave farmers more flexibility in relying on market forces to decide the type and amount of crops they produced.

Congress passed the Federal Agricultural Improvement and Reform (FAIR) Act of 1996 during a period of economic prosperity in the United States and reflected a desire to significantly lower the influence of government agricultural assistance programs. The FAIR Act discontinued payments to farmers based on differences between target and market prices and put an end to production-adjustment programs. The act established a schedule of declining payments given to farmers heavily dependent on government aid, which aided them in making a gradual transition toward relying on market forces instead of government programs to determine the extent and types of crops they produced.

Other important provisions of the act addressed conservation and rural development. Congress promoted more environmentally responsible farming not only by limiting government-subsidized production but also by increasing funds for U.S. Department of Agriculture conservation programs. The FAIR Act of 1996 also created the Rural Performance Partnership Initiative to provide states more flexibility in how they use federal agricultural aid money, and it allocated $300 million for rural development and agricultural research. The act cut back or simplified many complex federal government agricultural programs. However, many in Democratic and liberal circles criticized the bill for not being able to provide enough financial security to U.S. farmers in tougher economic times. In addition, Congress omitted from the final legislation more effective conservation measures, such as paying farmers directly for environmentally responsible farming practices.

—*Jonah Katz*

References

Clinton, William J. "Statement on Signing the Federal Agricultural Improvement and Reform Act of 1996." *Weekly Compilation of Presidential Documents* 32, no. 14 (1996): 614.

Smith, Katherine R. "Congress Again Considers 'Green' Payments to Farmers." *Issues in Science and Technology,* vol. 17, no. 3 (2001): 26.

See also Volume 1: Clinton, William Jefferson.

Federal Agricultural Mortgage Corporation (Farmer Mac)

Federally chartered secondary market for agricultural and rural housing mortgages, owned and capitalized privately, formed to attract financing for agricultural real estate and to provide liquidity to rural lenders.

The formation of the Federal Agricultural Mortgage Corporation (Farmer Mac) came about after the growing crisis occurring within the Farm Credit System through the 1980s, when increased land and interest prices were combined with lower agricultural prices. A secondary market for farm mortgage loans proved necessary to help ease the burden of the Farm Credit System by offering opportunities for commercial banks and insurance companies to buy high-quality agricultural and rural housing mortgages. Congress formed Farmer Mac through the Agricultural Credit Act of 1987 and modeled it after other federal mortgage programs such as the Federal National Mortgage Corporation (Fannie Mae) and the Federal Home Loan Mortgage Corporation (Freddie Mac). As an agricultural government-sponsored enterprise (GSE), Farmer Mac was granted specialized lending powers by Congress and allowed access to a credit line of more than $1 billion from the U.S. Treasury under certain conditions. Farmer Mac's share of the secondary market remained small after its inception, mainly because of regulatory constraints placed on it to use as little taxpayer money as possible for its activities. Farmer Mac was also criticized for only helping large-scale, financially healthy farmers. In 1990, it was authorized to form an additional market for farm and rural development loans guaranteed by the U.S. Department of Agriculture (USDA). This market, known as Farmer Mac II, tended to aid farmers who were more financially strapped. Dealing with the regulatory constraints blamed for Farmer Mac's tiny share of the secondary loan market, the Farm Credit System Reform Act of 1996 made major changes to Farmer Mac, establishing its current operating structure in order to attract more investors.

—*Jonah Katz*

References

Feldman, Ron. "Changes in Farmer Mac's Charter." *Choices: The Magazine of Food, Farm, and Resource Issues.* vol. 11, no. 3 (1996): 8–12.

U.S. Department of Agriculture Economic Research Service. "Lenders and Financial Markets: Farmer Mac." 2001. Available: http://www.ers.usda.gov/briefing/FinancialMarkets/LendersFarmerMac.htm; accessed January 18, 2002.

See also Volume 1: Farm Credit System Reform Act of 1996.

Federal Deposit Insurance Corporation (FDIC)

Independent agency of the federal government established in 1933 to restore and maintain confidence in the nation's banking system by insuring bank deposits.

Support for federal deposit insurance coalesced during the early 1930s when many banks failed, creating a liquidity crisis (a shortage of available funds) for thousands of communities throughout the United States. In an effort to reverse the economic hardships caused by these bank failures and to restore public confidence in the nation's financial institutions, Congress included the creation of the Federal Deposit Insurance Corporation (FDIC) as a key provision of the Glass-Steagall Banking Act of 1933.

Under a plan established by the Glass-Steagall Banking Act, the Temporary Federal Deposit Insurance Fund began insuring deposited funds on January 1, 1934, up to a maximum of $2,500 per depositor, with insurance protection increased to $5,000 on July 1, 1934 for most deposits. The positive effects on the battered banking system became immediately apparent: Only 9 insured banks failed in 1934, compared with more than 9,000 in the preceding four years, and total bank deposits increased by over 20 percent as people regained confidence in banking institutions.

In accordance with the recommendations of the FDIC, Congress passed the Banking Act of 1935 to finalize the terms of the permanent insurance plan. From 1934 though 1941, the FDIC handled 370 bank failures, with total insurance losses totaling nearly $23 million. Banking expanded during World War II, and the number of bank failures remained low during the 1950s and 1960s.

Increased fluctuation in the value of U.S. currency and interest rates and a higher threshold for risk in the banking industry during the 1970s and 1980s resulted in an increased number of bank failures. The greatest crisis of the modern era involved the savings and loan (S&L) associations, also known as thrifts, which were originally excluded from the FDIC system. The Federal Savings and Loan Insurance Corporation (FSLIC) had covered these institutions, but the failure of several thrifts in the late 1980s because of inflated loan values prompted Congress to grant the FDIC authority to regulate investments in savings and loan associations under the Financial Institutions Reform, Recovery, and Enforcement Act of 1989. These actions stemmed the tide of thrift failures and reassured S&L investors in the same way that FDIC insurance had reassured bank customers during the Great Depression.

Coverage limits increased during the life of the fund and kept pace with inflation. The individual insured amount rose from $5,000 to $10,000 in 1950, to $20,000 in 1969, and to $40,000 in 1974. In 1980 Congress raised the coverage limit to $100,000 over the objections of the FDIC. In 2002, Congress again considered raising the coverage threshold and also contemplated formally indexing the coverage level to inflation.

Some critics charged that the system of federal deposit insurance undermines the workings of the free market by creating a federal subsidy for poorly managed or inefficient banks. Despite these concerns, the FDIC system enjoyed widespread support from both the public and members of the business community.

—*Christopher A. Preble*

References

Federal Deposit Insurance Corporation (FDIC). *A Brief History of Deposit Insurance in the United States.* Washington, DC: FDIC, 1998.

See also Volume 1: Great Depression; New Deal.

Federal Emergency Management Agency (FEMA)

Federal agency established in 1979 responsible for emergency planning and for coordinating disaster relief efforts.

The origins of federal disaster relief can be traced to the Congressional Act of 1803, which provided financial aid to a New Hampshire town devastated by fire. In subsequent years, the federal government provided ad hoc legislative assistance to communities hit by hurricanes, floods, earthquakes, and other natural disasters.

Federal action widened in the 1930s, first when Congress granted authority to the Reconstruction Finance Corporation (an agency that provided assistance to banks and businesses) to provide loans to repair facilities damaged by natural disasters, and then when the Bureau of Public Roads and the Army Corps of Engineers assumed responsibility for repairing roads and bridges and for developing flood control projects.

Efforts to better coordinate federal relief efforts among executive agencies accelerated in the 1960s and 1970s in the wake of several major hurricanes and earthquakes in Alaska and California. By the late 1970s, more than 100 federal agencies participated in aspects of emergency planning and disaster relief.

Led by the National Governors Association, state and local officials appealed to President Jimmy Carter to centralize and consolidate federal disaster relief efforts. Prompted by these and other concerns, Carter issued an executive order in 1979 creating the Federal Emergency Management Agency (FEMA). FEMA absorbed the functions of many federal agencies responsible for dealing with natural disasters, such as fires, floods, and severe weather, and it also assumed responsibility for civil defense formerly held within the Defense Department's Defense Civil Preparedness Agency. The comprehensive nature of federal disaster planning continued into the twenty-first century, as FEMA planned to take a leading role in response to terrorist attacks such as those of September 11, 2001. FEMA is now part of the Department of Homeland Security, which was created after those attacks.

—*Christopher A. Preble*

References

FEMA: The Federal Emergency Management Agency. Washington, DC: FEMA, 2001.

See also Volume 1: New Deal.

Federal Emergency Relief Administration (FERA)

Government agency established to coordinate the relief effort during the early years of the Great Depression.

After his inauguration as president, Franklin D. Roosevelt initiated a shift in government involvement to end the Great Depression. He encouraged Congress to establish the Federal Emergency Relief Administration (FERA) in 1933. The agency, headed by Harry Hopkins, sought to provide relief for the unemployed masses through direct aid. After two years, the president and Hopkins agreed that a name change was necessary—that direct aid was not the most effective allocation of resources because it eliminated the motivation of workers, who wanted work rather than direct assistance. On May 6, 1935, Roosevelt issued an executive order renaming FERA, calling it instead the Works Progress Administration (WPA), and began providing jobs on public works projects instead of simply giving direct aid to unemployed people. The WPA became known as the Works Projects Administration on July 1, 1939.

FERA funds and the funds of its successor agencies were used for the white-collar and construction projects of the Civil Works Administration and the Civilian Conservation Corps as well as the WPA. During the Great Depression, the agency provided work for unemployed artists, writers, and teachers, as well as construction workers who helped build or repair airports, schools, playgrounds, bridges, and other infrastructure during the 1930s.

From 1935 on, Roosevelt focused on employment as a means of ending the Great Depression. The agency existed until 1943, when unemployment rates fell after the onset of World War II.

—*Cynthia Clark Northrup*

References

Carothers, Doris. *Chronology of the Federal Emergency Relief Administration, May 12, 1933, to December 31, 1935.* New York: Da Capo Press, 1971.

See also Volume 1: New Deal; Roosevelt, Franklin D.

Federal Highway Act of 1956

The act that funded the sprawling interstate highway system that crisscrosses the United States today.

The Federal Highway Act of 1956 authorized what was then the largest public construction project in U.S. history and ensured America's reputation as the most automobile-dependent society on earth. Even so, passage of the legislation involved intense political battles that dated back decades and became caught up in the cold war politics of the early 1950s.

Federal highway legislation before and during World War II recommended the construction of interstate highways but allocated no special federal funding. A 1952 highway act authorized $25 million in federal funds on a 50–50 matching basis with states. By the time President Dwight D. Eisenhower took office in 1956, more than 6,200 miles of interstate highway had been constructed. Eisenhower's military experience had made him a champion of modern highways. In 1919 he served in the U.S. Army's first transcontinental motor convoy, and as a World War II general he was impressed by Germany's autobahns. But several political issues stood in the way of easy congressional approval: whether the highways would be sited according to population, distance, or land area; the formula for state/federal cost sharing; whether construction would be financed mainly or exclusively by bonds or tolls; and wage rates for highway construction workers. Several competing bills were introduced and debated. Democratic Representative George H. Fallon of Maryland gained strong support for his plan by calling it a "National System of Interstate and Defense Highways," thereby linking it with cold war concerns about national security.

The final version of the bill was approved by the House and Senate June 26, 1956, and signed into law by Eisenhower three days later. It allocated more than $30 billion for construction of 41,000 miles of interstate highways with uniform design standards, limited access, and no highway or railroad crossings. The Highway Act was the first federal aid project to adhere to local wage standards as stipulated by the Davis Bacon Act of 1931, thus resolving the debate about construction wage rates.

The highway network profoundly influenced the American economy, society, and culture. Construction began almost immediately, employing tens of thousands of workers and consuming billions of tons of concrete and asphalt. Interstate trucking surged as the nation's fleet of long-haul trucks converted from gasoline to diesel engines and further eclipsed railroads in domestic freight shipping. The interstate highways also fostered the spread of American roadside culture—new franchise fast-food restaurants, hotels, and amusement parks sprang up at highway exits and interchanges to serve the millions of Americans who toured the country each year by automobile. By the 1960s, an estimated one in seven Americans was directly or indirectly employed in the automobile industry. Many historians consider the highway program President Eisenhower's most important legacy. Unlike President Franklin D. Roosevelt's similar but less ambitious public works projects, the highway program, once enacted into law, generated little political controversy. Along with roads, canals, railroads, shipping ports, and airports, the interstate highway system stands as a major component of the nation's transportation infrastructure.

—*David B. Sicilia*

References
Rose, Mark H. *Interstate Express Highway Politics 1941–1989.* Knoxville: University of Tennessee Press, 1990.
Seely, Bruce E. *Building the American Highway System: Engineers as Policy Makers.* Philadelphia: Temple University Press, 1987.
Weingroff, Richard F. "Federal-Aid Highway Act of 1956: Creating the Interstate System." U.S. Department of Transportation, Federal Highway Administration. April 28, 2003. Available: http://www.fhwa.dot.gov/infrastructure/rw96e.htm; accessed April 28, 2003.
See also Volume 2: Transportation Policy.

Federal National Mortgage Association (Fannie Mae)

Government-sponsored enterprise created to increase the supply of money available to lend to homebuyers.

Congress created the Federal National Mortgage Association, or Fannie Mae, in 1938 as a subsidiary of the Reconstruction Finance Corporation, which provided funds for banks and businesses. Fannie Mae initially focused on the purchase of long-term mortgages insured by the Federal Housing Authority. Fannie Mae does not lend money directly to homebuyers; the corporation buys mortgages from banks in order to increase the lending capacity of the banks.

After World War II, the corporation's mission expanded to include developing a secondary market for mortgages guaranteed by the Veterans Administration. Fannie Mae received a charter from Congress in 1948 that regularized its position as a government corporation. The Federal National Mortgage Association Charter Act of 1954 started the process through which the corporation became more reliant on private capital than funds from the federal Treasury. In 1968, Congress amended the 1954 law to make Fannie Mae a government-sponsored enterprise—a private company with stockholders and some government connections and protections.

Mortgage lenders have opposed the activities of Fannie Mae since World War II. They argue that the corporation has an unfair advantage because of its ties to the federal government. It does not have to register with the Securities and Exchange Commission like other publicly traded companies. In addition, Fannie Mae does not have to pay state and local corporate income taxes. The federal government also is willing to assist Fannie Mae in case of financial difficulty. In 2001, Representative Richard Baker, a Republican from Louisiana, introduced a bill that would restrict Fannie Mae's activities and place the corporation under the regulation of the Federal Reserve. Some critics argued for the privatization of the corporation and the severing of its lines of credit with the federal government. Baker's bill failed to pass.

—*John David Rausch Jr.*

References
Kosterlit, Julie. "Siblings Fat and Sassy." *National Journal,* May 13, 2000.
See also Volume 1: Federal Reserve Act; Securities and Exchange Commission.

Federal Reserve Act (Owen-Glass Act) of 1913

Financial system intended to "furnish an elastic currency [and] ... to establish a more effective supervision of banking."

The Aldrich-Vreeland Emergency Currency Act of 1908 created the National Monetary Commission to recommend reforms for the nation's banking system. In 1911 the commission, with Republican Senator Nelson Aldrich of Rhode Island as chair, issued a 49-volume report that called for the creation of a National Reserve Association run by private bankers and free of any real government control. The proposal never passed, and in 1912 the Democrats won control of the presidency and Congress. After his inauguration in 1913, President Woodrow Wilson called for extensive banking reforms. After a six-month debate, Congress passed the Owen-Glass Act on December 23, 1913, creating the Federal Reserve system. This system consisted of 12 regional banks coordinated by a central Federal Reserve Board. The act required all national banks to become members of the system, and state-chartered banks that met membership requirements could join. The act also required member banks to transfer a percentage of their capital for stock in the Federal Reserve system that holds members' deposits, creates new credit with additional reserves, and makes loans. After mid-1917, the Federal Reserve Bank required member banks to keep all of their reserves in their Federal Reserve district banks. The Federal Reserve raises and lowers the interest percentage that member banks must pay the Federal Reserve to borrow money, thus exercising great influence on the availability of credit for private borrowers.

The seven-member Federal Reserve Board assumed office in August 1914, and the Federal Reserve banks started to provide service three months later. By 1923 the Federal Reserve system controlled 70 percent of the banking resources in the United States. In 1933 and 1935 Congress passed acts that increased the Federal Reserve's power to control credit. In 1963 Congress amended the Federal Reserve Act to permit the Federal Reserve to increase the amount of money in circulation by issuing Federal Reserve notes instead of silver certificates. As a result, nearly all U.S. paper currency now consists of Federal Reserve notes backed by neither gold nor silver.

—*Steven E. Siry*

References
Moore, Carl H. *The Federal Reserve System: A History of the First 75 Years.* Jefferson, NC: McFarland, 1990.
See also Volume 1: Banking System; Volume 2 (Documents): Federal Reserve Act.

Federal Trade Commission Act (September 1914)

Act creating the Federal Trade Commission (FTC), which had the power to control monopolistic practices by corporations.

The introduction of the Clayton Bill in 1914 provided enforcement for the Sherman Anti-Trust Act regarding monopolies. The introduction of the Clayton Bill ended the "new freedom" phase of antitrust legislation (which had emphasized individualism and states' rights) during the presidency of Woodrow Wilson. Soon Wilson had major doubts that the Clayton Bill would provide an effective solution to unfair business competition and monopolies. Relying on advice from Boston lawyer Louis D. Brandeis, Wilson supported a Federal Trade Commission bill that embraced Theodore Roosevelt's "new nationalism" idea of a powerful commission to regulate business. The passage of the Federal Trade Commission Act served to kill monopolies at their

source. The president appointed the five members of the commission to seven-year terms with the Senate's approval. The act authorized the commission, which replaced the Bureau of Corporations, to use investigations and cease-and-desist orders to prevent people, partnerships, or corporations other than banks and common carriers from using unfair business practices. Banks and common carriers remained exempt because they were supervised by the Federal Reserve Board and Interstate Commerce Commission, respectively. Initially, however, the Federal Trade Commission suffered from poor leadership and Supreme Court rulings. Indeed, the Supreme Court would stay cease-and-desist orders because it did not accept the commission's facts, and in 1921 the Court ruled that the federal courts, not the commission, should define unfair competition. Nevertheless, many Americans often praise the Federal Trade Commission for improving business ethics and curtailing price fixing and false advertising.

—*Steven E. Siry*

References
Clements, Kendrick A. *The Presidency of Woodrow Wilson.* Lawrence: University Press of Kansas, 1992.
See also Volume 1: Wilson, Woodrow.

Federal Trade Commission (FTC) (1916)

Government agency charged with oversight of antitrust and consumer protection legislation passed by Congress.

Established in 1916 under the administration of President Woodrow Wilson, the Federal Trade Commission (FTC) is another example of the continuing emphasis that progressives placed on the dissolution of trusts and monopolies. The FTC assumed the role of the former Bureau of Corporations but with expanded powers that allowed it to examine all corporate records and to grant cease-and-desist orders. The commission consists of five members who are appointed for seven-year terms. Once a commissioner is appointed and confirmed, the president cannot remove him or her from office. To ensure that the FTC fulfills its functions, Congress appropriates its funds on a yearly basis.

The FTC scrutinizes the nation's corporations for antitrust activity through the examination of records, and it monitors mergers to provide the formation of future trusts. The FTC also examines trade practices to ensure that business is conducted without any unfair or deceptive tactics. If businesses threaten to adversely affect the consumer, the commission intervenes. Members also consult with the executive branch, Congress, and regulatory agencies.

—*Cynthia Clark Northrup*

References
Stone, Alan. *Economic Regulation and the Public Interest: The Federal Trade Commission in Theory and Practice.* Ithaca, NY: Cornell University Press, 1977.
Stuart, Pamela B. *The Federal Trade Commission.* New York: Chelsea House, 1991.
See also Volume 1: Antitrust Suits; Trusts; Wilson, Woodrow; Volume 2 (Documents): Federal Trade Commission.

Federalist Papers (1787–1788)

Series of essays by Alexander Hamilton, James Madison, and John Jay defending the Constitution.

Once the delegates to the Constitutional Convention in Philadelphia formally adopted the Constitution in September 1787, the battle over ratification began in earnest. The nation soon divided into two groups: the Federalists, who supported the Constitution, and the Anti-Federalists, who opposed it. The greatest battlegrounds between the two camps were in New York, Virginia, Massachusetts, and Pennsylvania. Some of the bitterest opposition to the Constitution could be found in New York. Like the other large states, New York had become a power in its own right under the Articles of Confederation. The state had grown rich by imposing tariffs on goods imported from other states and foreign nations.

Alexander Hamilton, a delegate to the Constitutional Convention from New York, decided that a newspaper campaign could persuade his fellow New Yorkers to support the Constitution. He enlisted John Jay of New York and James Madison of Virginia, both delegates to the convention, to help him write a series of essays defending the Constitution. Jay wrote only a handful of the 85 articles, and Hamilton and Madison wrote the vast majority. These essays ran several times a week in four out of the five New York newspapers throughout the spring of 1788. Collectively they became known as *The Federalist Papers*. Although the articles themselves had little direct effect on the ratification of the Constitution, they remain to this day the single greatest defense ever written of the Constitution and the government it brought to life.

The essays were constructed into two sections. The first half attacked the weak national government created under the Articles of Confederation. Hamilton and Madison reminded their readers that this weak government had led to the Constitutional Convention in Philadelphia. The Congress under the Articles of Confederation had few powers, whereas the individual states retained full sovereignty in almost every important political matter. The greatest flaw in the Articles of Confederation remained the inability of the Congress to lay (assess) taxes. This restriction meant that the national government could not raise an army or navy and thus could not provide for the common defense. Equally important, the Congress had little control over domestic or foreign trade, because each state could set its own policies. If this weak government continued, the essays theorized, the United States would soon be on the brink of foreign invasion, domestic unrest, and financial ruin.

In the second half of the essays, Hamilton and Madison emphasized the strengths of the new government formed under the Constitution. Both men stated that experienced and competent men had written the Constitution in a spirit of compromise. The new government they had created would provide the nation with the best form of republican government possible while preventing the worst abuses of uncontrolled democracy. They lauded the separation of powers into the legislative, executive, and judicial branches. Hamilton especially emphasized the fact that the bicameral national legislature would provide the checks and balances necessary for a stable government. The second half of *The Federalist Papers* profoundly influenced later interpreters of the Constitution, especially Chief Justice John Marshall during his Court tenure from 1801 through 1835.

—*Mary Stockwell*

References

Hamilton, Alexander, James Madison, and John Jay. *The Federalist Papers*. New York: Bantam Books, 1987.

See also Volume 1: Articles of Confederation; Constitution; Hamilton, Alexander.

FEMA

See Federal Emergency Management Agency.

FERA

See Federal Emergency Relief Administration.

Fletcher v. Peck (1810)

Supreme Court case leading to the custom of making states' laws subject to federal judicial review.

In 1795, the Georgia state legislature voted to sell 35 million acres in the Yazoo district in present-day Alabama and Mississippi to four land companies for 1.5 cents per acre. The land companies had bribed every member of the Georgia legislature, along with several senators and judges. After angry voters turned out the legislature in 1796, the newly elected representatives rescinded the original grant of land to the four companies. All subsequent sales made by the land companies were therefore nullified. Robert Fletcher had purchased land in the Yazoo district from John Peck and now sued in the hope that the Supreme Court would overturn Georgia's decision to rescind the original grant of land to the corrupt Yazoo land companies.

Chief Justice John Marshall ruled for the Supreme Court in favor of Robert Fletcher in a 4-to-1 decision. Although Marshall admitted that bribery had influenced the first vote on the Yazoo land grant, he argued that this could not be an issue for the Court when determining the constitutionality of Georgia's decision to rescind the original sale and nullify all subsequent sales. Marshall found that the state of Georgia had clearly violated the contract clause of the Constitution, which states in Article I, Section 10, that no state may pass laws "impairing the Obligation of Contracts." Along with upholding the vested rights of contracts, the chief justice also held in this decision that the Supreme Court had the right to rule on the constitutionality of all state laws. In fact, this case became the first time that the Supreme Court had declared a state law unconstitutional. Marshall's decision thus strengthened the power of the nation over the states by reminding them that they were not sovereign but were instead part of a union that existed under the rule of the Constitution.

—*Mary Stockwell*

References
Siegel, Adrienne. *The Marshall Court, 1801–1835*. Millwood, NY: Associated Faculty Press, 1987.
See also Volume 2: Judiciary.

Flex Acres

Key component of the 1990 and 1995 Farm Bills aimed at reducing government expenditures on agriculture by allowing farmers greater flexibility in production.

Federal expenditures on agriculture ballooned in the mid-1980s as exports and market prices declined across almost every agricultural commodity. The Food, Agriculture, Conservation, and Trade Act of 1990 (Farm Bill) sought to improve U.S. competitiveness in the international agricultural market while trimming the budget by giving farmers greater flexibility in their production decisions. The 1990 Farm Bill gave farmers greater freedom by allowing them to plant any crop on up to 25 percent of their base acres (land enrolled in commodity programs of the U.S. Department of Agriculture [USDA]). Farmers could then respond to the market by planting their designated crop, receiving deficiency payments if the market price fell lower than the government's target price, or planting a more profitable crop and thus forfeiting the government payments for that acreage. Previously farmers held rigidly to the historically determined commodity of their base acres. If they planted another crop, they permanently lost that amount of base acreage and thus government support. The Omnibus Budget Reconciliation Act of 1990 (Budget Act) followed the 1990 Farm Bill by cutting income support payments on 15 percent of base acres, regardless of whether the designated crops were planted. The 1990 Farm Bill and Budget Act thus jointly established the policy known as "flex acres." Proponents claim that flex acres reduce government costs, promote efficiency and crop rotation practices, and may increase farm income. Critics charge that flex acres hurt small and medium farms that lose a substantial portion of their income in the form of deficiency payments, whereas large farms have enough production to both farm flex acres and receive their maximum allotment of deficiency payments.

—*W. Chad Futrell*

References
Food, Agriculture, Conservation, and Trade Act of 1990. U.S. Statutes at Large 104 (1990): 1388.
See also Volumes 1, 2: Agricultural Policy.

Floating Exchange Rates

System of monetary exchange between countries.

The exchange rate is the rate charged for the changing of one currency for another one. Floating exchange rates vary depending on the market value of the currency on a daily basis instead of remaining at a fixed rate. Economist Milton Friedman constructed the classic case in favor of a system of floating exchange rates shortly after the establishment of the Bretton Woods system to stablilize the international movement of money in 1944. Friedman argued that the presence of flexible, or floating, exchange rates encourages multilateral trade and that such economic mechanisms would permanently solve the balance of payments problem created by the lack of a global standard currency value system, allowing rates to fluctuate wildly. He argued that laissez-faire government policies, in which the government only minimally regulated business, provided the best solution.

The supporters of the Bretton Woods system tended to deny that a floating exchange rate regime offered the best alternative to their system. In the Bretton Woods agreement, Robert Roosa argued that the alternative to Bretton Woods guaranteed "the anarchy of an entire world on flexible exchange rates, or (and this would be the more probable) the protectionism and economic autarchy of the sort of currency blocs that prevailed in the 1930s," an experience that was "all too searing still in our memories to forget." Roosa regarded the Bretton Woods system of fixed exchange rates as the peace treaty or "armed truce" that prevented a return to the anarchy of the 1930s. Countries could use flexible exchange rates as either a defensive barrier or as an aggressive instrument of economic warfare. The choice was not between fixed or floating but between stable or unstable rates. Indeed, Roosa denied that a market in foreign exchange would actually exist without fixed exchange rates. He predicted that large banks would create an undesirable situation for foreign exchange traders.

In early 1973, the crisis-prone par value system, which fixed the U.S. dollar value as $32 per ounce of gold, collapsed and was replaced by a generalized float of the major currencies. President Richard Nixon reflected that Friedman's solution of floating exchange rates provided an attractive solution. But subsequent events revealed that neither position proved entirely correct. During the 13 years of fixed exchange rates from 1960 to 1972 (the Bretton Woods system), the seven leading industrial countries experienced real growth rates at double the rate of the 1973–1990 period (floating exchange rate system), and as growth rates fell by 50 percent, inflation and unemployment more than doubled. Moreover, the post-1973 period also exhibited larger and more persistent inflation differentials than under the Bretton Woods system. But after the collapse of fixed exchange rates, governments failed to prevent jobs from being transferred to less-developed countries where labor received lower wages. Instead, the adoption of domestic monetarism (the reduction or expansion of the money supply to control inflation) led to soaring interest rates and, in effect, to competitive currency appreciations. At the beginning of the twenty-first century, questions relating to optimal currency areas (an area that uses one currency—for example, the European Union) and, at a practical level, to the nature of a future international monetary system potentially dominated by just a handful of major currencies (for example, the U.S. dollar, Eurodollar, German mark, and Japanese yen) have superseded the debate between floating and fixed currency exchange rates.

—*Robert Leeson*

References

Aldcroft, D. H., and M. J. Oliver. *Exchange Rate Regimes in the Twentieth Century.* Cheltenham, England: Edward Elgar, 1998.

Alogoskoufis, G. "Monetary Accommodation, Exchange Rate Regimes, and Inflation Persistence." *Economic Journal,* vol. 102 (May 1992): 461–480.

Bordo, M. D., and L. Jonung. *Monetary Regimes, Inflation, and Monetary Reform.* Stockholm: Stockholm School of Economics Reprint Series, no. 156, 1996.

Friedman, Milton. *Essays in Positive Economics.* Chicago: University of Chicago Press, 1953.

———. *Capitalism and Freedom.* Chicago: University of Chicago Press, 1962.

Friedman, Milton, and R. V. Roosa. *The Balance of Payments: Free versus Fixed Exchange Rates.* Washington, DC: American Enterprise Institute for Public Policy Research, 1967.

Nixon, R. M. *The Dollar and World Liquidity.* New York: Random House, 1967.

———. *The Real War.* New York: Warner, 1980.

Volcker, P., and T. Gyohten. *Changing Fortunes: The World's Money and the Threat to American Leadership.* New York: Times Books, 1992.

See also Volumes 1, 2: Monetary Policy.

FMD

See Foot and Mouth Disease.

Food and Drug Administration (FDA)

Agency of the executive branch that conducts research on the safety of and oversees the federal laws regarding the manufacture, transportation, and sale of food, drugs, and cosmetics.

Part of the Department of Health and Human Services, the Food and Drug Administration (FDA) regulates the supply of drugs and ensures the safety of manufactured and processed foods. The agency tests food for pesticide residues and harmful chemicals. Researchers also investigate medicated feed for livestock, the blood supply, and drugs. The agency ensures the safety of medical devices, insulin, and vaccines. Each must gain agency approval before being allowed on the market. Cosmetics and dyes undergo a rigorous testing process to prevent the possibility of adverse reactions among the American public.

In 2002 the FDA was operating with about 9,000 employees and was regulating roughly $1 trillion a year worth of products—or 25 percent of the nation's economy—at an annual cost to the taxpayer of about $3 per person. From district and local offices in 157 U.S. cities, 1,000 inspectors and investigators oversee 95,000 businesses and visit more than 15,000 facilities. In Washington, D.C., 2,100 FDA scientists, including 900 chemists and microbiologists, work in 40 laboratories to check approximately 80,000 products a year. If a company violates FDA rules, the agency can take the company to court, force it to stop selling the product, and charge it with criminal penalties. The FDA finds nearly 3,000 products a year detrimental to public safety, and most manufactures and distributors voluntarily withdraw the products from market. With one-quarter of the nation's economy under its jurisdiction, the FDA has a profound economic influence in the United States.

—*T. Jason Soderstrum*

References

Patrick, William. *The Food and Drug Administration.* New York: Chelsea House, 1988.

See also Volume 1: U.S. Department of Health and Human Services.

Foot and Mouth Disease (FMD)

A highly communicable viral disease of cattle, swine, sheep, goats, and deer that has caused great economic damage to agricultural and livestock operations throughout the world.

Foot and mouth disease (FMD) occurs in hooved animals and is characterized by blisterlike lesions around their mouths and hooves, which cause slobbering and lameness. Most adult animals recover but are left severely debilitated; having had the virus reduces their ability to produce milk and high-quality meat and leaves them commercially worthless. People who have had contact with infected animals or animal products can spread the disease through their equipment and clothing, and some studies have even shown that the virus can drift up to 40 miles on the wind. To contain the disease, exposed animals are typically destroyed; livestock markets and dairies are closed; premises and equipment are disinfected; and the transportation of livestock and livestock products is halted. A vaccine is also available.

One of the largest outbreaks of FMD in the United States occurred in California in early 1924. By the time the outbreak was eradicated in the summer of 1925, 17 California counties had been quarantined and more than 100,000 domestic animals destroyed. Moreover, 36 states, the territory of Hawaii, and several foreign countries placed embargoes against Californian goods. Ultimately, eradicating the outbreak cost the federal and state governments more than $6 million, not including the indirect losses to Californian businesses.

FMD has not occurred in the United States since 1929. However, when the disease broke out in Mexico in 1946, many people feared it might cross the border and infect American livestock. Thus, America and Mexico created a joint commission that eliminated the outbreak in 1951. FMD is currently widespread in Africa, Asia, South America, and Europe. In places where the disease is rare, tough import restrictions, mandatory quarantines, and effective inspection of livestock have prevented the disease from spreading.

—*David W. Waltrop*

References

Fox, Kel M. "Aftosa: The Campaign against Foot-and-Mouth Disease in Mexico, 1946-1951." *Journal of Arizona History,* vol. 38, no.1 (1997): 23–40.

Spear, Donald P. "California Besieged: The Foot-and-Mouth Epidemic of 1924." *Agricultural History,* vol. 56 (July 1982): 528–541.

See also Volumes 1, 2: Agricultural Policy.

Force Act (1833)

Act passed by Congress in 1833 authorizing President Andrew Jackson to use military force to override South Carolina's Ordinance of Nullification.

On November 24, 1832, South Carolina passed the Ordinance of Nullification to stop the enforcement of the Tariff of 1828 within its borders. This tariff, which placed a 41 percent tax on imports in the middle of a national economic depression, severely hurt the South. John Calhoun of South Carolina claimed that it amounted to the federal government taking one-third of the South's cotton crop in federal taxes, only for the benefit of Northern factory owners. This argument was based on the fact that the South depended on the sale of cotton to English textile mills since the Northern factories could not process all the cotton. In return, the South imported British manufactured goods but had to pay high tariff rates. When Congress only slightly modified the import duties in the Tariff of 1832, South Carolina took action and nullified the tariff.

President Jackson responded swiftly and decisively. First, on December 10, 1832, he issued a "Proclamation to the People of South Carolina" in which he denounced nullification as a threat to the Union and emphasized that the Constitution formed a government of the people, not a league of states. This Union remained perpetual, Jackson asserted; no state had the right to secede, and "disunion by armed force was treason." He ordered General Winfield Scott to go to Charleston and take command of the federal troops in the state and dispatched a navy warship and seven revenue cutters (government customs ships) to take up a position in the harbor. He then requested Congress for further authority to proceed with the collection of the tariff. Congress responded with the Force Bill—called the "Bloody Bill" in South Carolina—which the House Judiciary Committee sent to the Senate on January 21, 1833. The bill authorized the president to use the army and the navy to force South Carolina to pay the tariff if court action to achieve compliance failed.

But Jackson eagerly sought a compromise, because he and others in the administration believed that the entire South would stand against the Force Bill unless Congress enacted a tariff acceptable to South Carolina. Accordingly, when the Ways and Means Committee of the House reported out a compromise tariff on January 8 that reduced the tariff by 50 percent in one year, it received the support of a number of Jacksonian Democrats. But in the Senate, Henry Clay offered his own version of a compromise tariff, less dramatic that the House version. Introduced on February 12, 1833, it would have gradual reductions of the 1832 tariff at two-year intervals up to 1842 until all duties reached 20 percent. Despite some opposition in the House, where Democrats claimed that the Senate could not initiate a revenue bill because that remained the House's constitutional prerogative, the bill passed the House on February 26, 1833, by a vote of 119 to 85, and on March 1 the Senate approved the measure by a vote of 29 to 16. The next day Jackson signed both the compromise tariff and the Force Bill. South Carolina immediately accepted the tariff and repealed its Ordinance of Nullification. Then the South Carolina legislature promptly nullified the Force Bill, and the Force Act was never used by Jackson against South Carolina.

—*Robert P. Sutton*

References

Coit, Margaret L. *John C. Calhoun: American Portrait.* Boston: Houghton Mifflin, 1950.

Peterson, Merrill D. *Olive Branch and Sword: The Compromise of 1833.* Baton Rouge: Louisiana State University Press, 1982.

Remini, Robert V. *Henry Clay: Statesman for the Union.* New York: W. W. Norton, 1991.

Van Deusen, Glyndon G. *The Jacksonian Era 1828–1848.* Prospect Heights, IL: Waveland Press, 1992.

See also Volume 1: Clay, Henry; Jackson, Andrew; Protective Tariffs; *South Carolina Exposition and Protest*; Tariff of Abominations.

Ford, Henry (1863–1947)

American industrialist who invented the moving assembly line.

Born in Dearborn, Michigan, to Irish immigrant parents on July 3, 1863, Henry Ford displayed a mechanical proclivity at an early age through the repair of machinery including watches. In 1879 Ford started working as an apprentice in a machine shop. After working his way up to chief engineer for the Detroit Edison Company, Ford founded his own automobile company with other investors including the Dodge brothers. Ford's success hinged on the invention of the moving assembly line, which allowed him to reduce the cost of the Model T from $850 to $290. The reduction in price coincided with an increase in demand. In 1915 the Ford Motor Company sold one million automobiles. At this point Ford decided to increase the wages and decrease the hours of his workers so that they received $5 for an eight-hour workday. By paying higher wages than other employers, Ford ensured that he would attract reliable workers who could then purchase his product. The affordability of the automobile ushered in a new era in transportation. By the 1920s the industry had given rise to ancillary industries such as glassmakers, roadside restaurants, motels, and tire stores.

During World War I, Ford—a proponent of peace for political reasons and because war interfered with international trade—funded a peace mission to Europe that ultimately failed. After the United States entered the conflict, Ford's factories produced many of the war vehicles used, such as tanks, jeeps, and ambulances. In 1918 Ford ran for the U.S. Senate but lost. During the remainder of his life he devoted a large portion of his wealth to the Ford Foundation and also funded the establishment of Greenfield Village, a historical replica of his workshop in Dearborn, Michigan. Ford died on April 7, 1947.

—*Cynthia Clark Northrup*

References

Simonds, William Adams. *Henry Ford: His Life, His Work, His Genius.* New York: Bobbs-Merrill, 1943.

See also Volume 1: Automobile; Volume 2: Transportation Policy.

Fordney-McCumber Tariff (1922)

Tariff system created in 1922 to protect American products from foreign competition.

In response to the recession at the close of World War I, the administration of President Warren G. Harding sought increased tariff protection as part of a stimulus package to lower unemployment and reduce the number of bankruptcies. The Fordney-McCumber Tariff abandoned the pattern of reform set by the Democrats in the Underwood-Simmons Tariff—a tariff passed in 1913 that provided the first deep cuts in the tariff since the Civil War—and gave American products protection from foreign competition.

Conservative Republicans in Congress advocated a return to higher protection. Republican members of the Farm Bloc, who argued that tariff protection would bolster high prices for manufactured goods and favor urban businesspeople over workers and farmers, initially opposed an increase in duties. Fearing a divide between rural and urban constituencies, the Republican leadership in Congress offered substantial protection to agricultural goods.

This effort to placate rural concerns with a protective barrier for agricultural goods succeeded because of a shift in the balance of trade. After World War I, the American farmer faced substantial foreign competition for the first time. In an effort to protect key sectors of the agricultural economy, such as wheat, most Republicans from rural constituencies abandoned their reservations concerning tariff protection and supported passage.

The Fordney-McCumber Tariff protected established industries at about the same level as the earlier Payne-Aldrich Tariff (1909). In addition, it constructed substantial barriers against imported agricultural products and emerging industries, such as chemical dyestuffs. Its proponents pointed to the provisions for flexibility that allowed the president to raise or lower barriers on specified products as a response to changing patterns in international trade. Nonetheless, the Fordney-McCumber Tariff quickly became characterized as a conservative document that reversed the direction of progressive tariff reform.

—*Karen A. J. Miller*

References

Parrini, Carl P. *Heir to Empire: United States Economic Diplomacy, 1916–1923.* Pittsburgh, PA: University of Pittsburgh Press, 1969.

See also Volume 1: Agricultural Policy; World War I; Volume 2: Agricultural Policy.

Foreign Policy

American diplomatic relations with foreign powers traditionally stressing security, neutral rights, commercial reciprocity, and expansion of markets.

After gaining independence, the United States sought an end to the mercantile system, in which the colonies supplied raw materials for the mother country and operated for its benefit. Freed of British colonial restraints, foreign ships were able to enter U.S. ports freely, and the United States attempted to develop extensive trade that was as free as possible throughout the world. American merchants placed more focus on trade with the Spanish colonies in the Americas, and Asian trade grew after the first American ship reached China in 1784. Even so, England remained the principal trading partner of the United States despite the recent war for independence.

Although continuing to trade with America, the British government no longer allowed the United States the privileges of membership in the British Empire. England imposed tariffs on the new nation and forbade American trade with the British West Indies. Under the Articles of Confederation, each state created its own customs and tariff schedules, so the government was unable to coordinate commercial policy. The fragmentation kept the United States from being able to negotiate favorable commercial treaties.

Economic relations proved frustrating, and one goal of the 1789 Constitution was to place commercial power in the hands of a centralized federal government. Once the people ratified the new Constitution, the U.S. government gained greater control of commercial relations. With centralized control, the government sought commercial expansion while repaying the national debt created during the revolution. Import tariffs and a tax on shipping initially made funding the debt possible, and to promote commerce, early navigation laws discriminated only mildly against foreign merchants.

The French Revolution and the following Napoleonic Wars quickly brought American foreign relations into a new phase. In 1793, England and France went war. The United States maintained neutrality and desired trade with each power. Both sides seized American cargoes and ships that they determined to be in violation of trade with the enemy, and the United States vigorously defended neutral commercial rights. Ultimately, the United States had more trouble with Britain. Merchant ships seized within sight of the American coast and the impressment of American sailors into the British navy finally proved to be too much, and the United States declared war on Britain, thereby beginning the War of 1812. The war ended in 1815, but the British did not acknowledge neutral rights in the peace settlement. However, the United States had proved its willingness to fight to protect its rights, and British depredations did not continue.

After the War of 1812, the United States focused on events in Latin American as the Spanish colonies began fighting for their independence in the early nineteenth century. Fearful that other European powers would move into Latin America, the United States warned against new European colonization in the Americas and, with the Monroe Doctrine in 1823, forbade European intervention in the Americas. The United States issued the doctrine to prevent other European powers from taking over portions of the Spanish empire, and the United States increased its trade and influence in Latin America as the Spanish lost control.

Continental expansion was another major focus of American foreign policy in the nineteenth century. In 1803, the United States acquired the vast Louisiana Purchase from France, doubling the size of the nation for $15 million, and the nation subsequently added Florida, Texas, Oregon,

California, and the American Southwest to its territory in the decades before the Civil War. The United States purchased and made diplomatic arrangements for as much territory as possible, but in order to seize California and the Southwest, the United States fought a war with Mexico in the 1840s.

Following the Civil War, the United States grew as a regional power and expanded its influence in the Caribbean and the Pacific. After the Spanish-American War in 1898, the United States became an imperial power and gained Puerto Rico, Guam, and the Philippines as colonies. The United States did not annex Cuba after the war, but American power on the island increased dramatically after Cuban independence from Spain. Completion of the Panama Canal boosted American interest in the Caribbean and increased American commerce in Latin America and Asia. The United States also grew more involved in Asian trade at the turn of the century and vigorously promoted equal commercial access, or an "open door," for American and European merchants in China.

After issuing the Monroe Doctrine, the United States remained fairly aloof from European affairs until World War I. The British blockade of Germany and German submarine attacks on merchant shipping caused the United States to once again stress neutral commercial rights. The United States entered World War I in April 1917 on the side of the Allies primarily in protest of German submarine tactics. American economic and mercantile support helped the Allies achieve victory in 1919, and the United States emerged from the war as one of the great military and industrial powers of the world. But President Woodrow Wilson failed in his attempt to create a lasting international organization designed to prevent future wars through diplomacy when Congress rejected U.S. participation in the League of Nations. Congress feared that this supranational organization would lead to a loss of U.S. sovereignty and would be unconstitutional, even though Wilson had proposed the organization and worked tirelessly to secure its passage. The League of Nations operated from 1920 to 1946 and became primarily a tool of British and French foreign policy, so failing to achieve its larger objective; it was replaced in 1945 by the United Nations, in which the United States did participate.

Many Americans had been disillusioned by the bloody conflict of World War I (called then the Great War), and the United States entered a period of isolationism in the 1920s and 1930s. Although it stayed aloof from conflicts, the United States remained heavily involved with international trade during this period. The 1934 Reciprocal Trade Agreements Act promoted a policy of free trade and open markets and de-emphasized protectionism with its tariff barriers designed to eliminate or restrict foreign competition in trade. Freer trade has remained a vision of the United States since that time.

The rise of Nazi Germany and Japanese militarism ended American isolationism, and with the December 7, 1941, attack on Pearl Harbor, the United States entered World War II. American industrial power grew rapidly during the war, and American industry ensured an Allied victory. By 1945, the United States had become the world's foremost industrial and military power, and the United States and the Soviet Union emerged from the conflict as superpowers unrivaled by any other nation.

World War II changed the direction of American life and foreign policy in several ways. The conflict destroyed isolationist sentiment in the United States, and Americans believed more than ever in a U.S. mission to help the world through economic, social, and political programs and to prevent the spread of communism that would have produced a negative effect on American trade. The United States took an active part in the newly created United Nations, and American funds given through the Marshall Plan helped to rebuild Europe. The United States also sponsored closer international ties and the elimination of tariffs through the General Agreement on Tariffs and Trade (GATT) in 1947.

Vigorous opposition to the Soviet Union emerged as the second major direction of American foreign policy after World War II, when Eastern Europe fell under the Soviet sphere of influence and former Allies—the USSR, the United States, France, and Great Britain—divided Germany. U.S.-Soviet relations rapidly declined after the war and, driven by a desire to stop the spread of communism around the world, the United States entered the cold war.

During the cold war, the United States formed several international alliances. None proved more important than the North Atlantic Treaty Organization (NATO), which linked the United States and the nations of Western Europe in 1949. Even as the United States made alliances, international communism was rapidly spreading, and communists claimed control of China in 1949. Fearful that communism would soon spread all over the globe, the United States moved to oppose communist expansion. This rigid anticommunist stance would bring the United States to war in Korea and Vietnam, and caused the nation to increase its foreign aid budget dramatically to bolster anticommunist nations in Asia, the Middle East, and Latin America.

One of the most significant foreign policy developments after World War II was increased American activity in the Middle East. During the war, the United States realized that its own oil reserves would be insufficient in the case of a future conflict. As a result, the United States cultivated a relationship with Saudi Arabia and opposed Soviet expansion into the rich Middle Eastern oilfields.

When it sponsored the creation of Israel in 1948, the United States became even more heavily involved in Middle Eastern affairs. The close American relationship with Israel created difficulty for the United States in the heavily Arab Middle East. Arab nationalists resented the political and military presence of Western European countries and the United States, which exercised control over the region under mandates from the League of Nations. The situation grew worse following the 1956 Suez Crisis, when Egyptian ruler General Abdul Nasser nationalized the British and French–owned Suez Canal and the French, British, and Israeli governments responded with a military attack that President Dwight E. Eisenhower demanded be stopped. The Soviet Union developed diplomatic relations with Egypt, and the United States, in return, built up Israel. When Israel attacked Egypt with American military equipment in 1967, American-Arab relations plummeted. Despite Arab objections, the United States has maintained close relations with Israel, one of the chief recipients of U.S. foreign aid. As a result, U.S. relations with Arabic nations have remained poor.

With the collapse of the Soviet Union in 1991, the cold war ended, although the Middle East remains a troublesome area for the United States. In 1991 the United States went to war against Iraq, which had invaded Kuwait, to protect Kuwait and its oilfields. In 2003 the United States again invaded Iraq to topple the administration of Saddam Hussein because of his suspected production of weapons of mass destruction. Even so, American military funding was reduced until the presidency of George W. Bush, who increased the size of the military substantially, and fear of communist expansion no longer provides the basis for American aid commitments to developing nations. Free trade and an end of protectionism remain an American goal, and in 1994, the United States, Mexico, and Canada created the North American Free Trade Agreement (NAFTA), a free trade zone designed to offset the creation of the European Union.

After the terrorist attacks of September 11, 2001, the George W. Bush administration initiated a "war on terrorism." Its first battle was the 2001 invasion of Afghanistan, an effort to destroy terrorist bases. The 2003 invasion of Iraq was intended to topple Saddam Hussein's government, which had sponsored suicide bombers against Israel and which was suspected of possessing weapons of mass destruction that terrorists might use in future attacks. Since the end of the cold war, terrorism and the international drug trade have replaced communism as the chief global problems for the United States, and these concerns are increasingly shaping the direction of American foreign policy. Most countries have agreed with the United States' decision to fight global terrorism, although some countries such as France, Germany, and Russia have objected to the methods employed.

—*John K. Franklin*

References
Destler, I. M. *American Trade Politics.* 2d ed. Washington, DC: Institute for International Economics, 1992.
Ferrell, Robert H. *American Diplomacy: The Twentieth Century.* New York: Norton, 1988.
LaFeber, Walter. *The American Age: United States Foreign Policy at Home and Abroad since 1750.* 2d ed. New York: Norton, 1994.
Patterson, Thomas G., and J. Garry Clifford. *America Ascendant: U.S. Foreign Relations since 1939.* Lexington, MA: D. C. Heath, 1995.
See also Volume 1: Cold War; General Agreement on Tariffs and Trade; War of 1812; World War I; World War II.

Forest Reserve Act (1891)

A codification of land laws that created the first forest reserves, or national forests, in the United States.

The advent of national parks and growing concern over the alarming rate of timber resources consumption created a movement led by Bernhard E. Fernow, head of the Division of Forestry, that secured passage of the Forest Reserve Act in

1891. This act marked the beginning of the National Forest System. The act contained an inconspicuous provision that authorized the president at his discretion to withdraw public lands from private entry if "wholly or in part covered with timber." This provision would protect the forest areas from sale or homesteading by designating them as forest reserves (they were later renamed national forests). President Benjamin Harrison set aside 13 million acres including the Yellowstone Timber Reserve in western Wyoming and the White River Plateau Timberland Reserve in Colorado.

The Forest Reserve Act, however, only made the reserves into closed areas; it did not provide a plan of operation. Thus in 1896 the secretary of the interior proposed that the president of the National Academy of Sciences create a commission to report on issues concerning the protection and use of the reserves. When the National Forest Commission subsequently urged the expansion of the forest reserve, President Grover Cleveland set aside an additional 20 million acres despite strong opposition from many westerners. Before the end of his presidency in March 1897, Cleveland had substantially increased the number of acres in national forest reserves. Moreover, Congress passed the Organic Act in 1897 to establish a system of administration for the forest reserves and to declare the reserves secure for "favorable conditions of waterflows and to furnish a continuous supply of timber for the use and necessity of citizens of the United States." Between 1897 and 1901, President William McKinley withdrew 7 million acres from the public domain. But his actions were dwarfed by President Theodore Roosevelt, an ardent proponent of conservation, who withdrew 141 million acres of forest land, thus establishing the precedent of aggressive presidential leadership for conservation.

By 1974 the national forests, which included grazing areas, had grown to 184,276,463 acres. The Forestry Service in the Department of Agriculture administers both forests and grazing areas. As of 2002, more than 192 million acres of forests and grasslands are protected by the National Forest System.

—*Steven E. Siry*

References
Robbins, Roy M. *Our Landed Heritage: The Public Domain, 1776–1936.* Princeton, NJ: Princeton University Press, 1942.
See also Volume 2: Land Policies.

Fort Knox

Federal gold depository originally established in 1917 during World War I as an army base.

The U.S. Army base called Fort Knox lies 31 miles southwest of Louisville, Kentucky. Although the army's armored force calls this base home, the American public recognizes Fort Knox as the site of the U.S. Bullion Depository. The U.S. Mint, which is part of the Treasury Department, operates the facility, which was completed in December 1936 during the Great Depression. Construction cost the federal government more than $560,000. Materials used included 670 tons of structural steel, 750 tons of reinforcing steel, 4,200 cubic yards of concrete, and 16,000 cubic feet of granite. Fort Knox received most of its gold from storage sites around the country during the first six months of 1937. At the time, national financial systems operated on the gold standard, and so the government desired an inland storage facility relatively safe from foreign attack. During World War II, other important items were stored there as well, such as an original copy of the Magna Carta, President Abraham Lincoln's Gettysburg Address, the Declaration of Independence, the U.S. Constitution, and the Articles of Confederation. President Franklin D. Roosevelt visited the site on April 28, 1943. Except for some small samples, no gold has been transferred to or from the facility for many years. The most gold ever held there (on December 31, 1941) weighed 649.6 million ounces; the current gold holdings amount to more than 147 million ounces, with a value of $42.22 per ounce. (The balance was transferred to other vaults or to foreign countries in payment of U.S. debt.) Because of public rumors the gold had been secretly sold off, U.S. Mint Director Mary Brooks allowed a small group of congressional representatives to briefly visit the depository to inspect the gold supply in September 1974. Although closed to visitors, the public can take pictures from outside the fence. The Philadelphia Mint, the Denver Mint, the West Point Bullion Depository, and the San Francisco Assay Office also hold U.S. government gold supplies. Gold is now used to secure a portion of U.S. currency, but the currency is now valued on a floating exchange rate.

—*Daniel K. Blewett*

References

U.S. Army Armor Center, "History of Fort Knox." No date. Available: http://www.knoxarmy.mil/history.stm; accessed January 29, 2002.
See also Volume 1: Gold Reserve Act.

Forty Acres and a Mule

A post–Civil War idea, ultimately unsuccessful, that called for the heads of freedmen households (former slave households) to receive 40 acres of land and a mule.

On January 16, 1865, Union General William T. Sherman issued Special Field Order No. 15 calling for land that had been abandoned by displaced whites to be redistributed to black freedmen families. Sherman's plan was that each head of a freedman household would receive 40 acres of farmland and a government mule—a means of support after the abolition of slavery. Sherman's order referred to a 30-mile-wide, 274-mile-long plot of land along the Atlantic seaboard stretching from Charleston, South Carolina, to Jacksonville, Florida. Within two months after Sherman issued his order, former slave families—which found it safest to stay on the land because of strict vagrancy laws—had farmed 400,000 acres of land, raising mainly foodstuffs. Following the war, these families learned that Sherman's order had not had the support of the government and of law. In July 1865, Major General Oliver O. Howard of the Freedmen's Bureau proposed to remedy that by implementing Sherman's plan with

Circular Thirteen, which called for setting aside 40 acres of land for each freedman family and providing the freed slaves with economic tools for their survival. The problem was that the plan required the confiscation of private property from whites (who had fled from Sherman's army or been displaced by the war) and its redistribution to blacks. Many whites opposed this idea, and when President Andrew Johnson began to pardon prominent Confederate leaders, the idea faced increased opposition because it would have threatened the sanctity of property. The idea convinced many freedmen that they deserved land, but Johnson's policy of issuing pardons and preserving the sanctity of property meant that they did not receive any land. Instead, sharecropping arose, a form of tenant farming in which freed slaves farmed land in exchange for a percentage of the harvest. Under this system, blacks lacked the economic tools to escape dependency on white Southern landowners.

—*Ty M. Reese*

References

Oubre, Claude F. *Forty Acres and a Mule: The Freedmen's Bureau and Black Land Ownership.* Baton Rouge: Louisiana State University Press, 1978.
See also Volumes 1, 2: Slavery.

Fourteenth Amendment (1868)

Amendment to the U.S. Constitution that defined the rights of all federal citizens, both blacks and whites; prohibited states from abridging rights for citizens in the state; but did not define the relationship between citizens and private entities.

Congress submitted to the states the Fourteenth Amendment to the U.S. Constitution on June 13, 1866. The states ratified the amendment on July 9, 1868, and Congress officially made it part of the Constitution on July 18, 1868. This amendment overturned the Supreme Court ruling in *Dred Scott v. Sandford* (1857) that had declared blacks were not citizens. The Fourteenth Amendment provided citizens, both black and white, with the right of due process—that "no State shall make or enforce any law which shall abridge the privileges or immunities of citizens of the United States." It guaranteed equal protection under the law, and it excluded from federal office any state or federal official who violated his oath to the U.S. by participating in the Confederate rebellion.

However, the Supreme Court effectively nullified the provisions of the Fourteenth Amendment in 1873 with its decision in *The Butcher's Benevolent Association of New Orleans v. the Crescent City Live-Stock Landing and Slaughter-House Company* restricting the reach of the Fourteenth Amendment by severely limiting its due process clause to national citizenship, again lessening the rights of black citizens. (Although the Fourteenth Amendment declared that states could not discriminate against individuals, it did not prohibit private companies or individuals from doing so.) Then, in 1886 in *Santa Clara County v. Southern Pacific Railroad,* the Supreme Court asserted that the due process clause of the Fourteenth Amendment applied to corporations, which the Court defined as legal persons with rights that cannot be alienated.

This interpretation severely limited the ability of the federal government to pursue antimonopoly actions against corporations in the early twentieth century. Since the early twentieth century, the federal government has not been able to discriminate against citizens or entities (corporations).

—*James T. Carroll*

References

Schwartz, Bernard. *A History of the Supreme Court.* New York: Oxford University Press, 1993.

See also Volumes 1, 2: Slavery.

Free Market

An economic ideal dependent on free choice, private property, and the minimization of government intervention.

Synonymous with laissez-faire, a French term meaning "allow to act," the concept of the free market assumes that the collective, yet independent, decisions of individual buyers and sellers will determine the most efficient and just allocation of resources for a society. Free markets operate through freedom of choice and private ownership of the means of production and consumption: Owners of private property freely determine what is produced, how it is produced, who consumes what is produced, and at what price. Advocates of the free market consider this system not only just (because buyers and sellers exchange property at freely negotiated prices) but also economically efficient (because sellers meet buyer's needs by producing only demanded goods, services, and resources). The free market thus creates efficiency by encouraging a conflict between self-interested buyers and sellers. For instance, sellers compete to offer and produce goods, services, and resources for buyers who seek to obtain them at the lowest cost. Moreover, a free-market system functions most effectively when decisions remain decentralized and coordinated through markets rather than the government; government should be limited to maintaining the legal system and protecting property rights.

Although the United States has never had a completely free market, its economy remains free of government intervention compared with most other nations. Still, federal and state governments since the American Revolution have variously tried to regulate and encourage economic activity in hopes of improving economic justice or efficiency. For example, beginning in 1816, Secretary of the Treasury Alexander Hamilton tried to shield American businesses by promoting exports and establishing tariffs to protect native industries (textile mills, for example) and other manufacturers. On the other hand, taxation, immigration restriction, and fetters on domestic trade in the early American republic remained relatively minimal. Many Americans regard the nineteenth century as the height of laissez-faire or free-market economics. Yet, during this period, both the federal and state governments often directly interfered with markets. Governments invested heavily in transportation infrastructure and internal improvements, for example, the building of the Erie Canal in 1825. Moreover, the federal government temporarily erected protective tariffs and encouraged economic growth by distributing

nearly 300 million acres of land to citizens and businesses in the form of land grants. Land grants occurred primarily between 1861 and 1900, although some land grants continued until 1976 in remote areas such as Alaska. In the late nineteenth and early twentieth centuries, both federal and state governments hoped to regulate perceived economic injustices and inefficiencies by establishing sometimes competing and overlapping regulatory laws and agencies, such as the Interstate Commerce Commission (1887), the Sherman Anti-Trust Act (1890), the Federal Trade Commission (1914), and the Federal Reserve Act (1913). In the 1930s, the federal government's expansive New Deal used the crisis of the Great Depression to justify a great number of programs that variously tried to impose greater market efficiencies; protect various interest groups such as farmers, unions, and businesses; and redistribute wealth. The high point of federal involvement in the economy occurred during the 1960s with President Lyndon B. Johnson's Great Society, which provided for distribution of wealth through such programs as Medicaid, food stamps, Aid to Families with Dependent Children, and Head Start. Since then, Americans have increasingly debated whether the free market or government provides the more just and efficient way to order the economy. As a rule, Republicans prefer less government intervention and Democrats push for more government programs.

—*Eric Pullin*

References

Benedict, Michael Les. "Laissez-Faire and Liberty: A Re-Evaluation of the Meaning and Origins of Laissez-Faire Constitutionalism." *Law History Review,* vol. 3 no. 2 (Fall 1985): 293–332.

Fine, Sidney. *Laissez-Faire and the General Welfare State.* Ann Arbor: University of Michigan Press, 1966.

Hayek, Friedrich. *The Constitution of Liberty.* Chicago: University of Chicago Press, 1960.

———. *The Road to Serfdom.* Chicago: University of Chicago Press, 1980.

Free-Soil Party

Third-party political organization influential in the United States from 1848 to 1854.

During the 1840s, the Jacksonian Democrats in New York split over the issue of slavery. Many Northerners expressed concern over the annexation of Texas, which they feared would result in the creation of as many as six slaveholding states. The faction that supported slavery, the Hunkers, opposed the antislavery Barnburners. When the Democratic nomination for president in 1848 went to James K. Polk, a slaveholding Tennessean, the Barnburners left the Democratic Party and joined forces with the antislavery members of the Whig Party and the Liberty Party to form the Free-Soil Party. The coalition opposed the extension of slavery into the territories, advocated a revenue-only tariff, and promoted federal funding for internal improvements such as roads and canals as well as a homestead act. The Free-Soil Party nominated Martin Van Buren as its presidential candidate in 1848.

The group focused on preventing the expansion of slavery on the grounds that free labor would then have to compete with slave labor and that, because economically the two systems of labor remained incompatible, only a system of free men and free soil would guarantee the economic future of whites. Although the Free-Soilers failed to win the election, they did elect 9 members of Congress and helped secure a victory for Zachary Taylor because the free-soil Democrats split from the pro-slavery Democrats and supported Taylor. The Free-Soil Party continued for another six years, electing a senator and 13 congressional delegates between 1848 and 1854. By 1854 the Republican Party had absorbed most of the Free-Soil Party members and had co-opted the party platform.

—*Cynthia Clark Northrup*

References

Foner, Eric. *Free Soil, Free Labor, Free Men: The Ideology of the Republican Party before the Civil War.* New York: Oxford University Press, 1970.

Rayback, Joseph G. *Free Soil: The Extension of 1848.* Lexington: University Press of Kentucky, 1971.

See also Volumes 1, 2: Slavery.

Free Trade

A policy of minimal or zero trade barriers between countries—on the trade policy spectrum, at the opposite end from protectionism.

The idea of free trade was popularized by the classic liberal economist David Ricardo in his *Theory of Comparative Advantage.* Ricardo argued that the wealth of all nations would be greater if each country specialized in creating the goods and services it produced most cheaply and effectively and then traded those products for products that it did not make as efficiently. These ideas stand in sharp contrast to the mercantilist and imperialist policies that governed trade for most Western countries in Ricardo's lifetime (1772–1823).

The idea of free trade has been at the base of much of America's trade policy, especially since the close of the nineteenth century. Secretary of State John Hay's Open Door notes of 1899 were an early articulation of the American vision of free trade. Hay called for all powers with spheres of influence in China to relinquish their special trading privileges and allow the commerce of all countries to trade on terms equal to those of the power controlling the sphere. Although Hay's idea was rejected at the time, achieving a system in which no nation's trade was discriminated against became a cornerstone of American policy.

Since the 1934 passage of the Reciprocal Trade Agreements Act, which permitted President Franklin D. Roosevelt to reduce tariff rates by up to 50 percent, free trade has been the more or less dominant trend in American trade policy, although occasionally individual industries have been able to secure protectionist relief. Roosevelt's reciprocal trade program sought to bring about free trade through bilateral agreements to remove trade barriers between the United States and other countries. After World War II, the United States extended these agreements with a new approach to trade negotiations embodied in the 1947 General Agreement on Tariffs and Trade (GATT). Countries were invited to participate in rounds of multilateral negotiations to create tariff schedules and mutually-agreed-on trading rules. Most-favored-nation clauses ensured that all participating countries received the benefits of trade concessions given by any other member, allowing for a fairly comprehensive, but often slow, lowering of trade barriers.

Although many nonaligned and a few communist countries participated in GATT, the dynamics of the cold war limited GATT's ability to make free trade the universally accepted guiding principle of the world economy. The cold war's end in 1991 changed that. The eighth round of GATT negotiations, completed in 1994, created the World Trade Organization (WTO), a more comprehensive, permanent, and powerful body through which to coordinate the global adoption and regulation of free trade practices. By the beginning of the twenty-first century, most major countries including the People's Republic of China were well on their way to membership in the WTO. Although some critics of WTO emphasize the numerous exceptions that WTO allows to a strict interpretation of free trade principles, the WTO is expressly set up to facilitate the move to global free trade by offering a forum for discussing conflicts over trade barriers and methods for resolving or reducing them. In that sense, creation of the WTO and its wide acceptance around the world reflects the triumph of the American vision for a world economy operated along the principles of free trade.

—*G. David Price*

References

Irwin, Douglas A. *Free Trade under Fire.* Princeton, NJ: Princeton University Press, 2002.

Rogowsky, Robert A., et al. *Trade Liberalization: Fears and Facts.* Westport, CT: Praeger, 2001.

See also Volume 1: General Agreement on Tariffs and Trade; Mercantilism; Open Door Notes; Reciprocal Trade Agreement Act of 1934; ; World Trade Organization.

Free Trade Area of the Americas (FTAA)

Initiative to establish a free trade zone in the Western Hemisphere involving the United States, Canada, and all Caribbean and Latin American countries except Cuba and French Guiana.

A long-standing goal of U.S. trade policy has been the implementation of a trade system in the Western Hemisphere that would have a minimum of official barriers, promoting interhemisphere trade to the benefit of the United States. An early example of such a system is the the Pan-American schemes of the 1880s. Free trade principles in the hemisphere have advanced since the 1960s. The South American republics experimented extensively with various regional and subregional economic integration schemes, and in the 1980s they also experienced, for the most part, more or less successful political democratization and economic liberalization. Meanwhile, the United States tried to improve economic and political relations with Latin America by opening its market to its southern neighbors, particularly by lowering tariffs and nontariff trade barriers in the 1970s and 1980s.

In 1990, President George H. W. Bush declared his "Enterprise for the Americas" initiative aimed at promoting free trade within the hemisphere. This program evolved into the North American Free Trade Agreement of 1993, which was signed by the United States, Canada, and Mexico. By the end of the twentieth century, Western Hemisphere trade with its annual sum of $675.6 million accounted for 39 percent of U.S. foreign trade.

At a Summit of the Americas in Miami in December 1994, U.S. President Bill Clinton and leaders of 33 other American states declared their intention to create a free trade area in the Western Hemisphere within the next ten years. Summits of the Americas in Santiago (1998) and Quebec (2001), as well as conferences among trade ministers and other negotiations among American states, formalized the Free Trade Area of the Americas (FTAA). The initiative involves the United States, Canada, and all 31 countries of the Caribbean and Latin America except Cuba, which is communist, and French Guiana, which is under French authority. Participating nations hope to finalize the agreement by January 2005 and implement it by December 2005. Its objective is the establishment of a free trade zone encompassing (as of 2000) nearly 800 million people and more than $11 billion in gross domestic product.

The concept of the FTAA covers trade liberalization (including elimination of tariffs and nontariff trade barriers), transparency and market access, cooperation in the development of infrastructure, customs procedures, agriculture, investment policies, subsidies, intellectual property rights, and settlement of disputes. It envisages the establishment of a hemispheric common market—the world's largest trading block—based on economic integration and free exchange of goods, services, and capital. This concept, also closely linked with the development of a new kind of the hemispheric community, rested upon comprehensive cooperation, shared democratic values, and rule of law.

However, several economic, political, institutional, and cultural obstacles and difficulties exist in the process of developing the FTAA. Economic ties between North America and South America remain significantly unbalanced: U.S. trade with its NAFTA partners is substantially greater than U.S. trade with all of South America and the Caribbean. Political culture, institutions, legal systems, economic traditions, and values still differ between the United States and Canada in North America and the Central and South American nations. A huge gap in the well-being of populations between the Americas also exists. Some Latin American countries, particularly Brazil (which dominated MERCOSUR, the South American common market extant between 1991 and 1995) and Venezuela, have reservations about the FTAA. These reservations are motivated by political concerns about national sovereignty and the two nations' reluctance to open their markets to North American competitors, particularly in the chemical and papermaking industries as well as in

machinery and electronics. Some Latin American countries complain about U.S. antidumping rules (which prevent the sale of foreign products at below-cost prices) and farm subsidies (which provide funds for farmers who can then sell their products cheaply. Inclusion of provisions against dumping and farm subsidies allows participating countries to compete on an even basis.

Public and domestic political opposition to the FTAA continues both in the United States and other American countries. Impeding progress are a controversial antiglobalist movement against the World Trade Organization and other entities that promote global trade, environmental concerns raised by associations such as Greenpeace, rudiments of anti-Americanism in Latin America, and concern by organized labor in the United States about possible job losses to cheap foreign labor. To overcome these difficulties, the U.S. government has attempted to strengthen bipartisan domestic support for the FTAA, entice trading partners in the Americas by improving their access to the U.S. consumer market, and promote liberalization of bilateral trade.

—*Peter Rainow*

References

Carranza, Mario Esteban. *South American Free Trade Area or Free Trade Area of the Americas?* Burlington, VT: Ashgate, 2000.

Franko, Patrice M. *Toward a New Security Architecture in the Americas: The Strategic Implications of the FTAA.* Washington, DC: Center for Strategic and International Studies, 2000.

See also Volume 1: Clinton, William Jefferson; North American Free Trade Agreement.

French and Indian War (1754–1763)

Last in a series of conflicts between the British and French for control of the North American frontier, concurrent with the Seven Years' War in continental Europe.

During the early stages of the French and Indian War (1754–1763), French troops, with their Native American allies, overran British forts in the Ohio Valley, including Fort Necessity. A force led by British General Edward Braddock in 1755 to recapture the area was ambushed by the French and was a costly fiasco. The British also initiated an abortive invasion of French Canada. The tide only turned after the election in England of William Pitt as Prime Minister, who implemented a program to subsidize the Prussian effort in continental Europe, the primary theater of warfare.

This policy bore fruit at Fort Louisbourg in Canada and Fort Duquesne in western Pennsylvania, both French forts that were captured by the British, and proved correct when General James Wolfe captured Quebec in 1759. Meanwhile, in the backcountry, Roger's Rangers—American colonists fighting for the British—and Iroquois allies of the British regained ground. In 1763, the British forced the French to agree to an advantageous settlement that ceded Canada to Britain and removed the immediate threat of French encroachment into British colonial territory. However, the

British victory had also sown the seeds of colonial rebellion in the American colonies, as the massive war debt had led Parliament to tax the American colonies with acts such as the Stamp Act and the Sugar Act. The continuing presence of British troops in the colonies, although the French enemy was no longer present, annoyed colonists even more since they no longer needed the protection of the British army and were experiencing increased political and economic confidence. British attempts to incorporate French Canada through measures like the Quebec Act, which guaranteed French Canadians the right to practice the Catholic faith, horrified Protestant colonists and further undermined British authority among colonists who had just defeated the French with little assistance from regular British forces. The 1754 Albany Congress, arranged to coordinate war supplies and political support among the colonies as the British focused on the European military campaigns, also contributed to the developing sense of division from Britain. The French and Indian War gave Britain mastery of North America, but the victory also pushed the colonists toward rebellion.

—*Margaret Sankey*

References

Anderson, Fred. *Crucible of War*. New York: Alfred A. Knopf, 2000.

Jennings, Frances. *Empire of Fortune: Crowns, Colonies, and Tribes in the Seven Years' War in America*. New York: Norton, 1988.

Nester, William. *The First Global War*. Westport, CT: Praeger, 2000.

See also Volume 1: American Revolution; Stamp Act; Sugar Act of 1764.

FSA

See Farm Security Administration.

FTAA

See Free Trade Area of the Americas.

FTC

See Federal Trade Commission.

Fugitive Slave Acts (1793, 1850)

Controversial federal statutes dealing with the treatment of runaway slaves.

Following the American Revolution, Congress passed a Fugitive Slave Act (1793) to protect the property rights of slaveholders and to enforce Article 4, Section 2 of the U. S. Constitution, which states: "No person held to service or labor in one State under the laws thereof, escaping into another, shall, in consequence of any law or regulation therein, be discharged from such service or labor, but shall be delivered up on claim of the party to whom such service or labor may be due." The legislation gave legal support to owners seeking the return of runaway slaves who had fled into other states or into a federal territory. The law met with resistance in the North, where most states had already abolished slavery. Many Northerners contended that the law left free blacks vulnerable to false claims that they were actually runaways. Northerners also refused to accept the idea that Southern slaveholders had the right to recapture their property without the use of the court system. As a response, most Northern states during the antebellum period (1848–1861) passed so-called personal liberty laws that required judicial oversight of the process of returning runaway slaves.

The rise of the antislavery movement during the 1830s focused greater attention on the fugitive slave issue, and the Southern states soon began lobbying for stronger fugitive slave laws. Congress finally passed a stronger Fugitive Slave Act as part of the Compromise of 1850. The new law, which outraged many in the North, called for harsher penalties against runaways and against anyone who aided runaways in their escape. Many Northern states passed stronger personal liberty laws in response, and the fugitive slave issue became one of the most inflammatory sectional issues over which Northern and Southern states disagreed during the 1850s.

Because of Northern resistance and the difficult logistics involved in capturing runaways, the Fugitive Slave Act actually had little practical effect. If anything, its passage bolstered the resolve of antislavery factions in the North. The Civil War and the Emancipation Proclamation ultimately rendered the Fugitive Slave Act of 1850 moot, and Congress officially repealed it on June 28, 1864.

—*Ben Wynne*

References

Nye, Russell B. *Fettered Freedom: Civil Liberties and the Slave Controversy, 1830-1860*. East Lansing: Michigan State University Press, 1963.

See also Volume 1, 2: Slavery.

Full Employment

The absence of any excess supply of labor, so that any worker willing to work at prevailing wages can get a job.

In a fully employed economy, no unemployment would exist because of deficient demand—only frictional unemployment (workers investing time in search for better jobs), voluntary unemployment, or structural unemployment (workers lacking the skills or location now demanded by employers) would occur. Early drafts of the Employment Act of 1946, which established the president's Council of Economic Advisers and the Economic Report of the President, would have committed the U.S. government to a Keynesian policy of managing aggregate demand to maintain full employment, a proposal shaped by experience with mass unemployment in the 1930s. The final version of the Employment Act of 1946 only established high levels of employment as a goal. The Full Employment and Balanced Growth Act of 1978 (the Humphrey-Hawkins Act) set seven national goals: full employment and production, rising real income, balanced growth, a balanced federal budget, productivity growth, an improved trade balance, and reasonable price stability. It set numerical targets for unemployment (3 percent by 1983) and inflation, and it required a representative of the Federal Reserve Board to testify annually before congressional banking committees on how Federal Reserve policy for the coming year would achieve these goals. The stated numerical targets proved unrealistic, given the economic situation of the late 1970s (simultaneous high unemployment and high rates of inflation), and policymakers generally ignored them.

Beginning in the late 1960s, many economists—influenced by the future Nobel laureate Milton Friedman's argument that a natural rate of unemployment could not exist—accepted Friedman's argument that monetary policy can reduce unemployment below its natural rate only temporarily and at the cost of permanently higher inflation. During the 1970s another future Nobel laureate, Robert Lucas, argued that no systematic monetary policy could stimulate employment, even temporarily. Lucas's "new classical economics" held that monetary policy could reduce unemployment below its natural rate only by fooling workers into working for lower real wages than they expected (because higher prices reduced the purchasing power of their money wages), and that agents with rational expectations cannot be fooled systematically. These natural-rate theories persuaded many central bankers, including those who were part of the U.S. Federal Reserve system, to concentrate on price stability and abandon full employment as a policy goal. Keynesian economists including Nobel Prize winners James Tobin and William Vickrey continued to insist that to maintain full employment, active government management of aggregate demand must occur.

—*Robert Dimand*

References

Bailey, Stephen K. *Congress Makes a Law: The Story behind the Employment Act of 1946.* New York: Columbia University Press, 1950.

Spulber, Nicholas. *Managing the American Economy: From Roosevelt to Reagan.* Bloomington: Indiana University Press, 1989.

Stein, Herbert. *The Fiscal Revolution in America.* Rev. ed. Washington, DC: American Enterprise Institute, 1990.

Warner, Aaron W., Mathew Forstater, and Sumner M. Rosen, eds. *Commitment to Full Employment: The Economics and Social Policy of William S. Vickrey.* Armonk, NY: M. E. Sharpe, 2000.

See also Volume 1: Keynesian Economics; Unemployment.

G

G-7

See Group of Seven.

G-8

See Group of Seven.

Gadsden Purchase (1854)

Major land transaction between the United States and Mexico in 1854.

The Treaty of Guadalupe Hidalgo ended the Mexican-American War (1845–1848) and ceded vast western territory to the United States, but it left the precise boundary between the United States and Mexico vague. The area in dispute lay south of the Gila River and north of the current border. Hoping to settle the matter and at the same time secure the best route for a southern transcontinental railroad, President Franklin Pierce appointed James Gadsden, a railroad entrepreneur, as minister to Mexico and instructed him to negotiate the purchase of the disputed area.

Gadsden's original mission also included negotiating the purchase of lower California, but his abrasive personality offended Mexican authorities to such an extent that the country's president, Antonio Lopez de Santa Anna, refused to consider the sale of additional territory. Gadsden eventually reached a tentative agreement with the Mexican president, and the issue went before the U.S. Senate. After making some modifications and engaging in heated debate along North/South sectional lines, the Senate narrowly approved the purchase. Under the agreement the United States received 30,000 square miles that would form the southern portion of New Mexico and Arizona. In return, Mexico received $10 million, and both countries agreed to rescind or assume any additional claims against each other.

Although the Gadsden Purchase added significant territory to the United States, it generated a great deal of controversy. Many Americans, particularly in the North, viewed the entire episode as a brazen attempt by Southern politicians to advance their own interests. Debates in the Senate over the purchase further aggravated sectional tensions within the United States, and the issue did little to improve U.S.-Mexican relations. In Mexico the sale proved so unpopular that it helped topple Santa Anna's government.

—*Ben Wynne*

References

Faulk, Odie B. *Too Far North, Too Far South.* Los Angeles, CA: Westernlore Press, 1967.

See also Volume 1: Railroads; Volume 2 (Documents): Gadsden Purchase Treaty.

Gallatin, Albert (1761–1849)

Secretary of the Treasury during the administrations of Thomas Jefferson and James Madison.

Albert Gallatin was born January 29, 1761, in Geneva, Switzerland. He emigrated to the United States and settled in Pennsylvania in 1795, where he founded New Geneva. This colony was meant to house émigrés from the French Revolution and support itself with the production of glass products overseen by German glassmakers. Gallatin first made a name for himself as one of the moderate members of the Whiskey Rebellion in 1791, public protests and rioting that occurred after the federal government placed a tax on whiskey (a primary method of converting grain into a non-perishable commodity). He subsequently won election to the House of Representatives (where he served as chair of the House Ways and Means Committee) and the U.S. Senate from Pennsylvania. During the presidencies of Thomas Jefferson and James Madison, Gallatin served as secretary of the treasury (1800–1813), a post in which he planned to reduce the $80 million national debt in 1800 to $45 million in 1812 by the planned sale of federal lands and collection of customs revenue. The measure failed because of slow land sales and the cost of the War of 1812.

Gallatin strongly advocated building a federal infrastructure and pushed for the construction of the National Road—

built using federal monies exclusively—and the beginning of the canal network in the Northeast. (The National Road began in Cumberland, Maryland, and ended first at Wheeling, West Virginia; it was later extended to St. Louis, Missouri.) Gallatin supported the Louisiana Purchase and found the money necessary to pay for it without raising the national debt; he also pushed for the immediate exploration of the new area by Meriwether Lewis and William Clark and by Thomas Freemont, an experienced astronomer, and Peter Custis, a medical student, who mapped the Red River area of Louisiana. Lewis and Clark named rivers for Madison, Jefferson, and Gallatin. After 1813, Gallatin served as minister to France and Great Britain before retiring to found the National Bank of the City of New York in 1817 and the American Ethnological Society in 1842. A keen scholar of Native American languages, Gallatin wrote several books on ethnography, including the 1826 *Table of Indian Languages.* He died August 12, 1849.

—*Margaret Sankey*

References
Kuppenheimer, L. B. *Albert Gallatin's Vision of Democratic Stability.* Westport, CT: Praeger, 1996.
Walters, Ray. *Albert Gallatin.* New York: Macmillan, 1957.
See also Volume 1: U.S. Department of Treasury.

GATT

See General Agreement on Tariffs and Trade.

General Agreement on Tariffs and Trade (GATT)

Free trade agreement of the post–World War II period that initially included 25 countries.

Created in 1947 and guided by the United States, the General Agreement on Trade and Tariffs (GATT) reflected both the continuation of long-standing attitudes in U.S. trade policy and the realization of greatly changed circumstances necessitating a more involved and sustained role for the United States in world affairs. GATT represented many of the same concerns expressed at the Bretton Woods Conference in 1944—namely, the need to promote and to sustain postwar economic recovery generally and world trade specifically. GATT targeted tariffs, and European trade barriers particularly, as impediments to this process.

In all, GATT included eight rounds of negotiations: Geneva (1947), Annecy, France (1949), Torquay, England (1951), Geneva (1956), Geneva (1960–1962), Geneva (1962–1967), Tokyo (1973–1979), and Punta del Este, Uruguay (1986–1994). The final two Geneva rounds of the negotiations are sometimes referred to as the Dillon round (named for Undersecretary of State Douglas Dillon) and the Kennedy round (named for the recently assassinated President John F. Kennedy). Five rounds of negotiations between 1947 and 1962 reduced tariffs by 73 percent. Although primarily a U.S.-led initiative, GATT became affiliated with the United Nations

after the Geneva round in 1956. Subsequent rounds of negotiations in Geneva during the administrations of Presidents John F. Kennedy and Lyndon B. Johnson reduced tariffs by an additional 35 percent. Moreover, although negotiations were dedicated to tariff reduction, by the mid-1960s the final stages of the Kennedy round produced a preliminary, yet significant, antidumping agreement (an agreement that prohibits the sale of foreign goods at below-market prices and thereby eliminates unfair competition between countries).

Focused primarily on manufactured goods, the early rounds of GATT negotiations reached no agreement on agricultural subsidies and nontariff trade barriers. European agricultural interests successfully frustrated attempts to broaden the talks to address agricultural products. Additionally, Japan unabashedly maintained a series of procedural and structural barriers to foreign firms seeking to penetrate its market. The Tokyo round of GATT negotiations (1973–1979) involved more than 100 participating countries and represented a major attempt to address many of these nontariff trade barriers. These negotiations produced agreements (subsequently referred to as codes) on subsidies, technical barriers to trade, import licensing procedures, customs valuation, and other aspects of international trade. Wide disagreement continues over the actual effectiveness of these codes. The talks further reduced the average tariff on manufactured goods to 4.7 percent. However, the Tokyo round failed to reach any significant agreements on agricultural commodities. Also, technology issues created further problems, particularly with regard to copyright and other intellectual property issues.

The final round of talks, the Uruguay round (1986–1994), proved particularly problematic for these reasons. Nonetheless, this final round of negotiations proved successful in further reducing tariffs on manufactured goods. The Uruguay round also attempted to address some of the many issues pertaining to agriculture, services trade, and intellectual property rights. After the Uruguay round, the GATT was transformed into the World Trade Organization (WTO) in 1995.

—*Robert Rook*

References
Eckes, Alfred E. *Opening America's Market: U.S. Foreign Policy since 1776.* Chapel Hill: University of North Carolina Press, 1995.
Keylor, William R. *The Twentieth Century World: An International History.* New York: Oxford University Press, 2001.
Reynolds, David R. *One World Divisible: A Global History since 1945.* New York: W. W. Norton, 2000.
See also Volume 1: Protective Tariffs.

George, Henry (1839–1897)

American political economist and author of *Progress and Poverty* (1879) who proposed a single tax on land to eliminate rent monopolies and poverty and inspired American and European reformers.

Henry George was born September 2, 1839, in Philadelphia and sailed with his family for the Pacific Ocean and America's West Coast after the panic of 1873. Failing as a miner and publisher, he resorted to begging in San Francisco streets. His fortunes rebounded when he became a reporter. His article condemning Chinese immigration won Californians' praise and launched George's career as reformer and railroad critic. Though drawn to political economics, most of his ideas evolved before he wrote *Our Land and Land Policy, National and State* (1871), which owed more to Christ and Thomas Jefferson's ethics than to studies by economists David Ricardo and John Stuart Mill. Labor alone creates wealth, George insisted, when applied to land or resources. But if producers pay rent to idle landowners, that unearned increment will impoverish society unless completely taxed.

The 1870s depression and panic of 1873 strengthened his beliefs and led to his great work *Progress and Poverty* (1879). Expanding Ricardo's law of rent, George argued that economic misery results from social evils, not inevitable cycles. Only the product of labor or capital should compose property. That excludes land, to which all need access. But ground rents increase with the population, especially in cities. Income shrinks; overproduction and land speculation in increasingly marginal soils squeeze producers further. Conversely, a single tax absorbing rents—and financing services—would generate prosperity and brotherhood.

Speeches in Ireland (during rent boycotts there) and Britain increased George's fame; Europeans considered him to be land reform's main spokesman. He returned to New York in 1886, and Labor selected him as its candidate for mayor of New York City that year. He lost to Democrat Abram S. Hewitt but outpolled Republican Theodore Roosevelt. In 1887, followers organized an Anti-Poverty Society and a Single Tax League that claimed hundreds of clubs. Wanting the tools of production in private hands, George feuded with socialists and embraced the Democrats and William Jennings Bryan. After suffering a stroke, George concentrated on *The Science of Political Economy* (published posthumously). He also ran for mayor again in 1897 but died during the campaign on October 29, 1897.

Americans never adopted George's single tax. Yet his critique of plutocracy (government by the wealthy) galvanized reformers from George Bernard Shaw and Leo Tolstoy abroad to Tom Johnson, Frederic Howe, and Brand Whitlock, who were single-tax reformers, at home.

—*Everett W. Kindig*

References

Barker, Charles A. *Henry George.* New York: Oxford University Press, 1955.
Rose, Edward J. *Henry George.* New York: Twayne Publishers, 1968.
See also Volume 2: Taxation.

Gibbons v. Ogden (1824)

Supreme Court decision giving Congress control of interstate commerce and serving as a precedent for federal regulation of the economy.

In 1811, the New York legislature granted Robert Fulton, the inventor of the steamboat, and Robert Livingston, former ambassador to France, a monopoly on steamboat traffic in state waters. The two men gave Aaron Ogden, the former governor of New Jersey, a license to operate ferryboats from his state to New York. Thomas Gibbons set up a competing steamboat line from New Jersey to Manhattan seven years later. Although he had no license from Fulton and Livingston, he did have a coasting license, obtained from the United States government in 1793, that allowed him to operate coastal transportation vessels. Ogden sued Gibbons in the state courts of New York for interfering with his trade. The state courts consistently ruled in favor of Ogden.

When the case made it to the Supreme Court in 1824, Daniel Webster argued on behalf of Thomas Gibbons. He broadly interpreted the commerce power granted to Congress under Article 1, Section 8 of the Constitution. In contrast, lawyers for Aaron Ogden argued that a state's power to regulate interstate commerce is concurrent with the national government's power to regulate the same commerce. In a 6-to-0 decision, Chief Justice John Marshall ruled in favor of Gibbons. He broadly defined the commerce clause by stating that it meant Congress had the power to prescribe the rule that governed all business dealings between nations or parts of nations. With this definition in mind, Marshall concluded that the coasting license granted to Thomas Gibbons by the federal government took precedence over the license that Fulton and Livingston had granted to Aaron Ogden under the laws of the state of New York. Marshall's ruling has been credited with strengthening national business interests during rapid expansion in the nineteenth century and with serving as a precedent for federal regulation of the economy in the twentieth century.

—*Mary Stockwell*

References

Siegel, Adrienne. *The Marshall Court, 1801–1835.* Millwood, NY: Associated Faculty Press, 1987.
See also Volume 2: Judiciary.

G.I. Bill of Rights

See Servicemen's Readjustment Act.

Glass-Steagall Banking Act (1933)

Depression-era legislation that prohibited banks from underwriting or selling stocks and that created the Federal Deposit Insurance Corporation.

During the Great Depression, thousands of banks failed. In response, Senator Carter Glass, a Virginia Democrat, and Representative Henry Steagall, a Democrat from Alabama, crafted a bill to separate the commercial and savings banks from investment banking. The Glass-Steagall Act prohibited banks from underwriting or selling securities (stock) and remained virtually unchallenged for about four decades. In the 1970s, brokerage firms such as Merrill Lynch began to take on banking functions, offering money-market accounts that pay interest and allow check-writing privileges on the accounts.

As the differences between brokerages and banks began to disappear, the Glass-Steagall Act came under attack from the legislative and executive branches in the federal government. In 1983, President Ronald Reagan, a Republican, proposed that banks should be allowed to engage in securities, real estate, and insurance activities. Congress did not act on the proposal. Congress repealed a part of Glass-Steagall in 1988 by allowing banks to participate in securities activities while continuing to limit insurance activities. In 1991, the House of Representatives defeated a proposal to repeal parts of Glass-Steagall and to allow banks to establish nationwide branches. Legislation introduced in Congress in 1995 and reworked in 1996 failed because banks opposed the continued prohibition on insurance activities. Repeal efforts nearly succeeded in 1998; a bill passed the House by one vote but failed in the Senate.

President Bill Clinton, a Democrat, signed the Financial Modernization Act into law on November 12, 1999. The legislation, crafted by Senator Phil Gramm (R-Texas) and Representative Jim Leach (R-Iowa), repealed the Glass-Steagall prohibition on banks selling stocks and insurance. The financial services industry welcomed its new capability to provide one-stop shopping for consumers.

—*John David Rausch Jr.*

References

Kadlec, Daniel. "Bank on Change." *Time,* November 8, 1999.

See also Volume 1: Banking System; Clinton, William Jefferson; Great Depression; Reagan, Ronald; Volume 2: Banking.

Globalization

The highly controversial process by which the world economy is moving toward a more homogenous and unified structure dominated by the principles of capitalism and free trade.

The integration of the global economy has been under way for much of modern history, and the current incarnation of that process is called globalization. It is distinct from previous integration phases in several ways and has elicited a sizable amount of criticism.

Contemporary globalization involves spreading the economic structure of the industrial West—with capitalism and free trade as the underpinnings of that structure—to the rest of the globe. Not only are these principles quite different from the economic ideas and values traditionally practiced in much of the non-Western world, they are also different from the mercantilist policies (designed to economically benefit the mother country at the expense of a colony) and imperialist policies (which benefit the controlling national economy) used earlier by the West to control the world economy. Nevertheless, the effect of these policies is often similar to the effect of earlier policies, leading to a continuation of many of the earlier conflicts.

The contemporary phase of globalization emerged as the dominant force in international economic relations in the aftermath of World War II. American policymakers had great faith that capitalism and free trade would bring about the economic stability the industrial world so desperately craved after the deprivation and horrors of the Great Depression and World War II. Because the economy of the industrial world had long since become dependent on imported commodities and markets of the non-Western world, American policymakers believed that their ideals had to be extended to these areas as well. There was also an idealistic hope that the American way of organizing international trade would remake countries in the non-Western world into prosperous democracies that mirrored the United States in ways of living and political and economic values. To facilitate this, the United States helped create several international organizations and programs including the World Bank, International Monetary Fund, General Agreement on Tariffs and Trade (GATT), and the Marshall Plan.

The U.S. plan for globalization encountered opposition from the beginning. Communist countries balked at its presupposition that capitalism and market-directed free trade were the only acceptable bases for international economic activity. This disagreement became one of the underlying causes of the cold war. Other industrial countries were reluctant to give up special privileges they had in their empires or to reduce the tariff barriers that protected their domestic industries.

As the cold war came to dominate the tone of international relations, the United States was able to achieve limited success in its vision of globalization. The roughly one-third of the world's population that was communist formally rejected participation in the global economy; however, trade was never completely cut off between East and West during the cold war, and by the 1970s communist countries were allowing controlled marketing of Western-made consumer goods in their countries.

America's fellow capitalist countries proved reluctant about the U.S. plan as well. Many were slow to release their empires from the imperialist restraints they had established over them. Although they agreed in principle with the American idea of freer trade, they established economic blocs and customs unions like the British Commonwealth and European Economic Community (EEC), which went against the full spirit of the U.S. plan. Although the Europeans did not fully embrace the American vision of global free trade, they did take steps toward it. They cooperated with the tariff reduction agenda of GATT, and international organizations like the EEC—which became the European Union (EU) on November 1, 1993—did promote trade liberalization and economic integration among their members. Trade liberalization and economic integration were vastly different policies than the pre–World War II trade policy of industrial countries. Also, by the mid-1960s most colonial possessions of the industrial world had been granted at least formal independence, with some countries—for example, Australia and Canada—still functioning with the British monarch as head of state.

As the empires of the industrial world receded, new voices

emerged in the non-Western world that also questioned the American vision. One of the greatest objections to globalization was that those in the non-Western world did not agree that capitalism and freer trade would lead to industrialization and prosperity; rather they saw them as solidifying the existing inequities between the industrial and nonindustrial worlds. Under capitalism and free trade, they argued, areas with the most capital, most highly developed markets and technologies, and most diverse economies are in a much better position to grow than others. This attitude led to calls from the non-Western world for preferential treatment in trade, for economic and technological development assistance, and for other types of aid from the industrial world, to which the industrial world responded with both direct foreign aid programs and international organizations such as the World Trade Organization and the International Monetary Fund.

Human rights and environmental groups also criticized globalization. Access to Western markets often led to an increasing push by ruling elites or dictators in non-Western countries to force populations to move from subsistence agriculture to sweatshop-style wage labor. As this occurred, dramatic changes occurred in the daily lives of people that many claim adversely affected people's health and the environment. Urban areas swelled in population as people left rural areas to work in factories. Often governments paid little attention to housing and sanitation standards in these rapidly growing areas. In attempts to obtain much-needed foreign exchange (cash), some countries began aggressively exporting raw materials and engaging in large-scale slash-and-burn agricultural practices, wreaking havoc on sensitive ecosystems.

Toward the end of the twentieth century, criticism of globalization came even from within the industrial world. Social activists echoed many of the criticisms made by the non-Western world. Organized labor in industrial countries opposed the loss of jobs as some industries relocated factories to the non-Western world to take advantage of cheaper production costs.

It is difficult to make a normative judgment about whether globalization is a positive or negative development for the world. Certainly, for the industrial world, it has improved the quality of life in terms of diversity and quantity of goods available and living standards. Some non-Western countries have seen dramatic improvements in those measures as well, whereas others have experienced overwhelming social problems.

Despite these conflicts, globalization has pressed forward. The World Trade Organization, created in 1994 as a replacement for GATT, has become the primary vehicle driving the globalization process. At the same time, however, a trend toward regional, as opposed to global, economic integration has appeared, exemplified by NAFTA and the European Union. As the twenty-first century begins, scholars are torn as to whether globalization will triumph or there will be a retrenchment toward the development of regional economic blocs.

—*G. David Price*

References

Bairoch, Paul. *Economics and World History: Myths and Paradoxes.* Chicago: University of Chicago Press, 1993.

Barfield, Claude E. *Free Trade, Sovereignty, Democracy: The Future of the World Trade Organization.* Washington, DC: American Enterprise Institute, 2001.

Gilpin, Robert. *Global Political Economy: Understanding the International Economic Order.* Princeton: Princeton University Press, 2001.

Steger, Manfred B. *Globalism: The New Market Ideology.* Lanham, MD: Rowman and Littlefield, 2002.

See also Volume 1: Capitalism; Cold War; General Agreement on Tariffs and Trade; Great Depression; International Monetary Fund; Marshall Plan; Mercantilism; World Trade Organization; World War I; World War II.

GNP

See Gross National Product.

Gold Reserve Act (1934)

Federal law signed by President Franklin D. Roosevelt January 30, 1934, authorizing him to fix the price of gold in the United States after his controversial and ill-conceived gold-buying program failed to raise U.S. commodity prices.

Overproduction during the 1920s and the Great Depression of the 1930s drove farm prices in America to extremely low levels in the 1930s. Realizing that the economic situation facing American farmers in the 1930s had become desperate, President Franklin D. Roosevelt overruled the objections of his more conservative advisers, like Henry Morgenthau Jr., and embraced the highly questionable "commodity dollar" theories of economists Irving Fisher, George Warren, and Frank Pearson that large government purchases of gold would deflate the value of the dollar (because it was tied to the value of gold), which in turn would raise commodity prices and give American farmers a greater share of the world market.

On April 14, 1933, President Roosevelt abandoned the gold standard, and on October 19, 1933, he decided that the United States would begin buying gold. Each day the president met with Warren, Jesse Jones, Morgenthau, and other advisers to set the daily price of gold. However, the program was extremely controversial, and some of the president's closest advisers resigned in protest because of the program's deflationary effect.

Ultimately, the gold-buying program failed to open markets, and commodity prices continued to fall. In January 1934, the government stopped buying gold and on January 30, 1934, Roosevelt signed the Gold Reserve Act, which authorized the president to fix the price of gold. The next day, he set the price of gold at $35 an ounce, thereby fixing the value of the dollar at 59 percent of its pre-1933 level. Although it failed, the gold-buying program did satisfy farmers' desires for immediate federal action, emboldened monetary inflationists, and led to the Silver Purchase Act—which authorized the president to buy silver rather than gold to back U.S. currency—the following year.

—*David W. Waltrop*

References
Leuchtenburg, William Edward. *Franklin D. Roosevelt and the New Deal, 1932–1940.* New York: Harper and Row, 1963.
See also Volume 1: Great Depression; Roosevelt, Franklin D.

Gold Rush, California (1849)

Frantic search for gold in 1849 in the California Territory.

On January 24, 1848, James Marshall discovered gold on the American River while building a sawmill for John Sutter, who sought to create an agricultural empire in the California Territory. In December 1848 President James Polk verified the discovery and precipitated one of the largest human migrations in American history. By 1852 more than 200,000 gold seekers had traveled to the California Territory by sea around the tip of South America, by sea and land crossing at Panama, and by land via the Oregon Trail or California Trail. In addition to European Americans, the prospect of great wealth attracted Chinese, Chileans, Mexicans, Irish, Germans, French, and Turks in significant numbers. The initial success of the placer miners, who panned for gold in the rivers, ended when the surface gold disappeared and extraction was necessary, requiring advanced technology and significant financing.

The California Gold Rush lasted about six years, during which time California gained admittance to the Union; major businesses responded to the demands of the miners, including Wells Fargo (stagecoach) and Levi Strauss (clothing); cultural diversity created tensions and xenophobia; and miners extracted over $200 million in gold.

—*James T. Carroll*

References
Nugent, Walter. *Into the West: The Story of Its People.* New York: Alfred A. Knopf, 1999.
See also Volume 1: Gold versus Silver.

Gold Standard

Monetary system used by the United States during the nineteenth and early twentieth centuries that backed U.S. currency with gold.

Beginning in the nineteenth century, the United States backed its currency with gold. Investors or citizens could convert the currency for the precious metal at any time. The government relied on the gold standard to maintain stability in the currency system, both domestically and internationally. Nations with an unfavorable balance of trade (that is, where imports exceed exports) would settle the account by transferring gold to the other country (the one that is owed the money and that has the trade surplus); the increased amount of gold within the recipient country would cause prices to rise and lower the demand for exports, thereby creating a bal-

ance of trade once again. Problems with this system only arose when the discovery of a mother lode of gold would dramatically increase prices. The system worked well until after World War I when the United States adopted the gold bullion standard, in which nations agreed to no longer mint gold coins and fixed the price of gold. In 1934 Franklin D. Roosevelt modified the gold standard to prevent the outflow of gold. The Gold Reserve Act of 1934 ended the use of gold as a medium of exchange within the United States. Countries around the world fixed their currencies to the dollar instead of to gold. According to the Legal Tender Act of 1933, all debts could be paid with any American coin or paper money then in circulation, which then consisted of primarily Federal Reserve notes. This modified system continued into the 1960s, when inflation and diminishing gold reserves forced the government to adopt a two-tier system. Beginning in 1968, the price of gold was set at $34 an ounce, and the United States only transferred gold between central government (first-tier) gold bankers at this rate. Private investors paid the price established by supply and demand. As the drain of gold continued, President Richard Nixon decided to remove the United States from any future gold conversions—ending the gold standard. After 1976, the international economic system moved to a floating exchange rate monitored by the International Monetary Fund. In this system, the market determines the value of each currency.

—*Cynthia Clark Northrup*

References
Horman, Robert D. *Reforming the International Monetary System: From Roosevelt to Reagan.* New York: Foreign Policy Association, 1987.
See also Volume 1: Gold versus Silver; Volume 2: Currency.

Gold versus Silver

Nineteenth-century argument between Democrats and Republicans over the issue of bimetallism, the use of gold and silver to back currency.

In 1873 Congress decided to demonetize silver—that is, to make silver no longer legal tender for currency or debt—a shift that resulted in a constriction of the money supply. The two groups most adversely affected were silver miners and southern and western farmers. The debate over the use of silver as specie (coin currency) continued for the next two decades. During the administration of President William Henry Harrison, Congress passed the Sherman Silver Purchase Act of 1890, which required the U.S. Treasury to purchase 4.5 million ounces of silver per month. After the election of President Grover Cleveland, the country experienced a financial panic in 1893, in which hundreds of banks, railroads, and companies went bankrupt. Foreign investors feared the United States might abandon the gold standard and therefore rushed to convert their dollars into gold. Cleveland sought to repeal the Sherman Silver Purchase Act as a means of restoring confidence. With the drain on federal gold deposits reaching critical levels, the president authorized the sale of bonds to replenish the Treasury reserves. When the government failed to sell all of the bonds, Cleveland turned to financier J. P. Morgan, a decision that drew criticism from the American public. The public believed the president had sold out to banking concerns after Morgan purchased bonds with "greenbacks" (paper currency) and then exchanged the bonds for gold from the U.S. Treasury.

By 1895 Democrats in the South and the West, led by Senators William Jennings Bryan of Nebraska and Benjamin "Pitchfork" Tillman of South Carolina, began advocating a policy of free silver. They sought to establish the value of the dollar at 16 ounces of silver or 1 ounce of gold. Since the established rate of value was pegged at 32 to 1, this shift would have created rapid inflation and brought relief for debt-stricken miners and farmers as well as other groups, including labor. During the Democratic National Convention in 1896, Bryan (also supported by the newly formed Populist Party) delivered his rousing "cross of gold" speech, in which he stated that the people would not allow themselves to be crucified on the wealthy's cross of gold. The Republicans, with William McKinley as their candidate, campaigned in support of the gold standard. The Republicans won the election, and the United States remained on the gold standard. In the twentieth century, the financial difficulties of the Great Depression forced the country into modifying the gold standard, and eventually the system was abandoned in the 1970s.

—*Cynthia Clark Northrup*

References

Horwitz, Steven. *Monetary Evolution, Free Banking, and Economic Order.* Boulder, CO: Westview Press, 1992.

McElroy, Robert. *Grover Cleveland: The Man and the Statesman.* New York: Harper and Brothers, 1923.

See also Volume 1: Currency Act of 1900; Gold Standard; Volume 2: Currency.

Good Neighbor Policy

Term used to describe U.S. policy in Latin America in the 1930s and early 1940s employing mainly economic and political influence.

Early in the twentieth century, the United States was still following its traditional policy of direct intervention in and domination of other nations in the Western Hemisphere to maintain U.S. positions. Reversal of this policy toward a more flexible one employing mainly economic and political instruments of influence took shape under President Herbert Hoover, who introduced the term *Good Neighbor Policy.* Among early attempts to ease tensions with Latin American neighbors by renouncing earlier U.S. coercive protectionism and military control were Hoover's goodwill visit to several countries, withdrawal of U.S. Marines from Nicaragua, and ideas to repudiate the "Theodore Roosevelt corollary," which made the United States the policeman of the Western Hemisphere. However, the realities of American economic policy in the Western Hemisphere, particularly the high tariff policy including the protective Hawley-Smoot Tariff of 1930, precluded radical changes.

President Franklin D. Roosevelt, who usually receives credit for the shift to the use of economic and political influence, more clearly declared the new Latin American policy in his inaugural address of March 4, 1933, calling for abandonment of armed intervention in Western Hemisphere nations and for the recognition of equality, strengthening of confidence, and economic cooperation among republics in the Americas. The Roosevelt administration's devotion to concentrating resources domestically to combat the Great Depression rather than continuing expensive interventions in Latin America motivated this policy shift. At the Seventh Pan American Conference in Montevideo in 1933, U.S. Secretary of State Cordell Hull formally abandoned the interventionist policy by signing the Convention on Rights and Duties of States. Between 1934 and 1936 the United States terminated or limited its rights to intervene in Cuba and Panama and finally withdrew the Marines from Nicaragua, as well as from Haiti and the Dominican Republic, where they had been stationed to protect U.S. business interests. The government resolved land and railroad disputes with Mexico in 1936 and 1938 in a friendly manner and in 1938 restrained itself from intervening when the Mexican government nationalized the oil industry and vast holdings of American oil companies. Following the principles of the Good Neighbor Policy, the Roosevelt administration accepted the conflict as being between Mexico and the oil companies only.

The Reciprocal Trade Agreements Act passed by Congress in 1934 and Cordell Hull's persistent pursuit of a liberalized trade policy were formidable instruments for strengthening U.S. economic influence in Latin America. Under this new trade policy, an integral part of the Good Neighbor Policy, the U.S. share in the aggregate exports of Latin American countries grew from 31 percent in 1937 and 1938 to 43.7 percent in 1940 and 54.3 percent in 1941. At the same time, in 1938 the United States furnished about 35 percent of total Latin American imports. This figure rose to 54.6 percent in 1940 and 60.5 percent in 1941. At the Havana Pan American Conference of 1940, many Latin American countries remained unwilling to accept U.S. proposals to institutionalize new trade relations by establishing the Hemispheric Trade Cartel. For its part, the U.S. government created several new agencies to promote continental economic cooperation.

During World War II, the Good Neighbor Policy provided the inter-American strategic partnership with a solid economic foundation. The United States secured access to resources—particularly to the raw materials of Latin America that were critically important for its military efforts, while Latin American countries as a group received almost $263 million for armaments. By the end of the war, the United States had participated in some 50 multilateral and 25 bilateral agreements with the republics of Latin America.

—*Peter Rainow*

References

Curry, Earl R. *Hoover's Dominican Diplomacy and the Origins of the Good Neighbor Policy.* New York: Garland Publishing, 1979.

Pike, Frederick B. *FDR's Good Neighbor Policy: Sixty Years of Generally Gentle Chaos.* Austin: University of Texas Press, 1995.
See also Volume 1: Roosevelt, Franklin D.; Roosevelt, Theodore; Wilson, Woodrow.

Government Budgets

The balance sheets of national, state, and local governments displaying the relationships between government spending and tax revenues in one year.

Government budgets have two elements: spending (G) and tax revenues (T). A budget can be balanced (G = T), in deficit (G < T), or in surplus (G > T). The summation of all past federal budget deficits and surpluses constitutes the national debt. Three views on federal government budgets (and debt) are "deficit hawk," "deficit dove," and "functional finance." Deficit hawks view government deficits as causing inflation and/or high interest rates. Many argue that public spending crowds out private spending, because any increase in government spending must be financed through either taxes or bond sales, both of which would decrease private consumption and/or investment. In addition, deficit hawks view the national debt as a financial burden on future generations. Thus, deficit hawks recommend a balanced budget (or a surplus) in every single year, and many support a constitutional amendment to require a balanced budget.

Deficit doves believe deficits can be useful when used appropriately and responsibly. The government can run deficits during recessions, they believe, but it should also run surpluses during economic booms so that the budget is balanced over the business cycle. Deficit doves also argue that many measurement and accounting problems are related to deficits and the debt. The most important issue they emphasize in this regard is that the federal government keeps no capital account to hold a surplus of funds. Deficit doves argue that deficit/gross domestic product (GDP) ratios and debt/GDP ratios are more important than the absolute size of the deficit or the debt. According to deficit doves, high interest rates cause bigger deficits (not vice versa) because interest payments on the debt increase as interests rates rise. They also argue that there is no financial burden on future generations because government spending is simultaneously creating assets for the future. Furthermore, deficit doves point out that unemployment generates bigger deficits because of its association with lower tax revenues and higher government spending on things like unemployment compensation.

The functional finance view suggests that both hawks and doves are wrong. In a modern (state) money system in which government is the monopoly issuer of fiat currency (useless currency that is accepted as a medium of exchange), the state does not need the public's money in order to spend. Taxes and bond sales do not finance government spending. The purpose of taxes (and the requirement that taxes be paid in government money) is to create a demand for the fiat money. Bond sales drain the excess reserves created by deficit spending to maintain short-term (overnight) interest rates. In the functional finance view, the particular relation of G and T does not matter in and of itself; what matters are the effects of the budget stance. Deficit hawks treat the modern money system as though it were a gold standard, whereas deficit doves emphasize that the deficit is not really as big as it seems or that we can afford the deficit or the debt. According to the functional finance view, deficit and the debt are accounting information on the one hand and policy instruments on the other. Deficits can be too big, but they can also be too small, depending on the economic context. Debt is not a burden, because the monopoly issuer of the currency never has any problem settling an obligation denominated in that currency.

—*Fadhel Kaboub and Mathew Forstater*

References
Heilbroner, Robert, and Peter Bernstein. *The Debt and the Deficit: False Alarms, Real Possibilities.* New York: Norton, 1989.
Lerner, Abba. "Functional Finance and the Federal Debt." *Social Research,* vol. 10, no. 1 (1944): 10–51.
Peterson, Peter G. *Facing Up: How to Rescue the Economy from Crushing Debt and Restore the American Dream.* New York: Simon and Schuster, 1993.
See also Volume 1: Budget Deficits and Surpluses.

Gramm-Rudman-Hollings, Balanced Budget, and Emergency Deficit Control Act (1985)

Failed effort to legislate a balanced budget in response to a conservative movement that strongly opposed increased government spending.

Before 1985, congressional majorities necessary to pass a balanced budget amendment to the Constitution were lacking. The Gramm-Rudman-Hollings Act (GRH) was second best for some "deficit hawks," who recommended a balanced budget or surplus in every year and felt the legislation would provide the president and Congress with an important incentive to come to budget agreements. GRH, named for its sponsors, Senators Phil Gramm (R–Texas), Warren Rudman (R–New Hampshire), and Ernest Hollings (D–South Carolina), mandated a timetable of reduced budget deficits beginning in 1985 and ending with a balanced federal budget in 1991. In 1987, that target date changed to 1993. In 1990, the Omnibus Budget Reconciliation Act repealed GRH.

GRH required automatic spending cuts divided equally between defense and nondefense spending should the president and Congress not agree on a budget that reached that year's target. Social Security expenditures, interest on the national debt, and some programs targeted at the poor remained exempted from those automatic cuts.

In the mid-1980s, the administration of Republican President Ronald Reagan accused Congress of being unable to control spending. Congressional Democrats blamed the ballooning deficit on a big tax cut in 1981 (which lowered taxes for those in the highest tax brackets and was designed to produce a trickle-down effect in the economy) and a defense buildup. The GRH compromise promised Democrats that

Reagan would have to scale back defense spending if he wanted a balanced budget, and the Reagan administration thought it would force Democrats to be even more willing to cut nondefense expenditures. Meanwhile, some traditional Republicans thought Reagan might have to modify his refusal to raise taxes if he wanted a balanced budget.

As economic policy, GRH was a procrustean bed that made no distinction between useful and essential government activities on the one hand and government actions that were marginal at best, usually pork-barrel expenditures. Also, had it not been rescinded, GRH would have been bad policy in the face of a recession in 1985 and 1986. Although it had an escape clause that could be activated in response to recession, it called for spending cuts to resume in the first year of recovery. The first year of recovery is the worst possible year to reduce a deficit; a deficit reduction cuts the recovery short before the recovery has a chance to produce a long-term effect.

In 1986, the Supreme Court ruled unconstitutional the GRH mechanism for making automatic budget cuts, saying that the office of Comptroller of the Currency remained vested with this authority. The 1987 revision of GRH transferred that authority to the president. The old and new versions of the targets and the deficits that actually occurred are detailed in Table 1.

Table 1. Gramm-Rudman-Hollings Proposed and Actual Budget Reductions, 1985–1987

Fiscal year	1985 target ($ billion)	1987 target ($ billion)	Actual deficit ($ billion)
1986	$171.9 (billion)	$171.9	$221.2
1987	144.0	144.0	149.8
1988	108.0	144.0	155.2
1989	72.0	136.0	152.5
1990	36.0	100.0	221.4
1991	0	64.0	269.2
1992	0	28.0	290.4
1993	0	0	255.1

When Congress repealed GRH, the Council of Economic Advisers asserted that despite its failure to achieve its numerical goals, it had nevertheless restrained the growth of deficits. A much better epitaph is the tongue-in-cheek view of Warren Rudman, one of the bill's sponsors. He dubbed GRH a "bad law whose time has come." He was only half right, because the economic recession of the late 1980s forced an increase in taxes as well as an increase in spending.

—*Michael A. Meeropol*

References
Blinder, Alan. *Hard Heads, Soft Hearts: Tough-Minded Economics for a Just Society.* New York: Addison-Wesley, 1987.

Meeropol, Michael. *Surrender, How the Clinton Administration Completed the Reagan Revolution.* Ann Arbor: University of Michigan Press, 1998.

See also Volume 1: Reagan, Ronald.

Great Depression (1929–1941)

Worldwide economic slump characterized by international tariff barriers, the breakup of former empires, and destruction wrought by the loss of life and property during World War I in Europe that began, at least symbolically, with the collapse of stock prices on the New York Stock Exchange in 1929 and ended in the United States with widespread deficit spending on public works and rearmament in the late 1930s.

Owing to its severity, scope, and duration, the Great Depression has been the object of considerable debate among economists, sociologists, and historians in the United States and Europe. Although there is no consensus on how to explain the U.S. economic crisis, which had global repercussions, the following questions figure prominently in the literature on the subject: Did the Great Depression originate in the United States? If so, how did it spread to the rest of the world? Was the Great Depression a unique event? What, if anything, did the catastrophe reveal about the structure of the capitalist system?

The Federal Reserve Board adopted restrictive monetary policies as early as February 1929 aimed at curtailing speculation on the stock exchange, leading to a recession in the middle of 1929. However, the Great Depression itself began with a dramatic plunge in stock prices on October 24, 1929 (known thereafter as Black Thursday); the Federal Reserve Board continued to raise rates after that date. The crash not only produced widespread panic among firms and individual investors, but it also placed excessive strain on banks and other financial institutions. Within three years, stocks lost 80 percent of their value and 11,000 of the country's 25,0000 banks became insolvent. In the same period, the U.S. gross domestic product declined from an index of 163 to an index of 115, while unemployment climbed to 30 percent. Owing to the status of the United States as the world's most significant creditor and financier, the crisis soon spread to Europe (particularly Germany and Great Britain) and the rest of the world. Although the New Deal in the United States and similar public works programs in other countries reduced unemployment and increased purchasing power, the depression abated only with the preparations for war.

In retrospect, the period 1914 to 1945—which witnessed World War I, the failure to rebuild the European interstate system (a cooperative economic system that would have coordinated tariff rates and other trade issues), the Great Depression, and World War II—can be understood as the interregnum between the Pax Britannica (or British hegemony) and the Pax Americana (or U.S. hegemony). In *The World in Depression, 1929–1939*—an influential contribution to an ongoing debate between Keynesians (who favored deficit spending) and monetarists (who subscribed to the theory that market forces would control inflation, unemployment, and production)—Charles Kindleberger (1973) attributed the gravity, range, and length of the slump to the inability of the United States or Great Britain to achieve free market trade at a time when the international economy lacked a source of lending or a means of discounting.

After World War II, the lessons of the Great Depression were codified not only by Keynesian economics (with its emphasis on government intervention in the economy to prevent crises of underconsumption) but also by a set of new international institutions: the International Monetary Fund, the World Bank, the United Nations, and the General Agreement on Tariffs and Trade.

—*Mark Frezzo*

References

Bernstein, Michael A. *The Great Depression.* Cambridge: Cambridge University Press, 1987.

Galbraith, John Kenneth. *The Great Crash, 1929.* Boston: Houghton Mifflin, 1972.

Kindleberger, Charles. *The World in Depression, 1929–1939.* Berkeley: University of California Press, 1973.

Temin, Peter. *Lessons from the Great Depression.* Cambridge, MA: MIT Press, 1989.

See also Volume 1: Keynesian Economics; Public Works Administration.

Great Railroad Strike of 1877

The first national labor uprising in the United States, which alerted the federal government to its inadequacy in handling labor disputes.

On July 16, 1877, the day of a 10 percent wage cut, workers in Martinsburg, West Virginia, began a strike against the Baltimore & Ohio Railroad. In one week similar uprisings had immobilized rail hubs in Philadelphia, St. Louis, Indianapolis, Buffalo, Cincinnati, Columbus, and Kansas City. Strikers demonstrated by halting freight and passenger trains, but violence and rioting often broke out, as in Chicago, Pittsburgh, and Baltimore. Many state governors lacked sufficient militia to suppress the insurgents and quickly appealed to President Rutherford B. Hayes for federal military support.

Before 1877 the United States had no precedent or policy for dealing with labor disputes, which had been considered outside of federal jurisdiction. Hayes eventually deployed troops, but his action only restored law and order and did not deal with the underlying labor conflict. Federal Judge Thomas S. Drummond set the most significant legal precedents in the strike, holding Indianapolis strikers in contempt of court for obstructing the operation of federal receiverships (bankrupt railroads directed by federal courts for the public good). Hayes and his cabinet spurred other federal courts into similar action to restore railroad operation. By July 29, troops and judicial indictments had effectively ended the uprising. Railroad workers did not receive their wages, and many participants lost their jobs or ended up in jail. The strike resulted in no specific policy but set the precedent for federal executive and judiciary primacy in labor disputes. It also ushered in a decade of national labor struggles that culminated in the 1894 Pullman strike.

—*John Grady Powell*

References

Bruce, Robert V. *1877: Year of Violence.* Chicago: I. R. Dee, 1989.

Foner, Philip S. *The Great Labor Uprising of 1877.* New York: Monad Press, 1977.

See also Volume 1: Pullman Strike.

Great Society

Title given to the series of domestic programs during the presidency of Lyndon B. Johnson that tried to improve the quality of life for all Americans.

President Lyndon B. Johnson used the image and moniker of a Great Society to enlist support of Americans for his civil rights legislation, Medicare and Medicaid programs, environmental protection policies, and war on poverty and consumerism. The president first used the term in a speech at graduation ceremonies at the University of Michigan on May 22, 1964. He stated, "We have the opportunity to move not only toward the rich society and the powerful society, but upward to the Great Society." Using the highest ideals of society, he envisioned "an end to poverty and racial injustice," "a place where every child can find knowledge to enrich his mind and enlarge is talents," and "a place where the city of man serves not only the needs of the body and the demands of commerce but the desire for beauty and the hunger for community."

Johnson saw the role of the federal government as helping people overcome their disadvantages. He signed two major civil rights acts to help African Americans. The Civil Rights Act of 1964 prohibited discrimination in hotels, restaurants, and public facilities and authorized the Justice Department to initiate desegregation suits. The Voting Rights Act of 1965 outlawed discriminatory practices in elections and authorized programs for voter registration. Several other pieces of legislation tried to help those in poverty. The Economic Opportunity Act (1964) established the Office of Economic Opportunity to administer myriad poverty programs including the Jobs Corps for training young people, Work-Study Programs for low-income college students, a domestic Peace Corps called Volunteers in Service to America (VISTA), and a Work Experience Program to provide child day care and other services to the working class. Congress also created programs to increase food stamps and unemployment compensation during this time. Johnson established two new executive branch departments—the Department of Housing and Urban Development and the Department of Transportation. In 1965, his administration also sought to address the medical needs of the elderly through the Medicare and Medicaid programs. In addition, environmental protection legislation was a priority. Laws passed during these years including the Water Quality Act of 1965, the Clean Air Act of 1965, the Clean Water Restoration Act of 1966, and the Air Quality Act of 1967. Finally, several pieces of legislation designed to protect all Americans—such as the Highway Safety Act of 1966, the Fair Packaging and Labeling Act of 1966, and the Wholesome Meat Act of 1967—also passed.

Even though Johnson would have to give up or cut back on many of his programs in the face of the Vietnam conflict, the Great Society transformed the nation. In 1961, only 45 domestic social programs existed; when Johnson left office, 435 programs helped the American people. Spending on social programs increased from $9.9 billion at the beginning of the decade to $25.6 billion by the time Johnson left office. During his term the poverty rate fell from 22 percent to 13 percent of the population. The Great Society expanded the federal government, gave economic opportunities to a wide variety of Americans, and increased the standard of living of many stuck in poverty.

—*T. Jason Soderstrum*

References
Andrew, John A. *Lyndon Johnson and the Great Society.* Chicago: I. R. Dee, 1998.
See also Volume 1: Welfare Economics; Volume 2 (Documents): Lyndon B. Johnson's Great Society Speech.

Green Party

A national reform party formed in 1989 that rejects the political status quo (the Democratic and Republican parties) as dominated by corporate interests.

Green Party members stress environmental protection, social and economic justice, nonviolence, and participatory democracy. The party argues that treaties such as the North American Free Trade Agreement (NAFTA) and the General Agreement on Tariffs and Trade (GATT) limit the participation of individuals in trade and adversely affect the economic and environmental health of local communities. Inspired by the success of the German Green Party, American activists formed the Green Committees of Correspondence in 1984, which grew rapidly but evolved in many diverse directions. By the late 1980s, a grassroots movement had begun to unite these factions into a national political party, ultimately culminating in 1989 with the Green Congress in Eugene, Oregon. The following year in Estes Park, Colorado, the nascent Green Party adopted its first international platform, which reflected the demands of a worldwide reform constituency with allied parties in many countries. Holding to the vision of a just, peaceful, and environmentally safe society, the party grew rapidly throughout the early 1990s as a fragile coalition of liberal activists. In 1996, however, a schism occurred as several members left to form the Association of State Green Parties (ASGP). This group argued that the party had become too radical and activist and too harsh in its criticism of capitalism; it said the party should emphasize more conservative tactics such as legislation and lobbying. Although the two sides agreed in the nomination of Ralph Nader in the 2000 presidential election, an attempt by the ASGP to control the national convention failed. Today both groups lay claim to the title of Green Party. The original faction is known as "the Greens/Green Party USA" and in 1996 the ASGP filed with the Federal Elections Commission as a separate party, "The Green Party of the United States." The Green Party of the United States, which advocates more activism and grassroots involvement, supported more than 550 Green candidates in 2002.

—*Brooks Flippen*

References
Cherry, Shelia. "Green Machine." *Insight,* vol. 16, no. 45 (December 4, 2000): 24.
Confessore, Nicholas. "Green Herring." *The American Prospect,* vol. 43 (March 1, 1999): 41.
Culbert, Jeff. *The Open Mythology of the Green Party Politics.* North York, Ontario: York University, 1996.
MacKinnon, James. "It's Not Easy Being Green." *New Age Journal,* vol. 16, no. 6 (September 1, 1999): 76.
Paige, Sean. "Green Like Me." *Insight,* vol. 14, no. 46 (December 14, 1998): 16.
Poguntke, Thomas. *From Nuclear Building Sites to Cabinet: The Career of the German Green Party.* Keele, Germany: Keele University Press, 2001.
Silverstein, Ken. "Candidate Nader." *Mother Jones,* vol. 25, no. 4 (July 1, 2000): 60.
See also Volume 1: General Agreement on Tariffs and Trade; Nader, Ralph; North American Free Trade Agreement.

Greenpeace

An international organization dedicated to protecting and preserving the natural environment through direct action.

In 1971, members of the Don't Make A Wave Committee in Vancouver, Canada, gained extensive attention in their effort to stop the United States from conducting atmospheric nuclear tests on a small island off the Alaskan coast. The island, Amchitka, supported many endangered sea otters as well as eagles and falcons. A small group of volunteers in an old fishing boat eventually brought a halt to the testing in 1972 and established Amchitka as a bird sanctuary. The organization chose the new name Greenpeace to better reflect its mission.

Public interest sparked by the Vancouver organization led to the formation of Greenpeace groups in other countries. Together these independent groups formed a loose coalition. In 1977 the Canada group, the largest of the organizations, began to formalize ties with the other groups. The various Greenpeace groups tend to be autonomous and work together without the need for a strict hierarchy.

Using nonviolent direct action, Greenpeace focuses on six areas: preserving ancient forests, stopping global warming, exposing toxic pollutants, protecting the ocean, ending genetic engineering dangers, and halting the proliferation of nuclear production. The organization also conducts research and promotes educational programs that inform the public and government officials about environmentally sound solutions to current problems. Greenpeace has taken the lead in several "Earth-friendly" projects including the ozone-safe refrigerator, alternative fishing technologies, and alternative power sources (for example, its 1998 solar pioneers project in Canada promotes solar energy). Since 1971, Greenpeace's membership has swelled to 2.5 million members worldwide. The organization receives all of its support from its members; Greenpeace does not accept donations from governments or corporations.

—*Lisa A. Ennis*

References
"Greenpeace History." No date. Available: http://www.greenpeacecanada.org; accessed September 7, 2001.

"Inside Greenpeace: History and Mission." September 7, 2001. Available: http://www.greenpeaceusa.org; accessed September 7, 2001.

"London Greenpeace: A History of Peace, Protest, and Campaigning." No date. Available: http://www.mcspotlight.org/people/biogs/london_grnpeace.html; accessed September 7, 2001.

See also Volume 1: Environment.

Greenspan, Alan (1926–)

Since 1987 head of the nation's central bank with a pivotal role in the formulation of U.S. monetary policy.

Alan Greenspan was born March 6, 1926, in New York City and attended New York University, from which he received three economics degrees—a B.S. in 1948, an M.A. in 1950, and a Ph.D. in 1977 with published articles substituting for a dissertation. Greenspan also pursued graduate studies at Columbia University, where leading economist Arthur Burns influenced him. He entered the financial world as an economist with the National Industrial Conference Board and then partnered with bond trader William Townsend in 1954 to form the economic consulting firm Townsend-Greenspan and Company, which was financially successful for more than 30 years. Greenspan dissolved the company in 1987 after he failed to find a qualified buyer.

Although philosophically a Republican, Greenspan has never held an elected office; nonetheless, he has had an extended public service career. He first ventured into the political world as director of domestic policy research for Richard Nixon's presidential campaign team in 1968. He has advised Presidents Richard Nixon, Gerald Ford, and Ronald Reagan and served on several commissions including the Commission for an All-Volunteer Armed Forces and the National Commission on Social Security Reform, which he chaired. From 1974 through 1977, he was chair of the president's Council of Economic Advisers. Since 1987 he has been chair of the Board of Governors of the Federal Reserve Bank. With a reputation as an "inflationary hawk" who fought inflation and a proponent of laissez-faire economics, Greenspan became chair of the Federal Reserve Board in 1987. He was first nominated to that position by President Ronald Reagan and was renominated by President George H. W. Bush (1991 and 1996) and President Bill Clinton (2000). Since 1987, in his capacity as Federal Reserve Board chair, he has also chaired the Federal Open Market Committee of the Federal Reserve System, a group that determines economic policy.

The Federal Reserve Board of Governors chair, who is independent of both the president and Congress, has far-reaching powers in his function of directing monetary policy. Many perceive Greenspan as the second-most-influential person in the United States as demonstrated by his capacity to move markets simply by speaking at a press conference. His approach as chair has been marked by caution, pragmatism, and reliance on empirical evidence. Because he is a member of Washington, D.C., social circles and so is in the public eye, members of the public have become more aware of the Federal Reserve system than they once were.

—*John Marino*

References

Martin, Justin. *Greenspan, the Man Behind the Money.* Cambridge, MA: Perseus Publishing, 2000.

See also Volume 1: Federal Reserve Act of 1913; Volume 2: Federal Reserve Bank; Volume 2 (Documents): Federal Reserve Act.

Gross National Product (GNP)

Market value of the flow of final goods and services produced in a country.

The gross national product (GNP) measures a nation's output. A flow per unit of time (an annual or quarterly rate), the GNP equals the output of final goods and services produced in a nation valued at market prices. Final goods and services exclude intermediate products bought by firms and used up in the production of other goods and services within the period, so the GNP consists of goods and services sold to the final consumers plus additions to the initial capital invested to buy the stock of the company or bank. The government measures GNP either at current prices (nominal GNP or current-dollar GNP) or at the prices of some specified base year (real GNP or constant-dollar GNP). A related concept, gross domestic product (GDP), values the output of factors of production owned in a country rather than factors of production located in the country; it differs from GNP by the flow of investment income between countries. The net national product (NNP) equals the GNP minus depreciation (the cost of replacement investment needed to keep the capital stock constant by making up for wear and tear of machinery and buildings).

GNP has several well-recognized limitations as a measure of economic welfare and as a basis for economic and social policy. Its exclusion of nonmarket activities means that it undervalues housework and child care (except when these activities are bought in the market). GNP and NNP also neglect degradation of the environment and natural resources resulting from production and consumption. Changes in relative prices and the availability of new products complicate comparisons of real GNP over time. Gross private domestic investment, as measured in the national income and product accounts, counts only money spent on tangible, physical capital; it neglects spending on the acquisition of intangible human capital (knowledge and skills) through research and development and education, and it neglects government spending on physical capital (infrastructure investment such as highways and airports). Analysts have devoted considerable effort to improving the measurement of economic welfare—for example, by constructing "green accounts" for the environment and valuing housework—but traditional GNP figures continue to dominate political and journalistic debates over economic policy.

—*Robert Dimand*

References

Ahmad, J. J., E. Lutz, and S. El Sarafy. *Environmental Accounting for Sustainable Development.* Washington, DC: World Bank, 1989.

Eisner, Robert. *The Misunderstood Economy: What Counts and How to Count It.* Boston, MA: Harvard Business School Press, 1994.

Folbre, Nancy, and Wagman, Barnet. "Counting Housework: Revised Estimates of Real Product in the United States, 1800–1860." *Journal of Economic History,* vol. 53 (1993): 275–288.

See also Volume 1: Economic Indicators; Volume 2: Trade Policy.

Group of Seven (G-7)

An association of seven major industrialized nations of the world whose heads of governments meet annually to coordinate their economic policies.

The Group of Seven, or G-7, was formed in 1975 and includes the United States, the United Kingdom, Germany, France, Italy, Japan, and Canada (since 1976). Since 1977 the president of the European Commission has also attended the G-7 summits. By the end of the twentieth century, the other six members of the G-7 had accounted for 46 percent of U.S. foreign trade ($695.9 billion of U.S. exports to and $1,024.6 billion of U.S. imports from foreign countries, respectively). From 1975, when the first economic summit took place in Rambuillet, France, to 2001, the G-7 has held 27 summits. Four of these meetings were in the United States: San Juan, Puerto Rico (1976), Williamsburg, Virginia (1983), Houston, Texas (1990), and Denver, Colorado (1997).

In the 1970s and 1980s, the G-7 summits provided a high-level negotiating forum for discussion of numerous issues of mutual concern in international economic relations—for example, increased oil prices, inflation and economic stagnation, anticrisis economic measures, stabilization of finances including the U.S. dollar, liberalization of international trade, North-South relations in both the Western and Eastern Hemispheres, and the problem of debt of developing countries. The 1986 Tokyo summit established a framework for special consultations among finance ministers of the G-7 countries and the managing director of the International Monetary Fund to coordinate monetary policies of the industrialized world.

Since the 1978 Bonn summit, the United States and its industrialized trading partners Great Britain, France, Germany, and Japan have broadened the G-7 agenda, discussing topical political, strategic, and environmental issues. At the 1990 Houston summit, the G-7 began to develop a collective strategy to assist in the transformation of former communist economies. The G-7 invited the Soviet Union/Russia to participate in the 1991 London summit to discuss matters within Russia's competence, particularly its debt and economic reforms. The 1997 Denver summit institutionalized Russia's participation, and the Birmingham summit of 1998 officially renamed the group G-8, although the United States, its European trading partners, and Japan continue major economic and financial consultations within the traditional G-7 framework. With the progressive and expanding globalization of economy and trade in the information age, the G-7/G-8 has evolved from an informal economic forum to an effective directorate of leading powers, participation in which strengthens the global leadership of the United States. Even though globalization continues to progress, the meetings among the heads of state often draw protesters who oppose such globalization.

—*Peter Rainow*

References

Bergsten, C. Fred. *Global Economic Leadership and the Group of Seven.* Washington, DC: Institute for International Economics, 1996.

Putnam, Robert D., and Nichols Bayne. *Hanging Together: Cooperation and Conflict in the Seven-Power Summits.* Cambridge, MA: Harvard University Press, 1987.

See also Volumes 1, 2: Foreign Policy.

GSEs

See Agricultural Government-Sponsored Enterprises.

H

Hamilton, Alexander (1755–1804)

America's first secretary of the Treasury, an ardent supporter of the Constitution, and to that end coauthor of the *Federalist Papers.*

Born January 11, 1755, on the island of Nevis in the Caribbean Sea, the illegitimate son of a Scottish peddler, Alexander Hamilton spent his early life working as a clerk throughout the Caribbean. When he was still a boy, he sought his fortune in America. He attended King's College in New York and later served as an aide to General George Washington during the American Revolution. After the war, he became a lawyer in New York City. He attended the Consti tutional Convention in Philadelphia in 1787 and became an ardent supporter of the Constitution during the ratification process. Along with Constitutional Convention delegates James Madison of Virginia and John Jay of New York, Hamilton authored *The Federalist Papers,* a series of newspaper articles that brilliantly defended the principles underlying the Constitution.

In 1789, Hamilton became the first secretary of the treasury. In a series of important reports to Congress, he laid out his plans for the nation's economy. First he introduced a proposal that led to the 1791 Funding and Assumption Act, which made further provision for the payment of the debts of the United States under which the U.S. government would pay at full value all debts incurred by the nation during the American Revolution. The nation would also assume the remaining state debts. Next Hamilton called for the creation of the Bank of the United States ("Second Report on the Public Credit"). Both the American government and private investors would own stock in the new institution. The bank would control the nation's credit while its notes would serve as the nation's currency. Hamilton also proposed the establishment of a mint to coin money along with a duty on imported spirits and an excise on domestic whiskey to generate revenue. Finally, Hamilton laid out specific measures that the Congress should take to encourage manufacturing, including premiums, bounties, and protective tariffs.

Hamilton quickly made an enemy of Thomas Jefferson, secretary of state under President George Washington. He won Jefferson's support for the funding and assumption program by promising to build the national capital along the Potomac River in Virginia. However, Jefferson could never accept much of Hamilton's remaining financial program. He remained convinced that Hamilton sought only the good of the wealthiest Americans at the expense of farmers, tradesmen, and laborers. The conflict between these two men led to the creation of America's first two-party system. Hamilton's supporters became known as the Federalists, and Jefferson's followers became the Democratic-Republicans.

In 1796, Hamilton left public service and returned to private law practice in New York City. He remained interested in politics and defended many cases in the New York Supreme Court that guaranteed freedom of the press. When Thomas Jefferson and Aaron Burr deadlocked in the 1800 presidential race, Hamilton threw his support to Jefferson because he considered Burr a dangerous man. Burr later challenged him to a duel in the summer of 1804. Hamilton shot in the air, but Burr took deadly aim. After spending an agonizing day in terrible pain, Hamilton died on July 12, 1804. Though Hamilton was less well known than beloved leaders like George Washington and Thomas Jefferson, his economic nationalism has remained a model for politicians as different as Henry Clay, Abraham Lincoln, and Franklin D. Roosevelt.

—*Mary Stockwell*

References

Kline, Mary-Jo, ed. *Alexander Hamilton: A Biography in His Own Words.* New York: Newsweek Books, 1973.

See also Volume 1: Bank of the United States, First; *The Federalist Papers;* Volume 2 (Documents): *Report on the Subject of Manufactures.*

Harris Treaty (1858)

First commercial treaty between the United States and Japan.

Appointed by President James Buchanan as the U.S. consul to Japan, Townsend Harris arrived at his post in 1856. For two years the military rulers of Japan, the Tokugawa Shogunate, refused to welcome Harris into the diplomatic circle, but he stayed at a Buddhist temple in Shimoda while quietly establishing informal relations with some members of the Tokugawa government. Meanwhile, the British and the French had established military presences in Japan and had been pressuring the Japanese government to agree to trade terms that would be unfavorable to Japan. Harris persuaded the Japanese that a treaty under favorable terms with the United States would provide them with leverage in their negotiations with the European powers. On July 29, 1858, the United States and Japan signed their first commercial treaty.

Under the terms of the treaty, the United States gained access to five ports in Japan and received the right of extraterritoriality for American citizens, and Americans could worship without interference—a right that included the construction of churches and a pledge not to excite religious animosity. The terms concerning the tariff arrangements favored the United States with a low rate of 5 percent set for machinery and shipping materials as well as raw materials. The treaty also allowed the Japanese to purchase warships, whale ships, cannons, munitions, and other war matériel from the United States as well as to engage the services of mariners, scientists, and military experts.

The treaty became effective July 4, 1859. Each party reserved the right to revoke the treaty after giving the other party one year's notice. Terms could also be renegotiated after July 4, 1872. As a result of the treaty, the United States and Japan established commercial and diplomatic relations that lasted until 1937 and resumed after the Japanese surrender in 1945 that ended World War II.

—Cynthia Clark Northrup

References

Kelly, William Boland. *Studies in United States Commercial Policy.* Chapel Hill: University of North Carolina Press, 1963.
See also Volume 1: Japan; Japanese Oil Embargo.

Hawaii

South Pacific island kingdom that became the fiftieth state of the United States in 1959.

During the nineteenth century, the kingdom of Hawaii provided a substantial amount of sugar to the United States. U.S. planters controlled a large percentage of the island's production. During the 1840s the British and the French sought to incorporate the sugar-rich islands into their own empires. King Kamehameha III turned to the United States for assistance, and in 1851 the kingdom became a U.S. protectorate. After several failed attempts, the United States and the kingdom of Hawaii concluded a reciprocal trade agreement in 1885. Many Republicans opposed the agreement, which allowed the duty-free importation of Hawaiian sugar into the United States at the expense of domestic sugar producers and European sugar beet producers. The estimated loss of revenues for the United States from the tariff on Hawaiian sugar amounted to $12.8 million. The United States more than recouped this amount two years later when Hawaii granted the United States the right to establish a naval base at Pearl Harbor. During the first administration of Grover Cleveland (1885–1889), the United States attempted to annex the islands, and during the presidency of Benjamin Harrison (1889–1893) Americans in Hawaii briefly overthrew the government of Queen Lilioukaliani. However, the United States refused to recognize the new republic and the coup failed. Finally, in 1898, President William McKinley annexed Hawaii, and by the turn of the century the Pacific island kingdom had become a U.S. territory via the Treaty of Annexation of Hawaii.

During the first half of the twentieth century Hawaii continued to produce sugar and pineapples for American consumption, and it served as the naval base for the Pacific fleet during World War II. In 1959 Hawaii became the fiftieth state of the Union. Since the 1960s Hawaii has relied on tourism to boost its economy; most of its visitors are from Southeast Asia.

—Cynthia Clark Northrup

References

Tate, Merze. *The United States and the Hawaiian Kingdom.* New Haven, CT: Yale University Press, 1965.
See also Volume 1: Sugar.

Hawley-Smoot Tariff (1930)

Protective tariff on both industrial and agricultural products created as an initial response to the Great Depression.

Throughout most of the 1920s, the Fordney-McCumber Tariff protected the U.S. economy. The Hawley-Smoot Tariff of 1930 strengthened the provisions of Fordney-McCumber that protected medium-sized manufacturing concerns and agriculture.

During the 1928 presidential campaign, Herbert Hoover promised heightened protection for American farmers still suffering in connection with global surpluses of agricultural products. The Hawley-Smoot Tariff was part of an effort to placate Republican farmers, who had denounced Hoover's opposition to McNary-Haugen legislation. The McNary-Haugen legislation (1927) had attempted to establish agricultural parity based on 1919 agricultural prices.

The Hawley-Smoot Tariff marked a transformation of the debate over American tariff protection. Politicians from rural constituencies advocated its passage. Its opponents came from the American Bankers Association and from boardrooms of large corporations like General Motors and the Pennsylvania Railroad. Despite substantial pressure to the contrary from the business community, Herbert Hoover defended the Hawley-Smoot Tariff and signed it into law. In his arguments on its behalf, Hoover pointed to changes that would provide greater flexibility in altering barriers to trade. He had successfully requested provisions to enhance the capability of the bipartisan Tariff Commission to respond quickly to changes in international trade patterns: In the event a foreign government abandoned or initiated practices of unfair trade, the Tariff Commission could respond in kind. In this way, the United States could curb foreign government subsidies, which paid producers the difference between the producers' low selling prices and normal selling prices, and the formation of cartels, which controlled pricing by agreeing to restrict production. The administration of President Franklin D. Roosevelt strengthened the provision for flexible response with the passage of the Reciprocal Trade Agreements Act, an amendment to the Hawley-Smoot Tariff.

Provisions for tariff flexibility failed to allay the concerns of critics of the Hawley-Smoot Tariff. Foreign governments protested that high American tariffs slowed world trade and impeded recovery from the global recession. In particular, relations with agricultural exporters, such as Canada, suffered.

The reputation of the Hawley-Smoot Tariff deteriorated as the Great Depression continued. The early complaints by American businesses and foreign governments took on greater weight as economic nationalism lost its allure. By the presidential campaign of 1932, the Hawley-Smoot Tariff had become a target of derision. Democratic candidate Franklin D. Roosevelt claimed that Hoover's refusal to veto the bill caused the Great Depression. Hoover rebutted Roosevelt's argument, but the bad economy led to Roosevelt's election.

—*Karen A. J. Miller*

References
Goldstein, Judith. *Ideas, Interests, and American Trade Policy.* Ithaca, NY: Cornell University Press, 1993.
Kaplan, Edward S. *American Trade Policy, 1923–1995.* Westport, CT: Greenwood Press, 1996.
See also Volumes 1, 2: Agricultural Policy; Volume 2 (Documents): Franklin D. Roosevelt on Hawley-Smoot Tariff; Herbert Hoover's Response to Franklin D. Roosevelt on Hawley-Smoot Tariff.

Hay-Pauncefote Treaties (1900, 1901)

Two separate treaties signed by the United States and Great Britain that granted the United States the exclusive right to build, control, and fortify a canal across Central America.

American interest in an isthmian canal increased when the United States emerged from the Spanish-American War as a power in the Caribbean and the Pacific. A canal across Central America seemed necessary so that the U.S. fleet could participate easily in two-ocean operations and so Americans could take full advantage of trade opportunities in the Pacific. But the Clayton-Bulwer Treaty (1850) required a joint Anglo-American protectorate of any isthmian canal. In January 1900, a bill introduced into Congress called for the construction of a canal across Nicaragua despite the Clayton-Bulwer Treaty. British officials, involved in the Boer War in South Africa and facing several unfriendly European nations, deemed it unwise to jeopardize Britain's friendship with the United States. Thus on February 5, 1900, Secretary of State John Hay and British ambassador Sir Julian Pauncefote signed the first Hay-Pauncefote Treaty abrogating Clayton-Bulwer and giving the United States the sole right to build and control, but not fortify, a canal connecting the Atlantic and Pacific Oceans. Governor Theodore Roosevelt of New York and Republican Senator Henry Cabot Lodge of Massachusetts led the attack on the first treaty because it did not

give the United States the right to fortify the canal. Before ratifying the treaty on December 20, 1900, the Senate amended it to allow for fortification of the canal. But on March 11, 1901, Pauncefote informed Hay that the British government would not accept the treaty. In the following months, much talk in the United States called for the unilateral abrogation of the Clayton-Bulwer Treaty or even for going to war with Great Britain over the issue of the isthmian canal. British leaders, greatly disturbed by such talk, agreed to sign a second Hay-Pauncefote Treaty in November and December 1901, and both the U.S. Congress and British Parliament ratified the agreement that allowed the United States to build, control, and fortify a canal across Central America.

—*Steven E. Siry*

References
LaFeber, Walter. *The American Search for Opportunity, 1865–1913.* Cambridge: Cambridge University Press, 1993.
See also Volume 1: Panama and the Panama Canal; Volume 2 (Documents): Panama Canal Treaty of 1903.

Hepburn Railroad Regulation Act (1906)

A 1906 act that increased the power of the Interstate Commerce Commission over interstate common carriers such as railroads and ferries.

Under the leadership of Chief Commissioner Thomas M. Cooley, the Interstate Commerce Commission (ICC), which was established in 1887, attempted to halt harmful effects of competition such as rebates. Rebates were offered to large suppliers that were charged the same price for long-haul as smaller shippers received for short-haul; the large suppliers then received a rebate, which actually lowered their costs and allowed them to cut their prices and drive the smaller competitors out of the market. But during the late 1890s, the Supreme Court greatly circumscribed this type of regulation and, by 1900, the ICC was virtually powerless to end the abuses it was established to control.

In 1903, Congress began to strengthen the ICC with the Elkins Antirebating Act. This act prohibited rebates, or volume discounts, that benefited large shippers such as John D. Rockefeller, who would pay the same rate as a smaller shipper but would later receive a rebate from the railroad company. In 1904, the Supreme Court voided the railroads' solution to ruinous competition when it ordered the dismemberment of the Northern Securities Company (which monopolized the railroads in the Northwest and thereby controlled pricing). Thus, by 1905, shippers, railroads, politicians, and especially President Theodore Roosevelt began working toward a different approach to railroad regulation. With the active support of Roosevelt, whose ideas about the role of the federal government were consistent with expanding both regulatory and corporate power, Congress passed the Hepburn Act in 1906.

The Hepburn Act changed many regulations. Its "commodity clause" prohibited railways from transporting commodities in which they had an interest. This act attempted to eliminate unfair competition by railroads that hauled their own products, especially coal and iron ore. The act lengthened the time for notice of rate changes from 10 to 30 days. It established stiff monetary and prison penalties for rebating. It expanded membership in the ICC from five to seven members and lengthened the term of service to seven years. It required the railroads to standardize accounting practices and gave the ICC the right to inspect railroads' books, an essential power it needed to uncover rebating abuses, which often remained hidden through nonstandard accounting practices.

Most importantly, the act granted the ICC power to establish maximum rates that were "just, fair, and reasonable" (terms not defined in the act), and it granted the commission enforcement power. Thus railroads had to obey the ICC under penalty of fines or imprisonment, or bring suit. The act expanded the scope of the ICC to cover express (package-shipping) companies, sleeping car companies and other private car lines, and interstate pipelines. Finally, the ICC received the authority to control its own administration and to appoint agents and investigators. The ICC staff quickly ballooned.

The Hepburn Act signaled a change in U.S. regulatory policy toward one that recognized the monopolistic tendency of railroad transportation; the act regulated that monopoly, rather than attempting to control the harmful effects of a lack of competition, which had been Chief Commissioner Cooley's focus. Congress codified this view of the role of regulation in subsequent legislation. The Hepburn Act transferred regulatory power from the courts to the independent oversight commission. It transformed the ICC from a quasi-judicial body into an investigative agency and made it the dominant regulatory body of the U.S. government and the model for future regulatory agencies.

—*Russell Douglass Jones*

References

Berk, Gerald. *Alternative Tracks: The Constitution of the American Industrial Order, 1865–1917.* Baltimore, MD: Johns Hopkins University Press, 1994.

Stone, Richard D. *The Interstate Commerce Commission and the Railroad Industry: A History of Regulatory Policy.* New York: Praeger, 1991.

See also Volume 1: Interstate Commerce Commission; Railroads.

High-Tech Industries

Research-intensive industries that produce innovative technological products, formed in the 1980s with the invention of the personal computer and the rise of the Internet.

During the 1980s, high-technology (high-tech) industries in the United States grew rapidly. The average growth rate for four major research-intensive fields—aerospace, computers and office machinery, electronics and communication equipment, and pharmaceuticals—is twice that for other manufacturing firms. Since 1980 the average growth for high-tech companies has been 6 percent annually compared with 2.4 percent for other companies. Between 1992 and 1996, high-tech industries experienced an 8 percent annual growth rate—primarily because of the rise of the dot-com companies, which were entirely based on computer technology. By 1990, output from high-tech companies accounted for 13 percent of all U.S. manufactured goods.

The rise of high-tech industries coincided with the development of the personal computer (PC). Companies such as Microsoft, Dell, and Apple produced smaller computers for both office and home. Increased sales of PCs in turn stimulated the software industries. Video games and accounting, graphic design, and word processing packages allowed consumers to use the computer for more and more tasks. Manufacturers realized the need for backup data storage and addressed the problem with the development of the floppy disk, the zip drive, and the CD-ROM (compact disc read-only memory). The development of the CD-ROM in turn influenced other fields, such as music and movies. Each change in technology spurs the development of new products, which in turn stimulates the economy.

The high-tech industry created millions of jobs during the last two decades of the twentieth century. Although projections were that an additional 2 million jobs would be created between 2001 and 2006, that number may not be reached because of the recession that began in the United States in 2000. Some high-tech industries have been extremely hard hit, whereas others continue to show a more moderate growth and profit rate.

The U.S. government continues to encourage growth in this sector for several reasons. First, companies that produce innovative products generally increase their market share both domestically and internationally. New research-intensive products (for example, a software program) that support high value-added products (for example, a spreadsheet or word processing program), in which the original product is improved and the value is increased, do well overseas, and as profits increase, employees receive higher wages and subsequently have more disposable income and personal savings. New manufacturing processes generally are more efficient, resulting in the expansion of business and the creation of jobs—primary goals desired by the federal government, which then benefits from high tax revenues.

—*Cynthia Clark Northrup*

References

Nadiri, I. *Innovations and Technological Spillovers.* National Bureau of Economic Research (NBER) Working Paper no. 4423. Boston: NBER, 1993.

Tassey, G. *Technology and Economic Growth: Implications for Federal Policy.* National Institute of Standards and Technology (NIST) Planning Report 95-3. Washington, DC: U.S. Department of Commerce, 1995.

See also Volume 1: Aviation; Computer, Microsoft.

Homestead Act (1862)

First of a series of acts designed to encourage settlement on the western frontier.

Housing Act of 1949   145

On May 20, 1862, while the Civil War raged, the Northern Republican Congress passed "An Act to secure Homesteads to actual Settlers on the Public Domain." The federal government allowed U.S. citizens—or individuals who had immigrated to the United States and had applied for citizenship—to file a preemptive claim on a maximum quarter section of land in the public domain. Any man or woman who was the head of a household or had reached the age of 21 and who had never borne arms against the United States could reside on the property for five years, then receiving title, or could buy 160 acres of public land at $1.25 per acre or 80 acres for $2.50 per acre. If, at the end of five years, the person had moved his or her residence—that is, had left the land—for more than six months, the land reverted back to the government.

Between 1862 and 1986, the United States granted or sold more than 287.5 million acres to homesteaders. This figure represents approximately 25 percent of all public lands disposed of by sale or other means. The opening of western lands created a safety valve for Americans. Those from overcrowded cities or immigrants who had lived in the United States for several years had the opportunity for "free land." Many moved west who would not have otherwise. In the process, the U.S. government consolidated control over the area and new states were formed. Improvements in agriculture and the invention of barbed wire spurred the western movement.

Throughout the years, the Homestead Act has been modified often. For instance, veterans could deduct the time they served from the five-year requirement. Congress repealed the Homestead Act on October 21, 1976—extending, however, the effective ending date for public lands in Alaska 10 years to October 21, 1986.

—*Cynthia Clark Northrup*

References

An Act to Secure Homesteads to Actual Settlers on the Public Domain. U.S. Statutes at Large 12 (1863): 392–393.
See also Volume 2 (Documents): Homestead Act.

Horseshoe Bend, Battle of (1814)

Battle that opened Alabama and Mississippi to American settlement and led to the establishment of the southern Cotton Belt.

The Creek War was a war of the U.S. government against the Creek Indians, who had allied themselves with the British during the War of 1812. On March 27, 1814, Major General Andrew Jackson—leading the Tennessee militia and the 39th Regiment of the U.S. Army and accompanied by Native American allies from the Lower Creek and Cherokee tribes—had pushed the Muskogee tribe into a defensive position in a large bend in the Talapoosa River, across the neck of which the Muskogees constructed a barricade. In the early stages of the battle the allied Native Americans crossed the river upstream in stolen canoes and attacked the Muskogee village, taking the women and children prisoner, and then proceeded to attack the barricade from the rear. Jackson commenced a frontal assault on the barricade and succeeded in taking it after fierce fighting.

The subsequent Treaty of Fort Jackson, which Jackson negotiated without authorization from Congress, ended the Creek War and ceded to the United States 23 million acres of land owned by Creeks and other tribes, including some land belonging to tribes allied with the U.S. government. This victory opened much of the lower South to settlement by European Americans, and the white population of Alabama boomed from 9,000 in 1810 to 310,000 in 1830. This victory and the gain in territory cemented Jackson's popularity with the American public and contributed to his election as president in 1828.

—*Margaret Sankey*

References

Holland, James W. *Andrew Jackson and the Creek War.* Tuscaloosa: University of Alabama Press, 1990.
Horseshoe Bend National Military Park, Alabama: Official Guide and Map. Washington, DC: U.S. Department of the Interior, 1993.
Martin, Joel W. *Sacred Revolt: The Muskogees Struggle for a New World.* Boston: Beacon Press, 1991.
See also Volume 1: Indian Policy.

Housing Act of 1949

Federal legislation designed to fund inner-city urban redevelopment by razing existing slum structures and building new structures in urban areas.

The Housing Act of 1949 addressed issues related to urban redevelopment. After World War II, the white urban population moved to the suburbs, taking advantage of low-interest government-backed housing programs such as Fannie Mae, the Servicemen's Readjustment Act, and Veterans Administration mortgages. Inner-city housing was deteriorating and the private sector could not afford the costs of demolition and rehabilitation; therefore, to correct for market failure, Congress passed the Housing Act of 1949, creating a substantial federal subsidy for urban redevelopment. The act funded property acquisition, demolition of structures, and site preparation. To be eligible for federal funds, local governments had to take responsibility for one-third of a project's costs, a commitment they often realized by acquiring public works projects in local budgets.

The Housing Act of 1949 established a national legislative goal to provide "a decent home and a suitable living environment for every American family." The legislation equated housing with community development and the "general welfare and the security of the nation." Here, the concept of community development included the physical redevelopment of a community as an indicator of increased social welfare. This connection is cited as the rationale for legislation in the introduction to the act: "The Congress hereby declares that the general welfare and security of the Nation and the health and living standards of its people require housing production and related community development…"

—*Eileen Robertson-Rehberg*

References

Hays, R. Allen. *The Federal Government and Urban Housing: Ideology and Change in Public Policy.* 2d ed. Albany: State University of New York, 1995.

See also Volume 2: Urbanization.

Housing Act of 1954

Amendment to the Housing Act of 1949 that initiated city urban renewal projects and displaced poor residents.

The federal Housing Act of 1954 increased the flexibility of the Housing Act of 1949, specifying that the earlier act's funding for property acquisition, demolition of structures, and site preparation be expanded to include commercial and industrial development. The shift in emphasis from replacement residential housing (urban redevelopment) to commercial and industrial development (urban renewal) meant that poor neighborhoods could be demolished and replaced with businesses or apartments that did not necessarily provide residences for former neighborhood residents. After passage of the 1954 amendment, applications for federal funds increased significantly compared with what had been experienced after passage of the 1949 legislation, and politicians and business interests combined private funds with municipal and federal funds toward redeveloping core areas of big cities. These areas had experienced deterioration as new homes were built in the suburbs for young families seeking to live in their own homes rather than living with their parents. As more people moved to the suburbs, the inner city was abandoned and the tax base diminished, causing some areas to become slums.

Urban renewal legislation initiated a period of contention between advocates for the poor and local business interests. Frequently, cities pursued redevelopment plans that eliminated many poor neighborhoods and left others overcrowded. Poor inner-city neighborhoods were affected by practices such as redlining, a process of exclusion in which financial institutions denied development capital to neighborhoods designated as poor investments. Pockets of inner-city poverty and unemployment were increasingly evident within areas of relative prosperity. By the end of the 1950s, many large city governments were aggressively pursuing urban renewal in the interest of establishing more vital business districts rather than improving the living conditions of poor residents.

—*Eileen Robertson-Rehberg*

References

Hays, R. Allen. *The Federal Government and Urban Housing: Ideology and Change in Public Policy.* 2d ed. Albany: State University of New York, 1995.

See also Volume 2: Urbanization.

HUD

See U.S. Department of Housing and Urban Development.

Hull, Cordell (1871–1955)

Secretary of state under President Franklin D. Roosevelt from 1933 to 1945 who promoted reciprocal trade agreements.

Cordell Hull of Tennessee graduated from law school in his home state and then served as a captain during the Spanish-American War. He became a circuit judge after returning to the United States and in 1907 was elected to the House of Representatives, where he served until 1931, except for a hiatus between 1921 and 1923. He resigned from the House in 1931 to successfully run for the Senate. Two years into his Senate term he was appointed secretary of state by President Franklin D. Roosevelt.

While he was in Congress, Hull focused primarily on the tariff. His fascination with the subject began during the Mills Bill debate in 1888 on the reduction of tariff rates. Hull viewed the tariff as a domestic evil that contributed to the rise of big business, the loss of competition, and the cause of poverty among workers. He not only spoke out against high tariffs, but he proposed a series of "pop-gun bills"—pieces of legislation that addressed single tariff issues—and opposed passage of the Payne-Aldrich Tariff of 1909. After the election of President Woodrow Wilson, Hull helped draft the tax legislation that accompanied the Underwood-Simmons Tariff Act of 1913. The act decreased the tariff but added a personal income tax. Before the effects of the downward revision of the tariff could be realized, World War I disrupted international trade.

Hull realized that the high tariffs caused conflict, including World War I, in international affairs. He worked to lower rates in an effort to stabilize and improve foreign relations. He spoke out passionately against the proposed record-high Hawley-Smoot Tariff during congressional debates in 1929. After Congress passed it in June 1930, the Great Depression worsened and the country elected Franklin D. Roosevelt president after Herbert Hoover failed to implement policies to help individuals hit hard by the depression. Roosevelt appointed Hull as his secretary of state in 1933.

Hull attended the London Economic Conference in 1934 but could not cooperate with other European nations because of the restrictions placed on him by the Hawley-Smoot Tariff. When he returned to the United States, he persuaded Roosevelt to propose that Congress allow the administration to negotiate reciprocal trade agreements with individual countries in an effort to stimulate international trade. Congress passed the Reciprocal Trade Agreements Act of 1934, and Hull began negotiating agreements with countries that were willing to lower tariff barriers on a reciprocal basis with the United States. He continued to push for the reduction of tariffs throughout Roosevelt's presidency. His efforts set the United States on the course toward free trade. In recognition of his efforts to bring about peace and stability to the international community, Hull received the Nobel Peace Prize in 1945.

—*Cynthia Clark Northrup*

References

Butler, Michael A. *Cautious Visionary: Cordell Hull and Trade Reform, 1933–1937.* Kent, OH: Kent State University Press, 1998.

Hinton, Harold B. *Cordell Hull: A Biography.* Garden City, NY: Doubleday, Doran, 1942.

Hull, Cordell. *The Memoirs of Cordell Hull.* New York: Macmillan, 1948.

See also Volume 1: Great Depression; Protective Tariffs; Reciprocal Trade Agreements Act; Roosevelt, Franklin D.

I

ICC
See Interstate Commerce Commission.

IMF
See International Monetary Fund.

Immigration
The process of voluntary migration to the United States during the nineteenth and twentieth centuries.

During the late nineteenth and early twentieth centuries, immigrants to the United States tended to come from southern and eastern Europe. Although many chose to emigrate on the basis of cultural factors such as educational opportunities or political and religious freedom, immigrants generally benefited economically, having calculated the costs of emigrating, differences in the cost of living, and differences in wages and income between the home and host countries. However, during the late nineteenth and early twentieth centuries, many immigrants—often as many as half by nationality—returned to their native countries after realizing that temporary economic gains made in the United States would provide them with permanent investments back home.

The U.S. economy also benefited from immigration. The availability of relatively cheap, low-skilled immigrant labor helped fuel the rapid industrial expansion and development of the United States. Many immigrants' willingness to work longer hours for less pay reduced the price of labor for rapidly growing industries. However, the nation's economic gains did not come without social costs—anti-immigrant bigotry, racial tensions, and labor conflicts. The Know-Nothing (American) Party opposed immigration in the mid-1800s; the Molly Maguires (Irish coal miners) arranged for an end of Chinese immigration in the late 1800s; and the Ku Klux Klan of the 1920s was extremely anti-immigrant after World War I race riots occurred when returning veterans demanded jobs held by African Americans.

The Immigration Act of 1924, a result of the determination of the Ku Klux Klan and other groups to stop immigration after World War I, significantly diminished mass immigration until after World War II, when immigration resumed its steady increase. Like their predecessors, immigrants in the latter half of the twentieth century based the decision to emigrate on economic and cultural factors. For example, people were more likely to relocate to the United States if their native countries had less political freedom than the United States or if their country became involved in crisis or conflict. In addition, proximity to the United States, fluency in English, and levels of higher education increased the likelihood of immigration. On the other hand, immigration slowed when wages in source countries became higher than those in the United States. On arrival in the United States, immigrants often lagged behind in terms of earning potential, but they usually caught up with and sometimes surpassed native-born Americans of similar socioeconomic backgrounds within a generation.

After the passage of the Immigration Act of 1965, which removed restrictions on immigration to the United States from non-European nations, immigration began to increase from developing regions including India, China, the Middle East, and sub-Saharan Africa. In addition, the number of illegal Mexican immigrants looking for employment and a better life increased dramatically. Since the 1990s, the United States has offered amnesty programs allowing many illegal Mexican immigrants to file for citizenship. The increasing population of unskilled immigrants has sometimes burdened state and federal welfare systems and contributed to a decline in domestic unskilled wages. However, the number of highly skilled and educated immigrants from the same regions has also increased, a "brain drain" that has significantly benefited the United States. Taking into consideration both low-skilled and high-skilled immigrants, the United States has enjoyed a net benefit from immigration during the period since 1980.

—*Eric Pullin*

References
Borjas, George J. "The Economics of Immigration." *Journal of Economic Literature,* vol. 32, no. 4 (December 1994): 1667–1717.

Greenwood, Michael J., and John M. McDowell. "Differential Economic Opportunity, Transferability of Skills, and Immigration to the United States and Canada." *Review of Economics and Statistics*, vol. 73, no. 4 (November 1991): 612–623.

Higham, John. *Strangers in the Land: Patterns of American Nativism, 1860–1925*. New York: Atheneum, 1968.

Kessner, Thomas. *The Golden Door and Jewish Immigrant Mobility in New York City, 1880–1915*. New York: Oxford University Press, 1977.

World Bank. *World Bank Development Report 1999–2000*. Oxford: Oxford University Press, 2000.

See also Volume 1: Immigration; Volume 2: Labor.

Indentured Servants

European immigrants who were willing to trade a specific period of their life's labor in exchange for the opportunity to begin a new life in the Americas.

The system of indentured servitude originated in the English contractual systems of husbandry and apprenticeship, in which youths worked without wages in exchange for learning to care for animals or develop a specific skill. The system also developed in the American colonies because Britain, like other European states that attempted to colonize the Americas, quickly discovered that the New World contained a vast amount land that it hoped to make productive but had a dearth of willing laborers. The abundance of land, which the Europeans claimed because they believed the Native Americans did not own it, required settlers in British North America to develop effective labor systems to meet their needs. Colonial settlement in America coincided with the enclosure movement in Europe, which came about as farming became more efficient and forced many peasants off of the land and into overcrowded cities in search of jobs. Those displaced from European farms constituted a ready labor supply for the Americas, where as colonists and laborers they could become productive elements of society. However, because many could not afford to pay their passage across the Atlantic, they agreed that in exchange for passage they would labor for their employer in the colonies for a specific number of years to pay off their debt for passage. Many of these contracts included a benefit called "freedom dues," payable to the servant at the end of their contract. These dues might include tools of their trade or land. The servants' contracts could be bought and sold after their arrival in America if their services were no longer needed. As the number of English willing to become indentured servants diminished, the colonies started to accept indentured servants from throughout Europe. Virginia employed most of the indentured servants as field hands in the labor-intensive tobacco industry until the widespread use of slavery after the 1670s.

—*Ty M. Reese*

References

Morgan, Kenneth. *Slavery and Servitude in Colonial North America: A Short History*. New York: New York University Press, 2001.

See also Volume 2: Labor.

Indian Policy

Official treatment of Indians by the U.S. federal government.

The relationship between various Indian tribes and white settlers predated the formation of the U.S. government in 1781. Spanish, French, and English settlers followed different policies in relating to native populations: The Spanish advocated an aggressive approach to assimilation; the French sought a middle ground of mutual accommodation; and the English pursued the removal of native peoples from areas of white settlement.

After the Revolutionary War and the establishment of a government in the United States, federal authorities assumed responsibility for Indian policy under powers outlined in Article 1, Section 8, of the Constitution: "The Congress shall have power . . . to regulate Commerce with foreign nations, and among the several states, and with the Indian tribes." Since then, the Indian policy of the United States has been characterized by seven distinct and contradictory phases: annihilation, removal, concentration, assimilation, revitalization, termination, and self-determination.

Between 1789 and 1830, the federal government followed an unstated policy of annihilation of Indian tribes, although little such action by the federal government occurred because of extremely limited contact between white settlers and Indians. In 1830 the pressures of a growing European population and increasing demand for land prompted the promulgation of a removal policy by President Andrew Jackson, who wanted to move all native peoples to an Indian territory far from white settlement. This policy reached its zenith in 1838, when the U.S. government forced five civilized nations—the Cherokee, Chickasaw, Choctaw, Seminoles, and Creek—to move from North Carolina and Georgia to Indian territory in present-day Oklahoma along the Trail of Tears—a forced march during which a great many people, especially infants, children, and the elderly, died.

In 1850 the federal government responded to pressure from settlers by concentrating Indians on reservations and placing them under the jurisdiction of the Bureau of Indian Affairs (BIA). This policy opened vast tracts of Indian lands to white settlement and sparked tensions between settlers and Indians who were unwilling to live on reservations. In 1880, 141 Indian reservations existed in the United States.

In 1887 the Dawes Act altered policy by legislating private land ownership, formal education, and citizenship for Indians. The act's intent was to break up tribal power and culture and accelerate complete assimilation of Indians into the dominant culture. Most government officials and Indian rights organizations supported this policy, believing it would improve conditions for Indians. Ultimately it did not, and the result of the Dawes Act was that the Indian culture began to disappear and Indians began to be absorbed into mainstream U.S. culture.

The policy of assimilation persisted until the passage of the Wheeler-Howard Act in 1934, which called for the conservation of Indian lands and resources and limited home rule for Indians. Commissioner of Indian Affairs John Collier, a social worker with extensive involvement with Indian tribes, believed Indian culture could be revitalized by organizing tribal governments, holding reservations in common, promoting Indian traditions and practices, and ending the practice of allotment, which called for the provision of land to individual Indian families rather than to the tribe. The Indian New Deal, as it was known, was introduced by Collier and remained an idealistic and culturally sensitive policy that stayed in place as long as Collier served as the commissioner of Indian affairs. In 1945 Collier left office, and the most important policies of the Indian New Deal quickly disappeared.

President Harry S Truman and Commissioner of Indian Affairs Dillon Myer endorsed the policy of termination, which sought to end the reservation system, eliminate the trust relationship (in which the federal government was the trustee of Indian reservations), and terminate federal responsibility for Indian affairs. Between 1950 and 1970 the federal government and various Indian tribes became embroiled in legal battles over termination; only a small percentage of Indian tribes terminated their relationships with the federal government.

On July 18, 1970, President Richard Nixon ended termination and initiated the current policy of Indian self-determination. This approach called for reducing the influence of the Bureau of Indian Affairs in the daily lives of Indians, increasing the authority of tribal governments, and honoring treaties and annuity agreements (provision of a yearly income) between the federal government and Indian tribes. Since 1970 Native Americans have regained control over their educational system, pushed through legislation requiring the adoption of Native American children by Native American families, and gained more political and economic control of their affairs. Native Americans work in the Bureau of Indian Affairs and have helped ensure that their rights and grievances have been addressed more than they were in previous decades.

—James T. Carroll

References
Prucha, Paul. *The Great Father: The United States Government and the American Indians*. Lincoln: University of Nebraska Press, 1984.
See also Volume 1: Trail of Tears.

massive iron deposits of the Mesabi Range in northeastern Minnesota and the coalfields of southern Illinois, Indiana, and Ohio, and it contains the huge oil refineries of northwestern Indiana and northeastern Ohio.

Although the Industrial Revolution began in lower New England and the Middle Atlantic states early in the nineteenth century, it gradually expanded to include the industrial heartland encompassing Ohio, Michigan, Illinois, and Indiana, especially as the manufacture of iron and steel products, steam and electric engines, and automobiles became bellwethers of the industrial economy. By 1919, the Pennsylvania and New York region contained 21 percent of its manufacturing establishments, employed one-quarter of its wage earners, processed 27 percent of its raw materials, and accounted for 28 percent of the Industrial Heartland's product value and value added by manufacturing, outstripping New England by two or three to one in each category. Although the Middle Atlantic region actually enjoyed a moderate edge in all of these categories, the concentration of heavy industry in the East North Central states reinforced the area's popular reputation as the nation's "steel belt." During the past several decades, however, the area has declined significantly in economic importance, causing some to dismiss it as the "rust belt." The economy in this region continues to be depressed as U.S. steel companies compete with foreign steel companies. In 2002 President George W. Bush increased the tariff on imported steel in an effort to help the beleaguered industry.

—John D. Buenker

References
Madison, James H., ed. *Heartland: Comparative Histories of the Midwestern States*. Bloomington: Indiana University Press, 1990.
Sweet, William. *Great Lakes States: Trouble in America's Industrial Heartland*. Washington, DC: Congressional Quarterly Editorial Research Reports, 1980.
Teaford, Jon C. *Cities of the Heartland: The Rise and Fall of the Industrial Midwest*. Bloomington: Indiana University Press, 1994.
See also Volume 1: Industrialization.

Industrial Heartland
The Midwestern United States, where a major portion of industry is concentrated.

The term *industrial heartland* has been applied primarily to Ohio, Indiana, Illinois, Wisconsin, and Michigan—the area identified by the Census Bureau as the East North Central region. However, the concept has also been extended as far west as the Twin Cities (Minneapolis and St. Paul, Minnesota); as far south as St. Louis, Missouri; and as far east as Pittsburgh, Pennsylvania, and Buffalo, New York. According to urban historian Jon C. Teaford, the people of this region have in common their isolation from both the Atlantic and Pacific Oceans. The region's lifelines to that outside world have been primarily the Great Lakes, the Mississippi and Ohio Rivers, and the nation's railroad hub—Chicago. The industrial heartland remains strategically located between the

Industrial Revolution (1780s–1840s)
An economic process that started in England and also occurred in the United States that involved the introduction of technology into manufacturing.

Beginning in the 1500s, England's production of woolen textiles increased, and mechanized work became an important element of England's economic development. After 300 years, nonmechanical production capabilities had reached their limits. Growing demand for textiles and increased capital available for investment contributed to the introduction of technology into England's textile industry in the second half of the eighteenth century. England had already experienced other great changes in its modes of production, including the creation of small workshops and the putting-out system (cottage industries), and its agricultural system produced a surplus of food for a growing population. England's

Industrial Revolution saw the introduction of technology and the reorganization of labor under the factory system; the rise of new power sources, including water and the steam engine; and widespread social, economic, and political consequences of these revolutions. The introduction of technology allowed the English to produce more at lower cost, resulting in higher profits and a concerted effort to protect this technology through prohibition against exporting it.

The American colonies experienced the economic consequences of England's Industrial Revolution as Britain flooded colonial markets with cheap manufactured goods. Even after Americans gained their political independence from England, they remained, to the detriment of many, part of England's economic empire because of U.S. trade restrictions imposed by Great Britain.

Many of the earliest Americans saw the possibilities in England's Industrial Revolution and hoped to accomplish a similar revolution in the United States. President George Washington's secretary of the treasury, Alexander Hamilton, issued a series of reports promoting actions that would make America more economically independent and advanced, including improving public credit, paying off debt from the revolution, minting and standardizing currency, creating a national bank, and establishing tariffs designed to promote manufacturing. In the South, the postrevolutionary period saw a transformation to cotton production as English manufacturers demanded ever-increasing amounts of this raw material. The demand for cotton after the invention of the cotton gin in 1793 revitalized slavery in the South, where the economic system remained agrarian.

The economic and diplomatic problems caused by the Napoleonic Wars, coupled with the War of 1812, unleashed a fever of American nationalism that many citizens and politicians viewed as a call for economic independence and development. The War of 1812 and the expanding size of the United States clearly illustrated the need for an infrastructure, creating a boom in road and canal building followed shortly by steam-powered riverboats and railroads. The most important economic advancement for the United States in the early 1800s—and the one that would begin America's own Industrial Revolution—occurred when the Boston Associates, a group of wealthy New England entrepreneurs, decided to create their own textile mills. Their plan began when American entrepreneur Samuel Slater disguised himself as a sailor and set sail from England to the United States with the plans in his mind to build a spinning mill—plans he had memorized while in England to thwart England's attempts to keep its technological innovations secret. In 1813, the Boston Associates built their first mill in Waltham, Massachusetts, and then sent Francis Lowell, another member of the Boston Associates, to England to steal more technological secrets. In the early 1820s, the Boston Associates started to build a new state-of-the-art textile mill at Lowell, Massachusetts, hoping to improve on England's technology and to avoid the negative social consequences such as drinking and prostitution that were associated with the Industrial Revolution. Their business and social experiment—technological innovation paired with the attracting of qualified and devoted workers—

failed, but they had laid the foundations for America's own Industrial Revolution.

From this small beginning America's productive capacities expanded, and a second industrial revolution between the Civil War and World War II expanded the nation's manufacturing capability. The rise and dominance of big business during this period stemmed from continued territorial and demographic expansion, ever-increasing sources of raw materials, an expanding infrastructure, inventions that expanded and cheapened production, and new management techniques and methods of labor organization. The growing population created a ready supply of consumers and cheap labor, and the consolidation and expansion of business gave entrepreneurs increasing political power. John D. Rockefeller's Standard Oil Trust, Andrew Carnegie's steel empire, and J. P. Morgan's financial activities all serve as examples of the productive capabilities of the United States. This capability gave the United States a decided advantage when it entered World Wars I and II and made victory possible. In the twentieth century, this manufacturing solidified America's position as a world power. Since the mid-1990s, the United States and other industrialized nations have been moving into a post-industrial age in which mechanization is being replaced by a revolution in communications and service industries. This era is yet to be completely defined.

—*Ty M. Reese*

References
Berg, Maxine. *The Age of Manufacturers, 1700–1820: Industry, Innovation, and Work in Britain.* New York: Routledge, 1994.
Chandler, Alfred Dupont *The Visible Hand: The Managerial Revolution in American Business.* Cambridge, MA: Harvard University Press, Belknap Press, 1977.
Sellers, Charles. *The Market Revolution: Jacksonian America, 1815–1846.* New York: Oxford University Press, 1991.
See also Volume 1: Carnegie, Andrew; Rockefeller, John D.; Standard Oil.

Industrial Workers of the World (IWW)

A revolutionary labor organization founded in Chicago in 1905 that advocated the overthrow of capitalism by forcible means if necessary.

The Industrial Workers of the World (IWW), a labor union, received much attention and engendered substantial fear in early twentieth-century America among people who believed it was linked to socialism. It was established by William (Big Bill) Haywood, the radical secretary-treasurer of the Western Federation of Miners, with assistance from U.S. socialist leaders Daniel De Leon and Eugene Debs. The IWW welcomed members (known as Wobblies) regardless of race or gender as it tried to organize the skilled and unskilled American working class into a mammoth union that would promote social revolution. The IWW leaders also supported revolutionary movements in Russia and other countries.

Besides Haywood, IWW leaders included Mother Jones (Mary Harris), a famous veteran of labor conflict in the Illinois coalfields, and Elizabeth Gurley Flynn, who joined as a teenager and was a social organizer for the IWW. The IWW made major gains among miners and loggers in the South and Far West, migrant farm laborers on the Great Plains, and immigrant workers in the Northeast. At its peak, however, IWW membership probably amounted to no more than 100,000 at any given time. By 1908 Haywood had begun to promote violent class struggle, and in subsequent years the IWW led several major strikes, including strikes in 1912 at Lawrence, Massachusetts, and Paterson, New Jersey, that attracted national attention. IWW leaders incorrectly believed that capitalist repression of a series of local strikes would lead to a general strike throughout the United States and subsequently create a workers' commonwealth. The IWW's opposition to America's entry into World War I led to the federal government's prosecution of its leaders under the Espionage Acts of 1917 and 1918, which virtually destroyed the union's power. Haywood died in Moscow on May 18, 1928.

—*Steven E. Siry*

References

Dubofsky, Melvyn. *We Shall Be All: A History of the Industrial Workers of the World.* Urbana: University of Illinois Press, 1988.

See also Volume 2: Labor.

Industrialization

Process common to capitalist, socialist, and developing regimes that increases the proportion of the workforce engaged in manufacturing and the proportion of national income derived from manufacturing.

Industrialization, understood as the process by which Third World countries could catch up to the West technologically and economically, became the object of intense debate with the launching of the Bretton Woods organizations such as the International Monetary Fund designed to stabilize currency (1944), the United Nations designed to prevent future wars (1945), and Truman's Point Four Program based on his 1949 inaugural address calling for the provision of technological skills, knowledge, and equipment to poor nations (1949). In essence, the debate about industrialization centered on the interpretation of two historical events: the British Industrial Revolution (1780–1840) and Soviet industrialization (late 1920s to early 1950s).

Since the publication of historian Arnold Toynbee's lectures in 1884, which popularized the term "Industrial Revolution," economic historians have tended to conceptualize nineteenth-century Great Britain as the paradigmatic case of industrialization. Known as the "workshop of the world," Great Britain was presumed to have achieved a favorable position vis-à-vis France and other countries as a consequence of three factors: the implementation of the Enclosure Acts, which forced peasants off of the land and into the cities as laborers; the spread of the factory system, which transformed the division of labor into specialized occupations and jobs; and the employment of new machines (e.g., the spinning jenny and the steam engine) and new raw materials (e.g., coal

and iron ore). Thus, according to the conventional narrative, the Industrial Revolution began in the 1780s and ended in the 1840s. In the intervening period, Great Britain outstripped the rest of the world.

In *The Modern World-System III* (1989), Immanuel Wallerstein challenged the concept of the Industrial Revolution and by extension the so-called "English model" or path of development. Wallerstein argued not only that "there had been factories (in the sense of physical concentration under one roof of multiple workers paid by one employer) before this time," but also that "the extent of the introduction of the factory at this time can easily be overstated, even for Britain." If, as Wallerstein suggested, the process of industrialization began long before 1780 and ended long after 1840, it cannot be defined as a revolution. It would be preferable, therefore, to examine the uneven industrialization of the world over a longer period of time.

In the Soviet Union, two five-year plans beginning in 1929 and ending in 1938 emphasized the development of heavy industry and produced a dramatic increase in both the proportion of the labor force employed in manufacturing and the proportion of national income resulting from manufacturing. Owing the perceived success of its industrialization, the Soviet Union enjoyed considerable prestige in Africa, Asia, and Latin America. In the aftermath of World War II, the Soviet Union (with its socialist model) and the United States (with its Keynesian model) competed for influence over the industrialization of the Third World. However, as innumerable commentators on efforts to industrialize these regions have noted, there was considerable industrialization but very little wealth created. This remained the case as the twenty-first century began.

—*Mark Frezzo*

References

Braudel, Fernand. *The Perspective of the World: Civilization and Capitalism, 15th–18th Century.* London: Collins, 1984.

Hobsbawm, Eric. *The Age of Revolution, 1789–1848.* New York: Mentor, 1962.

Marglin, Stephen A., and Juliet B. Schor, eds. *The Golden Age of Capitalism: Reinterpreting the Postwar Experience.* Oxford: Clarendon Press, 1991.

Wallerstein, Immanuel. *The Modern World System III: The Second Era of Great Expansion of the Capitalist World-Economy, 1730–1840s.* New York: Academic Press, 1989.

Inflation

The collective increase in prices, money incomes, or the supply of money.

Compared with the less-developed world, the United States usually has enjoyed historically low rates of inflation, typically below 5 percent per year. But inflation is a politically charged issue and at times has been considered the nation's most serious economic problem. Price inflation generally benefits debtors (by allowing them to pay back debts with cheaper dollars) and those on fixed incomes, while harming creditors.

There are several widely accepted economic theories for the causes of inflation. According to quantity theory—dating back to the eighteenth century but made more sophisticated by Milton Friedman and other University of Chicago economists in the 1950s—when the total quantity of money in circulation is inadequate for the level of business activity, inflation results. Cost-push theory states that prices are chiefly determined by their costs, so that rising costs can set off a price-wage spiral. Conversely, demand-pull theory ascribes inflation to an overabundance of purchasing dollars chasing a relatively limited supply of goods. Other theories point to the undesirable wage rate declines and gaps between imports and exports that result in an unfavorable balance of trade and inflation. Most economists see an inverse relationship between inflation and unemployment (a theory known as the Phillips curve).

Since the 1930s, economic policymakers have used a variety of fiscal and, especially, monetary policies to sustain low levels of inflation. Most influential among these policies have been the actions of the U.S. Federal Reserve Bank, which controls the volume of money in circulation and the rate at which member banks can borrow from the central bank. But politics have often interfered with the type of sound macroeconomic management practiced by the Federal Reserve. A great inflation began in the mid-1960s, when the administration of President Lyndon B. Johnson refused to raise taxes while scaling up the Vietnam conflict in an economy with little excess capacity. Hyperinflation (above 10 percent) with slow growth, a combination called "stagflation," occurred in the late 1970s and was brought under control largely by Paul Volcker, chair of the Federal Reserve. His successor, Alan Greenspan, has sustained the policies controlling stagflation.

—*David B. Sicilia*

References
Samuelson, Paul A., William D. Nordhaus, and Michael J. Mandel. *Economics.* New York: McGraw-Hill, 1995.
Stein, Herbert. *Presidential Economics: The Making of Economic Policy from Roosevelt to Clinton.* Washington, DC: American Enterprise Institute, 1994.
See also Volume 1: Federal Reserve Act; Greenspan, Alan; Stagflation; Volcker, Paul.

Infrastructure

Services provided by physical or human capital along with indispensable social institutions that do not serve any one firm or person in particular.

Infrastructure yields benefits to all who use it. Typical infrastructure services include communications and transport such as roads, railways, harbors, airports, telephone and postal services; distribution systems for water, electric power, and natural gas; medical, educational, police, and correctional systems; and firefighting and other institutions. Most components of infrastructure are subject to economies of scale or scope. In general, one large provider can best organize provision of services, creating in the process a natural monopoly. Although this natural monopoly may cost the least, it can also result in poor service and less flexibility. Items of physical infrastructure include public goods, the use of which is not exclusive. Infrastructure differs from investment in plant and equipment, which generates direct, private benefit to its owner.

Services from infrastructure enable business firms to focus on their individual expertise rather than on providing for all of their basic needs. The private sector continues to provide many of the same infrastructure services but at a cost higher than that of public-sector services. The availability of privately funded infrastructure therefore makes investment by private firms more profitable and therefore more likely to occur. Once the government builds infrastructure such as a railway or highway, the additional cost to serve more firms remains small, encouraging further growth among manufacturing and transportation companies.

Components of American infrastructure have evolved in different ways. Municipal, state, or federal authorities have provided and maintained roads. Railways operate financially as separate entities, but the government often subsidized early construction because of high costs caused by the lack of prior infrastructure. Many harbors and airports are privately owned, though again government money frequently subsidizes construction. Telephone services continue under private ownership and postal services under partly private and partly public ownership, although the U.S. mail now has many private competitors for the more lucrative parts of its services. Water provision remains organized at the municipal level although it is sometimes contracted out to private companies, while electricity and natural gas are privately owned in most cases. Private companies provide medical services, although certain types of patients are directly subsidized by federal or state programs. Public primary and secondary education is available to all, though some choose private alternatives. Provision of tertiary education similarly is divided between public and private institutions. Police, justice, and firefighting systems are all publicly organized.

The many forms of infrastructure that are natural monopolies are not exposed to competitive forces. Such monopolies are frequently controlled by public regulatory bodies that themselves are not competitive, leading to inefficiencies. An important recent worldwide phenomenon has been the drive to privatize many items of physical infrastructure. Utilities and transportation systems, in particular, have been transferred from public to private ownership. The intention is to obtain greater efficiency by exposing the monopolies to competition.

—*Tony Ward*

References
Kessides, Christine. *The Contributions of Infrastructure to Economic Development: A Review of Experience and Policy Implications.* Washington, DC: World Bank, 1993.
See also Volume 1: Automobile; Railroads; Transportation Revolution.

Insular Cases

Series of Supreme Court cases determining the constitutional status—incorporated or unincorporated—of territorial possessions and dependencies outside of the continental United States.

As the nineteenth century ended, the United States embarked on a bold policy of overseas expansionism. The United States originally acquired territories like Hawaii, Guam, the Philippine Islands, and American Samoa in the Pacific, as well as Puerto Rico and the Virgin Islands in the Caribbean, for strategic purposes. In the case of the Pacific islands, Congress determined that such areas would serve as bases for the development of burgeoning American commerce with countries in the Far East. The United States acquired these territories at about the same time: Hawaii was annexed in 1898; the Philippine Islands, Puerto Rico, and Guam were added as a result of the Spanish-American War of 1898; American Samoa was added through a treaty with Great Britain and Germany in 1899; and the Virgin Islands were bought from Denmark in 1917. Collectively, these acquisitions became known as the Insular Possessions.

The new overseas possessions ultimately posed an important constitutional question: Can Congress exercise jurisdiction over American citizens living in these overseas possessions within the framework of the Constitution? In a series of rulings, the Supreme Court held that such possessions fall into two classifications: incorporated, in which all territories remain bound by the provisions of the Constitution; and unincorporated, in which certain territories are "bound only by certain 'fundamental' provisions of the same." The main issue was whether the revenue clauses of the Constitution and all rights pertaining to U.S. citizens extended to the newly acquired possessions and their inhabitants. In early 1901, in *De Lima v. Bidwell,* the Supreme Court held that "upon the ratification of the treaty of peace with Spain, Puerto Rico ceased to exist as a foreign country and became a territory of the United States, and that duties were no longer collectible upon merchandise brought from that island." However, on May 27, 1901, in *Downes v. Bidwell*—the key case in connection with the Insular Possessions—the justices ruled "that the provisions insuring jury trial and uniformity of tariff duties are not fundamental, but that the guarantee against deprivation of life, liberty and property without due process of law is fundamental and hence applicable in all the possessions of the United States." The Court held that certain fundamental rights guaranteed by the Constitution applied to all territories held by the United States, but it said many other provisions of the Constitution did not apply to possessions not "definitely incorporated as an integral part of the United States." Inhabitants of unincorporated territories lacked all the rights and privileges of American citizens, enjoying only those fundamental rights derived from natural law.

The Supreme Court rulings determined that the rights of inhabitants of the Insular Possessions included those relating to life, liberty, and property but that these inhabitants did not necessarily qualify under the constitutional provision "that all duties, imposts, and excises should be uniform throughout the United States." That is, they enjoyed the rights guaranteed under the constitution but, except in the case of U.S. possessions such as Puerto Rico and Guam, new territories such as Cuba would not be allowed to ship goods into the United States without paying duties. In *Hawaii v. Mankichi* (1903), the Court held that Hawaii and Alaska were incorporated territories. In *Dorr v. United States* (1904), the Court ruled that the Philippine Islands were unincorporated. Interestingly, despite passage of the Organic Act of 1917 granting U.S. citizenship to the people of Puerto Rico, the Court reasoned in *Puerto Rico v. Tapia* (1918) and *Balzac v. People of Puerto Rico* (1922) that the possession be classified an unincorporated territory. For commercial and strategic reasons, the Supreme Court backed the United States policy of overseas expansion while granting carte blanche privileges to certain territories and not others.

The Insular Cases provided a convenient way out of a situation that the Constitution did not address (that is, American expansionism) and enabled the United States to maintain its commercial and territorial expansion. Justice Henry B. Brown best expressed the Court's position by stating, "A false step at this time might be fatal to the development of what Chief Justice Marshall called the American empire."

—*Charles F. Howlett*

References

Bailey, Thomas A. "Was the Election of 1900 a Mandate on Imperialism?" *Mississippi Valley Historical Review,* vol. 24 (June 1937): 43–52.

Campbell, Charles S. *The Transformation of American Foreign Relations.* New York: Harper and Row, 1976.

Downes v. Bidwell, 182 U.S. 244 (1901).

Dulles, Foster Rhea. *America's Rise to World Power.* New York: Harper and Row, 1954.

Herman, Sondra R. *Eleven against Empire: Studies in American Internationalist Thought, 1898–1921.* Stanford, CA: Stanford University Press, 1969.

Pratt, Julius W. *The Expansionists of 1898.* Chicago: Quadrangle Books, 1964.

See also Volume 1: *De Lima v. Bidwell; Downes v. Bidwell.*

Interest Rates

Charge for the use of money or capital, usually calculated as a percentage of the principal (money being used) on an annual basis.

Prior to the creation of the Federal Reserve Bank, the federal government could not effectively control the interest rates. State banks and large financial firms like J. P. Morgan and Company set interest rates based on the amount of capital available and the relative demand for that money. During the panics of 1819, 1837, 1857, 1873, 1893, and 1907, interest rates rose dramatically, having the net effect of shrinking the money supply. Passage of the Federal Reserve Act in 1913 gave the Board of Governors of the Federal Reserve the task of setting the prime interest rate charged to banks and other lending institutions for loans. Consumers pay a higher rate than the prime rate—up to 25 percent. Anything over 25 percent is considered usury under U.S. law.

In recent times, credit cards continue to charge the highest overall rate—usually between 18 and 21 percent. Since the recession of 2000, and especially after the terrorist attacks on September 11, 2001, Federal Reserve Chair Alan Greenspan has continued to cut interest rates in an effort to stimulate the economy. During this time, manufacturers of large consumer items such as automobiles have offered 0 percent interest to entice buyers.

The Federal Reserve system has effectively controlled interest rates since its creation, except in one particular incident. After the stock market crash of 1929, the Federal Reserve increased rates at the same time that Congress elevated trade barriers by passing the Hawley-Smoot Tariff Act. The downturn in international trade coupled with a constricted money supply exacerbated the Great Depression. Since then, the Federal Reserve has maintained a policy of reducing rates during periods of financial difficulty.

—*Cynthia Clark Northrup*

References
Patinkin, Don. *Money, Interest, and Prices: An Integration of Monetary and Value Theory.* New York: Random House, 1965.
See also Volume 1: Banking System; Federal Reserve Act; Volume 2: Banking; Volume 2 (Documents): Federal Reserve Act.

International Monetary Fund (IMF)

An organization of 182 countries that facilitates international monetary cooperation throughout most of the world.

Established immediately after World War II, the International Monetary Fund (IMF) maintains stable exchange rates among currencies, thereby promoting the expansion of trade and economic growth. During the 1950s and 1960s, the IMF sought to maintain a system of fixed exchange rates, which would greatly reduce the individual risk encountered with international trade. The U.S. dollar was the key currency against which all others received valuation, with the dollar being convertible to gold at a fixed rate.

In 1971 President Richard Nixon suspended gold convertibility of the dollar because of inadequate U.S. gold reserves. This action resulted in the devaluation of the dollar, initially by 10 percent. Further convertibility adjustments by other countries led most countries to float their currencies based on market prices. The maintenance of fixed exchange rates proved unfeasible, but flexible rates also created substantial problems that included widely fluctuating values of currencies. The IMF adjusted its activities to accommodate these new needs, finding an important new role in stabilizing currencies.

The IMF continuously surveys member countries' exchange rate policies, and it steps in with credits and loans when a member experiences problems with exchange rates. Each member can borrow in units called "special drawing rights" (SDRs) from a combined total of $300 billion. The value of the SDR depends on a weighted combination of the French franc, the German deutschmark, the Japanese yen, the British pound, and the U.S. dollar. Each member nation contributes a quota of funds depending on its ability to pay. The United States contributes 18 percent of IMF total revenues, a significant amount for one nation, and so exerts a great deal of influence over the IMF's activities, but the U.S. does not draw loans from the IMF.

The IMF played an important role in helping many less-developed countries deal with the heavy indebtedness prevalent in the early 1980s. It still offers financial advice to debtor countries, advice that some developing countries consider intrusive. The IMF's promotion of the globalization of trade has led to continuing protests by groups that oppose global trade for reasons ranging from environmental concerns to issues raised by labor organizations.

—*Tony Ward*

References
Goldstein, Morris. *The Exchange Rate System and the IMF: A Model Agenda.* Washington, DC: Institute for International Economics, 1995.
See also Volume 1: Bretton Woods Agreement; United Nations.

International Trade Organization

Proposed organization to regulate world trade, for which a charter was drawn up in the 1940s, but which never came into being; a precursor of the World Trade Organization (WTO).

In 1916, Cordell Hull, Democratic congressional representative from Tennessee, proposed a permanent international trade congress to promote fair and friendly trade relations among nations. Only during World War II, however, did the question of creating such an organization become a matter of practical politics. During and immediately after the war, American and British planners drew up a blueprint designed to promote freer trade on a multilateral, nondiscriminatory basis and to regulate the use of devices such as trade preferences (by assigning most-favored-nation status) and international trade.

In a series of postwar international conferences culminating at Havana in 1947 and 1948, participants agreed to a draft charter for the organization. The agreement allowed exceptions to free trade rules for countries in balance-of-payments difficulties and for the purposes of economic development. All but 3 of the 56 participating countries signed the final act of the Havana conference, but individual nations including the United States still had to ratify the charter. In the United States, free trade purists, objecting to the concessions made at Havana, found themselves pushed into an "unholy alliance" with protectionists who opposed the International Trade Organization itself, in opposition to the charter. Accordingly, the administration of President Harry S Truman delayed putting the charter before Congress until 1950. In December of that year, with its attention distracted by the Korean War, the Truman administration finally announced it would not pursue the plan further. This rejection sounded the International Trade Organization's death knell.

However, the supposedly "interim" General Agreement on Tariffs and Trade (GATT), negotiated during 1947 in parallel with discussions of the charter, continued as the basis on which world trade was regulated until it was superseded by the World Trade Organization in 1995. Thus, the original attempt to create an International Trade Organization left a lasting legacy.

—Richard Toye

References

Gardner, Richard N. *Sterling-Dollar Diplomacy in Current Perspective: The Origins and the Prospects of Our International Economic Order.* New York: Columbia University Press, 1980.

Zeiler, Thomas W. *Free Trade, Free World: The Advent of GATT.* Chapel Hill: University of North Carolina Press, 1999.

See also Volume 1: General Agreement on Tariffs and Trade.

Interstate Commerce Commission (ICC)

A quasi-judicial body of the U.S. government established to regulate interstate common carriers.

Congress established the Interstate Commerce Commission (ICC) in 1887 under the Interstate Commerce Act to address the problem of rate instability in the railroad industry. Under the leadership of Thomas M. Cooley, its first chief commissioner, the ICC attempted to regulate competition. The Supreme Court circumscribed this approach to regulation in the 1890s, and the power of the ICC subsequently waned.

Congress attempted to strengthen the ICC during the Progressive Era. The Elkins Act (1903) outlawed rebating, a practice in which the shipping concern pays the large supplier the difference between the regular and an agreed-on price in exchange for the supplier's guarantee that it will ship a specific amount of goods under the contract. The Hepburn Act (1906) gave the ICC maximum rate-setting and enforcement authority. The Mann-Elkins Act (1910) gave the ICC power to initiate its own investigations and again outlawed long-haul versus short-haul discrimination in which farmers or manufacturers paid more per mile for short hauls than for long hauls. The Transportation Act of 1920 attempted to deal with the railroad network as a national monopoly; it ordered the ICC to protect weak railroads and establish a national plan of consolidation. It also introduced an ill-defined idea of "the public interest" into the deliberations of the ICC. It gave the ICC power over all railroad construction and service; expansions and abandonments required ICC approval. Last, it gave the ICC power to set minimum rates as well as maximum rates.

The powers of the commission have fluctuated over time. In 1906, it gained authority over private sleeping car companies (such as the Pullman Sleeping Car Company), express companies that shipped directly between cities or locations without intermediate stops, and interstate oil pipelines. In 1910, Congress gave the ICC power to oversee telephone, telegraph, and trans-Atlantic cable companies, but Congress later transferred this power to the Federal Communications Commission. In the Motor Carrier Act of 1935, Congress granted the ICC authority over the trucking industry, and the Transportation Act of 1940 added interstate water carriers to agencies regulated by the commission. In other areas, the ICC had gained authority over transportation safety and had power to order improvements. In 1920, it received power to regulate railroad securities (stocks, bonds, investment annuities, and mutual funds) owned by monopolistic railroad companies.

In 1958, Congress began to liberalize railroad regulation by making it easier for the railroads to abandon unprofitable service lines. But by this time the ICC had become ossified institutionally and was resistant to change. When the boards of directors of the New York Central Railroad and the Pennsylvania Railroad approved the merger of the two companies, the ICC initiated hearings in 1962. If the ICC had investigated both companies thoroughly, it would have found that the New York Central was already on the verge of bankruptcy. Instead, 14 months later, the ICC approved the merger. The ICC received the blame for the northeast railroad bankruptcy crisis brought on by the 1970 collapse of Penn Central—the largest bankruptcy in U.S. history until the twenty-first century. In 1976, Congress began to deregulate the railroad industry with the Railroad Revitalization and Regulatory Reform Act, but the ICC interpreted this action conservatively and rendered it ineffective. The bill, designed to increase competition and improve methods of enforcement, did little of either. During President Jimmy Carter's administration, the commission had a change of heart and voluntarily began to deregulate the industries under its jurisdiction.

In 1980 Congress completed the deregulation of the railroad industry in the Staggers Act, and it partly deregulated the trucking industry in the Motor Carrier Act. In 1994, Congress completed deregulation of the trucking industry, In 1995, Congress ordered the ICC disbanded and transferred all of its remaining functions to the Department of Transportation.

—Russell Douglass Jones

References

Hoogenboom, Ari, and Olive Hoogenboom. *A History of the ICC: From Panacea to Palliative.* New York: Norton, 1976.

Stone, Richard D. *The Interstate Commerce Commission and the Railroad Industry: A History of Regulatory Policy.* New York: Praeger, 1991.

See also Volume 1: Hepburn Railroad Regulation Act.

Intolerable Acts (1774)

Acts passed by England's Parliament designed to punish and divide the American colonies.

The British Parliament passed the Tea Act of 1773 to control that commodity in the American colonies. In December of that year, American patriots, who had been protesting taxation without representation committed a final act of defiance by throwing £15,000 worth of privately owned tea into Boston Harbor. Known as the Boston Tea Party, this act forced Lord Francis North and Parliament finally to take a tougher stance against the unruly colonists. In 1774, Parliament passed four acts—called in England the Coercive Acts and by the American colonists the Intolerable Acts—to punish Boston for its continued defiance. In addition, by only punishing Massachusetts, Parliament hoped to retain the loyalty of the other colonies and so divide the colonies. The first act, the Boston Port Act, closed Boston's harbor until the East India Company received reciprocity for its tea. Parliament designed this act to hurt Boston's economy, as the port served as an important entrepôt between the larger "Atlantic world" (England, Europe, Africa, and the Caribbean) and the New England hinterland, especially in regard to New England rum production. Parliament followed this measure with an Act for the Impartial Administration of Justice, which allowed Massachusetts's Governor General Thomas Gage to transfer to England the trial of any English official accused of committing a crime in the colony. The Massachusetts Government Act made many of the colonies' elected positions into Crown-appointed positions, and it limited town meetings, which served an important role in colonial organization and resistance. The final act, the Quartering Act, required local officials to find shelter in private homes for British soldiers who occupied Boston. These acts, designed to hurt Boston's economy, divide the colonies, and crush colonial resistance, produced the opposite result. The Bostonians successfully convinced colonists elsewhere in Massachusetts and in other colonies that such treatment by England could easily happen anywhere else in the colonies if it happened in Boston. Continued colonywide resistance led to the calling of the First Continental Congress.

—*Ty M. Reese*

References
Middlekauff, Robert. *The Glorious Cause: The American Revolution, 1763–1789*. New York: Oxford University Press, 1982.
See also Volume 1: American Revolution.

Iran-Contra (1986–1987)

Scandal in which the administration of President Ronald Reagan illegally provided money to Nicaraguan Contra rebels gained by covertly selling arms to Iran, weakening economic and legislative efforts of the executive branch.

The roots of the Iran-Contra scandal, which occurred during the presidency of Ronald Reagan, lie in the executive branch's reaction to the Boland Amendment Congress passed in 1982. Designed to prevent the president from continuing his support of the Contras in Nicaragua (rebels who opposed the communist-backed Sandinistas during the height of the cold war) the act banned governmental agencies, the Department of Defense, and the Central Intelligence Agency (CIA) from supporting, training, or equipping the rebels after September 1985. The administration decided to continue its aid and circumvented the Boland Amendment by using the National Security Council (NSC), which the amendment had not explicitly mentioned. The NSC covertly sold weapons to Iran and then used the profits to fund the Contras.

Robert McFarlane, former national security adviser, and later Rear Admiral John Poindexter directed administration efforts to uncover private and foreign sources of revenue for the Nicaraguan guerrillas. At about this time, the executive branch was also trying to make inroads with moderates in Iran, hoping to free seven American hostages held in Lebanon and to soften Iran's hard-line stance toward the West after the fundamentalist revolution of 1979. During NSC meetings, staffers came up with a plan to accomplish both of these objectives, because Iranian radicals controlled the terrorist groups that held the hostages. Via Israeli middlemen, the U.S. government would sell arms to Iran at a substantial markup starting in 1985 and divert some of the profit from these sales to the war in Central America. Marine Lieutenant Colonel Oliver North, who worked for the NSC, oversaw the program.

In November 1986, a Lebanese newspaper uncovered the arms deals. In the wake of that discovery, Poindexter resigned and North was fired. Select congressional committees held joint meetings, and Attorney General Edwin Meese uncovered the diversion of funds to Nicaragua. Lawrence E. Walsh, formerly a federal judge, acted as special prosecutor to look into the affair and the roles in it of public officials including President Reagan, Vice President George H. W. Bush, and Central Intelligence Agency (CIA) Director William J. Casey. After seven years of investigation and $47.5 million in costs, Walsh gained convictions only against McFarlane, North, and Poindexter; however, the latter two convictions were vacated because North and Poindexter had received immunity from prosecution in exchange for their testimony at Senate hearings. Secretary of Defense Caspar Weinberger and 14 officials from the Department of State and the CIA pleaded guilty to withholding information. George H. W. Bush who was elected to succeed Reagan as president, pardoned 6 of these officials in 1992; two other convictions were overturned on technicalities. During the last two years of the Reagan administration, the Iran-Contra scandal weakened the executive branch, affecting its economic and legislative efforts.

—*T. Jason Soderstrum*

References
Draper, Theodore. *A Very Thin Line: The Iran-Contra Affairs*. New York: Hill and Wang, 1991.
See also Volume 1: Reagan, Ronald.

Irrigation

System of supplying land with water by artificial means that transformed the American landscape and brought agriculture to areas previously unable to sustain it.

Fifty percent of the value of a farmer's crop is in the lands he or she has under irrigation. Irrigation accounts for 80 percent of the nation's consumptive water use and more than 90 percent in many western states. Although farmers have irrigated fields for more that 4,000 years, they did not use irrigation on a massive scale in the United States until the 1950s. In 1946, 250,000 acres received water from sprinkler irrigation in the United States, but by 1954, roughly 3 million acres received water by this method. Government sources estimate that 500,000 additional acres of land went under sprinkler irrigation each year throughout the 1950s. On the Great Plains, the center-pivot sprinkler had irrigated 400,000 acres by 1974, a fourfold increase since 1955. Other forms of irrigation had equally dramatic increases throughout the latter half of the twentieth century. Currently 10 million acres are under irrigation; 10 trillion gallons of water are used for irrigation annually. Sixty percent of the nation's vegetables and 25 percent of the nation's fruit and nut crops are irrigated.

Irrigation has allowed lands that were previously marginal or used for dryland wheat and grain sorghum to yield corn, sugar beets, alfalfa, and cotton. By 1954, the use of irrigation and fertilizer increased the per acre yield of crops such as alfalfa by 2.4 tons, forage sorghums by 9.5 tons, grain sorghum by 22 bushels, and wheat by 11 bushels. By 1990, tomatoes increased from 26 to 100 tons per acre and cotton jumped from 930 to 1,000 pounds per acre. These increases in yield brought greater farm income on the Great Plains and in the West. In Kansas alone, by 1966, irrigation had increased farm income by $24 million. This increased irrigation allowed farmers to expand their feedlots and develop a meatpacking industry on the Great Plains. In areas with little or sporadic rainfall, irrigation has led to a larger, more stable, agricultural industry and a cheaper food supply, although it has had environmental costs. One such area is Imperial Valley, California, where irrigation has yielded 115 million acres of annual vegetable production worth $350 million.

—*T. Jason Soderstrum*

References

Hurt, R. Douglas. *Agricultural Technology in the Twentieth Century.* Manhattan, KS: Sunflower University Press, 1991.

See also Volumes 1, 2: Agricultural Policy.

Isolationism

Stance on foreign relations that opts for noninvolvement in international affairs but nonetheless pushes for a nation's advancement and concerns through diplomatic means.

Isolationism, born when the United States was founded, originally emphasized America's estrangement from European wars and political intrigues to safeguard the young nation's republican virtue, free government, prosperity, and security. Thus, the republic needed to adopt a foreign policy advocating no permanent military and political alliance with foreign countries, save for commercial relations or temporary alliances to meet America's urgent needs, as President George Washington stressed in his farewell address of 1796. American foreign relations before the Civil War demonstrated this strong isolationist sentiment. When the United States became a major power in international affairs during the late nineteenth century, an isolationist tradition still influenced U.S. preference for going it alone in international affairs and for avoiding formal alliances with other nations.

During the Progressive Era, the United States took an internationalist course, but in response to that, isolationism gained momentum in the United States during the years between World War I and World War II (1919–1941). Basing their position on American exceptionalism (the belief that the wilderness transformed Europeans into Americans) and disillusionment with the American involvement in World War I, the isolationists expressed an abhorrence of war and strong aversion to assuming American responsibilities abroad. Plagued by the Great Depression, Americans in the 1930s expressed further isolationist feelings. Anxious to avoid trouble and restore the domestic economy, the United States was extremely passive in the face of expansionist drives undertaken by imperial Japan, Nazi Germany, and fascist Italy. The Neutrality Acts passed by the U.S Congress between 1935 and 1937 even reversed the traditional U.S. position on neutral rights and freedom of trade by forbidding arms sales to any belligerents. After the Japanese attack on Pearl Harbor in 1941, Americans who supported isolationism were perceived as unpatriotic. However, groups such as America First did influence a decision by Congress to restrict immigration. Isolationism as a doctrine has been losing its influence since the early years of the post–World War II era and the onset of the cold war. Since the 1950s, Americans have perceived the need to spread U.S. political and social values around the world in an effort to combat communism and strengthen the United States.

—*Guoqiang Zheng*

References

Cohen, Warren, ed. *The Cambridge History of American Foreign Relations.* London: Cambridge University Press, 1993.

See also Volume 1: World War I; World War II.

IWW

See Industrial Workers of the World.

J

Jackson, Andrew (1767–1845)

Seventh president of the United States (1828–1836) whose economic policies threatened the political and economic stability of the United States.

Andrew Jackson was born March 15, 1767. He lost his 1824 presidential bid in a disputed election against John Quincy Adams. He won the election of 1828, primarily because implementation that year of universal white male suffrage had opened the voting process up to the common man. During his eight years in office, Jackson faced several crises including the "bank war," the nullification crisis, the forced removal of five Indian tribes from the east to an area west of the Mississippi River, and problems within his own Cabinet over Washington society rejecting Peggy Eaton, the wife of his secretary of war, John Eaton.

During his first term in office, Jackson was forced to deal with the nullification crisis. After Congress passed the Tariff of 1828, South Carolina voiced its opposition to the increased duty rates, which hurt the South more than the North because of the trading relationship between the agricultural South and industrial England. Cotton would be shipped to England for processing in the numerous textile mills and, in exchange, the South would import cloth and other manufactured items. The increase in tariff rates made British goods cost-prohibitive when compared with American goods but New England factories did not require as much cotton as the South produced. Therefore, Southern farmers needed to sell their crops overseas. Vice President John C. Calhoun, a native of South Carolina, anonymously published the *South Carolina Exposition and Protest,* in which he argued that the tax was discriminatory and therefore illegal. As such, the state had the right and indeed the responsibility to nullify the law. The South Carolina legislature distributed copies of the document and also formally delivered it to Congress.

When Congress increased rates again with the Tariff of 1832, South Carolina passed the Ordinance of Nullification, in which the state refused to collect the tariff duties and threatened to secede if Congress did not repeal the act. Jackson responded by asking Congress to approve the use of military force if necessary to carry out the collection of duties and to prevent South Carolina from following through with its threat. Henry Clay, Speaker of the House, managed to persuade Congress to pass the Compromise Tariff of 1833 that reduced rates back down to 20 percent over a nine-year period, thereby protecting the interests of investors who had committed funds based on the existing rates. Jackson signed both the Compromise Tariff of 1833 and the Force Act, which authorized the use of military force in South Carolina to ensure the collection of tariffs, on the same day. South Carolina then repealed its nullification ordinance.

By the time the tariff issue was resolved, Jackson was dealing with another economic problem. During the 1832 election campaign Henry Clay—the Whig candidate and lawyer for the Second Bank of the United States (BUS)—had pushed through Congress a bill that authorized rechartering of the bank four years before the current charter expired. The bill was a blatant political move designed to force Jackson to sign the legislation into law or to veto it with the possibility of losing the election over the issue—the bank was extremely popular with the people. Jackson vetoed the measure and won the election anyway. He then instructed his secretary of the treasury, Louis McLean, to remove federal funds from the Second BUS and deposit them in state banks. McLean refused, citing lack of authority to do so, and Jackson received McLean's resignation. Jackson's next appointee also refused to remove the funds. Finally, Jackson appointed Roger B. Taney to the position, and Taney agreed to transfer the money. As the cash reserves of the Second BUS dwindled, bank officials were forced to call in loans to continue operations. Between 1833 and 1836 when the charter expired, the U.S. economy began to experience a contraction. When Martin Van Buren became president in 1837, the United States was plummeted into the panic of 1837, which lasted throughout Van Buren's presidency and earned him the nickname "Martin Van Ruin." Jackson retired to his home, the Hermitage, outside of Nashville, Tennessee, leaving the disastrous bank policy for his successor to handle. He died on June 8, 1845, at his home.

—Cynthia Clark Northrup

References

Remini, Robert V. *Andrew Jackson and the Bank War: A Study in the Growth of Presidential Power.* New York: W. W. Norton, 1967.

Somervill, Barbara A. *Andrew Jackson.* Minneapolis, MN: Compass Point Books, 2003.

See also Volume 1: Clay, Henry; Nullification Crisis.

Japan

Eastern Asian nation occupying an island chain east of the Korean Peninsula.

Japan placed heavy restrictions on trade with Europe and the United States until the Meiji Restoration in 1868, when the Meiji Emperor wrested control of Japan's government from the weakened Shogunate rulers. Under the Meiji Restoration, the Japanese government reorganized and made attempts to modernize the Japanese nation. During the late nineteenth century, following the lead of the West, Japan built railroads and improved its industrial infrastructure. This initiative led to moderate economic growth throughout the early twentieth century; even the Great Depression had little effect on the Japanese economy. However, in the 1930s, Japan began a program of imperialist expansion throughout Asia and put much of its industrial wealth to military purposes.

Japan's imperial expansion placed it on a collision course with its principal rival for influence in the Pacific, the United States. In an effort to stop Japanese expansion, the United States instituted an oil and scrap metal embargo against Japan in June 1941. Soon after, on December 7, 1941, the Japanese attacked Pearl Harbor, an action that resulted in the loss of 2,400 American lives and 200 naval ships and brought both Japan and the United States formally into World War II. Japan then took one island after another in the Pacific with little regard for prisoners of war or civilian lives. Six months after Pearl Harbor, the United States began to reclaim the islands in battles that caused extremely high death tolls for both sides. The United States was also striking the Japanese homeland by air, firebombing Tokyo and finally dropping atomic bombs on Hiroshima and Nagasaki in August 1945. The two bombs killed more than 110,000 people and destroyed two industrial cities that had been producing war material. After the bombings, Japan surrendered.

The destruction caused by World War II devastated the Japanese economy—the cost of the war to the Japanese amounted to $562 billion in actual outlays and destruction of infrastructure. In comparison, the United States spent $341 billion on the entire war, and its industrial capacity expanded to provide the needed war equipment and supplies. After the war, the United States helped rebuild Japan's crippled economy. The U.S. military occupied Japan from 1945 to 1952 and, with U.S. help Japan began to rebuild lost industrial capacity after the war. By the mid-1950s Japan's industrial output matched prewar levels. The economic alliance between Japan and the United States came about because of U.S. fears of Soviet communism during the cold war, which began after World War II ended.

The revised Japanese constitution adopted after World War II forbade the creation of another military force. Without military expenditures, Japan developed a diverse economy with varied industrial output including heavy industry, chemicals, automobiles, and shipbuilding. The Japanese economy began to compete internationally by the mid-1960s and, in the 1970s and 1980s, Japan became a major producer in the manufacture of high-tech products including consumer electronic equipment. Many of Japan's exports found their way into the American market, and although the United States developed a balance-of-payments deficit (in which imports exceed exports) in the late twentieth century, protectionist policies that restricted foreign manufacturers from selling in the Japanese market gave Japan a large balance-of-payments surplus (in which exports exceed imports). With a large number of Japanese automobiles being sold in the United States in the late 1970s, the U.S. trade deficit increased dramatically—primarily because Americans chose to buy these smaller, more efficient vehicles in response to the Arab oil embargoes. Despite recession in the 1990s, Japan's economy is one of the world's strongest, and Japan is one of the closest trading partners of the United States. In May 2003 the U.S.-Japanese market resulted in $4.46 billion in Japanese exports and $10.3 billion in imports, for a trade deficit of $5.83 billion. The Japanese government imported $48.42 billion dollars of U.S. products from January through May 2003.

—*John K. Franklin*

References

Dolan, Ronald E., and Robert L. Worden, eds. *Japan: A Country Study.* 5th ed. Washington DC: U.S. Government Printing Office, 1992.

U.S. Census Bureau. *U.S. Trade Balance with Japan.* 2003. Available: http://www.census.gov/foreign-trade/balance/c5880.html; accessed July 16, 2003.

See also Volume 1: World War II.

Japanese Oil Embargo (1940–1941)

Embargo that prohibited export of fuel and other war materials to Japan in the years preceding World War II.

In 1937 Japan and China began the second Sino-Japanese War, a war that would ultimately last until 1945. Because the fighting encroached on their trade and activities in the region, the Soviet Union, the United States, and Britain experienced a decline in their relations with Japan, and despite their protests Japan was determined to expand its territory. Moving outward from Manchukuo (the portion of Manchuria Japan had taken over in 1932), the Japanese also invaded eastern Mongolia. However, combined Soviet and Mongolian troops won a victory in 1939 that influenced Japan to instead move south toward China and Southeast Asia.

In 1940, Japanese Prime Minister Konoe Fuminaro called for the creation of a Greater East Asia Co-Prosperity Sphere to consist of Japan, China, Manchukuo, and Southeast Asia.

Under this plan, a Japanese-led Asia would be able to compete economically with the West. As a result of Japan's earlier expansion, in July 1940 the United States placed embargoes on war supplies destined for Japan. Specifically, the United States restricted the export of scrap metal and high-octane aviation fuel. Although the embargo was designed to stop Japanese expansion, it was incomplete and so proved ineffective.

Japan's relationship with the United States and Britain further deteriorated in September 1940, when Japan invaded Indochina and joined the Axis powers as a result of the Tripartite Pact. In April 1941, the Japanese signed a neutrality agreement with the Soviet Union and began making active war plans against the United States. Peace talks to avoid conflict deadlocked. Germany's invasion of the Soviet Union in June 1941 ended the Russian threat to Japan near Mongolia and, in July, Japan moved against the Dutch East Indies for its oil and rubber supplies. In response the United States froze Japanese assets in America and began a complete oil embargo against Japan. The British and Dutch did the same, and the cooperative embargo slashed Japanese oil imports by 90 percent.

Initially meant as a deterrent, the embargo rapidly led to economic warfare. Heavily dependent on outside petroleum sources, the Japanese felt pressured to confront the United States and to increase its supply of oil by capturing oil supplies in the East Indies before their stockpiles ran out. In response, the Japanese attacked Pearl Harbor on December 7, 1941, and full-fledged warfare broke out between Japan and the United States in the Pacific as the United States entered World War II against the Axis powers.

—*John K. Franklin*

References
Pastor, Robert A. *Not Condemned to Repetition: The United States and Nicaragua.* 2d ed. Boulder, CO: Westview Press, 2002.
See also Volume 1: World War II.

Jay's Treaty (1796)

First commercial treaty of United States with Great Britain.

Although the Treaty of 1783 had ended the American Revolution and secured the independence of the United States, serious issues remained unresolved between Britain and the new nation, particularly those regarding the status of American shipping, British presence in the old northwest forts in the Ohio Valley, and the commercial relationship between Britain and its former colony. As the French Revolution and the Napoleonic Wars loomed in Europe, President George Washington sent Chief Justice John Jay to London as a special envoy to negotiate a treaty with William Grenville, the British foreign secretary (1791–1801) and son of former prime minister George Grenville. The resulting agreement, Jay's Treaty, called for the British to evacuate the forts within two years, provided for commissions made up of both American and British members to decide matters of debts resulting

from confiscations and destruction during the Revolutionary War and between American and British merchants, and allowed for criminal extradition between the two nations.

However, the Americans protested Jay's Treaty. Jay was burned in effigy while Alexander Hamilton, the secretary of the treasury, and Washington pressed for the treaty's passage in the Senate. Americans felt humiliated by limits placed on U.S. trade with the British West Indies and angry that no restitution existed for slaves freed or taken by the British during the war. Americans also disliked that fact that the thriving British fur trade would continue in the old northwest in the Ohio Valley even after the British abandoned their forts. Additionally, the treaty avoided any agreement on the impressment of American sailors into the Royal Navy or the boarding of American ships in U.S. or international waters, a problem that was the main cause of the War of 1812. Despite these problems, on April 30, 1796, Jay's Treaty passed in a bill that provided appropriations to carry out its terms.

—*Margaret Sankey*

References
Johnson, Herbert A. *John Jay, Colonial Lawyer.* New York: Garland Publishing, 1989.
Morris, Richard B., ed. *John Jay.* New York: Harper and Row, 1975.
See also Volume 1: War of 1812.

Jungle, The (1906)

Novel by Upton Sinclair that prompted an investigation into the meatpacking industry and led to the passage of food safety laws.

To promote the cause of socialism, novelist Upton Sinclair decided to write a novel called *The Jungle* that told the story of an ordinary immigrant worker and the capitalist economic system that exploited his labor for profit. He set the story in the Chicago meatpacking industry—the "jungle" of the title. As part of his story, Sinclair described the stages involved in the processing of meat from the slaughter of the animal to its dismemberment, the transfer of body parts to different departments for subdivision, and the final packaging of the meat. He emphasized the inhumanity of conditions experienced by the working class by writing that workers occasionally fell into the huge vats, becoming part of the sausages along with rat dung, poisoned bread used to kill rats, and dead rats themselves. Not a literary masterpiece, the book nevertheless became a bestseller among readers who were more horrified by what might be in their dinners than by the tragedy of wage slavery. Seeking to avert a public relations disaster, representatives of the Beef Trust, a group of companies that monopolized the meat industry, argued that *The Jungle* was a fabrication of lies orchestrated by the author for his personal gain. The decision of the meatpacking producers to fight back against Sinclair's allegations further stimulated sales of the novel, and President Theodore Roosevelt was drawn into the melee. Investigators that Roosevelt sent to Chicago produced a report even more shocking than

Sinclair's novel had been and, in response to the growing clamor for the regulation of meatpackers, Congress hurriedly passed laws to guarantee the safety of the food supply. The Pure Food and Drug Act (1906) forbade the manufacture, sale, or transportation of adulterated or harmful foods, and the Meat Inspection Act (1906) imposed sanitation standards and required federal inspection of meats destined for interstate commerce.

—*Caryn E. Neumann*

References

DeGruson, Gene, ed. *The Lost First Edition of Upton Sinclair's* The Jungle. Memphis, TN: Peachtree Publishers, 1988.

See also Volume 1: Pure Food and Drug Act.

K

Keating-Owen Act (1916)

An act of President Woodrow Wilson's New Freedom program intended to regulate child labor.

The National Child Labor Committee initiated the Keating-Owen Act as a special project. The act prohibited the interstate shipping of goods made totally or partly by children younger than 14 or by children aged 14 to 16 who worked more than eight hours per day. It also forbade the interstate shipment of products from mines and quarries that involved the labor of children under 16. On February 2, 1916, the House of Representatives passed the bill. President Woodrow Wilson believed the measure created an unconstitutional invasion by the federal government into the police power of the states, and thus he made no effort for months to overcome opposition to the bill in the Senate because he doubted the constitutionality of the measure. But in mid-July the Congressional progressives (reform-minded Republicans and Democrats) warned him that they considered the bill a test of his progressive sympathies. Wilson had a change of heart because of the progressives' stance and subsequently persuaded Democratic senators that their party's future depended on the passage of the bill. As a result, the Senate passed the measure and Wilson signed it on September 1. In 1918, however, the Supreme Court in the case of *Hammer v. Dagenhart* ruled the Keating-Owen Act unconstitutional because the purpose of the law was not to regulate commerce but to regulate child labor, a power reserved to the states.

—*Steven E. Siry*

References

Link, Arthur S. *Woodrow Wilson and the Progressive Era, 1910–1917.* New York: Harper and Row, 1954.
See also Volume 1: Wilson, Woodrow.

Kennedy Round (1964–1967)

Sixth round of negotiations under the General Agreement on Tariffs and Trade (GATT).

After World War II, the United States pursued a policy of free trade to prevent future wars. To this end, several negotiations called *rounds,* part of the General Agreement on Tariffs and Trade (GATT), occurred between 1947 and 1960. The Kennedy Round, held in Geneva, Switzerland, from May 1964 through June 1967, continued the process of tariff reductions that began in 1947 after World War II. Issues discussed during these talks included eliminating nontariff barriers, reducing all rates by 50 percent across the board instead of negotiating individual items, and including additional agricultural and industrial products. At the conclusion of the talks, participants agreed to reduce rates on industrial items (excluding steel and textiles) by 35 percent over five years. In addition, the United States reduced its rates on chemicals by 50 percent, whereas Europeans only reduced their duties by 35 percent. For agricultural commodities, rates decreased by 15 to 18 percent. Negotiators also agreed to a strong antidumping resolution, which prohibited the sale of goods at below-cost prices, and forbade industrial nations from entering into reciprocal trade agreements with less-developed nations. The United States, which had previously enjoyed a trade surplus, gradually moved toward a trade deficit after the implementation of the Kennedy Round.

—*Cynthia Clark Northrup*

References

Preeg, Ernest H. *Traders and Diplomats: An Analysis of the Kennedy Round of Negotiations under the General Agreement on Tariffs and Trade.* Washington: Brookings Institution, 1970.
See also Volume 1: Free Trade; General Agreement on Tariffs and Trade.

Keynes, John Maynard (1883–1946)

British economist known best for his book *The General Theory of Employment, Interest and Money* (1936), which showed theoretically how decisions to consume and invest determine national income and employment.

Born in Cambridge, England, in 1883 and educated at Eton College and King's College, Cambridge, John Maynard

Keynes joined the civil service before becoming a Cambridge academic economist. He accepted a position at the British Treasury soon after the outbreak of World War I. Having resigned in disgust at the harsh Versailles peace settlement after that war, which placed heavy war reparations on Germany, he wrote *The Economic Consequences of the Peace* (1919) and achieved worldwide fame.

Keynes then returned to academe. Mass unemployment between the wars led him to reject strict laissez-faire economics, which is characterized by a hands-off approach from the government. He published several works, but only in *The General Theory of Employment, Interest and Money* (1936) did he show theoretically how decisions to consume and invest determine national income and employment. This revolutionary book attacked the orthodox view that governments could reduce unemployment by cutting wages. It also argued that money operated not as a neutral factor, but as something that could affect the underlying ways in which the economy worked. Keynes saw the rate of interest as a price like any other, but one set in the money markets rather than by the pressure to equate investment with savings. On these assumptions the economy could, Keynes showed, equilibrate below the full employment rate, given insufficient demand in areas such as consumption and investment plans backed by purchasing power. This possibility implied that governments should regulate aggregate demand to achieve full employment.

Keynes attracted followers in the United States among supporters of the New Deal, especially President Franklin D. Roosevelt, who used deficit spending as a means of ending the Great Depression. After the outbreak of World War II, Keynes returned to the British Treasury and, in negotiation with American officials, helped to design the Bretton Woods institutions (1945) to stabilize international currencies. His last major act prior to his death on April 20, 1946, was the negotiation of a U.S. loan to Britain.

—*Richard Toye*

References
Moggridge, D. E. *Maynard Keynes: An Economist's Biography.* London: Routledge, 1992.
Skidelsky, Robert. *John Maynard Keynes.* 3 vols. London: Macmillan, 1983–2000.
See also Volume 1: Bretton Woods Agreement; Deficit Spending.

Keynesian Economics

Paradigm devised by John Maynard Keynes that calls for deficit spending.

In *The General Theory of Employment, Interest and Money* (1936), Keynes argued that the classical paradigm (that supply and demand determine the market price) had been nullified by a series of historical events: World War I, the failure of the victorious Allies to reconstruct the international system, and the Great Depression. Because the classical paradigm assumed the validity of Say's law of markets (that is, the maxim that the balance between supply and demand would guarantee full employment), it could not explain the persistence of involuntary unemployment. Accordingly, Keynes proposed a straightforward but revolutionary remedy for chronic unemployment: deficit spending on public works to create jobs and augment purchasing power. More broadly, Keynes advocated government intervention in the economy not only to diminish the probability of a crisis but also to accommodate the demands of the working-class movement. It is worth noting, however, that Keynes did not influence the policies of the New Deal—a massive public works program instituted by President Franklin D. Roosevelt in response to the Great Depression—until the recession of 1937 and 1938. In effect, it was the 1937–1938 slump that convinced Roosevelt not only to use deficit spending as a means of "priming the pump," but also to take the *General Theory* seriously as a blueprint for managed capitalism. Keynesian ideas, having gained footholds in the Roosevelt brain trust (advisers from Ivy League schools) and the Harvard fiscal policy seminar held during the early 1940s, influenced both the financing of the American war effort for World War II and preparations for the Bretton Woods conference held in 1944 to stabilize international currencies that had abandoned the gold standard.

Keynesianism figured prominently in postwar reconstruction and recovery and the expansion of the world into the global economy. By incorporating the popular struggles of labor and the working classes into this expansion, the U.S.-sponsored "Keynesian consensus" of policymakers who supported Keynes's economic theories brought about a golden age in capitalist history. However, the consensus dissolved amidst fiscal crisis, deindustrialization, and stagflation (increased unemployment and inflation simultaneously) in the 1970s. In recent years, economists outside the mainstream have proposed global Keynesianism, a new Marshall Plan for reconstruction of national economies, and a renewed developmentalism or emphasis on social programs and domestic government efficiency as alternatives to neoliberalism (free trade and globalization).

—*Mark Frezzo*

References
Colander, David C., and Harry Landreth, eds. *The Coming of Keynesianism to America: Conversations with the Founders of Keynesian Economics.* Cheltenham, England: Edward Elgar, 1996.
De Angelis, Massimo. *Keynesianism, Social Conflict, and Political Economy.* London: Macmillan, 2000.
Singer, H. W. "Editorial: The Golden Age of the Keynesian Consensus—The Pendulum Swings Back." *World Development,* vol. 25, no. 3 (1997): 293–297.
See also Volume 1: Budget Deficits and Surpluses; Deficit Spending.

Keyserling, Leon (1908–1987)

A New Dealer and second chair of the Council of Economic Advisers who contributed to the policies and politics of the administrations of Franklin D. Roosevelt and Harry S Truman.

Born in Beaufort, South Carolina, on January 22, 1908, Leon Keyserling graduated from Columbia University with a bachelor's degree in economics in 1928. Rexford Tugwell (an American economist and political scientist) and John Dewey (an American philosopher and educator) significantly influenced his education. He received a law degree from Harvard in 1931 and completed all requirements except the dissertation for a Columbia doctoral degree when he joined the U.S. Department of Agriculture in 1933.

From 1933 to 1937, Keyserling served as the assistant to Democratic Senator Robert F. Wagner of New York, who was known as "the congressional Mr. New Deal" because of his support for the economic recovery programs of President Franklin D. Roosevelt during the Great Depression. For the next four years Keyserling contributed significantly to several pieces of legislation, writing them and lobbying for them. He wrote section 7A in the National Labor Relations Act of 1935; he also worked on the Social Security Act (1935) and the U.S. Housing Act (1937).

From 1937 to 1946, Keyserling served in various federal housing agencies. As general counsel of the National Housing Authority, he contributed to the establishment in 1965 of the Department of Housing and Urban Development. He wrote the National Housing Act of 1949 and guided that legislation through Congress.

Keyserling remained active in Democratic Party politics, writing speeches for President Roosevelt and Senator Wagner. He also crafted the Democratic Party's platform in 1936, 1940, and 1944. After Roosevelt's death and the assumption of the presidency by Harry S Truman, Keyserling was a major contributor at meetings of general counsel Clark Clifford's Monday night supper group, at which ideas and policies were generated that led to Truman's victory in 1948 following the Republican congressional victories in 1946.

Appointed vice chair of the Council of Economic Advisers by Truman in 1946, Keyserling became chair in 1949. He served as a close economic adviser to Truman during the Korean War and helped write NSC-68 (National Security Council 68), a basic document in the containment policy designed to prevent the expansion of communism. The Truman administration kept inflation under control and prevented any significant economic downturn with Keyserling's help.

In 1953, he established the Conference on Economic Progress, a liberal think tank and lobbying organization. He worked for New Frontier and Great Society legislation during the presidencies of John F. Kennedy and Lyndon B. Johnson, respectively. The Full Employment and Balanced Growth Act of 1977 (the Humphrey-Hawkins Act) was his last major contribution to public policy. Keyserling died in Washington, D.C., August 9, 1987.

—*Donald K. Pickens*

References

Brazelton, W. Robert. "The Economics of Leon Hirsch Keyserling." *Journal of Economic Perspectives*, vol. 11, no. 4 (Fall 1997): 189–197.

Pickens, Donald. "Leon Keyserling and Integrative Liberalism." *Red River Historical Journal*, vol. 1 (October 2000): 44–74.

See also Volume 1: Council of Economic Advisers; Housing Act of 1949; National Labor Relations Board; New Deal; Social Security Act of 1935.

Knights of Labor

Labor union that attempted to unite all American workers—skilled craft workers, white-collar employees, unskilled laborers, semiskilled workers, females, African Americans, and foreign-born—to improve working conditions.

On December 28, 1869, in Philadelphia, a group of garment cutters founded the Noble Order of the Knights of Labor and elected a tailor, Uriah S. Stephens, as its first president. Founders of the Knights denounced union emphasis on labor based on wages per hour and focused instead on the education of union members and working toward common goals. Their primary goal focused on securing a proper wage for laborers. The Knights favored an eight-hour working day and legislative abolition of child labor. They organized and operated their own cooperative stores and manufacturing plants, although most of their 135 cooperative enterprises failed because they lacked the money necessary to buy the best machinery and hire qualified managers.

The Knights' founders believed that labor organizations that were divided into craft divisions lacked unity and strength to fend off employer resistance, and so they decided to organize all workers regardless of skill. The only basic requirement for joining was the desire to work for their wages. For a period of time members swore an oath of secrecy, but later the group abandoned the oath.

Initially, the Knights of Labor organized on a geographic basis. In the early years it remained largely a local union with three assemblies—two in Philadelphia and one in Pittsburgh. The panic of 1873, when the government ended the use of silver as legal tender, and the accompanying collapse of many trade unions enabled the Knights to move beyond their original organizational structure. On January 1, 1878, in Reading, Pennsylvania, a representative assembly composed of members from Philadelphia and Pittsburgh took the first steps toward the formation of a national organization. In 1881, Stephens resigned to devote his full energies to the political arena. Terrance V. Powderly, a venturesome idealist, replaced him as president.

Powderly directed the affairs of the Knights for more than a decade of organizational highs and lows. Powderly opposed strikes, preferring instead to settle disputes between managers and laborers through industrial arbitration. He felt the organization could employ its resources more wisely in establishing cooperatives that, in turn, could bring an end to wage labor. In time, rank-and-file members forced him to accept the creation of a strike fund. An increasing split between the organization's reformists and hard-line trade unionists highlighted the strike issue.

The Knights' greatest success occurred in 1885 when, for the first time in American labor history, railroad operators met strike leaders on equal terms and acceded to labor's chief demands. The Knight's dramatic confrontation with the Wabash railroad, controlled by Jay Gould, swelled the union's ranks. When the strike started in 1885, the Knights numbered about 50,000 members, but within a year their membership had swelled to 700,000.

This rapid growth ultimately proved disastrous to the inexperienced union members, as a false sense of power permeated the rank and file. The decline of the Knights occurred almost as rapidly as the rise.

In 1886, the Knights lost an important strike against the Gould system of southwestern railroads. The strike alienated the public because of the violence involved and because shortages of food and coal resulted. An unsuccessful strike in the Chicago stockyards the same year—along with the general antilabor hysteria associated with the Haymarket Square Riot, in which both police and strikers were killed after someone threw a bomb into the crowd—further weakened the once-strong "noble order."

The failed strikes, coupled with the skilled craft unions dislike for and distrust of the all-inclusive policy of taking in unskilled workers, led a group of trade union leaders to form their own organization, the American Federation of Labor, in 1886. The newly created rival union argued for an immediate improvement in economic and working conditions rather than for political and reform measures.

By the summer of 1887, membership in the Knights had dwindled to 250,000. In 1890 membership was at 100,000, and three years later it fell to 75,000. In 1893, James R. Sovereign, an Iowa farm editor, replaced Powderly as president. When socialist members broke ranks and left the order, the Knights of Labor rapidly disintegrated. By the turn of the century, they no longer had an effective voice in the American labor movement.

—*Charles F. Howlett*

References

Fink, Leon. *Workingmen's Democracy: The Knights of Labor and American Politics.* Urbana: University of Illinois Press, 1983.

Foner, Philip S. *A History of the Labor Movement in the United States.* 4 vols. New York: International Publishers, 1955–1975.

Grobb, Gerald. *Workers and Utopia: A Study of Ideological Conflict in the American Labor Movement, 1865–1900.* Chicago: Quadrangle Books, 1961.

Montgomery, David. *The Fall of the House of Labor: The Workplace, the State, and American Labor Activism, 1865–1925.* New York: Cambridge University Press, 1987.

Rayback, Joseph G. *A History of American Labor.* New York: Free Press, 1966.

See also Volume 2: Labor.

L

Labor Contract Law

Laws governing union activity in the United States based first and foremost on policies and practices related to collective bargaining and its enforcement.

As industrialization began in early nineteenth-century America, courts considered union activity such as strikes, picketing, and reluctance to deal with various employers as equivalent to criminal activity. Courts dealt particularly harshly with workers and their efforts to organize to get higher wages. In *Commonwealth v. Pullis* (Philadelphia Mayor's Court 1806), the courts convicted workers of a criminal conspiracy "for refusing to work except at a specified wage rate and for attempting to prevent others from working at a lower rate." Subsequent cases held that union efforts to improve wages and working conditions represented criminal acts.

The celebrated case of *Commonwealth v. Hunt* (1842) represented a marked departure from criminal to civil liability as a means for controlling union activity. In its decision the Massachusetts Supreme Court permitted a group of workers to use economic weapons to prevent other workers from entering into individual contracts not compatible with the group's interests.

The key application in the *Hunt* decision involved an ends/means test: "The finding of a criminal conspiracy required proof of either an illegal purpose or the use of illegal means." Throughout the nineteenth century, state courts applied the ends/means test in civil suits for injunctions and damages "against concerted worker activity."

By the late 1800s, federal courts entered into judicial regulation of labor-management relations. The judiciary applied the 1890 Sherman Anti-Trust Act's restraint-of-trade provision to most union tactics dealing with organizing and economic pressure. Antitrust laws prohibiting unionizing efforts were highlighted in the Danbury hatters case (so called because it involved the first hatters' factory in the United States, in Danbury, Connecticut), *Loewe v. Lawlor* (U.S. 1908), when the Supreme Court declared the Sherman Act had been violated because a union instigated "a boycott of retail stores that sold hats produced by a struck manufacturer." The Clayton Anti-Trust Act (1914) sought to diminish the exposure of unions to antitrust liability, but in *Duplex Printing Press Co. v. Deering* (U.S. 1921), the Supreme Court narrowed the Clayton Act's provisions protecting labor activity. The Court injunction remained the most commonly used weapon by employers, and union activities were severely curtailed in this manner.

In 1932, however, passage of the Norris-LaGuardia Act withdrew the power of the federal courts to issue either temporary or permanent injunctions in nonviolent labor disputes. Congress declared that picketing and refusals to work remained "specifically immunized from injunctions." The act declared that the federal courts should not formulate "rules to govern labor policy" and that the government must remain neutral, thus permitting union growth. In 1935, the Wagner Act, or National Labor Relations Act, established new practices governing labor contracts. The act marked the beginning of strong support for organized labor and collective bargaining policies by the federal government. Specifically, with respect to unfair labor practices, members of the National Labor Relations Board (NLRB) served both the prosecutorial and adjudicator roles. The NLRB cited violations and then ruled on them under the law. The Wagner Act contained no restrictions on union activities. It functioned as the authority on issues of organized labor.

In 1947 the Taft-Hartley Act was passed in an effort to curb unions' practices including sympathy boycotts and strikes that forced employers to discharge workers because of their union affiliation. The act represented a shift in federal policy away from encouraging unionization to a more neutral posture while also protecting workers from employee coercion. In 1959 Congress passed the last major piece of legislation governing labor contracts. The Landrum-Griffin Act (Labor-Management Reporting and Disclosing Act) contained guarantees for union members and required that unions disclose the use of union funds. It also prescribed how union officers would be chosen and restricted financial abuse by officers. Congress passed the act in response to evidence related to looting of some union treasuries and denials of fundamental rights to members in some unions.

Today, laws regulating labor contracts address the following: organizational picketing, secondary boycotts, jurisdictional disputes, featherbedding (requiring employers to hire more employees than are needed), economic responses by employers to concerted employee activity, obligation to bargain, enforcing collective bargaining agreements, antitrust laws, and regulation of internal union affairs.

—*Charles F. Howlett*

References
Hunt, Commonwealth v. 45, Mass. (4 Met.) 111, 38 Amer. Dec. 346 (1842): 1, 2.
Leslie, Douglas. *Labor Law.* St. Paul, MN: West Publishing, 1986.
Millis, H. A., and E. C. Brown. *From the Wagner Act to Taft-Hartley.* Chicago: University of Chicago Press, 1950.
Tomlins, Christopher L. *The State and the Unions: Labor Relations, Law, and the Organized Labor Movement in America, 1880–1960.* Cambridge: Cambridge University Press, 1985.
See also Volume 1: *Commonwealth v. Hunt;* Sherman Anti-Trust Act; Wagner Act.

Labor-Management Relations Act (Taft-Hartley Act) (1947)

Congressional legislation guaranteeing unions the fundamental right of collective bargaining but substantially limiting their other powers.

During the late 1930s and World War II, unions enjoyed a considerable growth in membership and economic power as a result of the passage of the 1935 law sponsored by Republican Senator Robert F. Wagner of New York. The Wagner Act made it illegal for management to refuse to bargain with workers' representatives, encouraged workers to form unions and negotiate collectively through their elected officials, and focused attention on unfair management practices. In addition, the act established the National Labor Relations Board (NLRB) to help determine who "was to be the exclusive representative of all the workers in an appropriate bargaining unit" as well as "to investigate and draw up findings on charges of unfair labor practices." The new law received immediate criticism yet withstood a constitutional challenge in the Supreme Court. Many argued that unions would abuse their newfound strength.

Labor had expressly promised not to disrupt military efforts by calling strikes during World War II, and when the war ended in 1945 and wartime wage and price controls were lifted, a series of strikes ensued in which labor demanded increased wages to match the increase in prices. The public resented these disputes and, in 1947, after five months of deliberation and over President Harry S Truman's veto, Congress unanimously passed the Labor-Management Relations Act, better known as the Taft-Hartley Act. Republican Senator Robert Taft of Ohio, son of former President William H. Taft, sponsored the law along with Republican Representative Fred Hartley of New Jersey. The act upheld aspects of the National Labor Relations Act of 1935, including unions' fundamental right to collective bargaining, but it also stated specifically

that strikes that might cause a national emergency can be delayed for 80 days by presidential declaration.

The Taft-Hartley Act replaced the Wagner Act and focused on reducing the power unions had achieved as a result of New Deal programs to revitalize labor during the Great Depression. Specifically, the new law prohibited unions from contributing to political campaigns, restricted the union privilege of having management pay union dues of members without their consent (check-off), required union officials to swear that they were not communists in order to receive assistance from the NLRB, permitted management to seek court injunctions in times of strikes known as the "cooling-off period," allowed the government to sue union officials for violating contracts or engaging in strikes arising from jurisdictional disputes with rival unions, and forbade the closed shop, which prohibited the employment of nonunion workers. Section 301 of the act also made collective bargaining agreements enforceable in federal district court, and section 303 provided a civil damage remedy to private parties injured by secondary boycotts.

The Taft-Hartley or Labor-Management Relations Act marked a significant shift to a more neutral posture away from federal policy encouraging unionization while maintaining the right of employees "to be free from employer coercion." Organized labor attacked the new law and attempted to amend it or eliminate it altogether. Unions referred to it as the "slave labor law," while management insisted that the law appropriately balanced power between employees and employers. Despite union protestations to the contrary, the act did not wipe away the basic right of unions to exist, nor did it permit management to refuse to enter into collective negotiations with representatives of organized labor.

—*Charles F. Howlett*

References
Blum, Albert A. *A History of the American Labor Movement.* Washington, DC: American Historical Association, 1972.
Leslie, Douglas. *Labor Law.* St. Paul, MN: West Publishing, 1986.
Millis, H. A., and E. C. Brown. *From the Wagner Act to Taft-Hartley.* Chicago: University of Chicago Press, 1950.
Tomlins, Christopher L. *The State and the Unions: Labor Relations, Law, and the Organized Labor Movement in America, 1880–1960.* Cambridge: Cambridge University Press, 1985.
Zieger, Robert H. *American Workers, American Unions, 1920–1985.* Baltimore, MD: Johns Hopkins University Press, 1994.
See also Volume 2: Labor.

Laissez-Faire

Economic order free of government interference.

The canon of economics without government intrusion originated from the theory of classical economics that emerged and gained influence during European colonial expansion in the eighteenth century. According to the principal advocate of laissez-faire, Adam Smith, society could hardly prosper unless individuals enjoyed full freedom to pursue self-interests and personal welfare without state restrictions. Challenging mercantilism—a system that European powers adopted at the time to strengthen state controls over industry by restricting all trade between colonies and the mother country—Smith's laissez-faire concept underscored free trade demanded by a rising merchant class. In the U.S. Industrial Revolution of the post–Civil War era, the economic notion of laissez-faire, with its message of individualism and utilitarian ethics, appealed to capitalist entrepreneurs.

The laissez-faire dogma, embraced by the theory of social Darwinism (which justified the increased power of the fittest and the duplication of the political and social beliefs of "the fittest" nations on lesser nations for their benefit), provided a strong stimulus to and justification of America's Industrial Revolution and capitalist accumulation of wealth in the late nineteenth century. The dogma's proponents in the United States—for example, William Graham Sumner of Yale, a Darwinist sociology professor—believed that economic life functioned according to the theory of survival of the fittest, just as in nature, and that the "invisible hand" of competition would more effectively improve the economy than would state regulation. Proponents of laissez-faire believed everyone should have the absolute right to manage their personal property at their own pleasure and should be free to compete, to succeed, or to fail. Laissez-faire advocates also preferred that the law of supply and demand determine all economic variables such as prices, wages, rents, and interest rates. Yet the increasing pattern of monopoly, the social cost of industrialization (with labor living at mere subsistence levels), and entrepreneurs' demand for a well-structured economy made state intervention increasingly necessary. More recently, the laissez-faire approach (which began at the start of the twentieth century and increased, especially after the Great Depression, in the first part of the century) has become less and less feasible as the federal government takes a more active role in taxing and regulating businesses, although the government continues to give a moral boost to individuals' drive for personal prosperity by reducing government involvement, such as via tax cuts.

—*Guoqiang Zheng*

References
Tedlow, Richard S. *The Rise of the American Business Corporation.* Philadelphia: Harwood Academic Publishers, 1991.
See also Volume 1: Free Trade; Trusts.

Lee, Henry (1782–1867)

Author of the influential "Boston report," which challenged the ideas that the government should protect manufactures and that protective duties result in lowering prices.

Born in Beverly, Massachusetts, on February 4, 1782, Henry Lee dropped out of college early to enter business. He traveled to Calcutta in 1811 and, because of the War of 1812, he decided to remain in India, where he made trading acquaintances. A student of political economy, Lee opposed some of the viewpoints held by supporters of the American

System, which called for a national bank, protective tariffs, and government funding of internal improvements such as roads and canals. He also wrote for Condy Raguet's *Free-Trade Advocate,* a Philadelphia publication. In the 1820s, Lee turned his attention to the tariff—an issue that was very compelling in New England. Woolen manufacturers there supported protectionist tariffs because they faced strong competition from overseas. Merchants and traders who opposed these protectionist tariffs, fearing they would hinder trading relationships with foreign countries, chose Henry Lee to write the 200-word document *Report of the Committee of the Citizens of Boston and Vicinity, Opposed to a Further Increase of Duties on Importations,* sometimes called the "Boston report." First printed in 1827, it had four printings and was singled out by historian Edward Stanwood, who said in his *American Tariff Controversies in the Nineteenth Century* that "no more powerful document was ever produced in this country." The report challenged the ideas that the government should protect manufactures and that protective duties result in lowering prices, among other ideas. It also discounted the belief that the British government had suddenly altered its system of duties after the United States passed its tariff of 1824, thus undercutting American prices. Lee pointed out that the British had begun petitioning for this change in 1820 and passed legislation that lowered the tariff before they could even have heard of the American bill.

In 1828, Senator Daniel Webster of Massachusetts replied to the Boston report in a disappointing speech in the congressional debate on the proposed Tariff of 1828. He admitted that Britain did not lower its tariff in response to the American 1824 tariff, but he argued, "The effect of that reduction, on our manufactures, was the same precisely as if the British act had been designed to operate against them, and for no other purpose."

In the 1832 presidential election, South Carolina gave its 11 electoral votes for vice president to Henry Lee. He died February 6, 1867.

—*David E. Walker*

References
Register of Debates. Senate, 20th Cong., 1st sess., 1828.
Stanwood, Edward. *American Tariff Controversies in the Nineteenth Century.* New York: Russell and Russell, 1967.
See also Volume 1: Protective Tariffs; Tariff of Abominations.

Lend-Lease Act (1941)

Strategy calling for the United States to funnel armaments to the Allied powers to support Britain's struggle against Germany after the outbreak of World War II in Europe.

In late December 1940, President Franklin D. Roosevelt championed a strategy calling for the United States to funnel armaments and other materials to Great Britain, which was in a life-or-death struggle with Nazi Germany following the outbreak of World War II in 1939. Roosevelt's persuasion led Congress to pass the Lend-Lease Act—officially entitled "An Act to Promote the Defense of the United States, and for

Other Purposes"—in March 1941. This act anticipated the full use of America's industrial resources and military in World War II.

Roosevelt's lend-lease plan appeared as a resourcefully veiled reversal to a foreign policy of noninvolvement that Washington had been pursuing since the mid-1930s, when the Axis nations—militarist Japan, Fascist Italy, and Nazi Germany—intensified efforts for conquests in Asia, Africa, and Europe. Buttressed by a strong isolationist sentiment nationwide, the neutrality acts passed by Congress between 1935 and 1939 had kept the United States from being dragged indiscriminately into international crises or military conflicts regardless of circumstances. The U.S. propensity for neutrality remained firm even when the Nazi Germany regime, egged on by the British and French desire for appeasement and a Nazi-Soviet nonaggression pact, invaded Poland in September 1939 and catalyzed the eruption of World War II. In 1940, after France had capitulated to German aggression, Britain became the last line of defense against the Nazis. Preparing for its own national defense, a sympathetic U.S. government fine-tuned the neutrality acts to permit the supplying to Britain of arms essential for its survival. Given rampant domestic fear of war, however, the sale of arms to Britain was to be on a cash-and-carry basis. Despite its desperate situation, London depleted its U.S. dollar reserves for American purchases by fall 1940.

Because Britain needed more direct help than the cash-and-carry policy permitted, President Roosevelt contemplated a strategy of conveying armaments and goods to the British on a lend-lease basis. In a fireside chat broadcast December 29, 1940, Roosevelt explained to the American public that British survival was vital to America's own defense in view of the aim Nazi Germany and its allies had to achieve world domination. In his state of the union message on January 6, 1941, Roosevelt officially asked Congress for a lend-lease bill that would help ensure America's own national security as "an arsenal of democracy."

After much animated debate about whether this initiative would lead the United States toward war, Congress passed the Lend-Lease Act on March 11, 1941, and the president signed it the same day. The act authorized the president to implement when necessary immediate transfer—to a value of $1.3 billion—of war supplies (including weapons, munitions, aircraft, vessels, machinery, tools, materials, or any agricultural or industrial commodity) to any countries whose defense he considered critical to the safety of the United States. Altogether, the act appropriated $7 billion and stipulated the recipient nations' obligation to yield reciprocal (either military or commercial) advantages to the United States. The act also empowered Roosevelt to demand of the recipient governments payment or repayment in forms convenient or favorable to the United States.

As a foreign aid program, lend-lease assistance quickly enlarged American responsibility toward countries (at this point, Great Britain and the Soviet Union) fighting the Axis powers and soon led the United States toward direct participation in this international conflict. But the program also served American interests by upgrading Washington's role in influencing the course and direction of World War II and ultimately by helping to forge a postwar international order.

—Guoqiang Zheng

References
O'Neill, William L. *A Democracy at War: America's Fight at Home and Abroad in World War II.* New York: Free Press, 1993.
See also Volume 1: Roosevelt, Franklin D.; World War II.

Levittown

The paradigmatic post–World War II American suburb and product of a $50 million housing development constructed by Abraham, Alfred, and William Levitt.

Levittown was a development of mass-produced housing built beginning in 1947 in the Hempstead Plains of Long Island about 50 miles east of Manhattan. At first only returning World War II veterans and their families could purchase homes in the development. The town's progenitors, developer William Levitt and his architect brother, Alfred, capitalized on the housing crunch of the immediate post–World War II years and on their own mass-production know-how, learned from their father Abraham, to make home ownership a reality for the growing ranks of middle-class families. The planned community consisted of assembled homes, mostly Cape Cod and ranch-style single-family detached houses, along curvilinear drives off the parkways leading from New York City. Each unit included a 12-by-16-foot living room with a fireplace, one bath, and two bedrooms, with room for expansion upstairs or outward into the yard. Detractors ridiculed the raw, unfinished quality of Levittown's landscape and the homogeneity of its dwellings. But young, middle-income families responded enthusiastically to the prospect of home ownership made possible by the Levitts' novel approach to home building and new, more active government housing policies, such as mortgage guarantees by the Federal Housing Administration. The first 1,800 houses in Levittown were available only as rentals with an option to buy after a year's residence. Because the mortgage and taxes combined were less than the rent, almost all of the original Levittowners opted for purchase. After 1949, the developers sold all additional units. Levittown ultimately encompassed more than 17,400 separate houses and 82,000 residents. Levittown's restrictive racial covenant barring African Americans from purchasing homes stayed intact until the 1960s.

—Sayuri Shimizu

References
Gelfand, Mark I. *A Nation of Cities.* New York: Oxford University Press, 1975.
Jackson, Kenneth T. *Crabgrass Frontier.* New York: Oxford University Press, 1985.
Kelly, Barbara M. *Expanding the American Dream: Building and Rebuilding Levittown.* Albany: State University of New York Press, 1993.
See also Volume 2: Urbanization.

Lobbying

The act of influencing government decisions through pressure exerted on members of Congress by agents of special interest groups.

The term *lobbying* was first used in the 1830s when advocates of special legislative interests decided to meet in the lobby of the Capitol building. Since then the meaning of the term has expanded to cover all activities designed to influence the votes of representatives and senators. Most Americans accept the practice, although lobbying often leads legislators to introduce or vote for measures their constituents do not support. Lobbyists usually represent large corporations, financial institutions, educational organizations, medical professions, unions, or other industries. In addition, nationwide special interest groups such as Mothers Against Drunk Driving, the National Rifle Association, and Common Cause (a group of citizens formed to combat special-interest groups) push a single-issue or limited-issue program. Lobbyists often provide technical information to the legislators and occasionally draft resolutions for a legislator to introduce. The Regulation of Lobbying Act of 1946 required lobbyists to register—an attempt to limit their influence and reduce the opportunity for corruption. For example, lobbyists must report the gifts and contributions they give to lawmakers, which are limited by law.

Lobbyists use various tactics to ensure the passage of legislation favorable to their cause. Entertaining or becoming close friends with legislators and the use of promises for future favors such as campaign contributions often yield results. If these endeavors fail, lobbyists often turn to threats to withdraw financial support from legislators, mass media campaigns, or grassroots telephone and mail campaigns. The promise of funds from political action committees (PACs) often gets the attention of representatives who have to campaign for reelection every two years. Lobbyists control the funds of some PACs and therefore can use this tool to influence legislators.

Lobbyists have been successful over the decades, but Congress and U.S. citizens continue to monitor their activities to ensure that representatives keep the interest of the people as their primary focus. In 1995, Congress passed more stringent lobbying legislation that increased disclosure requirements.

—*Cynthia Clark Northrup*

References
Key, V. O. *Politics, Parties, and Pressure Groups.* New York: Crowell, 1964.
Wright, John R. *Interest Groups and Congress: Lobbying, Contributions, and Influence.* Boston: Allyn and Bacon, 1996.
See also Volume 1: Corruption.

Long, Huey (1893–1935)

Charismatic and flamboyant Louisiana governor who posed a significant political challenge to President Franklin D. Roosevelt by advocating sharing of wealth and hatred of the rich.

Born in Winnfield, Louisiana, August 30, 1893, Huey Long never attended college but worked as a salesman and attorney before entering politics. Quickly rising to the governorship of Louisiana in 1928, he established a program of public works and deficit spending. Louisianans loved the Democrat for the free textbooks that he provided for schoolchildren, paid for by severance tax on natural resources (a tax placed by states on extraction of natural resources used in other states). Elected to the U.S. Senate in 1930, Long supported high tariffs because he adamantly advocated protection for Louisiana products such as oil, cotton, and sugar. He generally voted slightly left of center on economic issues, although he never supporting the New Deal. In his most significant speech to the Senate, on April 4, 1932, Long concluded that modern mass production remained oppressive and that America must redistribute its wealth. He introduced a bill to limit annual income to $5 million, but, as happened with all of his proposals, it pulled only a handful of votes. Long believed that the nation possessed only a finite amount of economic resources and that the rich had acquired their wealth by taking it from the poor. He argued that the poor could only escape poverty by confiscating wealth. On February 23, 1934, Long began the Share Our Wealth Society, which grew rapidly and promised more than the New Deal. Through Share Our Wealth, Long proposed that the government confiscate any annual income above $1 million and wealth in excess of $5 million and that it provide each family with an annual income of at least $2,500 and also with a home, car, and a radio whose worth totaled at least $5,000. Long was shot September 8, 1935, in Baton Rouge, Louisiana, by a political opponent and bled to death a day later.

—*Caryn E. Neumann*

References
Jeansonne, Glen. *Messiah of the Masses: Huey P. Long and the Great Depression.* New York: Harper Collins, 1993.
See also Volume 1: Great Depression; New Deal; Roosevelt, Franklin D.; Share Our Wealth Plan; Share Our Wealth Society.

Louisiana Purchase (1803)

Purchase of the Louisiana Territory from France under Thomas Jefferson's administration.

In 1801, newly elected President Thomas Jefferson learned that Spain had surrendered the Louisiana Territory to the French under the secret Treaty of San Ildefonso. Like many other Americans, Jefferson feared that the French would rescind the right of American farmers to deposit their goods at New Orleans. He also worried that a reborn French empire across the Mississippi River would inspire the many Indian nations in the western country to rise up and attack settlements along the entire frontier. He even thought that Napoleon might send French settlers to the region to set up farms that would feed the slaves on the many plantations of France's sugar islands such as Haiti.

One year later, Jefferson instructed Robert Livingston, his

ambassador to France, to purchase New Orleans and western Florida from the French. If the French would not agree, then Livingston was instructed to purchase from them another tract of land along the Mississippi River, where America could build a new port for the deposit of western goods. Before Livingston could negotiate a purchase (and before Spain had surrendered Louisiana to the French), Spain closed New Orleans to American shipping. In response, Jefferson sent James Monroe to France in 1803 as a special minister with instructions to offer the French up to $10 million for New Orleans and western Florida.

Livingston and Monroe were stunned when French Foreign Minister Charles Maurice de Talleyrand offered in 1803 to sell the entire Louisiana Territory including New Orleans to the United States for $15 million. Napoleon, preparing to renew his military campaigns in Europe, needed money quickly. Livingston and Monroe agreed to the sale, and in 1803 Congress approved the Treaty between the United States of America and the French Republic, which made Louisiana, which stretched from the Mississippi River all the way to the Rocky Mountains, a territory of the United States.

—*Mary Stockwell*

References

Billington, Ray Allen. *Westward Expansion: A History of the American Frontier.* New York: Macmillan, 1967.

See also Volume 2: Land Policies; Volume 2 (Documents): Treaty between the United States of America and the French Republic with Conventions.

M

Macon's Bill No. 2 (1810)

Temporarily reversed Jeffersonian commercial policy and allowed trade with the warring states of England and France.

Passed into law May 1, 1810, following the failed Embargo of 1807 and the expiration of the Non-Intercourse Act of 1809, Macon's Bill No. 2 attempted to influence the policies of France and Britain. The measure continued the Jeffersonian policy of threatening to sever economic relations to force these nations to respect U.S. neutrality and shipping rights on the high seas. Sponsored by Republican Representative Nathaniel Macon of North Carolina, chair of the Foreign Affairs Committee, the bill lifted all restrictions on trade with France and England and promised to only bar war ships from American ports. It also stated that if either belligerent ended its restrictions against U.S. commerce before March 3, 1811, the president could authorize the resumption of nonintercourse against the nation that refused to change its policy within three months of the first country's declaration to end its restrictions against American shipping.

The bill enabled Napoleon Bonaparte to manipulate American policy to his own advantage, and it increased tensions between the United States and England. On November 1, 1810, Napoleon officially revoked the Berlin and Milan decrees that blockaded England and authorized the seizure of U.S. ships that refused to trade with France. According to the provisions of the bill, England was to revoke its restrictions by February 1, 1811. Although British officials did issue licenses to American ships to enter English ports, Parliament's unwillingness to officially renounce the Orders in Council that blockaded continental Europe forced the United States to reimpose nonintercourse against Britain. Even though Napoleon continued to seize American ships in French ports in violation of Macon's Bill No. 2, the actions of the British Navy proved more threatening and more damaging to U.S. shipping and neutrality and furthered the divide that resulted in the War of 1812.

—*Peter S. Genovese*

References

Horsman, Reginald. *The New Republic: The United States of America, 1789–1815.* New York: Longman, 2000.

See also Volume 1: Non-Importation Act; Non-Intercourse Act; War of 1812.

Macroeconomics

Economic analysis that deals with economy as a whole.

Two levels of analysis exist by which economists may derive laws concerning economic behavior—macroeconomics and microeconomics. The level of macroeconomics deals with the economy as a whole or with its basic subdivisions or aggregates such as the government, household, and business sectors. An aggregate consists of a collection of specific economic units, such as businesses, which are treated as if they were one unit—high-tech industries, for example. In dealing with aggregates, macroeconomics is concerned with obtaining an overview or general outline of the structure of the economy and the relationships among its major aggregates. Macroeconomics entails discussions of the magnitudes of total output, total level of employment, total income, total expenditures, general level of prices, and so forth, in analyzing various economic problems.

Unemployment and inflation are important factors that lead to macroeconomic instability. The United States seeks economic growth, full employment, and stable price levels. The broad spectrum of American economic history reflects remarkable economic growth: technological progress, rapid increases in productive capacity, and a standard of living that is a strategic facet of the dynamic character in the U.S. economy. The U.S. economy has been characterized by fluctuations (also called cycles) in national output, employment, and the price level. In addition, unanticipated inflation tends to arbitrarily redistribute income at the expense of fixed-income receivers, creditors, and savers. If inflation is anticipated, individuals and businesses may be able to take steps to mitigate or eliminate its adverse distributive effects.

Economists and researchers use economic models that help them understand why prices rise or fall, what causes unemployment, why shortages or surpluses of products occur, and so on. However, more importantly, economists view economic theory as the basis for economic policy. Further, economic principles attempt to prove models of reality and hence are abstract—their usefulness depends upon this abstraction. Nonetheless, it is not a simple matter to create specific policies designed to achieve the broad economic goals of the U.S. economy. Economic principles are particularly valuable as predictive devices; they are the bases for the formulation of economic policy designed to solve problems and control undesirable events.

—*Albert Atkins*

References
Stigler, George J. *The Theory of Price.* New York: Macmillan, 1947.
See also Volume 1: Microeconomics.

Mad Cow Disease

Progressive neurological disorder that afflicts the central nervous system of cattle, the spread of which the U.S. government continues to prevent in the United States.

Bovine spongiform encephalopahy (BSE) causes animals infected with it to die because no vaccine or treatment exists. The source of the epidemic apparently involved animal feed containing contaminated meat and bone meal in Britain in 1985. The disease has affected herds in Europe since 1985, but no case has been found in the United States.

BSE is a variant of transmissible spongiform encephalopathy (TSE). Some forms of TSEs—Creutzfeldt-Jakob disease (CJD), fatal familial insomnia, Gertsmann-Straussler-Seheinker Disease, kuru, and variant Creutzfeldt-Jakob Disease (vCJD)—afflict humans, whereas others affect animals and are often species-specific. In humans, TSEs cause slow degeneration of the central nervous system with dementia and loss of motor skills. According to the World Health Organization, the newly recognized vCJD is strongly linked to BSE and probably comes from consuming contaminated beef. All reported cases of BSE and vCJD have been in Europe, primarily in the United Kingdom. Since 1998 there has been a steady decline in the incidences of both types of cases.

BSE has had far-reaching economic consequences. The most visible outcome has been the destruction of hundreds of thousands of cattle throughout Europe. In addition, producers have experienced losses because of the ban on exporting beef or beef by-products. Other obvious costs include the establishment of government programs to monitor cattle production and to establish prevention programs. Much more difficult to assess are two consequences that are more subtle. The first is the effect of the loss of consumer confidence and the reduction in beef consumption. The second is the tension among nations with the imposition of trade barriers. For example, the United States has not imported beef from the United Kingdom since 1985, has barred importation of ruminant animals and at-risk products from nations with confirmed cases of BSE, has banned the inclusion of mammal-derived animal protein by-products in cattle feed, and has barred all imports of rendered animal protein from Europe without regard to species.

—*Susan Coleman*

References
World Health Organization. "Bovine Spongiform Encephalopathy Fact Sheet." Updated November 2002. Available: http://www.who.int/inf-fs/en/fact113.html; accessed September 4, 2001.
See also Volume 1: Food and Drug Administration.

Manifest Destiny

Phrase popular in the 1840s referring to an assumed divine intention that the United States should expand from the Atlantic to the Pacific Coast and used to justify American designs on the Pacific Northwest (Oregon), the American Southwest (Texas), and California.

Journalist John L. O'Sullivan coined the phrase *manifest destiny* in the July 1845 edition of the *United States Magazine* and *Democratic Review.* Although the term signifies American territorial expansionism in the 1840s, the concept of manifest destiny has roots deep in American culture and history. Manifest destiny reflected a dynamic and not always stable or consistent blend of Protestant millennialism (which preached the end of the world), ethno-racial attitudes, commercial agenda, and political pragmatism. Historian Anders Stephanson maintains that the term merely served as an expression, saying it involved "a whole matrix, manner of interpreting the time and space of America."

According to O'Sullivan and many like-minded Americans of the period, "providence" had determined America's future and required that the continent make room for the "multiplying millions" of Americans. This fusion of religiosity and demographic destiny can also be found in earlier political generations. Thomas Jefferson's purchase of Louisiana and desire for a continental, republican empire was partly grounded on these principles. Similarly, the widespread acceptance of Anglo-Saxon superiority among the white population in the United States reinforced religious and political motivations for territorial acquisition throughout the pre–Civil War period.

Manifest destiny transcended terrestrial and continental boundaries. The concept wedded American expansion to Western and Christian civilization spanning the Atlantic and the North American continent that, by the 1840s, stood ready to reach across the Pacific Ocean to Asia. Within this context, China merchant Asa Whitney and Whig politician William Seward cast the term in a decidedly commercial and global light. Although American farm families populated newly acquired territories, American entrepreneurs and businesses envisioned a vast financial and transportation network spanning the continent and underwriting U.S. penetration of foreign markets. To these interests, a transcontinental railroad served as the ultimate physical expression of manifest destiny. Within this vision, railroads channeled the agricultural and industrial products of the America's hinterlands through California seaports and on to the Far East, creating a commercial framework that promoted both profit and prophecy. Commerce became a vehicle for expansion of Christianity and Anglo-Saxon civilization. Other, particularly southern, versions of manifest destiny envisioned similar possibilities for Mexico, Central America, and the Caribbean basin.

—*Robert Rook*

References

Merk, Frederick. *Manifest Destiny and Mission in American History.* Westport, CT: Greenwood Press, 1963.

Stephanson, Anders. *Manifest Destiny: American Expansion and the Empire of Right.* New York: Hill and Wang, 1995.

See also Volume 1: Dollar Diplomacy.

Marshall, John (1755–1835)

America's greatest chief justice.

Born in Virginia on September 24, 1755, John Marshall became a devoted nationalist during his years as a soldier in the Continental Army. He rose to the rank of captain and fought in battles throughout New York, Pennsylvania, New Jersey, and Virginia in the Revolutionary War. Marshall often credited his years as a soldier as the turning point of his life. He was fond of saying that he joined the Continental Army as a Virginian, but he left as an American. His devotion to the nation led him to support the Constitution at Virginia's ratifying convention, and he later joined the Federalist Party. Marshall became a Federalist congressional representative from Virginia and also served as both minister to France and secretary of state under the administration of John Adams. As one of Adams's last acts in office, he appointed Marshall chief justice of the Supreme Court.

When Marshall assumed his new post, the Supreme Court still had no clear purpose. Article 3 of the Constitution gave few details concerning the Court's role in the new government. Justices had struggled for more than a decade with this problem. The new chief justice wasted little time in establishing the Court's precise role. He shaped it as an equal branch of the national government alongside both the legislative and executive branches. In the case of *Marbury v. Madison* (1803), Marshall established the principle of judicial review that allowed the Supreme Court to determine the constitutionality of laws. Later, in the case of *McCullough v. Maryland* (1814), he decided that the Congress did have the power to create the Bank of the United States. In this case, he also established the powerful principle that the nation must always take precedence over the states when their laws conflict. Marshall died July 6, 1835.

—*Mary Stockwell*

References

Smith, Jean Edward. *John Marshall: Definer of a Nation.* New York: Henry Holt, 1998.

See also Volume 1: *McCulloch v. Maryland;* Volume 2: Judiciary.

Marshall Plan (1948)

Comprehensive project designed and implemented by the Truman administration to underwrite restoration of Western Europe's World War II–ravaged economy.

The Marshall Plan to aid in rebuilding Europe after World War II was proposed in 1947 and signed into law in 1948 during the administration of President Harry S Truman. The Economic Cooperation Administration administered the plan, which also was known as the European Recovery Plan. It aimed to enhance America's long-term economic, political, and strategic interests at a time when Western European economies faced devastation following the end of World War II. U.S. policymakers believed that recovered Western European economies could provide a desired market for American goods and help make the United States a leading economic power in the postwar world. Also, they envisioned Western Europe as part of a multilateral system of world trade crucial to the liberal capitalist economy that Washington had in mind for itself and its allies. Unity in Western Europe would foster an American-type liberal capitalist order able to create high productivity, comfortable living standards, and political stability. Third, Washington saw the Marshall Plan as a means of strengthening shaky pro-American governments in Western European nations and a way of warding off rapid inroads being made by domestic communist parties and left-wing organizations leaning toward the Soviet Union. Thus did the European Recovery Plan emerge as an all-embracing effort for the economic revival of Western Europe as a whole.

U.S. Secretary of State George Marshall first publicized such a plan in a commencement speech at Harvard University on June 5, 1947. To avoid having the Marshall Plan viewed as anti-Soviet, Marshall subsequently invited the Soviet Union and its Eastern European satellite states to participate in its design; all the while, U.S. policymakers calculated Moscow's offhand rejection. The Soviet Union, together with Poland and Czechoslovakia, appeared at the first planning conference (convened in Paris on June 27, 1947) for Marshall's proposal, but as the United States had predicted it quickly withdrew, denouncing the plan as building an anti-Soviet bloc of Western capitalist powers. Lengthy negotiations followed without the Soviets; participants (17 Western European nations in all) laid the groundwork for a four-year recovery plan. On the plan's completion, the United States created the Economic Cooperation Administration and named Paul Hoffman the head. The Organization for European Economic Cooperation established by the 17 Western European states would coordinate the American effort.

From 1948 to 1952, $13.15 billion in Marshall Plan aid helped revitalize Western Europe and ushered it onto a path of durable economic growth and integration. The recharged economies that owed their lives to the Marshall Plan led to more stable political systems that discouraged communist encroachment in Western Europe. In addition, the United States buttressed its economic and political influence over Western Europe. Finally, the Marshall Plan widened the cold war gulf between the United States and the Soviet Union. Rather than surrender communism and its command economy to an American-dominated capitalist system, Moscow began its draconian policy of quarantining its Eastern European client states from the rest of Europe.

—*Guoqiang Zheng*

References
Hogan, Michael J. *The Marshall Plan: America, Britain, and the Reconstruction of Western Europe, 1947–1952.* New York: Cambridge University Press, 1987.
See also Volume 1: Cold War; Economic Cooperation Administration; Truman Doctrine.

Marxism

Array of social movements, political parties, theoretical tendencies, and doctrines descending from Karl Marx's writings in philosophy, political economy, and history; a doctrine that the United States spent much effort and money to oppose.

Karl Marx, who was born in 1818 and published his ideas during the 1860s, combined elements of German philosophy (Georg Wilhelm Friedrich Hegel and Ludwig Feuerbach), British political economy (Adam Smith and David Ricardo), and French socialism (Conte de Claude Henri de Rouvroy Saint-Simon and Pierre Joseph Proudhon) to form a coherent worldview that emphasized the inextricability of theory and practice in the struggle against capitalist exploitation. "The philosophers have only interpreted the world, in various ways," Marx said; "the point is to change it." Nevertheless, it was only after the fall of the Paris commune in 1871—the first successful proletarian revolution—and the ensuing dispute between the followers of Marx and Frederich Engels (i.e., the social democrats) and the followers of Mikhail Bakunin (i.e., the anarchists), that the term *marxism* gained currency. Thereafter, the founders of the German and Russian social democratic parties codified marxism as the official doctrine of the working-class movement.

One controversy in the history of marxism merits particular attention. The debate in the Soviet Union between Joseph Stalin and Leon Trotsky, who foresaw the expansion of communism throughout the world that began with Vladimir Lenin's death in 1924 and ended with Trotsky's expulsion in 1927 had its roots in the Soviet Union's ambiguous position as a territorial expansionist state and the "fatherland of the international proletariat." Whereas Stalin advocated "socialism in one country" (the idea that the Soviet Union could achieve socialism on its own), Trotsky advocated "world revolution" (the idea that the Soviet Union could not survive in the absence of revolutions in the West). Stalin's accession to power led not only to the bureaucratization of the Soviet government but also to the calcification of Soviet political doctrine.

After World War II, the term *western marxism* came to designate a range of alternatives to Soviet marxism: the rediscovered Hegelian and humanist marxism of the interwar period (Georg Lukács, Karl Korsch, and Antonio Gramsci); the existential marxism of Jean-Paul Sartre, Simone de Beauvoir, and Maurice Merleau-Ponty in France; the critical theory of the Frankfurt School in Germany; and cultural studies in Great Britain. These schools of thought, which shared an aversion to the economic determinism, objectivism, and scientism of Soviet marxism, revived interest in Marx's critique of alienation of workers and commodity fetishism (in which a commodity becomes so valued that the buyer develops a sense of love or devotion to it—the automobile, for example). Western marxism continues to exert considerable influence in European and American universities, especially in the domains of sociology, history, and literary studies.

—*Mark Frezzo*

References
Jay, Martin. *Marxism and Totality: The Adventures of a Concept from Lukacs to Habermas.* Berkeley: University of California Press, 1984.
Kolakowski, Leszek. *Main Currents of Marxism.* 3 vols. Oxford: Oxford University Press, 1978.
See also Volume 1: Socialism.

Maysville Road Bill of 1830

An act of Congress to fund internal improvements in Kentucky and a political battle over the federal financing of internal improvements.

In 1830, Congress approved a bill presented by Henry Clay, Whig Speaker of the House of Representatives, for federal payment of up to $150,000 in the Maysville, Washington, Paris, and Lexington Turnpike Road Company, a turnpike project in central Kentucky. The turnpike would constitute the first part of a planned larger road that would connect New Orleans via the Natchez Trace and Maysville Road with the National Road in Ohio. The bill also served as an expression of Clay's larger vision of economic nationalism, known as the American System, an aspect of which—the promotion of internal improvements—had strong popular support among westerners.

President Andrew Jackson vetoed the bill in a carefully crafted message designed to appease western Democrats who favored internal improvements. Although he rejected federal funding for transportation projects, he sought to maintain the political approval of westerners. Furthermore, both Jackson and Martin Van Buren, secretary of state, who wrote much of the veto, despised Clay and used the Maysville bill as a way to derail the American System. Thus, the veto remained more politically than economically inspired, an understanding shielded by the language of the veto message, which argued for a strict interpretation of the Constitution regarding federal funding of interstate projects and for fiscal responsibility.

Following the veto, Clay attempted to resurrect the American System by redefining the funding of internal improvements. Trying to circumvent Jackson's constitutional scruples, Clay turned to the idea of linking internal improvements with the sale of federal land, making the proceeds of land sales solely available for internal improvements. In later years, congressional opposition to this policy of monetary distribution to transportation companies solidified its support in favor of land grants, particularly railroad land grants. The Maysville veto marked the end of federal funding of state transportation projects. Americans had by the 1830s come to rely on state funding for transportation projects and had also lost their enthusiasm for Clay's American System.

—*Russell Douglass Jones*

References
Baxter, Maurice G. *Henry Clay and the American System.* Lexington: University Press of Kentucky, 1995.
Cole, Donald B. *The Presidency of Andrew Jackson.* Lawrence: University Press of Kansas, 1993.
See also Volume 1: American System; Clay, Henry.

McAdoo, William G. (1863–1941)

U.S. secretary of the Treasury from 1913 to 1918.

Born near Marietta, Georgia on October 31, 1863, William G. McAdoo began to practice law in New York City in 1892. In 1902, he became president of the Hudson and Manhattan Railroad Company and built the first traffic tunnel under the Hudson River. In 1912 McAdoo, who supported Democratic presidential candidate Woodrow Wilson, chaired the Democratic National Committee. During the 1912 presidential campaign, McAdoo wrote articles discussing and defending Wilson's economic policies, and he called for the election of new officials not affiliated with the monopoly of manufacturers. With Wilson's election, McAdoo became secretary of the Treasury, serving from 1913 to 1918. In 1914, he married Wilson's daughter, Eleanor Randolph Wilson. McAdoo served as director general of U.S. railroads, a wartime position, from 1917 to 1919. Dale Shook has contended that McAdoo's endeavors reflected his "ambition, a desire for prestige and respect, a sense of public service, and a secondary goal of making money."

As secretary of the Treasury, McAdoo revised the tariff law—a high-priority item in the Wilson administration. McAdoo believed that tariff laws were overprotective and discouraged the development of new industries. The tariff laws also resulted in higher prices and lower wages, he contended. The Underwood-Simmons Tariff Act of 1913 resulted in lower duties on imports and removed tariffs from (among other items) wool, sugar, steel rails, and iron ore. To replace the lost revenue, the bill proposed a graduated income tax, which the Constitution's Sixteenth Amendment, ratified in 1913, provided.

McAdoo also served as a leader in the creation of a Federal Reserve Board. Working with congressional leaders, he wanted a government bank that would diminish the power of Wall Street banking interests. At the same time, he believed government involvement should encourage individual initiative. McAdoo's ideas and actions raised his popularity and the trust of the public. Shook compared McAdoo's role to that of an assistant president in charge of both the creation of policy and the administration of nonpolitical affairs.

During World War I, McAdoo remained active in supporting the nation's efforts. In his speech "American Rights," he argued, "God has called us as a champion of freedom and democracy." In addressing economic needs, he contended that accepting Germany's attempt to create a zone of about 500 miles in which Americans could not sail their ships would bring disaster to America's farms, factories, mining interests, and labor interests.

McAdoo ran unsuccessfully for president in 1920 and 1924. When he and Attorney General A. Mitchell Palmer deadlocked at the 1920 Democratic convention, the delegates selected Governor James Cox of Ohio. When McAdoo and Governor Alfred E. Smith of New York deadlocked in 1924, the convention chose John W. Davis, former solicitor general of the United States under President Woodrow Wilson. McAdoo served as U.S. senator from California from 1933 to 1938. He is best remembered for having said, "It is impossible to defeat an ignorant man in argument." McAdoo died in Washington, D.C., February 1, 1941, and was buried at Arlington National Cemetery.

—*David E. Walker*

References
McAdoo, William Gibbs. "American Rights." *American Leaders Speak: Recordings from World War I and the 1920 Election, 1918–1920.* Sound recording, no date. Available: http://lcweb2.loc.gov/; accessed August 18, 2002.
Shook, Dale N. *William G. McAdoo and the Development of National Economic Policy: 1913–1918.* New York: Garland Publishing, 1987.
See also Volume 1: Wilson, Woodrow.

McCulloch v. Maryland (1819)

Case that established the constitutionality of the Bank of the United States.

The constitutionality of the Bank of the United States was debated beginning when Treasury Secretary Alexander Hamilton first proposed the institution in 1790. Hamilton argued that Congress could create the bank under the "necessary and proper" clause of the Constitution. In contrast, Secretary of State Thomas Jefferson had argued against founding the bank because the Constitution did not specifically grant this power to Congress. President George Washington and the Congress agreed with Hamilton and approved the establishment of the Bank of the United States in 1791. Twenty years later, President James Madison allowed the charter of the bank to lapse. But after the War of 1812, Congress chartered the Second Bank of the United States in the hope it would stimulate a failing economy. The directors of the new bank called in many outstanding loans, which helped to bring about the panic of 1819. Several states including Maryland retaliated by levying taxes on the national bank. James McCulloch, the cashier of the bank's Baltimore branch, refused to pay the $15,000 tax levied by Maryland and eventually took his case to the Supreme Court.

When Chief Justice John Marshall ruled in 1819 for a unanimous Court in favor of McCulloch, he made his strongest statement to date for the power of the nation over the states. He argued that the case posed the question of whether the bank was constitutional, and if yes, whether a state could tax the national bank. Closely following Hamilton's original argument, Marshall agreed that although the Constitution did not specifically grant the Congress power to establish a national bank, it nevertheless implied it. As to the second question, Marshall argued that a state could not use taxation to destroy a power rightly given to the Congress.

—*Mary Stockwell*

References
Siegel, Adrienne. *The Marshall Court, 1801–1835*. Millwood, NY: Associated Faculty Press, 1987.
See also Volume 2: Judiciary.

McKinley Tariff Act (1890)

Highest tariff in United States history to that point.

Despite a Treasury surplus attributable to previous tariffs, William McKinley, Republican member of the House of Representatives from Ohio and chair of the House Ways and Means Committee, introduced a tariff measure that increased duties on imports so substantially that it barred some foreign-made goods from entering the United States. Moreover, the measure had two other features that particularly differentiated it from previous tariffs: reciprocity (which allows for the reduction of duties charged a specific country in exchange for more favorable tariff rates from the other country) and the promotion of new industries, especially the tinplate industry, which made thin sheet iron or steel coated with tin. Republican Senator Matthew Quay of Pennsylvania, who had comanaged Benjamin Harrison's successful presidential campaign in 1888, strongly supported the passage of the tariff bill partly because of his many campaign promises to industrialists. Quay ensured passage of the bill by gaining Southern support through a compromise that prevented a vote on a federal elections bill concerning the right of African Americans to vote.

Many farmers and urban laborers called the 1890 McKinley measure a "rich man's tariff." Republicans asserted that the McKinley tariff would benefit workers through higher wages, but once the tariff was enacted, prices immediately rose faster than wages. Emphasizing the problems with the tariff, the Democrats soundly defeated the Republicans in the 1890 Congressional elections, and Grover Cleveland, the Democratic candidate, won the presidency in 1892. In 1894 the Wilson-Gorman tariff increased rates once again.

—*Steven E. Siry*

References
Terrill, Tom E. *The Tariff, Politics, and American Foreign Policy: 1874–1901*. Westport, CT: Greenwood Press, 1973.
See also Volume 1: Protective Tariffs.

McNary-Haugen Bill (1924, 1928)

Unsuccessful attempt to create a system of agricultural price supports in the mid-1920s.

To rectify the decline in farmers' purchasing power since 1913, in 1924 Congress passed legislation sponsored by Republican Senator Charles McNary of Oregon and Republican Representative Gilbert Haugen of Iowa. Their plan called for the creation of a Federal Farm Board that would define an equitable price for specified staple crops and guarantee that price to farmers. In return, farmers would pay an equalization fee to cover the costs of selling surpluses on the international market. Congress paired this system of price supports with a protective tariff on agricultural goods. Tariff protection remained relatively easy to achieve under the Fordney-McCumber Tariff of 1922. However, the creation of price guarantees failed to pass in the House in 1924.

Senator McNary and Representative Haugen based their support among congressional Republicans from rural states while encouraging the participation of Southern Democrats. In 1927 Congress passed a version of the McNary-Haugen Bill that would support prices for cotton, wheat, corn, rice, tobacco, and swine. However, President Calvin Coolidge vetoed the bill. Coolidge based his opposition on his belief that the plan would increase the surplus production of protected crops while discouraging diversification into areas of growing market demand such as fruit or threatening stable market sectors such as dairy and poultry. He also expressed concern over the appropriateness of government price fixing.

McNary and Haugen were unable to gain sufficient support to override the Coolidge veto. An adjusted version of the bill passed Congress in 1928 but once again without sufficient support to withstand a veto.

After he assumed the presidency in 1929, Herbert Hoover hoped to placate the supporters of McNary-Haugen legislation. He supported the successful passage of an alternative law, the 1929 Agricultural Marketing Act, which formed a Federal Farm Board, but the board had little authority to regulate prices.

—*Karen A. J. Miller*

References
Hansen, John Mark. *Gaining Access: Congress and the Farm Lobby, 1919–1981*. Chicago: University of Chicago Press, 1991.
See also Volumes 1, 2: Agricultural Policy.

Media

Agencies of mass communication that have influenced American economic and political development.

During America's first years as a nation, newspapers were the only form of communication. In addition to reporting general news, they helped to stimulate agriculture and business by providing information about new farming techniques and business news. By the late 1880s, foreign newspapers stimulated immigration by publishing ads from railroad companies and investors for cheap land. Foreign workers, enticed by these ads, provided the labor for the Industrial Revolution. Information about government land policies including the Homestead, Timber and Stone, and Timber Culture Acts was published in newspapers in the East and Midwest and encouraged farmers to move westward, resulting in the settling of the West and the use of millions of acres of land for crops or grazing. Editors addressed important economic issues of the post–Civil War period like the tariff and the use of silver as a medium of exchange.

The biggest influence the media had in the late nineteenth century was the result of a newspaper war involving two publishers, Joseph Pulitzer and William Randolph Hearst. Each newspaper attempted to generate more public sensation than the other. Hearst began a series of articles depicting the brutality and outrages committed by the Spanish against the Cuban people. As tensions among the American people against Spain escalated, President William McKinley dispatched the USS *Maine* to Havana's harbor, where an explosion sank the ship. Hearst claimed that divers had confirmed the cause of the explosion was a mine—this long before the invention of scuba gear, before which diving was impossible. Consequently, the United States declared war on Spain, and in the process of the Spanish-American War became an imperial power by ruling foreign peoples and controlling foreign markets. The United States acquired former Spanish-held territories the Philippines, Guam, Puerto Rico, and Guantanamo Bay in Cuba. Businesses turned their attention to foreign markets as never before.

During the Progressive Era—a period between 1900 and the beginning of World War I during which most middle- and upper-class Americans sought to address social and economic problems—many newspapers sponsored the development of urban areas by encouraging changes in transportation patterns, sanitation systems, and bridges and levee projects. City planning spread across the country as a result of newspaper editors' realization of the importance of clean, orderly communities. Newspapers also promoted the development of social programs, the construction of hospitals, and the establishment of universities, and they attracted potential investors to their communities.

The advent of radio extended the influence of the media throughout the country. Most of the first radio stations were owned by newspapers, which adopted the new technology to maintain their competitive advantage in disseminating the news and limit access to the market by competitors. The radio became very important during the Great Depression as Americans listened to President Franklin D. Roosevelt's fireside chats; the subject of the first one was the announcement of a four-day banking holiday to address the lack of confidence in banking institutions. Radio provided news, music, and other entertainment and was influential in establishing a sense of group identity among Americans. Eventually radio spawned an entire new industry, as entertainment broadcasts became part of the regular programming. Advertisers used radio to reach national audiences and increase their market share.

Television, which became a part of people's lives in the 1950s, has had a much greater influence than radio ever had. In addition to stimulating employment through the development of new jobs, television created a homogenous society whose members wanted what they saw portrayed on commercials and in programs, from clothing to toothpaste. The instantaneous dissemination of news about a new product or problem with a company could create a buying or selling frenzy on Wall Street. The role of the media in providing information as well as the continued display of new products will continue to influence the economic future of the United States.

In 2003 the Federal Communications Commission (FCC) loosened requirements that had restricted ownership by the same company of both newspapers and television stations in the same market area. Opponents contend that presentation of news by a limited number of companies eliminates the responsibility of media to provide all sides of the story. Proponents argue that the Internet and talk radio provide such a balance. By July 2003, a month after FCC announced the new rule, members of Congress were threatening to overturn the ruling through a resolution of disapproval.

—*Cynthia Clark Northrup*

References

Alexander, Alison, James Owers, and Rod Carveth. *Media Economics: Theory and Practice.* Hillsdale, NJ: L. Erlbaum Associates, 1993.

See also Volume 1: Immigration; Volume 2: Advertising; Land Policies.

Medicaid (1965)

Program established in 1965 and jointly funded by the state and federal governments to pay for medical care for eligible needy people to improve the health of this population.

Congress established Medicaid in 1965 through an amendment to the Social Security Act of 1935; it is part of the same legislation that created Medicare. The Medicaid legislation called for the federal government to establish guidelines that specify the minimum amounts of medical services covered by each state's Medicaid program and that may include inpatient and outpatient hospital services, physician services, laboratory tests, and X-rays. States may choose to cover additional services and to set the fees for the services they cover. Because states can limit the amount and duration of services offered, Medicaid benefits vary by state. Thus, citizens of one state may receive coverage for more days of inpatient hospitalization, doctor visits, and other services than citizens of an adjoining state.

Federal guidelines also specify minimum eligibility requirements for Medicaid benefits. States must cover pregnant women whose family income is below 133 percent of the federal poverty level (for instance, $13,874 for a family of three in 2000), individuals who would have qualified in July 1996 for a previous federal welfare program called Aid to Families with Dependent Children, recipients of a federal welfare program called Supplemental Security Income, and, as of 2002, all children under the age of 19 who are living in families whose incomes fall below the federal poverty level. Because states may elect to expand Medicaid coverage to other groups of financially or medically needy individuals, citizens of one state are sometimes eligible for Medicaid whereas similar citizens of an adjoining state remain ineligible. Under different eligibility guidelines that prevail nationally, in 2000 Medicaid covers about half of the nation's poverty-level population.

The federal government determines the share of each state's Medicaid expenses by comparing each state's average per-person income level with the national average. States with the highest average income levels may have 50 percent of their Medicaid costs paid for by the federal government, and states with the lowest average income levels may have up to 83 percent of their Medicaid outlays covered at the federal level.

Medicaid spends disproportionately more on some groups of beneficiaries. Spending on children, who make up 51 percent of all beneficiaries, averaged $1,150 per child in 1998. Beneficiaries in nursing homes and other facilities who are receiving long-term care receive 8.2 percent of Medicaid averaged at $12,375 per person in 1998.

—Saranna R. Thornton

References

Henderson, James W. *Health Economics and Policy.* Cincinnati, OH: South-Western Press, 2002.

Medicaid: A Brief Summary, Health Care Financing Agency. 2001. Available: http://www.medicaid.gov.

U.S. Census Bureau. *Poverty Thresholds in 2000, by Size of Family and Number of Related Children under 18 Years.* 2001. Available: http://www.census.gov/hhes/poverty/threshld/thresh00.html; accessed July 15, 2002.

See also Volume 1: Medicare.

Medicare (1965)

Provides health insurance for qualified elderly or disabled Americans who meet employment and tax-related qualifications or are married to someone who meets such qualifications.

In the mid-twentieth century, President Harry S Truman tried to establish a health insurance plan for Americans, but medical lobbyists caused his plan to fail. By 1965 spiraling medical costs associated with old age wiped out the savings of many of the elderly, leaving them impoverished. Because this trend was contrary to the goals of the 1935 Social Security Act, President Lyndon B. Johnson asked Congress in January 1965 to make Medicare legislation its first priority. Medicare provides medical coverage for those over the age of 65 and the permanently disabled. Most retired persons are covered under the program, as are the terminally ill. Medicare is different from Medicaid, which provides medical coverage for the poor. Johnson signed the Medicare bill into law in July 1965 and, as of 2000, 40 million Americans were receiving Medicare benefits.

Medicare's Part A hospital insurance program is provided at no additional cost to those who are eligible. Payroll taxes on employers and currently working employees, who each pay half the cost, fund the hospital insurance. In 2001, employers and employees contributed 1.45 percent of each worker's total salary to Medicare's hospital insurance trust fund. Subject to a yearly deductible and per-service copayments of $20 over the $100 deductible, the federal government, through Medicare's hospital insurance, covers inpatient hospital care, care in a facility that provides skilled nursing or by a home health agency following hospitalization, and hospice care for terminally ill beneficiaries with six or fewer months' life expectancy.

Anyone entitled to hospital coverage under Part A can enroll in Medicare Part B, a supplemental medical insurance program. After 2000, enrollment required payment of a monthly premium amounting to $45.50. The premiums paid 25 percent of Medicare Part B's expenses, and federal tax revenues paid the other 75 percent. Subject to deductibles and copayments, the federal government pays for doctors' services, services in the emergency room or an outpatient clinic, laboratory tests, X-rays, physical therapy, and durable medical equipment such as oxygen tanks or wheelchairs.

Despite the fact that Medicare does not cover all the medical needs of the elderly in areas such as prescription medications, the program has remained enormously successful in reducing poverty rates among the elderly. In 1959, 35.2 percent of Americans 65 or older lived in poverty. By 1999 only 9.7 percent of elderly Americans lived in poverty. This change can be attributed to Medicaid, Medicare, and social security.

Although Medicare has helped senior citizens in the past, the program is experiencing problems. Under current guidelines, Medicare Part A is funded by a 2.9 percent payroll tax that is placed in a hospital trust account. As the aging population increases this amount will be insufficient to cover the hospital care of the baby boom generation. By 2008 the program will be unable to meet the financial responsibilities of institutional care for the elderly. In addition, the ever-expanding Medicare bureaucracy, with its 111,000 pages of regulations and guidelines, denies 25 percent of all claims submitted by physicians on the basis that the treatment was not specifically approved under the program even if the doctor believed that it was medically necessary for the patient. Doctors faced increased liability, as fines for unauthorized procedures are $10,000 per incident. Fewer doctors are willing to accept Medicare because of the paperwork and liability placed on them. So the number of physicians using the program are decreasing as the number of elderly patients is increasing.

—Saranna R. Thornton

References

Johnson, Lyndon B. *The Vantage Point: Perspectives of the Presidency.* New York: Holt, Rinehart and Winston, 1971.

Medicare: A Brief Summary, Health Care Financing Agency. 2001. Available: http://www.medicare.gov.

U.S. Census Bureau. *Historical Poverty Tables—People.* Table 3. 2001. Available: http://www.census.gov/hhes/poverty/histpov/hstpov3.html; accessed June 12, 2002.

See also Volume 1: Medicaid.

Medicine

Practice of curing or preventing illnesses that substantially influences the economics of the United States in that more people are living longer lives and costs for their care are increasing.

The federal government got involved in the field of medicine in earnest for the first time after the Civil War in 1865. U.S. Army surgeons, faced with a staggering number of casualties, had only crude equipment and medicines to work with during the war. After the war ended, medicine assumed greater importance. Medical schools taught their students the latest treatments and procedures, and the practice of medicine was restricted to individuals who had completed formal training. The American Medical Association (AMA), founded in 1847, sought to standardize training and required physicians to be licensed. But it was not until the Spanish-American War in 1898 that breakthroughs in research netted substantial results, especially in the area of germ theory. The discovery of microscopic organisms opened up new avenues of research. The government has funded much of the medical research since the Spanish-American War.

At the beginning of the twentieth century, army surgeon Walter Reed and his medical team, funded by the U.S. Army and the federal government, discovered the cause of yellow fever—the mosquito. Government funding during the two world wars yielded a significant breakthrough in the discovery of penicillin. Throughout the cold war, the United States suspended support of research into medicine and the life sciences for the most part, resuming it when communism in the Soviet Union and Eastern Europe collapsed. From the 1960s throughout the 1990s, the percentage of federal dollars devoted to medical research has continued to increase, one reason being the spread of AIDS in the United States. By the late 1990s about 9 percent of the federal government's R&D budget was spent on drugs and medicine.

In addition to funding research programs, Congress also established the Department of Health and Human Services (HHS). With a 2002 budget of $460 billion and more than 65,000 employees, the HHS is the largest health care provider in the United States. Besides administering the Medicare programs for the elderly and the Medicaid program for the poor, the HHS also conducts medical and social science research, seeks to prevent the spread of infectious diseases through its immunization services, works to ensure food and drug safety, administers maternal and infant health programs, oversees the Head Start education of preschool students, provides in-home meals to elderly citizens, deals with substance abuse and treatment, and addresses child abuse, domestic violence, and mental health.

The high cost of medical insurance combined with the large number of uninsured Americans has sparked a debate over the development of a national health care system. The implementation of national insurance began in the mid-1960s with the creation of Medicare and Medicaid. During the administration of President Bill Clinton, proponents of a national health care system, in an effort spearheaded by first lady Hillary Rodham Clinton, attempted to pass legislation that would guarantee coverage for all Americans. The attempt failed, but the issue continues to be raised in Congress.

—*Cynthia Clark Northrup*

References

Gabe, Jonathan, David Kelleher, and Gareth Williams, eds. *Challenging Medicine.* New York: Routledge, 1994.

Huefner, Robert P., and Margaret P. Battin, eds. *Changing to National Health Care: Ethical and Policy Issues.* Salt Lake City: University of Utah Press, 1992.

See also Volume 1: Cold War; Medicaid; Medicare; Mental Illness.

Mellon, Andrew William (1855–1937)

U.S. secretary of the treasury serving from 1921 to 1932 and advocating federal government incentives to promote maximum efficiency and productivity of business and industry.

Born March 24, 1855, to a banker's family in Pittsburgh, Pennsylvania, Andrew Mellon graduated from the University of Pittsburgh. By controlling the family banking business with his brother and acquiring interests in coke, coal, aluminum, and iron enterprises, Mellon became one of the most important financial tycoons and wealthiest industrialists in the United States and the world. As U.S. secretary of the treasury—first appointed in 1921 by President Warren G. Harding—Mellon strongly supported the expansion of corporate industry. Believing that economic prosperity depended on the willing reinvestment of corporate profits into the economy, Mellon sponsored a federal policy of levying substantially low taxes on corporate profits, personal incomes, and inheritance. Largely because of his effort, Congress reduced personal income taxes by almost 50 percent for the top bracket of taxpayers earning more than $60,000 annually and deeply cut taxes on inherited wealth. The Treasury under Mellon returned considerable tax refunds to large corporations like U.S. Steel in the hope of encouraging the expansion of corporate business. To compensate for the loss in government revenues, Mellon preferred drastically slashing government spending. To pay for the unavoidable expenditures of government, he proposed to increase import duties and modestly raise regressive taxes (taxes that take a larger percentage of income from lower-income than from higher-income people). Aided by this policy, according to Mellon, business would create jobs and foster a better standard of living; economic prosperity, encouraged by government policy, would "trickle down" to the middle and lower classes. Such a government policy would also advance the spirit of enterprise in America, Mellon thought. Mellon died August 26, 1937.

—*Guoqiang Zheng*

References

Parrish, Michael. *Anxious Decades: America in Prosperity and Depression, 1920–1941.* New York: W. W. Norton, 1992.

See also Volume 1: Reaganomics; Supply-Side Economics.

Mental Illness

Disorders associated with the mind, the cost of the treatment of which is often borne by government.

Until the twentieth century, the cost of treating patients with mental illnesses—for example, depression, bipolar disorder (a manic depression that can result in death), schizophrenia, obsessive-compulsive disorder, and Alzheimer's disease—was the responsibility of families or the state in which the patient lived. For the past 100 years, however, more of the burden of treatment has shifted to the federal government. In terms of indirect costs, mental illness results in a loss to the U.S. economy of about $79 billion annually. This amount includes the loss of productivity for the patient, productivity lost by family members caring for the individual, the incarceration of mentally ill patients, and losses incurred by premature death because of accident or disease. The productivity loss accounts for more than 80 percent of the indirect costs.

The federal government, private insurance companies, and individuals absorb the direct costs for the treatment and care of persons suffering from mental illnesses. In 1996 the total spent on the treatment of mental illness exceeded $99 billion. Of this amount, $13 billion was spent for substance abuse and another $18 billion for the treatment of Alzheimer's disease. As the population in the United States ages, the amount appropriated for the prevention and care of Alzheimer's and other forms of dementia will continue to increase. The federal government pays about 53 percent of the direct costs for mental illness treatment; insurance companies cover more than 24 percent; and private individuals pay the remaining expenses out of pocket. In 1996 the total amount of expenditures on mental illness equaled 7 percent of the health care budget. The cost continues to increase at a rate of 7 percent annually; most of the additional expenses are because of higher costs for prescription drugs.

—*Cynthia Clark Northrup*

References
Barry, Patricia D. *Mental Health and Mental Illness.*
    Philadelphia: Lippincott-Raven, 1998.
See also Volume 1: Medicine.

Mercantilism

A body of economic doctrines and policies in the seventeenth and eighteenth centuries advocating government intervention to achieve a trade surplus.

Mercantilism—the "mercantile system" of political economy (named in 1776 by its opponent, the classical economist Adam Smith)—shaped European colonial policy in the seventeenth and eighteenth centuries. Its goal was to increase the power and wealth of the nation-state, notably through an inflow of gold and silver—the "sinews of war" designed to pay for armies and fleets. Nations sought colonies with gold and silver deposits in imitation of Spanish conquests in Mexico and Peru, and governments employed tariffs, embargoes, quotas, export bounties, and grants of monopolies to chartered companies to try to achieve trade surpluses (exports greater than imports). Such policies contributed to conflict between nations, because a country can have a trade surplus only if some other country has a trade deficit. Colonies provided raw materials for manufacturing in the home country and acted as captive markets for manufactures from the home countries. Thus, in the 1750s, Britain banned the manufacture of iron goods in its American colonies while admitting colonial pig and bar iron into England duty free since it was not a finished manufactured product. England restricted all such manufacturing within the Empire to the mother country to promote its industrial base.

The Molasses Act of 1733 attempted to protect planters in the British West Indies by imposing high tariffs on foreign sugar, molasses, and rum, but American colonial merchants who were importing the sugar largely ignored it. The Sugar Act of 1764, which raised the duty on sugar but lowered it on molasses in an effort to stop the smuggling, was enforced more effectively. However, it provoked resistance from the colonials, who vehemently opposed a provision that allowed smugglers to be tried in a military court instead of by a jury of their peers. England's Navigation Acts of 1651, 1660, and 1663 (extended to all of Britain after England's 1707 union with Scotland) provided that commodities originating in the British Empire, shipped between ports within the empire, or imported from Asia, Africa, or the Americas be shipped on British (including colonial) ships with a British captain and three-quarters of the crew made up of British subjects. One aim of the Navigation Acts, approved even by Adam Smith, focused on the maintenance of a naval reserve of ships and experienced sailors. The Navigation Acts raised the cost of shipping, benefiting colonial shipowners, shipbuilders, sailors, and producers of naval timber and tar, but burdening colonial trade in general, motivating some colonists to political activity in protest. But this form of control allowed the British to maintain their mercantile system, which benefited the mother country at the expense of the colonies.

Classical economists such as David Hume and Adam Smith argued that mercantilist policies, if they succeeded in increasing the stock of gold and silver in a country, would raise prices, eliminating the trade surplus, and that mercantilist interference with free trade would misallocate resources. In the twentieth century, John Maynard Keynes argued for the justified use of mercantilist policies to stimulate employment in an underemployed economy.

—*Robert Dimand*

References
Coleman, D. C., ed. *Revisions in Mercantilism.* London:
    Methuen, 1969.
McCusker, John J. *Mercantilism and the Economic History of
    the Early Modern Atlantic World.* Cambridge: Cambridge
    University Press, 2001.
See also Volume 1: American Revolution; Colonial
    Administration; Navigation Acts.

Merchants of Death

Term used to refer to American politicians and businesses that some claimed profited from arms sales during World War I.

When World War I broke out in Europe in 1914, the American public and President Woodrow Wilson insisted that the United States refrain from becoming a participant. After German U-boats sank several passenger ships carrying American civilians, including the *Lusitania*, and did not offer assistance to survivors, the United States moved closer to war. Arms and munitions left American ports bound for Great Britain. The United States profited from arms manufacturing during the first three years of the war until a telegram to Mexican officials from Arthur Zimmermann, the German foreign minister, revealed that Germany was plotting with Mexico to attack the United States—a strategy that would open a second front for the United States if it were to enter the conflict.

After World War I, the U.S. Senate held hearings chaired by Republican Senator Gerald P. Nye of North Dakota to examine American motives during the war. The Nye Committee argued that American businesses had postponed U.S. participation in the war until the Allies could no longer pay for additional supplies, and the U.S. government had then declared war so the same businesses could continue to profit from the loss of life and destruction in Europe. The committee's findings led to the passage of the Neutrality Acts of 1935 and 1936 just as Adolf Hitler, Benito Mussolini, and the Japanese empire began implementing expansionist plots to conquer their neighbors.

—*Cynthia Clark Northrup*

References
Cole, Wayne S. *Senator Gerald P. Nye and American Foreign Relations.* Westport, CT: Greenwood Press, 1980.
See also Volume 1: World War I.

MIC
See Military-Industrial Complex.

Microeconomics
The study of the decision-making processes of consumers and producers and their interaction in markets.

Since the 1930s, economists have contrasted microeconomics with macroeconomics. The latter focuses on the economy as a whole and the determination of aggregates including the price level, unemployment rate, and gross domestic product. Microeconomics is concerned primarily with determining the price of a good, the quantity of the good bought and sold, and the effect of the transaction on the well-being of consumer and producer. Microeconomic theory assumes that individuals act as rational maximizers—that they weigh costs against benefits in making decisions and that they implicitly or explicitly attempt to achieve the highest level of well-being possible in any given situation. Consumers generally maximize utility, whereas firms try to maximize profits. The discipline of microeconomics took its modern form in the late 1800s with the realization that rational maximizers weigh marginal costs against marginal benefits and with the understanding that supply (the quantity producers plan to sell at each price) and demand (the quantity consumers are willing to buy at each price) interact—like two blades of a scissors—to determine price and quantity. Microeconomic theory analyzes product markets ranging from perfect competition (in which there is no interference from government) to monopoly to input markets (markets for natural resources, labor, and capital) with attention to the conditions in which markets will achieve economic efficiency and those in

which markets fail to achieve efficiency. In recent decades microeconomics has dominated the social sciences, applying the paradigm of rational maximization to fields ranging from public choice (the decision-making of government itself) to criminal behavior.

During the twentieth century, policymakers increasingly called on microeconomists to assess and construct government policies. Microeconomic arguments and evidence have played important roles in the post–World War II move toward free trade, deregulation of industries such as the airline industry in the late 1970s and 1980s, and debates over the minimum wage, as well as in overhauling the welfare system, formulating antitrust rules, using marketable pollution permits designed to entice manufacturers to work harder for a cleaner environment, and a wide range of other policies.

—*Robert Whaples*

References
Perloff, Jeffrey. *Microeconomics.* Reading, MA: Addison-Wesley, 1999.
See also Volume 1: Macroeconomics.

Microsoft
Computer and software company that started the personal computer revolution.

In 1978 Bill Gates and Paul Allen, inspired by an article in *Popular Electronics,* developed the first BASIC computer language program for the Altair 8800, the first personal computer developed with 256 bytes of RAM and using an 8-inch floppy disk drive. They established their company, Microsoft, in 1978. Within three years the sales for the company exceeded $1 million. Gates and Allen set a goal of putting a personal computer (PC) in every home and office and decided that the way to achieve this goal was to create affordable, efficient software (programs that allow those who are not computer programmers to use the computer with minimal training). By the beginning of the 1980s, Americans began to see the first advances in software technology with the development of word processors. By 1981 Microsoft had developed an affordable PC that used the disk operating system (DOS). Development of additional software packages that included operating programs, language programs to create and build applications, and games made Microsoft a billion-dollar company. The introduction of Microsoft Office 95 (an integrated software that contains word processing and spreadsheet capabilities) increased sales once again, and by the mid-1990s there were more than 25 million PCs in homes and offices. Microsoft unveiled Internet Explorer, a program designed for access to and navigation of the Internet, in 1997. By 2000, more than 25 million people owned or used PCs and used the Internet. Microsoft continues to introduce new software and hardware products as communications technology continues its rapid change: Windows software for mobile phones; computer game systems such as XBox and a variety of XBox games; business software such as integrated card services, analytical and reporting software, and retail management software; and programs for the development of websites and other visual media.

The federal government has charged Microsoft with engaging in monopolistic practices, basing the charge primarily on the way the company "bundles" its software with hardware systems so that computers are sold with Microsoft programs instead of the competition's software. The case was settled in 2002 and the Supreme Court approved the settlement; Microsoft appointed a compliance officer to oversee the requirements of the Court. Microsoft's competitors doubt that the settlement will produce any substantial changes because Microsoft has already achieved market dominance, and breaking it into smaller companies will not reduce its net sales and control of market share.

Microsoft has had a tremendous influence on the U.S. economy. In addition to employing more than 50,000 workers, the company has provided investors with consistent dividends. The use of computers has streamlined business operation and expanded communications capabilities. This, in turn, has expanded business practices and increased company profitability. The explosion of the technology industry can be directly related to the rise of Microsoft as well.

—*Cynthia Clark Northrup*

References
Liebowitz, Stan J., and Stephen E. Margolis. *Winners, Losers, and Microsoft.* Oakland, CA: Independent Institute, 1999.
Microsoft. www.microsoft.com; accessed February 9, 2003.
See also Volume 1: Computer; Volume 2: Science and Technology.

Microsystems Technology Office (MTO)

Division of the Defense Advanced Research Projects Agency that coordinates the development of high-tech military equipment.

The Microsystems Technology Office, established in 1958 under the authority of the Defense Advanced Research Projects Agency (DARPA), works to reduce complex system applications that use multiple technologies (computers, for example) into chip-size packages. The three primary areas of focus are electronics, photonics, and microelectromechanical systems. Within these fields, the Microsystems Technology Office (MTO) has several featured programs that include advanced lithography, in which multiple beams of lights are condensed into one column to advance semiconductor technology that includes layered intelligence; distributed robotics based on biological features; microelectromechnical systems, which "merge sensing, actuating, and computing" to achieve "enhanced levels of perception, control, and performance to weapons systems and battlefield environments" (www.darpa.mil/mto); and the development of new technologies that integrate all three fields into advanced computer chips.

Although the advances developed by the Microsystems Technology Office are designed for military applications, many of them will affect businesses and consumers in the long term as the technology becomes available to the public (as transistors did after World War II).

—*Cynthia Clark Northrup*

References
Defense Advanced Research Projects Administration. www.darpa.mil/mto; accessed February 9, 2003.
See also Volume 1: Defense Advanced Research Projects Administration (DARPA).

Military-Industrial Complex (MIC)

Reciprocal relationship between government and industry.

Before 1945, America mobilized only after its wars began. During the cold war, however, Soviet capability to launch a surprise nuclear attack or to invade Western Europe required America to maintain large, combat-ready military forces in peacetime. The sum total of the academic, industrial, and government institutions that evolved to meet the requirements of cold war deterrence and defense is called the military-industrial complex (MIC). President Dwight D. Eisenhower first used the term in his 1961 farewell speech when he warned against excessive military and defense industry influence on the scientific world, academia, and democratic processes. Some observers describe the MIC as an "iron triangle" of beneficial relationships among the Defense Department, legislators with jurisdiction over defense programs and budgets, and defense contractors.

Creating and improving qualitatively superior military forces during the long cold war competition with the Soviets required relentless scientific, technological, and engineering innovation. To promote this innovation, the Defense Department sponsored basic and applied research, development, testing, evaluation, and experimentation in academic and industrial laboratories. Government funding of American research and development (R&D) exceeded private industry funding until the early 1980s, and defense generally dominated federal R&D funding after 1945, especially from 1945 until 1963. Defense research declined as a proportion of federal R&D after the Vietnam conflict, but jumped again (from 49 percent to 70 percent) between 1980 and 1987, largely because of research on the Strategic Defense Initiative (SDI), which is a space-based system designed to destroy incoming intercontinental ballistic missiles in space. Universities performed most of the basic defense research, and private industry conducted most of the applied research for SDI. Defense-related industries consistently received about 80 percent of all federal funding for manufacturing R&D from 1945 to 2002, with most of the funds concentrated among the largest contractors.

During the cold war, the U.S. government cooperated closely with defense industries, funding plant construction, providing guaranteed markets, protecting weak firms, and promoting exports. The government cultivated an oligopolistic defense industry in which relatively few aerospace, electronics, and communications firms provided small numbers of highly specialized products to a single customer that cared more about quality than cost. Defense projects represented about 6 to 10 percent of the private-sector workforce but employed more than half of the nation's aerospace engineers and one-quarter of all electrical engineers and physicists. Defense work also employed large numbers of highly skilled blue-collar workers, particularly aircraft and electronics assemblers, machinists, metalworkers, shipfitters, and aircraft mechanics.

Defense corporations usually hired retired military officers, who had excellent institutional knowledge and personal contacts inside the military, to market to the Pentagon. Defense corporations subsidized lobbying groups and contributed heavily to selected political campaigns. In the 1990s, defense lobbyists urged Congress to provide tax exemptions for arms exporters, to issue government-backed loans to countries importing American weapons, and to lift bans on arms sales to repressive regimes. Defense corporations often organized grassroots lobbying efforts for particular weapons systems that were in danger of cancellation.

The MIC conferred numerous benefits on the American economy and society. It created a military that deterred Soviet aggression and prevented nuclear war, and it ensured American leadership in aerospace, computer, communications, and electronics technologies. Commercial products or ventures that emerged from the MIC included jet engines, widespread civil aviation after the invention of radar, lasers, microchips, computers, satellites, robotics, and the Internet. However, the MIC imposed enormous financial, political, and environmental burdens on the nation. The MIC's costs impaired competitiveness in the post–cold war world and led to government neglect of social programs and the civilian industrial base.

—*James D. Perry*

References

Adams, Gordon. *The Iron Triangle*. New Brunswick, NJ: Transaction Books, 1982.

Hartung, William. *Corporate Welfare for Weapons Makers*. Washington, DC: Cato Institute, 1999.

Koistinen, Paul. *The Military-Industrial Complex*. New York: Praeger, 1980.

Markusen, Ann, and Joel Yudken. *Dismantling the Cold War Economy*. New York: Basic Books, 1992.

See also Volume 1: Cold War.

Minimum Wage

Minimum allowable wage to be paid to workers; first implemented by the U.S. government through the Fair Labor Standards Act of 1938, which set the rate at $.25 per hour.

The forces that led to minimum wage legislation took years to develop. Robert Pollin and Stephanie Luce have written that "one of the early works written on behalf of minimum wage legislation was a 1906 book by Monsignor John A. Ryan titled *A Living Wage: Its Ethical and Economic Aspects.*" Kansas enacted the first prevailing-wage law in 1891. In 1931 President Herbert Hoover signed the Davis-Bacon Act, an equivalent piece of national legislation written by Republican U.S. Senator James J. Davis of Pennsylvania, a former secretary of labor, and Republican U.S. Representative Robert L. Bacon of New York, a banker.

In 1932, Mary "Molly" Williams Dewson, director of the women's division of the Democratic National Committee, became a major advocate of establishing a minimum wage by advocating in a letter to the administration of President Franklin D. Roosevelt that no difference in minimum wage should exist between the sexes and that "time and one half should be paid for all time worked over and above 40 hours per week." The principles supported by Dewson were implemented in the Fair Labor Standards Act of 1938, which included minimum wage requirements. Conditions were auspicious for this national legislation at this time because the U.S. Supreme Court had upheld a state minimum wage law the previous year. The 1938 statute initially set a standard minimum wage of 25 cents per hour, and at first minimum wage laws were confined to government construction projects and referred to as efforts to establish prevailing wages.

The Fair Labor Standards Act was arguably the last major piece of New Deal legislation passed; the Democrats soon after sustained heavy losses in the November 1938 midterm elections, which gave rise in 1939 to a conservative coalition of Southern Democrats and Republicans that controlled the House and Senate. Additionally, World War II naturally shifted President Roosevelt's attention from the New Deal to efforts to win the war. Since 1950, when the minimum wage was $.75 per hour, Congress has increased the minimum wage at least 16 times to rates greater than $5.00 per hour in 1997 and $5.15 per hour in 2003.

—*Henry B. Sirgo*

References

Dewson, Mary W., to Mr. C. W. Dunning. Letter. "Objections to the Candy Manufacturing Code." Attached Testimony from Hearing of March 13, 1934. Democratic National Committee–Women's Division Correspondence–General (Box no. 5) Folder: Consumers' Advisory Board of NRA 1933–1935. Franklin D. Roosevelt Library, Hyde Park, New York, March 19, 1934.

Pollin, Robert, and Stephanie Luce. *The Living Wage: Building a Fair Economy*. New York: New Press, 1998.

See also Volume 1: Great Depression; Roosevelt, Franklin D.

Mixed Economy

An economy under which the government intervenes in certain sectors to compensate for perceived market failure—whether of growth, efficiency, or distribution.

A mixed economy occupies a position between an unplanned economy with no government interference and a command economy of the type that prevailed in the former Soviet Union. In a mixed economy, as in an unplanned economy, prices respond flexibly to supply and demand; competition ensures that firms make intensive use of resources; and financial constraints rather than quotas or production targets govern the decisions of firms. As under a command economy, however, a mixed economy nationalizes key industries (although fewer than under strict socialism) and imposes at least some central planning (although such planning remains aggregated at the industry or regional level rather than being firm-specific). Much coordination of supply and demand remains left to the market. Government intervention is exercised through control over expenditures, taxes, and social insurance such as Social Security; the use of regulatory authority; the ability to raise or lower barriers to market entry; and the ability to influence the allocation of investment.

Some economists consider that all Western countries including the United States have mixed economies, especially during the period between World War II and the 1980s when the public sector in all such countries expanded sharply. Other economists, though, apply the label to a narrower range of nations in which the government has asserted consistent leverage over economic growth. Under this latter definition, mixed economies include those of Taiwan, Singapore, South Korea, Japan, India, France, Italy, and Sweden—but not Canada, the United Kingdom, Australia, or the United States, because the planning that exists in the latter group is poorly coordinated. One may further distinguish between types of mixed economies: those under which government leverage comes from its welfare state role, as in Sweden, and those under which leverage lies elsewhere—such as a group or industry that exercises control over the economy.

—*Laura Seeley Pangallozzi*

References

Carson, Richard L. *Comparative Economic Systems.* Armonk, NY: M. E. Sharpe, 1990.
See also Volume 1: Government Budgets.

Monetary Policy

Effort to fight inflation or stimulate economy by controlling availability of spending money for consumers and businesses; used to attain stable prices with little or no inflation, maximum employment, and economic growth at the maximum rate the U.S. economy can sustain over a long time.

Most economists believe monetary policy requires stable prices because they are essential if the highest levels of employment and economic growth are to be achieved in the long run. In the United States, the Board of Governors of the Federal Reserve Board steers monetary policy. Increasing the amount of money and credit in the U.S. economy typically triggers a chain of events that causes interest rates to fall. Lower interest rates normally increase demand for items that most people buy on credit, such as new houses and cars. Lower interest rates also encourage businesses to invest in new factories, offices, and machines that they also pay for with credit.

The firms that produce these goods respond to the increased demand of consumers and businesses by increasing production and hiring more workers. The added income these workers earn is then spent on other goods, which other manufacturers must now produce in larger quantities. As they hire more workers to accomplish this, employment and economic growth both rise.

Problems result when the Federal Reserve lets the money supply grow too quickly or too slowly. If the Federal Reserve expands the money supply by too much, increased demand for products outstrips the ability of manufacturers to produce them, and inflation results. Higher rates of inflation ultimately choke off the economic expansion. Too little money growth results in high interest rates, reducing demand for interest-sensitive products and lowering levels of employment and economic growth.

—*Saranna R. Thornton*

References

Board of Governors of the Federal Reserve System. *The Federal Reserve System: Purposes and Functions.* Washington, DC: U.S. Government Printing Office, 1994.
See also Volume 2: Federal Reserve Bank.

Montgomery Bus Boycott (1955–1956)

Protest against racial segregation that led to a Supreme Court decision banning discrimination in intrastate transportation.

Angered by abusive bus drivers, leaders of the Montgomery, Alabama, African American community resolved to challenge the practice of reserving seats at the front of the bus for whites and, if additional whites boarded, forcing blacks to surrender their seats. Most bus patrons, about 80 percent, consisted of blacks. On December 1, 1955, police arrested Rosa Parks, an African American seamstress, for violating a local ordinance by declining to surrender her seat to a white man. Angered at the arrest, blacks called for a one-day bus boycott that proved a resounding success. The Montgomery Improvement Association (MIA), led by Martin Luther King Jr., then asked all Montgomery residents to refrain from riding buses until the conclusion of an agreement between MIA and the city of Birmingham concerning fare reductions, employment for black drivers, and a policy reserving five seats instead of ten for whites. Throughout the boycott, hundreds of people walked, while those with cars willingly served as chauffeurs. The MIA developed its own transportation service, hiring drivers and paying for the fuel used to transport people to work. Reluctant to lose household help, some white employers increased their employees' transportation stipend to cover taxi fare, while others increased wages. Because the business community had shown little support for the boycott, many black Montgomery residents decided to buy only essentials until the boycott ended because of the difficulty of carrying large purchases home without transportation. Many boycotters decided to trade only with black business operators. Beset by reduced sales, some white-owned businesses began closing early or going bankrupt. The bus company discontinued lines and laid off drivers. Rates were cut for the few buses still in operation, and buses ran much less frequently than they had in the past. The boycotters eventually won when in 1956 the Supreme Court let stand without review an opinion of a lower court mandating integration. The Court case was the deciding factor that ended the boycott on December 21, 1956.

—*Caryn E. Neumann*

References

Garrow, David J., ed. *The Montgomery Bus Boycott and the Women Who Started It: The Memoir of Jo Ann Gibson Robinson*. Knoxville: University of Tennessee Press, 1987.

See also Volume 1: Civil Rights Movement.

Morgan, John Pierpont (1837–1913)

American banker and financier.

Born April 17, 1837, in Hartford, Connecticut, John Pierpont (J. P.) Morgan grew up in a wealthy family. His father controlled J. S. Morgan and Company, an international banking enterprise that invested British funds in the United States and that provided a $50 million loan to the French government during the Franco-Prussian War (1870–1871). As a young man, J. P. Morgan studied in Europe before working for Duncan, Sherman and Company, a New York banking firm. In 1860 he became his father's agent in London. In 1869, the younger Morgan took on Jay Gould and Jim Fisk, gaining control over their Albany and Susquehanna Railroad. From there, Morgan targeted the railroad monopoly of Jay Cooke, who received funds from the United States government for the construction of his railways. Morgan's mastery of reorganization allowed him to consolidate control of the railroads and, in 1901, of the U.S. Steel Corporation. By 1890 Morgan had assumed control over the family business after his father's death.

His accumulation of wealth on such an unprecedented scale made Morgan the banker of last resort for the federal government. In 1895 and in 1907, Morgan provided loans to the United States, for which he was widely criticized because of the profit he gained from the transactions. During the trust-busting activity of the Progressive Era at the beginning of the twentieth century, Congress investigated the money trust (bankers who controlled the financial markets), targeting Morgan personally. In addition to his business activities, Morgan also engaged in philanthropy through donations designed to benefit the public and supported civic organizations. He also actively promoted the rights of women during his lifetime. He died March 31, 1913, leaving his extensive library and art collection to the people of New York. The items are housed in the Pierpont Morgan Library.

—*Cynthia Clark Northrup*

References

Forbes, John Douglas. *J. P. Morgan, Jr., 1867–1943*. Charlottesville: University Press of Virginia, 1981.

See also Volume 1: Panic of 1893; Panic of 1907; Railroads; Trusts.

Morrill Tariff Act (1861)

Important legislation that provided revenue for the Northern effort in the Civil War and expressed important principles of Republican political economy.

In the spring of 1860, Justin Smith Morrill, Republican of Vermont, proposed the tariff bill in the House of Representatives. Drafted to draw Northern industrial states to the Republican Party in that year's election, Morrill's bill was not an ordinary protective tariff that placed import duties on finished industrial goods. The act attempted to protect and support many sectors of the economy and all the regions of the country by placing tariff duties on agricultural, mining, fishing, and manufactured goods. Sugar, wool, flaxseed, hides, beef, pork, corn, grain, lead, copper, coal, and zinc all received protection by imposts, as did dried, pickled, and salted fish. In general, the tariff increased duties 20 percent on certain manufactured goods and 10 percent on specified raw materials. The bill reflected the Republican Party's commitment to general economic growth and expressed its belief that business interests interacted harmoniously and positively in the economy.

The tariff also differed in that it distributed the burden of protection across society rather than placing it on specific regions or poorer classes. Morrill instituted a graded system of duties on a series of enumerated goods. The bill placed a 10 percent duty on goods considered necessities and a 20 percent impost on products that were less necessary. Congress authorized a 30 percent tax on luxury items based on their value. Morrill believed that this system did not gouge consumers but taxed their ability and willingness to pay.

The House passed the bill May 10, 1860, when Western states rallied to it. However, Southern opposition defeated it in the Senate. After December 1860 when South Carolina seceded from the Union, Congress passed the tariff bill on March 2, 1861. The government enacted the tariff to raise revenues during the Civil War.

—*Peter S. Genovese*

References

Richardson, Heather Cox. *The Greatest Nation of the Earth: Republican Economic Policies during the Civil War*. Cambridge, MA: Harvard University Press, 1997.

See also Volume 1: Protective Tariffs.

MTO

See Microsystems Technology Office.

Multinational Corporations

Companies that operate in more than one country.

During the 1950s and 1960s, American firms of all kinds established offices abroad. According to the U.S. Department of Commerce Bureau of Economic Analysis, the book value of American foreign direct investment rose from $12 billion in 1950 to almost $80 billion in 1970. American companies sought to overcome trade barriers such as tariffs erected by most countries around the world that existed in the 1950s. As trade restrictions eased, however, American companies became more aggressive and tried to link technical, marketing, managerial and financial advantages with cheap overseas labor. During this period, "going multinational" became the fashionable thing to do, and American companies felt a need to develop global product portfolios to remain competitive.

In 1968, Jean-Jacques Servan Schreiber published *The American Challenge,* predicting that American multinational corporations would soon dominate world business. But large companies in other countries were also part of the international expansion, having begun in 1965 to set up or acquire foreign manufacturing operations at the same annual rate as American multinationals. The 1965 value of foreign direct investment in the United States totaled approximately $7.5 billion; by 1972 it had reached almost $15 billion. Although foreign investment in the United States remained small compared with U.S. investment abroad, the increase represented an important change in the organization of multinational companies, because funds from foreign investment exerted influence on the structure and operation of these entities.

By the 1970s, some of the glamour of internationalization started wearing off, resulting in a period of American divestment during the early 1970s. From 1971 to 1975, American companies sold 1,359 of their foreign subsidiaries (almost 10 percent). During the same period, a substantial decline occurred in the number of new subsidiaries being formed (3.3 for each divestment in 1971 compared with 1.4 in 1975). These divestments were largely in low-tech, high-competition industries such as textiles, apparel, leather, and beverages. Investment in high-tech industries such as pharmaceuticals, machinery, and office equipment increased during the same period. Thus, both investment patterns and the makeup of the multinationals themselves changed. European multinationals had largely caught up with American companies; Japanese firms began to expand internationally; and the developing countries spawned their own multinationals. By 2000, 62 percent of exports and 39 percent of imports involved multinational corporations. Total trade among multinational corporations equaled $363 billion.

—*Albert Atkins*

References
Ronen, Simcha. *Comparative and Multinational Management.* Washington, DC: Library of Congress, 1986.
See also Volume 1: Protective Tariffs.

Munn v. Illinois (1877)
U.S. Supreme Court case that established that states may regulate business for the public good.

In 1875, the Illinois legislature set the maximum rates that grain elevator operators could charge in Illinois cities of 100,000 or more. This action was in response to a movement among farmers known as the Grange that had asked lawmakers in Illinois and other Midwestern states to regulate the rates grain elevator operators and railroads could charge farmers; they charged low rates to large corporations but high rates to small farmers. Illinois grain elevator operators challenged the constitutionality of the 1875 law. The case came

before the Supreme Court, and lawyers for the operators argued that Illinois had surpassed the police power granted to it under the Constitution. They also argued that the law gave the state control over interstate commerce and deprived grain elevator operators of their private property without due process as guaranteed in the Fourteenth Amendment.

Chief Justice Morrison Waite ruled in favor of Illinois in a 7 to 2 decision. Citing England's Lord Chief Justice Sir Matthew Hale, renowned common-law jurist, Waite argued that private property ceases to be exclusively private when it is affected with a public interest. When private property is used in a public way, a state may regulate the property to protect its citizens. Waite admitted that states might abuse their police power over private property, but the best recourse was at the polls and not in the courts. He also dismissed the claim that the law interfered with interstate commerce since the relationship between farmers and grain elevators occurred primarily within the borders of Illinois. Although this decision and those from four other Granger cases set a precedent for future government regulation, most related decisions in the next 60 years followed the dissent of Justice Field, who argued that the Illinois law violated the Fourteenth Amendment.

—*Mary Stockwell*

References
Paine, Arthur Elijah. *The Granger Movement in Illinois.* Urbana: University of Illinois Press, 1904.
See also Volume 2: Judiciary.

Muscle Shoals (Tennessee Valley Authority)
Government hydroelectric project.

At Muscle Shoals in northern Alabama, the Tennessee River drops more than 140 feet along a 30-mile stretch, giving the area huge hydroelectric potential. The government began construction on two dams and two nitrate plants for hydroelectric power to manufacture nitrates for munitions during World War I. The war ended before engineers completed the projects, so the government no longer needed the nitrates for munitions. Since no agreements about postwar usage existed, President Warren G. Harding and Herbert Hoover, then secretary of commerce, developed plans to lease the installation to private companies that planned to use nitrates to manufacture fertilizer. Henry Ford expressed interest in the area and even proposed to build a "Detroit south" at Muscle Shoals.

The issue became heated after World War I when automaker Henry Ford attempted to buy the area and the dam from the federal government. Republican Senator George Norris of Nebraska, the chair of the Agriculture Committee, argued that the Muscle Shoals facilities should become the center of a public works project to develop fertilizer, flood control, and power for the welfare of the people. In 1925 President Calvin Coolidge appointed a committee, the Muscle Shoals Inquiry, to investigate whether private or public administration would operate more efficiently. The committee members, unwilling to entrench themselves in this controversial issue, declared the problem political rather than technical.

Norris would lead the fight to keep governmental control of the Muscle Shoals property. He demanded that the government administer the facility for the benefit of the people living in the Tennessee River Valley. Norris engineered the passage of two bills calling for governmental control of the facilities, one in 1928 and another in 1931. Both bills fell victim to presidential vetoes. Both Hoover and Norris refused to budge on the issue.

The Democrats remained committed to public ownership of the area, and the stalemate ended in 1933 with the election of Franklin D. Roosevelt to the presidency. Roosevelt visited Muscle Shoals and charged the Tennessee Valley Authority (TVA) with planning the usage, development, and conservation of the natural resources in the Tennessee River basin to the combined advantage of agriculture, forestry, and flood prevention. The TVA served as a model for the nation of re-vitalization of an area through government projects. Charges of unconstitutionality were lodged by private companies, which said that government ownership of utilities prevented private companies from entering the market. The TVA accomplished many of it goals and objectives and, as one of Roosevelt's most successful New Deal programs, TVA created three million jobs.

—*Lisa A. Ennis*

References

Clements, Kendrick A. *Hoover, Conservation, and Consumerism: Engineering the Good Life.* Lawrence: University Press of Kansas, 2000.

Hargrove, Erwin C. *Prisoners of Myth: The Leadership of the Tennessee Valley Authority 1933–1990.* Knoxville: University of Tennessee Press, 2001.

Olson, James Stuart, ed. *Historical Dictionary of the New Deal: From Inauguration to Preparation for War.* Westport, CT: Greenwood Press, 1985.

See also Volume 1: New Deal; Roosevelt, Franklin D.; Tennessee Valley Authority.

N

Nader, Ralph (1934–)

American consumer activist, renowned for spearheading a rise in consumer protection since the 1960s.

A lawyer trained at Princeton University and Harvard Law School, Ralph Nader made his first foray into the sphere of consumer advocacy with the appearance of the seminal work *Unsafe at Any Speed* in 1965. This book, the first of several he has written, induced a change in the market philosophy in the United States from "buyer beware" to more of a focus on consumer rights.

Before Nader began his campaigns, corporate aggression and government indifference had seriously eroded accountability of businesses to consumers. Nader was responsible for inducing policy changes during the 1960s and early 1970s in such areas as automobile safety, food and drug quality, pesticides, water pollution, energy consumption, cigarette content, and rates charged by the legal profession. He has also campaigned against government subsidies of nuclear power, aircraft development, and synthetic fuels. His main approach is to empower the consumer side of the market economy, which otherwise would remain fragmented and powerless, by developing citizen advocacy groups. These groups rely on a combination of publicity and court action to pressure firms and government bodies into mending their ways.

To encourage corporations and government agencies to reestablish their accountability, Nader has adopted the strategy of confronting corporate power via consumer activism and the exposing of information about the issue. This approach succeeded in 1974, for example, when Congress passed amendments to the Freedom of Information Act that opened up a wide variety of government data to citizen scrutiny. In 2002, Nader was the presidential candidate for the Green Party, an environmentally minded group, but he failed to win more votes than either major-party candidate.

Nader's legacy to American policymaking has caused many substantial firms and the government, knowing that their actions may be exposed to public scrutiny, to become obliged to more fully consider the interests of ordinary citizens. Newspapers and other media are more empowered to investigate business and government, holding them to account for their behavior.

—*Tony Ward*

References

Bollier, David. *Citizen Action and Other Big Ideas: A History of Ralph Nader and the Modern Consumer Movement.* Washington, DC: Center for the Study of Responsive Law, 1991.
See also Volume 1: Media.

NAFTA

See North American Free Trade Agreement.

NASA

See National Aeronautics and Space Administration.

Nasdaq

Over-the-counter stock exchange established in 1971.

Since the late 1700s, stock traders have transacted purchases on the New York and American Stock Exchanges. The advent and proliferation of computer technology in the 1950s and 1960s led to the first automated price quotation system that provides information on domestic securities not listed on the other stock markets, also called over-the-counter stocks. The Nasdaq, a subsidiary of the National Association of Securities Dealers (NASD), deals with these over-the-counter stocks and operates under the supervision of the Securities and Exchange Commission. In 1986, Nasdaq Europe opened in Great Britain after the deregulation of the securities industry in that country. Because investors and brokers use computers to transact purchases and sales, Nasdaq has had the capability of operating around the clock since 1999. In 1998, Nasdaq's transaction volume totaled $5.8 trillion, making the exchange second in the world only to the New

York Stock Exchange, which conducted $7.3 trillion in business the same year. During the economic decline of 2000, Nasdaq dropped significantly, because most of the computer stocks and dot-com businesses that were overinflated in value trade on this exchange.

—*Cynthia Clark Northrup*

References
Ingebretsen, Mark. *Nasdaq: A History of the Market That Changed the World.* Roseville, CA: Prima, 2002.
See also Volume 2: Stock Market.

National Aeronautics and Space Administration (NASA)

Government agency established for the exploration of space.

On October 1, 1958, Congress created the National Aeronautics and Space Administration (NASA) in response to the launching of the first satellite, *Sputnik,* by the Soviet Union during the cold war. As the successor of the National Advisory Committee for Aeronautics, NASA began to explore the feasibility of human space travel. The first flights of Project Mercury (1961–1963) were designed to explore the effects of space travel on humans. These were followed by the Project Gemini flights (1965–1966) in which humans explored space. Project Apollo (1968–1972) resulted in the landing of the first humans on the moon in 1969. Since then, NASA has focused on scientific experiments, the development of the international space station (involving cooperation among the United States, Canada, Brazil, Japan, Russia, and 11 nations of the European Space Agency), and exploring the far reaches of the galaxy using unmanned spacecraft—for example, the Hubble telescope and various unmanned missions to other planets.

Since its inception NASA has conducted experiments that have revealed valuable information on aerodynamics, wind shear, wind tunnels, flight testing, and computer simulations. Many biology and physics experiments have been conducted in space to explore the effect of weightlessness on objects. Long-range probes have explored the outer reaches of our universe, and the Hubble space telescope has revealed the existence of numerous astronomical bodies. In addition, communications satellites have enhanced the opportunities for technology used by telecommunications companies—for example, paging, cellular telephones, and global positioning systems.

NASA's goals include understanding the earth and its weather system in order to predict events such as flooding; exploring the fundamentals of physics, biology, and chemistry in the environment of space; understanding the origin and evolution of life on earth and searching for life elsewhere; encouraging the public, especially the younger generation, to explore space; and enabling revolutionary capabilities through the development of new technologies such as the personal computer.

As of 2003 NASA operates under a budget of $15 billion.

Since the space shuttle *Columbia* was destroyed on reentry February 1, 2003, opponents of NASA have argued for an increase in funding to ensure the safety of future missions.

—*Cynthia Clark Northrup*

References
Baker, Wendy. *NASA: America in Space.* New York: Crescent Books, 1986.
Bromberg, Joan Lisa. *NASA and the Space Industry.* Baltimore, MD: Johns Hopkins University Press, 1999.
See also Volume 2: Science and Technology.

National Bank Act of 1863

Legislation that prohibited the printing of paper money by anyone other than the federal government and established rules for banking structure in the United States.

Until the Civil War, currency was based on gold and silver. State banks printed "money," but it was not always accepted as legal tender or it might be discounted. The National Bank Act of 1863 began as a revision of the National Currency Act of 1863 by Hugh McCulloch, first comptroller of the currency. It was passed by Congress June 3, 1864. The new act granted more control to the federal government over the chartered banks than the original legislation had granted. State banks had not accepted the National Currency Act; they preferred the less-strict regulations of a noncentralized system. The new law raised the tax on state banknotes from 2 to 10 percent; this rate taxed the state banknotes out of existence and allowed for the new uniform currency called greenbacks or National Bank certificates. By 1865 most state banks had either become national chartered banks or had been dissolved.

The new banks had to comply with stricter federal regulations. Requirements included having at least five members on the board, having $50,000 to $100,000 in stable assets, and purchasing U.S. bonds equal in value to at least one-third of the bank's start-up capital. In exchange the Department of Treasury printed currency equaling 90 percent of the bonds' value, which the bank then used for transactions. Banks also received interest payments from purchased government bonds in the form of gold. This was an enticement to the remaining state-chartered banks to file for a federal charter and stop using private currency for daily business.

The National Currency Act and the National Bank Act served as the foundation for the United States banking system until the Federal Reserve Act was passed in 1913.

—*Deana Covel*

References
Zebib, Mohammad. "The Regulatory Road to Interstate Banking in the U.S.: Era of the National Bank Act, 1864–1900." *Delta Business Review,* vol. 5, no. 1. Available: http://cber.nlu.edu/DBR/ZEBIB.htm; accessed December 27, 2002.
See also Volume 1: Banking System; Federal Reserve Act; National Currency Act of 1863; Volume 2: Banking.

National Cordage Company

Monopolistic corporation that sparked the panic of 1893.

The National Cordage Company, the nation's leading manufacturer of rope and twine, became known as the first failed trust (or monopoly) in American history, one whose demise sparked the disastrous panic of 1893 and the ensuing depression. The company began as a group of rope manufacturers and experimented with the formation of trade associations that would negotiate agreements concerning production of the same or similar products and pools (which fixed prices) before uniting, in 1887, to form the National Cordage Company, a combination trust and corporation. It quickly bought up several smaller competitors, acquiring nominal control of 40 percent of the country's rope and twine production within three years. Reorganizing as a holding company (holding companies control smaller companies by holding the smaller companies' stock or controlling their operations) chartered in New Jersey and increasing its capital stock tenfold to $15 million, the company boasted effective control of about 90 percent of the country's cordage mills by early 1892. Financed by the leading New York banks, National Cordage was touted by the financial press as being one of the nation's rising industrial giants. However, the holding company borrowed large amounts of capital because four-fifths of its production remained in binder twine, a product that generated a cash flow only during harvest time. It also followed the dubious practices of purchasing the entire output of its suppliers on condition that the latter pledge not to equip its competitors, of buying out its competitors on condition that they retire permanently from the field, and of trying to corner the nation's hemp market.

With few actual economies of scale resulting from its reorganization in 1887, and with its recurring dependence on having escalating amounts of working capital, National Cordage encountered increasing difficulty paying its creditors. Adding insult to injury, several companies it had bought out used the proceeds from the sale to start new competing enterprises. During the early months of 1893, National Cordage boldly declared a 100 percent stock dividend in addition to making its usual payments to stockholders of 10 percent per annum. Happy stockholders received extra cash, but the financial press had no reaction. Just a few weeks later, however, the company announced its plans to file for receivership, touching off a selling frenzy among its stockholders. Over the next few months, the value of the company's stock plummeted from $138 to $20 per share. When the receiver put in charge of the company's finances discovered that the company treasury was empty, the *Commercial and Financial Chronicle* proclaimed, "Cordage has collapsed like a bursted meteor." Subsequent attempts to reorganize as the United States Cordage Company and as the Standard Cordage Company also failed by 1912.

—*John D. Buenker*

References

Dewing, Arthur S. *Corporate Promotions and Reorganizations.* New York: Harper and Row, 1969.

See also Volume 1: Panic of 1893.

National Currency Act of 1863

Act that imposed federal regulation on banks, the first such control since the dissolution of the Second Bank of the United States in 1837.

An economic crisis in 1857 caused several banks to fail because of the inadequacy of the banking system that had been established to replace the Second Bank of the United States. (The Second Bank had operated as the national bank and had provided some stability, but it closed in 1837. Between 1837 and 1857, state banks operated but were not regulated by the federal government.) Once the Civil War began, Abraham Lincoln proposed the first National Currency Act of 1863 to help finance the war by creating a system of national banks that were to issue the only legal paper currency. Congress passed the law on February 25, 1863. Its three main goals were to create a system of national banks, create a uniform national currency, and finance the Civil War.

The law intended to create a stable financial system though stricter supervision of banks by the federal government. The act established new operational standards for banks, established minimum amounts of capital to be held by banks in reserves, and defined how banks were to make and administer loans.

The law's second aim was to eliminate the more than 10,000 types of paper money issued by individual banks and to guarantee that legal paper currency could be exchanged for gold or silver currency. A uniform currency made transacting business easier. The new currency was issued against federally backed bonds, as is modern money. The government financed the war by selling these bonds and the limited printing of the new "greenback" banknotes.

The act established the Office of Comptroller of the Currency under the direction of the Treasury Department. Hugh McCulloch, the first appointed comptroller, wrote a revised version of the National Currency Act known as the National Bank Act of 1863. These two acts served as the foundation of the United States banking system until the Federal Reserve Act was passed in 1913.

—*Deana Covel*

References

Zebib, Mohammad. "The Regulatory Road to Interstate Banking in the U.S.: Era of the National Bank Act, 1864–1900." *Delta Business Review,* vol. 5, no. 1. Available: http://cber.nlu.edu/DBR/ZEBIB.htm; accessed December 27, 2002.

See also Volume 1: National Bank Act of 1863.

National Defense Education Act of 1958

Legislation enacted to provide financial assistance to students, states, and schools and so ensure a supply of people trained to meet future national defense needs.

In 1957, the Soviet Union launched the satellite *Sputnik* into space, spurring Congress to pass the National Defense Education Act of 1958. The bill, introduced by Senator Lister

Hill and Representative Carl Elliott, both Alabama Democrats, was an education bill framed as a measure to improve national defense. The act states, "The Congress hereby finds and declares that the security of the Nation requires the fullest development of the mental resources and technical skills of its young men and women. The present emergency demands that additional and more adequate educational opportunity be made available." Twenty-four Republicans voted for the expansive bill, although they had voted against similar legislation previously, before the *Sputnik* launch.

The act included provisions for the creation of the first federal student loan programs, as well as fellowships for graduate education in the sciences and engineering and increased federal assistance for teacher education. The act also called for the federal government to fund capital improvements at institutions of higher education, primarily the construction and renovation of science laboratories and buildings for expanded schools of education. Congress made money available for curriculum development in the sciences, mathematics, and foreign languages.

Public education benefited from additional money available to grade schools and high schools to improve science, mathematics, and foreign language instruction. The bill also expanded guidance, counseling, and testing in high schools. Although the act provided funding for kindergarten through twelfth grade education, its greatest influence was on higher education. Some observers argue that the National Defense Education Act, which is still in force, surpassed all other legislation for American higher education since the 1862 Morrill Land Grant Act.

—*John David Rausch Jr.*

References

Clowse, Barbara Barksdale. *Brainpower for the Cold War: The Sputnik Crisis and National Defense Education Act of 1958.* Westport, CT: Greenwood Press, 1981.

See also Volume 1: Agricultural and Mechanical (A&M) Colleges.

National Endowment for the Arts (NEA)

Government agency created to promote the arts.

In 1965 Congress established the National Endowment for the Arts, an agency proposed by President Lyndon B. Johnson under his Great Society program. The NEA sought to celebrate the rich cultural diversity of the United States, support artists demonstrating excellence in their particular medium, and promote learning in the arts, and it has been involved in development of the arts in local communities through a variety of programs. Since 1965 the agency has awarded more than 119,000 grants in the United States and its territories. In 1966 Congress appropriated $2.8 million for the NEA. Since that time the budget has increased substantially, reaching a peak in 1993 with more than $174 million and falling sharply in 1996 to $99 million. By 2002 the NEA budget had risen again to $115 million.

The NEA has achieved several successes since its inception. The agency sponsored the competition for the design of

the Vietnam veterans' memorial in Washington, D.C., funded the Celebration of Spirit memorial in Oklahoma City to honor victims of the bombing of the federal building there, and implemented the Healing Power of the Arts program at Columbine High School in Colorado after the fatal shooting of students and teachers. The NEA has also sponsored many writers who have gone on to win National Book Awards, National Book Critics Circle Awards, and Pulitzer prizes.

The agency often faces sharp criticism when it funds artists that deviate from accepted forms of art. Several artists who have received funding from the NEA have used the money to create projects that are offensive to a large portion of the American public. The lower level of funding in recent years may be attributed to the public outcry that resulted in these cases.

—*Cynthia Clark Northrup*

References

National Endowment for the Arts: 1965–2000: A Brief Chronology of Federal Involvement in the Arts. Washington, DC: National Endowment for the Arts, 2000.

See also Volume 1: Great Society.

National Endowment for the Humanities (NEH)

Government agency created to promote the humanities.

Established by Congress in 1965 under the Great Society program of President Lyndon B. Johnson, the National Endowment for the Humanities (NEH) promotes the study of history through education, by sponsoring research, by implementing public programs such as exhibits and television specials that convey the lessons of history, and by providing access to cultural resources. The agency provides grants to museums, educational institutions, public television and radio stations, and individuals engaged in teaching or researching the humanities.

Two of the most widely acclaimed achievements of the NEH include the King Tutankhamen traveling museum exhibition (and its corollary television program about the young king) and "The Civil War," the public television documentary by Ken Burns. The NEH also sponsors scholars who are conducting research for publication. Since the terrorist attacks of September 11, 2001, the NEH has renewed and strengthened its emphasis on the importance of history to our cultural heritage and democratic institutions. The agency has implemented a new program called "We the People: Special Initiative" to counter what it terms the "threat of historical amnesia." The goal of the program is to promote a greater understanding of American history and politics.

The proposed 2004 budget for the NEH totals $152 million. In addition to $25 million for the "We the People" program, the budget also includes $89.9 million for grants for education, research, preservation, and programming projects in the humanities. The NEH will allocate $10.4 million for matching funds and $5.6 million to encourage nongovernmental institutions to contribute to the humanities. The rest of the budget will pay for administration and miscellaneous programs.

—*Cynthia Clark Northrup*

References

Miller, Stephen. *Excellence and Equity: The National Endowment for the Humanities.* Lexington: University Press of Kentucky, 1984.

National Endowment for the Humanities. http://www.neh.fed.us; accessed February 15, 2003.

See also Volume 1: Great Society; National Endowment for the Arts.

National Grange of the Patrons of Husbandry (1867)

Farmer's organization begun as a social group that developed economic programs to increase the buying power of farmers.

In 1867 Oliver H. Kelly and six others developed the idea of a farmers' organization titled the National Grange of the Patrons of Husbandry, later simply called the Grange. The founders believed that the primary benefits of this organization for farmers should be social and intellectual, but by 1871 the group had become political and phrases such as "cooperation" (among Grange members) and "down with monopolies" were being heard at meetings.

The Grange started to grow vigorously in 1873 because an economic panic started that year that particularly affected farmers. Many farmers felt threatened by capitalistic changes after the Civil War such as larger railroad and industrial corporations. Organizational growth was strong in the northern Midwestern states and parts of the South, and more than 1,150 Granges were organized that year, compared with 132 in 1871. Membership peaked in 1875.

The two main forms of Grange activity centered on securing cheaper transportation rates for farmers, especially through the push for governmental regulation of railroads, and the introduction of cooperative schemes for farm products, supplies, and implements. Later, businesses advertised to Grangers in agricultural periodicals. Montgomery Ward, a department store, billed itself as the "original Grange supply house." Some Granges operated their own banks and offered mutual life and fire insurance policies. By 1876, some proposals even existed for international economic cooperation with other farming organizations.

Some Granges tried to cooperatively market crops with varying degrees of success during the last three decades of the nineteenth century. Most economic activity of the Grange centered around various schemes of cooperative buying and selling as a way to enhance the economic power of small individual farmers. These cooperative stores handled merchandise and farm implements for Grangers, but these business operations, successful or not, were never considered the main reason for the order's existence. By the late 1870s, many farmers left the Grange and joined the Farmer's Alliance, a more politically active group.

—*Lisa L. Ossian*

References

Buck, Solon Justus. *The Granger Movement: A Study of Agricultural Organization and Its Political, Economic, and Social Manifestations, 1870–1880.* Cambridge, MA: Harvard University Press, 1913.

Nordin, D. Sven. *Rich Harvest: A History of the Grange, 1867–1900.* Jackson: University Press of Mississippi, 1974.

See also Volume 1: Populist Party.

National Guard

Part-time trained state militias that also serve the federal government during times of crisis, allowing the nation to expand its trained fighting force without paying costs associated with the regular military.

The roots of the National Guard date back to 1636, when the early colonists formed militias (they were called the Minutemen in Lexington and Concord) to defend against Indian attacks and foreign troops. During the American Revolution, the militia was the first line of defense against the British until the formation of the Continental Army, and it continued afterward to defend the newly formed states. Because the United States did not have a large standing army throughout the nineteenth century, the state militias (in the early 1800s to be called the National Guard) provided the bulk of the forces that fought in the Mexican War and during the initial months of the Civil War. Guardsmen were also deployed in 1898 during the Spanish-American War. During World War I, more than 40 percent of the American forces were National Guard members. The National Guard also provided the first troops deployed during World War II, and the Air National Guard, created by the Department of Defense in 1947, also served during this conflict. Members of the National Guard served overseas during the Korean War and Vietnam conflict and have continued to do so in every major crisis since the 1960s. The president activated National Guard peacekeeping units destined for Iraq during the first Gulf War (1991), Haiti (1999), Kosovo (1999), and Bosnia (2002). Since the terrorist attacks of September 11, 2001, the National Guard has provided extra security at the nation's airports; it also assisted in the recovery of the space shuttle *Columbia,* which broke apart on reentry February 1, 2003. Many National Guard units were also deployed to Iraq again in 2003 for the second Gulf War.

—*Cynthia Clark Northrup*

References

Duncan, Stephen M. *Citizen Warriors: America's National Guard and Reserve Forces and the Politics of National Security.* Novato, CA: Presidio, 1997.

See also Volume 1: U.S. Department of Defense

National Income and Product Accounts (NIPA)

The quantitative basis for macroeconomic policymaking that deals with the overall economy.

The national income and product accounts (NIPA), a system

of measurement pioneered in the 1930s by the future Nobel laureate economist Simon Kuznets, measure the aggregate income levels in a country (and the components of national income such as wages and salaries, profits, and rent), the output of final goods and services produced for sale (both in aggregate and in each industry), and aggregate expenditure on the purchase of those goods and services (and the components of aggregate expenditure: consumption, investment, government purchases, and exports less imports). These data are indispensable for macroeconomic policymaking. A demand for data to guide policies to avoid a recurrence of the Great Depression of the 1930s and to manage resource mobilization during World War II fueled the development of NIPA.

Because they are shaped by these demands for data for specific purposes, the national income and product accounts have widely recognized limitations in measuring economic well-being or as guides to other types of policy. The exclusion of housework and child care (except when these services are purchased in the market) has distorted perceptions of women's contribution to the economy, with consequences for social policy. Unless the accounts are adjusted for the environmental and natural resource costs of production (the costs to clean up the environment or to remove resources from the ground and process them), they will continue to provide misleading data used to establish policies affecting the environment. Investment as measured in NIPA excludes acquisition of physical capital by the public sector (such as highways) and the acquisition of intangible capital by any sector (such as research and development expenditures and investment in human capital through education, training, and health spending). Much effort has been made to adjust NIPA for nonmarket activities, environmental changes, human capital formation, and government investment (see Eisner 1989 for a survey) and to incorporate such changes in new versions of the United Nations System of National Accounts, which has established global standards for its member nations. However, political and journalistic discussions of macroeconomic policy continue to rely on the NIPA measures of national income, investment, saving, and, especially, gross national product.

—*Robert Dimand*

References

Carson, Carol S. "The History of the United States National Income and Product Accounts: The Development of an Analytical Tool." *Review of Income and Wealth*, series 21 (1975): 153–181.

Eisner, Robert. *The Total Income System of Accounts.* Chicago: University of Chicago Press, 1989.

Kendrick, John W., ed. *The New System of National Accounts.* Boston: Kluwer Academic Publishers, 1996.

See also Volume 1: Economic Indicators.

(NIRA) in June 1933. The bill consisted of two components. First, it attempted to restore the "balance of production and consumption" by making various industries into cartels (businesses that form an organization to control prices, production, and wages). Prices and production increased through "codes of fair competition." Industrywide trade associations wrote these production codes to limit how much each member can produce—for example, yards of cloth—ensuring that prices remained truly representative of the entire industry and did not discriminate against small producers. In this way, the law attempted to increase the participation of small businesses in the recovery. With regard to increasing wages, the act's section 7(a) protected employees' rights to unionize and bargain collectively, and many of the codes specified minimum wage and maximum hours for workers. The National Recovery Administration (NRA), which was created by the National Recovery Act (1933), oversaw the operation of this aspect of the law.

The second important component of the act focused on stimulating wages and employment through a government-sponsored public works program. However, President Franklin D. Roosevelt created a Public Works Administration separate from the NRA, and as a result industrial recovery policy remained uncoordinated.

The National Industrial Recovery Act proved widely unpopular among manufacturers, who obeyed few of the production codes. Because of rampant price-cutting and other code violations, the act failed to achieve its primary aim of raising prices. The Supreme Court declared it unconstitutional May 27, 1935, in *Schechter Poultry Corp. v. U.S.* (295 US 495), stating that Congress had overstepped its authority in regulating the intrastate commerce of some manufacturers. Subsequently, through special legislation passed in 1935 and 1936, Congress reinstated the use of production codes in a few industries (apparel, airlines, bituminous coal, cotton textiles, lumber, trucking, and retail). Congress also reinstated many of the labor protection, wage, and hours provisions of section 7(a) of the act in the Wagner Act of 1937 and in the Fair Labor Standards Act of 1938.

—*Russell Douglass Jones*

References

Barber, W. J. *Designs within Disorder: Franklin Roosevelt, the Economists, and the Shaping of American Economic Policy, 1933–1945.* New York: Cambridge University Press, 1996.

See also Volume 1: Great Depression; New Deal; Wagner Act.

National Labor Relations Act

See Wagner Act.

National Industrial Recovery Act (NIRA) (1933)

New Deal legislation to promote industrial recovery after the Great Depression.

Congress passed the National Industrial Recovery Act

National Labor Relations Board (NLRB) (1935–Present)

Board that enforces the National Labor Relations Act, guarantees the right of collective bargaining, and sets rules for unions attempting to organize.

In 1935, Franklin D. Roosevelt signed the National Labor Relations Act, frequently called the Wagner Act after Democratic Senator Robert F. Wagner of New York, who championed the law. Designed to replace the National Industrial Recovery Act, which the Supreme Court had ruled unconstitutional, the Wagner Act created the National Labor Relations Board (NLRB). The NLRB guarantees labor the right to unionize and engage in collective bargaining. The board also conducts secret-ballot elections for workers who may wish to unionize. The NLRB differed from previous labor agencies because it enforced labor legislation rather than merely mediating disputes between business and labor. Critics challenged the Wagner Act's constitutionality before the Supreme Court in 1937. The National Labor Relations Act justified its provisions on the basis that the federal government had the constitutional power to regulate interstate commerce; the Court accepted the reasoning and upheld the law.

In 1947, Congress replaced the Wagner Act by passing the Taft-Hartley Act over the veto of President Harry S Truman. The Taft-Hartley Act turned the NLRB into a judicial body that had powers over unions as well as businesses. The new NLRB had the power to evaluate union practices that were considered unfair to businesses and employees. The Landrum-Griffin Act of 1959 further modified the operation of the NLRB by giving states jurisdiction over cases that the board declined to hear. Landrum-Griffin also outlawed "hot cargo agreements," in which unions forced employers to boycott groups having disputes with the union. The NLRB continues to regulate labor disputes, but labor organizations have often criticized it for being probusiness since the passage of Taft-Hartley.

—*John K. Franklin*

References
Lichtenstein, Nelson. *State of the Union: A Century of American Labor.* Princeton, NJ: Princeton University Press, 2002.
See also Volume 1: Great Depression; Roosevelt, Franklin D.; World War II.

National Marketing Quota (1938–Present)
Program to control domestic agricultural production created by the Agricultural Adjustment Act of 1938.

The federal government began programs to support farmers in the 1930s. The Agricultural Adjustment Act of 1933 first created a list of storable commodities that included tobacco, wheat, corn, peanuts, cotton, rice, and sugar. Farmers who voluntarily restricted their production of these products received government subsidies. In 1936, the Supreme Court declared the 1933 Agriculture Adjustment Act unconstitutional because a tax on processors (middlemen acting as agents) paid for the subsidies received by farmers. In response, the federal government instituted a stopgap measure to pay farmers for soil conservation until new legislation could be passed.

Congress passed another Agricultural Adjustment Act in 1938 (AAA), solving the constitutionality issue by specifying that subsidies were to be paid with general tax revenue. The 1938 act also provided for the use of national marketing quotas. Farmers could establish a marketing quota with a two-thirds vote of organization members who participated under the AAA. These quotas set limits on the amount of commodities that growers could market each year and established penalties for farmers that exceeded the limit. Each year, new quotas could be set, and farmers that participated received price supports based on parity pricing with 1910–1914 as the base period for most commodities.

National marketing quotas are subject to change each year, and pricing structures have undergone considerable change since their implementation in 1938. Supports for some agricultural products are no longer based on national marketing quotas, but quotas are still in place for some commodities—especially tobacco, which has been regulated by the quota every year since 1940.

—*John K. Franklin*

References
Lichtenstein, Nelson. *State of the Union: A Century of American Labor.* Princeton, NJ: Princeton University Press, 2002.
See also Volume 1: Great Depression.

National Oceanic and Atmospheric Administration (NOAA)
Federal agency responsible for gathering data on the environment.

President Richard Nixon proposed the creation of the National Oceanic and Atmospheric Administration (NOAA) in July 1970. The pollution of lakes, rivers, and the ocean had gained national attention in the late 1960s, prompting the administration to address the problem through a variety of means. In addition to creating the U.S. Environmental Protection Agency and promoting Earth Day, Congress authorized the creation of NOAA on October 3, 1970, and placed it in the U.S. Department of Commerce. By gathering scientific data over a long period of time, the agency has been able to effectively assess and manage information about oceans, the atmosphere, outer space, and the sun, and so it is better able to forecast the weather and issue severe-weather warnings to television and radio stations to help protect property and lives. Through its National Environmental Satellite, Data, and Information Service, NOAA gathers information about meteorology, oceanography, solid-earth geophysics, and solar-terrestrial sciences. In addition, it controls the Office of Marine and Aviation Operation, which comprises the NOAA ships and aircraft used to collect much of the data. The National Marine Fisheries Services, another division of NOAA, monitors fisheries along U.S. seacoasts to ensure the abundance of fish for the future. These fisheries export large quantities of fish overseas and help to maintain a favorable balance of trade. The National Ocean Service of NOAA oversees marine transportation, fishing, tourism, recreation, and home building along the nation's coasts. NOAA's Office of Oceanic and Atmospheric Research continues to analyze data with the mission of protecting life and property and promoting sustainable economic growth by assuring investors that their investments will be protected against natural disasters.

—*Cynthia Clark Northrup*

References

U.S. Department of Commerce. *NOAA's Climate Observations and Services.* Silver Spring, MD: National Oceanic and Atmospheric Administration, 2001.

See also Volume 1: U.S. Department of Commerce; Volume 2: Science and Technology.

National Recovery Administration (NRA)

A federal agency created by the National Industrial Recovery Act of June 13, 1933, to promote recovery during the Great Depression; abolished in January 1936 after the Supreme Court declared that its major provisions were unconstitutional.

When Franklin D. Roosevelt assumed the presidency in March 1933, more than 13 million people in the United States were unemployed as a result of the Great Depression, and the nation's financial and industrial systems were paralyzed. As a part of Roosevelt's New Deal to manage the economy and protect the public welfare, the National Recovery Administration (NRA) attempted to promote economic recovery by creating and administering a series of industrial codes—such as restricting manufacturers of cotton from producing rayon—that theoretically would allow the government to assist industries implement better business practices in the areas of trade, pricing, production, and labor relations. When the president approved such a code it had the force of law; if no codes were forthcoming, he could impose one himself.

Under the direction of Hugh S. Johnson, a member of the War Industries Board during World War I (which set prices, regulated manufacturing, and controlled transportation), the NRA wrote and approved a total of some 541 codes. To promote compliance with these codes, the NRA issued an emblem with the image of a blue eagle to businesses that abided by the codes, and it urged Americans, as part of their patriotic duty, to boycott businesses that lacked this emblem. Although noncompliance remained high, the NRA did reduce destructive competition through unfair business practices, promote better business practices, and—in accordance with section 7(a) of the National Industrial Recovery Act—help to ensure that labor could organize and bargain collectively.

Yet, despite these achievements, the NRA failed to bring about general economic recovery, and criticism of the agency increased. Opponents maintained that the NRA's code system promoted monopolies, hampered genuine unionization, and emphasized federal control over local control. This criticism crested in the summer of 1934 with a series of highly publicized hearings into the NRA, most notably a congressional hearing conducted by the National Recovery Review Board headed by lawyer Clarence Darrow, which found that the codes were injuring small businesses and gouging consumers.

With criticism and internal dissension within the NRA rising, Roosevelt approved a major reorganization of the National Recovery Administration. In September 1934, the National Industrial Recovery Board replaced Johnson as director of the NRA. This board attempted to make the codes less monopolistic, prevent abuses, and strengthen protections for small businesses, labor, and consumers. However, it had little success accomplishing these goals.

In early 1935, with the National Industrial Recovery Act approaching its expiration date, Roosevelt asked Congress to extend the act in a modified form. By that time, though, the NRA had few friends in Congress and the reauthorization debates quickly deadlocked. On May 27, 1935, in the midst of these debates, the Supreme Court ruled in the case of *Schechter v. United States* that the code system was unconstitutional on the grounds that it constituted an improper delegation of legislative authority to the executive branch. Consequently, the codes no longer had the force of law. Although the NRA attempted to implement voluntary codes, it quickly became a skeleton agency and spent the rest of its existence largely analyzing its failed code system.

—*David W. Waltrop*

References

Bellush, Bernard. *The Failure of the NRA.* New York: Norton, 1975.

Himmelberg, Robert F. *The Origins of the National Recovery Administration.* New York: Fordham University Press, 1976.

See also Volume 1: Great Depression; New Deal; Roosevelt, Franklin D.; *Schechter Poultry Corp. v. United States.*

National Technical Information Service (NTIS)

Branch of the U.S. Department of Commerce that serves as a central repository for scientific, technical, engineering, and business information collected as the result of government-funded research.

Established in 1950, the National Technical Information Service (NTIS) survived several attempts at privatization in the 1980s and fended off the threat of being eliminated in the late 1990s. Officials in the administration of President Ronald Reagan first proposed privatizing NTIS functions in 1981. Critics of that proposal noted that taxpayers funded many of the reports handled by the NTIS, and they questioned the shift toward a profit-based model for a government entity. Opponents to privatization expressed concern that any private solution would restrict access to NTIS materials.

Congress blocked further privatization initiatives in 1987 while ordering the NTIS to become self-sustaining. Sales at the NTIS declined dramatically from 1993 to 1999, however, as the Internet made millions of documents available free of charge, including many documents available for a fee from NTIS. When Congress balked at providing supplemental funds to close an estimated $2 million operating deficit for the NTIS, officials in the administration of President Bill Clinton proposed eliminating the NTIS entirely in October 1999.

Commerce Secretary William Daley offered the plan to eliminate the NTIS after the Clinton administration abandoned a fee-based service that had been expected to help restore NTIS's fiscal solvency. The plan ran counter to the administration's stated goal of maintaining free and open access to government documents and aroused the ire of regular users accustomed to paying for materials on a per-use basis. Opposition from Congress and NTIS users also prevented the elimination plan from being put into effect, however, and the NTIS remained within the Commerce Department.

By providing access to information, the NTIS has a mission of fostering economic growth by stimulating research and innovation. Librarians and researchers throughout the United States and abroad use the NTIS collection, which included more than two million publications covering 350 subject areas in 2002.

—*Christopher A. Preble*

References
McClure, Charles R. *Linking the U.S. National Technical Information Service with Academic and Public Libraries.* Norwood, NJ: Ablex, 1986.
See also Volume 1: U.S. Department of Commerce.

National Telecommunications and Information Administration (NTIA)

Agency within the U.S. Department of Commerce that manages the broadcast spectrum from radio to television to the Internet and that advises the president on issues related to telecommunications and information policy.

President Jimmy Carter established the National Telecommunications and Information Administration (NTIA) by executive order in 1978 as part of a major restructuring of the executive branch. The newly established NTIA assumed responsibility for the White House's Office of Telecommunications Policy (OTP) and the Commerce Department's Office of Telecommunications. Following this reorganization, the NTIA assumed control over the management of the telecommunications and radio broadcast spectrum, a function formerly under the purview of the OTP. In this capacity, the NTIA proved instrumental in urging the use of competitive bidding through auctions as a more efficient method for distributing FCC licenses during the early 1990s. The NTIA later worked with experts from the California Institute of Technology to develop a computerized bidding system also used by the Federal Communications Commission.

Under the terms of the NTIA Organization Act of 1992, the NTIA's assistant secretary for communication and information became the chief administrator for the NTIA. This individual reports to the Secretary of Commerce. Other offices within the NTIA that support the agency's mission include the Office of Telecommunications and Information Applications—which administers telecommunications grant programs including the Public Telecommunications Facilities Program and the Telecommunications and Information Assistance Program—and the Technology Opportunities Program.

The Institute for Telecommunications Services (ITS) provides research and engineering assistance to the NTIA and other federal agencies. Under the terms of the Federal Technology Transfer Act of 1986, the ITS also aids the private sector by encouraging the shared use of government facilities and resources to encourage the development of new telecommunications products and services.

—*Christopher A. Preble*

References
McClure, Charles R. *Linking the U.S. National Technical Information Service with Academic and Public Libraries.* Norwood, NJ: Ablex, 1986.
See also Volume 1: U.S. Department of Commerce.

National War Labor Board (NWLB) (1918–1919; 1942–1945)

Agency that mediated relations between labor and business to ensure wartime industrial production during World War I and World War II.

On March 29, 1918, in an effort to prevent labor strikes that would hamper military production during World War I, Woodrow Wilson created the National War Labor Board (NWLB) to mediate disputes between management and labor. The agency had little real power, but it recognized the right of workers to organize. The board, which included former President William Howard Taft, was also skilled at convincing each side to compromise. The NWLB prevented several strikes during the war. However, the government dissolved the agency after Germany's defeat, and major strikes in the steel and coal industries broke out in 1919.

When the United States entered World War II, the federal government recreated the National War Labor Board. To convince labor to uphold a no-strike pledge, the reincarnated agency also promoted collective bargaining, but the new NWLB had greater powers than its predecessor did. It could go beyond mere mediation and had the ability to force arbitration settlements on management and labor in order to ensure production. This power gave the NWLB indirect control over prices and wages.

With NWLB support, American union membership grew by about 40 percent from 1941 to 1945, and labor unions became less associated with political radicalism. The NWLB even increased workers' wages during the early years of the war. In response to complaints about wages from steelworkers, the NWLB instituted the Little Steel formula in July 1942. This method of wage control used pay rates in January 1941 as a base and gave steelworkers a 15 percent cost-of-living wage increase. Other industries involved in war production soon adopted the system, and it quickly became the standard. Initially the Little Steel formula pleased labor, but in April 1943 the federal government froze all workers' wages to control rising inflation. Therefore, labor unions lost the power to negotiate for wage increases for the rest of the war, and there were several small strikes, especially in the coal industry. The wartime strikes were typically short-lived, lasting no more than a few days because of NWLB intervention.

After the National War Labor Board was dismantled in 1945, there were several major labor strikes, just as there had been after World War I.

—John K. Franklin

References

Lichtenstein, Nelson. *State of the Union: A Century of American Labor.* Princeton, NJ: Princeton University Press, 2002.

See also Volume 1: World War I; World War II.

NATO

See North Atlantic Treaty Organization.

Navigation Acts (1651, 1660, 1672)

Series of restrictions passed by the English Parliament meant to restrict colonial American shipping to English ships and merchants, including colonies within the Empire, much to the frustration and anger of the colonists.

The first of the Navigation Acts, passed under the Protectorate of Oliver Cromwell in 1651, focused on the Dutch, who were then at war with England. The act prohibited shipping from the colonies except in English vessels, but allowed non-English goods that were transshipped through England. Officials barely enforced this act in the chaos surrounding the English civil war, but it set the pattern for further acts after the restoration of the monarchy in 1660. The second Navigation Act, this one promulgated under Charles II in 1660, was much the same but included measures for enforcement and enumerated a list of products including tobacco, sugar, cotton, wool, and dyes that would pay high duties when shipped to England. A third Navigation Act in 1672, also during the reign of Charles II during another period of hostilities against the Dutch, imposed additional colony-to-colony shipping restrictions and duties.

These policies operated as part of the widely accepted ideology of mercantilism, in which the British sought to ban other European countries from trading with the American colonies or gaining any benefit from their colonies' resources. The Navigation Acts also sought to maintain a favorable balance of trade between England and the colonies while restricting the manufacture of goods in the colonies by measures such as the 1733 Hat Act (which restricted the manufacture of felt hats to England) or 1750 restrictions on iron mills and bounties on raw materials. Although this appeared negative to many colonists, who turned to smuggling, these measures encouraged the American shipbuilding industry and protected American products like Southern tobacco against French and Dutch products in the English market. Key to the success of this mercantile system were the corn laws, which closed England to imported grain if the price of the domestic product fell below a certain level—a measure that persisted in English trade policy until 1846. Additionally, the Navigation Acts allowed the English to discipline Scotland and Ireland through restrictions on colonial trade, which had to be conducted through England, seriously affecting the growing ports of Glasgow and Belfast, which engaged in the slave and tobacco trade with the American colonies.

—Margaret Sankey

References

Dickerson, O. M. *The Navigation Acts and the American Revolution.* Philadelphia: University of Pennsylvania Press, 1951.

Harper, Lawrence A. *The English Navigation Laws.* New York: Octagon Books, 1964.

See also Volume 1: American Revolution; Stamp Act; Sugar Act of 1764.

NEA

See National Endowment for the Arts.

NEH

See National Endowment for the Humanities.

New Deal

System of managing the economy and protecting the public welfare that vastly enlarged the power of the federal government during the 1930s and eased the Great Depression.

On winning the Democratic nomination for president in 1932, Franklin D. Roosevelt pledged in his acceptance speech to give the American people a "new deal." He declined to discuss the specifics of his plan for pulling the economy out of the Great Depression and, when he took office in 1933, no one knew what to expect. To rebuild the economy, Roosevelt had to restore faith in the financial system. Five days into his presidency, he called Congress into session and pushed through his first reform, the Emergency Banking Bill, to provide help to private banks. The Glass-Steagall Banking Act (1933) again made banks safe repositories of money by separating commercial from investment banking and establishing the Federal Deposit Insurance Corporation to guarantee bank deposits. The Securities and Exchange Act, passed in June 1934, aimed to end the abuses that had led to the stock market crash by banning stock manipulation. Roosevelt concentrated on reform, recovery, and relief. The Tennessee Valley Authority (1933) brought recovery by building hydroelectric plants to allow the development of industry in Alabama, Kentucky, Mississippi, and Tennessee. The National Industrial Recovery Act (1933), the centerpiece of the First New Deal, focused on relief. It created the Public Works Administration to construct government projects, the Civil Works Administration to tide the unemployed over the winter of 1933–1934 with small projects, and the Civilian Conservation Corps to put young unmarried men to work in the wilderness. Farmers, who had been particularly hard hit by the depression, received help from the Farm Relief Act (1933), which provided lower mortgages through the Emergency Farm Mortgage Act. The farm bill also included the controversial 1933 Agricultural Adjustment Act (declared unconstitutional by the Supreme Court in 1935 because it included a tax on the middleman or agent), which paid farmers to reduce production. The program took effect in May 1933 after the growing season had begun. To the disgust of the many starving people in the cities, who could not afford food, farmers poured milk onto the ground and killed pregnant sows to receive government aid. To take land out of production, some growers evicted sharecroppers and tenant farmers, thereby worsening the misery of those already at the bottom of the economic ladder. As hard times continued, poor Americans turned politically leftward, and Roosevelt followed with the Second New Deal. In August 1935, Roosevelt won passage of the Social Security Act, which provided care for the aged and disabled. The National Labor Relations Act prohibited unfair practices by employers who sought to block unionization. The Works Progress Administration formed in 1935 provided workers who would add to the material and artistic wealth of the nation. Under the program, federal funds supported the arts in the form of the Federal Art Project, the Federal Music Project, the Federal Theatre Project, and the Federal Writers' Project. Following the defeat of many Democrats in the 1938 election, Roosevelt proposed no new reforms and instead focused on preserving the New Deal.

—*Caryn E. Neumann*

References
Davis, Kenneth. *FDR, the New Deal Years, 1933–37: A History.* New York: Random House, 1986.
Lash, Joseph P. *Dealers and Dreamers: A New Look at the New Deal.* New York: Doubleday, 1988.
See also Volume 1: Civil Works Administration; Civilian Conservation Corp; Glass-Steagall Banking Act; Great Depression; National Industrial Relations Act; National Industrial Recovery Act; New Deal; Public Works Administration; Roosevelt, Franklin D.; *Schecter Poultry Corp. v. United States;* Securities and Exchange Commission; Social Security Act of 1935; Tennessee Valley Authority.

New York Stock Exchange (NYSE)

Oldest stock exchange in the United States.

Formed in 1792, the New York Stock Exchange originally operated under a large buttonwood tree at 68 Wall Street. Twenty-four brokers subscribed to the agreement that established the exchange and traded stocks on a commission basis. In 1817 the group formally adopted the name *New York Stock and Exchange Board* and a new constitution. The final name change, to New York Stock Exchange (NYSE), occurred during the Civil War in 1863. After the war was over, the NYSE required that all securities be listed to prevent the overissuance of stocks. That same year, 1869, the market experienced a major crisis when Jay Gould and Jim Fish, two businessmen, attempted to corner the gold market. The crash of 1873 followed just four years later with numerous bank and company failures nationwide. Still, the New York Stock Ex-

change survived. In 1886 the NYSE traded more than one million shares—a record for the exchange in a given day. After the height of the panic of 1895, the NYSE recommended that companies publish and distribute annual financial reports to encourage investor purchases in their companies. In 1903 the NYSE moved to a new location at 18 Broad Street.

Operations ceased briefly at the onset of World War I. From July 31, 1914, through December 11, 1914, the NYSE remained closed. After the war Americans engaged in a buying frenzy—an act that ultimately led to the stock market crash of 1929. On October 29, 1929, the NYSE traded more than 16.4 million shares; brokers allowed purchasers to buy stocks on margin, that is, placing only 1 percent down. When President Franklin D. Roosevelt declared a banking holiday in March 1933, the market remained closed from the fourth through the fourteenth of March. Since 1933 the NYSE has operated under the supervision of the Securities and Exchange Commission. In 1971 the exchange was fully computer-automated, and it has since adapted new innovations such as 24-hour access via the Internet to buy and sell. Recent corporate scandals and insider trading resulted in the recommendation to the Securities and Exchange Commission by the NYSE's Stock Watch unit to freeze assets and impose fines and penalties totaling $8 million against 26 companies.

—*Cynthia Clark Northrup*

References
Geisst, Charles R. *100 Years of Wall Street.* New York: McGraw-Hill, 2000.
Sobel, Robert. *The Big Board: A History of the New York Stock Market.* New York: Free Press, 1965.
See also Volume 2: Stock Market.

Newlands Reclamation Act (1902)

Legislation passed by Congress to encourage the irrigation of western desert lands.

During the late nineteenth century, the United States government attempted to encourage the settlement and irrigation of western arid lands with the Desert Land Act of 1877. Having failed to entice both foreign immigrants and U.S. citizens to migrate to these difficult regions, by 1902 Congress passed another piece of legislation to stimulate migration—the Newlands Reclamation Act. Under the terms of the legislation, the federal government allowed for the western states to use up to 95 percent of the profits derived from sales of public land for irrigation projects with the understanding that the water users would pay off the cost of the irrigation works over ten years. The first two successful projects under this act involved the Carson and Salt River projects. The Carson project controlled the waters of the Carson and Truckee Rivers in western Nevada and resulted in the construction of the Lahontan Dam in 1915. The Salt River project provides electricity and water to the Phoenix, Arizona, area and encompassed the construction of the Roosevelt Dam in a canyon east of Phoenix. The dam provides a two-year supply of water to a region known for the growing of citrus fruits, lettuce, melons, and other crops. In 1914, Congress lengthened the time of repayment to two and then four years. During the Great Depression, the Roosevelt administration expanded the role of the U.S. Bureau of Reclamation, established in 1902 under the Department of the Interior. In addition to providing irrigation for these western states, the act also provides for the generation of hydroelectric power. Subsequent projects have included the Bonneville Dam and the Grand Couleee Dam, the Central Valley Project in California, the Colorado–Big Thompson Project, and the Missouri River Basin Project.

—*Cynthia Clark Northrup*

References

Hibbard, Benjamin Horace. *A History of the Public Land Policies.* Madison: University of Wisconsin Press, 1965.
See also Volume 2: Land Policies.

Nicaragua

Southern Central American nation marked by political instability since gaining independence in 1838.

The United States initially hoped that Nicaragua would be a suitable site for a transisthmian canal linking the Atlantic and Pacific Oceans. However, after American adventurer William Walker briefly took control of Nicaragua in the 1850s and requested its annexation to the United States as a proslavery state, Nicaraguans were suspicious of American motives. Because of mistrust related to this episode and Nicaraguan instability, the United States eventually selected Panama as the site for the canal.

By the end of the nineteenth century, Nicaragua had become a major exporter of coffee to the United States. Nicaragua also encouraged foreign investment to boost production, and Americans invested. Unfortunately, Nicaragua was politically unstable and U.S. Marines occupied Nicaragua in 1909 to protect U.S. interests. In an effort to lend stability, American troops remained and turned Nicaragua into a virtual protectorate until the complete U.S. withdrawal in 1933. During this period, American banks lent development money to Nicaragua, but the United States also controlled Nicaraguan customs duties and rail and steamship revenue.

After withdrawal in 1933, American relations with Nicaragua stabilized until the Sandinista National Liberal Front (FSLN) took control of the government in 1979. Fearful of Sandinista ties to communism, the U.S. government during the administration of President Ronald Reagan covertly supported anti-Sandinista rebels known as the Contras. During the ensuing Contra War of the 1980s, the Nicaraguan economy deteriorated because of warfare and an American embargo on Nicaraguan goods that began in 1985. In 1987, because of the publicity of the Iran-Contra scandal (in which Central Intelligence Agency arms were sold to Iran and the profits used to fund the Contras), the Congress stopped all military support for the Contras. Without American support the Contras were unable to keep fighting, and the groups negotiated. As a result of the negotiations, Nicaragua held free elections in 1991, the year the

war ended. Efforts to rebuild the Nicaraguan economy since the end of the war have met with limited success.

—*John K. Franklin*

References

Pastor, Robert A. *Not Condemned to Repetition: The United States and Nicaragua.* 2d ed. Boulder, CO: Westview Press, 2002.
See also Volume 1: Iran-Contra; Panama and Panama Canal; Reagan, Ronald.

NIPA

See National Income and Product Accounts.

NIRA

See National Industrial Recovery Act.

NLRB

See National Labor Relations Board.

NOAA

See National Oceanic and Atmospheric Administration.

Non-Importation Act (1806)

Legislation intended to stop England from violating the shipping rights of the United States through economic coercion.

The Non-Importation Act, passed by the United States in April 1806, had its intellectual foundations in the colonial protests that occurred in reaction to imperial policies and the belief that commercial discrimination by the United States could influence the course of British policy. In 1805, Britain changed its policy toward the "broken voyage"—which allowed ships to circumvent the British blockade by first stopping at an American port before continuing to their final destination—and began seizing American ships. Britain claimed that this action violated England's notion of neutral shipping.

The United States viewed Britain's acts as a violation of its rights, and in late January 1806, Congress began deliberating a response. Republican Representative Joseph Nicholson of Maryland proposed a measure that received majority support in Congress and would eventually develop into the Non-Intercourse Act. Rather than supporting a ban on all English imports, Nicholson proposed limiting nonimportation to goods that could be either produced in the United States or obtained from other countries. In the final act, this reasoning evolved into a long list of prohibited items that included hemp, flax, and certain woolen and metal goods. Also, Congress delayed the act, scheduling it to go into effect at the end of 1807.

The reason for this delay was Thomas Jefferson's belief that the administration could use the threat of nonimportation to gain favorable treatment for American shipping from the British. However, over the next year, both Britain and France intensified their efforts to thwart the trade of neutrals with the other state, and both nations preyed on American shipping. These actions forced Jefferson to take more drastic measures; in 1807 the United States rejected the concept of limited nonimportation embodied by the Non-Importation Act (which was never put in place) and passed the Embargo Act of 1807, which prohibited U.S. trade with France and England.

—*Peter S. Genovese*

References
Horsman, Reginald. *The New Republic: The United States of America, 1789–1815.* New York: Longman, 2000.
See also Volume 1: Embargo of 1807; Non-Intercourse Act of 1809.

Non-Importation Agreements, Colonial (1765–1776)

A technique of economic resistance used by the American patriots between 1765 and 1776 to oppose Britain's attempts to tax and control the colonies.

The end of the French and Indian War (1756–1763) left the British state deeply in debt, thus initiating a reexamination by England of the North American colonies' position in the British Empire. This state of affairs allowed George Grenville—Britain's minister of the Exchequer, who had assumed control because of the ill health of the prime minister—to push his Stamp Act through Parliament in 1765. The act was designed to raise revenue by taxing all printed materials in North America. The colonists quickly responded with ideological arguments examining the relationship between taxation and representation, but one of their most effective techniques involved the economic policy of nonimportation. As the North American colonies grew and developed in the eighteenth century, the American colonist came to consume increasing amounts of commodities manufactured in Britain or reexported (transshipped) from Britain. British merchants made credit easily available to these colonial consumers, facilitating their consumption. By 1765, many colonists found themselves deeply indebted to these British merchants. Thus, nonimportation was not only an act of colonial defiance but also a decision of economic policy. In these agreements, groups of citizens declared their mutual boycott of British goods until Parliament repealed the offending act. The colonists then stated their unwillingness to pay their debts until Parliament repealed the act. Nonimportation played an important role in the repeal of the Stamp Act, as the Marquis of Rockingham capitalized on the distress of British merchants brought about by colonial boycotts to convince Parliament to revoke the act. Nonimportation quickly became a favorite mechanism used by the American patriots against Britain's increasing tyranny. By the early 1770s, nonimportation came to serve as a motiva-

tion for developing domestic manufacturing. Many colonists demonstrated their patriotism by wearing homespun clothing and drinking herbal tea, and activities such as these laid the foundations for the development of North American manufacturing.

—*Ty M. Reese*

References
Maier, Pauline. *From Resistance to Revolution: Colonial Radicals and the Development of American Opposition to Britain, 1765–1776.* New York: Alfred A. Knopf, 1972.
See also Volume 1: American Revolution; Stamp Act.

Non-Intercourse Act of 1809

America's reaction to British and French attempts to restrict and seize American trade during the Napoleonic wars.

In 1806 and 1807, intending to create a "paper blockade" of Europe, Great Britain passed several Orders in Council that blockaded continental Europe and prohibited U.S. trade with France under the Rule of 1756. The Rule of 1756 stated that if a country had not traded with France in 1756, it could not trade with France during the French and Indian War. The United States was part of the British Empire in 1756 and was fighting against the French in that war. Although Great Britain lacked the naval power to completely blockade continental Europe, the Orders in Council made it illegal for trade between England and Europe to occur and gave Britain the power to regulate and inspect ships entering and leaving European ports. Napoleon responded with his Continental System, which created a paper blockade of the British Isles and allowed France to seize any ships that followed the British regulations. For the Americans, the Napoleonic Wars were an excellent economic opportunity for a young nation attempting to get its finances in order while paying off its revolution-related debt. The actions of both Britain and France made it so that both sides could stop, search, and seize American ships, and both sides did. In America, a debate raged over the issue of remaining neutral versus supporting France or Britain. President Thomas Jefferson responded to this situation in 1807 with the Embargo Act, which halted the American export trade and forbade American ships from leaving for foreign ports. The Embargo Act proved ineffective, and when James Madison became president the problem of American neutrality remained.

Madison and Congress continued Jefferson's policy of neutrality when they passed the Non-Intercourse Act of 1809. This act opened America's foreign trade with all nations except England and France and declared that trade would be resumed with either of these nations when they dropped their restrictions. The problem for Madison remained that of Jefferson's—trade with Europe, because of the war, remained too profitable, and American merchants and manufacturers continued to risk selling a variety of military and nonmilitary commodities and foodstuffs to both sides by maintaining its neutrality.

—*Ty M. Reese*

References
Stagg, J.C.A. *Mr. Madison's War: Politics, Diplomacy, and Warfare in the Early American Republic, 1783–1830.* Princeton, NJ: Princeton University Press, 1983.
See also Volume 1: American Revolution; Embargo of 1807.

North American Free Trade Agreement (NAFTA)

Agreement to create free trade zone among the countries of the North American mainland.

Congressional passage of HR 3450 in late November 1993 implemented a commitment to create the North American Free Trade Agreement (NAFTA) that President George H. W. Bush had made in 1992. If NAFTA works as planned, it should lead to the creation of a free trade zone between the United States, Canada, and Mexico by 2008. If NAFTA is successful in eliminating trade barriers among the three nations, the U.S. hopes to extend the idea throughout the Western Hemisphere through the Free Trade Agreement of the Americas.

NAFTA has to address and modify a great many policies and practices to achieve its goal of establishing a free trade zone. The agreement calls for elimination over a 15-year period (1993–2008) of tariffs on goods and restrictions on cross-border activity in service industries like telecommunications, trucking, and finance. It also calls for allowing businesses from any NAFTA country to set up operations in any other member country and be treated the same as if they were nationals of the country in which they established operations. The issue of health and environmental standards (which often serve as nontariff trade barriers) was addressed by asking that members "pursue equivalence" in those standards in a manner that did not weaken existing levels of protection.

Although both the Bill Clinton and George H. W. Bush administrations pushed for NAFTA approval, there was serious opposition both within and outside the mainstream of American politics. Opposition to NAFTA was one of the primary issues around which Ross Perot built his Reform Party movement, which garnered almost 20 percent of presidential votes in 1992. Opposition to NAFTA and freer trade policies in general would be a hallmark of third-party political campaigns throughout the 1990s on both ends of the political spectrum, from Perot and his successor Pat Buchanan to Ralph Nader, presidential candidate of the Green Party in 2000. Most Democratic leaders in Congress also opposed NAFTA, including Majority Whip David Bonior and Majority Leader Richard Gephardt.

This diverse group of opponents and the interest groups they represented were motivated by many considerations. Labor groups feared that NAFTA would cost American jobs, especially higher-paid unionized jobs, because businesses would relocate to Mexico in search of cheaper labor costs. Environmentalists and others were concerned that the United States would weaken environmental and health standards to comply with the agreement.

Aside from the executive branch, there were many supporters of NAFTA. Most major business organizations were anxious to see the expanded market. The Republican leadership was also very supportive, especially House Minority Whip Newt Gingrich. To encourage support for the measure, the Clinton administration negotiated some side agreements to give protection to labor unions and expanded markets to specific American industries such as the automobile industry. Clinton also obtained an amendment to the bill that would give money to those who lost jobs because of NAFTA to pay for retraining and provide income support during retraining. Those additions and hard lobbying efforts by the NAFTA supporters paid off, as NAFTA was approved and went into effect January 1, 1994.

—*G. David Price*

References
Clement, Norris C. *North American Economic Integration: Theory and Practice.* Northampton, MA: Edward Elgar Publishing, 1999.
Folsom, Ralph Haughwout. *NAFTA in a Nutshell.* St. Paul, MN: West Group, 1999.
See also Volume 1: Free Trade Area of the Americas; Nader, Ralph.

North Atlantic Treaty Organization (NATO)

A collective security alliance organized under the North Atlantic Treaty of 1949.

The North Atlantic Treaty Organization (NATO) was formed by the North Atlantic Treaty of 1949. Original members were the United States, the United Kingdom, Canada, France, Italy, Belgium, the Netherlands, Luxemburg, Norway, Denmark, and Iceland. Later several more European countries joined NATO: Greece and Turkey (1952); Germany (1955); Spain (1982); and Hungary, Poland, and the Czech Republic (1999). Russia joined in 2002, and NATO Allies decided at the 2002 summit in Prague to invite seven other countries to join: Bulgaria, Estonia, Latvia, Lithuania, Romania, Slovakia, and Slovenia. Over the years, NATO commitments have consumed the greatest share of America's defense budget. By the end of the twentieth century the NATO countries counted for some 40 percent of U.S. foreign trade ($684,478 million), including 44 percent ($308,478 million) and 37 percent ($376,000 million) of American exports from and imports to foreign countries, respectively.

The U.S.-sponsored European Recovery Program (the Marshall Plan) a massive financial aid package to Western Europe, laid a foundation for the collective security scheme by developing a shared belief that only an economically rehabilitated Europe could effectively resist potential communist subversion or Soviet aggression. Since January 1950 when NATO approved plans for integrated, or coordinated, defense against the Soviet Union, the United States has subsidized the massive buildup and rearmament of Western Europe. Additionally, by the end of the 1960s the United States contributed about $1 billion to NATO infrastructure (bases, airfields, pipelines, communications networks, and depots for military supplies).

Throughout NATO's history, the United States and its allies developed a much broader concept of the alliance, going beyond its immediate military and political functions to include security. According to Article 2 of the North Atlantic Treaty, the member states sought to eliminate conflicts and encourage economic collaboration among themselves. Members formed a special Economic Committee in March 1951 to reconcile the economic capabilities of the member states and coordinate efforts in security-related economic issues such as military spending, assessments of resources for defense planning, cooperation within the defense industries, and interalliance trade.

At the same time, several issues of an economic nature caused discord between the United States and its allies. NATO's acquisition of weaponry for use by the NATO armies occasionally intensified the economic rivalry between the United States and major Western European powers since the acquisition of weaponry originated in the United States. To manage the problem, the alliance established joint weapons production and licensing agreements. By the mid-1980s the United States licensed the production of main armaments (missiles, aircraft, warships, armored vehicles, and artillery) in ten NATO countries, and four allied powers licensed weapons production in the United States.

More frequently, the relocation or limitation of resources as well as the fact that the United States carried a disproportionate share of NATO defense expenses produced tensions within the alliance. These disputes became particularly fierce between the 1960s and 1980s. The United States, which had carried about two-thirds of NATO's financial burden for many years, repeatedly called for greater contributions from its allies. In the 1970s the U.S. Congress even pressured for scale-back of U.S. military commitments in Europe because of the federal budget and trade deficit. Although the NATO long-term defense programs and the rise of annual military spending by NATO countries between 1979 and 1983 gave some relief, the issue of uneven burden-sharing remained in the years to follow.

Indirectly, the economic considerations and concerns also influenced U.S. and NATO defense planning, particularly the doctrine of "massive retaliation" of the 1950s (which called for a massive counterattack against the USSR should the USSR attack a NATO member). Massive retaliation was implemented as a low-cost deterrence strategy, and the growth of NATO attention to "out-of area" operations in the 1970s and 1980s was motivated by unsecured Western vital economic interests in some regions.

Despite all economic and political difficulties within the alliance, the United States had succeeded in establishing and dominating a formidable international coalition based on superior economic and military might. The ability of the United States and NATO to concentrate greater economic weight and power contributed significantly to the final victory of the West in the cold war.

Since the 1990s, the NATO economic agenda has become an integral part of the alliance's broader approach to evolving security priorities. Developing closer security links with the new democracies (Latvia, Estonia, and Hungary) behind the old Iron Curtain (Eastern Europe under Soviet control), the United States and its allies set up several NATO programs to help these nations convert defense production and manage defense expenditures, thus contributing to the process of NATO expansion into Eastern Europe. NATO has also been involved in enforcing peace agreements in Bosnia since 1995. In 2002, NATO forces there were reduced from 18,000 to 12,000 as efforts to prevent continued conflict yielded positive results.

—*Peter Rainow*

References
Kaplan, Lawrence S. *NATO and the United States: The Enduring Alliance.* New York: Twayne Publishers, 1994.
Kunz, Diane B. *Butter and Guns: America's Cold War Economic Diplomacy.* New York: Free Press, 1997.
See also Volume 1: Cold War.

Northern Securities Company

A holding company charged with violating the Sherman Anti-Trust Act in 1901.

In early 1901, a battle erupted between E. H. Harriman, president of the Union Pacific Railroad, and James J. Hill, president of the Northern Pacific Railroad, for majority ownership control of the Northern Pacific. During April 1901 Edward Harriman, with the aid of investment bankers Otto Herman Kuhn, Solomon Loeb, and Jacob Schiff and silent partner financier William Rockefeller, began buying Northern Pacific stock. By early May, Hill had noticed the spikes in Northern Pacific prices and volume and took steps, with the aid of J. P. Morgan partner Roger Bacon, to secure control of the railroad. By May 8, 1901, Hill and Harriman had cornered the market on Northern Pacific stock and sent the market into a short-lived panic. Hill managed to gain majority ownership, but only barely.

To resolve the panic and retain his control over these western railroads, Hill created the Northern Securities Company (NSC) in November 1901. The Northern Pacific and Hill's other major lines—the Great Northern and the Chicago, Burlington, and Quincy Railroad—merged into the new holding company. As soon as the company formed, however, Minnesota Governor Samuel R. Van Sant charged that the owners had engaged in an anticompetitive merger and sought action in federal and state courts. In March 1902, U.S. Attorney General Philander Knox indicted the Northern Securities Company under the Sherman Anti-Trust Act, and the next month, the U.S. Circuit Court ruled in favor of the government. Hill appealed to the U.S. Supreme Court, which ruled on the case in March 1904. The Northern Securities Company followed a strategy similar to the one that prevailed in *United States v. E. C. Knight Co.* (Hill even hired John G. Johnson, Knight's lawyer. In the Knight case, the Supreme Court ruled that although the company controlled 98 percent of U.S. sugar production, it was not in violation of the Sherman Anti-Trust Act.) Northern Securities Company argued that the organization operated as a stock holding company and did not engage in commerce.

In a 5-to-4 decision, Justice John Harlan, writing for the Court, ruled that the mere existence of Northern Securities Company suppressed "competition between those companies" that formed it and that "to destroy or restrict free competition in interstate commerce was to restrain such commerce." The Court therefore ordered the company dissolved. Harlan had reversed the *Knight* decision and applied the Sherman Anti-Trust Act to companies instead of just labor unions such as the American Railways Union, where 100 percent of workers went out during the Pullman strike (1894).

The influence of the Northern Securities case, however, was short-lived. Beginning the following year with *Swift and Company v. United States,* Justice Oliver Wendell Holmes began further redefinition of the Sherman Anti-Trust Act that ultimately resulted in the "Rule of Reason"—defined in *Standard Oil Company v. United States* (1911)—for determining the benevolence or malevolence of monopolies.

—*Russell Douglass Jones*

References

Martin, Albro. *James J. Hill and the Opening of the Northwest.* New York: Oxford University Press, 1976.
Northern Securities Company v. United States, 193 U.S. 197 (1904).
Prager, Robin A. "The Effects of Horizontal Mergers on Competition: The Case of the Northern Securities Company." *Rand Journal of Economics,* vol. 23 (Spring 1992): 123–133.
See also Volume 1: Railroads; Trusts; *U.S. v. E. C. Knight Co.*

Northwest Ordinance (1787)

Act that allowed for the sale of lands under the Articles of Confederation.

In 1787, the Articles of Confederation Congress, which established the predecessor to the U.S. Constitution, faced the problem of settlement in the old northwest, opening the land north of the Ohio River and east of the Mississippi River to legal settlement under a specific plan engineered to allow the newly settled regions to mature into statehood after a period of territorial supervision. This plan—patterned after but more conservative than Thomas Jefferson's 1784 *Report of Government for Western Lands*—came at the insistence of lobbyists representing the Ohio Land Company, whose stockholders had deeply invested in speculation throughout the region.

Under the Northwest Ordinance, a territory operated initially under the leadership of a governor, secretary, and judges chosen by Congress. However, it could form an assembly and a congressionally named governing council when the free, male population of a territory reached 5,000. When the population reached 60,000, the territory could become a state equal with the original 13 states and could draft a constitution. This plan anticipated three to five new states, which eventually became Ohio, Illinois, Indiana, Michigan, and Wisconsin. The ordinance required the setting aside of land

in each region for schoolhouses, guaranteed the full exercise of constitutional freedoms, and, significantly, permanently forbade slavery in the expanding northwest. This ordinance was key to the orderly expansion of the United States and to the process by which new areas would become the equals of the original states.

—*Margaret Sankey*

References

Barrett, Jay Amos. *Evolution of the Ordinance of 1787.* New York: Arno Press, 1971.
Onuf, Peter S. *Statehood and Union: A History of the North-West Ordinance.* Bloomington: Indiana University Press, 1987.
Williams, Frederick D. *The Northwest Ordinance.* East Lansing: Michigan State University Press, 1989.
See also Volume 2: Land Policies; Volume 2 (Documents): Ordinance of the Northwest Territory.

NRA

See National Recovery Administration.

NTIA

See National Telecommunications and Information Administration.

NTIS

See National Technical Information Service.

Nullification Crisis (1832–1833)

The first serious confrontation between a federal law and states' rights since the crisis over the passing and enforcement of the Sedition Act, 1798–1801.

The confrontation of President Andrew Jackson with Vice President John C. Calhoun's defiant states' rights resistance to the enforcement of a federal tariff in South Carolina was the direct result of the presidential campaign of 1828. In this campaign, the Democrats planned to pass a tariff bill in the House of Representatives that had import duties so high on certain products vital to New England textile factories that Northern senators would defeat the bill. The plan to embarrass President John Quincy Adams backfired when Senator Daniel Webster of Massachusetts caught on to the scheme and convinced other Northern senators to join him in approving the bill. The resulting Tariff of 1828, known as the Tariff of Abominations, imposed a tariff wall of 41 percent, almost doubling the protective duties on the South, which then experienced severe economic difficulties trading with Great Britain because of the increased duties.

Although Calhoun hoped to negotiate an acceptable plan to lower the tariff from within the administration, he secretly wrote a states' rights tract against it. He sent the tract, called the *South Carolina Exposition and Protest,* to the South Carolina legislature, which adopted it December 19, 1828. Later, when President Jackson found out that his vice president had written what he considered a treasonous publication, he forced Calhoun to resign the vice presidency, the first man ever to do so. After his 1832 resignation, Calhoun returned to South Carolina, where the state legislature chose him as a state senator in the 1832 elections.

During the fall of 1832, the legislature called for a special convention to meet in the city of Columbia to adopt measures to resist the tariff. On November 24, this convention adopted the Ordinance of Nullification and declared the tariff null and void in South Carolina. The ordinance forbade any appeal to the federal courts and required all state officials to swear an oath to support the ordinance or resign. It declared that if the federal government attempted to collect the tariff, South Carolina would secede from the Union. President Jackson issued a "December proclamation" that denounced nullification and condemned disunion as treason. He sent General Winfield Scott to take command of federal troops in South Carolina and dispatched the navy to Charleston's harbor. Congress backed the president's threat to use military force against the "nullifiers" by passing the Force Bill.

Meanwhile, as Calhoun realized that other states had failed to support nullification, he returned to the nation's capital to arrange a compromise. Meeting with Henry Clay, Speaker of the House of Representatives, and others, he helped draft a new tariff bill that President Jackson signed on March 1, 1833. Called the Compromise Tariff, it provided for a gradual reduction of the tariff over a ten-year period to reach an overall rate of 20 percent, essentially the level of the first protective tariff of 1816. South Carolina accepted the compromise and rescinded the Ordinance of Nullification, and at the same time the legislature nullified the Force Bill. The Compromise Tariff ended the nullification crisis. This threat of secession was a precedent for the Civil War, in which states' rights was the primary issue, more important than slavery.

—*Robert P. Sutton*

References

Ellis, Richard E. *The Union at Risk: Jacksonian Democracy, States' Rights, and the Nullification Crisis.* New York: Oxford University Press, 1987.

Freehling, William W. *Prelude to Civil War: The Nullification Movement in South Carolina 1816–1832.* New York: Harper and Row, 1966.

Peterson, Merrill D. *Olive Branch and Sword: The Compromise of 1833.* Baton Rouge: Louisiana State University Press, 1982.

See also Volume 1: Clay, Henry; Jackson, Andrew; *South Carolina Exposition and Protest.*

NWLB

See National War Labor Board.

NYSE

See New York Stock Exchange.

OAS

See Organization of American States.

Occupational Safety and Health Act of 1970 (OSHA)

Also known as the Williams-Steiger Act, intended "to assure safe and healthful working conditions for working men and women."

The Occupational Safety and Health Act (OSHA) established three permanent federal agencies: the Occupational Safety and Health Administration (OSHA) to set and enforce standards, the National Institute for Occupational Safety and Health to conduct research on workplace hazards, and the Occupational Safety and Health Review Commission (OSHRC) to adjudicate enforcement challenges.

Factory inspection laws passed in a handful states in the last quarter of the nineteenth century provided the historical roots of OSHA. The first of these, enacted in Massachusetts in 1871, mandated the use of guards on machine belts, gears, and shafts; required the construction of adequate fire exits; and provided for public inspectors.

A broader but still limited commitment to workplace standards developed later during the passage of New Deal legislation including the National Recovery Act (1933) and the National Fair Labor Standards Act (1938). The need for workplace standards became clear because the patchwork of local inspection laws and state-based workers' compensation programs established in the Progressive Era at the beginning of the twentieth century, when reform-minded individuals attempted to address problems in society, had provided uneven and often inadequate protection. The Social Security Act of 1935 allowed the federal Public Health Service to underwrite state-based industrial health programs; the Walsh-Healey Public Contracts Act of 1936 enabled the Department of Labor to set standards for federal contract workers; and the Fair Labor Standards Act of 1938 empowered the Department to bar minors from "dangerous occupations."

The eventual OSHA reflects the turmoil of the 1960s.

Willard Wirtz, the secretary of labor in President Lyndon B. Johnson's administration, compared American casualties in Vietnam and in the workplace and, in remarks before a 1968 Congressional hearing, claimed that three out of four new entrants into the labor force would suffer work-related injuries at some point in their lives. President Johnson himself would describe the increased rate and seriousness of these "casualties" as "the shame of a modern industrial nation": at the time he spoke, in 1968, the annual number of deaths on the job had increased to 14,000, with another 2.2 million injured or made ill. The administration's own proposal, soon introduced as legislation, faced considerable opposition in Congress and from business, and it never reached a vote. Organized labor, on the other hand, would later oppose the Nixon administration's initial proposal. The bill that President Richard Nixon signed into law on December 29, 1970, functioned as a compromise of sorts between Senator Harrison Williams's (D–New Jersey) proposal (almost identical to the earlier Johnson plan) and Representative William Steiger's (R–New Jersey) more conservative plan.

OSHA published its first standards, which included permissible exposure limits (PELs) for more than 400 toxins, in 1971. This list included the asbestos PEL still in effect, for example, as well as the benzene PEL that the Supreme Court voided in 1980. The 1978 PEL for cotton dust that all but eliminated cases of "brown lung" remains one of OSHA's most important achievements. The 1978 and 1995 standards for lead, the 1991 standards for blood-borne pathogens, and the ergonomics standards issued in 2000 despite Congressional opposition—and repealed in 2001—are other well-known examples.

Other milestones include the defeat of the proposed OSHA Improvements Act in 1980, introduced by Senator Richard Schweiker (R-Pennsylvania), which would have restricted OSHA's inspection powers; the $1.4 million fine imposed on Union Carbide in 1986 for "egregious violations" at its plant in Institute, West Virginia, the first application of the "instance-by-instance" rule; IMC Fertilizer's $11.3 million fine in 1991, the largest ever imposed; and the Maine Top 2000 program initiated in 1993, a successful example of

OSHA's current emphasis on compliance assistance in high-risk industries.

OSHA assumed the transfer of workplace regulation to the states over time and provided for partial funding of state agencies that met federal guidelines. OSHA approved the first three state plans soon after Congress passed the act and issued its first "final approvals," which relinquished federal enforcement powers, in 1984. However, three decades after the act became law, only 24 comprehensive state plans exist. The California state legislature ended the largest state plan, CalOSHA, in 1987.

Since 1971, the number of workplace fatalities has decreased 60 percent, and the rate of injuries and illnesses has fallen 40 percent. OSHA has few inspectors, and the penalties for individual violations remain small. Fewer than 4,000 inspectors cover almost six million eligible establishments and, despite the previous cumulative penalties, until 1990 the maximum fine for a serious violation was just $1,000, after which it increased to $7,000. On the other hand, empirical evidence exists that OSHA's current focus on high-risk occupations and workplaces, its emphasis on compliance assistance and other forms of partnership, and its judicious use of VPPs or "voluntary protection programs"—which promote effective worksite-based safety and health—have proven successful.

—*Peter Hans Matthews*

References
Fleming, Susan Hall. "OSHA at 30." *Job Safety and Health Quarterly,* vol. 12 (Spring 2001): 23–32.
Gray, Wayne B., and Carol Adaire Jones. "Are OSHA Health Inspections Effective? A Longitudinal Study of the Manufacturing Sector." *Review of Economics and Statistics,* vol. 73 (August 1991): 504–508.
Lofgren, Don J. *Dangerous Premises: An Insider's View of OSHA Enforcement.* Ithaca: ILR Press, 1989.
Weil, David. "If OSHA Is So Bad, Why Is Compliance So Good?" *Rand Journal of Economics,* vol. 27 (Autumn 1996): 618–640.
See also Volume 2: Labor.

Office of Price Administration (OPA)

One of several federal agencies created during World War II to meet the exigencies of war production and to regulate the wartime economy.

Congress charged the Office of Price Administration (OPA) with the prevention of inflation. Near full employment achieved by war mobilization and the resulting extra earnings increased Americans' purchasing power, and the scarcity of goods available for civilian consumption added to this inflationary pressure. The federal government tried to offset the potentially baneful effects of the war-induced economic boom by several means. Alongside the indirect strategy of increased taxation, the administration of President Franklin D. Roosevelt adopted a set of policies to control wages and prices directly. In January 1942, Roosevelt signed the Emergency Price Control Act (later superseded by the Price Control Act of October 1942) and established the OPA

by executive order. Leon Henderson, an economist and Securities Exchange commissioner since 1939, became the OPA's inaugural administrator. Prentiss Brown (1943) and Chester Bowles (1944 to 1946) succeeded him in the position. In April 1942, the OPA issued the General Maximum Price Regulation policy (commonly known as "General Max"), which made prices charged as of March 1942 the ceiling prices for most commodities and consumer goods. Residential rents also came under the OPA's jurisdiction. At the peak of the OPA's price control program, the government froze approximately 90 percent of retail prices. The OPA also retained the power to ration scarce goods to civilian consumers. Items rationed by the OPA included tires, automobiles, sugar, gasoline, fuel oil, coffee, meats, and processed foods. The OPA received credit for the relative stability of consumer prices in the United States during the war years. With the end of World War II, rationing ended and price controls gradually disappeared. The OPA itself dissolved in 1947. Although most of the OPA-enforced controls ended after the war, the concept of greater government regulation of the economy survived into peacetime.

—*Sayuri Shimizu*

References
Campbell, Ballard C. *The Growth of American Government.* Bloomington: Indiana University Press, 1995.
Sparrow, Bartholomew H. *From the Outside In.* Princeton, NJ: Princeton University Press, 1996.
See also Volume 1: Roosevelt, Franklin D.

Office of Production Management (OPM)

Agency responsible for coordinating government purchases and wartime production.

As a result of the proliferation of economic agencies during World War II, the size of the federal bureaucracy nearly quadrupled. Frequent organizational changes and overlapping jurisdictional claims engendered numerous interagency conflicts. In January 1941, President Franklin D. Roosevelt established the Office of Production Management (OPM) to centralize direction of federal procurement programs and quasi-war production (that is, production taking place prior to the formal declaration of war). Under the executive order establishing the OPM, the armed services and the War Department cleared all contracts above $500,000 with the OPM's Division of Purchases. The OPM also spread government procurement contracts as widely as possible to alleviate the hardships of the small businesses whose peacetime lines of production had been either curtailed or prohibited. The armed services promoted subcontracting of government procurement by primary contractors (mostly large manufacturers) to small businesses. For this purpose, the OPM created the Defense Contract Service in February 1941 and established field offices in the Federal Reserve banks. The perceived interference by civilian officers of the OPM in military procurement elicited frequent protests from the military. The OPM's indirect involvement in government procurement programs in a supervisory capacity represented a model collaboration between the public and private sectors that contrasted with the model of the War Finance Committee, whose members (officials from the Department of the Treasury) worked directly with business and financial leaders in the sale of bonds.

In January 1942, about a month after the United States had formally entered World War II, Roosevelt issued Executive Order No. 9040, creating the War Production Board (WPB) to supersede the OPM. The WPB's chair, Donald Nelson, received sweeping powers over the economic life of the nation—now on an official war footing—to convert and expand the peacetime economy to maximum wartime production.

—*Sayuri Shimizu*

References

Campbell, Ballard C. *The Growth of American Government.* Bloomington: Indiana University Press, 1995.

Sparrow, Bartholomew H. *From the Outside In.* Princeton, NJ: Princeton University Press, 1996.

See also Volume 1: Roosevelt, Franklin D.

Office of War Mobilization (OWM)

An executive "super agency" created in 1943 to more effectively coordinate America's industrial and economic mobilization efforts during World War II.

On May 27, 1943, President Franklin D. Roosevelt issued an executive order establishing the Office of War Mobilization (OWM). Roosevelt took this action because many of the federal agencies that had been created to prepare America's resources for war were frequently at odds with each other and plagued by waste, inefficiency, and political self-interest. Realizing that he needed to reorganize America's entire mobilization effort into one strong agency, the president gave the OWM and its director, James F. Byrnes, considerable authority over America's wartime economy, so much so that people routinely called Byrnes the "assistant president."

However, unlike the directors of past mobilization agencies, Byrnes, who had served as a senator from South Carolina and Supreme Court justice before becoming director of the OWM, had extraordinary political and administrative skills. These skills allowed Byrnes to work with other agencies and played a large part in the success of the OWM. Byrnes ensured that the OWM did not encroach on the jurisdiction of other agencies or become too involved in the small details of wartime production and procurement. Instead he chose to set larger national goals and coordinate the activities of his subordinate agencies via the larger and stronger OWM.

Primarily because of the efforts of the OWM, American wartime production rose steadily after mid-1943, so that by 1944 the United States was producing 60 percent of all Allied munitions and 40 percent of the world's arms. The OWM formally ended in October 1944 when Congress converted it into the Office of War Mobilization and Reconversion (OWMR). Unlike the OWM, which helped mobilize America's resources for war, the OWMR was responsible for returning the United States to a peacetime economy.

—*David W. Waltrop*

References

Somers, Herman M. *Presidential Agency: The Office of War Mobilization and Reconversion.* New York: Greenwood Press, 1969.

See also Volume 1: Roosevelt, Franklin D.; World War II.

Oil

Any of a number of greasy combustible substances that are not soluble in water—a vital economic and strategic commodity.

Oil was the energy source that enabled the internal combustion engine to revolutionize industry, society, and the conduct of warfare in the twentieth century. Control of oil became a primary element of the national strategies of the great powers—the United States, Great Britain, France, Germany, and Russia—after 1900 and underpinned American hegemony after 1945.

Drilling first recovered subsurface oil in Pennsylvania in 1859. Until the late 1800s oil was primarily refined into kerosene, which was used for illumination. John D. Rockefeller's Standard Oil Company ruthlessly undercut competitors, and by 1880 Standard Oil controlled 90 percent of domestic production and 90 to 95 percent of refining capacity. Standard established a trust, or monopoly, to manage its domination of American oil production and distribution, but competition soon arose from new companies in Russia, Indonesia, and Texas. Legal challenges dissolved the trust in 1911 into 11 major companies: Standard Oil Company of New York, Atlantic Refining, Standard Oil of New Jersey, Standard Oil of Ohio, Standard Oil of Kentucky, Standard Oil of Indiana, Standard Oil Company of Louisiana, Waters-Pierce, Standard Oil of Nebraska, Continental Oil Company (Conoco), and Standard Oil of California (Socal). In addition, another 24 minor companies were spun off of Standard Oil, most of them either pipeline companies or tank lines.

Electricity replaced kerosene lamps after the 1880s, but internal combustion engines created a new market for oil in the 1890s. In 1911, Britain's Royal Navy converted to oil propulsion, and other navies and commercial fleets followed suit. Oil permitted at-sea refueling and greater speed and range than coal. The British government purchased 51 percent of the Anglo-Persian Company (later British Petroleum, or BP) to ensure an independent oil supply. World War I showed that future warfare would lavishly consume oil, and controlling oil became a major strategic objective. From 1918 until 1922, Britain and France dismembered the Ottoman Empire, installed client regimes (regimes they controlled) throughout the Middle East, and divided the region's oil.

Private ownership of automobiles exploded worldwide after 1920, and American oil production increased 430 percent from 1910 to 1930. Discoveries of large oil reserves in California, Oklahoma, Venezuela, and Mexico in the 1920s and in Kuwait and Saudi Arabia in the 1930s ensured that gasoline remained abundant and cheap. In 1928, the major oil companies created an informal global cartel to fix prices and allocate production quotas.

Oil decisively affected the course and outcome of World War II, which was characterized by vastly greater use of mechanized forces and aviation than World War I. Germany strove to capture Soviet oilfields and develop synthetic fuels, while Allied bombers attacked German oil production. America supplied 80 percent of Japan's oil until July 1941, when the American oil embargo forced Japan to enter the war with the goal of seizing the Indonesian oilfields. Fuel shortages seriously hampered Axis operations after 1944, and Allied access to U.S. oil ensured the ultimate victory of the Allies.

Rapid postwar economic growth required new sources of supply. Between 1945 and 1956, America replaced British influence in the Middle East, using cheap oil from huge new Middle Eastern fields to fuel postwar recovery and keeping Europe and Japan in the anti-Soviet camp through economic aid. World oil production increased nearly eightfold between 1940 and 1970 as industries converted from coal to oil power and suburban consumers bought automobiles and plastic products (plastic is an oil-based synthetic material). The dollar's role as an international currency (many commodities, including oil, were priced in dollars) and the dominant position of American oil companies were important sources of American economic power from 1945 until 1970.

Oil surpluses mounted in the 1960s with new discoveries in Libya and Nigeria, but by 1970, cheap oil no longer served American interests. Indeed, President Richard Nixon hoped to employ oil price increases to derail economic integration of European nations and brake post–World War II German and Japanese economic growth. Thus, the U.S. government restrained competition among oil companies by preventing other countries from raising their prices, and it refused to back the companies that opposed demands by the Organization of Petroleum Exporting Countries (OPEC) for higher prices and greater royalties. The 1973 Yom Kippur War and resulting oil embargo triggered a sharp price increase, but Germany and Japan compensated for higher energy costs with accelerated export-led growth throughout the 1970s. Prices jumped temporarily again after the 1979 Iranian revolution, but North Sea, Mexican, and Nigerian oil soon offset the loss of Iranian production. Oil prices plunged in the 1980s, partly because the administration of President Ronald Reagan sought to bankrupt the Soviet Union, which depended heavily on oil revenues. Prices spiked again after Iraq invaded Kuwait in 1990, but increased Saudi production stabilized the situation. The second Gulf War has reduced U.S. reliance on Saudi oil.

Global energy demand should double from 2002 to 2020, mainly because of Asian economic growth. Expanding production to stabilize prices may prove impossible, and therefore alternative energy sources should become increasingly cost-effective. Environmental concerns, particularly those relating to emissions of carbon dioxide, are certain to affect the industry significantly. Some analysts argue that world oil production will peak as soon as 2004, although the U.S. Geological Survey expects production to peak after 2037.

—*James D. Perry*

References

Blair, John M. *The Control of Oil.* New York: Pantheon, 1976.

Goralski, Robert, and Russell Freeburg. *Oil and War.* New York: William Morrow, 1987.

Sampson, Anthony. *The Seven Sisters.* New York: Viking, 1975.

Thornton, Richard C. *The Nixon-Kissinger Years.* New York: Paragon, 1989.

———. *The Carter Years.* New York: Paragon, 1991.

Yergin, Daniel. *The Prize: The Epic Quest for Oil, Money, and Power.* New York: Simon and Schuster, 1991.

See also Volume 1: Aviation; Oil Embargoes; Organization of Petroleum Exporting Countries; Rockefeller, John D.; Standard Oil; World War I; World War II.

Oil Embargoes

Action in which oil producers cut supplies to oil consumers in order to influence consumers' conduct.

Oil embargoes occur when producers cut supplies to consumers in order to influence the consumers' conduct. Oil embargoes are most effective when the victim heavily depends on a few producers and cannot increase domestic production or find alternative suppliers. Major embargoes occurred in 1941, 1956, 1967, and 1973.

In the 1930s, Japan imported some 80 percent of its oil from the United States. Japanese aggression in Asia raised the question of whether the United States should embargo this oil. President Franklin D. Roosevelt understood that an embargo would precipitate Japanese seizure of Indonesian oilfields, and he wanted to avoid this. But the situation changed in June 1941 when Germany invaded the USSR. Roosevelt knew the Japanese were debating an attack on Siberia, which might cause a Soviet collapse. To prevent this, he embargoed oil exports to Japan in July 1941. This embargo had the desired effect—Japan did not attack Siberia, and the USSR held out against Germany. In December 1941, Japan attacked the United States after the United States placed an embargo on oil and scrap metal to Japan.

In 1956, Britain and France attacked Egypt in order to regain control of the Suez Canal, the conduit for oil moving by ship from the Middle East to the Mediterranean. General Abdul Nasser of Egypt had nationalized the canal zone, denying Britain and France easy access to Middle Eastern oil. Saudi Arabia embargoed Britain and France, and Kuwait cut production. The British and French desperately needed American oil to prevent winter shortages, but President Dwight D. Eisenhower refused to provide emergency supplies until the two countries withdrew from the canal zone. This embargo and the financial pressure quickly induced a humiliating Anglo-French retreat.

In 1967, after Egypt forced the withdrawal of U.N. troops along its border with Israel and Egypt and Jordan signed a defense pact and began mobilizing troops,) Israel initiated a pre-emptive strike against Egypt, Syria, and Jordan in a brief military conflict that lasted for only five days and occupied the

Sinai Peninsula, the Gaza Strip, the West Bank, and the Golan Heights. In response, Arab oil producers embargoed the United States, Great Britain, and West Germany. However, the United States, Venezuela, Iran, and Indonesia increased production, and new supertankers quickly redistributed these supplies to prevent shortage. Arab oil producers lost significant oil revenues without influencing Western policy, and within a few months the Arabs rescinded their embargo.

In October 1973, Egypt and Syria attacked Israel, which they wished to see destroyed and replaced with an Arab state. Ten Arab oil producers decided to cut production 5 percent per month until Israel withdrew from territories it occupied in 1967, and these producers embargoed the United States, Portugal, the Netherlands, and South Africa. The oil embargo did not lead to any Israeli withdrawals, but it did produce a sharp price increase that persisted even after the embargo was lifted in March 1974.

For much of the twentieth century, American domination of world oil production and distribution enabled it to embargo others (1941, 1956) and to avoid embargoes on itself and its allies (1967). America's position weakened after 1970, but political influence in the Middle East has thus far mitigated the theoretical vulnerability to embargo. In 2003, President George W. Bush proposed a "Middle East map" that would allow for the creation of a Palestinian state that would coexist with Israel. A peaceful resolution of the Israeli-Palestinian problem would increase American influence in the Middle East, a development that may or may not lead to greater access to oil supplies or the control of oil prices.

—*James D. Perry*

References
Bromley, Simon. *American Hegemony and World Oil.* University Park: Pennsylvania State University Press, 1991.
Heinrichs, Waldo. *Threshold of War.* Oxford: Oxford University Press, 1990.
Yergin, Daniel. *The Prize: The Epic Quest for Oil, Money, and Power.* New York: Simon and Schuster, 1991.
See also Volume 1: Oil; Organization of Petroleum Exporting Countries; World War II.

OPA
See Office of Price Administration.

OPEC
See Organization of Petroleum Exporting Countries.

Open Door Notes (1899, 1900)
Diplomatic communications of the United States with European nations proposing an Open Door (free trade) policy in China.

Addressed, respectively, in 1899 and 1900 by U.S. Secretary of State John Hay, diplomatic notes known as the Open Door notes founded the Open Door policy that Washington pursued toward China during the first half of the twentieth century. The Open Door notes influenced U.S. relations with other imperial powers in East Asia until World War II.

While the United States was rising as a major world competitor during the late nineteenth century, American economic interests expanded in Asia. By taking over the Philippines in the Spanish-American War of 1898, the United States established a safeguard for U.S. trade in Asia and convenient proximity for American business to increase its commercial gains in China. A densely populated country of many millions of people, China was the largest potential market for American goods and investment. But the United States faced the danger of being frozen out of the Chinese market, given the separate and exclusive spheres of influences already carved out by Western powers and Japan. To preserve American interests without risking conflict, Hay delivered identical notes to England, Germany, Russia, France, Japan, and Italy on September 6, 1899, asking them to maintain their spheres of influence available to other nations, to respect China's tariff autonomy in all spheres and tariff duties indiscriminately on all foreign goods, to collect nondiscriminatory harbor dues on ships of other nationalities, and to impose fair railroad rates within the spheres. The major powers greeted the note with polite evasion but had to acknowledge a second Open Door note that Hay issued in July 1900, when the United States joined an international expeditionary force to quell the Boxer Rebellion (an antiforeigner movement) and thereby gained a voice in the settlement of the uprising. Hay's second note underscored the basic principles of the 1899 message but called for the major powers' commitment to uphold China's administrative and territorial integrity to prevent the country's dismemberment. Although acquiring an access to its China trade, the United States remained indisposed to backing the Open Door policy with the use of force.

—*Guoqiang Zheng*

References
Beisner, Robert L. *From the Old Diplomacy to the New 1865–1900.* Wheeling, IL: Harlan Davidson, 1986.
See also Volume 1: Boxer Rebellion; China.

OPM
See Office of Production Management.

Orders in Council (January 7, 1807; November 11, 1807)
England's response to Napoleon's Continental System, banning neutral trade with ports controlled by Napoleon and blockading trade with England.

On November 21, 1806, Napoleon issued the Berlin Decree, which placed England in a state of blockade and prohibited it from trading all British goods on the European continent. The decree played a key role in Napoleon's Continental System, by which the French emperor hoped to cut England off economically from the rest of Europe. On January 7, 1807, the British government responded with the first of two important decrees that prohibited neutral ships from carrying goods between ports within Napoleon's empire. Britain also declared that the Royal Navy would board any ship suspected of carrying on trade with French ports. The British would confiscate the contents of these ships and sell them as prizes of war.

Despite Britain's threats, ships from neutral nations, including the United States, continued to carry on trade between European ports controlled by Napoleon. England responded with a second important decree on November 11, 1807, that banned all neutral trade with any port on the European continent. All neutral ships trading with the French empire would be subject to searches and the confiscation of their goods. Napoleon responded with the Milan Decree on December 17, 1807, which declared that the French navy would capture all ships trading with England or its colonies and confiscate their goods.

During the next five years, England and France captured hundreds of American ships on the high seas. After British manufacturers protested the loss of American markets because of these measures, Parliament finally repealed the Orders in Council on June 23, 1812. However, the action came too late to restore peace with the Americans. The United States had already declared war on Great Britain five days before the repeal. Interference with American shipping along with Britain's apparent support for Native American resistance on the western frontier had led the Americans into the War of 1812.

—*Mary Stockwell*

References
Horsman, Reginald. *The Causes of the War of 1812.* New York: A. S. Barnes, 1962.
See also Volume 1: War of 1812.

Ordinance of 1785
America's first and most important land law.

As a result of the Treaty of Paris in 1783 between the United States and Great Britain, the United States of America came into possession of most of the land bounded on the east by the Appalachian Mountains and on the west by the Mississippi River. Congress soon began debating the best way to open this new western land for settlement. Many Northerners argued that the township system common in New England provided the best model to use. This method blocked out orderly sections of land for settlement by whole communities. Southerners called for a more individualistic system of random boundaries common throughout their region of the country.

Congress struck a balance in the Ordinance of 1785. This first land law of the new American nation ordered western lands to be sold in townships that were six miles square. Each township would be subdivided into 36 one-mile square sections. Every section would contain 640 acres. Alternating townships would be sold whole or in sections. Congress reserved four sections in every township for the future use of the American government, and it also set one section (section 16) aside in every township for education. Land would be sold at public auction in all the states for a minimum price of one dollar per acre. The sale of the land would begin in the Ohio Territory at the point where Pennsylvania's southwestern border ran north and intersected the Ohio River. A line drawn west from this point would become the northern boundary of the first seven columns of townships, known as the Seven Ranges.

At first glance, the law seemed to favor wealthy speculators and land companies, because 640 acres was the smallest tract of land open for sale and was more land than most farmers could afford. But in the long run, the law helped small farmers by opening the West for settlement in an orderly fashion under the rule of law.

—*Mary Stockwell*

References
Billington, Ray Allen. *Westward Expansion: A History of the American Frontier.* New York: Macmillan, 1967.
See also Volume 2: Land Policies.

Organization of American States (OAS)
Multilateral organization created in 1948 that settles inter-American disputes and promotes regional economic development in the Western Hemisphere.

On April 30, 1948, representatives of 20 Latin American nations and the United States met in Bogotá, Colombia, and created the Organization of American States (OAS). Members acknowledged that nations in the Western Hemisphere had common goals such as trade and security. They also pledged respect for the sovereignty of nations in the region. Since the founding of the organization, the OAS has expanded to 35 members and includes most Caribbean nations and Canada.

The OAS has a variety of functions. It provides a forum for member nations to air differences, denounces human rights violations in the Western Hemisphere, combats poverty in the region, and encourages inter-American trade. With the beginning of President John F. Kennedy's Alliance for Progress in 1961 and its promotion of economic progress in the Americas, the OAS became heavily involved in the economic affairs of member states and began to sponsor technical cooperation programs between them. In 1986 the OAS further expanded its responsibilities with the creation of the Inter-American Drug Abuse Control Commission (CICAD), which has the auspicious goal of ending the problem of illegal drugs in the Americas and has made some progress, although it has not fully succeeded. Since the adoption of the North American Free Trade Agreement (NAFTA) by the United States, Mexico, and Canada, the OAS has heavily promoted the establishment of free trade agreement for the Western Hemisphere known as the Free Trade Area of the

Americas (FTAA). Negotiations on the FTAA began in 1998 and have yet to be concluded.

—*John K. Franklin*

References

Gilderhus, Mark. *The Second Century: U.S.–Latin American Relations since 1889.* New York: Scholastic Resources, 1999.

See also Volume 1: Free Trade Area of the Americas; North American Free Trade Agreement.

Organization of Petroleum Exporting Countries (OPEC)

Organization of oil-exporting countries founded in direct response to a sudden price cut announced by several Western international oil companies.

The Organization of Petroleum Exporting Countries (OPEC) became the first in a series of steps by oil-producing nations to win greater control over oil production and pricing mechanisms. Original OPEC members included Iran, Iraq, Kuwait, Saudi Arabia, and Venezuela; all are still members today. The membership gradually expanded to include the United Arab Emirates, Algeria, Ecuador, Indonesia, Libya, Nigeria, and Qatar. An abundance of oil on the world market and difficulty in maintaining discipline within the ranks (especially concerning price controls) initially limited OPEC's effectiveness. By the early 1970s, market circumstances more than organizational and political prowess enhanced OPEC's influence. Increased worldwide demand for petroleum greatly increased OPEC's ability to influence oil pricing. An oil embargo by OPEC against the United States and Western European countries in response to the support of Israel by the United States during the 1973 Arab-Israeli War made OPEC a household name throughout the industrialized world. Contrary to popular myth, the 1973 oil embargo and production cutbacks took no oil off the market but rather provoked a wave of speculative buying of oil futures contracts that pegged oil prices at a specific level. This phenomenon demonstrated that a significant part of OPEC's power lay not in its members' oil reserves but in the public's perceptions of future circumstances in the Middle East. Suffering from recessions driven in part by greatly increased energy costs, the world's industrialized nations made substantial infrastructure improvements that lowered their energy demands. Moreover, OPEC-led increases in the price of oil fueled a worldwide quest for oil resources beyond OPEC's control. Ironically, high oil prices underwrote costly oil exploration and encouraged the expansion of oil production in Alaska, the Gulf of Mexico, and the North Sea. Ultimately, this increase in supply, together with increased fuel efficiencies, produced the 1986 oil price "collapse," which demonstrated that oil was simply one more commodity in the global economy and was beyond the control of a cartel. OPEC remains an important and influential actor in the world oil market, but it recognizes that its long-term health and its financial benefit to its constituent members depend on two critical factors. First, OPEC seeks to work cooperatively with competitors beyond its ranks, most notably a revived Russian oil industry. Second, OPEC recognizes that the economic success of the industrialized nations relies on its product, and it therefore works to maintain oil price stability. In this respect, OPEC has become a fully integrated member of the global economy.

—*Robert Rook*

References

Skeet, Ian. *OPEC: Twenty-five Years of Prices and Politics.* Cambridge: Cambridge University Press, 1988.

Yergin, Daniel. *The Prize: The Epic Quest for Oil, Money, and Power.* New York: Simon and Schuster, 1991.

See also Volume 1: Oil.

OSHA

See Occupational Safety and Health Act of 1970.

OWM

See Office of War Mobilization.

P

Pan American Union

Agency created by U.S. initiative in the late nineteenth century to encourage economic and cultural ties among Western Hemisphere nations, absorbed in 1958 by the Organization of American States.

The Pan American Union was initially created as a result of the Pan American Conference held in Washington, D.C., in 1889 and 1890. On April 14, 1890, the conference, presided over by U.S. Secretary of State James G. Blaine, set up the International Union of American Republics (referred to as the Pan American Union). The Commercial Bureau of American Republics was established as the central office of the International Union of American Republics in Washington, D.C. The Commercial Bureau of American Republics collected, exchanged, and disseminated economic, commercial, and juridical information—particularly on customs tariffs (which affect international trade), official trade and transport regulations, and statistics of production and commerce—for each country of the Western Hemisphere. The Washington conference placed the Commercial Bureau of American Republics (which was financed by annual contributions from all member countries according to their population) under the immediate supervision of the U.S. government. Aiming to foster economic, social, and cultural cooperation in the Western Hemisphere and especially attempting to standardize and simplify inter-American trade, the Commercial Bureau of American Republics became instrumental in promoting U.S. trade expansion in the Western Hemisphere.

Beginning in 1896, the scope of activities of the Commercial Bureau of American Republics broadened from merely collecting commercial statistics to include practically all subjects relating to social and economic development in the Western Hemisphere. In 1901 the name of the bureau changed to the International Bureau of American Republics.

In 1910 the International Union of American Republics changed its name to the Union of American Republics, and the bureau's name changed again, this time to the Pan American Union. At a 1928 meeting in Havana, members signed the Convention on Pan American Union, which defined the union as a nonpolitical permanent body of the Pan American conferences administered by a secretary general and assistant secretary general and supervised by special ambassadors of American republics. Delegates to the meetings of the Pan American conferences created divisions to deal with foreign trade, financial and economic information, statistics, intellectual matters, agricultural cooperation, labor and social welfare, and juridical issues. The Pan American Union published a *Monthly Bulletin* as well as special reports and pamphlets in English, Spanish, and Portuguese.

The Pan American Union also performed a wide variety of general and technical services in connection with issues dealt with by the Pan American conferences—issues of common concern such as arbitration of financial claims; copyrights, patents, and trademarks; construction of an intercontinental railway; and cooperation for the protection of industry, agriculture, and commerce. The annual budget of the Pan American Union in the 1940s totaled $500 million (the United States supplied more than 50 percent of it). At their meeting in Bogotá in 1948, members of the Pan American Conference formed the Organization of American States (OAS) and made the Pan American Union its central administrative branch. By 1958 the Pan American Union had finally been transformed into the general secretariat of the OAS. During its history the Pan American Union contributed significantly to multilateral international economic and commercial cooperation and was an effective tool promoting U.S. economic and trade interests in the Western Hemisphere.

—*Peter Rainow*

References

Pan American Union. *In the Service of the Americas: Fiftieth Anniversary of the Pan American Union, April 14, 1940.* Washington, DC: Pan American Union, 1940.
Rowe, Leo Stanton. *The Pan American Union and the Pan American Conferences, 1890-1940.* Washington, DC: Pan American Union, 1940.
See also Volume 1: Organization of American States.

Panama and the Panama Canal

Nation located on Isthmus of Panama between South America and Central America; location of the Panama Canal connecting the Atlantic and Pacific Oceans.

American interest in a transisthmian route between the oceans to facilitate trade began in the early nineteenth century. In the 1850s, American investors built a railroad across Panama (then Colombian territory) to facilitate trade between the U.S. East Coast and the state of California, but many, wishing to avoid the expense of unloading and reloading freight, desired a canal through which ships could pass. The Spanish-American War convinced the American government of the need for a canal to move battleships from one ocean to another quickly, and the United States began discussions with Colombia about taking over a canal project abandoned by France in 1889. The discussions with Colombia deadlocked, and the United States aided a Panamanian revolution against Colombia in 1903 in an attempt to conclude negotiations and begin construction of the canal. After Panama had achieved independence in 1903, the United States negotiated a treaty that gave America the right "in perpetuity" to build and operate a canal in a 10-mile-wide strip of land across Panama. American construction on the canal began in 1904 and was completed in 1914.

With the construction of the canal, Panama became a virtual protectorate of the United States. Panama did not even have its own paper currency; instead, the U.S. dollar became Panama's official currency. American control of the canal and its profits chafed Panamanian nationalists, and obtaining a more equitable canal arrangement was a goal of Panamanian foreign policy throughout the twentieth century. In 1977, the administration of President Jimmy Carter finally negotiated a new treaty with Panama that provided for complete Panamanian control of the canal beginning on December 31, 1999, and it provided for regular payments from the United States to Panama for use of the canal in the intervening period.

The canal has dominated the Panamanian economy since its construction, but since the 1950s Panama has sought diversification. The establishment of the Colón Free Zone (CFZ) in 1953 allowed foreign traders to unload and repackage cargo without customs duties, allowing them to comply with various tariff restrictions of both their home country and foreign destinations. A state-owned corporation provides warehousing, assembly, transshipment, and other services to merchants that use the CFZ. Since the 1970s, Panama has also become an international banking center. The nation's stringent secrecy laws attracted large assets to Panama's offshore banks. These offshore banks have been the subject of much debate between the United States and Panama since the 1980s. The United States alleges that the banks are used to launder drug money (that is, to attribute illegally gained money to a legitimate business without verifying the money's source) and has pressured Panama to end its secrecy laws, but the Panamanian government fears that an end to secrecy laws will end the attraction of Panamanian banking.

The United States, citing concerns about drug trafficking and the lack of democracy under Manuel Noriega, who had assumed control of the military and the country in 1983, took action, both economically and militarily, against Panama. In March 1988, the United States froze Panamanian assets in U.S. banks, withheld monthly payments for use of the canal, and suspended trade preferences on Panamanian imports. These measures nearly destroyed the Panamanian economy, already weak from government mismanagement and still reliant on U.S. currency. The United States followed with an invasion of Panama in 1989. Noriega was deposed in 1989 and brought to the United States for trial on drug trafficking charges; he was convicted and sent to a federal prison. Mireya Elisa has been president of Panama since September 1, 1999. Panama's economy remained poor after American troops left, but with international aid from other countries such as China, it has slightly improved. Despite the invasion, the United States passed control of the canal to Panama as scheduled.

—*John K. Franklin*

References

LaFeber, Walter. *The Panama Canal.* Rev. ed. New York: Oxford University Press, 1989.

McCullough, David. *The Path between the Seas: The Creation of the Panama Canal, 1870–1914.* New York: Simon and Schuster, 1977.

See also Volume 1: Roosevelt, Theodore; Volume 2 (Documents): Panama Canal Treaty of 1903.

Panic of 1819

First of many financial crises that occurred in the United States.

After the War of 1812 ended, the nation experienced a period of unprecedented economic growth. Part of this growth can be attributed to the sale of goods to war-torn Europe. In addition, after 1816, a moderately protective tariff, the Tariff of 1816, was instituted to protect infant industry developing in England. The charter of the First Bank of the United States (the nation's first central bank) had lapsed in 1811, so state banks operated as the primary financial institutions. Instead of conducting transactions with payments being made using gold and silver currency (in specie), state banks issued paper currency, a practice quickly followed by corporations and individuals. When Congress chartered the Second Bank of the United States in 1816, the use of paper currency continued. In 1819 when Langdon Cheves became president of the Second Bank of the United States, his conservative financial policies forced state banks to resume specie payments. At the same time, the United States paid a large portion of the $15 million price for the Louisiana Purchase. The draining of the gold reserves forced the Bank of the United States to demand the redemption of state notes in gold—a demand with which the state banks could not comply. Consequently, the state banks were forced to call in the loans of customers, many of them farmers in the South and West who had recently expanded their landholdings as the price of cotton continued to climb. Just as the banks called in the notes, European nations dumped their surplus goods on the American market at below-cost prices.

The panic of 1819 resulted in a rapid decline in land prices, numerous bank failures, bankruptcies, and high unemployment. One estimate claimed that more than 1 million

Americans—nearly 10 percent—were out of work. Bankruptcy sales occurred daily, with debtors being sent to prison—1,800 in Philadelphia and 3,500 in Boston alone. Land prices dropped, and loans were called in early to protect the banks. Northerners wanted a higher tariff to solve the financial problem, whereas Southerners wanted free trade. Western farmers and speculators wanted the Second Bank of the United States to ease credit practices. The panic ended in 1822 with more than 3 million Americans adversely affected economically.

Although several factors converged to create the panic of 1819, most Americans, including Major General Andrew Jackson, blamed the Bank of the United States for the problem. Jackson's distrust of the institution would mean that it was not rechartered during his presidency (nor was it ever rechartered). That, in turn, resulted in a second crisis, the panic of 1837.

—*Cynthia Clark Northrup*

References

Hammond, Bray. *Banks and Politics in America from the Revolution to the Civil War.* Princeton, NJ: Princeton University Press, 1957.

Knox, John Jay. *A History of Banking in the United States.* New York: Bradford Rhodes, 1903.

Rothbard, Murray N. *The Panic of 1819: Reactions and Policies.* New York: Columbia University Press, 1962.

See also Volume 2: Banking.

Panic of 1837

Panic with its roots in the nation's early banking system.

The abrogation in 1811 of the charter of the First National Bank of the United States, in addition to the growth stimulated by the War of 1812, led to the emergence of "wildcat" banks throughout the United States. The enormous growth of these banks, despite the chartering of the Second National Bank of the United States in 1816, led to a necessary contraction of the money supply in 1819, which created a decade of financial distress. In 1829, President Andrew Jackson, who believed the Bank of the United States was unconstitutional, removed government deposits from its coffers and placed them in state banks. He then vetoed a bill to renew the national bank's charter, which was to have passed in 1836. State banks initiated unprecedented discount rates, many more wildcat banks came into business, and a pattern of unregulated financial speculation ensued. Foreign goods poured into the country and, more importantly, in an effort to expand the money supply and reduce interest rates, industries set up operations on government land paid for with worthless paper money not backed by gold or silver. By 1836, government land sales had increased tenfold from only five years earlier. The Treasury Department, beginning to see the writing on the wall, issued a "specie circular" stipulating that after August 15, 1836, purchasers of government lands had to pay in gold or silver. A disastrous chain reaction followed. Expected gold and silver payments failed to appear, banks called in their loans and denied further discounts, prices declined,

and property lost value. A large minority of banks—343 out of 850—closed throughout the country. The dam broke completely in April 1837 when, over three weeks, 250 business houses failed in the state of New York alone. Mercantile interests crashed throughout the country as farmers, artisans, and laborers all suffered the panic's consequences. Politically, the panic doomed President Martin Van Buren's chances for reelection. His decision not to aid the business community during the panic subjected him to full rounds of criticism, even from his fellow Democrats. In 1840, the Whigs, with William Henry Harrison as their presidential candidate, gained the executive office. Recovery did not appear on the horizon until 1842, when Congress passed a tariff bill adding a 30 percent ad valorem tax (that is, a tax based on a percentage of the value of the product) on most imports.

—*James E. McWilliams*

References

Rezneck, Samuel. *Business Depressions and Financial Panics: Essays in American Business and Economic History.* New York: Greenwood Press, 1968.

See also Volume 1: Van Buren, Martin.

Panic of 1873

The first financial depression in the post–Civil War period.

The most important event of President Ulysses S. Grant's second term was the panic of 1873, which precipitated a four-year financial depression that stagnated the nation's economy and brought an end to a stretch of uninterrupted economic growth that had lasted almost 35 years. The panic had its roots in postwar inflated prices and expansive business growth that fueled an unprecedented level of speculative activity. This growth and speculation evolved alongside a contracting supply of currency, and so the preconditions for a crash existed. On October 1, 1873, the crash occurred when the prominent banking firm Jay Cooke and Company failed suddenly. The Philadelphia company had financed the Northern Pacific Railroad and handled most of the government's loans during the Civil War, and it had stood at the head of great banking concerns throughout the nation. The financial ruin of Cooke and Company reverberated throughout the economy, throwing the country into a tailspin even worse than that caused by the panic of 1837. After the fall of the company, the New York Stock Exchange closed for ten days. The panic touched not only the wealthy: Nearly every American suffered because the panic impaired credit, added pressure to pay back debts, and exhausted savings. With the closing of factories and adoption of half-time employment, labor bore a particularly heavy burden. As unemployment surged and productivity came to a halt, the nation experienced a surge in crime and violent protests by workers. The panic of 1873 also had clear political consequences. As the depression intensified, it diverted the nation's attention away from Reconstruction of the South in the post–Civil War period and was key in the Republican loss of 77 seats in Congress in the 1874 congressional elections. With the natural contraction of high wartime prices to low peacetime prices, the economy could not recover until 1878, when capital gradually began to overcome its timidity about investing.

—*James E. McWilliams*

References
Rezneck, Samuel. *Business Depressions and Financial Panics: Essays in American Business and Economic History.* New York: Greenwood Press, 1968.
See also Volume 1: Railroads.

Panic of 1893

Economic depression, one of the two worst in American history.

By the early 1890s, the foreign markets for American goods diminished, and foreign investments in the United States also declined. In addition, agricultural debt and foreclosures on farm property led to a substantial reduction of the purchasing power of a significant portion of the American population. These conditions made the overexpansion of America's transportation and manufacturing industries an even greater problem. As a result of these developments, in one day in February 1893 investors dumped 1 million overvalued shares of the Philadelphia and Reading Railroad, causing its bankruptcy. Soon banks cut back on loans for investments in the railroad and construction industries. Concerned about overproduction in many industries, investors quickly sold stocks and other assets to buy gold. This run on gold rapidly depleted the reserves of the U.S. Treasury, already reduced by the Sherman Silver Purchase Act's requirement that the government buy four million ounces of silver a month at the market price. On April 22, 1893, for the first time since the 1870s, the gold reserve fell below $100 million, the amount that stood for the federal government's commitment to maintain the gold standard, in which U.S. currency was backed by gold. The news shattered confidence in the economy, and on May 5, 1893, the stock market crashed when stock prices plummeted rapidly. It was Wall Street's worst day before the Great Crash of 1929. Banks subsequently called in loans and dried up credit, which greatly contributed to 16,000 businesses going bankrupt by the end of 1893. Despite the calling in of loans, 500 banks also failed by the end of the year.

By 1897 more than one-fourth of America's railroad tracks operated under receivership, which is when companies are placed under the control of a receiver during bankruptcy proceedings, and were very profitably recombined into new companies by the large banking houses of New York City. Although records are incomplete, it seems that nearly 20 percent of laborers lost their jobs for a significant time between 1893 and 1897, as the nation suffered its worst economic depression to that point. Wage cuts and layoffs more than offset the declining living costs. But by early 1897 the economy had started to revive. Early in his presidency, William McKinley supported the Dingley Tariff, which raised duties to an all-time high to protect additional American industries and to limit supply in the economy. Moreover, McKinley reaffirmed America's commitment to the gold standard. The discovery of gold in Alaska and Australia (1870–1877 and 1886, respec-

tively), together with the development of a new cyanide process for extracting gold from ore, increased the world's supply of gold and made more money available for investment in the American economy. By the end of 1897 the depression had ended.

—*Steven E. Siry*

References
Welch, Richard E. *The Presidencies of Grover Cleveland.* Lawrence: University Press of Kansas, 1988.
See also Volume 1: Depression of the 1890s; Depressions; Dingley Tariff.

Panic of 1907

Monetary crisis leading to banking reforms.

Following the recovery from the depression (panic) of 1893, the U.S. economy went into a period of sustained growth maintained by speculation and investments in merging and expanding corporations. Although new discoveries of gold and improved extraction technologies had increased the currency supply, the supply by no means expanded as quickly as the economy. The currency was funded by transfers of gold from European banks, but European bankers—wary of this steady drain on their gold reserves—raised their interest rates in 1906, thus reversing the flow of gold. This flow reversal caused the stock market to climax and begin a decline. The falling stock market affected businesses' confidence, and production slowed. In the autumn of 1907, when the harvest came in, banks found themselves already at or near their reserve limits and could make few loans. Interest rates therefore rose. Public confidence in the faltering economy collapsed in October, and runs occurred on eight of New York City largest trust or holding companies (which controlled other companies): Knickerbocker, Trust Company of America, and Lincoln were the hardest hit. Trust companies failed because of their low reserve requirements and, because they operated outside of clearinghouse institutions (which processed bank checks), they had no "lender of last resort," a lender to which banks turn in difficult times when their reserves drop.

J. P. Morgan, the wealthiest banker in the United States, intervened and prevented failure of the trust companies by making short-term loans to them. Taking advantage of the situation, Morgan informed President Theodore Roosevelt that the situation would stabilize once he controlled the Tennessee Coal and Iron Company. Roosevelt assented and promised no antitrust investigation when Morgan's U.S. Steel purchased the Tennessee company in 1907.

As a consequence of the panic of 1907, Congress passed the Aldrich-Vreeland Act in 1908, which created a national currency association consisting of banks with minimum capital reserves of $5 million. In the event of another crisis, association banks could issue notes using the reserves as collateral. The Aldrich-Vreeland Act also established a commission to study the U.S. banking industry and to make recommendations for its reform. The commission recommended the formation of a central bank having regional reserve associations. President William Howard Taft took no action on the commission's recommendations. But President Woodrow Wilson, early in his administration, urged Congress to act, and the commission's plan became the basis for the Federal Reserve system in 1913.

The Federal Reserve system established a bank controlled by the central government that, through its control of its member banks' gold reserves, could control the currency supply. Using the gold as collateral, the Federal Reserve's central bank could issue notes that would serve as day-to-day currency.

—*Russell Douglass Jones*

References

Kindleberger, Charles. *Manias, Panics, and Crashes: A History of Financial Crises.* New York: Basic Books, 1978.

Moen, Jon, and Ellis W. Tallman. "The Bank Panic of 1907: The Role of Trust Companies." *Journal of Economic History,* vol. 52 (September 1992): 611–630.

See also Volume 1: Trusts.

Parity

The quality of being equal; term applied to farmers' purchasing power compared with an established base.

For a five-year period from August 1909 to July 1914, farmers enjoyed a "golden age of American agriculture" in which their purchasing power reached an all-time high because agricultural prices increased more than the cost of production. After World War I, however, farm prices dropped dramatically to approximately two-thirds of parity—the word means "the quality of being equal" and was used in this case to compare farmers' purchasing power against an established base. When Congress considered farm legislation during the 1920s—a period of depression for many American farmers—it used farmers' purchasing power during the previous golden age as referent for "agricultural parity." In 1927, congressional legislators proposed the McNary-Haugen farm plan, which resulted in five unsuccessful bills during the 1920s. The idea seemed simple at first (establishing a ratio between the cost of what farmers produced and what they consumed) but became extraordinarily complex and attracted opposition from a variety of sources. A major aspect of the plan was the establishment of a government export corporation to bring the domestic prices of major crops up to a "ratio price," defined as the general price level before World War I. An all-commodity index would compare the price of wheat, for example, before the war and then set a price goal in a select year that would lead to parity. This proposal did not pass.

After several unsuccessful attempts to pass farm legislation, the stock market crashed in 1929, leading to the election of Franklin D. Roosevelt to the presidency in 1932. Roosevelt attempted to address the issue of farm parity upon assuming office. Part of the purpose of the Agricultural Adjustment Act, which established farm relief in 1933 during the Great Depression, focused on restoring farm parity purchasing power by creating a supply-and-demand situation that would restore prices to the goal of parity. This act redefined parity prices, creating a more precise formula that included interest payments, farm estate taxes, freight charges, and commodity prices.

During World War II, a time of sharply increased agricultural production determined by global needs, the existing parity legislation limited food production. In 1948 a new parity formula established set parity prices for any agricultural production at an adjusted base price—a ratio based on the previous ten years' of prices (1938–1948) as compared with the period between 1910 and 1914 as a base price. In the mid-1970s the government based target prices (or parity) on an index of production costs—taxes, interest rates, wages, and other production costs—to establish an even better ratio of parity.

In the 1970s, the government encouraged farmers to expand production through the continuation of parity payments under the 1973 Amendment to the Agricultural Adjustment Act. By 1970 the economy had become stagnant and government spending had skyrocketed. President Ronald Reagan, in an effort to bring spending down, sought to eliminate the parity system, which cost the federal government more than $21.8 billion annually. The Agricultural and Food Act of 1981 eliminated parity goals, and farm prices fell below parity levels. The next year Congress passed the Omnibus Budget Reconciliation Act of 1982, which required a reduction of parity levels if farm prices rose. In 1990, subsidies were cut again to farmers, and parity has been reduced to 65 percent—down from 90 percent in the 1970s.

—*Lisa L. Ossian*

References

Benedict, Murray R. *Farm Policies of the United States, 1790–1950: A Study of Their Origins and Development.* New York: Twentieth Century Fund, 1953.

Fite, Gilbert C. *American Farmers: The New Minority.* Bloomington: Indiana University Press, 1981.

Hurt, R. Douglas. *American Agriculture: A Brief History.* Ames: Iowa State University Press, 1994.

See also Volume 1: Agricultural Adjustment Act of 1938; McNary-Haugen Bill.

Patronage

Practice of appointing people to political or government offices.

During the administrations of George Washington and John Adams, the United States did not operate under a system of patronage. Although both presidents appointed people to political positions, the emphasis was on the appointees' qualifications. For example, Alexander Hamilton, a Federalist, was appointed secretary of the treasury by Washington because of his financial experience. When Thomas Jefferson, a Jeffersonian-Democrat whom Washington appointed as his secretary of state, defeated Adams in the presidential election of 1800, the Federalists feared that Jefferson would replace them with his own appointees. To prevent the complete loss of power, Adams issued "midnight appointments" at nine o'clock on the evening before he left office (some were hand-delivered up until midnight) to fill the judgeships created under the Judiciary Act of 1801. Jefferson did not initiate a widespread program to remove Federalists from office, but he refused to recognize the validity of any undelivered Adams appointments. Presidents between Jefferson, elected in 1800, and Andrew Jackson, elected in 1828, appointed individuals to office, but the practice of patronage proved limited because of the scarcity of government positions, the belief that one served out of duty to the country, and the lack of strong political parties. Jackson's election changed everything. Under the spoils system ("to the victor go the spoils"), presidents repaid political favors with government positions. Two key offices that offered both power and financial gain were postmaster general, with its thousands of offices to fill, and collector of the port, especially in cities like New York and New Orleans where customs officials received a percentage of the import duties as compensation for services.

The practice of patronage continued until after the Civil War, when corruption became so rampant that Americans began clamoring for civil service reform. Rutherford B. Hayes, elected president in 1876, advocated reform of the system but then appointed members of the Louisiana elections board, which had helped throw the election into dispute (thus guaranteeing Hayes' victory), to political positions. Hayes's successor, James A. Garfield, was shot four months after taking office and died three months later. Reform did occur under Chester Arthur, who then assumed the presidency. In 1883 Congress passed the Pendleton Civil Service Act, which placed 10 percent of government jobs under the merit system. Since then, the percentage of government positions that require a civil service exam has continued to increase. The primary positions that do not fall under this act are the Cabinet members, ambassadors, and judges, but because the Senate must confirm these appointments, the practice of distributing offices for political favors was effectively eliminated by the early twentieth century. Some scholars argue that a new form of patronage has developed with the rise of lobbyists and pork-barrel legislation (special projects that congressional members distribute to their constituents), but this form of patronage is associated with the legislative rather than the executive branch.

—*Cynthia Clark Northrup*

References
Prince, Carl E. *The Federalists and the Origins of the U.S. Civil Service.* New York: New York University Press, 1977.
See also Volume 1: Pendleton Act.

Payne-Aldrich Tariff Act (1909)
Measure that made the first change in the tariff schedules since the Dingley Tariff of 1897.

In March 1909, President William Howard Taft called Congress into special session for the purpose of revising the tariff schedules. Later that year the House of Representatives passed the Payne bill, put forth by New York Republican Sereno Payne, which reduced many rates. In the Senate, however, Nelson Aldrich, Republican from Rhode Island, had the Finance Committee make more than 800 changes to the bill,

which mostly increased the rates, although presidential authority to revise rates through reciprocity agreements (agreements between the United States and individual countries that called for favorable trade terms between both nations at rates lower than the current tariff schedule) continued. Aldrich wanted the Senate to pass the amended bill as a Republican measure without any discussion of its details. But insurgent Republican senators, mostly from the Middle West and led by Robert LaFollette of Wisconsin, forced a debate and a new examination of the bill. The insurgent Republicans divided the bill into separate parts of which several senators mastered the details. The insurgents, including Albert Beveridge of Indiana and Jonathan Dolliver of Iowa, discovered that Aldrich and his supporters had espoused the false idea that senators had cut rates significantly, and the insurgents also denounced the influence of lobbyists in shaping the tariff bill. Although the bill retained high rates on essential items like woolen cloth and raw wool, it also placed on the free or reduced list numerous articles that consumers neither wanted nor needed. These products included hog bristles, false teeth, stilts, skeletons, leeches, curling stones, silkworm eggs, and canary birdseed. As the cartoon character "Mr. Dooley" noted, "Th' new Tariff Bill puts these familiar commodities within th' reach iv all."

Despite the insurgents' criticisms, the Payne-Aldrich Tariff Act passed both Houses of Congress, and President Taft signed it on August 5, 1909. The president preferred more substantial reductions than those provided by the tariff rates, but he believed the new presidential power to revise rates offered a significant change. The tariff, however, greatly disappointed the insurgent Republicans, and the Republican disharmony received widespread exposure to the public, providing the Democrats with a powerful campaign issue for the 1910 congressional elections.

—*Steven E. Siry*

References
Cooper, John Milton, Jr. *Pivotal Decades: The United States, 1900–1920.* New York: W. W. Norton, 1990.
See also Volume 1: Wilson, Woodrow.

Pell Grant
Federally funded education grant started in 1973 and named for Senator Claiborne Pell because of his efforts in getting the grant established.

The Pell grant is a federally funded grant that requires no repayment. Its purpose is to help financially needy undergraduate college students meet the cost of their education at participating postsecondary institutions by providing direct grant assistance. Eligibility is based on household finances, not merit. Started in 1973 under the name Basic Educational Opportunity Grant, it was later renamed for Senator Claiborne Pell (D–Rhode Island) because of his efforts to get it established.

Pell grants have kept up with the rising costs of college over the years. In 2001 about 30 percent of undergraduates receive Pell grants; altogether, about 30 million students have benefited from it. The maximum Pell grant for the 2001–2002 academic year was $3,300 based on governmental funding; it typically increases each year. Pell operates as an entitlement grant, which means students are eligible any time during the year as long as they apply by the application deadline. Studies have shown that the use of the Pell grant helps students succeed in college and increases the employment and earning opportunities of disadvantaged populations.

To apply for the Pell grant, a student must complete a form called Free Application for Federal Student Aid to determine the family's financial need. Based on a congressionally specified formula and financial data about the student's family, an index is determined. Called the Estimated Family Contribution (EFC), it is the ability of the student's family to pay the cost of college. The Pell grant figure is then based on the EFC, how many credit hours of study the student enrolls for, and the cost of attendance at the specified college. The student must also meet other basic requirements to receive a Pell grant. The student must possess a high school diploma, GED or equivalent, enroll in an eligible degree program, be an undergraduate student and a citizen or eligible noncitizen, and possess a valid Social Security number. The student may not be in default on any federal loan programs, must be registered with Selective Service if a male 18 years or older, and must be making satisfactory academic progress set forth and evaluated by the school he is attending. Individual colleges are responsible for disbursing the funds for the Department of Education based on all the requirements.

—*Scott R. DiMarco and Julie A. Bogdan*

References

Federal Pell Grant Program. *Biennial Evaluation Report, FY 93–94*. Chapter 501. Available: http://www.ed.gov/pubs/Biennial/501.html; accessed November 27, 2002.

Mulhauser, Dana. "Student Aid Rose Sharply over the Past Four Years, Study Finds." *Chronicle of Higher Education*, July 31, 2001. Available: http://www.chronicle.com/daily/ 2001/07/2001073101n.htm; accessed June 3, 2002.

"Policy Analysis: Abstracts of the Chapters Memory, Reason, and Imagination: A Quarter Century of Pell Grants." The College Board. No date. Available: http://www.college board.org/policy/html/topics.html; accessed October 17, 2002.

The Student Guide: Financial Aid 2001–2002. Student Financial Assistance. U.S. Department of Education. Washington, DC: U.S. Government Printing Office, 2002.

See also Volumes 1, 2: Education.

Pendleton Act (1883)

Law authorizing the reform of the Civil Service System based on a program of selection rather than patronage.

President Andrew Jackson, elected in 1828, inherited a system of government service based on political patronage rather than merit, and his attempts to change this "spoils system" did little to correct the problem. In 1865, shortly before he was assassinated, President Abraham Lincoln observed that current government hiring practices would "ruin republican government." Job security became a way to make money out of the job, according to Lincoln, "by whatever means available before the return of the opposing party doomed one to departure." Tremendous time and effort had been consumed in dispensing favors to political allies.

As early as 1864, Senator Charles Sumner, a member of the Free-Soil Party from Massachusetts, had introduced a bill urging reform of the system. Three years later, Republican Representative Thomas Jenckes of Rhode Island tried to initiate reforms along British lines, basing positions on merit rather than political favors. In almost every instance reformers in Congress received mere lip service. In the 1870s leading proponents of civil service reform, such as *The Nation* editor E. L. Godkin and Republican Senator Carl Schurz of Missouri, encouraged the administration of President Ulysses S. Grant to initiate changes "in the manner of all appointments." Sparked by the Crédit Mobilier scandal (which involved the distribution of stocks at half their value to members of Congress to secure the representatives' support), the impeachment hearings of Secretary of War William Belknap for selling Indian trading posts, and other forms of corruption in government, Congress created a Civil Service Commission. However, the commission's efforts were merely cosmetic, and the government did little to carry out the needed reforms. President Rutherford B. Hayes, Grant's successor, supported efforts toward reforms but little changed.

The assassination of President James A. Garfield by a mentally disturbed, disgruntled government job seeker generated a public demand for civil service reform. On January 16, 1883, Congress passed the Pendleton Act on a bipartisan basis. Dorman B. Eaton, secretary of the Civil Service Reform Organization, drew up the act, and Democratic Representative George H. Pendleton of Ohio introduced it into Congress. The law specifically "classified" certain government jobs and established a bipartisan, three-member commission to draw up and administer competitive exams. The process established the procedure of filling civil servant jobs on a merit basis rather than on party affiliation. The law thus established an examination to determine qualifications and finally outlawed kickback contributions to political parties. The act also empowered presidents to add new positions to the classified service from time to time.

At first, the Pendleton Act covered fewer than 15,000 jobs, or about 12 percent of all federal employees. By 1897, when William McKinley assumed the presidency, 86,000 (almost half of all federal employees) fell under civil service classifications. By 1900 the number had grown to more than 100,000 and it would continue to grow throughout the twentieth century. The Pendleton Act aimed at ending corruption in government. In the process the quality of the federal bureaucracy steadily improved, and a major step had been taken toward making government more honest and efficient.

—*Charles F. Howlett*

References

Blodgett, Geoffrey. *The Gentle Reformers: Massachusetts Democrats in the Cleveland Era*. Cambridge MA: Harvard University Press, 1966.

Garraty, John A. *The New Commonwealth, 1877–1890*. New York: Harper and Row, 1968.

Hoogenboom, Ari. *Outlawing the Spoils: A History of the Civil Service Reform Movement, 1865–1883*. Urbana: University of Illinois Press, 1961.

McFarland, Gerald W. "Partisanship of Non-Partisan Dorman B. Eaton and the Genteel Reform Tradition." *Journal of American History*, vol. 54 (1968): 806–822.

White, Leonard D. *The Republican Era: A Study in Administrative History*. New York: Macmillan, 1965.
See also Volume 1: Corruption.

Personal Responsibility Act of 1996

First federal act to reform federal welfare system established by Great Society legislation of the 1960s.

For three decades, from 1965 to 1995, the federal government implemented a variety of programs designed to provide assistance for Americans in poverty. These programs were part of President Lyndon B. Johnson's Great Society program and included Medicaid, Food Stamps, Aid to Families with Dependent Children, and Head Start. By the 1990s, as many as three or four generations of families relied on the federal government for assistance. States beginning with Wisconsin began experimenting with ways to break this cycle of dependency. Many states limited the number of years recipients could receive benefits and encouraged them to participate in job assistance programs. In 1995, during the administration of President Bill Clinton, Congress considered HR 4, a welfare reform act, but did not pass it. Then, on August 22, 1996, the Personal Responsibility Act—a version of HR 4 that included deep budget cuts and provided for a way to move individuals off the welfare rolls and into the workplace ("welfare to work") became law. The measure required a two-year limit on assistance to welfare recipients. In addition, it required single parents to participate in job training at least 20 hours a week, increasing to 30 hours by 2000, and two-parent families to participate in job training at least 35 hours per week. During families' transition from welfare to the workplace, the federal program would continue to offer childcare assistance and medical coverage for at least one year.

To implement the Personal Responsibility Act, states received block grants from the federal government and could use the funds for the creation of new jobs if necessary. Stringent reporting and quota requirements forced the states to comply. Because many single mothers should have been receiving child support instead of welfare assistance, the bill required the establishment of paternity, the withholding of wages, and the revocation of drivers' and professional licenses for delinquent parents. In an effort to curb the large number of teenagers on welfare, the act required that teen mothers live with a responsible adult and attend school to receive benefits.

Since implementation of the act, more than 43 states have implemented 78 various welfare reform programs. Child support collections have increased by 50 percent, and 1.9 million people have left the welfare rolls.

—*Cynthia Clark Northrup*

References
Ewalt, Patricia L. *Social Policy: Reform, Research, and Practice*. Washington, DC: NASW Press, 1997.
See also Volume 1: Great Society; Medicaid; Medicare; Welfare Economics; Volume 2: Welfare State.

Personal Savings

Individual income set aside for future use.

Before 1929 the U.S. government did not collect information about personal savings. Individuals safeguarded a portion of their money either at home or in savings accounts at banks. The Bureau of Economic Analysis has compiled figures on personal savings since 1929. During the first three years of the Great Depression, 1929–1931, Americans saved between 4 and 5 percent of their disposable personal income per year. The percentages dropped dramatically in 1932 and 1933, when personal savings was negative 0.8 percent and personal disposable income was negative 1.5 percent. By 1936 and 1937 the percentage had increased again to more than 6 percent. The largest increases in personal savings occurred between 1941 and 1945 while the United States fought during World War II. Forced rationing and high employment meant that few consumer goods were available for workers purchase, so the rate of personal savings increased from 12.4 percent in 1941 to 26.3 percent in 1944. During the postwar period through the 1970s, the figures vary from 5.2 percent to 10 percent. Forced savings during the war provided the funds for Americans to purchase large quantities of consumer goods during the prosperous 1950s. Banks benefited from the use of these savings to offer low-interest loans for new housing, modern appliances, and automobiles. During the 1970s and 1980s, personal savings consistently averaged 10 percent. During the 1990s that trend reversed, and by 2000 the rate of personal savings had again dropped into the negative numbers (–0.7 percent). A recession coupled with higher unemployment has contributed to this development.

—*Cynthia Clark Northrup*

References
U.S. Bureau of Economic Analysis. www.bea.gov; accessed February 22, 2003.
See also Volume 1: Great Depression; Recession.

Philippines

Independent nation occupying an archipelago in the South Pacific.

The Spanish initially colonized the Philippines in 1565 as a base for Asian trade. To facilitate trade with North America, the Spanish opened the Philippines to free trade in 1834, and by the 1870s British and American merchants dominated the Filipino economy. By the end of the nineteenth century, the Philippines produced three major crops—tobacco, sugar, and hemp. Americans dominated hemp production and used it to manufacture rope in New England.

A war for Philippine independence from Spain began in

1896, and the guerrilla conflict upset American trade interests. In 1898, the United States went to war against Spain in order to gain independence for Cuba. The war spread to the Spanish Philippines, and the United States took advantage of the situation by deploying the U.S. Navy to attack the Spanish in the Philippines. After the Spanish-American War, Spain ceded the Philippines to the United States.

The United States kept the Philippines as a dependent colony until the Japanese invaded and conquered the islands in 1942 during World War II in an attempt to conquer all of Southeast Asia. After the defeat of Japan in World War II, the United States reoccupied the Philippines, granting it independence in 1946 but leasing several military installations from the Filipino government and maintaining a heavy military presence. The largest bases were the Subic Bay Naval Base and Clark Air Force Base. Negotiations to keep the bases open were often difficult. A volcanic eruption rendered Clark unusable in 1991, and the United States abandoned Subic Bay in 1992 when cold war tensions eased.

The Philippines remains a large producer of sugar, but in the 1970s, the economy began to diversify, especially into the textile and electronics industries. Since the 1970s, Japan has also been more active in the Philippine economy and has steadily challenged American dominance there. The United States continues to maintain a strong trading relationship with the Philippines. In 1998, 22 percent of the Philippines' imports were from the United States, and 34 percent of its exports went to the United States.

—John K. Franklin

References
Karnow, Stanley. *In Our Image: America's Empire in the Philippines.* New York: Ballantine Books, 1990.
See also Volume 1: Spanish-American War; Sugar.

Pinckney Treaty (Treaty of San Lorenzo) (1795)

Treaty between the United States and Spain that established the northern border of Florida.

Late in the eighteenth century, U.S. settlers in the territories of Kentucky and Tennessee, uneasy about Spanish claims on their region and agitated about restricted access to the Mississippi River (which had long been protected by Spanish forts), pressed the federal government for a legal treaty to resolve these issues amidst calls for secession and independence. Afraid that the United States would side with Great Britain against the Spanish after the conclusion of Jay's Treaty (a 1794 agreement designed to resolve differences concerning navigation and commerce that the Treaty of Paris, which formally ended the American Revolution, had failed to address), the Spanish anxiously sought an agreement.

Negotiated at the monastery of San Lorenzo el Real in Madrid by Charles Pinckney—a delegate to the Constitutional Convention and envoy to Spain from South Carolina—the resulting agreement set the southern border of the United States at the thirty-first parallel and guaranteed free navigation of the Mississippi River and the Gulf of Mexico,

with a right of deposit for American products in warehouses at New Orleans for three years. The agreement also contained a proviso in which the United States and Spain each promised not to incite Native American tribes against the other. Spain gained by this treaty a guarantee of the northern border of Florida, which had been established and expanded by the British in 1763. The treaty reassured settlers in Kentucky and Tennessee, who feared Spanish encroachment, while opening the Mississippi as a conduit for business. Popular in the United States, the treaty easily passed the Senate and became law in 1795, spurring the expansion of Americans into the Southeast.

—Margaret Sankey

References
Williams, Frances Leigh. *A Founding Family.* New York: Harcourt Brace Jovanovich, 1978.
Zahniser, Marvin R. *Charles Cotesworth Pinckney.* Chapel Hill: University of North Carolina Press, 1967.
See also Volume 2: Land Policies.

Pinkerton Detective Agency

Private detective agency that worked with the government and big business during the nineteenth and early twentieth centuries.

In 1842 Alan Pinkerton emigrated from Scotland to Illinois in the United States, where he became a cooper (barrelmaker). His shop became one of the many stations in the underground railroad that helped runaway slaves to freedom in the North in the pre–Civil War days. In 1846 Pinkerton discovered a counterfeiting ring and helped bring about the apprehension of the criminals. His efforts resulted in his election as sheriff in Dundee, Illinois, and then Chicago. In 1850 he formed his own private agency, the Pinkerton Detective Agency. At the beginning of the Civil War, he prevented several potential assassins from murdering President Abraham Lincoln, and for the duration of the war he operated a spy ring behind enemy lines in the South.

After the Civil War, the agency gained national recognition when it captured several notorious train robbers. It then focused on helping big business deal with labor strikes; in 1869 the Pinkerton Detective Agency helped break up the Molly Maguires, a group of Irish coalminers who had destroyed property while attempting to obtain concessions from the management. After Alan Pinkerton died, his two sons assumed control of the organization. Robert and William Pinkerton supplied armed Pinkerton guards to Andrew Carnegie during the Homestead Strike of 1892 for a shorter work week and increased wages, during which several strikers were killed. One of the agency's tactics was to place spies for the management in labor organizations. As the labor movement gained momentum and workers joined with angry farmers and miners to form the Populist Party (active between 1892 and 1908), one of the demands that labor placed on politicians was the prohibition of labor spies. Although the national government failed to pass such legislation, states eventually outlawed the use of spies within labor organizations. Ever since the early 1900s, the Pinkerton Detective Agency has provided bodyguards for individuals and detectives for corporations.

—*Cynthia Clark Northrup*

References

Horan, James David. *The Pinkertons: The Detective Dynasty That Made History.* New York: Crown Publishers, 1967.

Rowan, Richard Wilmer. *The Pinkertons: A Detective Dynasty.* Boston: Little, Brown, 1931.

See also Volume 2: Labor.

Piracy

Violent robbery of seagoing vessels or smuggling of illegal goods, hindering American trade from the colonial era until the U.S. wars with the Barbary states of North Africa along the southern shore of the Mediterranean Sea.

Pirates were most prevalent in North America during the latter half of the seventeenth century, when trade between the New World and Europe increased. Early pirates roamed the Caribbean but soon spread up the American coast, plundering ships and towns from Florida to New York. Although pirates harmed lawful trade, many colonial politicians willingly received them and their plundered goods because of British trade restrictions such as the Navigation Acts in 1651, 1660, and 1672. Additional legislation by Britain, beginning with the Sugar Act of 1764, aimed at curtailing piracy allowed colonial courts to try pirates, but it also provided Britain with the means to tighten its administrative reign in the colonies.

The development of well-organized navies by the British, French, and Spanish eliminated colonial piracy by the middle of the eighteenth century. After the American Revolution, though, Barbary pirates located along the Barbary Coast continued to attack American vessels in the Mediterranean. In 1784, Congress appropriated funds to pay tribute to the Barbary powers for safe passage, and the United States continued to pay annual tribute until 1801, when it refused the pasha of Tripoli's demand for more. Tripoli declared war against the United States, but by 1805, after an intense naval struggle, the pirates capitulated. In 1815 the United States went to war with Algiers because of repeated attacks by pirates on merchants and quickly exacted a treaty of tribute. The final action by the United States against piracy occurred in 1824 when a U.S. fleet went to the West Indies to eradicate bands of pirates around Cuba. Major world powers eventually condemned piracy in international law at the Nyon Conference held in Nyon, Switzerland, in 1936.

High-tech piracy is the new trend. Software piracy results in a loss of $10 billion a year to the U.S. economy.

—*John Grady Powell*

References

Griess, Thomas, ed. *Early American Wars and Military Institutions.* New York: Avery, 1986.

Lane, Kris E. *Pillaging the Empire: Piracy in the Americas, 1500–1750.* Armonk, NY: M. E. Sharpe, 1998.

See also Volume 1: Navigation Acts.

Poll Tax

Uniform state tax placed on individuals as a prerequisite for voting.

Following Reconstruction, during which Northern forces occupied the South after the Civil War and guaranteed the political rights of African Americans, the Democratic political establishment in the Southern states moved to consolidate Democratic power. Its greatest fear was that Democrats might one day be forced from office by a coalition of African American and poor white voters. Agrarian unrest of the 1880s and 1890s heightened these fears and led the existing Democratic power structure to take action. Particularly concerned with curtailing the African American vote, mainstream Democrats instituted several measures designed to circumvent the Fourteenth Amendment of the United States Constitution, which guarantees due process and prohibits states from denying citizens equal protection. By the end of the nineteenth century, the Southern states had amended their own constitutions or drawn up new ones that included disenfranchisement schemes including literacy tests, grandfather laws (which exempted whites who could not pass the tests because they had already exercised the right to vote), and poll taxes. The U.S. Supreme Court upheld such measures in *Williams v. Mississippi* (1898), which confirmed the validity of Mississippi's 1890 constitution. The poll tax was particularly effective in eliminating most of the African American vote along with the votes of many poor whites. Voters had to pay the tax months in advance of the actual election, before the issues or the identities of the candidates were clear. Poor citizens who fell behind in their payments soon found themselves owing more than they could ever afford to pay. As a result, voter turnout in the South, which had averaged 64 percent during the 1880s, fell to 30 percent by 1910.

The poll tax remained in place in several Southern states until the Civil Rights era in the 1960s. In 1964 the Twenty-Fourth Amendment to the Constitution struck down the poll tax in federal elections. Two years later, in *Harper v. Virginia Board of Elections,* the Supreme Court ruled that the poll tax in state elections violated the equal protection clause of the Constitution.

—*Ben Wynne*

References

Kousser, J. Morgan. *The Shaping of Southern Politics: Suffrage Restriction and the Establishment of the One-Party South, 1880–1910.* New Haven, CT: Yale University Press, 1974.

See also Volume 1: Fourteenth Amendment; *Williams v. Mississippi.*

Pollock v. Farmer's Bank & Trust (1895)

U.S. Supreme Court case in which national income tax was declared unconstitutional.

In 1894, Congress passed legislation instituting an income tax on all persons with a yearly income of $4,000 or more. The demand for a national income tax had come from the Populist Party, whose members believed that wealthy industrialists should share the tax burden with average Americans.

Supporters of the new income tax were hopeful that the law would not be challenged in the courts. The first income tax had been placed on the American people during the Civil War with little opposition. When that tax was finally challenged in *Springer v. United States* in 1881, the Supreme Court unanimously upheld the income tax as constitutional.

After the ruling, opponents of the new income tax launched a bitter campaign that declared the law to be part of the dangerous rise of socialism and communism around the world. They also argued that the income tax was a direct tax that Congress could only levy if apportioned among the several states according to population. After hearing *Pollock* twice, the Supreme Court finally ruled in 1895 in a 5-to-4 decision that all national income taxes were unconstitutional because direct taxes must be based on apportionment but personal income taxes are not apportional. Writing for the Court, Chief Justice Melville Fuller argued that an income tax was a direct tax. Ignoring former Court decisions, he followed former secretary of the Treasury Albert Gallatin's distinction between a direct tax levied on the people's capital or revenue and an indirect tax levied on their expenses. Because the income tax was a direct tax under Gallatin's definition, it must be apportioned among the states in accordance with Article I, Section 2 of the Constitution. In the most impassioned dissent of his career, Justice John Marshall Harlan called the decision a "disaster for the country" because it effectively crippled the power of the national government and placed the tax burden solely on the backs of average Americans.

The income tax was reinstated early in the twentieth century. The U.S. Congress passed a personal income tax amendment to the Constitution in 1909, and the states ratified the Sixteenth Amendment in 1913.

—*Mary Stockwell*

References

David, Andrew. *Famous Supreme Court Cases.* Minneapolis, MN: Lerner Publishing, 1980.
See also Volume 2: Judiciary.

Population

The number of people in a country or region.

The U.S. government monitors the population through the decennial census, established in 1790. The population of the United States increased from 3.9 million in 1790 to 272 million in 1999, and the Census Bureau projects that the U.S. population will reach about 392 million by 2050, an increase of 50 percent over the current figure. This population growth occurs through the natural increase because of more births than deaths and through net immigration. Immigration rates during the twentieth century varied from 10 percent per annum in the first decade of the century to 0.4 percent per annum in the 1930s. In 2000, the birth rate was 15.7 per thousand and the death rate was 8.6 per thousand, resulting in an annual increase of about 0.7 percent—low by historical standards. As health care has improved and longevity has increased, more people survive to older ages. This process will continue, increasing the number of older people in the United States, who may have savings but have passed the economically productive period of their lives and need increased medical and support services.

In less-developed countries (LDCs), population continues to grow more rapidly, and officials project that the world population will grow from the current six billion to around nine billion by 2070, subsequently declining. For many poor countries, the concern about rapid population growth involves their capability to build the necessary infrastructure to feed, house, and educate the increasing numbers. If population growth outstrips land and other resources, as has happened in many LDCs, poverty and malnutrition will increase. If that happens in the United States, the standard of living will decline and health care costs will soar. The United States does not have a formal population policy, but many other policies influence population levels. During the nineteenth century and the first decades of the twentieth century, the United States, to build up the frontier, encouraged immigration through its land policy. In the twentieth century an explicit population policy evaluated during the presidency of Richard Nixon focused on the issues of overpopulation in the United States, but the government abandoned the policy because it relied on the use of contraception and abortion—politically very sensitive issues. Currently the United States continues to restrict immigration and the Supreme Court continues to uphold *Roe v. Wade,* which guarantees the right of women to have abortions during the first trimester of pregnancy.

—*Tony Ward*

References

Rodgers, Harrell R. *American Poverty in a New Era of Reform.* Armonk, NY: M. E. Sharpe, 2000.
See also Volume 1: Immigration; Volume 2: Immigration Policy.

Populist Party

American political party active between 1892 and 1908.

The product of agrarian discontent during the late nineteenth century, the Populist Party represented the political culmination of years of attempts by American farmers to organize in defense of their livelihood. Drawing its support primarily from farmers in the West and the South, it succeeded the failed Greenback Party of the 1880s.

In the decades following the Civil War, farmers felt increasingly threatened by America's rapid industrialization. Crop prices fluctuated constantly and, particularly after the financial panic of 1873, many of those who made their living off the land found themselves mired in debt. They blamed their plight on the railroads, large corporations, and those in the government who controlled the nation's money supply. Discontent among the farmers gave rise to the National Grange and the Farmers' Alliance movement along with the short-lived Greenback Party. As agrarian discontent peaked during the early 1890s, farmers made a final attempt to forge a national political coalition that could compete with the two major parties, the Democrats and Republicans. They aligned themselves with the Knights of Labor and other groups to form the Populist (or People's) Party.

The party established its platform in 1892 at a convention in Omaha, Nebraska, calling for the free coinage of silver as a form of legal tender, the issuance of large amounts of paper currency, government ownership of the railroads, the abolition of the national banking system, a redistribution of the cost of government through a graduated income tax, the direct election of U.S. senators, and an eight-hour workday. The party nominated James B. Weaver for president in 1892 and made a good showing in its first national campaign. Weaver garnered more than 8 percent of the popular vote and 22 electoral votes. The party captured several state offices and immediately started work to consolidate its successes.

As the 1896 presidential contest approached, the Populists posed the greatest threat to the Democrats, whose constituency included many who could relate to the upstart party's platform. As a result, the Democrats adopted the free coinage of silver, a key Populist demand, as part of their agenda and nominated as their candidate William Jennings Bryan, who sympathized with Populist programs. By casting themselves as the party of reform, the Democrats sapped much of the Populists' strength. Although they nominated a different vice presidential candidate, the Populists also endorsed Bryan, but he subsequently lost the election to Republican William McKinley.

The fallout from the 1896 presidential campaign split the Populist Party and doomed it to extinction. Some Populists came to believe that they could best promote their agenda through the Democratic Party, while others believed that their goals could only be met with an independent organization. After McKinley's victory, the Populist Party went into sharp decline and by 1908 it had ceased to exist. Although the party did not survive, several Populist demands considered radical reforms when first proposed would become law during the Progressive Era during the first two decades of the twentieth century.

—*Ben Wynne*

References

Goodwyn, Lawrence. *The Populist Movement: A Short History of the Agrarian Revolt in America.* New York: Oxford University Press, 1978.

McMath, Robert C. *American Populism: A Social History, 1877–1898.* New York: Hill and Wang, 1993.

See also Volume 1: Congress; Protective Tariffs.

Poverty

Possession of inadequate resources to provide the necessities of life.

When a person's command of financial resources falls below a level that provides a secure, adequately comfortable lifestyle, then that person lives in poverty. What constitutes "comfortable" is very much a matter of opinion, which leads to widely diverse definitions of poverty. Poverty can be defined in absolute terms or relative terms. An absolute definition involves calculating the cost of a fixed bundle of goods, such as specific items of food or housing, and assigning to the poverty category those who cannot afford the bundle. The absolute definition has the advantage of being precise about applying the term "poverty." However, it can make internal comparison difficult because of fundamentally differing consumption patterns, and disagreement may occur over where to set the poverty line. The relative approach assigns to the poverty category those whose incomes fall below some fixed proportion of society's mean or median income. Economists find this easier to calculate, but the data are less clear. The United States uses an absolute income level to define poverty, unlike other Organization for Economic Cooperation and Development (OECD) countries, using levels equivalent to approximately one-third of median income—a very low standard.

Formal government policies to alleviate poverty have existed since the Great Depression of the 1930s. Yet as the twenty-first century begins only about one-third of the poor receive assistance, even though expenditure has increased over 400 percent over the period. In the late 1990s about three million Americans were poor, and 20 percent of the nation's children were living in poverty. Poverty remains unequally distributed across racial lines: 26 percent of African Americans, 24.3 percent of Hispanics, and 3.9 percent of Asians are poor, compared with 8.6 percent of white non-Hispanics. Family structure provides one of the most important determinants of poverty. Thirty-eight percent of all female-headed families live in poverty. This category has expanded rapidly as divorce rates and the rates of births to unwed mothers have risen.

American antipoverty policies developed later than those of other Western nations and have proven less generous in their scope. The first program began under President Herbert Hoover in 1929 with the Reconstruction Finance Corporation, which provided funds to banks and businesses so they would hire employers. President Franklin D. Roosevelt expanded that program in the 1930s during the Great Depression, and it culminated in 1935 with the Social Security Act, which included the Aid to Dependent Children (ADC) program. The issue of poverty almost disappeared as a social issue during World War II, but it grew again after the war. By 1960 still only 1.7 percent of all families received benefits, although 20.7 percent of families lived below the poverty line. In 1962, Congress changed the name of ADC to Aid to Families with Dependent Children (AFDC) and expanded the services to include caregivers (parents or guardians).

During the 1960s, several investigations revealed a widespread incidence of U.S. poverty and in that decade, as part of President Lyndon B. Johnson's Great Society legislation, several programs were created to address poverty, including the Food Stamp program (1964), Medicaid (1965), and Head Start (1965). In 1964, 17.4 percent of families lived in poverty. By 1973, that number had fallen to 9.7 percent. It climbed to 13 percent in 1993 before falling again to 9.9 percent in 2001. By 1996, medical programs formed 48 percent of outlays.

Cash, food, housing, and energy accounted for 46 percent. Job training and education accounted for only 6 percent of welfare assistance programs This approach supported those in poverty but did nothing to help lift them out of it. Other important programs intended to combat poverty include Supplementary Security Income (1956) and the Earned Income Tax Credit (1975).

A major overhaul of the American welfare system—which comprised primarily AFDC, food stamps, and Medicaid—began in 1996 with the passage of the Personal Responsibility and Work Opportunity Reconciliation Act (PRWORA). The most important aspect of this new legislation was the shift from supporting clients on inadequate benefits programs to helping poor people get back into the labor market. The legislation required that adults can be on welfare for a maximum of two years, after which they must begin to work. PRWORA placed all welfare programs under state rather than federal jurisdiction. Congress has also implemented better programs to help parents enter the workforce and to provide for childcare and the collection of child support. These new programs place a strong emphasis on birth control to reduce the perpetuation of poverty.

PRWORA has had significant but mixed effects. The number of people on welfare has fallen rapidly, from 14.1 million in 1996 when the Personal Responsibility Act began to 7.3 million in 1999. It is difficult to know how many people who were formerly on welfare have become employed. One estimate claims that 1.5 million people who were welfare recipients in 1997 had found employment by 1998. Many others, perhaps half, dropped out because they no longer qualified for assistance. Of those who dropped out, many have no visible means of support. Of those who have left welfare for employment, most do have higher incomes, but only marginally higher.

—*Tony Ward*

References
Rodgers, Harrell R. *American Poverty in a New Era of Reform*. Armonk, NY: M. E. Sharpe, 2000.
See also Volume 1: Medicaid; Medicare.

President's Commission on the Status of Women (1961)

Commission established by executive order of President John F. Kennedy charged with reporting on the status of women.

John F. Kennedy, after having won the 1960 presidential election by a narrow popular-vote margin, issued an executive order establishing the President's Commission on the Status of Women in December 1961. In October 1963 the commission produced its report, citing inequities that women—be they single or married, mothers or childless—confronted in the workplace. Noting that to date only 22 states had enacted equal pay statutes (requiring equal pay for men and women for the same job), the report supported equal pay legislation that was being advocated by the Women's Bureau of the U.S. Department of Labor. Not long

after the report was issued, Congress passed and President Kennedy signed the Equal Pay Act of 1963.

Despite a narrowing of pay differentials, women still make only about 75 percent as much money as men. Although it did not deal with several important related issues such as day care, the President's Commission on the Status of Women did contribute to a climate in which the policy concerns of women became increasingly expressed in the public discourse.

—*Henry B. Sirgo*

References
Conway, M. Margaret, David W. Ahern, and Gertrude A. Steuernagel. *Women and Public Policy: A Revolution in Progress*. Washington, DC: Congressional Quarterly Press, 1999.
See also Volume 1: Women.

Price Supports/Agricultural Adjustment

Government limitation on agricultural production to raise price per unit and a primary policy tool designed to stabilize agricultural commodity prices and thus farm income and closures.

The market dictated prices for agricultural commodities for much of U.S. history until the Agricultural Adjustment Act of 1933 (AAA), the most significant of President Franklin D. Roosevelt's New Deal policy interventions in the agricultural economy during the Great Depression. Among other interventions were the Emergency Farm Mortgage Act and the Farm Credit Act of 1933. The AAA, building on elements of both the McNary-Haugen Bill (which called for agricultural parity based on farm pricing in the early twentieth century) and the Domestic Allotment Plan (which paid subsidies to farmers not to plant certain crops), authorized the federal government to limit agricultural production in order to raise the price per unit and thus raise farmers' net income. The Supreme Court ruled the AAA unconstitutional in 1935. A modified version of the AAA was passed in 1938 and has evolved over time, with price supports extending from the 6 basic commodities (corn, wheat, cotton, tobacco, and peanuts) to the 14 so-called Steagall commodities (hogs, eggs, chickens, turkeys, milk, butterfat, certain dried peas, certain edible beans, soybeans, flaxseed and peanuts for oil, American-Egyptian cotton, potatoes, and sweet potatoes) during World War II. More nonbasic commodities were added in 1949.

The federal government controls market prices by aggressive export policies and by purchasing surplus production, storing it or redirecting it to domestic and international aid programs. The government controls production by setting target prices for each agricultural commodity and "base acreage"—historically determined acreage that is in production and the commodity being produced on it—for every farm. If the market price for crops produced on base acreage falls below the target price for that commodity, the government makes up the difference through deficiency payments. Price supports became practically inoperative from 1940 to 1951 because of high wartime prices. Since that time, however, government expenditures on price supports have fluctuated widely, depending on that year's output and global market. Agricultural adjustment policies were reformulated in the 1990 and 1995 Farm Bills toward greater flexibility in production, enabling farmers to respond to market signals. Since 1996, the federal government has moved away from price supports.

—*W. Chad Futrell*

References

Cochrane, Willard W. *The Development of American Agriculture: A Historical Analysis.* Minneapolis: University of Minnesota Press, 1993.

See also Volume 1: Agricultural Adjustment Act of 1938; McNary-Haugen Bill; New Deal.

Prigg v. Pennsylvania (1842)

U.S. Supreme Court case involving fugitive slaves and the Constitution.

In 1837, Edward Prigg, a professional slave catcher, attempted to seize a runaway slave named Margaret Morgan in Pennsylvania and to return Morgan and her children to Maryland. Prigg asked a justice of the peace in Pennsylvania for certificates of removal for Morgan and her family. These certificates were made necessary by Pennsylvania's personal liberty law of 1826. In accordance with the federal Fugitive Slave Law of 1850, the federal government required slave owners to prove that a slave actually belonged to them before the state would surrender the runaway. When the state justice of the peace refused to release Morgan and her children, Prigg ignored the ruling and took the slave woman and her family back to Maryland. Pennsylvania indicted Prigg for kidnapping, and Maryland extradited him only on the condition that the Supreme Court would quickly hear his case. The Court would determine what authority states had in fugitive slave matters.

Ruling for the Court in an 8-to-1 decision, Justice Joseph Story cited Article IV, Section 2 of the Constitution that clearly provided for the return of fugitive slaves to their owners. Story argued that the national government was bound by the Constitution to enforce the return of runaway slaves, and therefore the federal Fugitive Slave Law of 1850 was constitutional. He next reasoned that because this power was exclusive to the national government, Pennsylvania's personal liberty law of 1826 was unconstitutional. Although Story hoped his opinion would strengthen the power of the national government over the states, few people interpreted the ruling in this manner. Many Northerners condemned it as proslavery, while Southerners complained it had not gone far enough. Chief Justice Roger B. Taney echoed this sentiment in a separate opinion, arguing that states were bound under the Constitution to help capture runaway slaves.

—*Mary Stockwell*

References

Siegel, Martin. *The Taney Court, 1836–1864.* Millwood, NY: Associated Faculty Press, 1987.

See also Volume 2: Judiciary.

Prohibition (1919–1933)

Period during which the Eighteenth Amendment to the Constitution made the manufacture, sale, or transportation of intoxicating beverages illegal.

Hoping to end alcohol-related misery and boost the economic well-being of the nation, a growing number of citizens called for a ban on alcohol throughout the nineteenth century. Proponents of the law promised an end to problems historically associated with alcohol—family abuse, poverty, crime, illness, and low worker productivity. Their efforts were successful, culminating in 1920 in the ratification of the Eighteenth Amendment to the Constitution and its enforcing legislation, the Volstead Act.

Alcohol consumption virtually stopped in rural states, but the refusal of many people in cities to alter their drinking habits created a ready black market for illegal liquor and contributed to the rise of crime syndicates that trafficked in illegal liquor. People had to pay more for illegal alcohol, and many chose to buy products that were more potent, including dangerous homemade moonshine. Expenditures for distilled spirits as a percentage of all alcohol expenditures grew to between 70 and 87 percent as the price of spirits fell relative to the price of beer and, because buyers faced the risk of confiscation, because spirits were more compact and easier to hide. Crime patterns also shifted. Less-serious crime such as vagrancy and malicious mischief did diminish by half because of Prohibition, but crimes involving violence or theft of property increased by 13.2 percent during the Prohibition years. Homicides increased 16.1 percent and robbery rose 83.3 percent. The number of prisoners housed in federal prisons, reformatories, and camps grew from 3,889 in 1920 to 13,698 in 1932. Fewer than half of 287 surveyed industrialists noticed an improvement in absenteeism, one of the promised benefits of Prohibition, and a few claimed that the problem had worsened as workers needed more time to recover from drinking sprees.

By allowing the home production of nonintoxicating cider and fruit juices, Prohibition created an extremely strong demand for grapes suitable for shipping to urban ethnic neighborhoods. People accustomed to drinking wine with meals, for example, immigrants from Mediterranean countries, had to produce their own wine to ensure an adequate supply of what they viewed as a necessary commodity. In 1931, amid growing dissatisfaction with Prohibition, the National Commission on Law Observance and Enforcement (Wickersham Committee) issued a review of the first ten years of the law and noted that by June 1930, law enforcement agencies had dismissed more than 1,600 law enforcement personnel in the Prohibition unit for causes related to corruption. The days of the so-called "noble experiment" proved numbered, and passage in 1933 of the Twenty-First Amendment repealed the Eighteenth. In the midst of the Great Depression, many hoped that the return of alcohol industry jobs would assist recovery. The effects of Prohibition lingered for years. To gain access to illegal alcohol, women of good reputation had begun to patronize bars during Prohibition, and they continued to do so. Immigrants continued to home-produce their own wines after repeal, partly to avoid high taxes, and the demand for unfortified commercial table wine (less than 14 percent alcohol) remained low for some years.

—*Caryn E. Neumann*

References

Lapsley, James T. *Bottled Poetry: Napa Winemaking from Prohibition to the Modern Era*. Berkeley: University of California Press, 1996.

Thornton, Mark. *The Economics of Prohibition*. Salt Lake City: University of Utah Press, 1991.

See also Volume 1: Great Depression.

Protective Tariffs (1816–1930)

Tariff duties (taxes on imported goods) designed to generate revenue for the government and, more importantly, to protect domestic U.S. industries from foreign competition.

Between 1789 and 1816, Congress passed numerous tariff bills designed to simply generate funds for the Federal Treasury, which was running a deficit. As early as 1791, Secretary of the Treasury Alexander Hamilton had proposed that Congress consider protective tariffs as a means of stimulating industry so that the country could become economically self-sufficient. Legislators rejected the idea at the time, but after the War of 1812 against Great Britain, Congress accepted Hamilton's recommendations. The first protective tariff, passed in 1816, increased rates to 25 percent on wool, cotton, and manufactured iron; 30 percent on paper, leather, and hats; 20 percent on pig iron; and 15 percent on most other manufactured items. In addition, cheap Indian cotton was valued at a minimum cost of 25 cents per yard even though it was less expensive. Two years later, Congress raised rates again in response to Great Britain's practice of dumping goods on the American market at below-cost prices. In 1820, after the panic of 1819 hit, Congress once again increased rates to help stimulate the economy. Duties rose on iron, sugar, molasses, coffee, and salt. By 1824, Congress had established a pattern of approving protective tariffs.

The Tariff of 1824 resulted in higher duties on glass and paper. Congress also added numerous items to the list including leather, beef, bacon, cheese, wheat, flour, and most building materials. By this time the tariff had developed into a sectional issue. The debate over the Tariff of 1828 led Southerners to oppose the measure along with the Northern states until Massachusetts Senator Daniel Webster threw his support behind an amendment to increase the rate on woolen goods to 45 percent. Congress passed the tariff, but Vice President John C. Calhoun drafted the *South Carolina Exposition and Protest*, which argued for South Carolina's right to nullify the federal law if the hefty tariff proved detrimental to the people of South Carolina. The South Carolina legislature adopted the *Exposition* and issued a formal protest to the Senate demanding the reduction of rates. When Congress raised rates on most items again in 1832, South Carolina refused to collect the tariff duties and threatened secession. In 1833 President Andrew Jackson asked Congress to approve the Force Act, which would allow the use of military force if necessary to enforce U.S. laws. The Force Act reached Jackson's desk on the same day as the Compromise Tariff of 1833, a compromise worked out by Speaker of the House Henry Clay that gradually reduced the tariff rate to 20 percent over a nine-year period. The country had narrowly avoided a conflict. At the end of the nine years, the U.S. government owed $11 million in debts, and Congress began raising rates once again. Rates did decline in 1846 with the passage of the Walker Tariff but quickly rose again. Although the tariff had created sectional differences, by the 1850s the primary political issue had shifted to the extension of slavery. The protective tariffs had guaranteed the survival of the wool and textile industries in New England, as well as other manufacturing concerns, but the economy still struggled.

When the Civil War broke out in 1861, the Northern Republicans in Congress quickly passed the Morrill Tariff, which raised rates to pay for the cost of the war. From 1861 until the end of the nineteenth century, Congress continued passing protective tariffs. With Republicans in the White House the entire time except for the two presidencies of Grover Cleveland, the Democrats had little hope of reducing rates. As the tariff barriers rose, foreign competition found it difficult to compete with domestic manufactures, especially as companies began forming trusts (organizations combining similar companies) that dominated the oil, steel, beef, and sugar industries as well as many other industries. The lack of competition from abroad created a situation that encouraged the monopolistic practices of industrialists John D. Rockefeller and Andrew Carnegie. The expansion of the enumerated list included many everyday household items. Democrats charged that the wealthy could bring in luxury items for free but salt and cotton were taxed at very high rates—big business continued to grow at the expense of the average citizen. When Woodrow Wilson took office in 1913, Democrats managed to reduce tariff rates, but the outbreak of World War I altered the situation. Throughout the 1920s rates remained high to protect American industry as Europeans once again sought to dump goods on the U.S. market. European nations, some of which were newly formed out of former empires after the war, raised tariff barriers against the United States and other countries to protect their own industries. Finally, after the stock market crash in 1929, the United States responded by raising rates to a record level with the Hawley-Smoot Tariff of 1930. After Franklin D. Roosevelt became president, Congress authorized the executive branch to negotiate reciprocal trade agreements with countries on an individual basis. Not until after World War II did the United States abandon protective tariffs and pursue a policy of free trade under the General Agreement on Tariffs and Trade (1947).

—*Cynthia Clark Northrup*

References

Eckes, Alfred E. *Opening America's Market: U.S. Foreign Policy since 1776*. Chapel Hill: University of North Carolina Press, 1995.

Stanwood, Edward. *American Tariff Controversies in the Nineteenth Century*. New York: Russell and Russell, 1967.

See also Volume 1: Democratic Party; General Agreement on Tariffs and Trade; Reciprocal Trade Agreements Act of 1934; Republican Party; Revenue Tariffs; War of 1812.

Public Works Administration (PWA)

Federal agency established in 1933 to create jobs, augment purchasing power, and revive industry by funding large public works projects.

The Public Works Administration (PWA) was formed under the aegis of the New Deal's National Industrial Recovery Act on June 16, 1933, to fund public works projects including bridges, railroads, housing, hospitals, schools, and electricity-generating dams. An experimental institution, the PWA had the vague purview of "spending big bucks on big projects."

The idea of public works as a palliative for unemployment did not originate with the depression-fighting programs of the New Deal. Two previous debates on public works merit particular attention. During the "general glut controversy" in Europe in the early nineteenth century, economists Jeremy Bentham of England and Sismondi (Jean-Charles Leonard Simonde de Sismondi) of Switzerland dissented from British economist's David Ricardo's self-adjustment doctrine by advocating countercyclical public works. More significantly, during Lloyd George's electoral campaign for prime minister in Britain in 1929, the influential British economist John Maynard Keynes criticized the "Treasury view" that an increase in public expenditure would lead to a decrease in private expenditure (known as the "crowding out" problem). With Franklin D. Roosevelt's election to the presidency in 1933, Keynes hoped that the New Deal would prove his argument.

Initially proposed by Labor Secretary Frances Perkins, the first woman to hold a cabinet post, the PWA was directed by Interior Secretary Harold Ickes from 1933 to 1939. Placing particular emphasis on the construction industry, the PWA exemplified the idea of the "brain trust" (Roosevelt's Ivy League advisers) to prime the pump to stimulate economic growth. Although the PWA spent in excess of $6 billion during its tenure, it had only modest success in reducing unemployment and increasing industrial activity. It was constrained not only by Roosevelt's aversion to deficit spending but also by Ickes's desire to avoid corruption. Having been superseded by other recovery programs (most notably the Works Progress Administration), the PWA declined in importance in the late 1930s. It was officially abolished during the shift to a war economy in 1941.

—*Mark Frezzo*

References
Eden, Robert. *The New Deal and Its Legacy: Critique and Reappraisal.* New York: Greenwood Press, 1989.
Galbraith, John Kenneth. "Keynes, Roosevelt, and the Complementary Revolutions." In Harold L. Wattel, ed., *The Policy Consequences of John Maynard Keynes.* Armonk, NY: M. E. Sharpe, 1985.
See also Volume 1: Budget Deficits and Surpluses; Deficit Spending; Keynesian Economics.

Puerto Rico

Caribbean island with the status of United States commonwealth.

As a Spanish colony between 1492 and 1898, Puerto Rico principally exported sugar and sugar products such as rum. During the Spanish-American War of 1898, a U.S. military force seized Puerto Rico, which Spain then ceded to the United States. The United States had pledged in 1903 under the Platt Amendment not to annex Cuba, but it had made no such promises about Puerto Rico. Many Puerto Ricans saw American annexation as an attractive way to establish commercial and economic ties, and many islanders wanted to become a territory with an eye on possible statehood. Prior to World War II, Americans invested heavily in Puerto Rican sugar, and the industry boomed while other sectors in Puerto Rico languished.

Puerto Rico's status has been a bone of contention between the island and the United States since its annexation. In 1952, Puerto Rico drafted its own constitution and gained U.S. commonwealth status, which gives Puerto Rico a degree of autonomy over its own affairs. The Puerto Rican government has its own tax structure, and residents do not pay federal U.S. taxes. At the same time, Puerto Rico uses the U.S. dollar as its official currency and is exempt from U.S. customs duties. Furthermore, Puerto Rico is subject to American minimum wage laws, and Puerto Rican residents are free to enter, work, and travel within the United States. Because of tax breaks in Puerto Rico and freedom from U.S. customs duties, several American corporations have invested heavily in the island since the 1950s. As a result of American ties, Puerto Rico is the most industrialized and wealthy state in the Caribbean. However, Puerto Rican development pales in comparison to even the poorest states in the United States. In 2003 Puerto Rico remains a territory of the United States. Its people have all the privileges of U.S. citizens except the right to vote in national elections.

—*John K. Franklin*

References
Morales Carrión, Arturo. *Puerto Rico: A Political and Cultural History.* New York: Norton, 1983.
See also Volume 1: Spanish-American War; Sugar.

Pullman Strike (1894)

Violent union strike that occurred in Chicago in 1894.

Pullman, Illinois, was organized as a company-owned town for the workers of the Pullman Sleeping Car Company, which was owned by G. Pullman. During the heyday of the railroad, the company profited substantially, but when the panic of 1893 hit the United States, the company revenues declined. Consequently, the company laid off almost one-third of its employees. Those employees fortunate enough to remain on the payroll took a 25 percent wage reduction. However, the company refused to lower employees' rent or reduce the cost of items at the company-owned store. Workers who belonged to the American Railway Union tried to negotiate with management; when that failed, they voted to strike for lower rents and higher pay. Eugene V. Debs, the president of the union, called for a sympathy strike of all railway workers across the country. Citywide violence ensued as strikers rioted. When the state refused to intervene, railroad officials turned to the federal government because past presidents had always sided with management over labor during strikes. President Grover Cleveland deployed 12,000 troops to Chicago, and the attorney general issued an injunction against the union under the Sherman Anti-Trust Act. Government justification for intervening was that the mail trains had been interrupted. The government believed that the strike, which included all railroad employees, would fall under the authority of the Sherman Anti-Trust Act. The strike, which began on May 11, ended on July 20, 1894, when U.S. troops took over the operation of the railroads and the government arrested union officials. On August 3, 1894, the strike officially ended when workers returned to work. Eugene V. Debs, the president of the American Railway Union, went to prison for refusing to comply with an injunction that ordered an end to the strike (the injunction used the Sherman Anti-Trust Act as its authority; the labor union was considered a monopoly because 100 percent of the workers went out on strike). All union members were forced to sign an agreement not to reorganize. Just six days later, President Cleveland signed into law legislation that created a national Labor Day to appease the workers of the United States.

—*Cynthia Clark Northrup*

References

Papke, David Ray. *The Pullman Case: The Clash of Labor and Capital in Industrial America.* Lawrence: University Press of Kansas, 1999.
Warne, Colston E. *The Pullman Boycott of 1894: The Problem of Federal Intervention.* Boston: D. C. Heath, 1955.
See also Volume 2: Labor.

Pure Food and Drug Act (1906)

First law prohibiting the selling of adulterated or mislabeled food and drugs.

For years prior to 1906, Congress had considered a pure food bill, an idea staunchly supported by Harvey W. Wiley, the chief chemist in the Department of Agriculture. In December 1902 the House of Representatives passed a bill drawn up by Wiley. The National Association of Manufacturers, the American Baking Powder Association, and many individual food companies supported the measure. But by 1903 opponents to the measure had become organized, including primarily the patent drug and whiskey industries and some dissident growers who opposed this federal oversight. In 1905 the measure reached the Senate. President Theodore Roosevelt in his annual State of the Union address to Congress called for federal regulation of "misbranded and adulterated foods, drinks, and drugs." Congressional opponents blocked action on the measure, but this opposition collapsed in February 1906 when the American Medical Association warned Republican Senator Nelson Aldrich of Rhode Island that its 135,000 members would urge their patients to lobby senators for passage of the bill. The Senate quickly passed the measure, but it was soon buried deep in committee in the House of Representatives.

A month later, however, Upton Sinclair published *The Jungle*, a novel focused on socialist themes but which included a lurid description of Chicago's meatpacking plants. It revealed in great detail the revolting conditions under which beef and pork were processed. President Roosevelt appointed Charles P. Neill, the commissioner of labor, and James B. Reynolds, a Washington attorney, to conduct an investigation. Congress developed a compromise meat inspection bill, and the measure passed on June 30, 1906. Because of the impact of the meat inspection bill, the pure food and drug bill passed the same day. These precedent-setting laws in consumer protectionism initiated the emergence of the regulatory state in America. To enact the laws the president and Congress had to use the commerce clause of the Constitution, which allows the regulation of interstate commerce, because no power under the Constitution existed to regulate methods of manufacturing.

—*Steven E. Siry*

References

Kolko, Gabriel. *The Triumph of Conservatism: A Reinterpretation of American History, 1900–1916.* Chicago: Quadrangle Books, 1963.
See also Volume 1: Roosevelt, Theodore.

PWA

See Public Works Administration.

R

Railroads

Important mode of transportation popular in the nineteenth century linked to the economic development of the United States.

During the late nineteenth century, the steam locomotive was a dramatic influence in the United States. In 1869 the transcontinental railroad was completed, and the railroad industry revolutionized transportation of goods and people as it connected far-flung areas of the country and created a national economy. Before the Civil War the U.S. government greatly subsidized the railroad industry in an effort to promote economic development despite lawmakers' strict interpretation of the government's role in funding internal improvements. From 1850 to 1880, the federal government gave land grants to railroad companies totaling 131 million acres and provided other financial assistance, too, such as loans of up to $48,000 for each mile of railroad track built. By 1870 more than 93,000 miles of track had been laid—41,000 miles more than had existed at the beginning of the Civil War in 1860. By 1880 the number of miles had increased to 163,000, and it increased again to 193,000 miles by 1890. The total value of the government's assistance amounted to $707 million, yet the government had little oversight of the industry before 1887. Railroad executives became wealthy both from government funding and because they charged farmers high rates for short-haul trips to market and for grain storage in railroad-owned (unregulated) silos.

The federal government failed to implement economic policies beyond construction aid because of lawmakers' interpretation that the Constitution did not allow government control of transportation companies, especially in the case of intrastate trade. This interpretation was detrimental to the national economic interest because it put commercial agriculture at the mercy of numerous short-line railroads controlling an average of less than 40 miles of track. Regulating freight rates was critical to the economy if farmers were to produce commercially and move beyond subsistence farming.

Such regulation was supported by two Supreme Court rulings. In *Munn v. Illinois* (1877), the Court ruled that the government could regulate a private company whose business affected the public interest. In *Wabash, St. Louis, and Pa-cific Railway Co. v. Illinois* (1886), the Court ruled that laws passed by a Granger-controlled Illinois state legislature (the Grange was a farmers' group) violated the Constitution because they attempted to control interstate commerce—a responsibility that according to *Gibbons v. Ogden* (1824) belonged to the federal government. With these Court rulings as precedent, Congress passed the Interstate Commerce Act of 1887, banning railroads from discriminating against customers by charging lower freight rates for long hauls than for short hauls. The act required railroads to publish and file rates with the government. Furthermore, the newly created Interstate Commerce Commission (ICC) monitored the railroad industry to ensure that rates remained "reasonable and just." In short, the Interstate Commerce Act successfully remedied a situation in which railroads had taken advantage of small rural farmers in transporting goods to market, charging so much for hauling that it was difficult for the farmers to realize any profit.

The next significant legislation affecting the railroad industry occurred in 1890 with the passage of the Sherman Anti-Trust Act. This act, meant to end monopoly control of key industries, had little effect until Teddy Roosevelt became president and, in 1901, used the act to sue Northern Securities. Northern Securities was a holding company for the Great Northern and Northern Pacific Railroads and met the Interstate Commerce Act's definition of a monopoly. The government also passed the Heyburn Act (1906), giving the ICC power to set maximum freight rates that railroads could charge for shipping goods.

In 1920, the government reversed its policy with the Cummins Transportation Act, which encouraged railroad consolidation. The Cummins Act stipulated that the ICC must evaluate all railroad property, set rates of return for stockholders, and set costs for transporting passengers and freight. Congress designed the act to ensure that the policies enacted by the government would keep railroads profitable, yet operating cheaply enough to carry the nations' goods and benefit the economy. This act coincided with a reduction of railways after the advent of the automobile, highways, and the trucking industry. By 1920 the mileage of railroad tracks had declined from its height in 1900 of 193,346 miles; by the end of the twentieth century, railroad miles had further decreased to 131,984 miles. The interstate highway system and the airline industry have greatly reduced the need for and profitability of railroads in the United States, although railroads are still the primary method for shipping some bulk goods over long distances, and industries such as mining find the rates cheaper than other overland carriers.

—*Eugene Van Sickle*

References
Stover, John F. *American Railroads.* Chicago: University of Chicago Press, 1997.
See also Volume 1: Great Railroad Strike of 1877; Transportation Revolution.

Raw Materials
Agricultural or other unprocessed material that can be used in a manufacturing process.

Under the mercantilist system during colonial times, the American colonies served as a source of raw materials for Great Britain. Lumber, cotton, tobacco, rice, indigo, and foodstuffs comprised the bulk of the material shipped overseas for manufacturing in English factories. The British Parliament enacted a series of acts beginning in the mid-1600s to protect the fledgling industries in Britain. After the Enclosure Movement, when peasants were forced off the land and into factories, Parliament prohibited the importation of wool, but other items used in the textile industry—primarily cotton from the Americas—fueled the Industrial Revolution in Britain. Under the Navigation Acts (1651, 1660, and 1672), raw materials had to pass through the ports of England before being shipped to other countries, and the crews and ships had to be of British origin.

After the American Revolution, the United States found itself in much the same position as before the war—a source of raw materials. Secretary of the Treasury Alexander Hamilton, in his 1790 *Report on the Subject of Manufactures,* proposed the development and protection of infant industries in the United States as a means of competing with Great Britain. Finally, after the War of 1812, Congress implemented a protective tariff to encourage domestic manufacturing. As the countries of Western Europe industrialized, it became apparent that countries that continued to provide raw materials without industrializing would be relegated to a second-tier status among nations. During the Market Revolution from the 1820s through the 1850s, the United States slowly moved from simply providing raw materials to actually processing them into finished goods.

The real change occurred after the Civil War. American corporations began competing with other nations such as Germany, Japan, and Great Britain. However, the United States enjoyed an advantage over these countries in that it possessed a large reserve of raw materials available for domestic industries, whereas other countries relied on their colonial possessions to supply their industries. Since the early 1900s, the raw material requirements of industrialized nations have shifted to chemical and mineralogical resources, which the United States has in abundance. These items include coal, copper, lead, molybdenum, phosphates, uranium, bauxite, gold, iron, mercury, nickel, potash, silver, tungsten, zinc, petroleum, natural gas, and timber.

—*Cynthia Clark Northrup*

References
Manthy, Robert S. *Natural Resource Commodities—A Century of Statistics: Prices, Output, Consumption, Foreign Trade, and Employment in the United States, 1870–1973.* Baltimore, MD: Johns Hopkins University Press, 1978.
See also Volume 1: Industrial Revolution; Mercantilism; Volume 2 (Documents): *Report on the Subject of Manufactures.*

Raymond, Daniel (1786–1849)
Lawyer admitted to the bar in Baltimore in 1814 and known principally for his writings in political economy.

Daniel Raymond, born in 1786 in New Haven, Connecticut, first achieved notoriety with his pamphlet *The Missouri Question* (1819), which supported the abolition of slavery. In this work he pointed out the threat to white supremacy of black population growth under slavery. His *Thoughts on Political Economy* (1820), the first major work of economic theory by an American, is his principal contribution to policy development. His approach to the subject was very different from that of his contemporaries, classical economists in England and France. Raymond realized that national wealth does not simply equal the sum of all individual wealth. This realization led him to the belief that political economy should be more concerned with increasing the productive power of the nation than increasing its static wealth (property, for example).

Raymond saw national wealth as being increased by "effective" labor—labor that created permanent improvements, enhancing the nation's "capacity." He disagreed with economist Adam Smith, who believed that the wealth of a nation increased if the nation accumulated a surplus of produce in excess of consumption. Raymond felt that this surplus output does not contribute to wealth unless it is bought by consumers. If consumers fail to buy the output, it is the government's responsibility, Raymond believed, to amend the effects of the resulting downturn in the economy. Raymond saw the best way of achieving government responsibility as the creation of public monopolies through such devices as trade treaties and tariffs. The resulting increase in prices would, in Raymond's view, stimulate businesses, which would then hire more workers, and the labor force, in turn, would then buy up the accumulation of surplus goods. Tariffs raise prices, but the revenues from these high prices remain within the country and are not lost. Raymond believed that tariffs should be highest on goods the manufacture of which employed the largest number of people.

—*Tony Ward*

References
Dorfman, Joseph. *The Economic Mind in American Civilization.* New York: Viking Press, 1946.
See also Volume 1, Free Trade; Slavery; Volume 2: Slavery.

REA

See Rural Electrification Administration.

Reagan, Ronald (1911–)

Former actor and former governor of California who became fortieth president of the United States, 1981–1989.

Ronald Wilson Reagan won the presidential election in November 1980. At a time when the country's morale was quite low because of the Iranian hostage crisis and a bad economy, Reagan inspired the American people by arranging for the release of the hostages and by providing economic leadership for the country by pushing for a tax cut.

Contemporary writers described Reagan as an adherent to the supply-side economic theory, which became known as Reaganomics or the trickle-down theory. Supply-side economics calls for tax cuts for businesses and the wealthy, who, the theory goes, will then save money or invest for the benefit of the rest of society. Along with the tax cuts, Reaganomics was characterized by low spending for social services and increased military spending. This theory, according to Paul Roberts, Reagan's assistant treasury secretary for economic policy, focused on the economics of production rather than on the economics of consumption and spending. Such an economy was controlled by incentives for investment, which are directly affected by tax rates. Proponents of supply-side economics believed that cutting taxes and decreasing the federal budget would supposedly bring about noninflationary growth. In supply-side economics, production does not need to increase first; rather it increases supply of goods and services. Some argued that the tax cut would pay for itself by increasing revenue from increased sales.

In an address to the nation February 5, 1981, Reagan characterized the American economy as a "basket case" and argued that the nation was in the "worst economic mess since the Great Depression." He believed that government intervention and regulation should be kept to a minimum. In his 1981 inaugural address the previous month, Reagan had argued that "government is not the solution to our problem; government is the problem." He believed spending needed to be reduced, yet he also believed the military needed strengthening. The government must reduce inflation without creating a recession. A balanced budget, decreased reliance by individuals on the federal government, and high employment were other economic goals. Author Michael Boskin has described a sense of urgency in what the Reagan administration was doing—that the future was at stake.

David Stockman, a strong believer in supply-side economics, served as President Reagan's first director of the Office of Management and Budget. He believed in the need for a "frontal assault on the American welfare state." This assault included "risky and mortal political combat" with such groups as farmers, educators, students, Social Security recipients, and many others. Stockman criticized Reagan for not having the heart to carry out this phase of supply-side economics. He and other writers have characterized Reagan as a pragmatist who believed in a combination of monetarism (the belief that inflation can be controlled by controlling the money supply), supply-side economics, and traditional conservative orthodoxy.

Reagan's economic policy proved mostly negative. Federal deficits during his eight years in office were greater than those of all previous presidents combined. Some believed that his program would force Congress to cut social spending and end the "welfare state." Maximum income tax rates, cut from 70 to 33 percent, did not bring about the growth expected. Furthermore, tax cuts had taken away 30 percent of federal revenues. The size of government under Reagan grew by 30 percent in real terms rather than shrinking as had been hoped. President Reagan successfully motivated and inspired Americans, but his economic programs brought about considerable economic difficulties for some Americans.

Although Americans might disagree on the effectiveness of Reagan's economic programs, Reagan is credited with helping to bring about the end of the cold war between the United States and the Soviet Union. When he became president in 1981, Reagan stressed the need for increased military spending and assumed a strong stance against communism. In 1983 he proposed the Strategic Defense Initiative (SDI)—commonly known as Star Wars—which would protect the country from a nuclear attack by what Reagan called the "evil empire" (the Soviet Union). The largest government military project in American history, Star Wars was designed as an antiballistic space-based missile system that would destroy Soviet missiles before they reached the United States. The completion of such a project would have resulted in the end of the policy of mutually assured destruction that had maintained the peace between the two superpowers for the previous two decades.

SDI research began just as Mikhail Gorbachev assumed power in the Soviet Union. Gorbachev's new policy of openness and reform caused the United States to reevaluate its policy toward the Soviet Union. In 1985 Reagan and Gorbachev held their first meeting. No agreements were reached during the summit because of the Soviet insistence on an end to SDI. During the next four years the two leaders met three more times and finally concluded the Intermediate-Range Nuclear-Force Missile Treaty (INF) in 1987 when the Soviet's dropped their former demand. Many Americans believed that Reagan's insistence on the SDI program was designed to outspend and bankrupt the Soviet Union while others believe that the Soviet Union was already on the verge on collapse from internal forces. Regardless of the reason, the Soviet Union did collapse in 1991, effectively ending the cold war.

—*David E. Walker*

References

Boskin, Michael J. *Reagan and the Economy.* San Francisco: ICS Press, 1987.

Stockman, David A. *Triumph of Politics: How the Reagan Revolution Failed.* New York: Harper and Row, 1986.

See also Volume 1: Reaganomics; Supply-Side Economics; Volume 2 (Documents): Ronald Reagan's Remarks with Reporters on Air Traffic Controller's Strike.

Reaganomics

Name of economic program espoused by President Ronald Reagan.

When Ronald Reagan was elected president in 1980, largely on the basis of his economic program, the U.S. economy had been plagued with "stagflation" (a combination of high unemployment and high inflation) since the early 1970s. Reagan planned to restore growth and boost employment by cutting income taxes across the board, reducing nondefense spending, easing federal regulation of business and increasing the money supply slowly but steadily. He also promised to increase military spending and balance the federal budget within a few years. "Reaganomics," as it was called, thus would build on two elements of the economic program of the late 1970s under the previous administration of President Jimmy Carter—deregulation and monetary restraint—while adding aggressive new conservative measures. Most economists endorsed Reagan's monetary policy but doubted the overall feasibility of the program.

During his presidential campaign, Reagan increasingly claimed that tax cuts need not be offset fully by spending cuts. He was inspired in this view by an economic theory from economist Arthur Laffer, whose "Laffer curve" postulated that total federal tax revenues actually would increase if tax rates were reduced, because workers would be encouraged to work, save, and invest more. This notion—along with the idea that tax cuts would motivate the wealthy to invest in new plants and equipment (a theory known as trickledown), thereby creating new jobs for middle- and working-class Americans—were central tenets of supply-side economics. The promise of lower taxes without great sacrifice greatly appealed to stagflation-weary voters, who ushered Reagan into the White House by a wide margin.

Reagan followed through on most of his economic campaign promises by cutting taxes, easing economic regulation, and moderating economic growth. Following a severe but brief recession in the early 1980s, inflation plummeted. By that time, several of Reagan's top economic advisers, most notably Budget Director David Stockman, had resigned because they doubted the feasibility of Reaganomics. However, the president held firm, claimed his program was beginning to work, and won reelection in 1984. His successor and former vice president, George H. W. Bush, sustained Reagan's fundamental economic policies through 1992.

In retrospect, Reaganomics posted a mixed record. Inflation was controlled and economic growth rose moderately. Economic regulation was scaled back, boosting competitiveness in some sectors including the savings and loan industry, where this competitiveness led some individuals to engage in fraud to gain profits. Nondefense spending cuts were far outweighed by continually rising Medicare, Medicaid, and social security spending and by heavy defense spending. Nor did supply-side tax cuts prove effective; the largest (the Economic Recovery Tax Act of 1981) yielded an average annual net loss of roughly $250 billion per year from 1985 to 1991. Taken together, revenue losses and spending hikes boosted the national debt from 23 percent of GDP in 1981 to 69 percent in 1992. Reaganomics also increased the economic disparities between rich and poor; the income and wealth of the former rose dramatically while middle-class economic status changed little and the poor grew poorer. Under the administration of President Bill Clinton (1992–2000), many of Reagan's policies were reversed: Military spending was reduced and social programs were expanded. Reaganomics enjoyed a renaissance after the 2000 election of George W. Bush, who made a large income tax cut and deregulation central to his economic program.

—David B. Sicilia

References

Feldstein, Martin, ed. *American Economic Policy in the 1980s.* Chicago: University of Chicago Press, 1994.

Stein, Herbert. *Presidential Economics: The Making of Economic Policy from Roosevelt to Clinton.* Washington, DC: American Enterprise Institute, 1994.

See also Volume 1: Reagan, Ronald; Supply-Side Economics.

Recession

Downturn in aggregate output, income, and employment.

The National Bureau of Economic Research defines a recession as any period in which gross domestic product (GDP) has dropped for two consecutive quarters. The distinction between recession and depression is imprecise and depends on the severity of the unemployment increase and the length of the downturn of real GDP. In the post–World War II period, recessions occurred in 1945, 1949, 1958, 1961, 1970, 1975, 1980, 1982, 1991, and 2001 and usually lasted for one to two years.

In a "growth recession," there is a downturn in the rate of growth of real GDP, but the growth rate has not yet turned negative. Conditions for growth recession include a large decline in exports and a significant decrease in private expenditure relative to income. Most recently, these conditions became noticeable between the third quarter of 2000 and the second quarter of 2001. The government budget surplus plus the trade deficit equals the private-sector deficit—so if the government spends less than its income (tax revenue), thereby maintaining its surplus, and if the country buys more from abroad than it sells (spending more than its foreign income and thereby increasing its trade deficit) to keep GDP from falling, the private sector must also spend more than its income, thereby incurring a deficit. Thus, when the growth rate declines, a budget surplus cannot lead to a rise in private investment and a healthy long-run rate of profit.

Although the Federal Reserve may cut interest rates considerably in the face of excess capacity, the incentives to build more capacity remain few, even with cheap financing. Thus, increasing government spending and lowering taxes becomes necessary. Otherwise profits drop even farther than prices, while output shrinks and unemployment grows, and as a result the economy cannot run at or near full capacity. With reduced growth of disposable income, firms and households find it difficult to meet their payment commitments. Defaults and bankruptcies grow, and deflationary pressures occur.

—Zdravka K. Todorova and Mathew Forstater

References
Sherman, Howard J., and David X. Kola. *Business Cycles and Forecasting*. New York: Harper Collins, 1996.
See also Volume 1: Depressions.

Reciprocal Trade Agreements Act of 1934

Legislation passed by Congress that permitted the president to reduce tariff rates by up to 50 percent by a mutual agreement with a foreign country on a reciprocal basis.

The passage of the Republican-supported Hawley-Smoot Tariff Act of 1930 led to harsh criticism from the Democrats, who charged that President Herbert Hoover and the Republicans were responsible for the Great Depression. Hoover countered these accusations by pointing out that the international trade situation had already suffered as a result of the breakup of former European empires and the erection by these new European nations of high tariff walls. Nevertheless, Hoover lost the 1932 presidential election to Franklin D. Roosevelt. Roosevelt's secretary of state, Cordell Hull, long a proponent of free trade, advocated the passage of the Reciprocal Trade Agreements Act of 1934, legislation that allowed the executive branch to reduce or increase import duties by up to 50 percent from the rates established by Hawley-Smoot through mutually advantageous agreements with foreign nations. Hull worked diligently to conclude 25 reciprocal agreements by 1945. The reciprocal trade agreements signaled the acceptance of a freer trade policy and also shifted responsibility for conducting trade negotiations from the legislative to the executive branch, where it has remained ever since. Although Congress must approve trade agreements, the use of fast-track legislation—which Congress is prohibited from altering—has strengthened the power of the president in matters of foreign trade.

—*Cynthia Clark Northrup*

References
Pastor, Robert A. *Congress and the Politics of U.S. Foreign Economic Policy 1929–1976*. Berkeley: University of California Press, 1980.
See also Volume 1: General Agreement on Tariffs and Trade; Great Depression; Hawley-Smoot Tariff; Hull, Cordell; Protective Tariffs; Roosevelt, Franklin D.; World War II.

Relief Act of 1821

Legislation that adjusted debt repayment schedules for people who had bought public land before the federal government changed its method of selling public lands.

The United States government originally sold public lands through a credit or installment system that required repayment for the purchase over a four-year period. The Land Act of 1804 established a minimum purchase requirement of 160 acres and continued the price of $2 per acre for credit purchases. In 1820, Congress ended installment buying and required cash payments for future purchases. However, legislators lowered the minimum sale requirements to $1.25 an acre and 80 acres per purchase. The new policy placed an unfair burden on settlers that had bought land under the old system. Congress addressed this discrepancy by passing the Relief Act of 1821.

Congress had passed 12 such relief acts, which alleviated the burden on debtors from the requirements of the installment system, before 1820, and these acts generally extended the time of payment for settlers whose lands were scheduled for forfeiture within the year. The Relief Act of 1821 continued this principle but included additional provisions in response to the new policy of selling public land that Congress established in 1820. In addition to extending payment schedules, the act allowed settlers to return part of their land and retain the acreage that was equivalent to their payments. It also gave settlers a 37.5 percent discount off the original price of the land if they paid the whole amount. The act intended to lower the price of land purchased before 1820, to reduce an owner's existing debt to a level compatible with the new system, and to limit the number of forfeitures. These relief measures, although well intended, proved misguided. Settlers needed more than just time to pay off their debts, and the number of forfeitures did not diminish.

—*Peter S. Genovese*

References
Gates, Paul Wallace. *History of Public Land Law Development*. Washington, DC: U.S. Government Printing Office, 1968.
See also Volume 2: Land Policies.

Report on the Subject of Manufactures (December 5, 1791)

Treasury Secretary Alexander Hamilton's report on congressional aid to manufacturing.

On January 8, 1790, President George Washington spoke to Congress about the relationship between manufacturing and the national defense. He argued that manufacturing essential items like military supplies was necessary for the nation's safety. One week later, Congress ordered Secretary of the Treasury Alexander Hamilton to prepare a report on how the government could promote manufacturing in the United States. Hamilton worked on the report for nearly two years. He studied the economic ideas of Adam Smith and David Hume. The works of French Finance Minister Jacques Necker also greatly influenced him. After writing four drafts, Hamilton finally presented his *Report on the Subject of Manufactures* to Congress on December 5, 1791. (See Volume 2 for the full text of this document.)

In his opening remarks, Hamilton argued against those who believed America must remain a nation of farmers. He countered that manufacturing would bring more wealth to the nation than farming ever could. It would make use of the natural talent that most Americans had for invention. As Americans created new machines and other products, more and more people could find work. Women, children, and newly arrived immigrants would gladly work to make more money for themselves and their families. These new opportunities would allow all Americans to develop their individual talents.

Hamilton next argued against those who said that America must use all of its economic resources to expand westward and so must import its manufactured goods from Europe. He urged Americans to look at the political realities of the day; with each year it was becoming harder and harder to import goods from Europe. Constant war, along with the economic policies of most European nations, disrupted the free flow of trade across the Atlantic. Hamilton believed the United States must develop manufacturing simultaneously with its westward advance.

Hamilton concluded that manufacturing would not develop on its own in America. Only the national government could raise the massive amounts of capital necessary for manufacturing to take hold in the country. He advocated protective tariffs on rival foreign goods and establishment of a national board that would grant premiums or awards for excellence in manufacturing. Congress would grant bounties or cash payments to manufacturers that produced the most necessary items. Lastly, Hamilton said that Congress should take every measure to improve transportation in the country. Knowing that some might argue that these actions were unconstitutional (because the Constitution did not specifically state that Congress had such authority), Hamilton concluded that Congress had the power to promote manufacturing under the "necessary and proper" clause of Article 1 of the Constitution.

—*Mary Stockwell*

References

Hamilton, Alexander. *The Papers of Alexander Hamilton, Volumes VI–X*. New York: Columbia University Press, 1963.
See also Volume 1: Hamilton, Alexander; Volume 2 (Documents): *Report on the Subject of Manufactures*.

Report on Public Credit (January 1790)

Treasury Secretary Alexander Hamilton's plan to pay America's debts.

In January 1790, Secretary of the Treasury Alexander Hamilton presented his *Report on Public Credit*. He had prepared the report in response to Congress, which believed that solid support of the public credit (that is, the reputation of or confidence in the ability of the government to fulfill its obligations) was important to the "honor and prosperity" of the United States. Hamilton heartily agreed that the United States must place itself on a firm financial footing to win the world's respect. He worked diligently for nearly four months to prepare his 20,000-word report.

Hamilton calculated that the United States owed more than $11 million to foreign nations and more than $40 million to its own citizens. He argued that the government must repay the foreign debt according to the exact terms of the original loan agreements. He recommended the funding of the domestic debt at face value. He proposed to accomplish this goal by calling in outstanding government securities and issuing new bonds of the same value in their place. The national government would also assume the remaining debts of the individual states and pay them off under similar terms. Finally, he proposed the establishment of a sinking fund (which would be used to retire the debt) to guarantee payment of both the interest and principal of the national debt.

Hamilton recommended repaying the foreign debt by taking out new loans overseas. These loans would prevent a serious cash drain from the American economy. Increased duties on imports and tonnage (duties on ships based on their weight when loaded with cargo) could fund repayment of the domestic debt. The government could raise more money by placing new duties on imported wines, distilled spirits, tea, and coffee. He proposed a duty of 20 to 35 cents per gallon on Madeira and other wines, 20 to 40 cents per gallon on distilled spirits depending on the proof, 12 to 40 cents per pound on tea, and 5 cents a pound on coffee.

Republican Representative James Madison of Virginia led the Congressional opposition to Hamilton's recommendations. Madison favored "discrimination," a policy that would pay all the original as well as current owners of government securities. He also opposed the assumption of state debts, because Virginia and most of the other Southern states had already paid off their debts. Hamilton convinced most representatives that discrimination would not work, but Congress remained deadlocked over the assumption of state debts incurred before ratification of the Constitution in 1789. In July 1790, Hamilton offered to move the national capital from New York to Philadelphia for ten years and then to a site along the Potomac River in exchange for Madison's support. The compromise broke the deadlock, and Congress approved Hamilton's plans.

—*Mary Stockwell*

References

Hamilton, Alexander. *The Papers of Alexander Hamilton, Volumes VI–X*. New York: Columbia University Press, 1963.
See also Volume 1: Hamilton, Alexander; *Report on the Subject of Manufactures*.

Republican Party

Founded in February 1856 in opposition to proslavery forces in the Democratic and Whig parties.

The predecessors of the Republican Party included the Federalists (1789–1820) under the fiscal direction of Alexander Hamilton and the Whig Party (1836–1852) under the leadership of Speaker of the House Henry Clay. Both groups recognized the need for a protective tariff (in which tax revenues exceed expenditures; designed to reduce foreign competition) as opposed to a revenue-only tariff (which is only high enough to pay government expenses) and for federal funding of internal improvements. In the mid-1850s, the Whig Party split over the issue of extending slavery to new states and territories. Opponents of the spread of slavery formed a variety of parties including the Know-Nothings (a nativist, anti-immigrant group), the Free-Soil Party (which campaigned under the slogan "free soil, free labor, free men"), the abolitionists, and the Anti-Nebraska Democrats. By 1856 these groups merged to form the Republican Party. That same year the first Republican candidate for president, John C. Fremont, mounted a serious challenge against Democrat James Buchanan for the office of chief executive. Although Fremont lost, the Republican candidate in the 1860 presidential election, Abraham Lincoln, won. Opponents of the Republican Party (primarily Southern Democrats) thrust the nation into Civil War. In 1860, the Republican platform included a high protective tariff, free homestead land, and a transcontinental railroad, all of which appealed to Westerners, farmers, and eastern businesses. In the post–Civil War period, the Republican Party continued to support high tariffs and in the process encouraged the growth of big business by eliminating foreign competition. Because Republicans dominated politics during the late nineteenth century without much opposition, corruption permeated the political system. Cries for political reform finally led to the passage in 1883 of the Pendleton Civil Service Act, which sought to end patronage and initially placed 10 percent of federal jobs under a merit system. That percentage gradually increased and now includes most government positions.

Between the post–Civil War period and the early twentieth century, both major parties refused to address serious monetary issues, leaving the work to third-party candidates instead. But by 1896 the Republican Party became the standard-bearer for the continuation of the gold standard, which required that U.S. currency be backed with gold. During the presidency of Republican Theodore Roosevelt (1901–1908), the Republican Party moved toward a stronger foreign policy. As an imperialist power, the United States exerted its influence over the Philippines, Guam, Puerto Rico, and, to a lesser extent, Cuba. During the presidential administration of William Howard Taft, a Republican, foreign policy was dictated by "dollar diplomacy": Using dollars instead of bullets, Americans dominated much of Central and South America.

At the same time, Republicans initiated a policy of trust-busting at home designed to break up monopolies, a goal of Progressives who sought reform and better conditions for labor. With Democratic opponents arguing that the Treasury surplus called for a reduction of the tariff, Republicans agreed to lower duty rates if the states ratified a constitutional amendment that would allow a personal income tax. To the Republicans' surprise, the amendment was ratified in 1913. Although the tariff was initially reduced, during and after World War I rates climbed again on imports, culminating with the Hawley-Smoot Tariff of 1930 when rates reached an all-time high. Although Franklin D. Roosevelt and the Democrats claimed during the 1932 presidential election campaign that the Great Depression was the result of the passage of Hawley-Smoot, President Herbert Hoover said in numerous campaign speeches that the breakup of former European empires such as the Austro-Hungarian Empire, and the subsequent raising of tariff barriers overseas had caused the depression. Roosevelt won the 1932 election, and the Democrats maintained control over the White House and Congress until after World War II. In 1947 the United States moved toward free trade in an effort to avoid future international conflicts. As one of the original signatories of the General Agreement on Tariffs and Trade (GATT), the country pursued this goal during both Republican and Democratic administrations including those of Dwight D. Eisenhower, Richard Nixon, and Ronald Reagan. During the administration of President George H. W. Bush the United States signed the North American Free Trade Agreement (NAFTA), which opened up trade among the United States. Mexico, and Canada. The voluntary organization of GATT has since evolved to become the World Trade Organization. Republicans reversed their former protariff position after World War II because tariff barriers had been a major cause of the war.

Domestically, during the last 20 years the Republican Party has advocated tax cuts as a means of stimulating the economy, a philosophy originally called Reaganomics or supply-side economics. During the presidential administration of George W. Bush, a Republican who came to the White House in 2001, the Republicans have pushed for tax cuts to stimulate the economy following the recession of 2000 and the terrorist attacks of September 11, 2001. In addition to tax reform, the Republican Party has also pushed for welfare reform. (During the 1960s under Democratic President Lyndon B. Johnson, the country implemented a policy of wealth redistribution that created several generations of dependent recipients.) The Republican Party, beginning in the late 1990s in Wisconsin, started to reverse this trend by requiring welfare recipients to work while the government continues to provide childcare assistance for a specified period of time. During the administration of President Bill Clinton in 1996, the federal government made these changes to the entire welfare system nationwide.

—*Cynthia Clark Northrup*

References
Burdette, Franklin L. *The Republican Party: A Short History.* New York: Nostrand, 1972.
Schwengel, Fred. *The Republican Party: Its Heritage and History.* Washington, DC: Acropolis Books, 1987.
See also Volume 1: American System; Clay, Henry; General Agreement on Tariffs and Trade; Great Depression; Hamilton, Alexander; Protective Tariffs; Reaganomics; Supply-Side Economics; Whig Party; World Trade Organization; World War I; World War II.

Resumption Act (1875)

Monetary legislation that reversed inflationary government policies and restored specie payments (gold and silver) for the redemption of legal-tender notes.

Two views dominated the debate surrounding monetary policy in the decades following the Civil War. Conservatives feared depreciation (reduction of value of paper currency) and supported a return to specie—the use of gold and silver. Agrarian interests favored "cheap money" and wanted the government to increase the amount of currency in circulation. The panic of 1873 and the congressional elections of 1874 refocused the government's attention on the issue of currency. Resumption, that is, the return to specie payment, was popular among Republicans, many of whom were wealthy Northern industrialists. Party leaders expected that the issue would be settled sometime in the future, but loss of Republican majorities in Congress resulted in a resolution of the matter before the new Congress convened. The Senate passed the Resumption Act of 1875, a compromise measure authored and guided through Congress by Republican Senator John Sherman of Ohio, the chair of the Senate Committee on Finance.

Adopted on January 14, 1875, the act expanded the issuance of national banknotes (issued by state banks) and provided for the elimination of greenbacks (paper currency that had been printed during the Civil War to pay for the conflict) from circulation. However, the act effectively established a system that enabled the federal government to contract the money supply. The law required the Treasury to mint silver coins to replace fractional paper currency and removed the limitations placed on the amount of notes national banks could issue. It called for reduction in the amount of government notes from $382 to $300 million and enabled the Treasury to retire greenbacks equivalent to 80 percent of the banknotes issued. In addition, it authorized the resumption of specie payments for retiring greenbacks to begin on January 1, 1879. Theoretically, new issues of notes would keep pace with retirements. However, implementation of the act decreased the availability of cash, and prices continued to fall, creating a deflationary effect. Opposition to the Resumption Act led to the creation of the National Greenback Party, which supported inflationary policies. Inflation would have lessened the value of money, meaning that back debts would be repaid with cheaper money.

—Peter S. Genovese

References
Timberlake, Richard H. *Monetary Policy in the United States: An Intellectual and Institutional History.* Chicago: University of Chicago Press, 1993.
See also Volume 1: Congress; U.S. Department of Treasury.

Revenue Tariffs
Taxes on imports for the purpose of generating revenue only, not for the protection of domestic manufacturers.

A deficiency in planning for revenue generation led to the failure of the Articles of Confederation, a loose confederation of the states (1777–1789) that operated until the new constitutional government took effect. Thus a major problem the framers of the Constitution dealt with was the ability of the proposed federal government to generate revenue. Delegates to the Constitutional Convention agreed that Congress should have the power to tax but restricted tariffs to imports only. The first tariff, passed in 1789, placed a 5 percent duty on most imported items, but luxury items such as wines, dis-

tilled spirits, and tea carried a rate as high as 50 percent. An increase of 2.5 cents a gallon on molasses was also included in the first tariff. Congress passed the tariff to generate income to retire the Revolutionary War debt and to provide funds for the fledgling government. In 1790, Congress increased the rates by 50 percent, raising the average duty to between 7 and 10 percent ad valorem (rates based on the value of the goods). Although the duty on hemp decreased, the rate on steel increased.

By 1794, Secretary of the Treasury Alexander Hamilton reported that the government needed $24 million to cover losses from discontinued trade with Great Britain, pay current debts, and provide funds for General Anthony Wayne's army, which was fighting the Indians in the Ohio Valley. In addition to increasing rates on everyday items such as coal and salt, Congress also passed excise taxes (taxes on the manufacture or distribution of certain nonessential goods) on carriages, auctions, manufactured snuff, and sugar. Two years later, Congress approved further increases on a larger list of items including a 10 percent rate on sugar, molasses, tea, cocoa, velvet, and muslin. The high rates on wines, distilled spirits, and tea remained at that level, but Congress agreed that by 1797 the rates would decrease.

Before the Tariff of 1816 was passed, Congress twice increased rates to cover the cost of wars. In 1804 all duties increased by 2 percent to cover expenses associated with fighting the Barbary pirates. In 1812 rates doubled to pay for the cost of the War of 1812.

Each of these tariffs generated revenue for the government, which, however, continued to run a deficit. After the War of 1812, the United States experienced a period of prosperity that resulted in more proceeds for the government. At the same time, Congress decided to pass the first of a long series of protective tariffs designed to encourage domestic manufacturing.

—Cynthia Clark Northrup

References
Stanwood, Edward. *American Tariff Controversies in the Nineteenth Century.* New York: Russell and Russell, 1967.
See also Volume 1: Protective Tariffs.

Robber Barons
Pejorative term for wealthy industrialists apparently first employed by Carl Schurz, editor of the *New York Evening Post,* in a speech at Harvard University in 1882.

The term *robber barons* is part of a vociferous debate about the characters and motives of America's leading nineteenth-century industrialists. Historians question whether these men, such as the premier oilman John D. Rockefeller (1839–1937) or financier and railroad magnate Jay Gould (1836–1892), operated simply as monopolists or whether in spite of their faults they acted as the builders of America's industrial might with its attendant high standard of living for the wealthy made possible by the early twentieth century. Rockefeller, for instance, was painted in unflattering colors in

Henry Demarest Lloyd's *Wealth against Commonwealth* (1894) and Ida M. Tarbell's *The History of the Standard Oil Company* (1904). Allan Nevins, though, in *Study in Power: John D. Rockefeller: Industrialist and Philanthropist* (1953), presents Rockefeller in a basically sympathetic light. Much the same has happened for Jay Gould, who was once regarded as the prototype of a robber baron. Matthew Josephson in *The Robber Barons: The Great American Capitalists, 1861–1901* (1934) castigated Gould without mercy. Undaunted, however, by Josephson's marshaling of evidence against the man, Julius Grodinsky in *Jay Gould: His Business Career, 1867–92* (1957) defended him in important respects. This change in perception occurred after the large monopolies had been dissolved by order of the Supreme Court during the Progressive Era (1900–1920).

—*Keith L. Miller*

References
Bridges, Hal. "The Robber Baron Concept in American History." *Business History Review*, vol. 32 (Spring 1958): 1–13.
Folsom, Burton W., Jr. "Robber Barons Have Been Unfairly Denigrated." In William Dudley, ed., *The Industrial Revolution: Opposing Viewpoints*. San Diego, CA: Greenhaven Press, 1998.
Jones, Peter d'A., ed. *The Robber Barons Revisited: Problems in American Civilization*. Lexington, MA: D. C. Heath, 1968.
Solganick, Allen. "The Robber Baron Concept and Its Revisionists." *Science and Society*, vol. 49 (Summer 1965): 17–23.
See also Volume 1: Carnegie, Andrew; Rockefeller, John D.

Rockefeller, John D. (1839–1937)

Leading nineteenth-century industrialist and philanthropist who made his fortune in the oil industry.

John D. Rockefeller was born in 1839 to William A. Rockefeller and Eliza Davison at Richford, New York. His father, an itinerant businessman, often traveled away from home, and John developed a closer relationship with his mother, a devout Baptist. She instilled in the boy values of ethical conduct including discipline, thrift, and a belief in hard work.

Rockefeller put his upbringing to good use. After studying at Folsom's Commercial College in Cleveland (his family had moved to Ohio in 1853) and following a six-month job search, Rockefeller began his business career in September 1855 working as a clerk and bookkeeper in a wholesale commission house, which sold securities to dealers at wholesale prices. In 1859 he resigned from this position and, with a loan from his father, formed a partnership with Maurice B. Clark. From their commission house, the two men diversified into oil refining in 1863. At that time Samuel Andrews, an expert in refining crude, joined them. Rockefeller soon bought out Clark's interest and entered the oil industry full time. In 1864 Rockefeller married Laura Celestia Spelman, and the couple had four children. In 1867 Henry M. Flagler joined Rockefeller's firm, which they reorganized as Rockefeller, Andrews & Flagler. By 1870 the partnership had become Standard Oil of Ohio.

Beginning with refining, Rockefeller soon added the transporting of oil via pipelines, especially with the purchase of United Pipe Lines in 1877. He entered the production end of the business in 1889 with the acquisition of the Ohio Oil Company. From those origins and along with the establishment of the Standard Oil Trust in 1882, Rockefeller began to amass a great fortune, which peaked at $900 million in 1913. In 1911, the Supreme Court ordered the Standard Oil trust dissolved into smaller companies and forbade the continuation of the same board of directors for each smaller company formed. Much of the wealth (some $540 million) amassed by Rockefeller went into charities and his philanthropic foundations, particularly the Rockefeller Foundation. He created the foundation in 1913 after Andrew Carnegie convinced him to donate part of his wealth to quiet critics and socialists who might attempt to take it all by altering the U.S. economic and political system. Rockefeller died in 1937 at Ormond Beach, Florida.

—*Keith L. Miller*

References
Nevins, Allan. *Study in Power: John D. Rockefeller, Industrialist and Philanthropist*. New York: Scribner's, 1953.
Rose, Kenneth W. "John D. Rockefeller." In John A. Garraty and Mark C. Caernes, eds., *American National Biography*. New York: Oxford University Press, 1999.
See also Volume 1: Robber Barons; Standard Oil.

Rolfe, John (1585–1622)

First cultivator of marketable tobacco in Virginia.

John Rolfe was responsible for the development of a cash crop in the Virginia colony; he cross-pollinated tobacco plants to create a mild blend highly desired in Europe. Rolfe, his wife, and infant daughter traveled onboard the *Sea Venture* from England in 1609 and were stranded in Bermuda for almost a year with other settlers before being rescued by other ships of the Virginia Company—an event that inspired Shakespeare's *The Tempest*. Rolfe's wife and child died en route, and he arrived in the Virginia colony in 1610 a widower. The colony, meant to make profits for the Virginia Company, desperately needed a staple crop, but the tobacco grown by the region's Native Americans had a taste unfavorable in comparison to that grown by the Spanish in the Caribbean and Central America.

Between 1611 and 1612, Rolfe experimented with tobacco seeds smuggled from Spanish Surinam and developed a tobacco that, when tested in London, compared favorably with the Spanish product. In addition to being known for his work with tobacco, Rolfe also became famous as the husband of Pocahontas, whom he married in the spring of 1614 after she had converted to the Church of England and taken the name Rebecca. Rolfe and Pocahontas visited England in 1616 as part of a promotional tour on behalf of the Virginia

Company. Pocahontas contracted smallpox there and died, leaving Rolfe again a widower with a son, Thomas. After he returned to Virginia, Rolfe continued to plant tobacco. Virginia exported 20,000 pounds of it in 1617, and Rolfe was elected to the House of Burgesses, the colony's representative assembly. Rolfe died in 1622 after marrying for a third time, but the cause of his death, perhaps a devastating Indian raid that year, remains unknown.

—*Margaret Sankey*

References

Abrams, Ann Uhry. *The Pilgrims and Pocahontas: Rival Myths of American Origin.* Boulder, CO: Westview Press, 1999.

Bridenbaugh, Carl. *Vexed and Troubled Englishmen 1590–1642.* New York: Oxford University Press, 1968.

See also Volume 2: Trade Policy.

Roosevelt, Franklin D. (1882–1945)

Former governor of New York and thirty-second president of the United States, who served during the Great Depression and World War II.

Franklin Delano Roosevelt was born at Hyde Park, New York, on January 30, 1882, to James and Sara Delano Roosevelt. He graduated from Harvard University in 1904 and then studied at Columbia University law school before beginning his career as a lawyer. In 1905 Roosevelt married a distant cousin, Eleanor Roosevelt, who was the niece of former President Theodore Roosevelt. Together they had five children: Anna Eleanor, James, Elliott, Franklin D. Jr., and John A. Roosevelt. Both Franklin D. Jr. and John served terms in the House of Representatives.

Roosevelt began his political career in 1910 when he successfully ran for the New York Senate, where he gained a reputation as a reformer. In 1912 he supported Democratic candidate Woodrow Wilson for the presidency. Wilson appointed him as assistant secretary of the navy in 1913 and Roosevelt continued at that post until 1920, serving throughout World War I. In 1920 he ran as the Democratic vice-presidential candidate on the party ticket with James M. Cox, but they lost to Warren G. Harding and Calvin Coolidge. After he returned to New York, Roosevelt contracted polio, which left him crippled. He spent the next eight years working to regain the use of his legs and reemerged on the political scene in 1928, to win the governorship of New York. In 1932 he ran against Herbert Hoover, the incumbent Republican president. By this time, the country had been in a depression for three years.

President Franklin D. Roosevelt's approach to economic policy embodied both experimentation and pragmatism and was not a total break with Hoover's policies. The Roosevelt administration, for example, continued the Reconstruction Finance Corporation, which provided funds for banks and businesses so they could hire employees and invest in equipment. Both Roosevelt and his wife, Eleanor Roosevelt, had been admirers of Hoover in the early 1920s and had attempted to persuade Hoover to join the Democratic Party.

Franklin Delano Roosevelt came from old money. Indeed, the Delanos had made their initial fortune in the fur trade in the 1600s when New York was still New Amsterdam. Still, like his beloved cousin Theodore, Franklin D. Roosevelt did not worship money and thought little of the pursuit of wealth for its own sake. Roosevelt was no traitor to his class; he was a decent human being who had compassion for people and sought to ameliorate unnecessary suffering.

When Franklin D. Roosevelt became president of the United States in 1932 and intoned that "we have nothing to fear but fear itself," the Great Depression was in full swing. Unemployment stood at 25 percent of the workforce, and no suitable unemployment compensation program existed. During his famous first 100 days in office—which became something of a benchmark for his successors—he declared a banking holiday so that confidence in those vital institutions could be rebuilt. He also sent a torrent of legislative proposals to Congress, including legislation authorizing the creation of the Agricultural Adjustment Administration (to stabilize farm prices) and the National Recovery Administration (to coordinate industries, establish production quotas, and guarantee collective bargaining). The Supreme Court declared much of this early New Deal legislation, which was meant to restart the depressed economy, unconstitutional in 1935. The Court came around to the New Deal–style of thinking by 1937 and began upholding measures such as the National Labor Relations Act of 1935, which made it easier for labor unions to organize workers and to bargain collectively.

After declaring the banking holiday and taking other New Deal measures (including establishment of relief agencies such as the Civilian Conservation Corps, the Public Works Administration, and the Works Progress Administration) to get the nation's economy on an even keel, Roosevelt took steps to deal with some of the underlying causes of the Great Depression, for example, the rampant stock market speculation that had taken place in the 1920s. Emblematic of the problems on Wall Street was the fact that in 1938 the president of the New York Stock Exchange had been sent to Sing Sing, the penitentiary of the state of New York. Roosevelt signed legislation establishing the Securities and Exchange Commission to monitor and regulate the stock market and appointed Joseph P. Kennedy, later ambassador to Great Britain, as its first director. Following Kennedy in that position was William O. Douglas, who went on to serve on the U.S. Supreme Court for 36 years.

The influence on Roosevelt of economist John Maynard Keynes, with his emphasis on the utility of budget surpluses and deficits, is doubtlessly overstated. For one thing, much of Keynes' most influential work was not published until after Roosevelt had already taken action. Roosevelt's greatest economic miscalculation was probably his overconcern with deficit spending (in which the government spends more than its revenue) while the economy still operated far under capacity in the mid-1930s. By striving to reduce the deficit, he contributed to and perhaps unnecessarily caused the recession of 1937 and 1938. Putting people to work in productive pursuits became one of his most important goals, and he achieved this via the work of appointees Harold L. Ickes of the Works Progress Administration and Harry Hopkins of the Public Works Administration. Many of these organizations' projects still contribute to the strength of the U.S. economy, from the three original buildings on the campus of McNeese State University in Lake Charles, Louisiana, to the Riverwalk in San Antonio, Texas. These facilities continue to be used and have generated income for their respective communities through employment, fees, and tourism.

In foreign relations, Roosevelt, who blamed the high tariff rates established by the Hawley-Smoot Tariff Act for the Great Depression, implemented a policy of tariff reductions on an individual basis with foreign countries. In 1934 Congress passed the Reciprocal Trade Agreement Act, which allowed the president to reduce tariff rates by up to 50 percent for countries that would reduce tariff rates on American imports. Roosevelt also initiated the Good Neighbor Policy with Central and South America in an effort to open trade within the Western Hemisphere. He enjoyed less success in economically depressed Europe, where Adolf Hitler was already in control of Germany. When World War II broke out, Roosevelt tried to maintain American neutrality, which was required under the Neutrality Acts of 1935 and 1936 forbidding the sale of arms or the lending of funds to belligerent nations. By 1937 the acts were amended to allow for a "cash-and-carry" policy that required any nation at war that purchased U.S. goods to pay cash and to carry the goods on their own ships, not American ships that could be attacked.

After the fall of France and the bombing of England by Germany, Roosevelt implemented a new program called Lend-Lease that allowed the British and Russians to obtain goods without paying for them immediately. By that time the United States was on the verge of entering the war. On December 7, 1941, Japan attacked Pearl Harbor and the United States declared war on Japan. Funding of the war effort included the sale of war bonds and rationing at home. Roosevelt, a proponent of Keynesian economics (which called for deficit spending when necessary) later in the Great Depression, successfully coordinated business production and military requirements. As the war neared its conclusion in late 1944, the Roosevelt administration arranged for an economic conference held at Bretton Woods, New Hampshire, to discuss the postwar international economic system. The goal was to create a stable international system that would reduce the risk of future wars. Roosevelt also worked to lay the foundations for the United Nations.

On April 12, 1945, Roosevelt died in Warm Springs, Georgia, just a few weeks before Germany surrendered. Although he did not live to see the results of his efforts, the Bretton Woods system (which included the creation of the International Monetary Fund) and the United Nations served as the two principal international stabilizers of the postwar period.

—*Henry B. Sirgo*

References

Leuchtenburg, William Edward. *Franklin D. Roosevelt: A Profile.* New York: Hill and Wang, 1967.

See also Volume 1: Agricultural Adjustment Act of 1938; Great Depression; National Recovery Act; New Deal; Social Security Act of 1935; World War II; Volume 2 (Documents): Franklin D. Roosevelt on Hawley-Smoot Tariff; Herbert Hoover's Response to Roosevelt on Hawley-Smoot Tariff.

Roosevelt, Theodore (1858–1919)

Hero of the Spanish-American War; vice president under the twenty-fifth U.S. president, William McKinley; twenty-sixth president; leading Progressive; and groundbreaking conservationist.

Mark Hanna, the legendary moneyman in Republican Party politics around 1900, suggested that the rambunctious Theodore Roosevelt be put in the innocuous position of vice president on the ticket with William McKinley, who was elected president in 1901. Roosevelt had been the governor of New York from 1898 to 1900. He was well known by Americans because during the Spanish-American War, he had played a major role in taking the Philippines—as assistant secretary of the Navy in 1897 and 1898, he had ordered U.S. Commodore George Dewey to engage the Spanish fleet in the Philippines in the event of a war. He resigned his government position to form the Rough Riders, a volunteer unit, and gained a reputation as a war hero during the Spanish-American War (1898). Roosevelt became president in September 1901 after McKinley was assassinated by an anarchist at the Buffalo Pan-American Exposition.

Theodore Roosevelt transformed the office of the presidency and the nation's economy. He held a stewardship theory of the presidency, believing that the president should do all he can to promote the public's cause, save that which is prohibited by the U.S. Constitution. Roosevelt's initiatives resulted in the construction of the Panama Canal, pure food and drug legislation, the Tillman Act prohibiting corporate contributions to political campaigns (but which failed to limit personal contributions), trust-busting of monopolies, and a tremendous expansion of protection afforded to the nation's lands and forests. Roosevelt's vigorous use of executive orders to protect forests established a precedent used by other presidents to engage in economic environmental policymaking that restricted the sale and use of national lands. Franklin D. Roosevelt's New Deal (with its emphasis on government actively pursuing the public good) was greatly influenced by Theodore Roosevelt's Square Deal (which was based on corporate limitations on monopolistic activities, consumer protection, and conservation of natural resources for the benefit of the public). Roosevelt signed the Antiquities Act of 1906, which protected American historical and archaeological sites. It was invoked most recently in 1996 by President Bill Clinton to protect the Grand Staircase–Escalante National Monument in Utah.

After serving as president from 1901 to 1908, Roosevelt left office and went on safari with his son Kermit. William Howard Taft, Roosevelt's hand-picked successor, won the election of 1908, and Roosevelt believed Taft would continue the policies that he had implemented. However, during Taft's administration, two events transpired that created a rift between the two men. First, Roosevelt had advised Taft to avoid raising the issue of the tariff, but Taft called Congress into special session immediately after becoming president to address the issue. After Congress passed the Payne-Aldrich Tariff Act of 1909, Taft praised the measure as the best bill ever passed by Republicans—even though many in the party opposed the measure. The second issue involved one of Roosevelt's appointments. Roosevelt believed that the forestry department should be under the direction of a qualified individual who would use scientific management principles to protect the nation's forests. He chose Clifford Pinchot to head the department. During the Taft administration, Pinchot discovered that Secretary of the Interior Richard Ballinger had failed to investigate a fraudulent coal claim by a company on government lands in Alaska. He reported this to Taft, who did nothing. Pinchot then mentioned it to a reporter, who ran a story about the illegal mining, and Taft fired Pinchot for insubordination. Although Congress later exonerated him, Pinchot did not get his job back. The Ballinger-Pinchot controversy and the tariff issue led Teddy Roosevelt to seek the Republican nomination again in 1912. However, the Republican Party renominated Taft. Roosevelt then formed the Bull Moose Party, thereby splitting the Republican vote and ensuring the election of the Democratic candidate Woodrow Wilson.

Evidence of Teddy's greater ability to appeal to mass audiences manifested itself when, while settling a border dispute between the states of Louisiana and Mississippi in 1901, he refused to shoot a bear officials had tied to a tree for Roosevelt's "hunting" pleasure. A true sportsman, he refused to take unfair advantage of an animal that had been tied up. The teddy bear immortalizes this action. Roosevelt wrote a serious history of the American West and served as president of the American Historical Association following his presidential term.

—Henry B. Sirgo

References
Chessman, G. Wallace. *Theodore Roosevelt and the Politics of Power.* Prospect Heights, IL: Waveland Press, 1994.
See also Volume 1: Conservation; Panama and the Panama Canal; Protective Tariffs; Pure Food and Drug Act.

Rule of 1756

British naval doctrine that was the basis of Britain's definition of legal trade between neutrals and belligerents and the source of growing hostilities between England and the United States in the early 1800s.

The Rule of 1756, a British naval doctrine, emerged in a new commercial and imperial trading situation. During the Seven Years' War in the mid-eighteenth century, France could not supply its West Indian colonies in the face of British naval superiority, and so it relaxed its state monopoly on colonial trade and officially opened French ports to foreign ships.

Britain countered this action with the Rule of 1756, which stipulated that no trade closed to neutrals in a time of peace could remain opened in a time of war. According to the English, this self-serving doctrine legitimized their seizing of neutral vessels trading with French possessions, because they claimed that trade prohibited by municipal law in peace should be prohibited by international law in war.

When new hostilities between England and France emerged in the wake of the French Revolution (1789–1799), Britain regularly extended the limitations placed on neutral shipping and exceeded the original dictates of the Rule of 1756. Although the extension of this doctrine was aimed more at northern European nations than at the United States, the new measures drastically affected American shipping. In May 1793, Britain issued an Order in Council that blockaded continental Europe, prohibiting the carrying by any country of certain foodstuffs. In November of that year, Parliament extended the order to prohibit all neutral trade between France and its colonies. This course of action culminated with the Orders in Council of November 11, 1810, which blockaded all ports under French control. The new interpretations of the Rule of 1756 placed British naval forces at odds with American commercial shipping. Numerous seizures of U.S. vessels and cargoes and other abuses resulted, which increased tensions and eventually led to the War of 1812.

—Peter S. Genovese

References
Stagg, J.C.A. *Mr. Madison's War: Politics, Diplomacy, and Warfare in the Early American Republic, 1783–1830.* Princeton, NJ: Princeton University Press, 1983.
See also Volume 1: Embargo of 1807; Non-Importation Act; Non-Intercourse Act of 1809; War of 1812.

Rural Credit and Development Act of 1994

Legislation that expanded the role of the Farm Credit System (FCS) in rural areas.

By the 1990s, in the aftermath of the 1980s farm crisis during which low farm prices and high interest rates caused the loss of many family farms, younger farmers had left the land and the average age of rural citizens was in the sixties. Many rural areas had become poverty zones. The decrease in population and businesses also led to a crumbling tax base and infrastructure. In an effort to revitalize rural America and attract more young people into agricultural production, Congress passed the Rural Credit and Development Act of 1994 (HR 4129), which relaxed Farm Credit System (FCS) provisions regarding rural housing loans, enabling more people to qualify for them. In areas where the population numbered 2,500 or less, these loans could cover up to 85 percent of a home's appraised value. Also, by waiving the requirement that services by rural and agricultural businesses must be performed on the farm, it expanded these businesses' eligibility for loans. This allowed a host of companies that provided in-shop services to qualify for loans.

Congress designed the act to encourage local banks to operate more liberally in their lending policies to new businesses by authorizing the FCS to purchase all eligible loans. This not only decreased the risk to lending institutions, but it also provided more capital for loans in these areas. For the first time, rural communities also became eligible for FCS loans to finance community projects. Banks liberalized their lending policies to include local businesses that provide goods and services if such a loan would directly benefit a farm cooperative. Finally, rural water systems and power generating stations also qualified for FCS lending under the new rule. Rural borrowers and communities have benefited from expanded FCS lending activity and from access to FCS funds by rural banks.

—*T. Jason Soderstrum*

References

U.S. Department of Agriculture. *Credit in Rural America.* Washington, DC: U.S. Government Printing Office, 2001.
See also Volume 1: Farm Credit System Reform Act of 1996.

Rural Electrification Administration (REA)

Government-subsidized program to provide electricity to rural areas in the United States.

Beginning in the 1880s and through the 1920s, urban areas of the country moved from gas and coal energy to electric power. Industries that had been dependent on rivers for hydropower were able to move to other locations. Manufacturers began producing household goods such as refrigerators, washing machines, radios, telephones, and hot water heaters. As the standard of living increased in the metropolitan areas, a growing disparity appeared between rural and urban areas. Electric companies resisted cries for service from throughout the countryside, claiming that the low return on investment could not justify the high cost of capital required to hook rural residents to the electrical grid—that is, it would cost more than the consumer would be willing to pay. Several states including New York tried to establish programs that would encourage low-cost hydroelectric power, but the initiatives failed as states battled economic difficulties brought on by the Great Depression. When Franklin D. Roosevelt, the former governor of New York, became president in 1933, he appointed engineer Morris L. Cooke (who headed the Power Authority of the State of New York when Roosevelt was governor) to investigate the feasibility of a federal program to build electricity cooperatives in rural areas. In a report the following year, Cooke predicted that electricity could be provided by scattered small generating plants in rural areas at a cost of $400 per farm. Roosevelt signed Executive Order 7037 creating the Rural Electrification Administration (REA) on May 11, 1935, and Congress subsequently appropriated $410 million for the program. Electricity cooperatives received funds at the same rate of interest as U.S. loans (it was later changed to a fixed 2 percent rate), with members repaying the loans over a period of 10 to 25 years. By the end of 1938, more than 350 cooperative electrical generating plants had been constructed, and they had begun to provide electricity to 1.5 million farms. Over the next two decades, most farms joined the system. The REA later became responsible for programs that provided telephone, and most recently Internet, service to rural areas. In 1994 the REA became part of the Rural Utilities Service, which Congress created and made part of the U.S. Department of Agriculture.

Of all the legislation passed under Roosevelt's New Deal (his policy of using the government to assist people during the Great Depression), the REA proved the most successful and least controversial. Throughout its existence, the REA helped to establish 930 cooperatives that continue to supply 11 percent of Americans with electricity. Congress appropriated $57 million in federal loans to these nonprofit groups and in the process increased the standard of living for farmers and encouraged further agricultural development.

—*Cynthia Clark Northrup*

References

Brown, D. Clayton. *Electricity for Rural America.* Westport, CT: Greenwood Press, 1980.
Schurr, Sam H., Calvin C. Burwell, Warren D. Devine, and Sidney Sonenblum. *Electricity in the American Economy: Agent of Technological Progress.* Westport, CT: Greenwood Press, 1990.
See also Volume 1: Agricultural Policy; Great Depression; Roosevelt, Franklin D.; Volume 2: Agricultural Policy.

S

Schecter Poultry Corp. v. United States (1935)

"Sick chicken case" in which Supreme Court struck down the National Industrial Recovery Act, the legislative backbone of the New Deal.

During the Great Depression when Congress and President Franklin D. Roosevelt began implementing New Deal reforms to relieve individual and corporate economic problems, the Supreme Court's perception of congressional power under the Constitution's commerce clause was ambiguous. The issue hinged on the relationship between the regulation of intrastate business activity and the role of interstate commerce. The constitutional regulation of trade, reserved to the states according to the Tenth Amendment, became a source of judicial dispute between the Court and the New Dealers.

The Court called into question the validity of the National Industrial Recovery Act (NIRA), which Congress passed in 1933 authorizing Roosevelt to adopt "codes of fair competition" for various trades or industries. Specifically, the codes regulated items such as minimum wages and prices, maximum hours, and collective bargaining agreements. In 1934, in order to enforce NIRA codes, prosecutors charged the Schecter brothers, Brooklyn poultry owners, with violating the wage and hour provisions of the New York Metropolitan Live Poultry Industry Fair Competition Code. A lower court convicted them even though the vast majority of poultry sold in New York came from other states; Schecter Poultry brought the chickens to New York City but resold its stock exclusively to local dealers. The Schecters appealed, and the case eventually made its way to the Supreme Court.

On May 27, 1935, the Court rejected the government's arguments that the Schecters' activities fell within the "stream of commerce" and, though completely local, "affected commerce." In rejecting the government's arguments, the Supreme Court held the NIRA unconstitutional as applied to *Schecter.* The Court ruled that the Schecters' activities were not within the "current" or "stream" of commerce "because the interstate transactions ended when the shipments reached the Schecters' New York City slaughterhouses." Congress therefore had no authority to regulate their business because it was intrastate. The Court also stated that the Schecters' actions had an "indirect" effect on commerce—the company's "wage and price policies might have forced interstate competitors to lower their prices," but the actual "impact was much too indirect to allow for congressional control." The Court found that the Schecters' business occurred within the legal parameters of intrastate commerce and that the federal government "had no authority to regulate working conditions in the firm." Justice Benjamin Cardozzo, expressing the unanimous 9-to-0 decision, stated that the NIRA's legislative power operated as "delegation running riot."

Roosevelt appeared shocked and incensed. He expressed anger at liberal jurists like Cardozzo and Louis Brandeis, who had voted with the conservative members of the bench. The Court's narrow interpretation of the commerce clause destroyed Roosevelt's industrial recovery program and led him to proclaim that the country would become "relegated to the horse-and-buggy definition of interstate commerce." The Roosevelt administration had to reshape the New Deal as a result of the decision. Congress passed a new series of legislative enactments to conform to *Schecter.* Early in his second term, and still smarting from *Schecter,* Roosevelt sent a special message to Congress asking for an enlargement of the Court from 9 to a possible 15 members. Despite his arguments for change, Roosevelt's own party in Congress did not support the reorganization plan. The public, as well, did not endorse the proposal out of profound respect for the delicate balance in our constitutional system. The court-packing scheme died and so, too, did Roosevelt's attempt to restore completely the NIRA approach to government-business relations.

—Charles F. Howlett

References

A.L.A. Schecter Poultry Corp. et al. v. United States, 295 U.S. 495 (1935).

Corwin, E. S. "The Schecter Case—Landmark or What?" *New York University Law Quarterly Review,* vol. 13 (1936): 151–190.

Cushman, Barry. *Rethinking the New Deal Court: The Structure of a Constitutional Revolution.* New York: Oxford University Press, 1998.

Emanuel, Steven. *Constitutional Law.* Larchmont, NY: Emanuel Law Outlines, 1987.

Leuchtenburg, William Edward. *Franklin D. Roosevelt and the New Deal, 1932–1940.* New York: Harper and Row, 1963.
See also Volume 1: National Industrial Recovery Act; New Deal, Roosevelt, Franklin D.

School Busing

Controversial process of collecting children by bus from far-flung areas and driving them to a central school, used first to consolidate schools and capture efficiencies of scale and later to desegregate public schools and promote racial integration.

Policymakers have long sought to standardize education while cutting government expenditures per student. The lack of technological innovation and physical infrastructure in transportation, however, made school consolidation impossible until the 1930s. Since that time the number of schools and school districts has decreased by 67 and 91 percent, respectively, while the number of students has risen by 83 percent. Busing not only enabled this consolidation, it promoted it. States often passed laws consolidating schools at the same time as they passed laws to provide public funds for pupil transportation. School busing thus mollified rural critics of school consolidation. Economies of scale were captured in regard to both physical infrastructure (school buildings) and labor (teachers per student).

School busing later played a seminal role in desegregating schools after the Civil Rights Act. In this context, busing transferred children from all-black areas into white schools and white children into black schools to achieve a court-ordered ratio of black to white children. Symbolically tied to the bus boycotts, school busing became one of the most visible aspects of desegregation. The U.S. Supreme Court in 1971 backed the use of school busing as a policy tool to promote the consolidation and desegregation of schools.

The expansion of school busing has come at both an economic and social cost. Public expenditures on busing have risen enormously over the years, now costing more than $10 billion annually. Currently 60 percent of all schoolchildren ride the bus to school, covering 21 million miles every day on 400,000 buses. Rural schools spend a disproportionate amount of money on busing, while rural students spend far more time commuting to school than their suburban and urban counterparts. The influence of school consolidation and busing on communities and students is receiving growing attention from academics and policymakers. After whites fled to the suburbs to avoid school busing of their children to inner-city schools, the courts rejected an argument that would have allowed busing across district lines. With predominantly minority enrollment in big city districts, busing continued, but its intended effect was reduced. In 2003 school busing has become less of an issue for desegregation, with judges such as Barefoot Sanders (U.S. District Court of the Northern District of Texas) removing court orders for busing in Dallas, Texas.

—*W. Chad Futrell*

References
Killeen, Kieran, and John Sipple. *School Consolidation and Transportation Policy: An Empirical and Institutional Analysis.* Randolph, VT: Rural School and Community Trust, April 2000. Available: www.ruralchallenge.org; accessed May 30, 2001.
See also Volume 1: Civil Rights Movement; Education; Volume 2: Education.

SDI

See Strategic Defense Initiative.

Securities and Exchange Commission

Government commission created by the Securities and Exchange Act of 1934 designed to monitor and regulate the sale of securities.

The Securities and Exchange Commission (SEC) consists of five members appointed by the president and confirmed by Congress who enforce several acts designed to protect investors and to bolster confidence in the financial markets. At the height of the Great Depression, Congress passed the Securities Act of 1933. As a consequence of the stock market crash of 1929 and the subsequent Great Depression, the act required the full disclosure of all information to the SEC before registration for the sale of securities would be granted. If the SEC found that the firm omitted information or did not disclose sufficient information, then registration would be denied. The following year Congress passed the Securities Exchange Act of 1934, which required more disclosures from companies and was designed to prevent unfair practices in the U.S. stock exchanges. It also placed all exchanges under the authority of the SEC. In 1935 Congress charged the SEC with responsibility for enforcing the Public Utility Holding Company Act of 1935. The SEC then monitored all financial practices of electric and gas utilities but did not determine utility rates. The SEC was also charged with enforcing the Trust Indenture Act of 1939, the Investment Company Act of 1940, and the Investment Advisers Act of 1940. Congress also required that the SEC act as a participant in bankruptcy cases under the National Bankruptcy Act.

—*Cynthia Clark Northrup*

References
Manne, Henry G., ed. *Economic Policy and the Regulation of Corporate Securities.* Washington, DC: American Enterprise Institute for Public Policy Research, 1969.
Tyler, Poyntz, ed. *Securities, Exchanges, and the SEC.* New York: H. W. Wilson, 1965.
See also Volume 1: American Stock Exchange; Great Depression; Nasdaq; New Deal; New York Stock Exchange; Roosevelt, Franklin D.

Servicemen's Readjustment Act (G.I. Bill of Rights) (1944)

Legislation providing assistance to veterans returning to civilian life after military service during World War II.

President Franklin D. Roosevelt signed the Servicemen's Readjustment Act on June 22, 1944. The legislation emerged from Congress after months of intense debate and parliamentary maneuvering. Opposition in Congress came from those concerned about the possible effects the bill might have on admissions standards at American institutions of higher education. The eventual success of the legislation can be attributed to the American Legion, which publicized the legislation—both to veterans who would benefit from the bill and to the pubic—from its introduction in January 1944 until Congress passed it on June 13, 1944.

The bill provided five benefits to veterans: education and training; guaranteed loans for a home, farm or business; unemployment pay of $20 a week for up to one year; job-finding assistance; and review of dishonorable discharges. The act also called for the building of additional Veterans Administration hospitals. To be eligible for education benefits, a World War II veteran had to have served 90 days or more after September 1940 and had to be honorably discharged. A veteran received one year of full-time education plus a period equal to his or her time in service up to a maximum of 48 months.

The educational institutions received up to a maximum of $500 a year for tuition, books, fees, and other costs for each veteran admitted to educational programs. The Veterans Administration paid an unmarried veteran an allowance of up to $50 a month; veterans with dependents received more.

The World War II GI Bill program ended in July 1956. The program changed American higher education dramatically by increasing the number of students. In the peak year of 1947, veterans accounted for 49 percent of all college enrollments. Almost eight million veterans received training at a total cost to the government of $14.5 billion. The program helped control the unemployment rate after demobilization and allowed veterans to enter the labor market with additional skills.

—*John David Rausch Jr.*

References

Bennett, Michael J. *When Dreams Came True: The GI Bill and the Making of Modern America.* Washington, DC: Brassey's, 1996.

See also Volume 1: Education; World War II; Volume 2: Education.

Seward, William (1801–1872)

American statesman, radical antislavery politician, and secretary of state in the 1860s who paved the way for active foreign expansion of the United States.

Born May 16, 1801, in Florida, New York, William Henry Seward graduated from Union College in 1820 and commenced law practice in Auburn, New York, in 1822. During the 1830s he got involved in politics as a member of the Anti-Masonic Party and later as a Whig. William Seward served as a state senator in New York from 1830 to 1834. As a governor of New York from 1839 to 1843, he proposed a costly internal improvement program and advocated tax support for parochial schools. As conflict grew between the free North and slave South, he also endorsed radical antislavery principles, uncompromisingly stressing the socioeconomic over the human rights objections to slavery and emerging as a leader of the antislavery wing of the Whigs.

Seward carried his adamant antislavery stance into the U.S. Senate in 1849 where he served until 1861. He steadily contested compromise schemes of the political and economic settlement of the problem of slavery—such as the Missouri Compromise of 1820 and the Kansas-Nebraska Bill of 1854—and strongly supported the admission of California into the union as a free state without any concessions to the slavery system. This activity propelled him to the leadership of the newly formed Republican Party (1855), although his attempts to secure his party's nomination to the presidency during the campaigns of 1856 and 1860 proved unsuccessful.

In March 1861 Seward became secretary of state under President Abraham Lincoln. As a chief of American diplomacy during the Civil War, he advocated a strong and active foreign policy. He skillfully and firmly outmaneuvered attempts by the Confederacy to use economic leverage—particularly the dependence of the English and French textile industries on Southern cotton—to bring about intervention of England and France into the war on the Confederate side. Seward strongly advocated active U.S. expansion in the Western Hemisphere, Asia, and the Pacific, using mainly economic and commercial means. He supported rapid economic development of the American West and high tariffs to protect the growing domestic industry from European markets, and he actively promoted expansion of modern communications such as telegraph and railroads. Also, in 1868 and 1869, Seward unsuccessfully tried to obtain rights for the United States to built a canal across the Panamanian Isthmus. His ambitious projects to acquire key bases in the Caribbean and the Pacific to control trade routes there and annex some territories (including the Danish West Indies, Hawaii, and Alaska) received much serious opposition in Congress at that time as needless and extravagant. Congress rejected all of them except for the Alaska purchase, an agreement labeled "Seward's Folly" by his political opponents. William Seward died in Auburn, New York, on October 10, 1872.

—*Peter Rainow*

References

Taylor, John M. *William Henry Seward: Lincoln's Right Hand.* New York: Harper Collins, 1991.

Van Deusen, Glyndon G. *William Henry Seward.* New York: Oxford University Press, 1967.

See also Volume 1: Alaska.

Share Our Wealth Plan

Brainchild of Huey P. Long, popular Democratic Louisiana governor and U.S. senator, who proposed his plan to alleviate poverty and the Great Depression.

Dissatisfied with President Franklin D. Roosevelt's efforts to end the Great Depression, Huey P. Long developed his Share Our Wealth Plan to equalize the distribution of wealth in the United States. The core of Long's plan involved the government confiscating any surplus of personal wealth over $5 million accumulated by the few and redistributing it to the poor. Goods would also be redistributed: If someone had two houses, they would give one to someone who did not own a house, and someone with two cars would give one away. The plan also guaranteed nonworking families an annual income of $2,000 to $3,000 and working families at least $5,000. Further, Long proposed to shorten the workweek to 30 hours and the work year to 11 months, thereby increasing the need for workers. Other proposals included forgiveness of debt, free education, and a pension for those over age 60 without taking paycheck deductions. Procuring wealth from the very rich was to finance all of Long's proposals.

Although the plan had mass popular appeal, it also had its critics. Economist and politicians called the plan Marxist. Others claimed that Long designed the whole plan as a ploy to win presidential votes. Long defended his program at every chance offered, and popularity for the plan grew as Long's charisma, careful manipulation, and ardent defense of the plan reached more people. Share Our Wealth clubs began to form, and the movement gained significant momentum until Long was assassinated in 1935.

—Lisa A. Ennis

References
Hair, William Ivy. *The Kingfish and His Realm: The Life and Times of Huey P. Long.* Baton Rouge: Louisiana State University Press, 1991.
See also Volume 1: Long, Huey; New Deal; Roosevelt, Franklin D.; Share Our Wealth Society.

Share Our Wealth Society

Plan by Huey P. Long that gained currency during the Great Depression proposing redistribution of wealth.

Early in 1934, Louisiana Governor Huey P. Long made known his ideas about wealth and poverty, which became known as the Share Our Wealth Plan. The plan called for the redistribution of wealth from the very rich to the poor. On February 23, 1934, Long announced that the fight to equally distribute wealth would be conducted through the Share Our Wealth Society, a national political organization. With the motto "Every man a king," the society endeavored to promote Long's program of wealth redistribution. Long was elected to the U.S. Senate in 1931.

The first Share Our Wealth clubs were organized in Long's home state of Louisiana and were usually formed by Long's associates. Long used the radio to promote his plan and society. Supporters began flooding his office with requests for in-

formation on how to form a club. Long's staff eventually outgrew the allotted space given to senators, and he had to rent adjoining offices to accommodate extra clerical help just to keep up with demand. Each person who wrote in received a pamphlet entitled *Share Our Wealth: Every Man a King,* a copy of Long's autobiography, and a subscription to *American Progress* magazine, Huey Long's press.

Long's office reported that there were 7,682,768 names on the roster of club members. Long publicly supported African American membership in the program, and white supporters formed the first African Americans clubs in Louisiana. Most of the clubs formed in the South, followed by the north central states; 17 clubs were even formed in Ontario, Canada, by people who heard Long's radio addresses. After Long's assassination Gerald Smith, a longtime Long associate, tried to keep the movement alive, but without Long the plan and clubs dwindled. By the summer of 1936 the majority of the clubs had disbanded.

—Lisa A. Ennis

References
Hair, William Ivy. *The Kingfish and His Realm: The Life and Times of Huey P. Long.* Baton Rouge: Louisiana State University Press, 1991.
See also Volume 1: Long, Huey; New Deal; Roosevelt, Franklin D.; Share Our Wealth Plan.

Shelley v. Kraemer (1948)

Important property rights and equal protection case decided by the U.S. Supreme Court in 1948.

In 1911, 30 of the 39 property owners in a St. Louis residential area signed an agreement that prohibited the conveyance of property to anyone not of the Caucasian race, specifically "people of Negro or Mongolian Race," for a period of 50 years. At the time the agreement was signed, African Americans owned 5 of the 57 parcels in the area, and African Americans had occupied one parcel since 1882. The Shelleys, who were African Americans, purchased their home in 1945 without knowledge of the restrictive agreement. The successors to the original signers brought suit against the Shelleys. The Shelleys won at the trial level but lost in the Missouri Supreme Court. The U.S. Supreme Court agreed to hear the matter along with a similar companion case from Michigan, *McGhee v. Sipes.*

A basic principle of the American economic and political system involved private ownership of property. Property owners retained the right to set the terms, even discriminatory ones, for the sale of their property. However, even though these restrictive covenants were private agreements, the owners sought to enforce them in state courts. Under the Fourteenth Amendment, states cannot "deny to any person within its jurisdiction the equal protection of the laws" if state action is involved.

The Supreme Court held that the Fourteenth Amendment protected the owners' rights to "acquire, enjoy, own and dispose of property" and that the participation of the state in enforcing the restrictions was sufficient to bring the amendment into play. In effect, the Court ratified the validity of private discrimination but prevented the use of the state courts to enforce it under the equal protection clause. Because the state courts could not enforce the discriminatory residential agreements, landowners were not bound by them, and so *Shelley v. Kraemer* opened American neighborhoods to racial and religious diversity and served as a precursor to the Fair Housing Act of 1968.

—*Susan Coleman*

References
Shelley v. Kraemer, 334 U.S. 1 (1948).
See also Volume 1: Fourteenth Amendment.

Sherman Anti-Trust Act (1890)

Act passed in 1890 that made monopoly and restraints of trade illegal.

In the United States a sharp conflict of opinion has existed over the relative merits of business monopolies. Many believe that government policy toward business monopolies has been something less than clear-cut and consistent. Even to the present day, the major thrust of federal legislation and policy has focused on maintaining and promoting competition.

Historically, the U.S. economy, steeped in the philosophy of free, competitive markets, has been a fertile ground for the development of a suspicious and fearful public attitude toward business monopolies. This fundamental distrust emerged following the Civil War when local markets widened into national markets as transportation infrastructure improved, resulting in the growth of big business. Increasing mechanization of production and increasingly widespread adoption of the corporate form of business enterprise were important forces giving rise to the development of trusts, or business monopolies, in the 1870s and 1880s. Trusts developed in the petroleum, meatpacking, railroad, sugar, lead, coal, whiskey, and tobacco industries, among others, during this era.

In certain industries—the oil and steel industries, for example—market forces failed to provide adequate control to ensure socially tolerable behavior on the part of the company. High tariffs eliminated foreign competition and economies of scale vanquished domestic competition, and workers, paid low wages, suffered as a result of this lack of competition. To correct this situation, two techniques of regulation were adopted as substitutes for or supplements to the market. First, in those few markets where economic realities preclude the effective functioning of the market (that is, where the market tends toward a "natural monopoly"), the United States established public regulatory agencies to control economic behavior—by setting utility rates, for example. Second, in most other markets, social control has taken the form of antimonopoly or antitrust legislation designed to inhibit or prevent the growth of monopoly.

Acute public resentment of the trusts, which developed in the 1870s and 1880s, culminated in the passage of the Sherman Anti-Trust Act in 1890. The act made monopoly and restraints of trade—for example, collusive price fixing or the dividing up of markets among competitors—criminal offenses against the federal government. Either the Department of Justice or parties injured by business monopolies could file suits under the Sherman Act. The courts could dissolve firms found in violation of the act, or injunctions could be issued to prohibit practices deemed unlawful under the act. Fines and imprisonment were also possible results of successful prosecution. Further, parties injured by illegal combinations and conspiracies could sue for triple the amount of damages. The Sherman Act seemed to provide a sound foundation for positive government action against business monopolies.

The case against business monopoly centers on the contentions that business monopoly causes a misallocation of resources, retards the rate of technological advance, promotes income inequality, and poses a threat to political democracy. The defense of business monopoly revolves around the point that interindustry and foreign competition, along with potential competition from new industry entrants, makes American industries more competitive than generally believed. Also, supporters believe that some degree of monopoly may be essential to the realization of economies of scale and that monopolies are technologically progressive.

The cornerstone of antitrust policy consists of the Sherman Act of 1890 and later the Clayton Act of 1914. In summary, the Sherman Act specifies that "Every contract, combination . . . or conspiracy in the restraint of interstate trade . . . is . . . illegal," and that any person who monopolizes or attempts to monopolize interstate trade is guilty of a misdemeanor. The only successful prosecution under the Sherman Anti-Trust Act in the nineteenth century occurred not against big business, but against labor unions during the Pullman Strike of 1894, when 100 percent of the railroad workers agreed to strike. In 1895 when the U.S. Supreme Court heard the case of E. C. Knight Co., the sugar producer—the most prominent use of the act against big business in the nineteenth century—the Court ruled that this company, although controlling up to 98 percent of the market, did not violate the antitrust law because competition still existed. During the administration of President Theodore Roosevelt (1901–1908), the government finally won 45 cases against big business by using the Sherman Anti-Trust Act; during the administration of President William Howard Taft another 90 cases were successfully prosecuted, including one against Standard Oil in 1911. Congress reinforced the Sherman Anti-Trust Act with the passage of the Clayton Anti-Trust Act, which included fines or imprisonment for individuals who violated the act.

—*Albert Atkins*

References
Shepperd, William G. *The Economics of Industrial Organization.* Englewood Cliffs, NJ: Prentice-Hall, 1979.
See also Volume 1: Clayton Anti-Trust Act; Pullman Strike; *United States v. E. C. Knight Co.*; Volume 2: Labor; Volume 2 (Documents): Sherman Anti-Trust Act; Clayton Anti-Trust Act.

Sherman Silver Purchase Act (1890)

Late nineteenth-century act that authorized the U.S. Treasury to purchase a substantial amount of silver on a monthly basis.

During the post–Civil War period, the federal government attempted to take greenbacks (paper currency) out of circulation and restrict legal tender to gold only. A debate ensued as debt-ridden farmers and laborers fought to increase the money supply, thereby driving up inflation and decreasing the value of their debt. In 1890, during the administration of President Benjamin Harrison, Congress passed the Sherman Silver Purchase Act in which the government agreed to buy 4.5 million ounces of silver a month from silver miners in the West. Within three years a financial panic hit the country, and the gold reserve level dropped to a point that pushed the United States toward bankruptcy as foreign investors demanded payment for bonds in gold. President Grover Cleveland pushed in 1893 for the repeal of the act. He believed that foreign investors had stopped purchasing government bonds because they feared that the United States was abandoning the gold standard. The repeal of the act hurt western miners, southern and western farmers, and labor. These three groups found a common cause on the issue of silver and on that basis formed the Populist Party. Although the party disintegrated after the Spanish-American War because of its anti-imperialist position, the Progressives (reform-minded upper-class and upper-middle-class individuals) enacted the Populist Party's entire platform at the federal or state level over the next few decades.

—*Cynthia Clark Northrup*

References

Horwitz, Steven. *Monetary Evolution, Free Banking, and Economic Order.* Boulder, CO: Westview Press, 1992.

McElroy, Robert. *Grover Cleveland: The Man and the Statesman.* New York: Harper and Brothers, 1923.

See also Volume 1: Clayton Anti-Trust Act; Pullman Strike; Volume 2: Labor.

Sinclair, Upton Beal, Jr. (1878–1968)

Journalist, novelist, and unsuccessful politician whose socialist views found expression in the best-selling book *The Jungle.*

Born in Baltimore, Maryland, in 1878, Upton Sinclair and his family moved to the East Side of New York City when he was ten. Four years later Sinclair entered the College of the City of New York, graduating with a bachelor's degree in 1897. He then attended graduate school at Columbia University. He had intended to study law, but he changed his mind in favor of literature and contemporary politics. He supported himself and paid for graduate study by writing juvenile novels. Although he did not receive a graduate degree, his love for literature and writing quickly found expression in the form of social protest.

The prolific Sinclair became one of the most widely read writers in the United States. He wrote more than 80 books, many of which focused on social and economic issues. He also wrote numerous pamphlets that he published himself. In 1902 he moved to Princeton, New Jersey, where he joined the Socialist Party. Strongly influenced by the social and economic changes occurring in modern, urban-industrial America, Sinclair used his literary skills as a crusader for economic justice. He became an effective propagandist of the Progressive movement to address social and economic problems in the first two decades of the twentieth century. Along with Ida Tarbell, Lincoln Steffens, Frank Norris, and Jack London (he and London founded the Intercollegiate Socialist Society in 1905), Sinclair kept company with a select group of writers President Theodore Roosevelt disparagingly called "muckrakers."

Sinclair spent seven weeks in Chicago investigating the unsanitary conditions in the meatpacking industry and wrote about it, his observations initially appearing in the Socialist periodical *Appeal to Reason.* His work proved so compelling that Doubleday, Page and Company published it in novel form as *The Jungle* in 1905. The book became an immediate best-seller, established Sinclair's literary immortality and eventually led to passage in 1906 of federal legislation—first the Meat Inspection Act and later the Pure Food and Drug Act. To Sinclair's dismay, however, the socialist propaganda of the novel, aimed at the atrocious working conditions and harsh treatment of the immigrant workers, went largely ignored in favor of the "vivid descriptions of unsanitary food handling, contaminated meat, and generally dirty conditions." In Sinclair's own words: "I aimed at the public's heart and by accident hit it in the stomach."

In subsequent years Sinclair wrote several other novels depicting the negative effects of capitalism on American society including *The Metropolis* (1908) about upper-class New York society and its derision of the poorer people, *The Moneychangers* (1908) dealing with the economic consequences of the panic of 1907, and *King Coal* (1917) a criticism of working conditions in the coal mines. A nonfiction work, *Profits of Religion* (1918), continued his condemnation of the economic pitfalls of capitalism. For a brief period, he had resigned from the Socialist Party over its antiwar position, but he returned because of his disillusionment with President Woodrow Wilson's post–World War I policies.

In the 1920s Sinclair moved to California, where he ran unsuccessfully for numerous state and federal political offices. In 1933 during the Great Depression, he organized a political campaign for the governorship popularly called "End Poverty in California" that focused on his lifelong belief that poverty was at the root of America's capitalistic and political failures. Sinclair took direct aim at the New Deal's inability to provide economic relief to the masses in California. Rather than placing the unemployed on relief, Sinclair urged that they receive the chance to produce for themselves by having the state purchase land on which they could grow their own crops and make their own products. Seeking broader appeal among state constituents, Sinclair ran on the Democratic ticket. But his advocacy of government-owned factories and insistence that laissez-faire capitalism hurt all groups cost him the election. Republican incumbent Frank Merriam won handily.

In his later years Sinclair continued publishing works critical of American economic society. The third volume of his

11-volume Lanny Budd series, *Dragon's Teeth* (1942), won the Pulitzer Prize. Near the end of his life Sinclair became less enthusiastic about the nature of political reform. Whether or not literary critics consider him a serious novelist or quaint writer, Sinclair's works have a strong sense of social justice and economic reform. He remains "one of the original missionaries of the modern spirit." When he was 90 years old, he died in Bound Brook, New Jersey, on November 25, 1968.

—*Charles F. Howlett*

References

Bloodworth, William A., Jr. *Upton Sinclair.* New York: Macmillan, 1977.

Dell, Floyd. *Upton Sinclair: A Study in Social Protest.* New York: AMS Press, 1970.

Harris, Leon A. *Upton Sinclair: American Rebel.* New York: Thomas Y. Crowell, 1975.

Rideout, Walter B. *The Radical Novel in the United States, 1900–1951: Some Relationships of Literature and Society.* Cambridge, MA: Harvard University Press, 1956.

Scott, Ivan. *Upton Sinclair, the Forgotten Socialist.* Lewiston, NY: Edward Mellen Press, 1997.

Sinclair, Upton. *The Autobiography of Upton Sinclair.* New York: Harcourt, Brace and World, 1962.

See also Volume 1: Pure Food and Drug Act; Roosevelt, Theodore.

Sixteenth Amendment (1913)

Amendment to the United States Constitution sanctioning an income tax.

The Sixteenth Amendment (1913) revolutionized funding of the federal government by giving Congress the power to "lay and collect taxes on incomes, from whatever source derived, without apportionment among the several States, and without regard to any census or enumeration." Once ratified, Congress wasted no time in exercising its authority, and the graduated income tax quickly became the nation's chief source of revenue.

The Sixteenth Amendment developed during the Progressive Era (1900–1920) as Americans' concern grew over fiscal and social issues. By the turn of the twentieth century, an expanding federal government had rendered obsolete many traditional sources of funds; tariff revenues would no longer pay for expanding government agencies and programs. At the same time, the general public had become increasingly uncomfortable with disparities of wealth created by industrialization. Reformers sought to reduce protective tariffs, perceived by many as harmful to the lower classes, as a revenue measure and increase financial contributions from wealthier individuals and corporations. Many powerful businesses and manufacturers who supported high tariffs argued that an income tax would undermine traditional American democracy and transform the United States into a socialist or communist society. In addition to this type of resistance, reformers also had to wrestle with the legal implications involved in proposing an income tax. In 1895 the U.S. Supreme Court had ruled in *Pollock v. Farmers' Loan and Trust Company* that an income tax not apportioned according to the population of each state was a direct tax that violated Article 1, Section 9, Clause 4 of the Constitution. Because any income tax proposal would also be subject to judicial review, it seemed to many that a constitutional amendment offered the best course.

Ironically, a group of conservative Republican members of Congress actually introduced the proposal that would lead to the amendment. In 1909 antitariff Republicans and Democrats in Congress, most from the Midwest, aligned themselves in support of an income tax bill as an attachment to the current tariff measure. Hoping to neutralize this legislation, the conservatives presented a constitutional amendment legalizing the income tax. They hoped it would lead to the defeat of the bill and, more importantly, they felt confident that the states would never ratify the amendment. President William Howard Taft supported the amendment, and the short-term conservative strategy proved successful. Still believing that the amendment would fail, Congress sent it to the states. To the surprise of many, over the next four years 36 states ratified the Sixteenth Amendment, making it part of the Constitution. With the amendment ratified in 1913, Congress immediately passed a new income tax law using a progressive rate system based on ability to pay. The tax imposed a 1 percent tax on individuals and corporations earning more than $4,000, with rates ranging up to 6 percent on incomes over $500,000. The revenue generated by these new measures helped finance U.S. participation in World War I, and the Sixteenth Amendment had long-range social, economic, and political consequences for the nation, with income tax rates reaching heights of 65 percent to 70 percent and debates about tax cuts occurring from the John F. Kennedy administration through the presidency of George W. Bush.

—*Ben Wynne*

References

Grimes, Alan P. *Democracy and the Amendments to the Constitution.* Lexington, MA: Lexington Books, 1978.

U.S. Senate. *Report of the Subcommittee on the Constitution, Committee on the Judiciary.* Washington, DC: U.S. Government Printing Office, 1985.

See also Volume 1: Protective Tariffs; Volume 2: Taxation.

Slavery

Ownership of humans as a labor force and cornerstone of the economy of the South until its defeat in the Civil War.

The first slaves arrived in North America from Africa in 1619. They helped cultivate and harvest crops such as coffee, tobacco, sugar, rice, and later, cotton. For the most part, slavery was unprofitable in the North, where smaller farms were cultivated by families themselves, and by the nineteenth century it had mostly disappeared from the North. The Constitution prohibited the importation of slaves after 1808, but in the 1850s Southerners began to discuss the reopening of the slave trade.

Although there were few slaves in the North during colonial times as early as the 1680s Samuel Sewall wrote a book called *The Selling of Joseph* in which he warned of the potential problems of slavery and encouraged those in the New

World to stop the practice before it became a formal institution. However, Northerners made few attempts to address the issue. In the 1830s, the balance of power in the Senate between free and slave states was threatened when Missouri applied for statehood as a slave state. Henry Clay, the Whig Speaker of the House of Representatives, negotiated the Missouri Compromise allowing the admission of Missouri as a slave state and Maine as a free state and establishing 36 degrees, 30 minutes latitude as the dividing line—all new states below the line would be slave states, and those above the line would be free states. That appeared to have resolved the issue until Texas won its independence from Mexico and applied for statehood in 1836. Northerners protested the extension of slavery and the admission of Texas as a slave state. During the 1830s several incidents involving slavery gained national attention. A ship carrying slaves left Virginia bound for New Orleans; the slaves took over the ship and landed at Nassau in the British Caribbean, where British authorities declared them free since slavery was illegal throughout the British Empire. American owners claimed the slaves were property obtained before the end of the slave trade in 1808 under the Constitution and should therefore be returned. The British refused, and no compensation was paid. In another famous case, the judge ruled in the *Amistad* trial in 1840 that the Africans on board the ship had been taken from Africa and therefore must be released because the slave trade had ended almost 30 years earlier.

Slavery became a frequent political issue during the 1840s and 1850s. During the Mexican-American War, Congress debated the Wilmot Proviso in 1846 and 1847, which would have required all new territory gained during the war to be free. The proviso was attached to an appropriations bill for military funding. Although the proviso never passed, the debate it sparked politicized the slavery issue: Northerners advocated the containment of slavery, and Southerners wanted to expand slavery to new territories. The Compromise of 1850 settled the issue temporarily, with California being admitted as a free state and Texas as a slave state. In 1850 Congress also passed a stronger Fugitive Slave Act that placed responsibility for returning runaway slaves with federal authorities instead of the states—many of which had passed personal liberty laws making it difficult for slaves to be returned to the South. To placate Northerners, Congress also passed a law that banned the sale of slaves in Washington, D.C.

The slavery issue emerged again as a national issue in 1854 when Stephen Douglas proposed the construction of a transcontinental railroad from Chicago to California. Southerners wanted the railroad to go from Atlanta to California along a southern route. To gain support for the northern route, Douglas proposed a repeal of the Missouri Compromise and advocated popular sovereignty, which would have allowed people in the new territories of Kansas and Nebraska (through which the railroad would run) to determine if their state would be free or slave. Both territories were located north of the Missouri Compromise line. Proslavery and antislavery forces engaged in fighting over Kansas. Kansas sent a proslavery constitution to Congress in 1858, and Congress returned it because of voting irregularities, requesting a second vote. The state constitutional convention then removed the proslavery clauses and the slavery advocates refused to participate since they believed the first election to be valid. A new constitution was drafted and sent to Congress in 1859; the House of Representatives approved it, and the Senate rejected it. After Southern states left the Union in December 1860 and February 1861, Congress finally approved the constitution and Kansas became a free state.

Between 1854 and 1860 the issue of slavery gained further attention. In a Senate race in Illinois, Republican candidate Abraham Lincoln and Democratic Senator Stephen Douglas engaged in several debates, during which Lincoln argued that slavery should not extend into new territories and that it was morally wrong. Southerners remembered his words during the election of 1860, and South Carolina threatened to leave the Union if he was elected president. It followed through on its threat. Southerners were also paranoid of Northern efforts to end slavery after John Brown's raid on Harper's Ferry, in which Brown, a white abolitionist from Kansas, attempted to seize weapons from the federal arsenal to arm slaves for an insurrection. The government prevented the insurrection but Southern fears continued to grow. While these events were transpiring, a few (fewer than 1,000) slaves managed to escape captivity through the Underground Railroad, a network of individuals who hid runaway slaves or assisted them to their freedom in the North or Canada.

The South considered that the perpetuation of slavery was necessary to support its agrarian civilization. During the Civil War, Vice President Alexander Stephens of the Confederate States of America described slavery as the "cornerstone of the Confederacy," whose plantation wealth was usually dependent on land and "property of persons." Senator John Calhoun, speaking in the U.S. Senate on December 27, 1837, argued that "domestic slavery . . . composes an important part of their [the South's] domestic institutions, inherited from their ancestors, and existing at the adoption of the Constitution." James Henry Hammond, governor of South Carolina and later U.S. senator, supported the economic necessity of the institution of slavery in his book *Cotton Is King*. In an 1858 speech in the Senate, Hammond argued that blacks constituted an inferior class that could perform the drudgeries of the Southern agrarian economy. Southerners believed that slavery allowed white slaveholders to pursue intellectual and cultural interests.

George Fitzhugh, in his 1850 pamphlet *Slavery Justified, by a Southerner,* argued that blacks benefited economically from slavery. He contended that they could not take care of themselves, but that their masters ensured that they were "well fed, well clad, have plenty of fuel, and are happy. They have no dread of the future—no fear of want."

Edmund Ruffin, one of the Southern Fire-Eaters (an organization of people who would rather eat fire than give in to the Northern antislavery position) and also the man who fired the first shot at Fort Sumter, which began the Civil War, argued extensively for the need for Southern slavery. Abolition, he believed, would destroy the South economically. In contrast with the economic system of the North and its "wage slavery," Ruffin argued that the concept of "free labor" should really be called the "slavery of labor to want," because Northern workers received mere subsistence wages most of the time. Ruffin subscribed to the philosophy of the inferiority of the African slave. He also argued that Southern slaves enjoyed not only employment but also housing, comforts of family and health, and old age care. Ruffin did admit, however, that free laborers had more incentive to work hard and that slaves attempted to work only as much as was necessary to avoid being punished. Ruffin also noted that the North had the advantage of constant shiploads of immigrants adding to the labor pool.

Benjamin Morgan Palmer's "Thanksgiving Sermon, 1860" at the First Presbyterian Church in New Orleans, Louisiana, contended that Southern whites had received a "providential trust" to continue slavery as it existed. He reasoned that slavery supported the South's material interests and that the principle of self-preservation forced the South to continue it. He also argued that only a tropical race could survive working in the tropical climate of the South and that slavery was part of the social fabric of the South. Palmer further argued that if masters freed their slaves and transported them back to Africa, the slaves would starve rather than return to "their primitive barbarism."

Palmer argued that slavery benefited the North as well as the South, because the North had profited from the South's need for its products (textiles and iron, for example). Palmer also reasoned that the wealth of England and other countries had increased as a result of the products of Southern soil, because cotton (a duty-free product because it was domestic) was used in the textile mills.

During 1861 and much of 1862, the North did not fare well militarily and lost several battles. The South was able to use slaves to continue farming while the white masters fought in the war. Furthermore, the Confederate states had tried to work out alliances with Great Britain and France, which they believed needed Southern cotton for manufactured products, although the strategy backfired because of a glut on the English cotton market. President Abraham Lincoln developed a strategy that would strike a blow at the Southern economy with the Second Confiscation Act. This legislation, which passed July 17, 1862, freed slaves belonging to anyone who rebelled against the U.S. government. Previously Lincoln had attempted to strike a balance between the abolitionists who sought the abolition of slavery and those in the North and the Union border states of Kentucky, Missouri, Delaware, and Maryland who opposed freeing the slaves. Lincoln's role in the war had been to save the Union, and to bring that about he initially accepted the compromise on the slavery issue by signing the second Confiscation Act (1862), but the act could not be enforced because Union forces did not control any of the South. In the latter part of 1862, Lincoln began drafting his Emancipation Proclamation, which would abolish slavery in rebellious states under Union control. He signed the document January 1, 1863, in an effort to block England's support of the Confederacy—support that seemed imminent. After the adoption of the Emancipation Proclamation, England could no longer afford to support the Southern cause. It announced its opposition to slavery, and said it could not support a regime dedicated to upholding this institution.

During much of the war slaves had been fleeing the Confederate states, but after the Emancipation Proclamation, the number of slaves escaping to the North increased. Blacks fought in the Northern armies, strengthening the Northern military, which by then had begun to experience a manpower shortage.

By autumn of 1863, the Confederate economy had started to disintegrate. Consumer products were scarce, as the North had established a successful blockade of the South, and the agrarian South could not manufacture these items at home. Costs rose to extremely high levels, and Southern currency became virtually worthless. In April 1865, the bloody conflict ended. The most devastating blow to the South was the abolition of slavery, which had been the foundation of the Southern economy. Congress abolished slavery with the passage of the Thirteenth Amendment in 1865 and protected the rights of African American citizens with the Fourteenth Amendment in 1868.

—*David E. Walker*

References
Heisey, D. Ray. "Slavery: America's Irrepressible Conflict." In Dewitte Holland, ed., *America in Controversy: History of American Public Address.* Dubuque, IA: W. C. Brown, 1973.

Mitchell, Betty Lou. "Prophet without Honor: A Biography of Edmund Ruffin." Ph.D. dissertation, University of Massachusetts, 1979.

Perritt, H. Hardy. "Robert Barnwell Rhett's Speech, July 4, 1859." In J. Jeffery Auer, ed., *Antislavery and Disunion, 1858–1861: Studies in the Rhetoric of Compromise and Conflict.* New York: Harper and Row, 1963.

See also Volume 1: Emancipation Proclamation; Volume 2: Slavery; Volume 2 (Documents): Emancipation Proclamation.

Smith-Connally Act (War Labor Disputes Act) (1943)

Legislation that defined the relationship between labor unions and the federal government during World War II and would later influence anti-union forces.

Congress passed the Smith-Conally Act over President Franklin Roosevelt's veto on June 25, 1943, after John L. Lewis, union president, and his United Mine Workers defied the federal government by going on strike in May 1943. Also called the War Labor Disputes Act, the bill required unions to give formal notice of intention to strike, to observe a 30-day cooling-off period, and to secure majority support for the strike from the rank-and-file membership. It also gave the president the power to seize war plants and to impose penalties for illegal work stoppages. President Franklin D. Roosevelt used this act to federalize the railroads between December 27, 1943, and January 18, 1944, when the unions representing the Locomotive Firemen, Railway Conductors, and Switchmen refused to withdraw a strike order. The act expired in June 1947.

—*James T. Carroll*

References
Dulles, Foster Rhea, and Melvyn Dubofsky. *Labor in America: A History.* Wheeling, IL: Harlan Davidson, 1993.
See also Volume 2: Labor.

Smith-Lever Act (1914)

Established the Cooperative Extension Service to communicate new agricultural methods and technologies to farmers.

At the turn of the twentieth century, the rural population was the poorest segment of American society. The U.S. Department of Agriculture (USDA) sought to improve farmers' lives through education regarding agricultural practice. The Smith-Lever Act, introduced by Democratic Senator Hoke Smith of Georgia and Democratic Congressman Asbury F. Lever of South Carolina, authorized the federal government to support, with matching state funds, the creation of a Cooperative Extension Service at the land grant colleges, where higher education was provided in agricultural and mechanical subjects.

Signed into law by President Woodrow Wilson on May 8, 1914, this system of county extension agents sought to empower rural inhabitants through the acquisition of new skills, attitudes, knowledge, and aspirations. Agents were affiliated with land grant colleges but provided their services off-campus for rural residents; they taught practical skills for both farmers and homemakers through publications and demonstrations. The USDA, the land grant institutions, and county governments determined the program priorities. The Smith-Lever Act helped transform rural America into a more prosperous place.

The act also provided federal funds to the states to organize agricultural clubs for boys and girls. Through such organizations as 4-H, young people would learn through doing by undertaking agricultural and home economics projects. Children would not only carry the improved practices back to their farms but would gain self-confidence, leadership skills, and a commitment to community service.

During the New Deal, a series of programs and agencies established to assist individuals during the Great Depression, the Cooperative Extension Service became the means through which many government programs were implemented to help preserve the family farm. During World War II, it educated rural America about rationing and how to deal with shortages. In the 1960s, extension agents expanded their services to include minorities and urban programs, creating boys' and girls' clubs in cities in an effort to prevent crime.

—*T. Jason Soderstrum*

References
Rasmussen, Wayne D. *Taking the University to the People: Seventy-five Years of Cooperative Extension.* Ames: Iowa State University Press, 1989.
See also Volumes 1, 2: Agricultural Policy.

Smithsonian Agreement (1971)

Agreement designed to reestablish international fixed currency exchange rates.

Currencies are valued on either a fixed rate set by the government or on a floating rate, in which the free market determines the value of the currency. Fixed rates are usually more stable; floating rates can fluctuate wildly. Meeting in December 1971 at the Smithsonian Institution, ten industrialized nations voted to establish the Smithsonian agreement, which resurrected the system of international fixed currency exchange rates (although without the backing of the currencies by gold or silver). International fixed currency exchange rates—from the Bretton Woods agreement in 1945 (which, based on the gold standard, stabilized currencies and established the International Monetary Fund) to President Richard Nixon's New Economic Policy of August 1971—provided the postwar foundations of international monetary arrangements. Tension had long existed within the Nixon administration between the veterans of the Bretton Woods discussions and staffers including George Shultz, Nixon's secretary of labor, who believed passionately in the price mechanism and a floating exchange rate system. Others, such as Secretary of State Henry Kissinger and Federal Reserve Chair Arthur Burns, successfully persuaded Nixon of the need to return to a par value system based on a fixed rate. The International Monetary Fund (IMF) likewise determined to strengthen the Bretton Woods system that had created it, and the IMF remained committed to establishing a once-and-for-all currency realignment based on its own internal computations. As a result, the Smithsonian agreement reestablished the par value system and allowed the devaluation of the U.S. dollar by about 8 percent. The price of gold rose to $38 per ounce, and the permitted variation around par values was increased to 2.25 percent. The agreement removed the 10 percent import surcharge that had been introduced in Nixon's 1971 New Economic Policy.

Nixon hailed the negotiated realignment as "the most significant monetary agreement in world history." He also recalled that the Federal Reserve had launched an aggressive rearguard action in 1971 to preserve the par value system. In that rearguard action, Burns of the Federal Reserve declared that the Senate must pass the Par Value Modification Act, 1972 legislation that called for compliance with the Smithsonian agreement. The act passed.

In just over a year, the Smithsonian edifice collapsed, primarily because of domestic U.S. difficulties that led Nixon to remove the United States from the gold standard. Burns extolled the Smithsonian agreement as "solidly based," describing the alternative of wildly fluctuating rates and devaluations as "not pleasant to contemplate." In July 1972, the Federal Reserve began for the first time since August 1971 to intervene in support of the dollar against the German currency, the deutsche mark.

Nixon supported floating rates and showed no interest in defending the Smithsonian agreement. In June 1972 Bob Haldeman, chief of staff at the White House, informed Nixon that the British pound was floating—that is, removed from the gold standard—but Nixon replied, "I don't care about it."

Haldeman pressed Nixon to take an interest in the international monetary crisis, telling him that Burns was particularly concerned about the Italian lira, which was also fluctuating in value. But Nixon retorted that he did not care about the lira. By March 1973, the major world currencies were floating. The final collapse of an international system of fixed currency exchange rates arrived unexpectedly.

Shultz later recalled that the administration hoped for a more fundamental reform and that the Smithsonian agreement merely functioned as a prelude to such a reform. Defending the par value system was, he believed, "a futile effort." Shultz bemoaned the fact that economic policy had often adversely affected the market economy and said that reliance on the market system offered the best alternative. He noted that "the price of money is the most important price in an economy" and recalled that in supporting floating rates, he had helped to "achieve a major transformation in the international monetary system," the emergence of "a flexible rate system." Insiders believed that conservative economist Milton Friedman had influenced Shultz between 1969 and 1971. In December 1971, Friedman campaigned without noticeable effect to "keep the dollar free." When the pound began to float in 1972, Friedman argued that the "sooner the Smithsonian agreement is undermined the better."

In retrospect, the Smithsonian bargain among the top ten industrialized nations merely delayed the rendezvous with the political, economic, and intellectual forces pushing hard against the system of fixed exchange rates. The demise of the par value system in 1973 initiated a new episode in international monetary arrangements, and by 1975 many countries had started to experiment with floating rates. Thus the international policy revolution in which the Smithsonian agreement was abandoned and floating rates were embraced acted as a forerunner of—and precondition for—the domestic monetarist policy revolution that removed the United States from the gold standard.

—*Robert Leeson*

References

Burns, A. F. "Some Essentials of International Monetary Reform." *Federal Reserve Bulletin*, vol. 58, no. 6 (June 1972): 545–549ff.
_____. *Reflections of an Economic Policy Maker: Speeches and Congressional Statements 1969–1978*. Washington, DC: American Enterprise Institute, 1978
Coombs, C. A. *The Arena of International Finance*. New York: John Wiley and Sons, 1976.
de Vries, G. M. *Balance of Payments Adjustment, 1945 to 1986: The IMF Experience*. Washington, DC: International Monetary Fund, 1987.
Emminger, O. "The D-Mark in the Conflict between Internal and External Equilibrium, 1948–75." Princeton, NJ: International Finance Section, Department of Economics, Princeton University, 1977.
Friedman, Milton. *An Economist's Protest*. Glen Ridge, NJ: Thomas Horton, 1972.
James, Harold. *International Monetary Cooperation since Bretton Woods*. New York: Oxford University Press, 1996.
Kirshner, O., ed. *The Bretton Woods–GATT System: Retrospect and Prospect after Fifty Years*. London: M. E. Sharpe, 1996.
Shultz, G. P., and K. W. Dam. *Economic Policy beyond the Headlines*. New York: W. W. Norton, 1977.
Volcker, P., and T. Gyohten. *Changing Fortunes: The World's Money and the Threat to American Leadership*. New York: Times Books, 1992.
Williamson, J. *The Failure of World Monetary Reform*. London: Nelson, 1977.
See also Volume 1: Wage and Price Freeze.

Smuggling

Illegally importing items into a country.

From colonial times to the present, Americans have engaged in smuggling. The extensive coastline and the limited number of customs officers mean that arrests and convictions have always been few. Under the British mercantile system, in which all trade was centralized for the benefit of the mother country, American colonists smuggled goods in from the French and Spanish Caribbean. Molasses (for the production of rum) and sugar (because of demand in the colonies) became the two most smuggled items. If a smuggler was caught, which happened infrequently, he was tried in a court of law in the colonies before a jury of his peers—most of whom were also smugglers. Consequently, the verdict would almost always be "not guilty." After the British defeated the French in the Seven Years' War (also known as the French and Indian War, 1754–1763), the British Parliament, for the first time ever, increased control over the colonies. The Sugar Act (1763), the first in a series of such acts, lowered duties on English molasses while raising the rate on sugar. By lowering the molasses tax, Parliament hoped to remove the incentive for smuggling; some tax revenue would be preferred to none. The inclusion in the Sugar Act of a clause that moved smuggling cases from the civil courts to the vice admiralty courts angered the colonists, who viewed the act as a direct violation of a basic English right because English common law required a trial by a jury of peers.

After America gained its independence and mindful of the hated 1765 British Stamp Act (which taxed legal documents as well as newspapers, dice, and so on, and required that the tax be paid in gold or silver), the founding fathers adopted a low-revenue tariff under the Constitution. This tariff, which would generate only enough revenue to meet current government operating expenses and debt payments, was intended to make smuggling less attractive and would therefore result in collection from importers of more duties. Most Americans paid the duty on imported items as much for patriotic reasons as to avoid prosecution. But with the purchase of the Louisiana Territory from France in 1803, smuggling once again flourished. Pirates, often using letters of marque (documents from a foreign government authorizing them to prey on the ships of nations at war with them), plied the waters of the Gulf of Mexico. Men like Jean Lafitte and his gang sailed under letters of marque from the newly declared independent republics of Central and South America, regions that broke the bonds of European domination during and after the Napoleonic Wars. After the War of 1812, the federal government cracked down on these pirates, forbidding American citizens from operating under letters of marque in the future.

As the government erected a high tariff barrier during the middle to late nineteenth century, smuggling continued but on a limited basis. At the same time, the Customs Department increased the number of revenue officers available for securing the coast. The next major challenge to these collectors came during Prohibition, which began in 1919. When the customs officers realized that they could not gather enough evidence to convict men like Al Capone for the distribution of alcohol, they began working with the Treasury Department to charge bootleggers with income tax evasion. The problem of smuggled alcohol seemingly disappeared overnight when Prohibition was repealed in 1933.

Since the 1960s, the primary mode of transportation used by smugglers is the airplane. Flying low enough to avoid detection by radar, modern-day smugglers usually deal in contraband weapons and drugs. In addition, from south of the U.S. border, smugglers now find it more profitable to smuggle illegal aliens across the Rio Grande River than to deal in goods like drugs. To diminish the loss of tax revenues and to stem the tide of drugs and illegal immigrants, Congress continues to increase appropriations to the Customs Service. Particular attention has been paid to the problem of smuggling since the terrorist attacks of September 11, 2001. In 2003 the Customs Service became part of the Homeland Security Agency and now has greater authority, granted by Congress, to prevent suspected future terrorists from entering the country.

—*Cynthia Clark Northrup*

References

Paxton, John, and John Wroughton. *Smuggling.* London: Macmillan, 1971.

Williams, Neville. *Contraband Cargoes: Seven Centuries of Smuggling.* New York: Longmans, 1959.

See also Volume 1: Mercantilism; Protective Tariffs; Revenue Tariffs; Sugar.

Social Security Act of 1935

Legislation enacted in 1935 as part of New Deal aimed at creating an insurance fund for the elderly.

The Social Security Act of 1935 was an important stabilizer for the U.S. economy at a time when the nation had high unemployment during the Great Depression (1929–1941). The objective of the act was to allow senior citizens to retire with a small guaranteed income so younger unemployed workers could fill their positions. A small percentage of workers' wages are held in a trust and distributed on a monthly basis to seniors. Social Security embodies the concept of social insurance or putting money aside for a rainy day—in this case the end of people's productive working years and the onset of old age, although additional amendments in 1956 and 1965 provided for disability benefits and the Medicare program, respectively. (Roosevelt had quickly dismissed the idea of adding national health insurance benefits to the original package because he feared that the American Medical Association would attack it as "socialized medicine" and sink the entire program.) Congress also authorized the extension of unemployment compensation benefits under provisions of this act. The original legislation requires states to set up unemployment compensation programs or have the U.S. government establish one for them. The states all chose the former course.

The Social Security Act came out of deliberations by the Committee on Economic Security, which President Franklin D. Roosevelt established via Executive Order No. 6757 on June 29, 1934. The committee was chaired by U.S. Secretary of Labor Frances Perkins, and Roosevelt appointed U.S. Secretary of the Treasury Henry Morgenthau as one of its members. Edwin Witte, professor of economics at the University of Wisconsin–Madison, served as executive director of the committee. Roosevelt acted under pressure from such potential opponents as Dr. Francis E. Townsend, who favored a national pension plan, and Democratic U.S. Senator Huey Long of Louisiana, who promoted his own plan called "Share Our Wealth." The House Ways and Means Committee held hearings from January 21 through February 12, 1935, on the economic feasibility of the plan and came up with the name *Social Security.*

After George W. Bush assumed the presidency in January 2001, Republicans in Congress began pushing for a policy to phase in the privatization of Social Security. Some of the discussion stemmed from concern that the fund as currently constituted will have more outgo than income by 2036 at the latest, when the number of employees paying into the fund will have declined to 1.9 for every retiree. Privatizing retirement funds would allow the worker to determine where the funds are invested and in what amounts. Some argue that by allowing the private investment of retirement money in the stock market, the returns will be greater and the burden on Social Security reduced. However, opponents argue that private investment of these funds will hurt many Americans because benefits now available to them under Social Security would no longer be an option. (For example, under Social Security, women are guaranteed payment based on the benefits of their husband [or former husband if married for at least 10 years]). Discussions of privatization were suspended in the immediate aftermath of the terrorist attacks on September 11, 2001. With the economy experiencing difficulty and employers releasing thousands of workers, Social Security is the source for expanded unemployment money made available to people after their state unemployment benefits run out. The duration of the post-2001 recession and the high number of unemployed in many states has resulted in Social Security unemployment benefits being extended from 26 weeks to 36 weeks.

—*Henry B. Sirgo*

References

Schieber, Sylvester J., and John B. Shoven. *The Real Deal: The History and Future of Social Security.* New Haven, CT: Yale University Press, 1999.

See also Volume 1: Great Depression; Roosevelt, Franklin D.

Socialism

Philosophy calling for the replacement of capitalism (which is predicated on private ownership of the means of production) with a more egalitarian system predicated on collective ownership of the means of production.

The concept of socialism—a collection of social movements, political organizations, theoretical currents of thought, and doctrines—did not originate in the writings of Karl Marx. An inchoate idea of socialism inspired not only the Levellers and Diggers (religious-economic movements that advocated egalitarianism and communist philosophy) during the English Civil War (1642–1652) but also Gracchus Babeuf's "conspiracy of equals" during the French Revolution (1789–1799). (This conspiracy was a secret society in France that sought to overthrow the French government and replace it with a communist regime; the plot was discovered and Babeuf was executed.) However, the term *socialism* was first used in the early 1830s by disciples of Robert Owen (an innovative English industrialist) and Claude-Henri de Saint-Simon (a radical French aristocrat). With a view to converting their elite peers to the new creed, Owen and Saint-Simon drafted detailed blueprints of socialist society.

In contrast, Marx endeavored not only to influence the growing working-class movement but also to ground his vision of socialism in a concrete analysis of capitalist development. In the *Critique of the Gotha Programme* (1875), Marx sketched two phases of revolutionary transformation: the socialist phase, which would be characterized by the dictatorship of the proletariat (understood as a transitional workers' state); and the communist phase, which would be characterized by the withering away of the state and the realization of classless society. Owing to his aversion to utopian speculation, Marx refrained from describing the socialist and communist phases in detail. It remained for the Second International (the term used to describe a series of meetings between 1889 and 1914 of socialist organizations in Europe that advocated socialism and social democracy) spearheaded by the German Social Democratic Party, to debate Marx's intentions.

A debate between Edward Bernstein and Karl Kautsky on socialist strategy merits particular attention. Whereas Bernstein's revisionists advocated the parliamentary path to socialism, Kautsky's orthodox Marxists advocated the revolutionary path to socialism. Although the Bernstein-Kautsky debate ended abruptly with the collapse of the Second International (it collapsed because of World War I and its opposition to the war) and the division of the working-class movement into socialist and communist factions, revisionism remained influential. In the aftermath of World War II, labor, social-democratic, and socialist parties rose to prominence in Western parliaments, emphasizing the principles of the "mixed economy," or the socialist management of capitalist expansion.

—*Mark Frezzo*

References
Haupt, Georges. *Aspects of International Socialism, 1871–1914.* Cambridge: Cambridge University Press, 1986.

Sassoon, Donald. *One Hundred Years of Socialism: The West European Left in the Twentieth Century.* New York: New Press, 1996.
See also Volume 1: Marxism.

Soil Conservation and Allotment Act (1936)

Government agency that paid farmers to plant soil-building crops.

Franklin D. Roosevelt was not the first president aware of the need for soil conservation. President George Washington—whose approach to managing Mount Vernon was a model for how Roosevelt modeled his home, Hyde Park—used sophisticated crop rotation techniques because he knew that certain crops including tobacco were hard on soil. Still, it was in Roosevelt's day that the ramifications of damaged soil on people's lives and the economy became most readily apparent. In an address to Congress June 3, 1937, the president observed: "Nature has given recurrent and poignant warnings through dust storms, floods, and droughts that we must act while there is yet time if we would preserve for ourselves and our posterity the natural sources of a virile life." Although President Roosevelt believed that final coordination at the national level was important, he believed that national planning had to start at the level of "townships, counties, and states." The travesty of the dust bowl during the 1930s, which at times caused the noon sky to grow dark because what had once been fine topsoil blotted out the sun, was the stuff of tragedy. The concomitant plight of the Okies—Oklahoma residents hit hard by severe drought and dust storms who fled to California and elsewhere—was written about by John Steinbeck in *The Grapes of Wrath*, which was made into a motion picture in 1939. Because of the influx from Oklahoma, the California legislature even enacted an "anti-Okie" statute in 1937 that made it a misdemeanor to assist or bring an indigent into California. The U.S. Supreme Court found the statute unconstitutional as violating the fundamental right of travel.

A U.S. Supreme Court ruling in 1936 held that the government did not have the right to regulate agricultural production by restricting crop production, as the Agricultural Adjustment Administration had been doing by paying farmers cash not to plant crops in an effort to improve soil condition. Using a proposal prepared by an Agricultural Adjustment Administration economist, Congress promptly passed the Soil and Conservation Domestic Allotment Act in 1936, which, heeding the eighteenth-century insights of George Washington, paid farmers to cut back on the production of soil-depleting crops such as wheat and instead plant soil-building crops such as legumes.

Soil conservation measures were also implemented in more recent times. In 1982, Congress passed the National Conservation Program to reduce soil erosion and protect surface and underground water quality. In 1985, the Farm Bill paid farmers to plant cropland with grasses, legumes, trees, windbreaks, wetlands, or wildlife cover. In the late 1980s, as mayor of Weatherford, Texas, Jim Wright—who eventually served as Speaker of the U.S. House of Representatives—observed the ruin wrought by seven years of drought. Wright became a disciple of soil conservation after seeing farms devastated by the loss of topsoil. He observed that, in light of this experience with soil depletion, "I became friendly with a man named Frank White, [Wright's county extension agent] who was a district supervisor of soil conservation activity, introduced a bill in the state legislature which passed, giving money to soil conservation districts to match local efforts to acquire equipment, and carry out soil conservation activities such as terracing, cover cropping, and so forth."

—*Henry B. Sirgo*

References

Nixon, Edgar B. *Franklin D. Roosevelt and Conservation.* Hyde Park, NY: Franklin D. Roosevelt Library, 1957.

Wright, Jim. Interview with Henry Sirgo. Fort Worth, Texas, April 10, 1998.

See also Volume 1: Roosevelt, Franklin D.

South Carolina Exposition and Protest (1828)

Document by Vice President John C. Calhoun that was South Carolina's rationale in its states' rights resistance to the federal government.

In the document *South Carolina Exposition and Protest,* written in 1828, John C. Calhoun, who was vice president from 1824 to 1832 under both Presidents John Quincy Adams and Andrew Jackson, "solemnly" protested "against the system of protecting duties, lately adopted by the federal government." Calhoun gave eight reasons for his position. Summarized briefly, they were that the powers of Congress were specified in the Constitution and any statute that went beyond these limits was "unwarrantable as the undisguised assumption of substantive, independent powers not granted or expressly withheld." Citing the Virginia Resolution of James Madison (1798) and the Kentucky Resolutions of Thomas Jefferson (1798 and 1799), both of which argued against the constitutionality of the 1798 Sedition Act, Calhoun argued that the Union had been formed by state governments and hence was a "compact" in which the powers of Congress were precisely limited. Any law that exceeded these enumerated powers could be nullified by a state to prevent the law's enforcement within the state's borders. Calhoun said the Tariff of 1828 (Southerners called it the Tariff of Abominations) was "unconstitutional, unequal, and oppressive, and calculated to corrupt the public virtue and destroy the liberty of the country." It had made Southerners "the serfs" of the system of manufacturing and imposed a protective tax on planters exclusively for the benefit of Northern factory owners, which was the "despotism of the many" that made the rich richer and the poor poorer. Calhoun described an unavoidable economic conflict between the industrial North and the agricultural South. The South's condition after the Tariff of 1828 proved intolerable—Congress

appropriated the money equivalent of one-third of the South's cotton crop (the South's main cash crop), and because the region could not raise the price of cotton in a world market because of foreign competition, it remained helpless. Congress, Calhoun warned, if not restrained, might pass other laws designed to ruin the agrarian South. Finally, Calhoun reasoned that South Carolina had the power to nullify such unconstitutional laws because this power remained with the states, as specified in the Tenth Amendment. The South Carolina legislature then issued a formal protest to the U.S. Congress. When Congress raised rates again in 1832, South Carolina used the arguments of the *Exposition* to justify its passing of the Ordinance of Nullification at the Columbia Convention on November 24, 1832, in which the state threatened to leave the Union if the tariff rates were not reduced by February 1833. The resulting crisis, known as the Nullification Crisis, ended when Congress passed the Compromise Tariff of 1833 lowering rates over a nine-year period. Although the *Exposition* failed in its purpose (because no other Southern state endorsed nullification), it became the foundation of a states' rights resistance to federal power, especially as related to slavery, for the next three decades. After passage of the Ordinance of Nullification, Calhoun resigned as vice president. He returned to Washington as the Senator from South Carolina in 1833.

—*Robert P. Sutton*

References

Ellis, Richard E. *The Union at Risk: Jacksonian Democracy, States' Rights, and the Nullification Crisis.* New York: Oxford University Press, 1987.

Latner, Richard B. *The Presidency of Andrew Jackson.* Athens: University of Georgia Press, 1979.

Peterson, Merrill D. *Olive Branch and Sword: The Compromise of 1833.* Baton Rouge: Louisiana State University Press, 1982.

Remini, Robert V. *Andrew Jackson.* New York: Harperennial, 1999.

See also Volume 1: Clay, Henry; Force Act; Jackson, Andrew.

Spanish-American War (War of 1898)

Conflict between Spain and the United States that resulted in Cuban independence and the cession of the Philippines, Guam, and Puerto Rico to the United States.

In February 1895, Cuban revolutionaries began a war for independence against Spain. The war had humble beginnings, but by mid-1896, a 50,000-man army battled against Spain in an attempt to attain freedom. In August 1896, as Spain fought in the Caribbean, another insurrection against it broke out in the Philippines. In the face of domestic dissatisfaction, the Spanish government struggled to maintain its empire. In late 1897, the Spanish instituted colonial reforms and made provisions to allow for Cuban home rule. Cubans denounced the reforms and called for complete independence.

Because of rioting throughout Havana in 1898, the U.S. consul there requested that the American government send naval support to protect American interests in Cuba, and the administration of President William McKinley sent the battleship *Maine* to Havana's harbor. Meanwhile, the United States attempted to mediate in the conflict between Cuba and Spain, but in February a letter critical of President McKinley written by Enrique Dupuy de Lôme, the Spanish minister in Washington, D.C., found its way into American newspapers and strained U.S.-Spanish relations. One week later, the *Maine* exploded in Havana's harbor. U.S. newspaper editors such as William Randolph Hearst and Joseph Pulitzer claimed a Spanish mine in the harbor caused the explosion. (In the 1970s, divers discovered that the munitions had been stored adjacent to the ship's boiler room and a spark ignited the explosion.) The United States demanded that Spain begin an immediate armistice, and the Spanish seemed ready to comply. The Cubans were not ready to comply and continued fighting.

Cuban independence seemed certain, but the McKinley administration coveted Cuba and knew the United States would be unable to ever acquire it if Spain granted it independence. On April 11, 1898, McKinley asked Congress for permission to intervene in the war between Cuba and Spain in order to establish "a stable government." There was no express mention of Cuban independence in McKinley's message. However, members of Congress passed a joint declaration known as the Teller Amendment that prohibited annexation of Cuba, and the United States declared war against Spain on April 18, 1898.

The United States actually fought its first battle against the Spanish in the Philippines rather than in Cuba. In an effort to eliminate Spanish naval forces, U.S. Commodore George Dewey arrived in Manila Bay and sank the Spanish fleet at anchor there on May 1, 1898. Six weeks later, U.S. troops arrived in Cuba and, with Cuban aid, quickly routed the Spanish. An armistice began in August, and on December 10, 1898, Spain and the United States signed the Treaty of Paris, ending the war. The treaty granted Cuban independence, but Spain ceded the Philippines, Guam, and Puerto Rico to the United States for $20 million.

After the war, American troops remained in Cuba until 1902, ostensibly to oversee the creation of a stable government. The United States fought a guerrilla war against Filipino insurgents (who had been fighting against the Spanish), subduing the rebels in March 1901. The Spanish-American War transformed the United States into a colonial power and created an American presence in the Caribbean and the Western Pacific.

—*John K. Franklin*

References
Pérez, Louis A. *Cuba: Between Reform and Revolution.* New York: Oxford University Press, 1988.
See also Volume 1: Cuba; Philippines; Puerto Rico; Spanish-American War.

Stagflation
Simultaneous unacceptably high inflation and high unemployment.

Before 1970 the American economy seemed to be characterized by a stable trade-off between unemployment and in-

flation. This relationship (described by the Phillips curve) held for most of the 1950s and 1960s (see Table 1).

Table 1 Unemployment and inflation in the United States, 1961–1969

Year	Rate of inflation (consumer price index)	Civilian unemployment rate (percent)
1961	1.0	5.5
1962	1.0	6.7
1963	1.3	5.5
1964	1.3	5.2
1965	1.6	4.5
1966	2.9	3.8
1967	3.1	3.8
1968	4.2	3.6
1969	5.5	3.5

During the 1970 recession, policymakers appeared surprised to see the rate of inflation rise to 5.7 percent. Economist Paul Samuelson dubbed this *stagflation* (high unemployment combined with high inflation and stagnant economic growth). The problem vexed policymakers. Expansionary fiscal or monetary policy raises aggregate demand, reducing unemployment but increasing inflation. Restrictive fiscal or monetary policy restrains demand, decreasing inflation but often causing unemployment increases. Stagflation required tools to fight both.

In 1971, President Richard Nixon tried wage and price controls, which cut the rate of inflation while permitting expansionary policies with lower interest rates in 1972. Critics of wage and price controls point to high inflation in both 1973 and 1974, but others argued that this occurred as the result of supply shocks or surges in the prices of strategically important commodities. In the United States in 1973 and 1974 this commodity was oil, although prices of certain food products also rose. Theory predicted that price hikes in individual products, even important ones, would be balanced by relative price declines in others. Mainstream economists argued that prices and wages in the United States had become resistant to those declines. Thus, the rate of inflation rose. Areas of the economy experiencing falls in demand would suffer unemployment and business losses, while everyone in the economy except the producers of the favored products would suffer because of inflation. The government had the unenviable choice of using expansionary policy to raise money incomes so the population could afford the higher prices or permitting unemployment to rise so that price increases on important products would not spread to all products.

At times during this period the government flip-flopped in its focus. In 1974, officials focused on inflation. Rising interest rates and a virtually balanced federal budget combined to restrain the economy and, in fact, helped to cause a recession. Yet President Gerald Ford went before Congress in the fall of 1974 and pleaded for a tax increase as part of a program he supported that would "whip inflation now." In January 1975, he asked for a large tax cut to combat the recession of 1974–1975. His tax cut passed, the recession ended, and the inflation rate came down from its 1974 level. However, inflation did not fall below the 1970 rate before it resumed its rise. Between 1976 and 1978 as unemployment fell slowly toward 6 percent, inflation rose (see Table 2). This pattern occurred before the last oil price shock of the decade in 1979.

Table 2   Unemployment and inflation in the United States, 1970–1979

Year	Rate of inflation (consumer price index)	Civilian unemployment rate (percent)
1970	5.7	4.9
1971	4.4	5.9
1972	3.2	5.6
1973	6.2	4.9
1974	11.0	5.6
1975	9.1	8.5
1976	5.8	7.7
1977	6.5	7.1
1978	7.6	6.1
1979	11.3	5.8

This experience damaged the reputation of the Keynesian philosophy of aggregate demand management (increased government expenditure to stimulate the economy) and led to the Federal Reserve's brief "monetarist experiment" from 1979 to 1982 (an increase in interest rates that created difficult financial problems for many Americans) and the flirtation by some politicians with supply-side economics, also known as trickle-down economics and characterized by tax cuts for the wealthy, who would theoretically save or invest the extra money for the benefit of the working class. With the institution of stringent anti-inflationary policies by the Federal Reserve during Paul Volcker's tenure and the deep recession of 1981 and 1982, the "-flation" part of stagflation disappeared from U.S. economic life. The defeat of inflation occurred because of the willingness to accept high levels of unemployment over a long period of time.

—*Michael A. Meeropol*

References
Blinder, Alan. *Economic Policy and the Great Stagflation.* New York: Academic Press, 1979.
Meeropol, Michael. *Surrender, How the Clinton Administration Completed the Reagan Revolution.* Ann Arbor: University of Michigan Press, 1998.
See also Volume 1: Reagan, Ronald; Wage and Price Freeze.

Stamp Act (1765)

One of a series of British taxes imposed on the colonies that sparked the American Revolution.

To help pay off the huge war debt from the French and Indian War left after 1763, the British Parliament passed the Stamp Act, a measure that would apply to the colonies a tax that had been in place in Britain for nearly a century: the purchase of a royal stamp for all diplomas, newspapers, playing cards, and legal documents. The colonists, infuriated at this first attempt of the government to tax them directly, had to pay for the stamps in cash, a restriction that cut most of the colonists, short on specie (gold or silver) and using a barter system, out of the transaction. The Stamp Act had the secondary effect of pricing newspapers out of the range of many

colonists and thus restricting the flow of information and the prized idea of a free press.

Because the Stamp Act affected all colonists in every region of North America, it quickly sparked protests. The Sons of Liberty in Boston hung stamp sellers in effigy, harassed officials, and began a boycott of British goods. James Otis, writing *Letters of a Pennsylvania Farmer,* circulated an ideological attack against the Stamp Act—that Parliament included no American representatives and therefore should not tax the colonies. George Grenville, who had championed the Stamp Act, retired as British prime minister in 1765 because of differences with the king, and his successor, the Marquis of Rockingham, under pressure from British merchants hurt by the colonial boycott, repealed the act in 1766. However, in the 1766 Declaratory Act, Parliament insisted that Britain had the right to tax its colonies in any form in the future. The Declaratory Act was largely ignored because of the celebration over repeal of the Stamp Act.

—*Margaret Sankey*

References
Morgan, Edmund S., and Helen Morgan. *The Stamp Act Crisis.* New York: Collier, 1962.
Weslager, C. A. *The Stamp Act Congress.* Newark: University of Delaware Press, 1976.
See also Volume 1: American Revolution; Sugar Act.

Stamp Act Congress

Meeting of colonists convened in 1765 to protest British taxation acts.

As part of the protest rising against the implementation of the 1765 Stamp Act, which placed a tax on legal documents, newspapers, and several products in the American colonies, the Massachusetts House of Representatives invited delegates of the other colonies to meet in New York and formulate an official protest to the British Parliament. Encouraged by the continuing success of the boycott of British goods (in response to the Stamp Act), the widely read arguments of James Otis (who declared that there should be "no taxation without representation"), and the charge of Patrick Henry that Virginians deserved the rights of Englishmen, nine of the colonies sent delegates.

Twenty-seven representatives from Massachusetts, New York, Connecticut, Rhode Island, New Jersey, Pennsylvania, Delaware, Maryland, and South Carolina met in New York from October 7 to 25, 1765. This meeting resulted in a polite acknowledgement that the colonies owed allegiance to the king and were subject to Parliament, but it also included a statement of grievances in which they asked the king for relief from oppressions including the lack of representation, trial by jury, shortage of hard currency, and the imposition of taxes. Taxes, they felt, were a gift freely given by the people to the Crown through elected representatives, not imposed. Parliament repealed the Stamp Act the following year under pressure of the boycott and the new administration of the Prime Minister Marquis of Rockingham. Through the Stamp Act Congress, colonists articulated the growing colonial sentiment that they deserved the full rights of English citizens and could successfully demand them.

—*Margaret Sankey*

References

Morgan, Edmund S., and Helen Morgan. *The Stamp Act Crisis.* New York: Collier, 1962.

Weslager, C. A. *The Stamp Act Congress.* Newark: University of Delaware Press, 1976.

See also Volume 1: American Revolution; Sugar Act.

Standard Oil

Oil company founded in 1870 that transformed the business world by implementing economies of scale based on integration of related companies to form one monopoly.

Standard Oil of Ohio was founded by John D. Rockefeller in 1870 and incorporated in 1882 in New York as the Standard Oil Trust (a trust is a holding company that constitutes a monopoly). The company became a vertically integrated oil company in that it engaged in two or more of the following functions: producing, transporting, refining, and marketing. Standard Oil fit the definition of a vertically integrated company. It had acquired Ohio Oil Company, which produced crude oil, in 1889, an action that complemented its original nature as a combination of refineries in Cleveland.

Forward integration of a company occurs when the organization takes on functions closer to the consumer. Backward integration takes the company away from the consumer. By the time Standard Oil Company (New Jersey) dissolved in 1911, it had already operated as an integrated company (forward and backward) in the four functions of producing, transporting, refining, and marketing. In fact, by 1907 that company owned or controlled 67 subsidiary businesses, which included 3 producing companies, 12 pipeline companies, 9 refining companies, and 6 marketing companies.

As the company grew, journalists, historians, and government officials, not to mention an embittered general public consisting of low-wage laborers who witnessed the extravagances of the Rockefellers, attacked Standard Oil Company (New Jersey). Its size alone had aroused suspicion regarding its conduct and had fostered a belief that it was monopolistic in character. Even before Standard Oil became Standard Oil Company (New Jersey) under a law of that state in 1882, while it existed as the Standard Oil Trust, it eventually controlled 80 percent of the country's refineries and 90 percent of the nation's pipelines. As a result, Standard Oil had become the world's leading industrial organization.

Such a concentration of power invited attacks. The U.S. Congress, mainly in response to the Standard Oil Trust's stranglehold on refining and transporting activities, passed the Sherman Anti-Trust Act of 1890, the very law on which the Supreme Court would base its dissolution decree of 1911 dissolving the company. Before that, in 1892, the Ohio Supreme Court had forbidden Standard Oil Trust from operating Standard Oil of Ohio, which had been founded in 1870. Interestingly enough, this divestiture prompted the organization of the Standard Oil Company (New Jersey) in 1892.

Although some practices of Standard Oil and its founder, John D. Rockefeller, appeared unscrupulous, the company made major contributions to the American economy. It improved the quality of petroleum products, especially kerosene; through its large storage facilities, it was able to stabilize the price of crude oil; by means of chemical research it made possible the marketing of the highly sulfurous oil from the Lima-Indiana oilfield in northwestern Ohio; and by aggressive marketing it protected American interests abroad.

By 1911 Standard Oil had for some time fought a losing battle against competition both at home and abroad. Beginning in the 1880s and 1890s, Russian and Dutch East Indian oil competed with American crude for markets in Europe and the Orient. At home, following the discovery of oil at Spindletop near Beaumont, Texas, in 1901, new companies and prodigious new deliveries of crude also reduced Standard Oil's market share, especially for gasoline.

After the breakup of Standard Oil, the company divided into several smaller companies, most of them using the Standard name (for example, Standard Oil of Ohio, Standard Oil of New Jersey, and so on). Standard Oil and other U.S. oil companies benefited during the oil crisis of the 1970s when restricted supplies from abroad in connection with the Arab oil embargo increased oil prices domestically. Standard Oil modified its business plan by opening Exxon and Mobil gas stations and selling convenience products from them. Standard Oil also opened Marathon gas stations and merged with Quaker State to develop the Pennzoil–Quaker State brand. Standard continues to operate tankers as well.

—*Keith L. Miller*

References

Hidy, Ralph W., and Muriel E. Hidy. *Pioneering in Big Business 1882–1911.* New York: Harper and Brothers, 1955.

Larson, Henrietta M. "The Rise of Big Business in the Oil Industry." In *Oil's First Century: Papers Given at the Centennial Seminar on the History of the Petroleum Industry,* comp. and ed. staff of *Business History Review.* Boston: Harvard Graduate School of Business Administration, 1960.

Martin, Jonathan. "Exxon." In Adele Hast, ed., *International Directory of Company Histories.* Chicago: St. James Press, 1988–1996.

McLean, John G., and Robert William Haigh. *The Growth of Integrated Oil Companies.* Boston: Division of Research, Graduate School of Business Administration, Harvard University, 1954.

See also Volume 1: Energy; Rockefeller, John D.

Steel

Commercially produced iron that contains carbon as an alloying constituent, and an industry initially important to the U.S. economy as the nation reconstructed itself after the Civil War.

During the industrial and transportation revolutions of the early 1800s, a need for a metal stronger than iron developed.

The Bessemer steel process (named for British inventor Henry Bessemer), which was developed during the 1850s and removes impurities from iron to make steel, proved critical to rail transportation. It was used to make the stronger and more durable track that railroads lay to connect areas of the nation; the friction and wear of the railroad cars was otherwise too great to make railroad transportation feasible. Great steel magnates like Andrew Carnegie constructed large steel corporations that controlled every aspect of production, thus creating monopolies that controlled this vital industry.

After passage of the 1914 Clayton Anti-Trust Act, the United States government acted as mediator and guarantor of competition. Using the Clayton Anti-Trust Act, the government sought to prevent monopolies in the steel industry. Unlike other industries, steel had not received government subsidies or assistance during the late 1800s. Beginning in 1968, however, the government passed antidumping and countervailing-duty laws that aimed to limit growth of steel imports and protected U.S. steel producers and the domestic market from foreign competitors selling steel below the cost of production.

Exceptions were made to general steel policy and were applied during times of crisis. During World War II and the Korean War, the U.S. government intervened to ensure that production continued to meet demand. The United States acted in 1973 and 1974 during a worldwide steel shortage by freezing wages and prices. The shortage collapsed the U.S. market in 1976—that is, market prices rose so high that there was a lack of liquidity and trade, and the market price fell rapidly—forcing the government to address the rapid growth of steel imports. To deal with antidumping suits filed against Japanese companies by U.S. producers, the administration of President Jimmy Carter established the Solomon Task Force, which proposed the trigger price mechanism (in which the government investigated any steel priced below trigger prices) to offset dumping by foreign producers. The problem of import growth did end as the trigger price mechanism, like previous trade policy, proved a reactionary, unstable way to deal with the issue. Problems continued under the administration of President Ronald Reagan, which thus entered into repeated negotiations and arrangements, particularly with the European Community, limiting steel imports to the United States. These arrangements had the temporary effect of preserving the domestic market for U.S. producers.

Traditional economic policy toward steel has been that of mediator, arbiter, and protector. Nevertheless, critics have attacked the U.S. government for its often soft and contradictory policies regarding steel when compared with other nations' policies to assist steel producers. U.S. economic policy regarding steel has been reactionary, placing the burden on domestic steel producers to prove injury to their business before the government intervenes. Only then has government acted to maintain the economic feasibility of the industry—such as in March 2002, when President George W. Bush raised tariff rates on steel from 8 to 30 percent to assist the ailing U.S. industry.

—Eugene Van Sickle

References
Howell, Thomas R., et al. *Steel and the State: Government Intervention and Steel's Structural Crisis.* Boulder, CO: Westview Press, 1988.
See also Volume 1: Carnegie, Andrew; Protective Tariffs.

Strategic Defense Initiative (SDI) (1983)

Government program designed to develop a space-based defense against intercontinental ballistic missiles.

The Strategic Defense Initiative (SDI) emerged from President Ronald Reagan's March 23, 1983, speech calling for long-term research into ballistic missile defense technologies (a defense system to identify and destroy incoming nuclear warheads delivered by ballistic missiles). SDI precipitated intense controversy over the goals, costs, technical feasibility, survivability, effectiveness, and diplomatic implications of missile defense. SDI originally imagined layered defenses against a massive Soviet missile attack, but after the collapse of the Soviet Union in 1991, SDI focused on limited national missile defenses (NMD) and theater (city or regional) missile defenses (TMD).

The Defense Department united its existing missile defense programs under the SDI Organization (SDIO) in 1984. SDIO researched sensor, battle management, directed energy, and kinetic energy technologies. Research initially stressed long-term technologies to destroy incoming missiles like space-based lasers and particle beams, but proponents worried that SDI could not survive as a pure research program. Thus, in 1986 SDIO shifted emphasis to technologies that would be deployable in the near term. In 1987, SDIO proposed deploying a large "Phase I Architecture," which included space-based kinetic-kill interceptors designed to destroy the target with one hit. In 1988, SDIO reassessed this ambitious plan and advocated deploying only a modest number of ground-based interceptors in this phase. In 1989, SDIO promoted the "brilliant pebbles" concept, which involved thousands of small space-based kinetic-kill interceptors, each with sufficient sensing and computing power to detect and intercept an enemy missile independently.

During the 1980s, the Soviet Union attempted to persuade the United States to abandon SDI and at the same time began researching a similar program of its own. However, the costs were too great for the fragile Soviet economy to endure. These efforts helped contribute to the collapse of the Soviet Union in 1991. With a massive Soviet attack seeming increasingly improbable, President George H. W. Bush decided that SDI should concentrate on TMD and limited NMD against rogue nation strikes or unauthorized launches by terrorists who gain access to missiles.

In 1993, SDIO became the Ballistic Missile Defense Organization (BMDO). BMDO shifted resources from NMD into TMD programs including Theater High Altitude Area Defense (THAAD), Patriot Advanced Capability 3 (PAC-3), Navy Lower Tier, Navy Theater Wide, and the airborne laser in order to protect forward American forces and allied nations. President Bill Clinton continued NMD research and resisted strong Republican pressure for NMD deployment until 1996. He then proposed to develop an NMD system within three years and to deploy it three years after that if threats justified it. Subsequent reviews and technology tests indicated that this "three plus three" plan was highly risky and prompted Clinton repeatedly to postpone a deployment decision. Nevertheless, ominous estimates of rogue nation missile threats, such as an estimate emerging from 1998 Rumsfeld Commission of a greater-than-expected threat from rogue nations within five years, sustained pressure for rapid deployment.

BMDO became the Missile Defense Agency in 2002. Plans under the administration of George W. Bush envision upgrading radar installations and fielding 100 ground-based interceptors in Alaska by FY2007. MDA would add further interceptor sites, radars, and space-based sensors by 2015.

Analysts disagree on the cost of SDI. SDIO claimed it spent $33 billion from 1983 to 1993, but the Congressional Research Service estimated the true expenditure as $71 billion. SDI did not achieve Reagan's dream of an impenetrable shield, but it generated major advances in electronics, sensors, propulsion, communications, and power technologies and in understanding of systems engineering and integration. BMDO spent about $4 to $5 billion a year under Clinton, but President George W. Bush requested about $8 billion per year in fiscal year 2002 and fiscal year 2003. Future costs are difficult to estimate and depend on the type of system constructed. The Congressional Budget Office considers that NMD would cost about $29.5 billion (in 2001 dollars) from 1996 to 2015 for the deployment of an initial capability. SDI research is now part of the Homeland Security Agency.

—*James D. Perry*

References

Cordesman, Anthony. *U.S. Government Efforts to Create a Homeland Defense Capability: Program Budget and Overview.* Washington, DC: Center for Strategic and International Studies, December 2000.

Fitzgerald, Frances. *Way Out There in the Blue.* New York: Simon and Schuster, 2000.

Graham, Bradley. *Hit to Kill.* New York: Public Affairs, 2001.

Nolan, Janne. *Guardians of the Arsenal.* New York: Basic Books, 1989.

See also Volume 1: Cold War; Reagan, Ronald.

Sugar

A commodity used as a sweetener derived from sugar cane or sugar beet and one of the highest-priced commodities during the eighteenth and nineteenth centuries.

Throughout much of the nineteenth and twentieth centuries, the United States imported much of its sugar from Hawaii and Cuba. The primary domestic mainland source of sugar was Louisiana. During the mid-nineteenth century American businesses invested heavily in sugar plantations in Hawaii. In 1875 the United States signed a reciprocity agreement (mutual reduction of tariff rates) with Hawaii that Congress failed to renew in 1884. When the agreement was finally renewed in 1887, Congress added an amendment that granted the United States the exclusive right to establish a naval base at Pearl Harbor. Thereafter U.S. businesses increased their control over the Hawaiian Islands until the reign of Queen Liliuokalani (1891–1895). During her reign, Americans with business interests in Hawaii overthrew the monarchy and applied for statehood. In 1894, President Grover Cleveland refused to annex Hawaii, so the Hawaiian revolutionaries elected Sanford B. Dole, owner of a large sugar plantation, as the president of the newly formed republic. In 1898, during the administration of President William McKinley (1897–1901) the United States finally annexed the Hawaiian Islands. The Hawaiian Islands remained a territory of the United States until 1959, when they became the fiftieth state.

The sugar industry also influenced the American relationship with the island of Cuba. During the Civil War between the U.S. states, Cuban rebels fought for independence from Spain. Because the United States was distracted with domestic problems, the rebels received no assistance. During the late 1890s Cuban rebels again were fighting the Spanish for independence, and this time the United States, to protect American sugar interests, sent the USS *Maine* to Havana. When the battleship sank in Havana harbor, the United States found provocation for war against Spain, believing a Spanish mine had sunk the ship. (In the 1970s, divers discovered that the munitions had been stored adjacent to the ship's boiler room and a spark ignited the explosion.) The Cubans finally achieved their independence at the conclusion of the Spanish-American War. Between 1898 and 1959 the Cuban economy supplied the majority of the sugar imported into the U.S market. When in 1959 Fidel Castro assumed power in Cuba and the country fell under communist control, the United States placed an embargo on Cuban products, an embargo that still stands in 2003. (Current sources for sugar for the United States include Hawaii, the Caribbean, Canada, and Argentina.)

During the 1830s, sugar trade equaled 800,000 tons at $200 per ton. That amount increased to 8 million tons by 1900 and 115 million tons by 2000. The sugar industry continues to play an important role in the world and U.S. economies.

—*Cynthia Clark Northrup*

References

Abbott, George C. *Sugar.* New York: Routledge, 1990.

See also Volume 1: Cuba; Hawaii; Spanish-American War.

Sugar Act of 1764

First in a series of taxes imposed by the British Parliament that sparked the American Revolution.

After the Seven Years' War (1754–1763), the British government faced a war debt of more than £140 million and sought ways to include the colonies in the upkeep of the British forces in North America. The Sugar Act of 1764 modified the 1733 Molasses Act, which charged a duty on molasses of sixpence per gallon, changing the duty to a reduced three-pence in an attempt to curb smuggling of French molasses from the Caribbean and thus boost the customs revenue on British molasses. This product, crucial to the thriving rum distilleries of New England, had been a continuing source of friction between New England merchants and the British government, and Parliament assumed that reducing the duty while strengthening customs administration would improve relations between Britain and its American colonies.

Although the act also included unpopular new duties on wine, coffee, pimentos, cambric, and calico print fabric, the colonies especially resented that the Sugar Act regulated the export of lumber and iron from the colonies, restricting the ability of the colonies to produce anything but raw materials and to engage in trade with the French or Dutch. Increased naval patrols by the Royal Navy of the French West Indies seriously disrupted the smuggling trade and harmed the colonial economy. James Otis, who linked the new taxation with the hated Quartering Act, in which Parliament required the housing of British soldiers in private colonial homes, led the protests in Boston. Because the Sugar Act reduced the duties on molasses, Parliament kept the duties in place despite colonial protests. Opposition to the duties was one of the causes of the American Revolution.

—*Margaret Sankey*

References
Doerflinger, Thomas. *A Vigorous Spirit of Enterprise: Merchants and Economic Development in Revolutionary Philadelphia.* Chapel Hill: University of North Carolina Press, 1986.
Maier, Pauline. *From Resistance to Revolution: Colonial Radicals and the Development of American Opposition to Britain, 1765–1776.* New York: Alfred A. Knopf, 1972.
See also Volume 1: American Revolution; Stamp Act; Stamp Act Congress.

Supply-Side Economics

Balance or equilibrium between volume of goods and services produced (the supply side) and level of demand for those goods and services (the demand side).

Government economic policies that give incentives to investors and producers to increase the supply of goods and services are supply-side measures. Common examples are investment tax credits, reductions in capital gains taxes, rapid depreciation allowances, universal tax-deferred investment retirement accounts, and tax cuts for corporations and individuals with high levels of wealth and income.

A key supply-side principle in classical economics was that business cycles were caused by a lack of credit rather than weak demand. The administration of President Calvin Coolidge followed essentially supply-side economic policies, although former chair of the Council of Economic Advisers

Herbert Stein did not coin the term until decades later. Beginning in the 1950s, Milton Friedman and other University of Chicago economists made great strides in monetary theory, arguing that business cycles correlated closely with the volume and velocity of money in circulation. In the 1970s, Harvard economist Martin Feldstein and others did important work on the influence of taxation rates on savings and investment rates.

Supply-side economics was the centerpiece of the presidential administrations of Ronald Reagan and George H. W. Bush in the 1980s. Reagan embraced a theory put forward by University of Southern California economist Arthur Laffer that reducing tax rates actually would increase federal tax revenues by increasing work, savings, and investment. According to legend, Laffer sketched out the first version of his "Laffer curve" on a cocktail napkin in a Wall Street restaurant. Laffer's idea was embraced by a handful of Republican politicians including New York Congressman Jack Kemp and was popularized by influential journalists Robert Bartley and Jude Wanniski of the *Wall Street Journal* and by conservative pundit Irving Kristol, among others. Promising to dramatically reduce taxes without making correspondingly deep spending cuts, Reagan handily won election in 1980.

The rising popularity of supply-side economics reflected growing disillusionment with Keynesian economics, with its emphasis on monetary controls and government spending to boost consumer spending during recessions. Supply-siders believed that tax relief for investors would create new investment and new jobs by boosting capital formation. Benefits from new job creation and increased economic growth would in turn "trickle down" to middle-class and poor Americans.

Reagan's supply-side promises were embodied in the Economic Recovery Tax Act (ERTA) of 1981 and in subsequent tax legislation. But rather than increasing federal tax revenues, the ERTA created shortfalls of $200–300 billion per year for several years. Laffer's curve illustrated a basic economic principle, but demonstrated neither optimal tax rates nor whether current tax rates were above or below them. Nevertheless, tax-cut-based supply-side economics has remained popular among many conservatives and was the centerpiece of the economic platform of George W. Bush during and after the 2000 presidential election.

—*David B. Sicilia*

References
Brooks, David. "Supply-Side Squabbles." *National Review,* vol. 38 (October 24, 1986): 28–33.
Feldstein, Martin, ed. *American Economic Policy in the 1980s.* Chicago: University of Chicago Press, 1994.
Krugman, Paul. *Peddling Prosperity.* New York: W. W. Norton, 1994.
See also Volume 1: Reagan, Ronald; Reaganomics.

T

Taft-Hartley Act

See Labor-Management Relations Act.

Tariff of 1828

See Tariff of Abominations.

Tariff of Abominations (Tariff of 1828)

Protective tariff that led to the development of the principle of nullification in the South.

The presidential election of 1824 was decided in the House of Representatives for John Quincy Adams, even though Andrew Jackson won the popular vote. After the election, congressional Representative Martin Van Buren meticulously organized support for Jackson in the next presidential election. In 1828, Van Buren drafted a tariff bill designed to undermine the political base of the Adams administration. The bill raised duties on iron, hemp, flax, molasses, and distilled spirits, which benefited Western and mid-Atlantic interests, and lowered rates on finished woolen goods, which adversely affected New England textile manufacturers. Van Buren hoped Adams would veto the bill and make it appear that he sought to protect New England and his own political position. However, Adams held to his belief that protective tariffs promoted national economic development and signed the Tariff of 1828, which raised the duty on some European products by almost 50 percent.

The new tariff infuriated Southerners, who believed Congress had favored Northeastern industrial interests at the South's expense by raising the cost of goods the South could not manufacture for itself. The new rates raised prices on all sorts of imported products in the South and practically destroyed any hope for Adams's reelection. One Southern legislature after another denounced the tariff as unconstitutional, unjust, and oppressive. The Virginia legislature called it the "Tariff of Abominations." The most outspoken opposition arose in South Carolina. Vice President John C. Calhoun anonymously voiced Southern discontent by publishing the

South Carolina Exposition and Protest, an essay that advanced the principle that a single state might overrule or nullify federal law within its own territory, unless three-quarters of the states deemed the law constitutional. Jackson's attempt to enforce the tariff in the state led to a constitutional crisis and resulted in the passage of the Force Act of 1833 authorizing the use of force against South Carolina if it continued to refuse to collect the tariff. At the same time, Henry Clay, Speaker of the House, negotiated a compromise Tariff of 1833 that reduced the tariff incrementally over nine years—a bill South Carolina accepted.

—*Peter S. Genovese*

References

Feller, Daniel. *The Jacksonian Promise: America, 1815–1840.* Baltimore, MD: Johns Hopkins University Press, 1995.
See also Volume 1: Clay, Henry; Force Act; *South Carolina Exposition and Protest.*

Taxation, Confederation

Taxation system under the Articles of Confederation that demonstrated the young nation's commitment to republican ideology and a decentralized government.

The sole method of government taxation for the fledgling United States was a requisition system. Article 8 of the Articles of Confederation granted the power to levy and collect taxes to the individual states rather than to Congress. Under this system, Congress would send a request for funds to the states, and the state assemblies would then pass legislation that complied with this request. State officials collected the money and forwarded the required amount to Congress. The taxation policy of the Articles of Confederation made the national government completely dependent on the states for revenue.

This fiscal policy reflected the eighteenth-century republican notion of the proper power relationship between the people and their government. In the late 1700s, most Americans believed the power to tax was the right and responsibility of a sovereign state and that the location of this power within the structure of a government determined the nature of society. They argued that popular (or local) control of taxation provided the very foundation of representative government. Jeffersonian Republicans believed that local control of taxation ensured the rights of the citizen and acted as a check on the arbitrary authority of the state.

The political traditions and experiences of the colonies under the British imperial system provided another source of resistance to centralized taxation. In the colonial period, state assemblies operated their own fiscal systems and, in many ways, functioned as independent states. In the conflict that emerged between the colonies and England after 1763, when England began taxing the colonies directly for the first time, colonists argued that the British Parliament did not have the right to tax the colonies because the colonies were not represented in that body. This strong sense and tradition of localism combined with republican ideology to determine the nature of taxation under the Confederation.

Although the requisition system protected the interests and powers of the states, it proved crippling from the perspective of the national government. Congress was regularly short of funds and unable to pay its expenses. Frequently states assemblies either refused to send the full amount of a requisition or completely ignored the request. The Revolutionary War with England exacerbated these faults as Congress grew deeper in debt, fell behind in paying military salaries, and halted interest payments to its creditors. The shortcomings of the requisition system stimulated attempts to amend the Articles of Confederation and the call for a new government.

—*Peter S. Genovese*

References

Ferguson, E. James. *The Power of the Purse: A History of American Public Finance, 1776–1789.* Chapel Hill: University of North Carolina Press, 1961.

Rakove, Jack. *The Beginnings of National Politics: An Interpretive History of the Continental Congress.* New York: Alfred A. Knopf, 1979.

See also Volume 1: American Revolution; *The Federalist Papers.*

Tea Act of 1773

Tax measure by the British government that led to the Boston Tea Party.

By 1773, the British East India Company was experiencing serious financial trouble and required an emergency loan from the British government to continue operating. The British Parliament not only sought to regulate the company through the Regulating Act for India, it also wanted to remedy the company's financial situation through economic aid in the form of a tax cut on tea the company had stockpiled in its warehouses. The Tea Act of 1773 actually reduced the duty on tea shipped to America from 9 to 3 English pennies per pound, a rate that made English tea cheaper than smuggled Dutch tea—especially because the British East India Company paid the duty in London rather than at the colonial ports. Under the Tea Act, Parliament consigned the tea to a

few major importers in the colonies and shipped the tea, hoping it would sell quickly, pay the British East India Company's debts, and discourage smuggling.

However, the colonists, for whom tea had become a household staple, still resented that tea had remained taxed after the repeal of the Townshend duties (in effect from 1767 to 1773) on lead, glass, paper, and tea to raise money for the British Treasury. Merchants complained that only a few well-connected importers could sell tea. Protests occurred in Philadelphia and New York when the tea arrived, and in Boston the Sons of Liberty led the Boston Tea Party, in which Bostonians destroyed tea aboard the *Dartmouth, Eleanor,* and *Beaver.* Instead of solving a problem by making a commodity more accessible to the colonies, the Tea Act of 1773 sparked only resentment of the British East India Company's privileged position and of continued taxation of the colonies by the British Parliament.

—*Margaret Sankey*

References

Griswold, Wesley S. *The Night the Revolution Began.* Brattleboro, VT: Stephen Green Press, 1972.

Labarre, Benjamin Woods. *The Boston Tea Party.* New York: Oxford University Press, 1964.

See also Volume 1: American Revolution; Stamp Act; Sugar Act.

Technology Transfer

The acquisition of advanced or strategic technology by purchasing it rather than developing it—the U.S. government has ongoing efforts to prevent technology transfer to its political adversaries.

Although technology transfer was a concern between 1880 and 1945, it emerged as an important issue in U.S. economic diplomacy during the cold war, which pitted the United States and its allies against the Union of Soviet Socialist Republics (USSR) and its client states. In February 1949, Congress approved the Export Control Act authorizing the Commerce Department to restrict exports via a system of licenses. That November, the United States expanded its policy of denying military hardware and technologies to the USSR by forming the Coordinating Committee for Multilateral Export Controls from among noncommunist industrialized nations.

The government and the press widely debated the technology transfer issue when Congress renewed the 1969 Export Administration Act (EAA) in 1979. J. Fred Bucy of Texas Instruments, who chaired the Defense Department's Science Task Force on the Export of U.S. Technology, suggested the premise of the legislation. The Bucy report noted that the Soviet Union did not want Western goods as much as it wanted Western know-how to permanently improve its economic and strategic capabilities. The report differentiated between technology and goods and recommended strengthening regulations governing the former while lessening export restrictions on the latter.

Thus the EAA of 1979 focused on controlling processes, not products, especially the "critical technologies" on which

America's military superiority over the USSR presumably rested—for example, in the realm of microelectronics. The EAA embodied this notion in the form of the Military Critical Technologies List, a classified document generated and kept by the U.S. Defense Department. With the collapse of the Soviet bloc in 1989 and the Soviet Union in 1991, technology transfer became a secondary issue in the public forum. Nevertheless, in one sense, the arguments presented in the Bucy report persisted in influencing American economic diplomacy. In the post–cold war world, the U.S. government continued to restrict—and encouraged its allies also to restrict—the transfer of critical technologies to perceived or potential adversaries. For example, Congress reauthorized the EAA in 1999 to prevent the proliferation of weapons of mass destruction and their means of delivery to the nations of Iran, Iraq, Libya, and North Korea.

—*James K. Libbey*

References

An Analysis of Export Control of U.S. Technology, a DOD Perspective: A Report of the Defense Science Board Task Force on Export of U.S. Technology—The "Bucy Report." Washington, DC: U.S. Government Printing Office, 1976.

Bertsch, Gary K., ed. *Controlling East-West Trade and Technology Transfer.* Durham, NC: Duke University Press, 1988.

House Committee on International Relations. *Implementation of the Iran Nonproliferation Act of 2000.* Washington, DC: U.S. Government Printing Office, 2001.

Libbey, James K. *Russian-American Economic Relations.* Gulf Breeze, FL: Academic International Press, 1999.

See also Volume 1: Cold War; Coordinating Committee for Multinational Export Controls.

Tennessee Valley Authority (TVA)

Independent government agency responsible for developing the Tennessee River basin to control flooding and provide hydroelectric power.

During World War I, the U.S. government constructed a plant at Muscle Shoals, Tennessee, for the production of nitrate, a primary component in munitions. After the war, automobile manufacturer Henry Ford attempted to purchase the plant with the hope of transforming the area into an industrial center. Republican Senator George William Norris of Nebraska opposed Ford's purchase and counterproposed that the government continue to operate the facility and other projects in the region, including the Wilson Dam. Presidents Calvin Coolidge and Herbert Hoover rejected Norris's plan because it would involve government interference in private business. Norris finally convinced President Franklin D. Roosevelt to support the project.

Created by Congress in 1933, the Tennessee Valley Authority (TVA) addressed the problems of flooding, soil erosion, and poverty throughout the 41,000-square-mile basin of the Tennessee River, which ran through seven states. Governed by a three-person board with its headquarters located locally, the TVA constructed and maintained dams that generated inexpensive hydroelectric power to the people of the area, controlled flooding, initiated a program of reforestation to stop soil erosion, addressed the problem of malaria, developed fish and wildlife resources, built recreational facilities along the banks, and conducted environmental research. The availability of cheap electrical power attracted businesses to the area. Since the 1930s, industries such as coal, grain, petroleum, chemicals, forest products, and construction materials have provided additional employment for local inhabitants. The TVA addressed the poverty of the area by providing employment and conducting home demonstrations on subjects such as canning food, sewing clothes, and making butter and cheese, as well as personal hygiene and prenatal care.

Until 1959, the government provided the funding for the TVA. As expenses continued to climb, Congress authorized the sale of bonds and notes to fund the project. Eventually, the sale of electricity placed the TVA on a self-sufficient basis, and in the 1990s it paid back more than $2.5 million to the U.S. Treasury. The project had also achieved success in raising the per capita income in the area. Since the 1970s the TVA has shifted its focus to environmental protection, specifically how the growing human population will affect the ecosystem and how to prevent the destruction of plant and wildlife.

—*Cynthia Clark Northrup*

References

Callahan, North. *TVA: Bridge over Troubled Waters.* South Brunswick, NJ: A. S. Barnes, 1980.

Chandler, William U. *The Myth of TVA: Conservation and Development in the Tennessee Valley, 1933–1983.* Cambridge, MA: Ballinger, 1984.

McCraw, Thomas K. *TVA and the Power Fight, 1933–1939.* Philadelphia: Lippincott, 1971.

See also Volume 1: Great Depression; Muscle Shoals; Roosevelt, Franklin D.

Thirteenth Amendment (1865)

Constitutional amendment that outlawed slavery.

After South Carolina seceded from the Union in December 1860, several attempts at reconciliation occurred. One proposal was an amendment, the Thirteenth Amendment, that would have guaranteed the continuation of slavery. After Civil War fighting commenced, the Northern Republican Congress passed two Confiscation Acts declaring slaves in areas of open rebellion to be free. President Abraham Lincoln finally issued the Emancipation Proclamation on January 1, 1863, declaring that all slaves in areas of open rebellion were free. (Confiscation Acts passed between 1861 and 1864 had stated that all slaves in all states, including those loyal to the Union, were free, and Lincoln did not enforce those acts.) After the Civil War, Congress quickly passed the Thirteenth Amendment outlawing slavery altogether and submitted it to the states for ratification on January 31, 1865. The states ratified it on December 6, 1865. Congress issued an official proclamation to that effect on December 18, 1865. This amendment outlawed slavery and involuntary servitude in the United States, thus ending a system of involuntary labor that divided the states and became an issue of the American Civil War. By the time the states ratified this amendment all but two states had outlawed slavery, and most slaves had already gained their freedom. New Jersey, Delaware, and Kentucky initially rejected the proposed amendment but later accepted it. Only Mississippi has never ratified this constitutional change. Passage of this amendment signals the beginning of Reconstruction and the process of unifying the nation.

In 1918 in *Arver v. United States*, the Supreme Court ruled that the "involuntary servitude" clause of the Thirteenth Amendment did not extend to the military draft.

—*James T. Carroll*

References
Foner, Eric. *Reconstruction: America's Unfinished Revolution, 1863–1877*. New York: Harper and Row, 1988.
See also Volumes 1, 2: Slavery.

Timber and Stone Culture Act (1878)

Act that made cheap public land available for lumber interests.

In March 1877, Congress passed the Desert Land Act, which allowed individuals to claim up to 640 acres of arid western land at only $1.25 per acre if they attempted to irrigate the land within three years. The law applied to the states of California, Oregon, and Nevada as well as to the territories of Washington, Idaho, Montana, Utah, Wyoming, Arizona, New Mexico, and the Dakotas. Nearly nine million acres of arid public land were affected by the act. Most of the property went to cattle ranchers.

A year later, lumbermen lobbied for a similar act that would benefit their industry, and Congress passed the Timber and Stone Culture Act in 1878 to meet their demands. The law offered tracts of public land unfit for agriculture in the states of California, Oregon, and Nevada and in the Washington Territory at only $2.50 per acre. The size of any one tract could not exceed 160 acres. Individuals who purchased the land had to swear that they were buying the land for their own use or benefit and that they had made no agreements to transfer the land to anyone else. Lawmakers added these provisions fearing that lumbermen would hire individuals to claim small tracts, only to transfer their titles immediately to a large lumber company.

In 1878, the U.S. Supreme Court ruled that individuals could transfer their titles immediately after acquiring the land to any person or company. As a result, large lumber companies became the major beneficiaries of the new law. The acquisition of nearly one-third of the privately owned forests in the Pacific Northwest occurred through the Timber and Stone Culture Act. In 1892, the law extended to public land in all the states. Eventually Americans purchased over 13 million acres under the provisions of the Timber and Stone Culture Act.

—*Mary Stockwell*

References
Billington, Ray Allen. *Westward Expansion: A History of the American Frontier*. New York: Macmillan, 1967.
See also Volume 2: Land Policies; Volume 2 (Documents): Timber and Stone Culture Act.

Timber Culture Act (1873)

Legislation that offered free land in exchange for planting trees.

The Homestead Act of 1862 allowed any adult citizen or resident alien the right to claim 160 acres of newly surveyed land in the public domain, mostly in the Great Plains. The claimant paid a $10 fee and then had to live on the land or improve it in some way over a five-year period. After that time, the land belonged to the claimant free of charge. Many Americans living in the East wanted the Great Plains opened to small farmers; many westerners knew that 160 acres could not support either farming or ranching in the arid land between the Mississippi River and the Rocky Mountains.

Congress made the first attempt to give settlers in the Great Plains more land through the passage of the Timber Culture Act in 1873. The law allowed individuals to claim another 160 acres of free land if they planted at least one-quarter of the property with trees over a four-year period. Later amendments to the act reduced the amount of trees to ten acres and allowed up to eight years to complete the planting.

The Timber Culture Act had three main purposes. Scientists hoped that more trees on the Great Plains would bring plentiful rainfall into the arid country. The trees would also serve as a renewable source of fuel, homes, and fences. Finally, settlers could acquire a bigger piece of property and so better survive in the harsh conditions of the Great Plains. Some settlers combined their timber culture rights along with their homestead and preemption rights to set up farms and ranches of 480 acres. Eventually the government granted 11 million acres of western land through the Timber Culture Act.

—*Mary Stockwell*

References
Billington, Ray Allen. *Westward Expansion: A History of the American Frontier*. New York: Macmillan, 1967.
See also Volume 2: Land Policies; Volume 2 (Documents): Timber Culture Act.

Townsend, Francis E. (1876–1948)

Originator of the Social Security Act who initially advocated a monthly check for elderly citizens as a means of opening jobs for younger, unemployed workers during the Great Depression.

During the Great Depression, several individuals achieved national recognition for their proposals to end the nation's economic problems. One of them was Francis E. Townsend. Townsend was born August 13, 1876. He attended medical school at the University of Nebraska early in the twentieth century and practiced medicine for many years before settling in Long Beach, California. When the Great Depression hit, Dr. Townsend, concerned with the growing population of aging unemployed workers, devised the "old age revolving pension." A political activist, he promoted at enormous rallies nationwide that the government should issue monthly checks for $200 to individuals over the age of 60 years on the condition that they spend the money in order to receive the next month's check. This spending would stimulate the economy. Townsend employed charismatic speakers like Gerald L. K. Smith, who changed the name to the Townsend Plan, to promote the idea across the nation. He also coordinated efforts with Father Charles E. Coughlin, a popular priest from Royal Oak, Michigan. The three men formed the Union Party to oppose President Franklin D. Roosevelt, who sought a second term in the 1936 presidential election. Disagreements among the three founders during the election resulted in the decline of the party afterward. Roosevelt feared the continued efforts of Townsend, who was an increasingly popular opponent nationwide during the election campaign. In 1935, prior to the election, Roosevelt persuaded Congress to pass the Social Security Act to silence his critics, including Townsend. Townsend continued to modify his plan into the 1940s in an effort to retain national notoriety. He died November 30, 1948.

—*Cynthia Clark Northrup*

References
Conway, Thomas A. *The ABC of the Townsend Plan.* New York: H. W. Wilson, 2000.
See also Volume 1: Great Depression; Roosevelt, Franklin D.; Townsend Plan.

Townsend Plan

Proposal that resulted in the Social Security Act after Franklin D. Roosevelt coopted the plan during his 1936 reelection campaign.

In 1933, as the Great Depression continued unabated, Francis E. Townsend of Long Beach, California, a politically active doctor, called for the establishment of the Old Age Revolving Pension. Under his plan every American over the age of 60 years would receive a monthly check from the government in the amount of $200 on the condition that all of the money would be spent every month. The funds would be generated by a 2 percent federal sales tax. This plan, designed to provide income for the aging unemployed population, would open up jobs for younger workers while providing older citizens a means of continued financial support. Promoted across the nation by dynamic promoters like Gerald L. K. Smith (Townsend's adviser, who named the idea the Townsend Plan), the idea became extremely popular. Franklin D. Roosevelt added it to his platform during his 1936 presidential campaign for a second term, in which he faced the Union Party that Townsend and Smith had helped to found. In 1935, Roosevelt persuaded Congress to pass the Social Security Act.

—*Cynthia Clark Northrup*

References
Conway, Thomas A. *The ABC of the Townsend Plan.* New York: H. W. Wilson, 2000.
See also Volume 1: Great Depression; Roosevelt, Franklin D.; Townsend, Francis E.

Townshend Duties (1767–1773)

Series of restrictive acts by the British Parliament that taxed the American colonies and restricted residents' rights as English citizens.

After the British government under pressure from American colonists repealed the 1765 Stamp Act, which placed a duty on newspapers, legal documents, and other items including dice, it still faced a looming war debt from the Seven Years' War and the continuing cost of keeping troops in North America. Charles Townshend, England's chancellor of the Exchequer, proposed a new set of customs duties on lead, glass, tea, paint, and paper from Britain, with the taxes going to support not only the English military presence in the colonies but to pay the salaries of customs commissioners, making them independent of colonial politics. The bill also included provisions for the existence of admiralty (military) courts in Halifax, Nova Scotia, to try smugglers without juries, and for writs of assistance—warrants that authorized customs officials to impound ships and cargo.

The colonial population hated these measures and quickly mobilized the same protests it had successfully used against the Stamp Act, including a 1765 nonimportation agreement spearheaded by the Sons of Liberty in Boston and the Daughters of Liberty, colonial women who vowed not to purchase British products. The British government responded to colonial refusal to rescind inflammatory circular letters by dismissing the Massachusetts General Court and sending 4,000 soldiers to Boston to quell riots in 1768. Although the new government of British Prime Minister Lord North rescinded the Townshend Duties in 1770, it kept the tax on tea as part of the 1773 Declaratory Act, which insisted that Britain had a right to tax its colonies. Troops remained in Massachusetts, leading to the Boston Massacre (an incident on March 5, 1770, in which five colonists were killed by British soldiers and six others were wounded after colonists taunted a lone British sentry) and further clashes with the colonists including the Boston Tea Party in 1773.

—*Margaret Sankey*

References
Forster, Cornelius P. *The Uncontrolled Chancellor: Charles Townshend and His American Policy.* Providence: Rhode Island Bicentennial Foundation, 1978.
Knight, Carol Lynn H. *The American Colonial Press and the Townshend Crisis 1766–70.* Lewiston, NY: Edward Mellen Press, 1990.
See also Volume 1: American Revolution; Stamp Act; Sugar Act; Tea Act of 1773.

Trademark Act of 1947

Legislation designed to increase protection of trademarks.

On July 5, 1946, Congress passed the Trademark Act of 1947, known as the Lanham Act, making the effective date July 5, 1947. The bill increased the protection of trademarks already provided under earlier legislation: the Trade-Mark Act of March 3, 1881; "An Act relating to the registration of trade marks" (August 5, 1882); and the Trade-Mark Act of

1905. Legislators strengthened provisions against the deceptive and misleading use of trademarks in commerce and provided protection from unfair competition. Of particular importance, the Trademark Act of 1947 provided remedies in cases involving the fraudulent use of trademarks through the use of "reproductions, copies, counterfeits, or colorable imitations of registered marks." The act defined requirements for application, service of process (in which court documents are served on individuals or agencies), court appeals, and jurisdiction. Under the act the federal government prohibited states from infringing on the rights of persons or entities using a registered trademark and placed jurisdiction in the federal courts. Trademark certificates were valid for ten years, but after six years the commissioner could revoke the certification unless the party notified the patent office that the mark was in actual use or satisfactorily explained why it was not. The act remained in effect until 1999, when Congress passed an updated law that addressed the liability of the federal government and modern technological advances (Trademark Amendments Act).

—*Cynthia Clark Northrup*

References

Long, Doris E. *Unfair Competition and the Lanham Act.*
Washington, DC: Bureau of National Affairs, 1993.
See also Volume 1: Trademark Amendments Act of 1999.

Trademark Amendments Act of 1999

Amendments clarifying the trademark protections established in the Trademark Act of 1947.

The Trademark Amendments Act of 1999 clarified American trademark law established in 1946 by the Trademark Act of 1947, also called the Lanham Act. It expanded the protection of famous trademarks, like Coca-Cola®, by prohibiting the dilution (erosion of the selling power) of those marks. The act took effect in August 1999 when President Bill Clinton signed the bill.

Under the Trademark Amendments Act, dilution justifies opposition to someone's application to register a new mark or to petition to cancel a trademark already registered. The legislation specified a process for determining whether or not a trademark is famous. The U.S. Patent and Trademark Office will consider how long the register has used the mark, how distinctive and recognizable the mark appears, and whether or not other companies use similar marks.

The legislation also eliminated the federal government's immunity from lawsuits for violating the Lanham Act. Representative Howard Coble, a Republican from North Carolina, introduced the House version of the legislation. He argued, "The federal government cannot be sued for trademark infringement by a private citizen or corporate entity. Yet, the federal government enters the marketplace as a competitor to private business and is in a position to sue others for infringement." According to Coble, allowing holders of trademarks to sue the federal government would level the playing field.

The administration of President Bill Clinton opposed the legislation in part because of the removal of the federal government's immunity. The Clinton administration also believed that the bill would increase the workload at the Patent and Trademark Office. Despite the opposition, Congress easily approved the legislation and President Clinton signed it.

—*John David Rausch Jr.*

References

Welch, John L. "Modernizing for the Millennium: The 1999 Amendments to the Trademark Law." *Intellectual Property Today*, vol. 7, no. 1 (January 2000): 24–33.
See also Volume 2: Intellectual Property.

Trail of Tears (1838)

Forced march of Indian tribes from the eastern United States to Oklahoma.

During the early years of the U.S. Republic, Native Americans continued to live among Europeans in the eastern part of the United States. Five of the tribes became known as the "civilized tribes"—the Cherokee, Creeks, Choctaw, Chickasaw, and Seminoles. By the 1830s, these tribes had adopted white ways including establishing schools for their children, plowing fields and cultivating crops, and even owning slaves. Yet President Andrew Jackson believed that as long as the Indians remained among the U.S. population, the possibility of problems existed. He stated, "Humanity weeps over the fate of the Indians, but true philanthropy reconciles the mind to the extinction of one generation for another." Earlier attempts to persuade the Indians to voluntarily move west of the Mississippi River failed, and after the discovery of gold on tribal lands, Congress passed the Indian Removal Act of 1830 at Jackson's request. Threatened with forced removal, the Indians attempted to resist it in the courts. Many whites believed the policy flawed and tried to assist the Indians in their legal battle. On July 15, 1831, a Christian missionary from New England named Samuel A. Worcester crossed into Indian territory to help them, and the state of Georgia had him arrested. Worcester took his case to the U.S. Supreme Court, which that ruled against Georgia in *Worcester v. Georgia*. Still, the Court lacked the power to enforce its decision. Consequently, Jackson ordered the forced removal of the Indians.

The U.S. Army organized 13 separate groups of Indians and then hired contractors to move them west toward the setting sun. These contractors received $65 per person from the government to provide food and medicine for the Indians during the 1,000-mile forced march. At gunpoint, these Indians moved along a trail that extended across Tennessee, Kentucky, Illinois, and Missouri to present-day Oklahoma. The U.S. government failed to monitor the situation, and many of the contractors provided bad meat and no medicine, choosing to keep the money as part of their profit. As a result, approximately one-quarter of the Indians perished along the Trail of Tears. When the remaining Indians reached Oklahoma, the tribes established their own governments. Not surprisingly, when the Civil War broke out, most of the survivors of the Trail of Tears supported the Confederate States of America.

—*Cynthia Clark Northrup*

References
Foreman, Grant. *Indian Removal: The Emigration of the Five Civilized Tribes of Indians.* Norman: University of Oklahoma Press, 1953.
See also Volume 1: Indian Policy.

Transcontinental Railroad

Railroad link between the Mississippi River Valley and the Pacific coast.

By the early 1850s, many Americans were calling for the construction of a transcontinental railroad that would link the Mississippi River Valley to the Pacific coast. In the spring of 1853, Congress ordered the Army Corps of Engineers to survey the best possible routes west. The army proposed four possible pathways. The first ran from Lake Superior to Portland, Oregon; the second followed the South Pass through the Rocky Mountains to San Francisco; the third ran from the Red River Valley in Texas to southern California; and the fourth headed west from Texas through the Gila River Valley in Arizona.

Democratic Senator Stephen Douglas of Illinois, knowing that sectional rivalries would prevent the construction of any of the routes, proposed instead, in 1854, construction of three transcontinental railroads, which he called the Northern Pacific, the Central Pacific, and the Southern Pacific. Both Northern and Southern members of Congress agreed that sectional rivalries made it impossible to choose one route over another, but they turned down his counterproposal as simply too expensive. However, once the Civil War broke out, sectional rivalries no longer mattered because construction would only occur in the North. Northern congressional representatives passed the Transcontinental Railroad Act July 1, 1862, authorizing construction of a railroad along the central route.

The Union Pacific Railroad would be built west from the 100th meridian—the boundary between the moist East and the arid West—and the Central Pacific Railroad would head east from California. Two private companies built these lines, but both needed financial help from the U.S. government to complete their routes. Each company received a 400-foot right-of-way along the tracks as well as ten alternate sections of free land for each mile of track laid. The companies could make a profit by selling land along their routes as well as by carrying goods and selling passenger tickets. The government also paid the companies a premium of $16,000 for every mile of track laid in level country, $32,000 for every mile of track laid in foothills, and $48,000 for every mile of track laid in mountain ranges.

At first, construction of both routes proceeded slowly, but within four years, the pace picked up. Irish immigrants laid most of the Union Pacific track across the Great Plains, and Chinese laborers did the backbreaking work of pushing the Central Pacific over the Sierra Nevada mountain ranges. By 1867, the Union Pacific had reached Cheyenne, Wyoming, and was about to enter the South Pass of the Rocky Mountains. The Central Pacific had already crossed the Nevada deserts. The pace of construction increased even more when Congress classified the plains of Utah as mountain ranges. This designation meant that each company now received a $48,000 premium for every mile of track it laid.

During 1868, crews building the Union Pacific laid 360 miles of track, and those constructing the Central Pacific put down 425 miles. The race became so hectic that neither side paid attention to the fact that on their present courses the trains would not meet but would instead pass by each other somewhere in northern Utah. Congress solved the problem by ordering the two lines to meet at Promontory Point near Ogden, Utah. The last railroad tie, made of laurel and wrapped in silver, was finally laid in May 1869. Leland Stanford, president of the Central Pacific Railroad, hammered the last golden spike into the tie. People throughout the United States celebrated the completion of America's first transcontinental railroad—a symbol of the unity the nation desperately needed in the aftermath of the Civil War.

Soon more transcontinental railroads appeared. The Kansas Pacific Railroad linked Kansas City to Denver. The Atchison, Topeka and Santa Fe connected Kansas to New Mexico. The Southern Pacific Railroad linked San Francisco to the Colorado River. The line soon extended south across Texas to Galveston on the Gulf of Mexico. The Northern Pacific, built in 1883, was the last transcontinental railroad. It connected the Upper Great Lakes to the Puget Sound. After some 20 years of construction, the many transcontinental railroads had finally opened the Great Plains for settlement.

—*Mary Stockwell*

References
Billington, Ray Allen. *Westward Expansion: A History of the American Frontier.* New York: Macmillan, 1967.
See also Volume 2: Transportation Policy.

Transportation Revolution

Early nineteenth-century technological innovations in transportation that began with the invention of the steam engine.

The steam engine was invented in 1698 and was used to pump water out of coal mines. James Watt improved the design in 1763. In 1830, it came into common use in the United States to pull trains. Before that time, roads, sailing vessels, and canals dominated transportation in the United States. Turnpikes connecting the Atlantic states dominated interior travel, which was by horse and buggy. Sailing vessels dominated coastal transport, but steamboats displaced them after 1815. By the 1830s railroads replaced canals as an important mode of transportation; using the new steam engines, railroads connected the country and revolutionized transportation.

Before 1824, the federal government played a limited role in transportation. Congress granted one exception and helped with construction of the National Road by funding it via sales revenues from 5 percent of Ohio land that the federal government owned and sold to settlers or investors. However, transport over roads remained slow. The federal government, partly because of opposition to its involvement with the National Road, stayed out of the road-building business until 1916 after the invention of the automobile, when another revolution in transportation occurred.

Strict constructionists argued that the Constitution did not grant the federal government power to fund internal transportation improvements. This perspective changed when the Supreme Court issued its decision in the 1824 case of *Gibbons v. Ogden*. Although the case involved steamboat travel in New York, the decision strengthened the power of the U.S. government because it established national supremacy in regulating interstate commerce. Based on the Court's ruling, the government could support transportation as a matter of interstate commerce. The decision also became the basis for government regulation of railroads in 1887.

The government used subsidies to encourage the transportation revolution in the nineteenth century. The United States bought stock in canal, steamship, and turnpike companies and funded the building of telegraph lines so station masters could communicate about arrival and departure times and conduct other railroad business. Western states granted free land to railroad companies, which sold the land at a profit so it could fund construction of the railroad tracks. Congress provided government surveyors to help companies lay out transportation routes, and it reduced tariffs on materials such as iron used to build railroad tracks. In 1850, Congress gave land grants to three railroads—Illinois Central, Mobile, and Ohio—to connect Illinois with the South. Such subsidies helped to connect the continent by the 1870s and allowed farmers to take part in a national economy. Being able to transport their produce to distant markets via railroads allowed farmers to move from subsistence to the market economy.

The land grant also set a precedent for the next two decades. Based on the 1850 act, Congress passed the Pacific Railway Act in 1862, authorizing land grants and cash premiums up to $48,000 per mile of track for the Union Pacific and Central Pacific Railroad companies, which were building a transcontinental railroad. Congress issued a similar grant in 1864 to the Northern Pacific. The government transferred 131 million acres to railroad companies and through their efforts connected the continent by the 1870s.

The era of railroads ended after another transportation revolution occurred in the early twentieth century. The invention of the automobile led to passage of the Federal Highways Act in 1916. This act provided for construction of a national road system connecting far-flung areas of the country and furthering economic development. In the 1920s, passenger travel began a steady decline, and by 1971 Congress created Amtrak to serve intercity and passenger train travel. The government has continued to provide assistance to Amtrak, which had never operated profitably.

The most recent form of transportation to develop was the airplane. Limited passenger travel started in 1912 with the zeppelin airship. The U.S. government began subsidizing the airline industry in 1919 by sending mail by air. As a result of these subsidies the airline industry expanded; new companies such as Pan Am, United Airlines, American Airlines, and Delta formed between 1928 and 1931. In 1930 only a few thousand people traveled by air; that number increased to 2 million passengers per year by 1930. Passenger travel boomed after World War II; 16.7 million passengers per year traveled by air in 1949. The development of jet airliners reduced flight times and fares, and by 1988 more than 455 million passengers per year traveled by air. The airline industry continued to enjoy prosperity until the terrorist attacks of September 11, 2001. The dramatic decline in air travel since then has forced many airlines close to bankruptcy, and they compete for passengers by slashing fares. In 2002 Congress authorized a $15 billion bailout package for the airlines.

—*Eugene Van Sickle*

References
Fehrenbacher, Don E. *The Era of Expansion, 1800–1848.* New York: John Wiley and Sons, 1969.
See also Volume 1: Automobile; Railroads.

Treaty of 1783

Treaty between Britain and the United States that ended the Revolutionary War and secured American independence; also known as the Treaty of Paris.

During the Revolutionary War following the Battle of Yorktown in 1782, the British chose to make peace rather than continue the fight to keep the colonies. The American negotiators were already in Europe on diplomatic missions—John Jay was in Spain, and Benjamin Franklin and John Adams were in France—so talks began immediately in Paris. By beginning treaty talks with Britain, the United States violated its agreement with France not to make a separate peace, which would mean that France, Spain, and the Dutch would remain at war with Britain in India and the Caribbean.

The treaty itself was signed on October 8, 1782, and ratified in January 1783. It guaranteed the independence of the new nation, the United States, and fixed its western boundary at the Mississippi River. Florida, which had been in British hands since 1763, was returned to Spain. The United States received the right to fish off the Grand Banks of Newfoundland and to navigate the St. Lawrence River, and the British received a guarantee that the Confederation Congress (the current American government) would recommend that U.S. states pay reparations to loyalists who had lost property in the war and repay debts to British merchant houses. The northern and southern borders of the United States remained vague in this treaty, particularly in the stretch of land between Canada and the United States in the north, and two further treaties were required to solidify them. Most importantly, the Treaty of 1783 accomplished the British withdrawal of troops from the United States and the diplomatic recognition of the United States as a separate country from Great Britain.

—*Margaret Sankey*

References
Bemis, Samuel Flagg. *The Diplomacy of the American Revolution.* Bloomington: Indiana University Press, 1957.
Hoffman, Ronald. *Peace and the Peacemakers.* Charlottesville: University Press of Virginia, 1986.

Schoenbrun, David. *Triumph in Paris: The Exploits of Benjamin Franklin.* New York: Harper and Row, 1976.

See also Volume 1: American Revolution.

Treaty of 1867

Treaty that arranged the purchase of Alaska from Russia.

In 1741 the Russian explorer Vitus Bering crossed the straits that separated Russia from the North American continent, a distance of 55 miles. He discovered Alaska, mapped the region, and claimed the land for Russia. In 1784 Russian fur traders established a trading post at Three Saints Bay on Kodiak Island. In 1866, the Russian czar instructed his foreign minister to negotiate the sale of the land to the United States. U.S. Secretary of State William Seward signed the treaty on March 30, 1867. The terms of the treaty called for the United States to receive 586,000 square miles of land in exchange for $7.2 million. The purchase was unpopular in the United States; critics labeled the land acquisition "Seward's Folly" or "Seward's Ice Box." Then, in the 1880s and 1890s, prospectors discovered gold in Alaska. The U.S. government encouraged expeditions into the region to map the geography and catalog the wildlife and cultures. The Harriman Expedition of 1899 designated many of the geographic features including Mt. McKinley, named for William McKinley, who was president at the time. Alaska became a territory in 1884 and a state on January 3, 1959. Even more important than the discovery of gold was the discovery of oil in 1968 at Prudhoe Bay, Alaska. At first the cost of transporting oil restricted exploration for it, but that problem was solved with the construction from 1973 to 1977 of the Alaskan pipeline. Exploration in Alaska stepped up because of the Arab embargo in the 1970s, when the price of oil was high, and because of continued concerns about political volatility in the Middle East, from which the U.S. imports 22 percent of its oil (2002 data). At the same time, environmentalists have fought to preserve Alaskan wildlife, claiming that such exploration would be detrimental to the local ecology. After the terrorist attacks of September 11, 2001, President George W. Bush proposed additional drilling in Alaska, but Congress rejected the measure.

—*Cynthia Clark Northrup*

References

Sgori, Peter P. *The Purchase of Alaska, March 3, 1867: Bargain at Two Cents an Acre.* New York: Franklin Watts, 1975.

See also Volume 1: Oil; Volume 2: Land Policies.

Treaty of Ghent (December 24, 1814)

Treaty that concluded the War of 1812 and ended the policy of economic warfare between the United States and Great Britain.

Hostilities between Britain and the United States had begun in 1812, and peace negotiations to end the war opened between delegates from the United States and Great Britain in Ghent, Belgium, on August 8, 1814. The American delegation, which included John Quincy Adams, Henry Clay, Albert Gallatin, James A. Bayard, and Jonathan Russell, insisted that the British abandon the policy of impressing U.S. seamen (claiming they were deserters and forcing them into service in the Royal Navy), respect international law in operating blockades, and pay indemnity for their illegal seizure of American ships. The demands of the United States intended to redress the causes of the war. The British delegation included James Lord Baron Gambier, Henry Goulburn, and William Adams. These men, under strict instructions from London, proposed demands designed to protect Canada from American aggression and expansion. The British wanted territorial concessions in New York and Maine, the surrender of American control on the Great Lakes, the creation of an autonomous Indian buffer state, the right to navigate the Mississippi River, and the relinquishment of American fishing rights off the coasts of Newfoundland and Labrador.

As negotiations proceeded, the diplomats dropped one demand after another and eventually agreed to a peace treaty that settled nothing but simply restored conditions to their prewar status. Completed and signed on December 24, 1814, the treaty, referred to as the Peace of Christmas Eve, outlined the agreements made in the settlement. Each side agreed to evacuate all enemy territory, not to carry off any enemy property, and to return all prisoners as soon as practicable. Each nation also promised to make peace with Native American groups and agreed to establish future joint commissions to address the issues of impressment and neutral rights, the demilitarization of the Great Lakes, the definition of the Canadian-American border, and disputed fishing rights. Although the treaty achieved the most important objective and concluded hostilities, neither delegation felt truly satisfied because neither succeeded in having its demands met.

The provisions of the treaty, however, had important ramifications for the future development of the United States. It established a pattern of improving relations between the two nations, and England's abandonment of an Indian buffer state placed the destiny of the old northwest frontier solely in the hands of the U.S. government. This aspect of the agreement freed Americans from the fear of British intrigues in the West and hastened settlement.

—*Peter S. Genovese*

References

Engelman, Fred L. *The Peace of Christmas Eve.* New York: Harcourt, Brace and World, 1962.

Hickey, Donald R. *The War of 1812: A Forgotten Conflict.* Urbana: University of Illinois Press, 1989.

See also Volume 1: War of 1812.

Treaty of Greenville (1795)

Treaty under which Indians agreed to open Ohio for settlement.

In 1790, the Native American tribes of the old northwest in the Ohio River Valley region joined together to stop the advance of the Americans north of the Ohio River. Their leaders included the Wyandot Chief Tarhe the Crane, the

Shawnee Chief Bluejacket, and the Miami Chief Little Turtle. These men successfully led their warriors against the armies of General Josiah Harmar in 1790 and General Arthur St. Clair in 1791. Desperate to open the West for settlement, President George Washington sent a third army into Ohio under General Anthony Wayne in 1792. Wayne took two years to train his forces before heading north to meet the Indians along the rapids of the Maumee River. His army defeated the combined tribes at the Battle of Fallen Timbers on August 20, 1794.

One year later, in 1795, General Wayne called the defeated tribes together to negotiate a treaty. They met at Fort Greenville in western Ohio. Wayne had built the fort during the march to Fallen Timbers and had named it in honor of General Nathaniel Greene. After weeks of debate, the chiefs of the major Ohio tribes finally signed the Treaty of Greenville. They agreed to divide Ohio by a line that started at the mouth of the Cuyahoga River and ran south to Fort Laurens on the Tuscaroras River, west to Fort Loramie on a branch of the Great Miami River, and finally southwest to the Ohio River. The Indians promised to live north of the line; Americans could settle south of it and in 16 smaller plots set aside in Indian territory. The Native Americans could also cross south of the line to hunt, while Americans received a guarantee of safe passage through Indian country. In exchange for agreeing to the terms of the Treaty of Greenville, the U.S. government promised the Indians yearly payments of up to $1,000 per tribe.

—*Mary Stockwell*

References
Knepper, George W. *Ohio and Its People.* Kent, OH: Kent State University Press, 1997.
See also Volume 1: Indian Policy; Volume 2: Land Policies.

Treaty of Guadalupe Hidalgo (February 2, 1848)

Treaty that ended the Mexican-American War.

After the United States passed a joint resolution annexing Texas, the Mexican army began attacking Americans just north of the Rio Grande River. Congress declared war on Mexico in retaliation. After U.S. forces occupied Mexico City in 1847 at the end of the Mexican War (1845–1848), the two countries signed the Treaty of Guadalupe Hidalgo on February 2, 1848. In addition to ending the hostilities, the treaty renounced future war as a means of settling conflicts. John Trist, the U.S. minister to Mexico, disregarded the president's instructions to return to Washington after being rebuffed by the Mexican government and instead negotiated the terms of the treaty. According to the agreement, which ratified by the Senate March 1, 1848, by a 38-to-14 vote, the two countries recognized the Rio Grande River as the boundary between the United States and Mexico. In addition, all land that encompasses present-day Arizona (except for the Gadsden Purchase, in which the U.S. bought Mexican land to use in building the transcontinental railroad), New Mexico, Colorado, Utah, Wyoming, and California was ceded to the United

States for $15 million. The United States also assumed responsibility for any claims by American citizens against the Mexican government. The Mexican government ratified the treaty May 3, 1848, and U.S. forces withdrew from Mexico City. As a result of the Mexican-American War, the United States gained 338,680,960 acres of land and another 78,926,720 acres from the acquisition of Texas through a joint resolution of Congress that admitted the Republic of Texas into the Union as a state. Much of this land became available to settlers under the Homestead, Timber Culture, Timber and Stone Culture, and Desert Land Acts.

—*Cynthia Clark Northrup*

References
Griswold del Castillo, Richard. *The Treaty of Guadalupe Hidalgo: A Legacy of Conflict.* Norman: University of Oklahoma Press, 1990.
See also Volume 1: Timber and Stone Act; Timber Culture Act; War and Warfare; Volume 2: Land Policies; Volume 2 (Documents): Treaty of Guadalupe Hidalgo.

Treaty of Paris

See Treaty of 1783.

Treaty of San Lorenzo

See Pinckney Treaty.

Triangular Trade

Term referring to a key component of the colonial mercantilist economy, a series of established trade routes that linked Europe, Africa, and the Americas.

Begun by the Portuguese and Dutch as early as the sixteenth century and perfected by the French and British as late as the early nineteenth century, the complex system of commerce called *triangular trade* involved the transport of European manufactured items to Africa for the purchase of slaves, the transport of these slaves to America in exchange for the products of slave plantations, and, in the third and final leg, the transport of the American cash crops to Europe. In later years, a second pattern emerged that involved American slavers. New England slave ships sailed to Africa with rum for the purchase of slaves, who were transported to the West Indies and sold for molasses, which, in turn, was brought back to New England and distilled into rum.

Triangular trade was largely a private endeavor. Although a few investors lost money because of the risks involved in trans-Atlantic trade, the cost of European goods such as guns, cheap cloth, and trinkets remained negligible compared with the value of the slaves, and thus most investors profited immensely. Triangular trade was by its very nature brutally harsh. In the second leg of the journey—the infamous "middle passage" from Africa to America—slaves were chained and regimented into overcrowded quarters. Racked with disease and malnutrition, thousands died. As a complex system of industrial interdependency linked by transportation, dependent on communication, and financed by investment capital, triangular trade represented an early form of a global economy. Each leg of the trade was integrated with the others, and the same people were often involved. Investors in a cargo of slaves were often plantation owners, who might also be involved in shipbuilding. Plantation profits might be invested in a factory to produce the trinkets necessary for the acquisition of slaves. A slaver might use his profits to purchase a plantation.

By helping to make colonization a profitable enterprise, triangular trade spurred on further development in America, including aspects of the economy not directly related to the slave industry (such as production of textiles from Southern cotton). In addition, reinvestment of profits in England helped provide the capital for the Industrial Revolution, which started in England and then spread to the United States.

—*Brooks Flippen*

References

Emert, Phyllis Raybin. *Colonial Triangular Trade: An Economy Based on Human Misery.* Carlisle, MA: Discovery Enterprises, 1995.

Findlay, Ronald. *The Triangular Trade and the Atlantic Economy of the Eighteenth Century.* Princeton, NJ: International Finance Section, Department of Economics, Princeton University, 1990.

See also Volumes 1, 2: Slavery.

Truman Doctrine

Policy of containment of communism enunciated by President Harry S Truman in 1947 that laid the cornerstone for several decades of U.S. confrontation with the Soviet Union.

The Truman Doctrine braced the United States for a campaign to check communist expansion and secure predominance in the postwar world. The doctrine shaped up between 1945 and 1947 when Washington's relations with Moscow—an ally during World War II but by 1947 a dominant communist power—became increasingly acrimonious. Throughout this two-year period, the U.S. government displayed a strong repugnance toward Moscow's authoritarian control over Eastern Europe (albeit a Soviet sphere recognized by the United States and its Western allies) and its growing ideological animosity toward the capitalist West. At the same time, American policymakers were anxious about the rising influence of domestic communists and pro–Soviet Union radicals in a war-devastated Western Europe, an area essential to the liberal capitalist international order the United States desired to build. Washington was also becoming ever more vigilant and wary of Soviet intentions in the Middle East, an oil-rich and strategically important region, as Moscow attempted territorial inroads into Iran and Turkey. To the further dismay of the United States, from 1944 through 1949 civil war ran rampant in Greece—the British sphere of influence—between the oppressive government in place and guerrillas supported by the communist regimes of Bulgaria, Yugoslavia, and Albania. A communist victory in Greece would not only create a

vacuum for the Soviets to fill but would menace American economic and strategic safety. American policymakers came to believe that expansion was innate to Soviet communism and knew no bounds, and that only the United States had the material resources to contain the Soviet Union until it eventually collapsed. Such a line of thinking produced Truman's policy to assist pro-American governments against the thrust of communist expansion.

Truman declared this U.S. position in an address to Congress on March 12, 1947, following Britain's decision the previous month to relinquish its support for the Greek government. Truman asked Congress for $400 million to fortify the Greek regime and help Turkey, which also faced the Soviet threat. He argued that a struggle between the free and the nonfree ways of life now dictated history—the United States, leader of democracy, had the moral obligation and material strength to support free peoples in their resistance to "subjugation by armed minorities or by outside pressures" and help the free nations toward self-determination. The new policy worked to buttress Greece and Turkey and, along with the Marshall Plan, it helped to assist the economic recovery in Western Europe and to strengthen its strategic alliance with the United States. By mobilizing an anticommunist crusade, the Truman Doctrine also helped raise the Truman administration's popularity at home. Yet, the United States, as the administration itself recognized, was incapable of accomplishing all that the Truman Doctrine promised. In the years to come, Washington had to make strategic adjustments, focusing on strategic areas instead of peripheral regions to avoid overstretching American resources.

—*Guoqiang Zheng*

References

Cohen, Warren, ed. *The Cambridge History of American Foreign Relations.* London: Cambridge University Press, 1993.

See also Volume 1: Cold War; Communism.

Trusts

Combination of companies with a single board of trustees formed to reduce competition and control prices.

Samuel Dodd, an attorney for Standard Oil Company, created the first trust on January 2, 1882. Under the Standard Oil Trust, a nine-member board of trustees controlled all of John D. Rockefeller's oil-related companies. Rockefeller had worked hard to establish Standard Oil and used methods that reduced his costs to increase profits. Stockholders received shares in the trust, to which all profits from the various companies were transferred. The board then determined the amount of dividends paid to the stockholders. The nine trustees served as director or officers of the various companies, in essence creating a monopoly. Over the next few years, as Standard Oil dominated the petroleum industry and drove out the competition, the public began to agitate against the monopolies—not just the oil trust, but also the sugar, beef, and steel trusts. In 1890 Congress addressed the issue by passing the Sherman Anti-Trust Act.

Designed to prevent the restraint of trade, the Sherman Anti-Trust Act was ineffective against the giant conglomerates of the day because of its lack of an enforcement clause and because of the Supreme Court's interpretation of a monopoly. (For example, when the federal government tried to prosecute the sugar trust, the Supreme Court ruled in *United States v. E. C. Knight Co.* that control over 98 percent of the market did not constitute a monopoly.) Because Standard Oil did not control 100 percent of the oil market, the company escaped prosecution. However, when the railroad workers all struck against the Pullman Sleeping Car Company in 1894, the government threatened the union under the Sherman Anti-Trust Act because 100 percent of the workers had joined the strike.

The ineffectiveness of the Sherman Anti-Trust Act did not deter President Theodore Roosevelt from pursuing trusts. During his seven years in office from 1901 to 1908, Roosevelt instructed his attorney general to file charges against the largest trusts, starting with Northern Securities Company, the controlling entity for the Great Northern and Northern Pacific Railroads. After the Supreme Court ordered the dissolution of Northern Securities, the Roosevelt administration prosecuted another 40 cases before William Howard Taft became president in 1908. Taft proved a greater trust-buster than Roosevelt, successfully dismantling 70 trusts during his short four-year term. During Taft's administration, the U.S. Supreme Court ruled against Standard Oil and dissolved the interlocking directorate that had allowed the company to monopolize the industry. In 1914 during Woodrow Wilson's term (1913–1921), Congress passed the Clayton Anti-Trust Act, legislation that provided enforcement provisions.

Since the early twentieth century, companies have refrained from monopolistic practices, an important exception being the computer software company Microsoft, which started in 1978. The rise of Microsoft, with its monopolistic practice of eliminating competition by packaging its operating system with personal computers, forced the U.S. government to reexamine the issue of monopolies. In 1998 in *United States v. Microsoft*, the government charged Microsoft with monopolistic practices. The case against Microsoft continues as both sides attempt to work out acceptable arrangements to comply with antitrust legislation. The government has reached an agreement with Microsoft, and compliance officers continue to monitor the company, which must comply with the Court's final judgment concerning its business practices in regard to its competitors.

—*Cynthia Clark Northrup*

References

McKenzie, Richard B. *Trust on Trial: How the Microsoft Case Is Reframing the Rules of Competition.* Cambridge, MA: Perseus Publishing, 2001.

Meyer, Balthasar Henry. *A History of the Northern Securities Case.* New York: Da Capo Press, 1972.

Russell, Charles Edward. *The Greatest Trust in the World.* New York: Ridgway-Thayer, 1905.

See also Volume 1: Microsoft; Rockefeller, John D.; Standard Oil; *United States v. E. C. Knight Co.*

Truth-in-Lending Act (1968)

Legislation designed to protect consumers who buy on credit.

In 1968 Congress passed the Consumer Credit Protection Act. Title I of that act became known as the Truth-in-Lending Act. Designed to protect consumers by providing them with information about finance charges and additional fees that are tacked on to loans, the act covers all financial transactions of any business that extends credit on a regular basis to customers. Under the act, a lender must disclose the finance charge, the annual percentage rate, the amount financed, the total number of payments, and the total sale price. With this information, the buyer can compare the total loan cost among various lenders regardless of the method the lenders use to compute the finance charge. Confusion had arisen in the past over the various methods of computing interest—simple, compounded (on a daily, weekly, or monthly basis), and whether interest was computed on the highest, lowest, or average balance. The Truth-in-Lending Act also required the disclosure of all loan origination fees (charged to process the paperwork for the loan).

Many federal agencies exercise oversight authority under the Truth-in-Lending Act. The Federal Reserve Board deals with the majority of the financial institutions. Under regulation Z, the Federal Reserve deals with credit offered to consumers on a regular basis. These transactions include purchases for personal, family, or household use and are usually conducted with a credit card or via consumer loan. Regulation M deals with consumer leasing transactions when the term of the lease exceeds four months and the amount financed is less than $25,000. Other agencies besides the Federal Reserve also deal with truth-in-lending requirements: The Department of Transportation, the Veterans Administration, the Department of Housing and Urban Development, the Federal Home Loan Bank Board, and the National Credit Union Administration enforce these regulations.

The penalty for violating the Truth-in-Lending Act includes the ability of the injured party to sue for two times the amount of the finance charges. Congress simplified the Truth-in-Lending Act with the Depository Institutions Deregulations and Monetary Control Act of 1980. The latter act phased out ceilings on interest rates, established uniform cash reserve requirements for institutions, added liability for firms, and offered assistance to troubled institutions.

—*Cynthia Clark Northrup*

References

Keest, Kathleen E. *Truth in Lending.* Boston: National Consumer Law Center, 1995.

See also Volume 1: Credit; Federal Reserve Act; Interest Rates.

Truth in Securities Act (Securities Act of 1933)

Depression-era legislation providing for registration of securities (stocks) and full disclosure of information about their issuers.

Investment bankers had a low public image in 1933, primarily because of the financial dealings that took place at the beginning of the Great Depression. That year the U.S. Senate's Banking Committee had completed an investigation into the shadowy Wall Street operations of the 1920s, finding that bankers and their associates regularly dipped into special funds to protect themselves from losses during times of economic decline. Congress responded to the public's anger by passing several new regulations affecting the financial industry, including the Securities Act of 1933, usually referred to as the "Truth in Securities Act."

The law had two basic objectives. First, the legislation required that investors receive financial and other significant information concerning securities, or stocks, being offered for public sale. The second objective was to prohibit deceit, misrepresentations, and other fraud in the sale of securities. The key element of the law made Wall Street operations transparent to investors. For this reason, most Wall Street bankers opposed the legislation as it made its way through Congress.

Despite its opposition to the Securities Act of 1933, the investment community credits it with the growth of stock market activity between the 1930s and the end of the twentieth century. Before the market crashed in 1929, average folks viewed Wall Street as a murky world of insider information and rigged stocks. Only about 1.5 million people out of a population of 120 million (just over 1 percent of the population) invested in the market in the 1920s. By the 1990s, nearly 80 million people out of a population of 248.7 million (32 percent of the population) invested in stocks. The law also re-

sulted in the growth of brokerage firms like Merrill Lynch, whose founder believed that the information required by the Securities Act could be used to market stocks to small investors.

According to Wall Street historian Ron Chernow, the Truth in Securities Act changed the face of Wall Street. Whereas power once flowed from the top down and the prestigious firms did not work with small investors, after passage of the Truth in Securities Act brokerages had to market their services and products much like soap and cereal. The growth of the Internet (a high-speed method of computerized information and communication that became widely used by the public in the 1990s) and the ready availability of information companies are required to provide have made it easier for investors to control their portfolios having only limited contact with a stockbroker.

—*John David Rausch Jr.*

References

Chernow, Ron. "The New Deal's Gift to Wall Street." *Wall Street Journal,* November 11, 1999.

Seligman, Joel. *The Transformation of Wall Street: A History of the Securities and Exchange Commission and Modern Corporate Finance.* Rev. ed. Boston: Northeastern University Press, 1995.

See also Volume 1: Securities and Exchange Commission.

TVA

See Tennessee Valley Authority.

U

UN

See United Nations.

Underwood-Simmons Tariff Act (1913)

Legislation that reduced tariffs on more imports than had any tariff act since the Civil War and that included a rider establishing the first income tax since passage of the Sixteenth Amendment had allowed for such a tax.

A commitment to reform of the tariff laws dominated the 1912 presidential election, in which Democrat Woodrow Wilson was elected. One of the first items on Wilson's New Freedom legislative agenda included restructuring "the system of privileged tariff protection that the Republican party had carefully erected since 1861." In dramatic fashion, shortly after his inauguration, Wilson delivered a personal message to both houses of Congress calling for tariff reform. In the eyes of reformers, the high protective tariff that had existed during the period of rapid industrial growth following the Civil War symbolized privilege. Tariff reform had proved a tough political issue to resolve: President Grover Cleveland (who had two terms, 1886–1890 and 1894–1898) almost wrecked the Democratic Party by trying to lower rates, and the promise by Republican President William Howard Taft (1909–1913) of tariff revision "had hastened the disruption of his party."

Oscar W. Underwood, chair of the House Ways and Means Committee, introduced the House bill for tariff revision on April 22, 1913. Protection of wool and sugar became the sticky issue among some Democratic house members, who did not want those commodities protected, and President Wilson skillfully maneuvered the committee to accept the adoption of free wool and sugar. The House version failed to establish a free tariff; it "aimed only at striking down the special advantages that the protectionist policy had conferred upon American manufacturers."

The Underwood Bill—the initial bill in the House of Representatives—sought to establish moderate protection "by placing domestic industries in a genuinely competitive position with regard to European manufacturers." The tariff measure that finally became law lowered duties on nearly 1,000 items including cotton and woolen goods, iron, steel, coal, wood, agricultural tools, and many other agricultural products. Congress reduced the average of all duties from 41 percent—the average ad valorem rate of the Payne-Aldrich Tariff of 1909—to 29 percent. Certain items moved to the free list or received "incidental protection."

Before the act's final adoption by both houses of Congress in October 1913, the Senate attached to it a graduated income tax, anticipating a decrease in customs receipts of about $1 million due to the lower tariff rates—the first income tax passed under the Sixteenth Amendment, which established the personal income tax and had been adopted in 1913. Although Democratic Representative Cordell Hull of Tennessee had initially drafted the income tax proposal, Senate Finance Committee Chair Furnifold M. Simmons introduced the approved compromise surtax charge. A section of the Underwood-Simmons Tariff Act provided for a graduated tax ranging from 1 to 6 percent on incomes greater than $4,000 per year.

The Underwood-Simmons Tariff Act passed against strong opposition from Republicans, who objected to the lower tariff rates. It did, however, answer the widespread call for tariff reform while also establishing the principle that those with more income had the responsibility of paying a heavier share of government expenses. The "ability to pay" principle of taxation became firmly established. Additionally, the new law demonstrated the ability of the Democratic Party to pull together and free itself from special privilege.

In 1922, Republican President Warren G. Harding signed into law the Fordney-McCumber Act, wiping out the reductions made in the Underwood-Simmons Tariff. It set considerably higher rates on hundreds of manufactured products. The new tariff also authorized the President to raise or lower tariff rates by as much as 50 percent. Naturally, most adjustments increased rates. This short-lived victory for Democratic advocates of tariff reform encouraged those wishing to tear down the wall of special privilege.

—Charles F. Howlett

References

Crunden, Robert M. *Ministers of Reform: The Progressives' Achievement in American Civilization, 1889–1920.* New York: Basic Books, 1982.

Link, Arthur S. *Woodrow Wilson and the Progressive Era, 1910–1917.* New York: Harper and Row, 1954.

Link, Arthur S., and Richard L. McCormick. *Progressivism.* Arlington Heights, IL: Harlan Davidson, 1983.

Mitchell, Broadus. *A Preface to Economics.* New York: Henry Holt, 1932.

Taussig, Frank W. *Tariff History of the United States.* 8th ed. Cambridge, MA: Harvard University Press, 1931.

See also Volume 1: Sixteenth Amendment; Wilson, Woodrow.

Unemployment

The proportion of the labor force out of work but actively seeking jobs, a long-standing concern of economic policy.

The Massachusetts Bureau of the Statistics of Labor, in its 1887 survey of workers involuntarily without employment, coined the noun "unemployment." The measured percentage of unemployment always remains positive because of frictional, structural, and seasonal unemployment. Frictional unemployment describes workers who seek better-paying jobs that make the best use of their skills rather than taking the first available position, and it contributes to efficient matching of jobs and workers. Structural unemployment occurs when the skills of workers no longer match those demanded by employers because of technological change or when workers live in depressed areas (inner cities or Appalachia, for example) where jobs are scarce. The seasonal nature of much work contributes to unemployment at certain times of year.

Policymakers focus most on unemployment due to macroeconomic fluctuations, with high unemployment in the depression years of 1873–1878, 1883–1885, 1893–1897, 1921, and 1929–1940. The coincidence of declining prices under the gold standard (in which currency is completely backed by gold) from 1873 to 1896 with three panics led to Populist Party agitation for bimetalism, which would establish gold and silver as legal tender, thereby increasing the money supply and causing a decline in inflation and an increase in employment. Retrospective estimates of unemployment range from less than 2 percent of the civilian labor force in the boom years of 1906, 1918, and 1919 to more than 18 percent in 1894 (although Christina Romer has argued that a somewhat narrower range of fluctuation existed). Before the Great Depression of the 1930s, public policy response to unemployment concentrated on relief to the unemployed (including public works and unemployment insurance programs of individual states, as well as private charity) and on labor exchanges to speed the matching of jobs and workers.

The Great Depression, with its high unemployment from late 1929 to 1940 peaking at one-quarter of the civilian labor force in 1933, changed the focus of policy from amelioration of the condition of the unemployed to the use of counter-cyclical monetary and fiscal policy to prevent recurrence of high levels of unemployment. These policies included interest rate adjustments along with tax increases and government spending, and they remained in place during the immediate postwar period (1945–1970). From the 1970s onward, monetarists (for whom the supply of money is the most important economic measure) and new classical economists (who believe that prices and wages adjust quickly according to the natural cycle of supply and demand) increasingly influenced policy, arguing that there exists a natural rate of unemployment and that aggregate demand management (increased government expenditure to stimulate the economy) cannot achieve any lasting reduction of unemployment below this natural rate. Both monetarists and new classical economists stressed instead the supply-side effects of tax rates and minimum wages on the natural rate of unemployment. New Keynesian economists, on the other hand, have continued to insist on a role for aggregate demand management in controlling fluctuations in output and employment.

—*Robert Dimand*

References

Garraty, John A. *Unemployment in History: Economic Thought and Public Policy.* New York: Harper and Row, 1978.

Keyssar, Alexander. *Out of Work: The First Century of Unemployment in Massachusetts.* Cambridge: Cambridge University Press, 1986.

Lebergott, Stanley. *Manpower in Economic Growth: The American Record since 1800.* New York: McGraw-Hill, 1964.

Nelson, Daniel. *Unemployment Insurance: The American Experience, 1915–1935.* Madison: University of Wisconsin Press, 1969.

Romer, Christina D. "New Estimates of Prewar Gross National Product and Unemployment." *Journal of Economic History,* vol. 46 (1986): 341–352.

Weir, David. "The Reliability of Historical Macroeconomic Data for Comparing Cyclical Stability." *Journal of Economic History,* vol. 46 (1986): 353–365.

See also Volume 1: Keynesian Economics.

Unemployment Insurance

Federal-state income replacement program for temporarily unemployed workers.

Like similar programs in Western Europe, unemployment insurance in the United States is decentralized (handled by the states) and experience-rated (the amount paid to the unemployed person is based on amount of time worked throughout the year). It provides shorter-term benefits than do programs in Europe. The program originated in Titles III and IX of the Social Security Act of 1935.

Unemployment insurance was decentralized because the administration of President Franklin D. Roosevelt, concerned that the Supreme Court would find the national program unconstitutional, continued its commitment to "unemployment and old-age insurance under State laws." To this end, the Social Security Act established a tax-offset mechanism, the details of which are sometimes attributed to

Justice Louis Brandeis. The federal government imposed a 3 percent tax on wages, with a promise to refund 90 percent of the revenues to states that enacted unemployment insurance programs, subject to minimal guidelines. By 1937, every state had done so.

One requirement stipulated that premiums be experience-rated in the sense that firms would be penalized in the form of a higher tax rate for benefits paid to their own workers, with states free to set both the minimum and maximum tax rates. The rationale then and now is that seasonal businesses would have an incentive to smooth production and that firms with low turnover rates should not subsidize firms with higher rates. This is distinct from the more important stabilization function of unemployment insurance—limiting fluctuations in aggregate demand.

Decentralization of unemployment insurance has meant that even now, wide variations exist among states in benefit amounts and in the structure of premiums. During the first quarter of 2001, for example, the average weekly benefit amount varied from $160.51 in Mississippi to $314.28 in Massachusetts. Measured as a share of wages in "covered employment"—jobs covered by the program—it varied from 22.8 percent in California to 44.4 percent in Iowa. In the United States as a whole, however, the ratio of benefits to covered wages has remained constant over long periods. The degree of experience rating is more difficult to measure, but Hawaii, for example, has less than most, and New York more.

Two other historical trends deserve note. First, the percentage of workers covered by unemployment insurance has increased over time, from less than 60 percent to more than 90 percent, as state laws expanded to include workers in the public and nonprofit sectors and at small establishments. Second, the fraction of insured unemployment—the percentage of unemployed workers who collect unemployment insurance benefits—has declined over time, with substantial reductions in the mid-1960s and first half of the 1980s. Labor economists have attributed the first of these reductions to demographic changes and the second to a decline in the take-up rate: that is, for reasons both economic and political, fewer eligible workers now submit unemployment insurance claims.

—Peter Hans Matthews

References

Baicker, Katherine, Claudia Goldin, and Lawrence F. Katz. "A Distinctive System: Origins and Impact of U.S. Unemployment Compensation." In Michael D. Bordo, Claudia Goldin, and Eugene N. White, eds., *The Defining Moment: The Great Depression and the American Economy in the Twentieth Century.* Chicago: University of Chicago Press, 1998.

Blank, Rebecca M., and David E. Card. "Recent Trends in Insured and Uninsured Unemployment: Is There an Explanation?" *Quarterly Journal of Economics,* vol. 106 (November 1991): 1157–1189.

Nelson, Daniel. *Unemployment Insurance: The American Experience, 1915–1935.* Madison: University of Wisconsin Press, 1969.

See also Volume 2: Labor.

UNICEF

See United Nations Children's Fund.

United Nations (UN)

Prominent global governance system set up after World War II.

The United Nations (UN) has promoted peace-building strategies based on direct, collective economic assistance to developing countries that advocate an international economic order based on free market economies. UN methods often conflict with traditional U.S. economic policy.

The UN was formed in 1945 with the primary purpose of maintaining international peace and security. Its charter states that part of the pursuit for world peace involves promoting "higher standards of living, full employment, and conditions for economic and social progress and development." The charter created the Economic and Social Council (ECOSOC) to handle international relations in the social and economic spheres by coordinating the efforts of specialized agencies more directly involved with fostering economic growth and sustainable development. But U.S. support of ECOSOC emphasized the specific functional roles of these growing agencies as having prominence over a highly centralized international economic order led by the United Nations. Even more importantly, the United States preferred to rely on the Bretton Woods institutions rather than the United Nations as the appropriate channel for economic assistance to developing countries. The Bretton Woods institutions were created by the Bretton Woods agreements in 1945 to stabilize world economies and currencies. These institutions include the World Bank (which lends to foreign governments to reduce these governments' national debt and so make domestic money available for programs such as health care or education) and the International Monetary Fund (IMF), which stabilized international currency rates.

In the early 1960s, membership in the United Nations skyrocketed because a number of independent countries emerged from their former colonial status. The universality of membership in the United Nations allowed for a majority of members representing the interests of developing countries, and these countries' dissatisfaction with the domination of Western private markets in international economic affairs led them to use their majority power to form a caucusing group, the Group of 77 (G-77), at the 1964 United Nations Conference on Trade and Development. Through the mid-1970s, the G-77 worked on the development of a new international economic order that demanded greater economic sovereignty for developing countries through the restructuring of markets, increased developmental assistance, and a greater role for developing countries in the Bretton Woods institutions. The political leverage given to developing countries in the United Nations created a rift between the developed and developing countries over the proper ways to channel developmental aid. Beginning in the late 1970s and continuing through the administration of President Ronald Reagan in the 1980s, the United States began to distance itself from the UN's multilateral style of collective action aid measures, dropping its membership in several UN specialized agencies and supporting budget cuts in many UN programs. Support from the United States and the West instead shifted to restructuring the IMF and World Bank's terms for loans and credit to developing countries.

The early 1990s revealed more points of conflict between U.S. economic interests and UN ideals of collective action with the addressing of global environmental problems. Industrialized countries including the United States attacked proposals to limit global warming and other similar proposals as seriously restricting their economic growth and negatively affecting their industries disproportionally compared with the proposals' effect on economic and industrial growth in developing countries. Other recent UN initiatives have attempted to bring the private business sectors of developed countries into an internationalist fold as globalization of the economy brings with it opportunities for positive development as well as increasing inequities between rich and poor countries. Although the inherent weakness of the United Nations makes its effects on the economic policies of independent member states minimal, the global organization provides a strong forum where countries can voice their concerns about the negative effects of traditional American economic policy in the world marketplace. Between 1995 and 2000, the United States placed a 25 percent cap on contributions to UN peacekeeping costs. In 1999 the Helms-Biden Act lowered U.S. contributions to the UN from 30 percent to 25 percent of the UN budget, resulting in an arrearage of $671.4 million in U.S. payments. Since 2001, President George W. Bush has asked Congress to pay these fees, and two of three large payments have been made.

—*Jonah Katz*

References
Jeong, Ho-Won. "The Struggle for Wider Participation." In Chadwick F. Alger, ed., *The Future of the United Nations System: Potential for the Twenty-first Century*. Tokyo: United Nations University Press, 1998.
Weiss, Thomas G., D. P. Forsythe, and Roger A. Coate. *The United Nations and Changing World Politics*. Boulder, CO: Westview Press, 1994.
See also Volume 1: Bretton Woods Agreement; International Monetary Fund.

United Nations Children's Fund (UNICEF)

UN association that focuses on child welfare worldwide.

The United Nations Children's Fund, or UNICEF (it was originally called the United Nations International Children's Emergency Fund), was created in 1946 at the first meeting of the United Nations General Assembly. Its initial focus was primarily on assisting child welfare programs in countries ruined by World War II. After the early 1950s, its emphasis expanded to other numerous developing nations. UNICEF not only aids in emergency situations, it also devotes a large portion of its assistance to the support of long-term developments. The organization gives governmental aid to children in emergency situations, villages with low water supplies, and families with few or no resources. UNICEF also assists with education and social welfare in countries with few opportunities for a basic education system or social justice. In 1965, UNICEF received the Nobel Peace Prize for its efforts to help those in need.

UNICEF is run by countries selected by the United Nations Economic and Social Council, and numerous members of the United Nations govern the organization. Members include but are not limited to the United States, the United Kingdom, New Zealand, and Spain. An executive director heads the association and maintains responsibility for distributing funds, developing programs, and obtaining further resources. Voluntary contributions from individuals, governments, activists, and other organizations financially support UNICEF. In 1969, 128 governments contributed $33.4 million to UNICEF's causes. Financial allocations to this organization have increased, and other sources of financing (occasional corporate sponsorships and sales of UNICEF items such as greeting cards) have proved essential to UNICEF's survival.

In 1997, the United Nations Children's Fund reinforced coordination with governments and other organizations to ensure that children receive a fair percentage of a nation's resources and that their rights remain protected. Specific areas of concern include reducing maternal and infant mortality, improving basic education, providing immunizations, controlling diseases such as polio and AIDS among children, addressing problems of malnutrition, and providing a constant and sanitary water supply. During this period, UNICEF program expenditures exceeded $822 million. The organization has continued to respond to the HIV/AIDS epidemic by cosponsoring the United Nations Program on HIV and AIDS. The top priorities for UNICEF include issues such as the search for affordable ways to prevent HIV transmission; the prevention of infection; and the strengthening of affordable community-based programs to help children and adults with HIV/AIDS. The United Nations Children's Fund continues to search for other ways to assist nations in need of assistance during long-term and emergency situations.

—*Sandra L. Willett*

References
"The United Nations Children's Fund." *Yearbook of the United Nations*. New York: United Nations, 2000.
See also Volume 1: United Nations.

United States v. E. C. Knight Co. (1895)

Supreme Court decision distinguishing between manufacturing and commerce as the two activities relate to the definition of a monopoly.

In 1890, Congress passed the Sherman Anti-Trust Act outlawing all business combinations in restraint of trade—that is, monopolies. Two years later, the American Sugar Refining Company took control of 98 percent of the nation's sugar refining industry. When the national government attempted to break up the sugar monopoly, the American Sugar Refining

Company sued to retain its control of the industry. Lower courts decided in favor of the sugar monopoly and, in 1894, the case made it to the Supreme Court, which was asked to decide whether the Constitution gave the national government power to regulate monopolies.

Ruling for the Court in an 8-to-1 decision, Chief Justice Melville Fuller distinguished between manufacturing and commerce. He argued that as part of its police powers, a state could control a monopoly in manufacturing that took place solely within the state's own borders. In contrast, the national government could only regulate monopolies involved in interstate commerce. Fuller next posed the question of whether a monopoly in manufacturing could be considered a monopoly in interstate commerce because manufactured items were usually sold across state lines. He answered that commerce follows manufacturing but is not a part of it. Because the refining of sugar took place solely in one state, the national government had no power to break up the sugar monopoly under the Sherman Anti-Trust Act. Fuller warned that if manufacturing and commerce were considered identical, then the national government would be involved in every sector of the American economy. In his dissent, Justice John Marshall Harlan argued that no state had the power to regulate national monopolies and that the Sherman Anti-Trust Act had been effectively dismantled. Although the Court later upheld the breakup of Standard Oil and the American Tobacco Company, Fuller's distinction between manufacturing and commerce survived until the late 1930s.

—Mary Stockwell

References

Duggan, Michael A. *Antitrust and the U.S. Supreme Court, 1829–1980: A Compendium of Supreme Court Decisions Dealing with Restraint of Trade and Monopoly.* New York: Federal Legal Publications, 1981.
See also Volume 2: Judiciary.

Urban Policy

Economic and social plan that sets priorities and regulates resources for city development.

The term *urban policy* is used for a wide range of concerns and activities in connection with issues of economic development, social development, housing and neighborhoods, and community services in federal and local governments. Urban policy also includes city planning issues such as spatial relationships in the city, transport, the environment, parks, and the urban infrastructure. According to Fainstein, urban policy is a state activity that affects "urbanism." Urbanism is "the distribution of investment and consumption activities in real space, the character and form of the built environment, and the distribution of population groupings in relation to both."

Prior to the New Deal legislation of the 1930s, when the federal government established relief and work programs for the poor and unemployed, urban policy was often addressed as local solutions to planning problems. City planning strived for more orderly, efficient, and racially segregated urban development as cities expanded. By the 1920s, more than half of the nation's population lived in cities, a development that led to housing problems, migrating populations, racial and ethnic diversity, and land use issues. In many cases, planning was de facto policy in urban practices such as school segregation and racial zoning.

Urban policy changed the landscape of cities. Changes included the development of roads and highways to accommodate the increasing popularity of automobile transportation in a period that included suburban development. Slum clearance and the erection of skyscrapers characterized federally subsidized post–New Deal changes, and the federal government built public housing projects for low-income families. However, in some areas local politicians opposed federally funded urban housing for the poor, basing their rhetoric on the claim that government interference in housing issues smacked of socialism and a planned economy. Business interests and local politics did, however, support federally subsidized slum clearance and urban commercial redevelopment, which were part of the urban renewal legislation in the Housing Acts of 1949 and 1954. The 1949 act called for urban renewal, defined as the construction of public housing to alleviate housing shortages and the clearing of slums. The 1954 act modified the 1949 law to include code enforcement; it also established Federal Housing Administration mortgages to help low-income homeowners buy homes and provided builders with tax credits to encourage urban renewal programs.

Antipoverty Great Society legislation during the 1960s provided federal support for urban social and economic development, including a new Cabinet-level Department of Housing and Urban Development (HUD). Although HUD and federal funding for cities continued in the 1970s, the administration of President Richard Nixon (from 1969 to 1974) shifted from the Great Society philosophy to a "new federalism" that returned decision-making power to municipal governments. The emphasis of new federalism was revenue sharing, in which federal funds were granted to local communities but the federal government placed restrictions on how the funds could be used. These developments were supported by the political and social analyses of urban problems by Democratic Senator Patrick Moynihan of New York, Nixon's urban policy advisor, and by conservatives who were critical of Great Society programs. The administration of President Ronald Reagan (1981–1989) continued to support the concept of new federalism and increased deregulation. Reagan further retreated from social welfare programs and generally encouraged free market activity as opposed to government intervention. The result was increased commercial redevelopment of inner-city business districts and a policy emphasis on jobs for the poor.

In the 1990s during the administration of President Bill Clinton, empowerment zone legislation (which called for economic revitalization through development of businesses in depressed communities) and other forms of federally supported community development programs were available to local governments. Since the 1990s the role of the federal government in urban affairs has been to encourage local municipal comprehensive planning for jobs and housing and to provide incentives for private-sector business and home ownership.

—Eileen Robertson-Rehberg

References
Fainstein, S. *Restructuring the City: The Political Economy of Urban Development.* New York: Longman, 1983.
Kleinberg, Benjamin. *Urban America in Transformation: Perspectives on Urban Policy and Development.* Thousand Oaks, CA: Sage Publications, 1995.
See also Volume 2: Urbanization.

U.S. Agency for International Development (USAID)

Federal agency established under the aegis of the Foreign Assistance Act to administer economic, as opposed to military, assistance to developing nations.

The U.S. Agency for International Development (USAID), established on November 3, 1961, was designed to unify the International Cooperation Agency, the Development Loan Fund, the Export-Import Bank, and the Food for Peace Program. It established both a Development Loan Fund to increase productive capacities and a Development Grant Fund to cultivate human resources in the Third World. Exempt from military and political obligations, USAID became the first U.S. organization that had as its sole function to oversee long-term development projects in the Third World.

USAID had its precursors in the Marshall Plan (1948–1951), the Mutual Security Act (1951), and other postwar reconstruction, recovery, and development programs. In his inaugural address in 1949, President Harry S Truman promised "to help the free peoples of the world, through their own efforts, to produce more food, more clothing, more materials for housing, and more mechanical power to lighten their burdens." Truman's speech, which proposed "a program of development based on the concept of democratic fair dealing," envisioned a competition between the superpowers—the United States and the USSR—for influence on underdeveloped nations. In accordance with Truman's Four Point agenda, the United States began to distribute economic, technical, and military assistance across the noncommunist world. Designed to cultivate friendly regimes, foreign aid remained an important feature of U.S. strategy throughout the cold war.

A dozen years later, faced with waning congressional enthusiasm for foreign aid, President John F. Kennedy revived Truman's vision of economic assistance as a means of mitigating the threat of communism. More precisely, Kennedy warned that "widespread poverty and chaos [would] lead" not only "to a collapse of existing political and economic structures," but also to "the advance of totalitarianism" in the Third World. Accordingly, Walt Rostow's *The Stages of Economic Growth: A Non-Communist Manifesto* (1960), which emphasized macroeconomic planning and programmed industrialization, became the handbook of USAID.

With the breakdown of the Keynesian consensus (an agreement among economists that Keynesian economics

worked) in the early 1970s, Congress altered the purview of USAID. Since then, USAID has aimed not to help developing countries to catch up with the West but rather to cater to the "basic human needs" of the world's poor.

—Mark Frezzo

References
Hirschman, Albert O. *A Propensity to Self-Subversion.* Cambridge, MA: Harvard University Press, 1995.
Sachs, Wolfgang. "The Archaeology of the Development Idea." *Interculture,* vol. 23, no. 4 (1990).
U.S. Department of State. *Foreign Assistance Act of 1961.* Washington: U.S. Government Printing Office, 1982.
See also Volume 1: United Nations.

USAID

See U.S. Agency for International Development.

U.S. Chamber of Commerce

Advocacy group formed in 1912 to represent the interests of independent businesses, local chambers of commerce, and affiliated business associations.

The U.S. Chamber of Commerce was formed in 1912 by business leaders seeking an organization to represent the interests of the business community. Members held the first meeting January 21, 1913. During World War I, the Chamber of Commerce sought greater cooperation between government and the business community in the planning and allocation of materials for the war effort. To this end, it assisted the Council of National Defense by organizing more than 400 War Service Committees. After the war ended, the chamber lobbied for an end to wartime regulations. During the 1920s, the organization worked closely with President Herbert Hoover's Department of Commerce to establish voluntary guidelines governing fair competition.

The Chamber of Commerce was an early supporter of the National Recovery Administration (NRA), an agency established in 1933 as part of President Franklin D. Roosevelt's New Deal that encouraged production quotas and guaranteed unions the right of collective bargaining. After the Supreme Court declared the NRA unconstitutional, Congress passed the Wagner Act (also known as the National Labor Relations Act) in 1935 to guarantee the rights of labor to form unions. Later, the Chamber of Commerce became an outspoken critic of many of President Franklin D. Roosevelt's other New Deal programs, including the National Labor Relations Act, the Banking Acts, and the Social Security Act. The chamber criticized Roosevelt for failing to resolve the economic crisis of the depression and urged a return to fiscal balance to restore the nation's economic health. Despite these tensions, the chamber cooperated with the Roosevelt administration during World War II, assisting it in administering production, wage, and price regulations. In the postwar period, the chamber resumed its crusade for reduced government spending and lower taxes.

Recognized as one of the leading voices for business interests in the United States, the Chamber of Commerce lobbies in support of probusiness legislation, and it challenges regulations deemed unfair to business. The Chamber of Commerce has traditionally supported free-trade policies, has favored lower taxes and reduced government spending as an engine for economic growth, and has opposed environmental and employment regulations because it believes they increase operating costs for its members.

—*Christopher A. Preble*

References
Wolman, Paul. *Most Favored Nation: The Republican Revisionists and U.S. Tariff Policy, 1897–1912.* Chapel Hill: University of North Carolina Press, 1992.
See also Volume 1: Great Depression; New Deal.

U.S. Customs Service

Agency founded in 1789 charged with revenue collection and prevention of smuggling; formerly part of the U.S. Department of Treasury but now part of the Department of Homeland Security.

The U.S. Customs Service, founded in 1789, has the responsibility of classifying and designating products for purposes of implementing tariffs, and it also is responsible for searching for contraband. Customs inspectors have the longest lineage of any government officials in the United States working in law enforcement. Today, we most often think of customs inspectors in airports, but long before the Orville and Wilbur Wright took wing at Kitty Hawk, North Carolina, Custom Service inspectors performed their duties at the many points of entry into the country. The U.S. Customs Service, with centuries-old responsibilities of levying excise taxes and tariff revenues until the second decade of the twentieth century (at which point the income tax took effect and lessened the need for tariff revenue), guarded the major source of revenues for the U.S. government. It is part of the U.S. Department of Homeland Security and, in carrying out its missions of revenue collection and the prevention of smuggling, it frequently works with other departments as well, including the U.S. Department of Agriculture. Customs inspectors are located at all major points of entry—harbors, airports, and major highways. Airports that house U.S. Customs Service inspectors are designated as international airports.

The activities of customs officials can be highly varied. A typical area of concern early in the twenty-first century is the smuggling into the United States from the Netherlands of a drug called *ecstasy.* Another case involved the arrest by undercover agents of a Pennsylvania State University graduate student for having three videos of young girls in inappropriate sexual poses even though they were clothed. Renewed emphasis has been given to funding and staffing the U.S. Customs Service in the aftermath of terrorists' use of commercial airliners to destroy the World Trade Center and damage the Pentagon. Having instituted tighter security in the aftermath of these attacks, in 2002 the U.S. Customs Service reported an 80 percent drop in the amount of drugs confiscated along the 1,962-mile U.S.-Mexico border.

—*Henry B. Sirgo*

References
Daynes, Byron W., and Glen Sussman. *The American Presidency.* Upper Saddle River, NJ: Prentice-Hall, 2001.
See also Volume 1: Smuggling; U.S. Department of Treasury.

U.S. Department of Commerce

Agency formed in 1789 to regulate commerce and collect economic data.

The U.S. Department of Commerce comprises 13 bureaus charged with the responsibility of collecting and disseminating economic information from demographics to business transactions. The U.S. Census Bureau conducts a census every ten years as required by the Constitution. The information from the census is used in a variety of ways, including the determination of how many representatives a state has in Congress and the appropriation of certain funds. The agency also has the Bureau of Industry and Security (BIS) under its current organizational structure. The BIS focuses on national security issues such as preventing the spread of weapons of mass destruction while promoting U.S. exports. The Economics and Statistics Administration (ESA) collects and analyzes vital economic and demographic information. The Bureau of Economic Analysis (BEA) provides the most current statistical information on the U.S. economy. Another bureau, the Economic Development Administration (EDA), provides funding to economically distressed communities to ensure the retention of jobs and industry. The International Trade Administration (ITA) promotes U.S. exports abroad. The Minority Business Development Agency (MBDA) promotes the development of minority businesses. The National Oceanic and Atmospheric Administration (NOAA) focuses on protecting the environment while collecting information that can be used to also protect the public safety. The National Telecommunications and Information Administration (NTIA) advises the president on issues concerning telecommunication and worked with Congress to establish the Internet. The Patent and Trade Office protects inventors and encourages the development of new products through the issuances of patents and trademarks. The Technology Administration (TA) focuses on promoting civilian technology. The National Institute of Standards and Technology (NIST) works with industry under the TA, and it also helps businesses apply measurements and standards. The National Technical Information Service (NTIS) is a repository of commerce-related research from both governmental and private sources.

Throughout the years the Commerce Department has experienced change. In 1903 the department was merged with the Department of Labor until 1913. During the 1800s the Bureau of Immigration operated under the Commerce Department but was transferred to the Bureau of Immigration and Naturalization in 1906 and is currently under the Department of Homeland Security. The Patent Office was transferred to Commerce in 1925 from the Department of the Interior, as was the Bureau of Mines that was later returned to the Department of Interior. When radio was first invented stations operated under the direction of the Federal Radio commission but those responsibilities were transferred to Commerce in 1927. In 1932 these responsibilities were transferred to the Federal Radio Commission. In 1940 the Weather Bureau became part of the Commerce Department. The Federal Highway Act of 1956 was administered by Commerce. The development of the St. Lawrence Seaway beginning in 1957 also fell under the responsibilities of this agency. From the 1970s to the present the current organizational structure developed. Commerce currently focuses on all aspects of the economy, weather, communication, and research that impact the economic conditions of the United States.

—*Henry B. Sirgo*

References

Wray, J. Harry. *Sense and Non-Sense: American Culture and Politics.* Upper Saddle River, NJ: Prentice-Hall, 2001.
See also Volume 1: Census; National Oceanic and Atmospheric Administration.

U.S. Department of Defense (DOD)

Government agency established to direct and coordinate military affairs and issues of national security.

Created in 1947 by the National Security Act, the Department of Defense (DOD) is a Cabinet-level agency. Prior to its creation, the Department of War and Department of the Navy (both established in 1789) coordinated the military establishment. Based in the Pentagon, the department is divided into three sections—the Army, the Navy, and the Air Force. The DOD also supervises several other agencies including the Advanced Research Projects Agency, the Ballistic Missile Defense Organization (Strategic Defense Initiative), the Defense Intelligence Agency, the Defense Mapping Agency, and the National Security Agency. The Department of Defense also operates the National War College.

The Department of Defense coordinated military planning efforts for the first time during the Korean War, which lasted from 1950 to 1953. During the administration of President Dwight D. Eisenhower (1953–1961), the DOD relied on the threat of massive nuclear retaliation against the Soviet Union and communists. Under the Kennedy and Johnson administrations between 1961 and 1969, the DOD shifted toward more conventional warfare (instead of relying primarily on nuclear warfare), using land forces in Vietnam. Throughout the cold war between 1945 and 1991, the Department of Defense allocated much of its budget to research and development, and its massive purchases have stimulated computer, software, and associated technologies. In 1958 Congress established the agency that became known as DARPA (Defense Advanced Research Projects Agency) under the DOD, an agency that funds research on artificial intelligence as well as microelectronics. After the cold war the DOD

budget was streamlined, but annual military spending increased once again because of the Persian Gulf War in 1991 and the response to the terrorist attacks on September 11, 2001. With operations in Afghanistan and Iraq as well as numerous other regions of the world, the DOD will continue to maintain an important position within the Cabinet.

—*Cynthia Clark Northrup*

References

Cohen, Andrew, and Beth Heinsohn. *The Department of Defense.* New York: Chelsea House, 1990.
See also Volume 1: Defense Advanced Research Projects Agency; War and Warfare; Volume 2: Science and Technology.

U.S. Department of Health and Human Services

Agency originally known as the U.S. Department of Health, Education and Welfare that is responsible for protecting the health of Americans.

In 1953 President Dwight D. Eisenhower proposed and Congress approved the establishment of the U.S. Department of Health, Education and Welfare (HEW). Eisenhower appointed Oveta Culp Hobby to serve as the first HEW secretary. The final HEW secretary, Joseph Califano, served until July of 1979 when he was dismissed by President Jimmy Carter, who was concerned that his 1980 reelection bid would be undermined by Califano's antismoking activities.

Not surprisingly, HEW emerged as one of the departments most important to U.S. economic policy. Social scientist Harold Wilensky has observed that the most important predictor of government expenditures is the age of a polity's population. Thanks to advances in public health, many of which were supported by HEW, the average age of the U.S. population has increased considerably. In the late eighteenth century, the average American was 14 years old. In 2003, the average American is 50 years old. An aging population relies more greatly on benefits from the Social Security retirement fund, which provides an income for retirees out of money contributed by individuals who are currently working.

Following the establishment of the U.S. Department of Education in 1979, HEW was renamed the U.S. Department of Health and Human Services. Patricia Roberts Harris, former Secretary of Housing and Urban Development and the first African American woman to serve in the Cabinet, was appointed in 1979 by President Jimmy Carter as Secretary of Health and Human Services. Recent Health and Human secretaries have hailed from Wisconsin, the state most strongly associated with the pioneering efforts that led to the Social Security Act of 1935. Donna Shalala of that state held the post from 1993 to 2001.

The Department of Health and Human Services is responsible for the health of all Americans and administers several programs that deal with health-related legislation. The agency conducts medical and social science research, oversees immunization programs for children, administers the Medicaid and Medicare programs, provides financial assistance for low-income families, coordinates the Head Start program for disadvantaged children, attempts to prevent substance and child abuse, administers programs for the elderly such as Meals on Wheels, and offers a health care program for Native Americans.

The 2003 budget for the Department of Health and Human Services amounted to $502 billion, and the department currently employs more than 65,000 people. The agency's operating divisions include the National Institutes for Health, which supports medical research on a broad range of illnesses from Alzheimer's disease to diabetes; the Food and Drug Administration, which ensures the safety of food, pharmaceutical, and other consumer products; the Centers for Disease Control and Prevention, which monitors outbreaks of diseases and analyzes national health statistics; and the Indian Health Service, which provides health care services to 1.5 million Native Americans.

The Department of Health and Human Services also provides health care for the poor and elderly through the Health Resources and Services Administration, the Centers for Medicare and Medicaid Services, Administration for Children and Families, and the Administration on Aging. The Agency for Healthcare Research and Quality continues to conduct research on improving health care, reducing costs, and other medical issues.

With the issue of the health of Americans as its core objective, the Department of Health and Human Services strives to keep the national population healthy and strong and in the process protects workers and employers from spiraling health costs and lost wages, which adversely affect the U.S. economy.

—Henry B. Sirgo

References
Wray, J. Harry. *Sense and Non-Sense: American Culture and Politics.* Upper Saddle River, NJ: Prentice-Hall, 2001.
See also Volume 1: Baby Boom, Social Security Act of 1935; Volume 2: Education.

U.S. Department of Housing and Urban Development (HUD)
Government agency created in 1965 to provide safe, affordable housing for Americans.

As early as 1934, Congress addressed the issue of housing in the United States by passing the National Housing Act and establishing the Federal Housing Administration. Three years later the U.S. Housing Act of 1937 created the United States Housing Authority to create low-income rental housing and to coordinate the clearing of slums. Under President Lyndon B. Johnson's Great Society, a series of programs to eliminate poverty, Congress established the Department of Housing and Urban Development (HUD) in 1965 as a Cabinet-level agency. For three years, promises for improved housing and government assistance were not fulfilled, and Congress attempted to resolve the problem by passing the Civil Rights Act of 1968, which outlawed housing discrimination. HUD was the agency responsible for enforcing this act and for im-

plementing the Housing Act of 1968, which established the Government National Mortgage Association (Ginnie Mae)—legislation that provides federally backed mortgage loans for moderate- and low-income families. Beginning in the 1970s, HUD focused on community development by establishing low-income housing and educating the public about the nation's housing laws through advertising and a mail campaign. With the assistance of HUD and private incentives (for example, tax benefits for housing contractors that develop affordable homes in the city), the number of Americans who own homes reached a record level of 71.6 million households in 2000.

—Cynthia Clark Northrup

References
Lapidus, Nancy. *HUD House.* Bloomington, IN: First Books Library, 2002.
McFarland, M. Carter. *Federal Government and Urban Problems: HUD: Successes, Failures, and the Fate of Our Cities.* Boulder, CO: Westview Press, 1978.
See also Volume 1: Great Society; Housing Act of 1949; Housing Act of 1954; Volume 2: Urbanization.

U.S. Department of Labor
Agency established in 1913 responsible for promoting welfare of workers through improving working conditions, protecting benefits, and tracking changes in employment-related economic factors; originally part of the Department of Commerce and Labor during the administration of Theodore Roosevelt between 1901 and 1909.

In 1913, the first year of the administration of President Woodrow Wilson, the Department of Commerce and Labor separated into two departments. The Department of Labor became a natural home for resolution of immigration policy issues, particularly in the early decades of the twentieth century as the nation experienced concurrent massive industrialization and immigration. The Bureau of Immigration and Naturalization was part of the Department of Labor until 1940, when it was transferred out of Labor and into the Department of Justice. Congress established the Women's Bureau in the department in 1918, and since then it has been a particularly important department for gender issues such as equal pay, family leave, and maternity-related issues. The department also includes the Bureau of Labor Statistics, created in 1884 to collect information about economic issues that affect workers.

Historically, the Department of Labor has gained influence when national security is in jeopardy (in wartime, for example), and its influence has waned during prosperous times. When the United States entered World War I in 1917 and great numbers of men joined the armed services, production output of military equipment and supplies coincided with a labor shortage. The Labor Department played an instrumental role in coordinating labor-management relations to prevent strikes and supply the needed war material. This effort included bringing in 3 million workers from abroad, who were quickly processed through the agency's Bureau of

Immigration. At the conclusion of World War I in 1919, returning veterans found that their jobs had been filled by these immigrants or by Southern blacks who had migrated to the Northern industrial areas in search of jobs during the conflict. Race riots and general strikes threatened the domestic peace, and the Labor Department once again helped to defuse the conflict between labor and management. By 1920 the manufacturing sector shifted from military to consumer production, and as jobs became available tensions decreased. Throughout the prosperous 1920s, the Department of Labor focused primarily on immigration and naturalization. After the stock market crash of October 1929, the department's role greatly expanded as the number of laborers out of work increased.

Under the direction of the first woman Cabinet member, Francis Perkins, who was labor secretary from 1933 through 1945, the Department of Labor implemented many of President Franklin D. Roosevelt's New Deal economic relief policies. One direct relief program for the unemployed was the Civilian Conservation Corps, created in 1933, which employed millions of young men in soil conservation efforts. Roosevelt's National Recovery Administration, designed to coordinate and limit manufacturing production to raise prices, included section 7(a) guaranteeing the rights of unions to engage in collective bargaining. When, however, the Supreme Court declared the National Recovery Administration unconstitutional in 1935, the Labor Department worked to pass in that same year the National Labor Relations Act (also known as the Wagner Act), which gave labor the right to engage in collective bargaining through unions. It also worked to pass the Fair Labor Standards Act of 1938, which guaranteed a minimum wage and overtime for any time worked over the 40-hour weekly limit.

When World War II started and U.S. production started to climb, the New Deal relief programs were abolished. After the United States entered the war in 1941, there was another labor shortage. Once again the Department of Labor stepped in to coordinate labor-management relations. During World War II the government suspended the right to bargain collectively because the shortage of workers gave labor the potential to demand much higher pay or threaten to strike, which the government sought to avoid. After World War II, labor unions initiated strikes in response to the wage freezes of the war period. This led Congress to pass the Taft-Hartley Act of 1947 restricting union activities. The act prohibited the existence of closed shops (where only union members could work) and allowed the president to order a "cooling-off period" before a strike could occur in industries deemed vital to national interests. During the 1950s labor prospered as the economy rebounded and jobs remained available. During the 1960s and 1970s, however, labor once again became an issue. During the 1970s the United States experienced stagflation (simultaneous high unemployment and high inflation). Many workers found that they were unemployed or that their wages were insufficient to keep up with inflation. In 1971 President Richard Nixon imposed a 90-day wage and price freeze to address the situation, but throughout the 1970s the problem remained unresolved. During this time the Depart-

ment of Labor greatly expanded and assumed its current organizational structure.

The Labor Department has many bureaus and departments under its jurisdiction. The largest bureau is the Employment Standards Administration (ESA), which enforces labor-related laws. The bureau's Wage and Hour Division enforces minimum wage, child labor, overtime, family leave, and medical leave laws. The Office of Federal Contract Compliance enforces legislation that requires equal employment opportunity for federal contract employers. The Office of Workers' Compensation Programs hears appeals on certain workers' compensation cases. The Office of Labor-Management Standards works to protect the rights of workers and unions. The Labor Department also has several bureaus that deal with benefits—among them the Benefits Review Board, which administers the Longshore and Harbor Worker's Compensation Act and deals with black lung benefits for coal miners. The Department of Labor also regulates pension and welfare benefits under the Employee Benefits Security Administration. The Bureau of Labor Statistics continues to act as the department's fact-finding agency. The Mine Safety and Health Administration, Occupational Safety and Health Administration, and Office of Congressional and Intergovernmental Affairs, as well as many other bureaus, also operate under the Labor Department.

The Department of Labor continues to focus on labor-related issues by attempting to balance labor and management objectives in an effort to act as a conciliatory agency whose mission is to "foster, promote and develop the welfare of working people, to improve their working conditions, and to enhance their opportunities for profitable employment." By fulfilling its mission, the Department of Labor works to ensure economic prosperity and domestic labor peace in the United States—an accomplishment that ensures the stability of the U.S. economy.

—Henry B. Sirgo

References
Ware, Susan. *Beyond Suffrage: Women in the New Deal.* Cambridge, MA: Harvard University Press, 1981.
See also Volume 1: Women; Volume 2: Labor.

U.S. Department of Treasury
Agency established by the Constitution in 1789 responsible for fiscal policy.

The aspirations of the first secretary of the U.S. Treasury, Alexander Hamilton, and his Federalist followers to lay the foundation for a unified commerce within the newly formed U.S. government were realized when Congress passed Hamilton's proposals to establish the U.S. Mint, create the Bank of the United States, and sell U.S. lands to pay off U.S. debts.

The position of U.S. Treasury Secretary is one of four Cabinet positions that date back to 1789. The other three positions are secretary of state, secretary of defense, and U.S. attorney general. (The State Department as originally called the Department of Foreign Affairs, and the Defense Department was originally called the War Department.)

The Department of the Treasury consists of several bureaus that serve a variety of functions pertaining to the collection and disbursement of funds and financial data. The largest Treasury bureau is the Internal Revenue Service (IRS), which currently collects more than $2 trillion annually in all forms of income tax. The IRS is also responsible for collecting and disseminating data about the internal revenue of the nation. The Financial Management Service, also under the Treasury Department, receives the $2 trillion from the IRS and places it in federal accounts, disbursing it at a rate of $50 billion per day. This bureau processes all government payments, including the $1.6 trillion paid annually to Social Security recipients and veterans. It is also charged with collecting money owed to the government from other sources, an amount that equals $2.3 trillion annually. The Bureau of Public Debt borrows the money needed to pay the national debt by selling government bonds and securities. In June 2003 the U.S. debt stood at $6.598 trillion, with $3.820 trillion of that debt held by the public in U.S. bond treasury notes and $2.778 trillion held by intergovernmental holdings (Social Security funds that have been used by the government). The Treasury Department also collects excise taxes from the sale of alcohol, tobacco, firearms, and ammunition under the recently renamed Alcohol and Tobacco Tax and Trade Bureau, which was previously part of the Bureau of Alcohol, Tobacco, and Firearms (ATF). The ATF's law enforcement functions were transferred to the Department of Justice in 2003.

In addition to the collection and disbursement of funds, the Treasury Department also deals with the production of currency. The Bureau of Engraving and Printing is responsible for the design of official treasury certificates and of the currency; it has redesigned the paper currency since the mid-1990s to prevent counterfeiting. The U.S. Mint manufacturers coins as well as commemorative medals and is responsible for protecting the silver and gold assets of the United States. Through the Office of the Comptroller of the Currency and the Office of Thrift Supervision, the department oversees the nation's banking and thrift institutions. The Federal Crimes Enforcement Network supports law enforcement in the investigation and prosecution of financial crimes, both domestically and internationally. Finally, the Community Development Financial Institution (CDFI) provides funds to economically distressed areas for the development of small businesses, low-income housing projects, and rural projects. Since 1994 the CDFI has awarded $543 million in grants.

In connection with the reorganization of government agencies after the September 11, 2001, terrorist attacks, several Treasury Department bureaus were transferred to the newly created Department of Homeland Security. These include the U.S. Secret Service (created in 1789 when the Treasury Department was founded to protect the president and other government officials), the Customs Service (which uses air, land, and naval resources to protect the nation's borders against smuggling, illegal contraband, and now potential terrorists), and the Federal Law Enforcement Training Center.

—*Henry B. Sirgo*

References
Bryan, Frank, and John McClaughry. *The Vermont Papers: Recreating Democracy on a Human Scale.* Post Mills, VT: Chelsea Green Publishing, 1989.
Warshaw, Shirley Anne. *The Keys to Power: Managing the Presidency.* New York: Longman, 2000.
See also Volume 1: Hamilton, Alexander.

U.S. Environmental Protection Agency (USEPA)

Agency established to safeguard the environment.

Congress officially brought the U.S. Environmental Protection Agency (USEPA) into existence in 1970, but its roots go back as far as 1962. The impetus for the USEPA was a best-selling book by Rachel Carson, a bird watcher, titled *Silent Spring.* The carefully researched and wonderfully written work focused on the indiscriminate use of pesticides. Her book was to the environmental movement what Harriet Beecher Stowe's *Uncle Tom's Cabin* was to the abolitionist movement and brought together more than 14,000 people, who formed a grassroots effort to protect the environment.

From 1962 to 1970, the environmental movement gained strength and support. In a nation disillusioned by the war in Vietnam and civil rights struggles, the environmental movement was something positive for people to concentrate on. Further, the environmental movement has had staying power in the politics and culture of the United States.

In May 1969, President Richard Nixon called for the establishment of a Cabinet-level Environmental Quality Council and a Citizens' Advisory Committee on the environment. But he was criticized for the weakness of these agencies, and so that December he appointed a White House committee to investigate whether there was a need for a separate environmental agency. In the meantime Congress had developed a bill called the National Environmental Policy Act (NEPA) sponsored by Senator Gaylord Nelson, Democrat from Wisconsin. Nixon signed the act on New Year's Day 1970, establishing the USEPA.

The popularity and support for USEPA and the success of the first Earth Day celebration in April 1970 (when Americans of all backgrounds took part in activities that improved the environment) helped to strengthen a recommendation from Roy L. Ash, director of the Office of Management and Budget, who argued that the environmental agency must operate independently. Originally reluctant, Nixon eventually accepted the two arguments that if the environmental agency operated under another agency it would remain biased toward that agency and that such a situation would affect objectivity. Satisfied, Nixon called for "a strong, independent agency." The mission of the USEPA included establishing and enforcing environmental protection standards, conducting research, providing assistance to other environmental groups, and helping to develop and recommend new policies. One of the most important charges of the new USEPA involved becoming the enforcement arm for federal environmental legislation.

Component parts of the USEPA originated in the Department of Health, Education, and Welfare; the Food and Drug Administration; the Atomic Energy Commission; and various other agencies and departments. Nixon named William D. Ruckleshaus as the USEPA's first administrator, an excellent choice. Ruckleshaus immediately began gaining headlines and publicity for the fledgling agency. Only nine days after opening its new offices, the USEPA gave the mayors of three cities six months to bring their water supplies into compliance with government standards or come to court. By the end of its first year, the USEPA had tackled other problems large and small. It ended the year with the Clean Air Act of 1970, an effort to reduce polluting emissions from American automobiles, among other things. The USEPA's mission and its focus of protecting human health and the environment have remained stable and constant throughout its 39-year history. In 2003 the USEPA employs about 18,000 people and has an annual budget of more than $7 billion. As such, it ranks as one of the largest federal agencies, and its regulatory functions are emulated by similar agencies at the state level.

—*Lisa A. Ennis*

References
"EPA Timeline." January 10, 2003. Available: http://www.epa.gov/; accessed February 2, 2003.
Lewis, Jack. "The Birth of EPA." November 1985. Available: http://www.epa.gov/; accessed September 17, 2001.
See also Volume 1: Environment.

U.S. Housing Authority

Federal authority for public housing and predecessor of the Department of Housing and Urban Development.

The U.S. Housing Authority and the Public Housing Program were outgrowths of President Franklin D. Roosevelt's economic recovery programs during the Great Depression in the 1930s. Initially, the National Recovery Act of 1933 authorized the use of federal funds to finance low-cost housing and slum clearance projects under the Public Works Administration (PWA), a federal agency that provided jobs for the unemployed. However, PWA housing construction was successfully challenged in a 1936 lawsuit, *United States v. Certain Lands,* which disputed the proposed use of certain land for public purposes such as building low-income housing. The result was an alternative provision in the Wagner-Steagall Act (1937) that, combined with the U.S. Housing Act of 1937, created the U.S. Housing Authority. Congress authorized the U.S. Housing Agency to extend long-term, low-interest loans to local housing authorities to finance slum clearance and build low-rent public housing units and also to provide aid to communities for such construction through annual cash contributions. To qualify for the funds, communities were required to do two things: to exempt such housing from real and personal property taxes; and to provide to the project and its tenants public services such as fire and police protection, water, sewer, and other public services at the same level provided to other residents in the community.

Local governments had the option whether or not and where to build public housing units, and the U.S. Housing Authority reserved the right to approve or reject selected sites. Amendments to the U.S. Housing Act of 1937 ensured that public housing units would be provided only to the lowest-income group and that costs per room and per unit were minimal. These provisions were made in response to opposition from lobbyists representing powerful business interests that opposed government intervention in the private housing market. At the same time, however, these special interests did not oppose government subsidies for private housing development or mortgage loans.

The insufficient production of public housing units before the 1950s meant that local housing authorities had ample numbers of applicants to choose from for each unit available. Therefore U.S. Housing Authority public housing units were often provided to applicants it considered to be more desirable, usually traditional working-class families who lived in public housing temporarily until they could find alternative housing. Many single-parent families and families on direct relief were not accepted for public housing. Since the 1970s, this trend has changed, with many one-parent families living in federal housing. Low-income families qualify even after they return to work under the welfare reform measures instituted during the administration of President Bill Clinton.

—*Eileen Robertson-Rehberg*

References
Meehan, Eugene J. "The Evolution of Public Housing Policy." In J. Paul Mitchell, ed., *Federal Housing Policy and Programs: Past and Present.* New Brunswick, NJ: Center for Urban Policy Research, 1985, pp. 287–318.
Pit, Fenna, and Willem Van Vliet. "Public Housing in the United States." In Elizabeth Huttman and Willem Van Vliet, eds., *Handbook of Housing and the Built Environment in the United States.* New York: Greenwood Press, 1988.
See also Volume 2: Urbanization.

USIA

See U.S. Information Agency.

U.S. Information Agency (USIA)

Independent foreign affairs agency active during the latter half of the twentieth century that supported American foreign policy and promoted U.S. interests abroad.

During World War I, the Committee on Public Information, also known as the Creel Committee, became the first federal entity responsible for coordinating U.S. government information. Cultural and informational exchange programs, including radio broadcasts and news summaries sent to diplomatic missions abroad, continued on an ad hoc basis during the 1930s and then in a more formalized way during World War II.

Information and cultural programs were consolidated after World War II within the Office of International Cultural Affairs and the International Press and Publication Division, both operating within the State Department. To train the Germans and Japanese in democratic ways, the State Department also conducted reorientation and reeducation programs in Germany and Japan after World War II. Recognizing the need for a comprehensive approach to the coordination and dissemination of information, President Dwight D. Eisenhower created the U.S. Information Agency (USIA) on August 3, 1953, by executive order, in accordance with the provisions of the Smith-Mundt Act of 1948.

The USIA's cultural programs included education exchanges, the most famous of these being the Fulbright Scholars program. Named for Democratic Senator J. William Fulbright of Arkansas, who sponsored the legislation that created them, the Fulbright scholarships facilitate international exchanges between students, researchers, and academicians. The Fulbright Scholars program operated within the State Department from its inception in 1946, but after 1953 USIA personnel were responsible for supervising the administration of the program. The program officially transferred to the USIA in 1978.

The primary broadcasting component within the USIA was the Voice of America (VOA). Broadcasting during World War II in 27 languages to countries throughout the world, the VOA survived after the war ended after a committee of private citizens recommended that the government maintain an active role in managing how the United States was portrayed abroad. VOA was active worldwide during most of the cold war (1945–1991), and expanded broadcasting operations in the 1980s. The Radio Broadcasting to Cuba Act, passed in October 1983, established Radio Marti, which began broadcasting to Cuba in May 1985. The VOA also resumed broadcasting in Europe in 1985 after a 25-year hiatus.

The USIA ceased operations on October 1, 1999 in accordance with the Foreign Affairs and Restructuring Act of 1998. Most of its functions were folded into the Department of State. The Voice of America continued to operate under the International Broadcasting Bureau.

—*Christopher A. Preble*

References

U.S. Information Agency (USIA). *United States Information Agency: A Commemoration.* Washington, DC: USIA, 2000.

See also Volume 2: Communications.

The U.S. Mint has its headquarters in Washington, D.C., and has or has had locations in other major cities including Denver, San Francisco, and New Orleans. The old New Orleans Mint on Esplanade Avenue in the French Quarter is now a museum. A radical change in the nature of the money supply came when the U.S. Constitution replaced the Articles of Confederation. Before the Constitution was ratified, debtors were pleased that the individual states printed paper money, because it made it easy for them to pay creditors with inflated currency. Cheap paper money was naturally repugnant to the creditors as well as to advocates of the development of a strong national economy. However, the debtors, mostly small yeoman farmers, cared little about such development.

Congress granted the U.S. government the exclusive right to coin money in Article I, Section 8 of the Constitution in 1787. Paper currency was not issued until well into the nineteenth century. The authority of the U.S. government to issue paper currency is based on the "necessary and proper" clause of the Constitution: Because the economy was expanding but the gold supply was limited, the introduction of paper money was necessary to meet the demands of the economy.

The phrase *e pluribus unum* (of many, one) appears on all U.S. currency. On the back of the dollar bill is a Masonic symbol—appropriately enough in light of George Washington's affiliation with the Masons—the pyramid with an eye at its top. Occasional changes in currency design over the years have reflected security efforts and perhaps changing social mores—in the middle of the nineteenth century in the aftermath of a religious movement known as the "first great awakening," the phrase "in God we trust" was added to U.S. currency and remains there today. To make counterfeiting more difficult, paper money issued since the early 1990s has been redesigned: clearly visible changes include larger, off-center portraits of George Washington, Abraham Lincoln, Alexander Hamilton, and Benjamin Franklin. Although the dollar coin issued in the late 1970s featuring the likeness of Susan B. Anthony (an advocate for women's rights) proved generally unsuccessful, the more recent dollar coin featuring Sacagawea (a guide for the Lewis and Clark expedition) has fared well.

—*Henry B. Sirgo*

References

Ware, Susan. *Beyond Suffrage: Women in the New Deal.* Cambridge, MA: Harvard University Press, 1981.

See also Volume 1: U.S. Department of Treasury; Volume 2: Currency.

U.S. Mint

Innovative, self-funding government agency in charge of manufacturing U.S. coins and paper currency.

Van Buren, Martin (1782 –1862)

Former U.S. senator and governor of New York, eighth president of the United States.

Nicknamed "the magician" in tribute to his political acumen, Martin Van Buren grew up in Kinderhook, New York, studied law in New York City, and was admitted to the bar in 1803. He won election to the state senate in 1812 and quickly rose in the leadership ranks of the Democratic-Republican Party in New York. He served as state attorney general from 1816 to 1819 and won election to the U.S. Senate in 1821. After seven years in the Senate, Van Buren became the governor of New York. He secured his rise to national prominence through his support of Andrew Jackson's successful campaign for the presidency in 1828.

Jackson appointed Van Buren secretary of state, and as part of the Cabinet the New Yorker eventually supplanted rival John C. Calhoun (former vice president and current South Carolina senator) as a presidential intimate. He resigned his State Department post in 1831 and Jackson selected him as foreign minister to England. After Calhoun and others blocked the appointment in the Senate, Jackson secured for Van Buren the Democratic vice presidential nomination in 1832.

Van Buren served as Jackson's vice president from 1833 to 1837, and with Jackson's endorsement won the presidency in 1836. He vowed to continue Jackson's policies, but the economic depression of 1837 weakened him politically. Van Buren received the Democratic nomination again in 1840 but, shouldering the blame for the country's financial woes, lost the election to Whig war hero William Henry Harrison. In 1844 a falling-out with Jackson over the annexation of Texas cost Van Buren the Democratic nomination, and his political fortunes began to decline. He ran for president a final time in 1848 as the candidate of the Free-Soil Party but failed to capture a single electoral vote. Van Buren later retired to Kinderhook, where he died in 1862 at the age of 79.

—*Ben Wynne*

References

Niven, John. *Martin Van Buren: The Romantic Age of American Politics.* New York: Oxford University Press, 1983.
See also Volume 1: Panic of 1837.

Vietnam Conflict (1954–1973)

War in Southeast Asia that helped lead to skyrocketing inflation and economic stagnation in the 1970s in the United States because of the way the administrations of Presidents Lyndon B. Johnson and Richard Nixon chose to manage the economy.

In an effort to prevent the spread of communism, the United States became involved in the Vietnam conflict in 1954. Vietnam had been controlled by the French before World War II and was conquered by Japan in 1940. Ho Chi Minh led a nationalist group that fought the Japanese and gained control over most of northern Vietnam by 1945. The French returned after World War II and attempted to regain power, but they met resistance from Ho Chi Minh's forces as they moved north. Both Great Britain and the United States denied French requests for military assistance, but the United States, believing that Ho Chi Minh had communist leanings and fearing the spread of communism, sent military advisers. The policy of providing advisers was expanded by President John F. Kennedy, who sent U.S. Army Green Berets to Vietnam in 1961, and finally by President Lyndon B. Johnson, who refused to be the first American president to lose a war and sent as many as half a million troops into the fighting during the 1960s. The United States withdrew its forces from Vietnam in 1973, and it is generally agreed that American forces lost the war.

Estimating the costs and impact of the Vietnam conflict is difficult because of how the U.S. government financed it. Official estimations at the time excluded many costs and, under the administration of President Lyndon B. Johnson, officials recorded expenses in a misleading manner or purposely underestimated them. In fact, the government did not begin to officially estimate the costs of the war until 1965.

From 1954 to 1963, the early years of U.S. involvement in Vietnam under the administrations of Presidents Dwight D. Eisenhower and John F. Kennedy, the conflict had virtually no effect on the nation's economy. Over the first dozen fiscal years of the war, the nation spent nearly $2.4 billion—only 0.04 percent of the gross national product and 0.53 percent of the nation's defense spending. The cost in manpower, not figured in this total, proved even more insignificant. Throughout the

1950s, the salaries of military personnel cost the nation $15 million annually, rising to $18 million in 1961. Although economic growth in the United States during Eisenhower's term in office (1952–1960) totaled less than in the post–World War II era (1945–1952) and the nation had experienced mild recessions in 1945, 1949, and 1958, the economy continued to grow at 2.4 percent.

The 1960 recession helped John Kennedy become president. His financial advisers decided to combat this slowdown using the Keynesian method of stimulating the economy, thus leading to high employment and economic growth through increasing deficit spending, tax cuts, and increasing the money supply. In theory, the right combination of these elements would ignite the sluggish economy. Yet, such a monetary policy runs the risk of causing a rise in prices. Thus, defense spending rose to $52 billion in 1963, or 9.1 percent of the gross national product. Still, Vietnam only cost the American taxpayers $414 million in 1963.

Scholars have debated this monetary policy's effect, but it did stimulate the economy. Economic growth revived, growing by 5.5 percent in 1964 and 6.3 percent in 1965. Unemployment fell from 5.4 percent in December 1964 to 4.4 percent in December 1965. The price index (an inflation indicator that measures how prices vary for a fixed group of products and services) remained stable, rising by 1.6 percent in 1964. By 1965, unemployment dropped down to 4.2 percent and gross domestic product grew at slightly under 5 percent. According to Keynesian thought, there would be time in 1966 to restrain the economy through decreased government spending, increasing taxes, and a tighter monetary policy; otherwise, the economy would be at risk of burning out of control.

President Johnson pursued almost the opposite track. Deeply involved in his Great Society domestic programs (welfare programs based on income redistribution), he increased deficit spending to finance the Vietnam conflict. This combination of "guns and butter" helped lead to economic inflation. As Johnson increased the U.S. presence in Southeast Asia—from 200,000 troops in 1965 to 536,000 troops three years later—the budget deficit grew. The president's spending on the war increased from $100 million in 1965 to $28.8 billion by 1969. With the economy in full swing, the annual inflation rate rose to 4.7 percent in 1968. With the influx of cash and a limited number of goods, the consumer market experienced inflation, which would continue into the 1970s.

Some economists also believe that the Vietnam conflict created an atmosphere that affected the entire society. It altered people's decisions, investments, and trust in the government. It also affected the career choices of young people, marriage rates, the number of children couples decided to have (in 1965 the average household had three children; by 2002 that rate had declined to 2.5 children per household), the divorce rate (which has increased since the 1960s), and home ownership (which has decreased). From the gloom of the Tet offensive (in which North Vietnamese soldiers attacked the U.S. embassy in the southern capital of Saigon before being repelled, the act that turned U.S. public opinion against the war) to the social instability of war protests on college campuses and in cities nationwide (often characterized by clashes between citizens and police and sometimes—as at Kent State University in Ohio and Jackson State University in Mississippi—in students' deaths at the hands of U.S. National Guardsmen or local police, respectively), Americans changed how they lived their lives, and the effects on the economy cannot be estimated. Because the Vietnam conflict cost more than $500 billion and perhaps as much as $900 billion, Johnson would have to make sacrifices in his Great Society, whose costs in urban problems also cannot be calculated because housing shortages and substandard housing continued into the late 1960s and became one cause of urban riots in 1966 and 1967. The total cost of the Vietnam conflict to the economy will remain unknown.

—T. Jason Soderstrum

References
Campagna, Anthony S. *The Economic Consequence of the Vietnam War.* New York: Praeger, 1991.
See also Volume 1: Great Society.

Virgin Islands, Purchase of (1917)

Caribbean islands purchased from Denmark because of their strategic position en route to the Panama Canal.

The 1917 U.S. acquisition of the Danish part of the Virgin Islands archipelago (Danish West Indies) consisted of the islands of St. Croix, St. John, St. Thomas, and some 50 smaller islets and cays, with a total area of 133 square miles and population of 26,000 inhabitants. The story of the purchase demonstrates a complex and multifaceted interplay between economic and budgetary concerns on the one hand and political and strategic considerations on the other.

By the mid-nineteenth century, the Danish West Indies became a liability for Copenhagen, mainly because of the progressive decline of sugar plantations after the emancipation of local slaves and disappearance of cheap labor. Despite the evident economic nonprofitability of the colony, the United States became increasingly interested in acquiring the islands as a strategic asset guarding eastern approaches to the Isthmus of Panama and later to the Panama Canal. Additionally, the United States feared the potential annexation of the islands by foreign powers in the 1860s, first by Austria and Prussia and later by Germany. Such an annexation would constitute a clear violation of the Monroe Doctrine and establish a foreign military presence in the excellent harbor of Charlotte Amalie on St. Thomas, an ideal site for a naval base. The Danes could not defend the islands from such a threat.

The United States had tried several times to negotiate the purchase of the Danish West Indies. Between 1865 and 1867, Secretary of State William Seward conducted negotiations for the purchase of the islands with the Danish minister in Washington, and Seward agreed to buy the archipelago for $7.5 million. The two countries signed the treaty October 24, 1867. Later that year the Danish Parliament approved the treaty, which the king then ratified. In addition, island residents voted overwhelmingly to transfer the Danish West Indies to U.S. control. Coincidentally, in November 1867, the colony experienced a devastating earthquake, tidal wave, and tropical hurricane, which ravaged much of the local economy. These natural cataclysms reinforced the reluctance of Congress to approve the deal, and suspicions continued about Seward's annexation schemes following the $7.2 million Alaska purchase, which was highly controversial. Additionally, the U.S. government remained financially preoccupied with the reconstruction of the South and development of the West. In November 1867 the House of Representatives rejected the Virgin Islands Treaty, and the Senate never voted on it.

In 1902, Secretary of State John Hay negotiated a new treaty with the Danes, only to have the agreement rejected by Copenhagen because of the compensation (only $5 million) pledged by the United States. During World War I the fear of German penetration into the Caribbean revived the idea of the purchase. In 1915 the American minister in Copenhagen, Maurice F. Egan, and the U.S. secretary of state arranged the final $25 million deal. Representatives signed the treaty August 4, 1916, and Congress approved it January 17, 1917. On March 31, 1917, the United States officially took possession of the islands and renamed them the Virgin Islands of the United States. Although economically the islands remained unprofitable until the development of the tourist industry, their acquisition proved to be strategically sound, strengthening U.S. control over the Caribbean. Citizens of the U.S. Virgin Islands have U.S. citizenship and have a nonvoting representative in the U.S. House of Representatives.

—*Peter Rainow*

References

Tansill, Charles C. *The Purchase of the Danish West Indies.* Baltimore, MD: Johns Hopkins University Press, 1932.

See also Volume 1: Panama and the Panama Canal; Seward, William; World War I.

Volcker, Paul A. (1927–)

Chair of the Board of Governors of the Federal Reserve System from 1979 to 1987.

In 1979, President Jimmy Carter's job approval rating had reached a low point, and Americans continued to express their anxiety about spiraling inflation. Carter nominated Paul A. Volcker to chair the Board of Governors of the Federal Reserve system. Born in Teaneck, New Jersey, Paul Volcker held a master's degree in political economy from Harvard University and had also studied at the London School of

Economics and Political Science. He worked as an undersecretary in the Treasury Department before becoming president of the New York Federal Reserve Bank. On July 30, 1979, the Committee on Banking, Housing, and Urban Affairs of the U.S. Senate, chaired by U.S. Democratic Senator William Proxmire of Wisconsin, held a confirmation hearing. Volcker brought a wealth of experience from service rendered in the banking industry as well as in both Democratic and Republican administrations beginning with the administration of President John F. Kennedy. Senator Proxmire expressed concern that Volcker would be out of touch with the concerns of average workers and too attuned to the desires of Wall Street, but Volcker was approved over Proxmire's objections.

When Volcker was confirmed as chair of the Board of Governors of the Federal Reserve Board, he added stability to the board's membership, promulgated innovative policies, and arguably doomed the reelection bid of President Jimmy Carter in 1980. Although real income grew over the course of the Carter administration, the gross domestic product actually shrank during the first six months of 1980. No incumbent presidential party has ever retained the White House under such circumstances. Volcker's (1980) policy of historically high interest rates made recovery by the first Tuesday after the first Monday in November highly unlikely. Walter Dean Burnham has observed that Jimmy Carter had contributed to his own loss by nominating Volcker, who "executed a revolutionary policy change: targeting money supply rather than interest rates—thus producing the highest extended real rates of interest since the post–Civil War Great Deflation of 1865–1880, and in time quite effectively killing the inflation dragon, as it was intended to do."

Volcker was reconfirmed as chair during the administration of President Ronald Reagan (1981–1987). He and his successor Alan Greenspan are the only two people to chair the Board of Governors of the Federal Reserve Board since 1979.

—*Henry B. Sirgo*

References

Burnham, Walter D. "The Legacy of George Bush: Travails of an Understudy." In Gerald M. Pomper, ed., *The Election of 1992*. Chatham, NJ: Chatham House Publishers, 1992.

U.S. Senate. *Nomination of Paul A. Volcker*. Hearing before the Committee on Banking, Housing, and Urban Affairs. 96th Cong., 1st sess., July 30, 1979.

See also Volume 1: Federal Reserve Act.

W

Wage and Price Freeze (1971)

New economic policy designed by President Richard M. Nixon in August 1971 that imposed a 90-day freeze on wages, prices, rents, and dividends.

Following a weekend crisis consultation with his economic advisers at Camp David, President Richard M. Nixon announced a policy imposing a 90-day freeze on wages, prices, rents, and dividends in a television broadcast August 15, 1971. This "Nixon shock" came only 11 days after an impromptu press conference in which Nixon declared that he was "unalterably opposed . . . to the Galbraithian scheme . . . of permanent price and wage controls . . . the extremists on the left of the economy spectrum have always favored a totally government controlled economy."

The new economic policy proved not as unexpected as the rhetoric suggested. Nixon decided not to jeopardize his reelection chances by tolerating higher than necessary levels of unemployment. He attributed his 1960 defeat by John F. Kennedy to an insufficient degree of political sensitivity within President Dwight D. Eisenhower's Cabinet with respect to the forthcoming election. Unemployment increased to 452,000 (5.8 percent) in October 1960 and, said Nixon, "All the speeches, television broadcasts and precinct work in the world could not counter that one hard fact."

In 1970, as president, Nixon bluntly instructed his Federal Reserve chair Arthur Burns to ensure that no recession occurred, but by that time inflation had become a major societal problem. Burns argued, "We should not close our minds to the possibility that an incomes policy, provided that it stopped well short of direct price and wage controls and was used merely as a supplement to overall fiscal and monetary measures, might speed us through this transitional period of cost-push inflation." Stagflation (high unemployment and high inflation) undermined the traditional remedies, and the situation now required other tools to counter rising costs. One of Nixon's top priorities was to make businesses in the private sector aware of and accepting of the fact that the economy was in desperate straits and so wage and price freezes—which would guarantee that workers' earning power would not be reduced—were necessary. In November 1970, Nixon again urged Burns to expand the money supply at a faster rate; Burns replied that the economy required some form of policy that limited wage increases. In December 1970 Burns publicly argued for such a policy in a speech at Pepperdine College. Nixon began to appeal to labor and management to fight against inflation.

Initially, the new economic policy appeared to restrain some wage and price pressures. In the policy's second phase, a 15 percent wage increase was granted for coal miners. In February 1972, two prominent trade unionists withdrew from the supervisory panels created by the administration. Nixon had begun to alienate his own constituency. Milton Friedman regarded the "jerry-built freeze" and the controls as "deeply and inherently immoral . . . [they] threaten the very foundations of a free society." In May 1973, Nixon announced another 60-day price freeze.

Later, Nixon reflected that the controls contradicted his own philosophy, noting the economy involved spiritual as well as accounting issues. He concluded that a direct link existed between civil liberties and economic freedom—a relationship strained by wage and price controls. As a consequence of the disappointing results of attempting to freeze prices, policymakers looked more sympathetically upon anti-inflation policies that proved less frustrating to those who administered them. Thus in the mid-1970s, Americans perceived monetarism (forces that cause inflation, unemployment, and fluctuating production) temporarily as a less exhausting and more reliable method of controlling inflation.

—*Robert Leeson*

References

Burns, A. F. *Reflections of an Economic Policy Maker: Speeches and Congressional Statements 1969–1978*. Washington, DC: American Enterprise Institute, 1978.

Diamond, R. *Nixon: The Third Year of His Presidency*. Washington, DC: Congressional Quarterly Press, 1972.

Friedman, M. *There's No Such Thing As a Free Lunch*. LaSalle, IL: Open Court, 1975.

Nixon, R. M. *Six Crises*. London: W. H. Allen, 1962.

———. *The Real War*. New York: Warner, 1980.

Stein, Herbert. *On the Other Hand . . . Essays on Economics, Economists, and Politics*. Washington, DC: American Enterprise Institute, 1995.

Wells, Wyatt C. *Economist in an Uncertain World: Arthur F. Burns and the Federal Reserve, 1970–78.* New York: Columbia University Press, 1994.
See also Volume 1: National Income and Product Accounts.

Wagner Act (1935)

Also known as National Labor Relations Act, this law, passed by the U.S. Congress in 1935, empowered organized labor by granting working people numerous rights and privileges that improved their standard of living.

Senator Robert F. Wagner, Democrat of New York, introduced this legislation for federal regulation of labor relations in 1935, after the U.S. Supreme Court declared the National Recovery Act (NRA) unconstitutional. Sponsored by President Franklin D. Roosevelt and the New Dealers and enacted by Congress in 1933, the NRA had aimed to regulate and restore prosperity to the depression-shattered economy of the United States by eliminating waste, inefficiency, and destructive competition among business. The statute applied the code of fair competition industrywide and made the federal government the referee among companies and between capital and labor. Section 7(a) of NRA broke a new path for labor by requiring employers to allow workers to engage in collective bargaining (on wages, hours, and working conditions) through the trade unions of their own choosing. This provision boosted labor unionization and gained popular support, but as counterbalance, employers formed company-dominated unions.

In an effort to broaden labor's rights, oversee labor disputes, and counter employer intransigence, the Wagner Act reclaimed the principle of section 7(a) by continuing to guarantee the right of collective bargaining through the labor union that workers freely selected by majority vote. More important, the act outlawed unfair labor practices used by employers, among them retaining company-controlled unions, blacklisting union activists, coercing or firing workers who sought to join an independent union, and using industrial spies. The act established the National Labor Relations Board (NLRB) as a crucial enforcement mechanism to hear employee complaints, determine union authority, direct on-site union elections, and issue cease-and-desist orders to employers found responsible for any unfair labor practice the act defined.

—*Guoqiang Zheng*

References
Gordon, Colin. *New Deals: Business, Labor, and Politics in America, 1920–1935.* New York: Cambridge University Press, 1994.
See also Volume 1: New Deal; Volume 2: Labor.

War and Warfare

State of armed conflict between states or nations that has complex economic consequences for all involved.

War and economics are deeply interconnected. Some theorists assert that economic factors lead to war. War causes inflation, higher taxes, destruction of human and physical capital, and misallocation of resources. Economic strength can determine the duration and outcome of war. Military victory can bring economic benefits—including plundering the defeated, controlling markets and trade routes, and making the rules that govern international trade and finance.

In the nineteenth century, some believed that aggressive mercantilism (in which all trade benefits the mother country) led to war and thus that free trade would promote peace. Karl Marx asserted that war was the inevitable result of capitalism. Other Marxists argued that the imperialist struggle for increased profits and markets for surplus goods caused war. After 1918, some blamed war on individual capitalists such as munitions makers and on interest groups such as the military-industrial complex (military organizations and manufacturers that have an economic relationship). Some modern theorists contend that war can emerge from disparities in economic development (the "North-South divide") and long-term economic cycles ("Kondratieff waves"). Others argue that competition for valuable resources such as oil, water, or diamonds engenders war.

War is expensive. For defense in peacetime, modern states typically devote 5 to 10 percent of the national income or gross national product (GNP) and 50 to 90 percent of government spending, which results in deficit spending—and they spend much more than that during wartime. To finance war, governments borrow, raise taxes, and debase (or devalue) currency. Spending vast sums of money has raised prices and caused inflation (which is sometimes called an indirect tax). In earlier eras, governments lowered the purity of metal coins, and later—after the invention of paper money—simply printed more banknotes. Significant inflation occurred as a result of the American Civil War, World Wars I and II, and Vietnam.

Warfare provoked much financial innovation throughout history. For example, during the financial revolution of the late 1600s, England created the banking, credit, and financial institutions that enabled it to prevail in the hegemonic struggle against France from 1688 until 1815. Warfare also stimulated technological innovations that profoundly affected the world economy. For example, jet aircraft engines, lasers, microchips, and satellites all emerged from military research programs.

The side that mobilizes the greatest economic resources usually achieves victory in war, although as the Vietnam conflict demonstrated, weak powers can use guerrilla warfare to exhaust superior opponents, and superior resources cannot ensure victory when military strategy is faulty. The two world wars galvanized the entire economies of the major participants, and in each case the victors comprehensively outproduced the defeated in terms of military equipment and supplies. Neither war was a foregone conclusion, but in both cases, superior economic power permitted the Allies to recover from early defeats and secure ultimate victory.

Victory brings economic benefit in the form of plunder or reparations. Before 1914, war could pay for itself, but since then, the costs of war have far exceeded the direct profits thereby gained. Territorial conquest brought great economic benefit during the age of mercantile empires, when international trade remained restricted and internal development was slow. During the modern era (since 1900), nations had to increase national wealth and power by conquering new lands to provide resources and markets. As international trade increased, territorial conquest became less attractive than making the rules that governed the international economic system—and military hegemony guaranteed the right to make the rules. For example, American military power underwrote the Bretton Woods system (which stabilized international economies by establishing exchange rates and the International Monetary Fund) from 1944 to 1970, and it has also ensured access to Middle Eastern oil. Warfare brings great economic benefit when rival powers exhaust or destroy each other. For example, European warfare from 1789 to 1815 and 1914 to 1945 contributed to U.S. economic growth, and the Vietnam War undermined American economic power relative to that of Germany and Japan.

Paul Kennedy has argued that over the long term, immoderate diversion of resources from investment to military power and the acquisition of excessive security commitments ("imperial overstretch") weaken states and lead to a shift in the balance of economic power. However, Niall Ferguson has contended that economic power influences—but does not determine—history. He claimed that hegemonic decline actually results from "understretch"—the political unwillingness to mobilize sufficient resources quickly enough to deter potential aggressors.

—*James D. Perry*

References

Blainey, Geoffrey. *The Causes of War.* New York: Free Press, 1988.

Brewer, John. *The Sinews of Power: War, Money, and the English State, 1688–1783.* Cambridge, MA: Harvard University Press, 1990.

Brodie, Bernard. *War and Politics.* New York: Macmillan, 1973.

Davies, Glyn. *A History of Money from Ancient Times to the Present Day.* Cardiff: University of Wales Press, 2002.

Ferguson, Niall. *The Cash Nexus.* New York: Basic Books, 2001.

Kennedy, Paul. *The Rise and Fall of the Great Powers.* New York: Vintage Books, 1987.

Milward, Alan S. *War, Economy, and Society 1939–1945.* Berkeley: University of California Press, 1977.

Strachan, Hew. *The First World War: Volume 1.* Oxford: Oxford University Press, 2001.

See also Volume 1: War of 1812; World War I, World War II.

War Labor Disputes Act

See Smith-Connally Act.

War of 1812

America's second War of Independence.

In June 1812, President James Madison asked Congress to declare war on Great Britain. Madison and his supporters in Congress, known as the war hawks, had many complaints against the British. First, England had interfered with America's trade on the high seas for nearly two decades. In an effort to stop all commerce with Napoleon, the British navy had captured hundreds of American ships. Equally important, many American sailors had been forcibly impressed into the Royal Navy. British officers boarded American ships at gunpoint and forcibly removed any sailors thought to be English citizens. Finally, Americans suspected the British army in Canada of helping the Shawnee chief Tecumseh organize his Indian confederation against the United States along the western frontier. Tecumseh had united dozens of tribes in his effort to stop America's westward advance. He hoped that the British would help him win a separate Indian nation north of the Ohio River for all the tribes.

The opening year of the War of 1812 proved disastrous for the United States. The city of Detroit fell to the British and Indians, while the American invasion of Canada by way of upstate New York collapsed. But by 1813, the tide had turned in favor of the Americans. U.S. troops turned back an invading army of British and Indians led by Tecumseh at Fort Meigs along the Maumee River in Ohio by the summer of 1813. Oliver Hazard Perry's fleet soundly defeated the British navy at Put-in-Bay on Lake Erie in September 1813. In October, Tecumseh lost the Battle of the Thames in western Ontario. Tecumseh died in the fighting, and Indian resistance in the northwest broke. Later in Alabama, Tecumseh's last Indian allies met defeat in the brutal Creek War.

Despite these American victories, Great Britain launched a three-pronged attack against the United States in 1814. The first British army turned back at Plattsburgh on Lake Champlain in September 1814. The second army invaded Washington, D.C., and burned many government buildings including the White House. But the British met stiff opposition at Baltimore and retreated to the Caribbean to join the third army gathering for the attack on New Orleans. General Andrew Jackson soundly defeated the British at the Battle of New Orleans in January 1815.

As Americans celebrated the great victory at New Orleans, word arrived that the peace treaty ending the war had already been signed on Christmas Eve in 1814. Minister to Russia John Quincy Adams, Speaker of the House Henry Clay, and former secretary of the Treasury Albert Gallatin had worked tirelessly for nearly a year to prepare the Treaty of Ghent. At first, the British demanded a separate Indian state in the old northwest territory but finally agreed to return to the status quo before the war. Although the United States lost many battles in the War of 1812, the nation had finally won the respect of Great Britain. England would never again interfere with American trade on the high seas or help the Indians in their long war against the advancing Americans.

—*Mary Stockwell*

References

Horsman, Reginald. *The War of 1812.* New York: Alfred A. Knopf, 1969.

See also Volume 1: Treaty of Ghent.

War of 1898

See Spanish-American War.

War Production Board (WPB)

Government agency established in 1942 to direct war production and procurement of materials for World War II.

To organize American economic mobilization for World War II, President Franklin D. Roosevelt created the War Production Board (WPB) in January 1942 under Sears Roebuck executive Donald Nelson. The WPB was theoretically a "superagency" that controlled war production and procurement and allocated materials and production facilities. In practice, Nelson proved a poor bureaucratic infighter, and rival agencies constantly outmaneuvered the WPB. His worst decision was to permit the armed services to set priorities and clear contracts. Thus, the WPB could not determine overall production priorities and ensure compliance with them.

Nelson converted many civilian industries to war production. For example, he banned civilian automobile production in February 1942. Automobile manufacturers subsequently produced vast quantities of planes, aircraft engines, tanks, trucks, and munitions.

Nelson, an idealist, wanted to give contracts to small businesses even though the approach would have increased costs, created delays, and resulted in administrative inefficiencies. The military preferred working with large corporations, which had the plant, equipment, managerial expertise, trained workers, and mass production techniques to procure immense quantities of complex equipment quickly. Congress created the Smaller War Plants Corporation under Nelson to convert small businesses to war work, but the military preference for big business generally prevailed. The Smaller War Plants Corporation increased the small business share of War Department contracts from 12.6 percent in 1943 to 27.4 percent in 1945, but these contracts were mainly for commercial-type items procured for the Quartermaster Corps.

The WPB's chief duty involved administering the Controlled Materials Plan established in November 1942 to ration steel, copper, and aluminum. Claimant agencies (initially the War and Navy Departments, Maritime Commission, Aircraft Resources Control, Lend-Lease Administration, Board of Economic Warfare, and Office of Civilian Supply) estimated their needs each quarter, and the WPB allocated to them a proportion of the available total to distribute to prime contractors.

Roosevelt created many rival agencies that duplicated WPB functions, such as the Office of War Mobilization, and refused to support Nelson in the inevitable disputes. Nelson's bitter fights with the military eventually led to his downfall. Nelson wanted to begin reconverting defense plants to civilian production as early as 1943, but the Joint Chiefs of Staff violently resisted this idea. Roosevelt sided with the Joint Chiefs of Staff, and Nelson resigned in August 1944. Julius Krug replaced Nelson and lifted wartime economic controls in April 1945. In sum, the WPB's charter envisioned total control over the wartime economy, but Nelson's failure to bend the military and big business to his will helped ensure that the WPB never achieved this objective.

—*James D. Perry*

References

Blum, John Morton. *V Was for Victory*. San Diego, CA: Harcourt Brace Jovanovich, 1976.

Gropman, Alan, ed. *The Big L: American Logistics in World War II*. Washington, DC: National Defense University Press, 1997.

Smith, R. Elberton. *The Army and Economic Mobilization*. Washington, DC: U.S. Government Printing Office, 1959.

War Production Board. *Industrial Mobilization for War*. Westport, CT: Greenwood Press, 1970.

See also Volume 1: Office of War Mobilization; World War II.

Wealth Distribution

The pattern of wealth-holding in a society.

Wealth consists of a stock of any asset that has a money value in exchange. Economists measure the distribution of wealth by sorting all members of society in order from those with no wealth to the wealthiest, then dividing that list up into equal-sized groups. The proportion of total wealth held by each group then gives an indication of the equality wealth holding. In most societies, the majority of people have only small amounts of wealth, while a few are very rich.

Strong links exist between income and wealth, but two factors distinguish them. The first, inheritance, consists of wealth passed from one generation to the next. The second focuses on the point in the lifespan of the individual. Most people begin their adult lives with little, but they accumulate wealth during their years of work. They then spend their savings during their retirement. Most individuals hold their wealth in assets not easily converted to cash—particularly homes, which account for 46 percent of all wealth, followed by interest-bearing assets and then motor vehicles.

Given the high degree of wealth inequality in the United States, administrations between 1960 and 2003 have sought to achieve a more equitable distribution. Redistribution achieves a more socially desirable distribution of wealth, and in doing so transfers wealth to the poor, who have a greater propensity to spend, thereby increasing demand. The most common method of redistribution is through the use of income and consumption taxes.

Prior to World War II, there were few attempts to redistribute wealth in the United States. In October 1942 Roosevelt imposed a progressive income tax—one that taxes the rich more than the poor. Such taxes continue to form the mainstay of wealth redistribution efforts, together with programs to alleviate poverty.

—*Tony Ward*

References

Rodgers, Harrell R. *American Poverty in a New Era of Reform*. Armonk, NY: M. E. Sharpe, 2000.

See also Volume 1: Medicaid; Medicare.

Welfare Economics

System that uses economic theory to analyze the desirability of one situation over another.

Most economic theory focuses on positive analysis by simply measuring and understanding people and firms. The main purpose of welfare economics involves the development of mechanisms that enable us to compare alternative situations and obtain a social ordering. This process inevitably relies on the use of value judgments to decide which situation is preferable.

Welfare economics relies on the market-based tools of neoclassical economics to support two basic theorems. The first fundamental theorem of welfare economics states that if individual preferences obey certain regulatory restrictions, the outcome of a free-market system will achieve efficiency—a condition when resources cannot be reallocated to make anyone better off without making someone else worse off. Such equilibria remain quite common, and the theorem does not necessarily help us to decide which of two situations is preferable in some global sense. This first theorem constitutes a formal proof of Adam Smith's propositions in the *Wealth of Nations* (1776). If the situation does not meet the necessary technical conditions, any outcome is by definition optimal, so this theorem does not help us to distinguish between alternative states.

There are many possible criticisms of the first theorem, which lessen its effectiveness. Apart from several (critical) technical problems, the theorem has no concern for the distribution of income or wealth, and an outcome that is highly unequal is just as satisfactory as one of perfectly equal distribution. This strong objection to the usefulness of the first theorem is at least partly answered by the second theorem.

The second fundamental theorem of welfare economics states that inequalities of distribution can be dealt with efficiently through the use of lump-sum taxes and transfer payments. A benign government can therefore enjoy the advantages of an efficient competitive economy whilst also achieving equity. Although not dealing with the important technical problems, this provides strong support for the use of a competitive market system.

The two theorems together then provide a logical underpinning to today's market economic system. If all the required regularity conditions hold true in the real world, then that support would be valid. The "second best theorem" then shows that if any of the stringent conditions does not hold true, the overall results are not correct. Not only does the overall result not hold, but assuming that the other conditions are satisfied, does not necessarily improve the outcome.

There are many situations, such as the provision of public goods that do not result in efficient provision by a competitive economy. In such cases government needs to intervene to ensure provision, and needs the welfare economics tools of benefit-cost analysis to evaluate how much to provide.

—*Tony Ward*

References
Rodgers, Harrell R. *American Poverty in a New Era of Reform.* Armonk, NY: M. E. Sharpe, 2000.
See also Volume 1: Great Society; Medicaid; Medicare.

Whig Party

American political party popular from 1836 to 1854.

Taking its name from the eighteenth century British and American opponents of the monarchy, the Whig Party formed out of opposition to President Andrew Jackson, who some disparaged as "King Andrew the First" because of his overbearing political methods. Direct political successors to the old National Republicans, the Whigs drew the bulk of their support from New England and the Upper Midwest. They remained ardent nationalists and promoted the American System, a plan designed to unite the country economically through a national bank, high protective tariffs, federally sponsored internal improvement, and a conservative public land sales policy. Their programs proved especially attractive to manufacturers, merchants, and commercial farmers. Two of the great statesmen of the era, Henry Clay of Kentucky and Daniel Webster of Massachusetts, ranked among the party's leadership.

The Whigs began organizing in 1834 in response to Jackson's veto of the National Bank, which killed the institution. They brought members of the Anti-Mason party into their coalition, and fallout from the nullification crisis (which threatened dissolution of the Union over discriminatory tariffs in 1828 and 1832) allowed them to forge an uneasy alliance with John C. Calhoun and his states' rights followers in the South. Though Jacksonian Democracy dominated the Southern states, many among the region's planter class held the Whig point of view. Jackson's retirement coupled with the financial panic of 1837 weakened the Democrats and allowed the Whig candidate, war hero William Henry Harrison, to win the presidency in 1840 over incumbent Martin Van Buren. The Whig victory proved short-lived, as Harrison died only one month into his term. John Tyler, a states'-rights former Democrat, replaced Harrison and subsequently vetoed key Whig economic legislation.

The Whig Party claimed the presidency again in 1848 with another war hero, Zachary Taylor, but he served only 16 months. Taylor's death in 1850 left Millard Fillmore as the nation's chief executive at a time of increasing sectional tensions over slavery and western expansion. Although the Compromise of 1850 was not entirely a Whig undertaking, the Whig leadership played a prominent role in its passage. (The Compromise of 1850 admitted California as a free state and Texas as a slave state, and it established the Fugitive Slave Act placing recovery of runaway slaves under federal jurisdiction and ending slave trade in Washington, D.C.) Soon after 1850, though, the party began to crumble. Fillmore was an ineffective leader, and the deaths of Clay and Webster in 1852 were blows from which the Whigs would never recover. As sectional tensions became more acute, many party leaders defected to the Free-Soil Party, and suspicions over its association with antislavery elements never allowed the Whigs to gain a strong foothold in the South. The rise of the Republican and Know-Nothing parties in 1856 completed the Whig collapse as a viable political entity.

—*Ben Wynne*

References

Holt, Michael F. *The Rise and Fall of the American Whig Party: Jacksonian Politics and the Onset of the Civil War.* New York: Oxford University Press, 1999.

Howe, Daniel W. *The Political Culture of the American Whigs.* Chicago: University of Chicago Press, 1979.

See also Volume 1: Clay, Henry; Nullification Crisis; Panic of 1837.

Whiskey Rebellion (1794)

Popular revolt in western Pennsylvania brought about by a federal tax on distilled spirits.

Since 1791, back-country farmers in all of the states had been seething about the federal excise tax on distilled alcohol, proposed by Alexander Hamilton, secretary of the treasury. The tax charged small producers nine cents a gallon on their product while taxing larger distillers only six cents. This measure made the alcohol almost impossible to sell at a profit, cut into the hard currency available to the farmers, and became the focus of rural discontent across the western frontier. In 1794, efforts to more strongly enforce the tax sparked violent protest in Pennsylvania, where angry farmers attacked, tarred, and feathered a tax inspector and then burned his house. The government, afraid of the violence contemporaneously sweeping the French Revolution, quickly summoned 13,000 militia from Pennsylvania and the surrounding states, under the command of General Henry Lee, but with George Washington riding at their head to confront the protesters.

Meanwhile, the "whiskey rebels" in Pennsylvania had elected an assembly to broadcast their grievances, and although many members were moderates like Albert Gallatin, the violence continued until the militia arrived. Faced with federal force, the protesters melted away, although the forces arrested 12 men who they sent to Philadelphia for trial. All but one received presidential pardons shortly thereafter. The Whiskey Rebellion tested the new constitutional government of Washington for the first time, required the initial use of the 1792 Militia Act, and resulted in the widespread outpouring of anti-Federalist sentiment from the western counties of every state but New York.

—*Margaret Sankey*

References

Clouse, Jerry A. *The Whiskey Rebellion.* Harrisburg: Pennsylvania Historical and Museum Commission, 1994.

Slaughter, Thomas P. *The Whiskey Rebellion: Frontier Epilogue to the American Revolution.* New York: Oxford University Press, 1986.

See also Volume 2: Taxation.

Williams-Steiger Act

See Occupational Safety and Health Act of 1970 (OSHA).

Williams v. Mississippi (1898)

Landmark Supreme Court case dealing with minority voting rights.

Handed down in the shadow of *Plessy v. Ferguson* (1896), this decision upheld measures designed to curtail black voting in the South. In 1896 an all-white grand jury in Washington County, Mississippi, indicted Henry Williams, a black man, for murder, and an all-white petit jury subsequently convicted him and imposed a death sentence. Williams argued that both the indictment and trial violated the Equal Protection Clause of the Fourteenth Amendment because the laws of the state of Mississippi disqualified blacks from jury service. Franchise provisions in Mississippi's 1890 Constitution included a poll tax and literacy test, which had greatly reduced the number of black voters in the state and effectively eliminated blacks from the jury pool. (Williams had failed to pass the literacy test.) The Court rejected Williams's argument by a vote of 9 to 0 (including Justice John Marshall Harlan, who had previously cast the only dissenting vote in the *Plessy* case). In writing the opinion, Justice Joseph McKenna stated that the poll tax and literacy test provisions of the Mississippi Constitution "do not on their face discriminate between the races, and it has not been shown that their actual administration was evil; only that evil was possible under them." Coupled with the *Plessy* decision, the outcome of the Williams case was a great victory for the Jim Crow South, and white politicians throughout the region moved quickly to consolidate their position. Armed with legal sanction from the nation's highest court, other southern states soon adopted similar laws that would keep blacks away from the polls for decades. Minority voting would remain unusually low in the South until after passage of the Civil Rights Act of 1964 and the Voting Rights Act of 1965.

—*Ben Wynne*

References

Furer, Howard B. *The Fuller Court, 1888–1910.* Vol. 5, *The Supreme Court in American Life.* Millwood, NY: Associated Faculty Press, 1986.

See also Volume 1: Poll Tax; Volume 2: Judiciary.

Wilson-Gorman Tariff (1894)

Democratic tariff reform bill that included a federal income tax.

Tariff questions played a key role in the election of Democratic President Grover Cleveland to a second (nonconsecutive) term in 1892. The Democratic Party included a tariff reduction plank in its platform. In a special session called by President Cleveland in 1894, the House, with a significant Democratic majority, moved quickly to enact tariff reductions through legislation written by the chair of the Ways and Means Committee, Democratic Representative William L. Wilson of West Virginia. The Democrats enjoyed a smaller majority in the Senate, and so the tariff reduction bill became loaded with protectionist amendments favoring high tariffs. Because the Senate bill differed from the House bill, a conference committee of members from both chambers had to reach a compromise. The House and Senate approved the compromise legislation, but President Cleveland indicated his dissent by not signing the bill. It became law without his signature in August 1894.

The Wilson-Gorman Tariff included the first federal income tax enacted since the Civil War. Persons with incomes over $4,000 paid a 2 percent tax. The U.S. Supreme Court ruled the income tax provision unconstitutional in 1895. The Wilson-Gorman Tariff removed the tariff on wool and simplified the rates on woolen products imported to the country. Many of the other rate changes involved slight reductions from the McKinley Tariff of 1890; the protectionists in the Senate blunted more significant reductions. The Wilson-Gorman Tariff reinstituted the tariff on sugar, resulting in an increase in revenue. The change also wreaked havoc on economic conditions in Cuba, which relied heavily on the American market for its sugar exports. Cuban exports to the United States fell more than 50 percent, leading to political strife that resulted in the Spanish-American War.

The Democratic Party lost much of its electoral support because of the lack of significant rate reductions in the Wilson-Gorman Tariff. The Democrats lost their majorities in both houses of Congress as voters swept many Democrats, including Representative Wilson, from office.

—*John David Rausch Jr.*

References

Summers, Festus. *William L. Wilson and Tariff Reform.* New Brunswick, NJ: Rutgers University Press, 1953.
See also Volume 1: McKinley Tariff Act; Sugar.

Wilson, Woodrow (1856–1924)

Former governor of New Jersey and twenty-eighth President of the United States (1913–1921) who advocated the progressive reforms of the New Freedom to promote free enterprise.

Wilson was born December 28, 1856, and raised in a southern family of Presbyterian pastors. In 1879, he graduated from Princeton University and entered the Law School of the University of Virginia. In 1883, he attended Johns Hopkins University for a doctorate in political science and history. He then took successive professorships at Bryn Mawr College in Pennsylvania, Wesleyan University in Connecticut, and Princeton University. From 1902 to 1910, Wilson served as president of Princeton University.

Wilson began his political career as reform governor of New Jersey (1911–1913). He supported comprehensive reform legislation that included a corrupt practice act prohibiting monopolies and insider trading, the Workingmen's Compensation Act, municipal reform, reorganization of the school system, passage of antitrust laws, and the implementation of the direct election primary. With his record as a reformer, Wilson won the Democratic nomination for the White House in 1912 and won the presidency by campaigning for the New Freedom, a national program to unleash American economic dynamism and boost individual energies for creative competition.

As president, Wilson strengthened executive authority by endorsing an ambitious legislative agenda and securing its approval from a Democratic Congress. He called for tariff reform and, by battling both lobbyists who represented special interest groups and opposition from within his own party, he forced through Congress the Underwood Tariff Act of 1913, the first substantial downward revision of duties since before the Civil War. To reorganize the banking and credit system to free them from monopolistic control, he pushed through Congress the Federal Reserve Act of 1913 and strengthened antitrust laws to address unfair trade practices. The New Freedom ideals also found expression in Wilson's foreign policy, which aimed to construct new international relations along liberal-internationalist lines by calling on foreign nations to copy American-type democracy and capitalism. Such diplomacy met severe challenges and almost brought the United States into war with Mexico in 1916 (after Mexico accepted correspondence from Germany that suggested a joint attack by Mexico and Germany on the United States, which would open a second front and keep the United States out of the European War). This diplomacy was partly responsible for U.S. entry into World War I in 1917 because the United States publicly revealed the correspondence and declared war on Germany before Mexico had a chance to act on the German suggestion. After the war's end, Wilson failed to implement his Fourteen Points for international peace—save for the League of Nations, which the United States failed to participate in because it would have supranational authority over the United States, and over which he fought a losing battle against the Republican opposition in Congress. Other points that failed included one calling for self-determination for all people, a "no war guilt" clause for the German government, and a system of war reparations that would have required Germany to pay for the entire cost of World War I. Wilson suffered a nervous collapse in September 1919 while on a national speaking tour touting support for the League of Nations and never fully recovered. In December 1920, Wilson won the Nobel Peace Prize for his efforts at Versailles in 1919. He died in Washington, D.C., on February 3, 1924.

—*Guoqiang Zheng*

References

Saunders, Robert M. *In Search of Woodrow Wilson: Beliefs and Behavior.* Westport, CT: Greenwood Press, 1998.
See also Volume 1: Federal Reserve Act; World War I; Volume 2: Trade Policy.

Women

Largest segment of the U.S. population long denied economic and political rights.

Throughout most of U.S. history, women have been subservient to men when it comes to conducting business transactions, controlling property and wealth, and making decisions concerning politics. During the 1600s, when the number of men far exceeded the number of women, society placed women in a position to have more control of their situations: Men died young, and women usually remarried several times.

Each time a woman remarried, her wealth increased, providing her with the choice of taking another husband or remaining on her own. The rigors of frontier life usually meant she opted for the former. As the balance between the sexes reached a balance in the colonies, the rights of women declined rapidly. Later individual states would pass laws granting men authority to control all of a woman's assets. At the same time, men assumed responsibility for any legal consequences of their decisions.

During the early years of the republic, women stayed home and cared for the household and the children. As men began leaving family farms for wage-paying jobs in skills trades or factories during the market revolution (1815–1849), when the U.S. economy shifted from a subsistence to a cash economy, women's work remained uncompensated. This trend continued throughout the rest of the 1800s, even though women fought for the right to vote. During the last few decades of the nineteenth century as American industry expanded, many newly arrived female immigrants found themselves forced into the lowest-paying jobs in factories. Still women remained economically restricted.

By the outbreak of World War I, women's rights were still limited, although a few states had finally passed legislation that allowed women to control their own economic affairs. During the war, women filled factory jobs vacated by men who had joined the armed services and worked as nurses, teachers, and in other traditional female occupations. Congress rewarded their efforts after the war—and after years of political agitation in which women pushed for political participation—by passing the Nineteenth Amendment, an act that granted women the right to vote. More economic opportunities arose during World War II as women once again returned to the factories in large numbers. After the United States defeated Germany and Japan, however, most women returned to their traditional roles as housewife and mother. The 1950s witnessed the apex of this trend. By the 1960s, women began once again to agitate for their rights—this time for their economic rights. Demands for an Equal Rights Amendment to the Constitution met stiff resistance from many special interest groups, which argued that the amendment would encompass all groups (including women, gays, and other groups), making the law unpalatable. In 1961, President John F. Kennedy appointed Eleanor Roosevelt to head the President's Commission on the Status of Women. The commission reported that women received less pay than men for performing the same job, and a movement began to equalize pay. By the 1970s women fought to eliminate the "glass ceiling,"—a term used to describe the invisible barrier that prevented women from achieving promotions from middle management to top executive positions. Although women have since attained a measure of success in this area, most professional women still receive lower compensation than their male counterparts, and fewer women than men fill top positions in corporations. During the last few decades of the twentieth century, the government began to address other issues that affect women in the workplace, such as employer day-care facilities and family leave for personal reasons such as illness or the birth of a child. The poorest women, often stuck in a cycle of poverty and dependent on government welfare assistance, received job and day-care assistance in an effort to elevate their economic position while reducing the number of Americans on the government welfare rolls. Although disparities still exist between the sexes economically, the trend continues to move forward as more women move into politics and the workforce.

—Cynthia Clark Northrup

References
Chesler, Phyllis, and Emily Jane Goodman. *Women, Money, and Power.* New York: William Morrow, 1976.
Tilly, Louise A., and Patricia Gurin, eds. *Women, Politics, and Change.* New York: Russell Sage Foundation, 1990.
See also Volume 1: Aid to Dependent Children; Aid to Families with Dependent Children; Equal Pay Act of 1963; Family Assistance Plan; President's Commission on the Status of Women; World War I; World War II.

Workers' Compensation

State programs that provide cash and/or medical services to workers injured on the job or, in cases of workplace fatalities, survivor benefits.

Workers' compensation endures as one of the most important and durable contributions of the Progressive Era: in the short time between 1910 and 1921, all but four states—Arkansas, Florida, Mississippi and South Carolina—established programs. These plans provided the first form of social insurance in the United States and, as such, foretold such New Deal initiatives as old age pensions and unemployment insurance. Throughout the nineteenth century, disabled workers had to prove strict negligence under the common law of industrial accidents, which afforded employers three defenses—contributory negligence (in which the employer fails to ensure safe working conditions), the negligence of fellow servants (in which employees create a safety hazard), and assumption-at-risk (referring to jobs with inherent foreseeable hazards). Workers often found the costs of a protracted court case prohibitive, however, and under these rules, positive verdicts or settlements often proved difficult to achieve. In some states, for example, fewer than half the families of men and women killed on the job received compensation. The problem was underscored in several well-documented catastrophes. Following the infamous Triangle Shirtwaist fire on March 26, 1911, for example, in which 146 workers died, the owners settled a small number of civil cases, but the courts acquitted them in the criminal case. The dramatic rise in the accident rate over previous decades further served to galvanize the reform movement. The rate of nonfatal accidents for railroad workers, for example, had more than doubled between 1894 and 1910.

All 50 states as well as the District of Columbia, Puerto Rico, and the Virgin Islands now have workers' compensation laws based on the principle of no-fault liability (in which it is not necessary to establish fault). There are also two national programs, one for federal government workers and the other for longshoremen and harbor workers. In all states but New

Jersey and Texas, where participation remains elective, eligible employers must purchase sufficient insurance to provide mandated benefits, though most allow self-insurance, either alone or in small groups. Public and private insurance funds coexist in 21 jurisdictions and, in 8 of these, an exclusive state carrier exists. In most cases, premiums are both class-rated (based on income) and experience-rated (firms are penalized at a higher tax rate for benefits paid to their own workers).

The decentralization of workers' compensation in the United States explains its most distinctive (and sometimes problematic) feature: the wide variation in plans. Differences in access to care, coverage of agricultural workers, treatment of small firms, and, most important, the amount and duration of benefits, continue to exist even within a single region. In 2001, for example, a worker who lost his or her hand in an industrial accident in New England could receive $21,690 in Rhode Island but $138,250 in Vermont. Similar variations occur in the maximum survivor benefit: Over all states, it varied from $223 per week in Idaho to $1,031 per week in Iowa.

—*Peter Hans Matthews*

References

Fishback, Price V., and Shawn Everett Kantor. *A Prelude to the Welfare State: The Origins of Workers' Compensation.* Chicago: University of Chicago Press, 2000.

Goldin, Claudia. "Labor Markets in the Twentieth Century." In Stanley L. Engerman and Robert E. Gallman, eds., *The Cambridge History of the United States.* Vol. 3. New York: Cambridge University Press, 1996.

See also Volume 2: Labor.

World Intellectual Property Organization (WIPO)

International organization established in 1970 for the protection of intellectual property.

The roots of the World Intellectual Property Organization (WIPO) go back to the late nineteenth century. During the Gilded Age, writers, composers, and inventors had to deal with the theft of their ideas. Fearing that others would copy their industrial designs, many scientists refused to participate in the International Exhibition of Invention in Vienna in 1873. In response, 14 nations signed the Paris Convention in 1883 to safeguard patents, trademarks, and industrial designs. Three years later they agreed to the Berne Convention, which extended copyright privileges to writers, composers, and artists. In 1893 the two groups merged and became the United International Bureaux for the Protection of Intellectual Property (BIRPI), the predecessor of the WIPO. In 1960, the BIRPI moved from Berne to Geneva, Switzerland, to be closer to the United Nations agencies. A decade later the organization became known as the World Intellectual Property Organization. Seeking greater participation and recognition, the organization became a specialized agency of the United Nations in 1974. After the establishment of the World Trade Organization (WTO) in 1996, the agency signed an agreement of cooperation with the WTO.

The WIPO allows for the application of protection of intellectual property that covers the work in all 179 member states. For instance, if an American writer copyrights his or her book, short story, poem, or other form of writing through the WIPO, the piece is protected internationally throughout all participating countries. If disputes arise, the WIPO facilitates resolutions, and it provides legal assistance to developing countries. The formation of the WIPO has protected Americans in both the arts and the sciences and has stimulated industries by providing accessibility to important information.

—*Cynthia Clark Northrup*

References

World Intellectual Property Organization. *The First Twenty-five Years of the World Intellectual Property Organization, from 1967 to 1992.* Geneva: International Bureau of Intellectual Property, 1992.

———. www.wipo.org; accessed September 2, 2002.

See also Volume 2: Intellectual Property.

World Trade Organization (WTO)

International organization that deals with the rules of trade between nations.

Established on January 1, 1995, the World Trade Organization (WTO) replaced the General Agreement on Tariffs and Trade (GATT). Created during the Uruguay Round of GATT (1986–1994), the WTO differs from its predecessor in scope and authority. Headquartered in Geneva, Switzerland, the WTO consists of 144 member countries. The organization administers WTO agreements, operates as a forum for trade negotiations, and handles disputes among members. It also monitors national trade policies and provides technical assistance for developing countries.

A primary criticism of the WTO in the United States revolves around the expanded authority of the new organization. Under GATT, signatories were not bound to the agreement. Countries joined voluntarily and could leave voluntarily. Under the terms of the World Trade Organization agreement, signatories are bound to the agreement. For instance, section 16 states that "each member shall ensure the conformity of its laws, regulations and administrative procedures with its obligations as provided in the annexed Agreements." In addition, trade panels, instead of magistrates, decide disputes that arise between members. For example, in 2003 the trade panel ruled against India's claim that the United States was not abiding by the WTO's Rules of Origin for Textiles and Apparel Products. The decision of the panel is binding, and heavy fines are imposed if the judgment is ignored. Many opponents argue that these clauses violate the sovereignty of the nation and usurp domestic legislation. As a result of U.S. participation in the WTO, Congress has relegated some of its authority over trade to a supranational organization with potentially far-reaching consequences for the future economic well-being of the country.

Even as the WTO expands its role, opposition to it continues. Various labor activists, religious groups, environmentalists, and academics have created havoc in demonstrations at WTO meetings in Seattle, Prague, Melbourne, New York,

Philadelphia, and Los Angeles. These groups oppose economic globalization, saying that it will mean a loss of jobs in industrialized countries as manufacturers move to countries where labor is cheap and that less developed countries are more lax on environmental controls.

—*Cynthia Clark Northrup*

References

Eckes, Alfred E. *Opening America's Market: U.S. Foreign Policy since 1776.* Chapel Hill: University of North Carolina Press, 1995.

See also Volume 1: General Agreement on Tariffs and Trade; Volume 2: Trade Policy.

World War I (1914–1918)

Early-twentieth-century war primarily fought in Europe that pitted the German, Austro-Hungarian, and Ottoman Empires against Britain, France, Russia, and, in the end, the United States.

In the decades prior to the outbreak of World War I, the nations of Europe vied for economic dominance. Britain began the Industrial Revolution, but its rivals were not far behind. Increased industrial output created a need for more markets. At the turn of the century, Germany, France, and Britain struggled to develop colonies in Africa and Asia. The United States, with its victory in the Spanish-American War of 1898, dominated the Caribbean and was making strides in the Pacific.

The economic struggles of these nations turned into open warfare after the assassination of Austrian Archduke Franz Ferdinand by a Serbian nationalist on June 28, 1914. Diplomatic solutions broke down, and by August 4, 1914, all of Europe was at war. Britain, France, and Russia led the Allied powers in opposition to the Central Powers comprising Germany, Austria-Hungary, and the Ottoman Empire.

Europe was at war, but the United States remained neutral. Initially, it seemed that supplying both sides during the war would create an economic boom for the United States, but in October 1914, the British began a naval blockade of Germany. The British issued an expansive contraband list that all but prohibited American trade with the Central Powers. The British heavily mined the North Sea in November to further ensure that merchant vessels could not reach Germany. The blockade had a detrimental effect on the American economy, and the United States vigorously protested. Britain did not wish to antagonize the United States, but cutting off trade to the enemy seemed a more pressing goal. As a result, the United States quickly settled into a pattern of trading with Britain and France.

Fearing economic strangulation, Germany began using its large submarine fleet to blockade merchants destined for Britain or France. Initially, German submarines surfaced before stopping a neutral merchant, but surfacing made the submarines too vulnerable to the British navy. As a result, German submarines began sinking vessels suspected of carrying military material into Britain or France. The Germans justified the attacks by arguing that the Allied blockade starved the German population, but the United States had a greater interest in its own ships and complained bitterly about German tactics. Because of American pressure after Germany had sunk several passenger ships, notably the British cruise ship *Lusitania,* the Germans ended submarine warfare against nonmilitary vessels in March 1916.

The United States continued trading with the Allied powers, and the trade grew despite the 1916 British publication of a blacklist that prevented trade with American merchants suspected of trading with the Central Powers. Meanwhile, the British blockade was having a serious effect on Germany. Faced with food riots and fearing economic strangulation, the Germans announced a resumption of unrestricted submarine warfare on January 31, 1917. The United States broke diplomatic relations with Germany on February 3, and after German submarines sank several American merchant ships, the United States went to war on April 6, 1917.

The United States sent troops to Europe, but America's chief contribution came in helping end the submarine threat. German submarines wreaked havoc on British merchant vessels, and the United States helped institute a convoy system that escorted merchants across the Atlantic and greatly reduced the submarine threat.

The United States also made a large financial contribution to the Allied effort and loaned about $10 billion to Britain and France. The United States supplied food, weapons, and munitions for the Allies, but the United States initially had difficulty coming up with supplies. No centralized system for purchasing military goods existed in America. Therefore, the U.S. military had to compete for goods in the open market. Additionally, the government did not order factories to convert to war production, and American labor threatened strikes. To deal with these difficulties the government created the War Industries Board to increase industrial efficiency and the National War Labor Board to prevent strikes by meeting with management and labor.

The cost of war and of supplying the Allies was tremendous. The federal budget skyrocketed from $1 billion in 1916 to $19 billion in 1919, and the national debt grew from $1 billion in 1915 to $24 billion in 1920. The federal income tax, which started in 1913, and corporate taxes funded about one-third of the war, and the American people made up the difference by purchasing bonds known as "liberty loans." As a result, the federal government owed the bulk of its debt to its own citizens.

Although the United States was just gearing up to fight, Russia was nearly out of the war. Russia's Bolshevik Revolution took place in November 1917, and the new communist leadership made peace with the Central Powers in March 1918. Even without Russia's help, the Allies proved victorious and signed an Armistice with Germany on November 11, 1918.

In the ensuing peace process, President Woodrow Wilson represented the United States and pushed for a treaty based on his Fourteen Points. The most famed of these was the idea of creating a League of Nations, an international organization designed to mediate national disputes. However, the Fourteen Points also touched on economic issues and urged an end to colonialism and the removal of trade barriers between nations. Wilson abandoned many of his goals and focused on the League of Nations (which the United States never even joined). In the post–World War I negotiations over the Treaty of Versailles, the Allies forced harsh reparations on Germany.

World War I was a golden era for American farmers as they supplied Europe with food, and the war encouraged industrialization and mass production in the United States. As Europeans struggled to obtain American supplies, the United States managed to double its overseas investments while European investments in the United States diminished. In short, participation in the war and the realization of American industrial capacity earned the United States a position as a world power.

—*John K. Franklin*

References
Hardach, Gerd. *The First World War, 1914–1918*. Berkeley: University of California Press, 1977.
Keegan, John. *The First World War*. New York: Alfred A. Knopf, 1999.
Tucker, Spencer C. *The Great War, 1914–1918*. Bloomington: Indiana University Press, 1998.
See also Volume 1: War and Warfare.

World War II (1939–1945)

Mid–twentieth century war fought primarily in Europe, North Africa, and the Pacific that pitted the Axis powers (Germany, Italy, and Japan) against the Allied powers (Britain, the Soviet Union, and the United States).

The deteriorated economic condition of Europe during the Great Depression coupled with German anger over the punitive peace terms of World War I created international tension that led to general war in Europe after Germany invaded Poland in September 1939. War also wracked Asia as Japanese expansionists fought a series of wars against China beginning in 1931. Despite war around the globe, the United States initially attempted to remain neutral. Even so, American neutrality was not impartial; the United States clearly favored the Allies over the Axis powers.

However, the United States was initially unable to supply Britain with a great deal of aid. A series of U.S. Neutrality Acts passed in the 1930s prohibited loans to nations at war and forbade American vessels from shipping arms to belligerents. Instead, the United States abided by a policy known as "cash and carry," whereby belligerents could purchase goods in the United States and ship them home in their own ships. Such a policy made acquiring arms in the United States difficult for the European powers. The strength of the British navy prevented German merchants from picking up goods in the United States, and by the end of 1940, British credit was running out. To aid Britain and circumvent the Neutrality Acts (which prohibited the sale of arms, or even the making of loans, to belligerent nations), the United States initiated the Lend-Lease program in March 1941 to provide military supplies without requiring the payment of cash. Lend-lease allowed the U.S. government to loan military hardware to any

nation considered vital to American security. The program clearly demonstrated American support for Britain and the Allies. Over the course of the war, lend-lease was the principal method of U.S. economic and industrial support for the Allies. By the war's end, the United States had distributed more than \$50 billion in lend-lease assistance. Britain received the most aid with more than \$31 billion. The Soviet Union, which entered the war in the summer of 1941 and ultimately received about \$11 billion in aid, was a distant second.

The United States also maintained an interest in the fighting between Japan and China. By 1940, Japan had become increasingly expansionistic. The Japanese government stressed the creation of a Greater East Asia Co-Prosperity Sphere, in which Japan would lead Asia into political and economic competition against the industrialized Western nations. The United States favored China in the conflict and attempted to pressure Japan through a Japanese oil embargo that began in July 1940. In September 1940, U.S.-Japan relations deteriorated further when Japan forged an alliance with Germany and joined the Axis powers. As a result, the United States steadily increased economic pressure on Japan until the Japanese finally retaliated with the December 7, 1941, attack on Pearl Harbor.

The attack on Pearl Harbor brought the United States fully into World War II. The scale of the fighting in World War II vastly surpassed anything the United States had ever experienced, and during the conflict, the United States military fought in North Africa, Europe, and the Pacific. The Allies finally won after the United States dropped two atomic bombs on Hiroshima and Nagasaki in Japan in August 1945. However, American industrial capacity with its development of new technologies contributed as much to the victory as did military action.

When the United States entered the war, mobilization became a key issue—the scale of World War II required total economic and industrial commitment. Anticipating a need for readiness, President Franklin D. Roosevelt had created the War Resources Board and the Office of Production Management to carry out planning and to stress military production, but without the threat of immediate war, these agencies were largely ineffective in persuading industry to prepare. The attack on Pearl Harbor generated the required willingness to participate, and American industry, led by the newly created War Production Board, began converting to military production. Conversion was difficult, but once it was complete the United States churned out military equipment at an impressive rate. The American auto industry was probably the industry most affected by the war. Auto factories turned to the production of a wide range of military vehicles, from supply trucks and tanks to fighter planes and heavy bombers. By the war's end, former auto producers had manufactured thousands of tanks, armored cars, and airplanes.

Increased industrial production created huge labor demands, and World War II eradicated the unemployment problems created by the Great Depression. With the need for large numbers of workers, labor concerns were an important issue, and the federal government created the National War

Labor Board to help ensure labor's loyalty throughout the war. Production rates were so high and so many men served in the military that businesses also hired women in large numbers for jobs traditionally reserved for men.

The war provided millions of Americans with jobs and money, but it nonetheless created problems with the domestic economy. Industries involved in military production required a great deal of raw material, especially metals, rubber, and fabric. Consequently consumers experienced shortages of several products. In response, the government created the Office of Price Administration to oversee the rationing of consumer goods such as fuel, food, and tires.

Despite the irritation of shortages and rationing, the American economy boomed during World War II. Heavy industrial output ensured an Allied victory but it also put the United States at full production and ended the Great Depression. Indeed, by 1945, the United States had become the world's leading industrial power. A significant factor in the rise of the United States was its separation from the fighting; it is the only major industrialized nation that did not suffer a significant attack on its industrial base. Warfare ravaged Europe and Japan but American factories emerged from the war unscathed. World War II reduced the industrial capacity of the other powers in Europe and Japan even as American industry expanded.

—*John K. Franklin*

References

Harrison, Mark, ed. *The Economics of World War II*. New York: Cambridge University Press, 2000.

Milward, Alan S. *War, Economy, and Society 1939–1945.* Berkeley: University of California Press, 1977.

Nash, Gerald. *The Crucial Era: The Great Depression and World War II, 1929–1945.* 2d ed. New York: Waveland Press, 1998.

Winkler, Allan M. *Home Front U.S.A: America during World War II.* 2d ed. Wheeling, IL: Harlan Davidson, 2000.

See also Volume 1: Great Depression; Japanese Oil Embargo; National War Labor Board.

WPB

See War Production Board.

WTO

See World Trade Organization.

Y

Yazoo Land Companies

Four companies involved in a fraudulent claim on western lands that resulted in the U.S. Supreme Court decision *Fletcher v. Peck.*

On January 7, 1795, Governor George Matthews of Georgia signed into law the Yazoo Land Act, which granted more than 40 million acres of land in present-day Alabama and Mississippi to the Georgia Company, the Georgia-Mississippi Company, the Upper Mississippi Company, and the Tennessee Company for $500,000. Several Georgia legislators owned stock in these companies. When the public learned of the bribery and corruption that secured the passage of the Yazoo Land Act, political turmoil ensued and a newly elected legislature, led by the bombastic Georgia Senator James Jackson (part of the loyal opposition to President George Washington led by Thomas Jefferson), repealed the act February 18, 1796. Georgia offered to refund the price of the land, but many purchasers refused to accept the payment and pressed their claims. On April 26, 1802, Georgia sold its western lands to the United States for $1.25 million. In the settlement the Yazoo claimants could have received five million acres or the money received from their sale. They rejected this offer as well.

The issue rose to national importance and caused conflict between President Thomas Jefferson and Virginia Representative John Randolph. Jefferson wished to settle the matter by compensating the claimants. Randolph opposed any settlement and accused the administration of helping to perpetrate the fraud, and his political connections allowed him to prevent congressional action. In 1810 the U.S. Supreme Court settled the matter by rendering a decision on *Fletcher v. Peck.* The Court ruled that the repeal of the act of 1795 by Georgia was unconstitutional and argued that the act constituted a legal contract binding the state to the land deal even if fraudulent. The decision established the legal notion of the inviolability of contracts and eventually led to Congress awarding the Yazoo claimants more than $4 million.

—*Peter S. Genovese*

References

Magrath, C. Peter. *Yazoo: Law and Politics in the New Republic, Case of* Fletcher v. Peck. Providence, RI: Brown University Press, 1966.
See also Volume 2: Judiciary.